Lecture Notes in Computer Science 1702

Edited by G. Goos, J. Hartmanis and J. van Leeuwen

T0222122

Springer
Berlin
Heidelberg
New York
Barcelona
Hong Kong
London
Milan
Paris
Singapore
Tokyo

Gopalan Nadathur (Ed.)

Principles and Practice of Declarative Programming

International Conference PPDP'99
Paris, France, September 29 – October 1, 1999
Proceedings

Springer

Series Editors

Gerhard Goos, Karlsruhe University, Germany
Juris Hartmanis, Cornell University, NY, USA
Jan van Leeuwen, Utrecht University, The Netherlands

Volume Editor

Gopalan Nadathur
The University of Chicago, Department of Computer Science
1100 East 58th Street, Chicago, IL 60637, USA
E-mail: gopalan@cs.uchicago.edu

Cataloging-in-Publication data applied for

Die Deutsche Bibliothek - CIP-Einheitsaufnahme

Principles and practice of declarative programming : proceedings / International Conference PPDP '99, Paris, France, September 29 - October 1, 1999. Gopalan Nadathur (ed.). - Berlin ; Heidelberg ; New York ; Barcelona ; Hong Kong ; London ; Milan ; Paris ; Singapore ; Tokyo : Springer, 1999
(Lecture notes in computer science ; Vol. 1702)
ISBN 3-540-66540-4

CR Subject Classification (1998): D.3, D.1, F.3

ISSN 0302-9743
ISBN 3-540-66540-4 Springer-Verlag Berlin Heidelberg New York

Typesetting: Camera-ready by author
SPIN: 10704567 06/3142 – 5 4 3 2 1 0 Printed on acid-free paper

Preface

This volume contains the papers presented at the 1999 International Conference on Principles and Practice of Declarative Programming (PPDP'99) held in Paris from September 29 through October 1, 1999. PPDP'99 participated, together with the International Conference on Functional Programming (ICFP) and several related workshops, in a federation of colloquia known as Principles, Logics and Implementations of high-level programming languages (PLI'99). The overall event was organized by the Institut National de Recherche en Informatique et en Automatique (INRIA) and the ACM Special Interest Group for Programming Languages (ACM/SIGPLAN).

PPDP represents the union of two conferences that had been in existence for about a decade: Programming Languages, Implementations, Logics and Programs (PLILP) and Algebraic and Logic Programming (ALP). These conferences were held as one for the first time under the name PLILP/ALP in their tenth and seventh respective incarnations last year. The present rendition follows a decision by the combined steering committees to adopt a simpler name for the conference that also reflected the union. Continuing the tradition of PLILP/ALP, PPDP aims to stimulate research in the use of declarative methods in programming and on the design, application, and implementation of programming languages that support such methods. Topics of interest include the use of type theory, logics, and logical methods in understanding, defining, integrating, and extending programming paradigms such as those for functional, logic, object-oriented, constraint, and concurrent programming; support for modularity; the use of logics in the design of program development tools; development of implementation methods; and the application of the relevant paradigms and associated methods in industry and education. Many of these themes are reflected in the papers appearing in the present collection. Of particular note in these proceedings is the broad interpretation of declarative programming and the emphasis on both principles and practice in this area of research.

A few words about the selection of papers. Fifty-one full-length papers were received in response to the call for submissions. Each of these papers was reviewed by at least four individuals. The program committee met electronically in the last two weeks of April 1999 and, based on the reviews, selected 22 papers for presentation at the conference. A decision was also made during this meeting to include invited talks by Georges Gonthier (INRIA-Rocquencourt, France), Simon Peyton Jones (Microsoft Research, UK) and Pascal van Hentenryck (Catholic University of Louvain, Belgium), and tutorials by Chris Okasaki (Columbia University, USA) and Frank Pfenning (Carnegie Mellon University, USA) in the scientific program. These proceedings include all 22 contributed papers that were accepted, revised in accordance with the suggestions of the reviewers. Also included are papers that complement the presentations of Simon Peyton Jones and Pascal van Hentenryck and an abstract of the tutorial by

Frank Pfenning. Papers accompanying the remaining invited talk and tutorial were not received by the time of going to press.

Many people and institutions are to be acknowledged for their contributions to PPDP'99. The organization of this conference and PLI'99 would not have been possible but for the efforts of François Fages and Didier Rémy, the chairs of PPDP'99 and ICFP'99, and Annick Theis-Viemont and the INRIA staff. The quality of the technical program owes much to the diligence of the program committee members and the several referees whose help they enlisted. In addition to providing careful reviews of submitted papers, many of these individuals participated in extended discussions at the PC meeting towards ensuring consistency and accuracy in the selection process. At a financial level, PPDP'99 benefitted from a grant from the European Commission program for Training and Mobility of Researchers; this grant was mediated by the European Association for Programming Languages and Systems (EAPLS). Additional financial support was provided by the Centre National de la Recherche Scientifique (CNRS), CompulogNet, Microsoft Research, Ministère de l'Education Nationale, de la Recherche et de la Technologie (Gouv. France), Trusted Logic, and France Telecom. Finally, the meeting received an endorsement from the Association for Logic Programming.

July 1999 Gopalan Nadathur

Conference Organization

Conference Chair

François Fages, CNRS, ENS, Paris, France

Program Chair

Gopalan Nadathur, University of Chicago, USA

Program Committee

Martín Abadi	System Research Center, Compaq, Palo Alto, USA
Maria Alpuente	Universidad Politécnica de Valencia, Spain
Mats Carlsson	SICS, Sweden
Iliano Cervesato	Stanford University, USA
Bart Demoen	Katholieke Universiteit Leuven, Belgium
Sandro Etalle	Universiteit Maastricht, The Netherlands
François Fages	CNRS, ENS, Paris, France
Manuel Hermenegildo	Universidad Politécnica de Madrid, Spain
Patricia Hill	University of Leeds, UK
Joxan Jaffar	National University of Singapore, Singapore
Bharat Jayaraman	SUNY Buffalo, USA
Xavier Leroy	INRIA, Rocquencourt, France
Pierre Lescanne	ENS Lyon, France
Eugenio Moggi	University of Genova, Italy
Gopalan Nadathur	University of Chicago, USA
Tobias Nipkow	Technische Universität München, Germany)
Francesca Rossi	University of Padova, Italy
Harald Søndergaard	University of Melbourne, Australia
David S. Warren	SUNY Stony Brook, USA
Nobuko Yoshida	University of Sussex, UK

List of Referees

The following individuals and a few others who wished to remain anonymous have participated in the assessment of the manuscripts submitted to the conference:

Martín Abadi
Elvira Albert
Maria Alpuente
Roberto Bagnara
Richard Banach
Françoise Bellegarde
Zine-El-Abidine Benaissa
Brandon Bennett
Nick Benton
Roberto Bruni
Maurice Bruynooghe
Francisco Bueno
Daniel Cabeza
Mats Carlsson
Manuel Carro
Iliano Cervesato
Michael Codish
Vítor Santos Costa
Baoqiu Cui
Rowan Davies
Danny De Schreye
Pierpaolo Degano
Giorgio Delzanno
Bart Demoen
Marc Denecker
Rachid Echahed
Jesper Eskilson
Sandro Etalle
François Fages
Moreno Falaschi
Antonio J. Fernandez
Maribel Fernández
G. Ferrari
Cormac Flanagan
Matthew Flatt
Cedric Fournet
Fabio Gadducci
María García de la Banda
Simon Gay
Vincente Gisbert
Michael Hanus
Andrew Heaton
Nevin Heintze
Martin Henz
Manuel Hermenegildo
Angel Herranz
Carlos Herrero
Patricia Hill
Kohei Honda
Zhenjiang Hu
Joxan Jaffar
Gerda Janssens
Bharat Jayaraman
Wolfram Kahl
Antonios Kakas
Andy King
Shinji Kono
Per Kreuger
Frédéric Lang
Xavier Leroy
Pierre Lescanne
Francesca Levi
Mark D. Lillibridge
Luigi Liquori
Pedro López-García
Salvador Lucas
Luc Maranget
Julio Mariño
Kim Marriott
Michel Mauny
Guy McCusker
Aart Middeldorp
Dale Miller
Eugenio Moggi
Eric Monfroy
Juan José Moreno-Navarro
Gines Moreno-Valverde
Gopalan Nadathur
Wolfgang Naraschewski
Tobias Nipkow
Michael J. O'Donnell
Hitoshi Ohsaki
Mehmet Orgun
Catuscia Palamidessi
Benjamin C. Pierce
Enrico Pontelli
Frédéric Prost
Germán Puebla
María José Ramírez
Rafael Ramirez
Gianna Reggio
Pedro Resende
Christophe Ringeissen
Francesca Rossi
Salvatore Ruggieri
Claudio Vittorio Russo
Konstantinos Sagonas
David Sands
Ralf Schweimeier
Bernhard Schätz
Laura Semini
Manuel Serrano
Peter Sewell
Konrad Slind
Jan-Georg Smaus
Sylvain Soliman
Zoltan Somogyi
Harald Søndergaard
Fausto Spoto
Leon Sterling
Christopher A. Stone
Peter Stuckey
Péter Szeredi
Walid Taha
Vincent Tam
Héléne Touzet
Henk Vandecasteele
Wim Vanhoof
Femke van Raamsdonk
Sofie Verbaeten
German Vidal
David S. Warren
Markus Wenzel
Benjamin Werner
Roland Yap
Nobuko Yoshida
Zhang Yuanlin
Hans Zantema

Table of Contents

C--: A Portable Assembly Language that Supports Garbage Collection

Simon Peyton Jones[1], Norman Ramsey[2], and Fermin Reig[3]

[1] Microsoft Research Ltd
simonpj@microsoft.com
[2] University of Virginia
nr@cs.virginia.edu
[3] University of Glasgow
reig@dcs.gla.ac.uk

Abstract. For a compiler writer, generating good machine code for a variety of platforms is hard work. One might try to reuse a retargetable code generator, but code generators are complex and difficult to use, and they limit one's choice of implementation language. One might try to use C as a portable assembly language, but C limits the compiler writer's flexibility and the performance of the resulting code. The wide use of C, despite these drawbacks, argues for a portable assembly language. C-- is a new language designed expressly for this purpose. The use of a portable assembly language introduces new problems in the support of such *high-level run-time services* as garbage collection, exception handling, concurrency, profiling, and debugging. We address these problems by combining the C-- language with a C-- *run-time interface*. The combination is designed to allow the compiler writer a choice of source-language semantics and implementation techniques, while still providing good performance.

1 Introduction

Suppose you are writing a compiler for a high-level language. How are you to generate high-quality machine code? You could do it yourself, or you could try to take advantage of the work of others by using an off-the-shelf code generator. Curiously, despite the huge amount of research in this area, only three retargetable, optimizing code generators appear to be freely available: VPO [6], ML-RISC [16], and the gcc back end [33]. Each of these impressive systems has a rich, complex, and ill-documented interface. Of course, these interfaces are quite different from one another, so once you start to use one, you will be unable to switch easily to another. Furthermore, they are language-specific. To use ML-RISC you must write your front end in ML, to use the gcc back end you must write it in C, and so on.

All of this is most unsatisfactory. It would be much better to have one portable assembly language that could be generated by a front end and implemented by any of the available code generators. So pressing is this need that it has

G. Nadathur (Ed.): PPDP'99, LNCS 1702, pp. 1–28, 1999.

become common to use C as a portable assembly language [2,5,25,37,18,22,30]. Unfortunately, C was never intended for this purpose — it is a *programming* language, not an *assembly* language. C locks the implementation into a particular calling convention, makes it impossible to compute targets of jumps, provides no support for garbage collection, and provides very little support for exceptions or debugging (Section 2).

The obvious way forward is to design a language specifically as a compiler target language. Such a language should serve as the interface between a compiler for a high-level language (the *front end*) and a retargetable code generator (the *back end*). The language would not only make the compiler writer's life much easier, but would also give the author of a new code generator a ready-made customer base. In an earlier paper we propose a design for just such a language, C-- [24], but the story does not end there. Separating the front and back ends greatly complicates run-time support. In general, the front end, back end, and run-time system for a programming language are designed together. They cooperate intimately to support such high-level features as garbage collection, exception handling, debugging, profiling, and concurrency — *high-level run-time services.* If the back end is a portable assembler like C--, we want the cooperation without the intimacy; an implementation of C-- should be independent of the front ends with which it will be used.

One alternative is to make all these high-level services part of the abstraction offered by the portable assembler. For example, the Java Virtual Machine, which provides garbage collection and exception handling, has been used as a target for languages other than Java, including Ada [36], ML [7], Scheme [12], and Haskell [39]. But a sophisticated platform like a virtual machine embodies too many design decisions. For a start, the semantics of the virtual machine may not match the semantics of the language being compiled (e.g., the exception semantics). Even if the semantics happen to match, the engineering tradeoffs may differ dramatically. For example, functional languages like Haskell or Scheme allocate like crazy [14], and JVM implementations are typically not optimised for this case. Finally, a virtual machine typically comes complete with a very large infrastructure — class loaders, verifiers and the like — that may well be inappropriate. Our intended level of abstraction is much, much lower.

Our problem is to enable a *client* to implement high-level services, while still using C-- as a code generator. As we discuss in Section 4, supporting high-level services requires knowledge from *both* the front and back ends. The insight behind our solution is that C-- should include not only a low-level assembly language, for use by the compiler, but also a low-level run-time system, for use by the front end's run-time system. The only intimate cooperation required is between the C-- back end and its run-time system; the front end works with C-- at arm's length, through a well-defined language and a well-defined *run-time interface* (Section 5). This interface adds something fundamentally new: the ability to inspect and modify the state of a suspended computation.

It is not obvious that this approach is workable. Can just a few assembly-language capabilities support many high-level run-time services? Can the front-end run-time system easily implement high-level services using these capabilities? How much is overall efficiency compromised by the arms-length relationship between the front-end runtime and the C-- runtime? We cannot yet answer these questions definitively. Instead, the primary contributions of this paper are to identify needs that are common to various high-level services, and to propose specific mechanisms to meet these needs. We demonstrate only how to use C-- to implement the easiest of our intended services, namely garbage collection. Refining our design to accommodate exceptions, concurrency, profiling, and debugging has emerged as an interesting research challenge.

2 It's Impossible — or it's C

The dream of a portable assembler has been around at least since UNCOL [13]. Is it an impossible dream, then? Clearly not: C's popularity as an assembler is clear evidence that a need exists, and that something useful can be done.

If C is so popular, then perhaps C is perfectly adequate? Not so. There are many difficulties, of which the most fundamental are these:

- The C route rewards those who can map their high-level language rather directly onto C. A high-level language procedure becomes a C procedure, and so on. But this mapping is often awkward, and sometimes impossible.
  For example, some source languages fundamentally require *tail-call optimisation*; a procedure call whose result is returned to the caller of the current procedure must be executed in the stack frame of the current procedure. This optimisation allows iteration to be implemented efficiently using recursion. More generally, it allows one to think of a procedure as a labelled extended basic block that can be *jumped to*, rather than as sub-program that can only be *called*. Such procedures give a front end the freedom to design its own control flow.
  It is very difficult to implement the tail-call optimisation in C, and no C compiler known to us does so across separately compiled modules. Those using C have been very ingenious in finding ways around this deficiency [34,37,25,18], but the results are complex, fragile, and heavily tuned for one particular implementation of C (usually `gcc`).
- A C compiler may lay out its stack frames as it pleases. This makes it difficult for a garbage collector to find the live pointers. Implementors either arrange not to keep pointers on the C stack, or they use a conservative garbage collector. These restrictions are Draconian.
- The unknown stack-frame layout also complicates support for exception handling, debugging, profiling, and concurrency. For example, an exception-handling mechanism needs to walk the stack, perhaps removing stack frames as it goes. Again, C makes it essentially impossible to implement such mechanisms, unless they can be closely mapped onto what C provides (i.e., `setjmp` and `longjmp`).

– A C compiler has to be very conservative about the possibility of memory aliasing. This seriously limits the ability of the instruction scheduler to permute memory operations or hoist them out of a loop. The front-end compiler often knows that aliasing cannot occur, but there is no way to convey this information to the C compiler.

So much for fundamental issues. C also lacks the ability to control a number of important low-level features, including returning multiple values in registers from a procedure, mis-aligned memory accesses, arithmetic, data layout, and omitting range checks on multi-way jumps.

In short, C is awkward to use as a portable assembler, and many of these difficulties translate into performance hits. A portable assembly language should be able to offer better performance, as well as greater ease of use.

3 An Overview of C--

```
/* Ordinary recursion */
export sp1;
sp1( bits32 n ) {
  bits32 s, p;
  if n == 1 {
      return( 1, 1 );
  } else {
      s, p = sp1( n-1 );
      return( s+n, p*n );
  }
}

/* Tail recursion */
export sp2;
sp2( bits32 n ) {
  jump sp2_help( n, 1, 1 );
}

sp2_help( bits32 n, bits32 s, bits32 p ) {
  if n==1 {
      return( s, p );
  } else {
      jump sp2_help( n-1, s+n, p*n )
  }
}

/* Loops */
export sp3;
sp3( bits32 n ) {
    bits32 s, p;
    s = 1; p = 1;

  loop:
    if n==1 {
      return( s, p );
    } else {
      s = s+n;
      p = p*n;
      n = n-1;
      goto loop;
    }
}
```

Fig. 1. Three functions that compute the sum $\sum_{i=1}^{n} i$ and product $\prod_{i=1}^{n} i$, written in C--.

In this section we give an overview of the design of C--. Fuller descriptions can be found in [24] and in [28]. Figure 1 gives examples of some C-- procedures that give a flavour of the language. Despite its name C-- is by no means a subset of C, as will become apparent; C was simply our jumping-off point.

3.1 What is a Portable Assember?

C-- is an *assembly language* — an abstraction of hardware — not a high-level programming language. Hardware provides computation, control flow, memory, and registers; C-- provides corresponding abstractions.

- C-- expressions and assignments are abstractions of computation. C-- provides a rich set of computational operators, but these operators work only on machine-level data types: bytes, words, etc. The expression abstraction hides the particular combination of machine instructions needed to compute values, and it hides the machine registers that may be needed to hold intermediate results.
- C--'s `goto` and `if` statements are abstractions of control flow. (For convenience, C-- also provides structured control-flow constructs.) The `if` abstraction hides the machine's "condition codes;" branch conditions are arbitrary Boolean expressions.
- C-- treats memory much as the machine does, except that addresses used in C-- programs may be arbitrary expressions. This abstraction hides the limitations of the machine's addressing modes.
- C-- variables are an abstraction of registers. A C-- back end puts as many variables as possible in registers; others go in memory. This abstraction hides the number and conventional uses of the machine's registers.
- In addition, C-- provides a procedure abstraction, the feature that looks least like an abstraction of a hardware primitive. However, many processor architectures provide direct support for procedures, although the nature of that support varies widely (procedure call or multiple register save instructions, register windows, link registers, branch prediction for return instructions, and so on). Because of this variety, calling conventions and activation-stack management are notoriously architecture dependent and hard to specify. C-- therefore offers prodedures as a primitive abstraction, albeit in a slightly unusual form (Section 3.4).

Our goal is to make it easy to retarget front ends, not to make every C-- program runnable everywhere. Although every C-- program has a well-defined semantics that is independent of any machine, a front end translating a single source program might need to generate two different C-- programs for two different target architectures. For example, a C-- program generated for a machine without floating-point instructions would be different from a C-- program generated for a machine without floating-point instructions.

Our goal contrasts sharply with "write once; run anywhere," the goal of such distribution formats as Java class files, Juice files [15], and ANDF or TenDRA [20]. These formats are abstractions of high-level languages, not of underlying machines. Their purpose is binary portability, and they retain enough high-level language semantics to permit effective compilation at the remote installation site.

Even though C-- exposes a few architecture-specific details, like word size, the whole point is to hide those details, so that the front end job can largely independent of the target architecture. A good C-- implementation therefore must do substantial architecture-dependent work. For example:

- Register allocation.
- Instruction selection, exploiting complex instructions and addressing modes.
- Instruction scheduling.
- Stack-frame layout.
- Classic back-end optimisations such as common-subexpression elimination and copy propagation.
- If-conversion for predicated architectures.

Given these requirements, C-- resembles a typical compiler's intermediate language more than a typical machine's assembly language.

3.2 Types

C-- supports a bare minimum of data types: a family of `bits` types (`bits8`, `bits16`, `bits32`, `bits64`), and a family of floating-point types (`float32`, `float64`, `float80`). These types encode only the size (in bits) and the kind of register (general-purpose or floating-point) required for the datum.

Not all types are available on all machines; for example, a C-- program emitted by a front-end compiler for a 64-bit machine might be rejected if fed to a C-- implementation for a 32-bit machine. It is easy to tell a front end how big to make its data types, and doing so makes the front end's job easier in some ways; for example, it can compute offsets statically.

The `bits` types are used for characters, bit vectors, integers, and addresses (pointers). On each architecture, a `bits` type is designated the "*native word type*" of the machine. A "*native code-pointer type*" and "*native data-pointer type*" are also designated; exported and imported names must have one of these pointer types. On many machines, all three types are the same, e.g, `bits32`.

3.3 Static Allocation

C-- offers detailed control of static memory layout, much as ordinary assemblers do. A data block consists of a sequence of labels, initialised data values, uninitialised arrays, and alignment directives. For example:

```
data {
  foo:  bits32{10};        /* One bits32 initialised to 10 */
        bits32{1,2,3,4};   /* Four initialised bits32's */
        bits32[8];         /* Uninitialised array of 8 bits32's */
  baz1:
  baz2: bits8              /* An uninitialised byte */
  end:
}
```

Here `foo` is the address of the first `bits32`, `baz1` and `baz2` are both the address of the `bits8`, and `end` is the address of the byte after the `bits8`. The labels `foo`, `baz1`, etc, should be thought of as addresses, not as memory locations. They are all immutable constants of the native data-pointer type; they cannot be assigned to.

How, then, can one access the memory at location `foo`? Memory accesses (loads and stores) are typed, and denoted with square brackets. Thus the statement:

```
bits32[foo] = bits32[foo] + 1;
```

loads a `bits32` from the location whose address is in `foo`, adds one to it, and stores it at the same location. The mnemonic for this syntax is to think of `bits32` as a C-like array representing all of memory, and `bits32[foo]` as a particular element of that array. The semantics of the address is not C-like, however; the expression in brackets is the *byte address* of the item. Further, `foo`'s type is always the native data-pointer type; the type of value stored at `foo` is specified by the load or store operation itself. So this is perfectly legal:

```
bits8[foo+2] = bits8[foo+2] - 1;
```

This statement modifies only the byte at address `foo+2`.

Unlike C, C-- has no implicit alignment or padding. Therefore, the address relationships between the data items within a single `data` block are machine-independent; for example, `baz1` $=$ `foo` $+ 52$. An explicit `align` directive provides alignment where that is required.

C-- supports multiple, named data sections. For example:

```
data "debug" {
  ...
}
```

This syntax declares the block of data to belong to the section named `"debug"`. Code is by default placed in the section `"text"`, and a `data` directive with no explicit section name defaults to the section `"data"`. Procedures can be enclosed in `code "mytext" { ... }` to place them in a named section `"mytext"`.

C-- expects that, when linking object files, the linker concatenates sections with the same name. (For backwards compatibility with some existing linkers, front ends may wish to emit an alignment directive at the beginning of each

C-- section.) C-- assigns no other semantics to the names of data sections, but particular implementations may assign machine-dependent semantics. For example, a MIPS implementation might assume that data in sections named "rodata" is read-only.

3.4 Procedures

C-- supports procedures that are both more and less general than C procedures — for example, C-- procedures offer multiple results and full tail calls, but they have a fixed number of arguments. Specifically:

- A C-- procedure, such as sp1 in Figure 1, has *parameters*, such as n, and *local variables*, such as s and p. Parameters and variables are mapped onto machine registers where possible, and only spilled to the stack when necessary. In this absolutely conventional way C-- abstracts away from the number of machine registers actually available. As with registers, C-- provides no way to take the address of a parameter or local variable.
- C-- supports fully general tail calls, identified as "jumps". Control does not return from jumps, and C-- implementations must deallocate the caller's stack frame before each jump. For example, the procedure sp2_help in Figure 1 uses a jump to implement tail recursion.
- C-- supports procedures with multiple results, just as it supports procedures with multiple arguments. Indeed, a return is somewhat like a jump to a procedure whose address happens to be held in the topmost activation record on the control stack, rather than being specified explicitly. All the procedures in Figure 1 return two results; procedure sp1 contains a call site for such a procedure.
- A C-- procedure call is always a complete statement, which passes expressions as parameters and assigns results to local variables. Although high-level languages allow a call to occur in an expression, C-- forbids it. For example, it is illegal to write

  ```
  r = f( g(x) );                /* illegal */
  ```

  because the result returned by g(x) cannot be an argument to f. Instead, one must write two separate calls:

  ```
  y = g(x);
  r = f(y);
  ```

  This restriction makes explicit the order of evaluation, the location of each call site, and the names and types of temporaries used to hold the results of calls. (For similar reasons, assignments in C-- are statements, not expressions, and C-- operators have no side effects. In particular, C-- provides no analog of C's "p++.")
- To handle high-level variables that can't be represented using C--'s primitive types, C-- can be asked to allocate named areas in the procedure's activation record.

```
f (bits32 x) {
  bits32 y;

  stack { p : bits32;
          q : bits32[40];
  }
  /* Here, p and q are the addresses of the relevant chunks
     of data. Their type is the native data-pointer type. */
}
```

`stack` is rather like `data`; it has the same syntax between the braces, but it allocates on the stack. As with `data`, the names are bound to the addresses of the relevant locations, and they are immutable. C-- makes no provision for dynamically-sized stack allocation (yet).

- The name of a procedure is a C-- expression of native code-pointer type. The procedure specified in a call statement can be an arbitrary expression, not simply the statically-visible name of a procedure. For example, the following statements are both valid, assuming the procedure `sp1` is defined in this compilation unit, or imported from another one:

```
bits32[ptr] = sp1;            /* Store procedure address */
...
r,s = (bits32[ptr])( 4 );     /* Call stored procedure */
```

- A C-- procedure, like `sp3` in Figure 1, may contain `goto`s and labels, *but they serve only to allow a textual representation of the control-flow graph.* Unlike procedure names, labels are not values, and they have no representation at run time. Because this restriction makes it impossible for front ends to build jump tables from labels, C-- includes a switch statement, for which the C-- back end generates efficient code. The most efficient mix of conditional branches and indexed branches may depend on the architecture [8].
  Jump tables of procedure addresses (rather than labels) can be built, of course, and a C-- procedure can use the `jump` statement to make a tail call to a computed address.

3.5 Calling Conventions

The calling convention for C-- procedures is entirely a matter for the C-- implementation — we call it the *standard* C-- *calling convention.* In particular, C-- need not use the C calling convention.

The standard calling convention places no restrictions on the number of arguments passed to a function or the number of results returned from a function. The only restrictions are that the number and types of actual parameters must match those in the procedure declaration, and similarly, that the number and types of values returned must match those expected at the call site. These restrictions enable efficient calling sequences with no dynamic checks. (A C-- implementation need not check that C-- programs meet these restrictions.)

We note the following additional points:

- If a C-- function does not "escape" — if all sites where it is called can be identified statically — then the C-- back end is free to create and use specialised instances, with specialised calling conventions, for each call site. Escape analysis is necessarily conservative, but a function may be deemed to escape only if its name is used other than in a call, or if it is named in an `export` directive.
- Support for unrestricted tail calls requires an unusual calling convention, so that a procedure making a tail call can deallocate its activation record while still leaving room for parameters that do not fit in registers.
- C-- allows the programmer to specify a particular calling convention (chosen from a small set of standard conventions) for an individual procedure, so that C-- code can interoperate with foreign code. For example, even though C--'s standard calling convention may differ from C's, one can ask for a particular procedure to use C's convention, so that the procedure can be called from an external C program. Similarly, external C procedures can be called from a C-- procedure by specifying the calling convention at the call site.
  Some C-- implementations may provide *two* versions of C's calling convention. The lightweight version would be like an ordinary C call, but it would be useful only when the C procedures terminate quickly; if control were transferred to the run-time system while a C procedure was active, the run-time system might not be able to find values that were in callee-saves registers at the time of the call. The heavyweight version would keep all its state on the stack, not in callee-saves registers, so the run-time system could handle a stack containing a mix of C and C-- activations.

3.6 Miscellaneous

Like other assemblers, C-- gives programmers the ability to name compile-time constants, e.g., by

```
const GC = 2;
```

C-- variables may be declared `global`, in which case the C-- compiler attempts to put them in registers. For example, given the declaration

```
global {
  bits32 hp;
}
```

the implementation attempts to put variable `hp` in a register, but if no register is available, it puts `hp` in memory. C-- programs use and assign to `hp` without knowing whether it is in a register or in memory. Unlike storage allocated by `data`, there is no such thing as "the address of a global", so memory stores to unknown addresses cannot affect the value of a global. This permits a global to be held in a register and, even if it has to be held in memory, the optimiser does not need to worry about re-loading it after a store to an unknown memory address. All separately compiled modules must have *identical* `global` declarations, or horribly strange things will happen.

global declarations may name specific (implementation-dependent) registers, for example:

```
global {
  bits32 hp    "%ebx";
  bits32 hplim "%esi";
}
```

We remarked in Section 2 that the front end may know a great deal about (lack of) aliasing between memory access operations. We do not yet have a way to express such knowledge in C--, but an adaptation of [21] looks promising.

4 The Problem of Run-Time Support

When a front end and back end are written together, as part of a single compiler, they can cooperate intimately to support high-level run-time services, such as garbage collection, exception handling, profiling, concurrency, and debugging. In the C-- framework, the front and back ends work at arm's length. As mentioned earlier, our guiding principle is this:

> C-- should make it *possible* to implement high-level run-time services, but it should not actually *implement* any of them. Rather, it should provide just enough "hooks" to allow the front-end run-time system to implement them.

Separating *policy* from *mechanism* in this way is easier said than done. It might appear more palatable to incorporate garbage collection, exception handling, and debugging into the C-- language, as (say) the Java Virtual Machine does. But doing so would guarantee that C-- would never be used. Different source languages require different support, different object layouts, and different exception semantics — especially when performance matters. No one back end could satisfy all customers.

Why is the separation between front and back end hard to achieve? *High-level run-time services need to inspect and modify the state of a suspended program.* A garbage collector must find, and perhaps modify, all live pointers. An exception handler must navigate, and perhaps unwind, the call stack. A profiler must correlate object-code locations with source-code locations, and possibly navigate the call stack. A debugger must allow the user to inspect, and perhaps modify, the values of variables. All of these tasks require information from both front and back ends. The rest of this section elaborates.

Finding roots for garbage collection. If the high-level language requires accurate garbage collection, then the garbage collector must be able to find all the *roots* that point into the heap. If, furthermore, the collector supports compaction, the locations of heap objects may change during garbage collection, and the collector must be able to redirect each root to point to the new location of the corresponding heap object.

The difficulty is that neither the front end nor the back end has all the knowledge needed to find roots at run time. Only the front end knows which source-language variables, and therefore which C-- variables, represent pointers into the heap. Only the back end, which maps variables to registers and stack slots, knows where those variables are located at run time. Even the back end can't always identify exact locations; variables mapped to callee-saves registers may be saved arbitrarily far away in the call stack, at locations not identifiable until run time.

Printing values in a debugger. A debugger needs compiler support to print the values of variables. For this task, information is divided in much the same way as for garbage collection. Only the front end knows how source-language variables are mapped onto (collections of) C-- variables. Only the front end knows how to print the value of a variable, e.g., as determined by the variable's high-level-language type. Only the back end knows where to find the values of the C-- variables.

Loci of control A debugger must be able to identify the "locus of control" in each activation, and to associate that locus with a source-code location. This association is used both to plant breakpoints and to report the source-code location when a program faults.

An exception mechanism also needs to identify the locus of control, because in some high-level languages, that locus determines which handler should receive the exception. When it identifies a handler, the exception mechanism unwinds the stack and *changes* the locus of control to refer to the handler.

A profiler must map loci of control into entities that are profiled: procedures, statements, source-code regions, etc.

At run time, loci of control are represented by values of the program counter (e.g., return addresses), but at the source level, loci of control are associated with statements in a high-level language or in C--. Only the front end knows how to associate high-level source locations or exception-handler scopes with C-- statements. Only the back end knows how to associate C-- statements with the program counter.

Liveness. Depending on the semantics of the original source language, the locus of control may determine which variables of the high-level language are visible. Depending on the optimizations performed by the back end, the locus of control may determine which C-- variables are live, and therefore have values. Debuggers should not print dead variables. Garbage collectors should not trace them; tracing dead pointers could cause space leaks. Worse, tracing a register that once held a root but now holds a non-pointer value could violate the collector's invariants. Again, only the front end knows which variables are interesting for debugging or garbage collection, but only the back end knows which are live at a given locus of control.

Exception values. In addition to unwinding the stack and changing the locus of control, the exception mechanism may have to communicate a value to an exception handler. Only the front end knows which variable should receive this value, but only the back end knows where variables are located.

Succinctly stated, each of these operations must combine two kinds of information:

- *Information that only the front end has:*
  - Which C-- parameters and local variables are heap pointers.
  - How to map source-language variables to C-- variables and how to associate source-code locations with C-- statements.
  - Which exception handlers are in scope at which C-- statements, and which variables are visible at which C-- statements.
- *Information that only the back end has:*
  - Whether each C-- local variable and parameter is live, where it is located (if live), and how this information changes as the program counter changes.
  - Which program-counter values correspond to which C-- statements.
  - How to find activations of all active procedures and how to unwind stacks.

5 Support for High-Level Run-Time Services

The main challenge, then, is arranging for the back end and front end to share information, without having to implement them as a single integrated unit. In this section we describe a framework that allows this to be done. We focus on garbage collection as our illustrative example. Other high-level run-time services can fit in the same framework, but each requires service-specific extensions; we sketch some ideas in Section 7.

In what follows, we use the term "variable" to mean either a parameter of the procedure or a locally-declared variable.

5.1 The Framework

We assume that executable programs are divided into three parts, each of which may be found in object files, libraries, or a combination.

- The front end compiler translates the high-level source program into one or more C-- modules, which are separately translated to *generated object code* by the C-- compiler.
- The front end comes with a (probably large) *front-end run-time system.* This run-time system includes the garbage collector, exception handler, and whatever else the source language needs. It is written in a programming language designed for humans, not in C--; in what follows we assume that the front end run-time system is written in C.
- Every C-- implementation comes with a (hopefully small) C-- *run-time system.* The main goal of this run-time system is to maintain and provide access to information that only the back end can know. It makes this information available to the front end run-time system through a C-language run-time interface, which we describe in Section 5.2. Different front ends may interoperate with the same C-- run-time system.

To make an executable program, we link generated object code with both run-time systems.

In outline, C-- can support high-level run-time services, such as garbage collection, as follows. When garbage collection is required, control is transferred to the front-end run-time system (Section 6.1). The garbage collector then walks the C-- stack, by calling access routines provided by the C-- run-time system (Section 5.2). In each activation record on the C-- stack, the garbage collector finds the location of each live variable, using further procedures provided by the C-- runtime. However, the C-- runtime cannot know which of these variables holds a pointer. To answer this question, the front-end compiler builds a statically-allocated data block that identifies pointer variables, and it uses a `span` directive (Section 5.3) to associate this data block with the corresponding procedure's range of program counter values. The garbage collector combines these two sources of information to decide whether to treat the procedure's variable as a root. Section 5.4 describes one possible garbage collector in more detail.

5.2 The C-- Run-Time Interface

This section presents the core run-time interface provided by the C-- run-time system. Using this interface, a front-end run-time system can inspect and modify the state of a suspended C-- computation. Rather than specify representations of a suspended computation or its activation records, we hide them behind simple abstractions. These abstractions are presented to the front-end run-time system through a set of C procedures.

The state of a C-- computation consists of some saved registers and a logical stack of procedure activations. This logical stack is usually implemented as some sort of physical stack, but the correspondence between the two may not be very direct. Notably, callee-saves registers that logically belong with one activation are not necessarily stored with that activation, or even with the adjacent activation; they may be stored in the physical record of an activation that is arbitrarily far away. This problem is the reason that C's `setjmp` and `longjmp` functions don't necessarily restore callee-saves registers, which is why some C compilers make pessimistic assumptions when compiling procedures containing `setjmp` [17, §19.4].

We hide this complexity behind a simple abstraction, the *activation*. The idea of an activation of procedure P is that *it approximates the state the machine will be in when control returns to P.* The approximation is not completely accurate because other procedures may change the global store or P's stack variables before control returns to P. At the machine level, the activation corresponds to the "abstract memory" of [27, Chapter 3], which gives the contents of memory, including P's activation record (stack frame), and of registers.

The activation abstraction hides machine-dependent details and raises the level of abstraction to the C-- source-code level. In particular, the abstraction hides:

- The layout of an activation record, and the encoding used to record that layout for the benefit of the front end runtime,

- The details of manipulating callee-saves registers (whether to use callee saves registers is entirely up to the C-- implementation), and
- The direction in which the stack grows.

All of these matters become private to the back end and the C-- runtime.

In the C-- run-time interface, an activation record is represented by an *activation handle*, which is a value of type `activation`. Arbitrary registers and memory addresses are represented by variables, which are referred to by number.

The procedures in the C-- run-time interface include:

`void *FindVar( activation *a, int var_index )` asks an activation handle for the location of any parameter or local variable in the activation record to which the handle refers. The variables of a procedure are indexed by numbering them in the order in which they are declared in that procedure, starting with zero. `FindVar` returns the address of the location containing the value of the specified variable. The front end is thereby able to examine or modify the value. `FindVar` returns `NULL` if the variable is dead. It is a checked runtime error to pass a `var_index` that is out of range.

`void FirstActivation( tcb *t, activation *a )`. When execution of a C-- program is suspended, its state is captured by the C-- run-time system. `FirstActivation` uses that state to initialise an activation handle that corresponds to the procedure that will execute when the program's execution is resumed.

`int NextActivation( activation *a )` modifies the activation handle `a` to refer to the activation record of a's caller, or more precisely, to the activation to which control will return when `a` returns. `NextActivation` returns nonzero if there is such an activation record, and zero if there is not. That is, `NextActivation(&a)` returns zero if and only if activation handle `a` refers to the bottom-most record on the C-- stack.

Notice that `FindVar` always returns a pointer to a memory location, even though the specified variable might be held in a register at the moment at which garbage collection is required. But by the time the garbage collector is walking the stack, the C-- implementation must have stored all the registers away in memory somewhere, and it is up to the C-- run-time system to figure out where the variable is, and to return the address of the location holding it.

Names bound by `stack` declarations are considered variables for purposes of `FindVar`, even though they are immutable. For such names, `FindVar` returns the value that the name has in C-- source code, i.e., the address of the stack-allocated block of storage. Storing through this address is meaningful; it alters the contents of the activation record `a`. Stack locations are not subject to liveness analysis.

5.3 Front-End Information

Suppose the garbage collector is examining a particular activation record. It can use `FindVar` to locate variable number 1, but how can it know whether that variable is a pointer? The front end compiler cooperates with C-- to answer this question, as follows:

- The front end builds a static initialised data block (Section 3.3), or *descriptor*, that says which of the parameters and local variables of a procedure are heap pointers. The format of this data block is known only to the front-end compiler and run-time system; the C-- run-time system does not care.
- The front end tells C-- to associate a particular range of program counters with this descriptor, using a span directive.
- The C-- run-time system provides a call, GetDescriptor, that maps an activation handle to the descriptor associated with the program counter at which the activation is suspended.

We discuss each of these steps in more detail. As an example, suppose we have a function f(x, y), with no other variables, in which x holds a pointer into the heap and y holds an integer. The front end can encode the heap-pointer information by emitting a data block, or *descriptor*, associating 1 with x and 0 with y:

```
data {
  gc1: bits32 2;        /* this procedure has two variables */
       bits8  1;        /* x is a pointer */
       bits8  0;        /* y is a non-pointer */
}
```

This encoding does not use the names of the variables; instead, each variable is assigned an integer index, based on the textual order in which it appears in the definition of f. Therefore x has index 0 and y has index 1.

Many other encodings are possible. The front end might emit a table that uses one bit per variable, instead of one byte. It might emit a list of the indices of variables that contain pointers. It might arrange for pointer variables to have continuous indices and emit only the first and last such index.[1] The key property of our design is that *the encoding matters only to the front end and its runtime system.* C-- does not know or care about the encoding.

To associate the garbage-collection descriptor with f, the front end places the definition of f in a C-- *span*:

```
span GC gc1 {
  f( bits32 x, bits32 y ) {
    ...code for f...
  }
}
```

A span may apply to a sequence of function definitions, or to a sequence of statements within a function definition. In this case, the span applies to all of f.

[1] This scenario presumes the front end has the privilege of reordering parameters; otherwise, it would have to use some other scheme for parameters.

There may be several independent span mappings in use simultaneously, e.g., one for garbage collection, one for exceptions, one for debugging, and so on. C-- uses integer *tokens* to distinguish these mappings from one another; GC is the token in the example above. C-- takes no interest in the tokens; it simply provides a map from a (token, PC) pair to an address. Token values are usually defined using a `const` declaration (Section 3.6).

When the garbage collector (say) walks the stack, using an activation handle a, it can call the following C-- run-time procedure:

`void *GetDescriptor( activation *a, int token )` returns the address of the descriptor associated with the smallest C-- span tagged with `token` and containing the program point where the activation a is suspended.

There are no constraints on the form of the descriptor that `gc1` labels; that form is private to the front end and its run-time system. All C-- does is transform `span` directives into mappings from program counters to values.

The front end may emit descriptors and spans to support other services, not just garbage collection. For example, to support exception handling or debugging, the front end may record the scopes of exception handlers or the names and types of variables. C-- supports multiple spans, but they must not overlap. Spans can nest, however; the innermost span bearing a given token takes precedence. One can achieve the effect of overlapping by binding the same data block to multiple spans.

5.4 Garbage Collection

This section explains in more detail how the C-- run-time interface might be used to help implement a garbage collector. Our primary concern is how the collector finds, and possibly updates, roots. Other tasks, such as finding pointers in heap objects and compacting the heap, can be managed entirely by the front-end run-time system (allocator and collector) with no support from the back end. C-- takes no responsibility for heap pointers passed to code written in other languages. It is up to the front end to pin such pointers or to negotiate changing them with the foreign code. We defer until Section 6.1 the question of how control is transferred from running C-- code to the garbage collector.

To help the collector find roots in global variables, the front end can arrange to deposit the addresses of such variables in a special data section. To find roots in local variables, the collector must walk the activation stack. For each activation handle a, it calls `GetDescriptor(&a, GC)` to get the garbage-collection descriptor deposited by the front end. The descriptor tells it how many variables there are and which contain pointers. For each pointer variable, it gets the address of that variable by calling `FindVar`. If the result is `NULL`, the variable is dead, and need not be traced. Otherwise the collector marks or moves the object the variable points to, and it may redirect the variable to point to the object's new location. Note that the collector need not know which variables were stored on the stack and which were kept in callee-saves registers; `FindVar` provides the location of the variable no matter where it is. Figure 2 shows a simple copying collector based on [1], targeted to the C-- run-time interface and the descriptors shown in Section 5.3.

```
struct gc_descriptor {
  unsigned var_count;
  char heap_ptr[1];
};

void gc(void) {
  activation a;

  FirstActivation(tcb, &a);
  for (;;) {
    struct gc_descriptor *d = GetDescriptor(&a, GC);
    if (d != NULL) {
      int i;
      for (i = 0; i < d->var_count; i++)
        if (d->heap_ptr[i]) {
          typedef void *pointer;
          pointer *rootp = FindVar(a, i);
          if (rootp != NULL) *rootp = gc_forward(*rootp);
                /* copying forward, as in Appel, if live */
        }
    }
    if (NextActivation(&a) == NULL)
      break;
  }
  gc_copy(); /* from-space to to-space, as in Appel */
}
```

Fig. 2. Part of a simple copying garbage collector

A more complicated collector might have to do more work to decide which variables represent heap pointers. TIL is the most complicated example we know of [38]. In TIL, whether a parameter is a pointer may depend on the value of another parameter. For example, a C-- procedure generated by TIL might look like this:

```
f( bits32 ty, bits32 a, bits32 b ) { ... }
```

The first parameter, `ty`, is a pointer to a heap-allocated type record. It is not statically known, however, whether `a` is a heap pointer. At run time, the first field of the type record that `ty` points to describes whether `a` is a pointer. Similarly, the second field of the type record describes whether `b` is a pointer.

To support garbage collection, we attach to `f`'s body a span that points to a statically allocated descriptor, which encodes precisely the information in the preceding paragraph. How this encoding is done is a private matter between the front end and the garbage collector; even this rather complicated situation is easily handled with no further support from C--.

5.5 Implementing the C-- Run-Time Interface

Can spans and the C-- run-time interface be implemented efficiently? By sketching a possible implementation, we argue that they can. Because the implementation is private to the back end and the back-end run-time system, there is wide latitude for experimentation. Any technique is acceptable provided it implements the semantics above at reasonable cost. We argue below that well-understood techniques do just that.

Implementing spans The span mappings of Section 5.3 take their inspiration from table mappings for exception handling, and the key procedure, `GetDescriptor`, can be implemented in similar ways [10]. The main challenge is to build a mapping from object-code locations (possible values of the program counter) to source-code location ranges (spans). The most common way is to use tables sorted by program counter. If suitable linker support is available, tables for different tokens can go in different sections, and they will automatically be concatenated at link time. Otherwise, tables can be chained together (or consolidated) by an initialisation procedure called when the program starts.

Implementing stack walking In our sketch implementation, the call stack is a contiguous stack of activation records. An activation handle is a static record consisting of a pointer to an activation record on the stack, together with pointers to the locations containing the values that the non-volatile registers[2] had at the moment when control left the activation record (Figure 3). `FirstActivation` initialises the activation handle to point to the topmost activation record on the stack and to the private locations in the C-- runtime that hold the values of registers. Depending on the mechanism used to suspend execution, the runtime might have values of all registers or only of non-volatile registers, but this detail is hidden behind the run-time interface. [27] discusses retargetable stack walking in Chapters 3 and 8.

The run-time system executes only when execution of C-- procedures is suspended. We assume that C-- execution is suspended only at a "safe point." Broadly speaking, a safe point is a point at which the C-- run-time system is guaranteed to work; we discuss the details in Section 6.2. For each safe point, the C-- code generator builds a statically-allocated *activation-record descriptor* that gives:

[2] The non-volatile registers are those registers whose values are unchanged after return from a procedure call. They include not only the classic callee-saves registers, but also registers like the frame pointer, which must be saved and restored but which aren't always thought of as callee-saves registers.

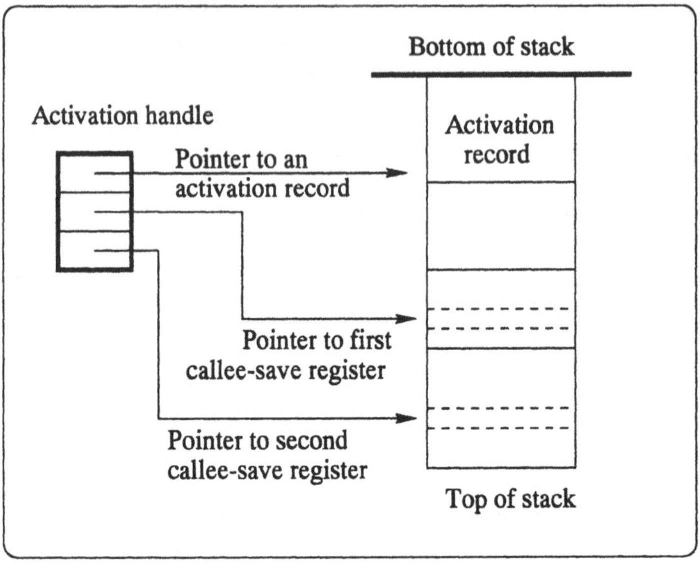

The activation handle points to an activation record, which may contain values of some local variables. Other local variables may be stored in callee-saves registers, in which case their values are *not* saved in the current activation record, but in the activation records of one or more called procedures. These activation records can't be determined until run time, so the stack walker incrementally builds a map of the locations of callee-save registers, by noting the saved locations of each procedure.

Fig. 3. Walking a stack

- The size of the activation record; `NextActivation` can use this to move to the next activation record.
- The liveness of each local variable, and the locations of live variables, indexed by variable number. The "location" of a live variable might be an offset within the activation record, or it might be the name of a callee-saves register. `GetVar` uses this "location" to find the address of the true memory location containing the variable's value, either by computing an address within the activation record itself, or by returning the address of the location holding the appropriate callee-saves register, as recorded in the activation handle (Figure 3).
- If the safe point is a call site, the locations where the callee is expected to put results returned from the call.
- The locations where the caller's callee-saves registers may be found. Again, these may be locations within the activation record, or they may be *this* activation's callee-saves registers. `NextActivation` uses this information to update the pointers-to-callee-saves-registers in the activation handle.

The C-- runtime can map activations to descriptors using the same mechanism it uses to implement the span mappings of Section 5.3. The run-time interface can cache these descriptors in the activation handle, so the lookup need be done only when `NextActivation` is called, i.e., when walking the stack. An alternative that avoids the lookup is to store a pointer to the descriptor in the code space, immediately following the call, and for the call to return to the instruction after the pointer. The SPARC C calling convention uses a similar trick for functions returning structures [32, Appendix D].

The details of descriptors and mapping of activations to descriptors are important for performance. At issue is the space overhead of storing descriptors and maps, and the time overhead of finding descriptors that correspond to PCs. [19] suggests that sharing descriptors between different call sites has a significant impact on performance. Because these details are private between the back end and the back-end run-time system, we can experiment with different techniques without changing the approach, the run-time interface, or the front end.

6 Refining the Design

The basic idea of providing a run-time interface that allows the state of a suspended C-- computation to be inspected and modified seems quite flexible and robust. But working out the detailed application of this idea to a variety of run-time services, and specifying precisely what the semantics of the resulting language is, remains challenging. In this section we elaborate some of the details that were not covered in the preceding section, and discuss mechanisms that support run-time services other than garbage collection. Our design is not finalised, so this section is somewhat speculative.

6.1 Suspension and Introspection

All our intended high-level run-time services must be able to suspend a C-- computation, inspect its state, and modify it, before resuming execution.

In many implementations of high-level languages, the run-time system runs on the same physical stack as the program itself. In such implementations, walking the stack or unwinding the stack requires a thorough understanding of system calling conventions, especially if an interrupt can cause a transfer of control from generated code to the run-time system. We prefer not to expose this implementation technique through the C-- run-time interface, but to take a more abstract view. The C-- runtime therefore operates as if the generated code and the run-time system run on separate stacks, as separate threads:

- The *system thread* runs on the *system stack* supplied by the operating system. The front-end run-time system runs in the system thread, and it can easily inspect and modify the state of the C-- thread.
- The C-- *thread* runs on a separate C-- *stack*. When execution of the C-- thread is suspended, the state of the C-- thread is saved in the C-- *thread-control block*, or TCB.

We have to say how a C-- thread is created, and how control is transferred between the system thread and a C-- thread.

- The system thread calls InitTCB to create a new thread. In addition to passing the program counter for a C-- procedure without parameters, the system thread must provide space for a stack on which the thread can execute, as well as space for a thread-control block.
- The system thread calls Resume to transfer control to a suspended C-- thread.
- Execution of a C-- thread continues until that thread calls the C-- procedure yield, which suspends execution of the C-- thread and causes a return from the system thread's Resume call. The C-- thread passes a *yield code*, which is returned as the result of Resume.

For example, garbage collection can be invoked via a call to yield, when the allocator runs out of space. Here is how the code might look if allocation takes place in a single contiguous area, pointed to by a heap pointer hp, and bounded by heap_limit:

```
f( bits32 a,b,c ) {
  while (hp+12 > heap_limit) {
              yield( GC );     /* Need to GC */
  }
  hp = hp+12;
  ...
}
```

It may seem unusual, even undesirable, to speak of two "threads" in a completely sequential setting. In a more tightly-integrated system it would be more usual simply to *call* the garbage collector. But simply making a foreign call to the garbage collector will not work here. How is the garbage collector to find the top of the C-- portion of the stack that it must traverse? What if live variables (such as a, b, c) are stored in C's callee-saves registers across the call to the garbage collector? Such complications affect not only the garbage collector, but any high-level run-time service that needs to walk the stack. Our two-thread conceptual model abstracts away from these complications by allowing the system thread to inspect and modify a tidily frozen C-- thread.

Using "threads" does not imply a high implementation cost. Though we call them threads, "coroutines" may be a more accurate term. The system thread never runs concurrently with the C-- thread, and the two can be implemented by a single operating-system thread.

Another merit of this two-thread view is that it extends smoothly to accommodate multiple C-- threads. Indeed, though it is not the focus of this paper, we intend that C-- should support many very lightweight threads, in the style of Concurrent ML [29], Concurrent Haskell [23], and many others.

6.2 Safe Points

When can the system thread safely take control? We say a program-counter value within a procedure is a *safe point* if it is safe to suspend execution of the procedure at that point, and to inspect and modify its variables. We require the following precondition for execution in the front-end run-time system:

> A C-- thread can be suspended only at a safe point.

A call to `yield` must be a safe point, and because any procedure could call `yield`, the code generator must ensure that every call site is a safe point. This safe point is associated with the state in which the call has been made and the procedure is suspended awaiting the return. C-- does not guarantee that every instruction is a safe point; recording local-variable liveness and location information for every instruction might increase the size of the program by a significant fraction [35].

So far we have suggested that a C-- program can only yield control voluntarily, through a `yield` call. What happens if an interrupt or fault occurs, transferring control to the front-end run-time system, and the currently executing C-- procedure is not at a safe point? This may happen if a user deliberately causes an interrupt, e.g., to request that the stack be unwound or the debugger invoked. It may happen if a hardware exception (e.g., divide by zero) is to be converted to a software exception. It may happen in a concurrent program if timer interrupts are used to pre-empt threads. The answer to the question remains a topic for research; asynchronous pre-emption is difficult to implement, not only in C-- but in *any* system. [11] and [31] discuss some of the problems. One common technique is to ensure that every loop is cut by a safe point, and to permit an interrupted program to execute until it reaches a safe point. C-- therefore enables the front end to insert safe points, by inserting the C-- statement

```
safepoint;
```

6.3 Call-Site Invariants

In the presence of garbage collection and debugging, calls have an unusual property: *live local variables are potentially modified by any call.* For example, a compacting garbage collector might modify pointers saved across a call. Consider this function, in which a+8 is a common subexpression:

```
f( bits32 a ) {
  bits32[a+8] = 10;   /* put 10 in 32-bit word at address a+8 */
  g( a );
  bits32[a+8] = 0;    /* put 0  in 32-bit word at address a+8 */
  return;
}
```

If g invokes the garbage collector, the collector might modify a during the call to g, so the code generator must recompute a+8 after the call — it would be unsafe to save a+8 across the call. The same constraint supports a debugger that might change the values of local variables. Calls may also modify C-- values that are declared to be allocated on the stack.

A compiler writer might reasonably object to the performance penalty imposed by this constraint; the back end pays for compacting garbage collection whether the front end needs it or not. To eliminate this penalty, the front end can mark C-- parameters and variables as *invariant across calls*, using the keyword invariant, thus:

```
f( invariant bits32 a ) {
  invariant bits16 b;
  bits32 c;
  ...
  g( a, b, c );        /* "a" and "b" are not modified
                          by the call, but "c" might be */
  ...
}
```

The invariant keyword places an obligation on the front-end run-time system, not on the caller of f. The keyword constitutes a promise to the C-- compiler that the value of an invariant variable will not change "unexpectedly" across a call. The run-time system and debugger may not change the values of invariant variables.

If variables will not be changed by a debugger, a front end can safely mark non-pointer variables as invariant across calls, and front ends using mostly-copying collectors [3,4] or non-compacting collectors [9] can safely mark *all* variables as invariant across calls.

7 Exceptions and Other Services

In Section 4 we argued that many high-level run-time services share at least some requirements in common. In general, they all need to suspend a running C-- thread, and to inspect and modify its state. The spans of Section 5.3 and the run-time interface of Section 5.2 provide this basic service, but each high-level run-time service requires extra, special-purpose support. Garbage collection is enhanced by the invariant annotation of Section 6.3. Exception handling requires rich mechanisms for changing the flow of control. Interrupt-based profiling requires the ability to inspect (albeit in a very modest way) the state of a thread interrupted *asynchronously*. Debugging requires all of the above, and more besides. We believe that our design can be extended to deal with these situations, and that many of C--'s capabilities will be used by more than one high-level service. Here we give an indicative discussion of just one other service, exception handling.

Making a single back end support a variety of different exception-handling mechanisms is significantly harder than supporting a variety of garbage collectors, in part because exceptions alter the control flow of the program. If raising an exception could change the program counter arbitrarily, chaos would ensue; two different program points may hold their live variables in different locations, and they may have different ideas about the layout of the activation record and the contents of callee-saves registers. They may even have different ideas about which variables are alive and which are dead. In other words, unconstrained, dynamic changes in locus of control make life hard for the register allocator and the optimiser; if the program counter can change arbitrarily, there is no such thing as dead code, and a variable live anywhere is live everywhere.

Typically, handling an exception involves first unwinding the stack to the caller of the current procedure, or its caller, etc., and then directing control to an exception handler. Many of the mechanisms used for garbage collection are also useful for exception handling; for example, stack walking and spans can be used to find exactly which handler should catch a particular exception. But the mechanisms we have described so far don't allow for changes in control flow. C-- controls such changes by requiring annotations on procedure calls.

The key idea is that, in the presence of exceptions, *a call might return to more than one location, and every* C-- *program specifies explicitly all the locations to which a call could return.* In effect, a call has many possible continuations instead of just one. When an activation is suspended at a call site, three outcomes are possible.

- The call returns normally, and execution continues at the statement following the call.
- The call raises an exception that is handled in the activation, so the call terminates by transferring control to a different location in that activation.
- The call raises an exception that is not handled in the current activation, so the activation is aborted, and the run-time system transfers control to a handler in some calling procedure.

C--'s call-site annotations specify these outcomes in detail.

We are currently refining a design that supports suitable annotations, plus a variety of mechanisms for transfer of control [26]. Exception dispatch might unwind the stack one frame at a time, looking for a handler, or it might use an auxiliary data structure to find the handler, then "cut the stack" directly to that handler in constant time. Our design also permits exception dispatch to be implemented either in the front-end run-time system or in generated code. The C-- run-time system provides supporting procedures that can unwind the stack, change the address to which a call returns, and pass values to exception handlers.

8 Status and Conclusions

The core design of C-- is stable, and an implementation based on ML-RISC is freely available from the authors. This implementation supports the features described in Section 3, but it does not yet include the **span** directive or a C-- run-time system.

Many open questions remain. What small set of mechanisms might support the entire gamut of high-level language exception semantics? How about the range of known implementation techniques? Support for debugging is even harder than dealing with exceptions. Exactly what is the meaning of a breakpoint? How should breakpoints interact with optimization? What are the primitive "hooks" required for concurrency support? How should C-- cope with preemption?

These questions are not easily answered, but the prize is considerable. Reuse of code generators is a critically important problem for language implementors. Code generators embedded in C compilers have been widely reused, but the nature of C makes it impossible to use the best known implementations of high-level run-time services like garbage collection, exception handling, debugging, and concurrency — C imposes a ceiling on reuse.

We hope to break through this ceiling by taking a new approach: design a low-level, reusable compiler-target language *in tandem with* a low-level, reusable run-time system. Together, C-- and its run-time system should succeed in *hiding* machine-dependent details of calling conventions and stack-frame layout. They should eliminate the distinction between variables living in registers and variables living on the stack. By doing so, they should

- Permit sophisticated register allocation, even in the presence of a garbage collector or debugger.
- Make the results of liveness analyses available at run time, e.g., to a garbage collector.
- Support the best known garbage-collection techniques, and possibly enable experimentation with new techniques.

Although the details are beyond the scope of this paper, we have some reason to believe C-- can also support the best known techniques for exception handling, as well as supporting profiling, concurrency, and debugging.

Acknowledgements

We thank Xavier Leroy, Simon Marlow, Gopalan Nadathur, Mike O'Donnell, and Julian Seward for their helpful feedback on earlier drafts of this paper. We also thank Richard Black, Lal George, Thomas Johnsson, Greg Morrisett, Nikhil, Olin Shivers, and David Watt for feedback on the design of C--.

References

1. Appel, Andrew W. 1989 (February). Simple generational garbage collection and fast allocation. *Software—Practice & Experience*, 19(2):171–183.
2. Atkinson, Russ, Alan Demers, Carl Hauser, Christian Jacobi, Peter Kessler, and Mark Weiser. 1989 (July). Experiences creating a portable Cedar. *Proceedings of the '89 SIGPLAN Conference on Programming Language Design and Implementation, SIGPLAN Notices*, 24(7):322–329.

3. Bartlett, Joel F. 1988 (February). Compacting garbage collection with ambiguous roots. Technical Report 88/2, DEC WRL, 100 Hamilton Avenue, Palo Alto, California 94301.
4. Bartlett, Joel F. 1989a (October). Mostly-copying garbage collection picks up generations and C++. Technical Report TN-12, DEC WRL, 100 Hamilton Avenue, Palo Alto, California 94301.
5. Bartlett, Joel F. 1989b. SCHEME to C: A portable Scheme-to-C compiler. Technical Report RR 89/1, DEC WRL.
6. Benitez, Manuel E. and Jack W. Davidson. 1988 (July). A portable global optimizer and linker. In *ACM Conference on Programming Languages Design and Implementation (PLDI'88)*, pages 329–338. ACM.
7. Benton, Nick, Andrew Kennedy, and George Russell. 1998 (September). Compiling Standard ML to Java bytecodes. In *ACM Sigplan International Conference on Functional Programming (ICFP'98)*, pages 129–140, Balitmore.
8. Bernstein, Robert L. 1985 (October). Producing good code for the case statement. *Software Practice and Experience*, 15(10):1021–1024.
9. Boehm, Hans-Juergen and Mark Weiser. 1988 (September). Garbage collection in an uncooperative environment. *Software Practice and Experience*, 18(9):807–820.
10. Chase, David. 1994a (June). Implementation of exception handling, Part I. *The Journal of C Language Translation*, 5(4):229–240.
11. Chase, David. 1994b (September). Implementation of exception handling, Part II: Calling conventions, asynchrony, optimizers, and debuggers. *The Journal of C Language Translation*, 6(1):20–32.
12. Clausen, LR and O Danvy. 1998 (April). Compiling proper tail recursion and first-class continuations: Scheme on the Java virtual machine. Technical report, Department of Computer Science, University of Aarhus, BRICS.
13. Conway, ME. 1958 (October). Proposal for an UNCOL. *Communications of the ACM*, 1(10):5–8.
14. Diwan, A, D Tarditi, and E Moss. 1993 (January). Memory subsystem performance of programs using copying garbage collection. In *21st ACM Symposium on Principles of Programming Languages (POPL'94)*, pages 1–14. Charleston: ACM.
15. Franz, Michael. 1997 (October). Beyond Java: An infrastructure for high-performance mobile code on the World Wide Web. In Lobodzinski, S. and I. Tomek, editors, *Proceedings of WebNet'97, World Conference of the WWW, Internet, and Intranet*, pages 33–38. Association for the Advancement of Computing in Education.
16. George, Lal. 1996. MLRISC: Customizable and reusable code generators. Unpublished report available from http://www.cs.bell-labs.com/ george/.
17. Harbison, Samuel P. and Guy L. Steele, Jr. 1995. *C: A Reference Manual.* fourth edition. Englewood Cliffs, NJ: Prentice Hall.
18. Henderson, Fergus, Thomas Conway, and Zoltan Somogyi. 1995. Compiling logic programs to C using GNU C as a portable assembler. In *ILPS'95 Postconference Workshop on Sequential Implementation Technologies for Logic Programming*, pages 1–15, Portland, Or.
19. Liskov, Barbara H. and Alan Snyder. 1979 (November). Exception handling in CLU. *IEEE Transactions on Software Engineering*, SE-5(6):546–558.
20. Macrakis, Stavros. 1993 (January). *The Structure of ANDF: Principles and Examples.* Open Systems Foundation.
21. Novack, Steven, Joseph Hummel, and Alexandru Nicolau. 1995. *A Simple Mechanism for Improving the Accuracy and Efficiency of Instruction-level Disambiguation*, chapter 19. Lecture Notes in Computer Science. Springer Verlag.

22. Pettersson, M. 1995. Simulating tail calls in C. Technical report, Department of Computer Science, Linkoping University.
23. Peyton Jones, Simon L., A. J. Gordon, and S. O. Finne. 1996 (January). Concurrent Haskell. In *23rd ACM Symposium on Principles of Programming Languages (POPL'96)*, pages 295–308, St Petersburg Beach, Florida.
24. Peyton Jones, SL, D Oliva, and T Nordin. 1998. `C--`: A portable assembly language. In *Proceedings of the 1997 Workshop on Implementing Functional Languages (IFL'97)*, Lecture Notes in Computer Science, pages 1–19. Springer Verlag.
25. Peyton Jones, Simon L. 1992 (April). Implementing lazy functional languages on stock hardware: The spineless tagless G-machine. *Journal of Functional Programming*, 2(2):127–202.
26. Ramsey, Norman and Simon L. Peyton Jones. 1999. Exceptions need not be exceptional. Draft available from `http://www.cs.virginia.edu/nr`.
27. Ramsey, Norman. 1992 (December). *A Retargetable Debugger.* PhD thesis, Princeton University, Department of Computer Science. Also Technical Report CS-TR-403-92.
28. Reig, F and SL Peyton Jones. 1998. The `C--` manual. Technical report, Department of Computing Science, University of Glasgow.
29. Reppy, JH. 1991 (June). CML: a higher-order concurrent language. In *ACM Conference on Programming Languages Design and Implementation (PLDI'91).* ACM.
30. Serrano, Manuel and Pierre Weis. 1995 (September). Bigloo: a portable and optimizing compiler for strict functional languages. In *2nd Static Analysis Symposium*, Lecture Notes in Computer Science, pages 366–381, Glasgow, Scotland.
31. Shivers, Olin, James W. Clark, and Roland McGrath. 1999 (September). Atomic heap transactions and fine-grain interrupts. In *ACM Sigplan International Conference on Functional Programming (ICFP'99)*, Paris.
32. SPARC International. 1992. *The SPARC Architecture Manual, Version 8.* Englewood Cliffs, NJ: Prentice Hall.
33. Stallman, Richard M. 1992 (February). *Using and Porting GNU CC (Version 2.0).* Free Software Foundation.
34. Steele, Guy L., Jr. 1978 (May). Rabbit: A compiler for Scheme. Technical Report AI-TR-474, Artificial Intelligence Laboratory, MIT, Cambridge, MA.
35. Stichnoth, JM, G-Y Lueh, and M Cierniak. 1999 (May). Suppport for garbage collection at every instruction in a Java compiler. In *ACM Conference on Programming Languages Design and Implementation (PLDI'99)*, pages 118–127, Atlanta.
36. Taft, Tucker. 1996. Programming the Internet in Ada 95. In Strohmeier, Alfred, editor, *1996 Ada-Europe International Conference on Reliable Software Technologies*, Vol. 1088 of *Lecture Notes in Computer Science*, pages 1–16, Berlin. Available through `www.appletmagic.com`.
37. Tarditi, David, Anurag Acharya, and Peter Lee. 1992. No assembly required: compiling Standard ML to C. *ACM Letters on Programming Languages and Systems*, 1(2):161–177.
38. Tarditi, D, G Morrisett, P Cheng, C Stone, R Harper, and P Lee. 1996 (May). TIL: A type-directed optimizing compiler for ML. In *ACM Conference on Programming Languages Design and Implementation (PLDI'96)*, pages 181–192. Philadelphia: ACM.
39. Wakeling, D. 1998 (September). Mobile Haskell: compiling lazy functional languages for the Java virtual machine. In *Proceedings of the 10th International Symposium on Programming Languages, Implementations, Logics and Programs (PLILP'98)*, Pisa.

On Formalised Proofs of Termination of Recursive Functions *

Fairouz Kamareddine and François Monin

Department of Computing and Electrical Engineering,
Heriot-Watt University,
Edinburgh EH14 4AS, Scotland,
fairouz@cee.hw.ac.uk, monin@cee.hw.ac.uk

Abstract. In proof checkers and theorem provers (e.g. Coq [4] and *ProPre* [13]) recursive definitions of functions are shown to terminate automatically. In standard non-formalised termination proofs of recursive functions, a decreasing measure is sometimes used. Such a decreasing measure is usually difficult to find.

By observing the proof trees of the proofs of termination of recursive functions in *ProPre* (the system used in Coq's proofs of termination), [14] finds a decreasing measure which could be used to show termination in the standard non-formalised way. This is important because it establishes a method to find decreasing measures that help in showing termination. As the *ProPre* system made heavy use of structural rather than inductive rules, an extended more powerful version has been built with new proof trees based on new rules.

In this article, we show that the ordinal measures found in [14] lose the decreasing property in the extended *ProPre* system and then, set out to show that the extended *ProPre* system will still be suitable for finding measures required by other systems (e.g. NQTHM). We do this by showing that exist other measures that can be associated to the proof trees developed in the extended *ProPre* system that respect the decreasing property. We also show that the new parameterised measure functions preserve the decreasing property up to a simple condition.

1 Introduction

In the verification of programs defined on recursive data structures, that use automated deduction, an important property is that of termination. A recursively defined function terminates if there is a well-founded order such that each recursive call of the function decreases with respect to this order. Though the termination problem is undecidable, several methods have been proposed for studying the termination of functional programs. For example, measures are used in the well-known NQTHM system of Boyer-Moore [2,3], and in [6] the system can deal with measures based on polynomial norms. Though efficient, these methods need however the measures to be given by the user. Other automated

* Supported by EPSRC GR/L15685.

G. Nadathur (Ed.): PPDP'99, LNCS 1702, pp. 29–46, 1999.

systems [18,15,19] have been developed, these are fully automated but they use only fixed ordering or a lexicographic combinations of the ordering.

Another approach has been developed in the termination procedure of the Coq prover [4] implemented in the *ProPre* system [11]. The method is automated and builds formal proofs because it is based on the Curry-Howard isomorphism from which lambda-terms are extracted which compute the algorithms. In contrast with other methods as for instance in [3,6], a notion of right terminal state property for proof trees is introduced in the procedure instead of measures. It has been shown in [14] that once a termination proof is made, it is then possible to find a decreasing measure related to each proof tree. The measures characterize in some sense the orders found by the *ProPre* system (called *ramified measure*) which differ from the lexicographic combinations of one single fixed ordering. Moreover it has been shown that these measures could be automatically given for the NQTHM system.

However a difficult task for the system of [11] is to be able to establish the termination of the automated construction of the proof trees. A drawback of that system is that it is not easy to derive efficient rules in a formal context. More particularly, the method in [11] is restricted to one general structural rule and this implies the right terminal state property of proof trees to be limited.

To circumvent these drawbacks, the formal logical framework behind the method in [11], has been extended to give rise to a new system [12] using other rules and accommodated with a generalized induction principle. Furthermore an order decision procedure on terms has been introduced outside the proof trees that alleviate the search of right terminal state properties. As a consequence, the termination method can be used by the system in a far more efficient way and the class of formal termination proofs made in the system has been considerably enlarged.

The measures coming from the previous system can be also defined in the new system. But unfortunately they do not enjoy the decreasing property anymore. Therefore, the method of [14] cannot be used in the new *ProPre* system [12] to find suitable measures required by other systems such as NQTHM. We solve this problem in this paper by showing that there exist other measures that can be associated to the proof trees developed in the system respecting the decreasing property.

Moreover, the order decision procedure mentioned above, that is external to the formal proofs in the *ProPre* system, is based on the so-called size measure. So, this measure function could be easily changed or parameterised in the extended *ProPre* system. We also show that, up to a simple condition (Property 4.11), the decreasing property of measures will still hold.

Our work has the following advantages:

- We establish a method to find the measures needed to establish termination for recursive functions. We extend the system to a more powerful version while retaining the decreasing property of measures. This is important because non-formalised termination proofs usually rely on the decreasing property.

- As the extended version of *ProPre* used the advantageous order decision procedure which was isolated from the formal proofs (in contrast to being intertwined with them as in the earlier version of *ProPre*), this implied that the measure functions could be easily parameterised or changed. In this paper we show that those measure functions preserve the decreasing property up to a simple condition. This means that the measures (now in a larger class) found by the method of this paper can be used by systems such as NQTHM.

2 Preliminaries

We assume familiarity with basic notions of type theory and term rewriting. The following definition contains some basic notions needed throughout the paper.

Definition 2.1.

1. **Sorts, Functions, Sorted Signature** We assume a set S of *sorts* and a finite set $\mathcal{F}$ of *function symbols* (or *functions*). We use s, s_1, s_2, ..., s', s'', ... to range over sorts and $f, f_1, f_2, \dots, f', f'', \dots$ to range over functions. A *sorted signature* is a finite set $\mathcal{F}$ of functions and a set S of sorts.
2. **Types, Arities of functions and Constants** For every function $f \in \mathcal{F}$, we associate a *type* $s_1, \dots, s_n \to s$ with $s, s_1, \dots, s_n \in S$. The number $n \geq 0$ denotes the arity of f. A function is called *constant* if its arity is 0.
3. **Defined and Constructor Symbols** We assume that the set of functions $\mathcal{F}$ is divided in two disjoint sets $\mathcal{F}_c$ and $\mathcal{F}_d$. Functions in $\mathcal{F}_c$ (which also include the constants) are called *constructor symbols* or *constructors* and those in $\mathcal{F}_d$ are called *defined symbols* or *defined functions.*
4. **Variables** Let $\mathcal{X}$ be a countable set of variables disjoint from $\mathcal{F}$. We assume that for every variable is associated a sort.
5. **Terms over F and $\mathcal{X}$ of sort s: $\mathcal{T}(F,\mathcal{X})_s$** If s is a sort, F is a subset of $\mathcal{F}$ and $\mathcal{X}$ is a certain set of variables, then the set of terms over F and $\mathcal{X}$ (simply called terms) of sort s denoted $\mathcal{T}(F,\mathcal{X})_s$, is the smallest set where:
   (a) every element of $\mathcal{X}$ of sort s is a term of sort s,
   (b) if $t_1, \dots, t_n$ are terms of sort $s_1, \dots, s_n$ respectively, and if f is a function of type $s_1, \dots, s_n \to s$ in F, then $f(t_1, \dots, t_n)$ is a term of sort s.
   We use $t, l, r, u, v, t_1, l_1, r_1, t_2, \dots, t', l', r', t'', \dots$ to range over $\mathcal{T}(F,\mathcal{X})_s$. If $\mathcal{X}$ is empty, we denote $\mathcal{T}(F,\mathcal{X})_s$ by $\mathcal{T}(F)_s$. $\mathcal{T}(F,\mathcal{X}) = \bigcup_{s \in S} \mathcal{T}(F,\mathcal{X})_s$.
6. **Constructor Terms, Ground terms and Ground Constructor Terms** Recall the set of variables $\mathcal{X}$ and the set of functions $\mathcal{F} = \mathcal{F}_c \cup \mathcal{F}_d$.
   (a) Elements of $\mathcal{T}(\mathcal{F}_c,\mathcal{X})_s$, i.e., terms such that every function symbol which occurs in them is a constructor symbol, are called *constructor terms.*
   (b) Elements of $\mathcal{T}(\mathcal{F}_c \cup \mathcal{F}_d)_s$, i.e., terms in which no variable occurs, are called *ground terms.*
   (c) Elements of $\mathcal{T}(\mathcal{F}_c)_s$ i.e., terms which do not have any variables and where every function symbol which occurs in them is a constructor symbol, are called *ground constructor terms.*

7. **(Sorted) Equations** A *sorted equation* is a pair $(l, r)_s$ of terms l and r of a sort s. We always assume that the equation is sorted and hence, we may drop the term *sorted* and speak only of equations. An equation $(l, r)_s$ gives rise to a *rewrite rule* $l \rightarrow r$. Although a pair $(l, r)_s$ is oriented it will also be written $l =_s r$. When no confusion occurs, the sort may be discarded from the equation and we write (l, r), $l \rightarrow r$ and $l = r$. l (resp. r) are called the left (resp. right) hand side of the equation.
8. **Left-Linear Equations** An equation is *left-linear* iff each variable occurs only once in the left-hand side of the equation.
9. **Non-Overlapping Equations** A set of equations is *non overlapping* iff no left-hand sides unify each other.
10. **Specification or Constructor System** A *specification* of a function $f : s_1, \ldots, s_n \rightarrow s$ in $\mathcal{F}_d$ is a non overlapping set of left-linear equations $\{(e_1, e'_1)_s, \ldots, (e_p, e'_p)_s\}$ such that for all $1 \leq i \leq p$, e_i is of the form $f(t_1, \ldots, t_n)$ with $t_j \in \mathcal{T}(\mathcal{F}_c, \mathcal{X})_{s_j}$, $j = 1, \ldots, n$, and $e'_i \in \mathcal{T}(\mathcal{F}_c \cup \mathcal{F}_d, \mathcal{X})_s$. We use $\mathcal{E}$, $\mathcal{E}'$, ... to range over specifications.
11. **{Constructor, Ground, Ground Constructor} Substitution** A substitution σ is a mapping from the set $\mathcal{X}$ of variables to the set of terms $\mathcal{T}(\mathcal{F}, \mathcal{X})$, such that for every variable x, $\sigma(x)$ and x are of the same sort. A substitution σ is called a *constructor substitution* (respectively *ground substitution*, *ground constructor substitution*) if $\sigma(x)$ is a constructor term (respectively ground term, ground constructor term) for any variable x.
12. **Recursive Call** Let $\mathcal{E}$ be a specification of a function f with type $s_1, \ldots, s_n \rightarrow s$. A *recursive call* of f is a pair $(f(t_1, \ldots, t_n), f(u_1, \ldots, u_n))$ where $f(t_1, \ldots, t_n)$ is a left-hand side of an equation of f and $f(u_1, \ldots, u_n)$ is a subterm of the corresponding right-hand side.

3 The Extended *ProPre* System

The extended *ProPre* system deals with inductive types that are defined with second order formulas using first and second order universal quantification, implication and a general least fixed point operator on predicate variables. The last connective aims at improving the efficiency of the extracted programs (see [16]).

Unlike the previous system [11], a connector symbol $\upharpoonright$ is added whose meaning is a connective conjunction used with some restrictions but without any algorithmic counterpart. The last property is interesting because it first allows the programs not to carry out some unnecessary computations, and secondly it can easily support inductive methods (which was not the case in the previous system). Combined with the connector $\upharpoonright$, a binary relation symbol $\prec$ is added. It corresponds to a well-founded ordering on terms which is used for the inductive rule defined in the section.

Definition 3.1. The language is defined as follows:

1. **Terms** The terms of Definition 2.1.6 constitute the first order part.

2. **Data Symbols** For each sort s_i is associated a unary second order predicate said also data symbol and denoted by D_{s_i} or D_i, whose meaning is: $t \in \mathcal{T}(\mathcal{F}_c)_{s_i}$ iff $D_{s_i}(t)$ holds.
3. **Formulae** A formula is built as follows:
   (a) if D is a data symbol and t is a term then $D(t)$ is a formula,
   (b) if A is a formula and x is a variable, then $\forall x A$ is a formula,
   (c) if A is a formula and u, v are terms, then $A \upharpoonright (u \prec v)$ is a formula,
   (d) if A and B are formulas, then $A \to B$ is a formula.
   We use $A, B, P, F, F_1, F_2, \ldots$ to range over formulae.

Notation 3.2. We will use some convenient conventions:

1. $Du_{\prec t}$ is a shorthand for $D(u) \upharpoonright (u \prec t)$,
2. $\forall x A \to B$ denotes $\forall x(A \to B)$.
3. $F_1, \ldots, F_n \to F$ denotes $F_1 \to (F_2 \to \ldots \to (F_n \to F)) \ldots)$.
4. Let $P = F_1, \ldots, F_k, \forall x D'(x), F_{k+1}, \ldots, F_m \to D(t)$ be a formula, then $P_{-D'(x)}$ denotes the formula $F_1, \ldots, F_k, F_{k+1}, \ldots, F_m \to D(t)$.

Note that the later notation is correct as it will be used with Definition 3.4.

Definition 3.3. Let $f : s_1, \ldots, s_n \to s \in \mathcal{F}_d$. The *termination statement for f* is the formula: $\forall x_1(D_{s_1}(x_1) \to \ldots \to \forall x_n(D_{s_n}(x_n) \to D_s(f(x_1, \ldots, x_n))) \ldots)$, also written by Notation 3.2 as: $\forall x_1 D_1(x_1), \ldots, \forall x_n D_n(x_n) \to D(f(x_1, \ldots, x_n))$.

In the previous *ProPre* system, the proofs relied on two fundamental notions: the distributing trees and the right terminal state property. In the extended version, the distributing trees now include two new rules, said *Struct* and *Ind* rules defined in the section. The definition of the right terminal state property (Definition 3.8) is now more sophisticated due to the introduction of these rules.

The *ProPre* prover makes termination proofs, said I-proofs, with the help of some macro-rules (or *tactics*, or *derived rules*) of Natural Deduction for Predicate Calculus (see [9]). The set of the rules and the definition of I-proofs is described in [12]. Due to Proposition 3.9 below, we will only need here to define the *Struct*-rule and the *Ind*-rule which constitute the distributing trees in *ProPre*.

Although the earlier *ProPre* system can prove the termination of many algorithms, there are numerous interesting algorithms for whose there exist no proof trees. For instance, the example below illustrates that the use *Rec*-rule defined in [11] can lead to loss of efficiency. Let Tr be the sort *tree*, with the *leave* constant $le : Tr$ and the *branch* constructor $br : Tr, Tr \to Tr$. Consider the specification of the *flatten* function $flat : Tr \to Tr$ given by the following equations:

$$flat(le) = le$$
$$flat(br(le, a)) = br(le, flat(a))$$
$$flat(br(br(a_1, a_2), a)) = flat(br(a_1, br(a_2, a))).$$

While the specification cannot be proven to terminate in the previous system [11], the termination proof is now easily done in the extended system due to the new rules presented below. Note that a single ordering using for instance the size measure [18] is not sufficient for the termination proof because of the presence of the second recursive call. The $flatten$ can be proved to terminate using polynomial ordering [10], but these have to be given by the user [1]. Therefore methods have been developed in [5,17] that aim at synthesising polynomial orderings.

We now introduce the rules that are used in the extended system. Let be given a sort s. We then consider all the constants $c_1, \dots, c_p$ of type $:\rightarrow s$, and all the constructor functions $C_i : s_{i_1}, \dots, s_{i_k} \rightarrow s$, $(i_k \geq 1)$, $i \leq q$, whose range is s. Note that the above distinction between constants and the other constructors just corresponds to a question of presentation. Let also $F(x)$ be a formula where x, of sort s, is free in F. Then:

1. $\Phi_{c_i}(F)$ denotes $F[c_i/x]$, $i \leq p$,
2. $\Phi_{C_i}(F)$ denotes $\forall x_{i_1} D_{i_1}(x_{i_1}), \dots, \forall x_{i_k} D_{i_k}(x_{i_k}) \rightarrow F[C_i(x_{i_1}, \dots, x_{i_k})/x]$, $i \leq q$, where $x_{i_1}, \dots, x_{i_k}$ are not in F,
3. $\Psi_{C_i}(F)$ denotes $\forall x_{i_1} D_{i_1}(x_{i_1}), \dots, \forall x_{i_k} D_{i_k}(x_{i_k}), \forall z(Dz_{\prec C_i(x_{i_1},\dots,x_{i_k})} \rightarrow F[z/x]) \rightarrow F[C_i(x_{i_1}, \dots, x_{i_k})/x])$, $i \leq q$, where $z, x_{i_1}, \dots, x_{i_k}$ are not in F.

Definition 3.4. Let P be of the form $F_1, \dots, F_k, \forall x D(x), F_{k+1}, \dots, F_m \rightarrow D'(t)$. The induction rule for the sort s is a choice between the two following rules:

$$\frac{\Gamma \vdash \Phi_{c_i}(P_{-D(x)}) \; i \leq p, \; \Gamma \vdash \Phi_{C_j}(P_{-D(x)}) \; j \leq q}{\Gamma \vdash P} \; Struct(x)$$

$$\frac{\Gamma \vdash \Phi_{c_i}(P_{-D(x)}) \; i \leq p, \; \Gamma \vdash \Psi_{C_j}(P_{-D(x)}) \; j \leq q}{\Gamma \vdash P} \; Ind(x)$$

For instance the induction rule *Ind* on integers is:

$$\frac{\Gamma \vdash P_{-N(x)}(0) \quad \Gamma \vdash \forall y N(y), \forall z(Nz_{\prec sy} \rightarrow P_{-N(x)}(z)) \rightarrow P_{-N(x)}(sy)}{\Gamma \vdash P} \; Ind(x)$$

The *Struct* has to be considered as a reasoning by cases. The above rules lead the following

Definition 3.5. A formula F is called an *I-formula* iff F is of the form $H_1, \dots, H_m \rightarrow D(f(t_1, \dots, t_n))$ with D a data symbol and $f \in \mathcal{F}_d$ such that for all $i = 1, \dots, m$, H_i is of the form either $\forall x D'(x)$ or $\forall z(D'z_{\prec u} \rightarrow F')$, with D' a data symbol, F' an I-formula and u a term.
Furthermore a formula of the above form $H_i = \forall z(D'z_{\prec u} \rightarrow F')$ is called *a restrictive hypothesis* of F.

Note that the above definition is a recursive definition whose initial case can be obtained with "$H_i = \forall x D'(x)$". The *heart* $C(F)$ of the formula F will denote the term $f(t_1, \dots, t_n)$.

Though a restrictive hypothesis is not an I-formula, we will also say that H' is a restrictive hypothesis of another restrictive hypothesis $\forall z(D'z_{\prec s} \rightarrow F')$ if H' is a restrictive hypothesis of the I-formula F'. Finally $C(\forall z(D'z_{\prec s} \rightarrow F'))$ will be $C(F')$.

Definition 3.6. Let $\mathcal{E}$ be a specification of a function f of type $s_1, \ldots, s_n \rightarrow s$. $\mathcal{A}$ is a *distributing tree for* $\mathcal{E}$ iff $\mathcal{A}$ is a proof tree built only with the *Struct* rule and *Ind* rule such that:

1. its root is $\vdash \forall x_1 D_1(x_1), \ldots, \forall x_n D_n(x_n) \rightarrow D(f(x_1, \ldots, x_n))$ (termination statement).
2. if $\mathcal{L} = \{\Gamma_1 \vdash \theta_1, \ldots, \Gamma_q \vdash \theta_q\}$ is the set of $\mathcal{A}$'s leaves, then there exists a one to one application b: $\mathcal{L} \hookrightarrow \mathcal{E}$ such that $b(L) = (t, u)$ if and only if $L = (\Gamma \vdash \theta)$ where θ is an I-formula with $C(\theta) = t$.

One can see that the antecedents remain unchanged in the definition of the rules *Struct* and *Ind* in the *ProPre* system. Though this is not so usual, it turns out that the antecedent formulas are embedded in the consequents. So, as the context (i.e. the set of antecedents) is empty in the root of a distributing tree, there is no antecedent in each node of the tree. Therefore we will use the notation θ both for $\vdash \theta$ and for the formula itself. One notes that any formula in a distributing tree is an I-formula.

Before stating the right terminal state property that enjoy the distributing trees in the I-proofs developed in the *ProPre* system, we assume that there is a well founded ordering $\sqsubset$ on term corresponding to the interpretation of the relation symbol $\prec$ defined in the language. This ordering is made explicit in the next section. We also need the

Definition 3.7. We say that an I-formula or restrictive hypothesis P can be applied to a term t if $C(P)$ matches t according to a substitution σ such that for each variable x occurring free in P we have $\sigma(x) = x$.

Definition 3.8. Let $\mathcal{E}$ be a specification of a function f and $\mathcal{A}$ be a distributing tree for $\mathcal{E}$. We say that $\mathcal{A}$ satisfies *the right terminal state property* (r.t.s.p.) iff for all leaves $L = \theta$ of $\mathcal{A}$ with $e \in \mathcal{E}$ the equation such that $b(L) = e$ (b given in Definition 3.6) and for all recursive calls (t, v) of e, there exists a restrictive hypothesis $P = \forall z D z_{\prec s}, H_1, \ldots, H_k \rightarrow D(w)$ of θ and a such that P can be applied to v according to a substitution σ with:

1. $\sigma(z) \sqsubset s$ and
2. for all restrictive hypothesis H of P of the form $\forall y D' y_{\prec s'} \rightarrow K$ there is a restrictive hypothesis H_0 of θ of the form $\forall y D' y_{\prec s_0} \rightarrow K$ such that $\sigma(s') \sqsubseteq s_0$.

This characterization is due to the following proposition (see [12] for proof).

Proposition 3.9. There exists an I-proof for f iff there exists a distributing tree for f with the right terminal state.

Proposition 3.9 says that one can only focus on distributing trees that satisfy the right terminal state. So, as already mentioned, we do not explicit I-proofs here but we only consider distributing trees and the right terminal state properties.

4 Synthesising Ordinal Measures

The earlier system built proof trees which have the right terminal state property defined in [13]. It has been shown in [14] that one can extract an ordinal measure, which will be called R-measure, from each proof tree. The R-measure has the decreasing property if the proof tree satisfies the right terminal state property. This measure can be also defined against a proof tree with the new context. But the decreasing property of the R-measure is not valid anymore. A reason is that, as the system *ProPre* corresponds to an extension of the `Recursive Definition` of the Coq system, the existence of suitable measures does not correspond any longer to the R-measures. It turns out that if we want to retrieve the decreasing property, we need to extend the class of measures to other measures.

In this section we recall the definition of the R-measures but in the context of the extended system, and we present the theorem on the decreasing property of the measures that fails but which will be re-established. We then introduce the extended measures for which Theorem 1 holds again.

4.1 The R-measures

Before giving the ordinal measures we first introduce some definitions concerning the judgments in distributing trees.

Definition 4.1. Let $\mathcal{A}$ be a distributing tree. A branch $\mathcal{B}$ from the root θ_1 to a leaf θ_k will be denoted by $(\theta_1, x_1), \dots, (\theta_{k-1}, x_{k-1}), \theta_k$ where x_i $(1 \leq i < k)$, is the variable for which either the rule *Struct* or *Ind* is applied on θ_i.

Definition 4.2. Let $\mathcal{A}$ be a tree and θ a node of $\mathcal{A}$. The *height* of θ in $\mathcal{A}$, denoted by $\mathcal{H}(\theta, \mathcal{A})$, is the height of the subtree of $\mathcal{A}$ whose root is θ minus one.

According to the definition of a distributing tree $\mathcal{A}$, we have the two following straightforward facts.

Fact 4.3. Let $\mathcal{E}$ be a specification of a function f of type $s_1, \dots, s_n \to s$ and $\mathcal{A}$ be a distributing tree. For each $(t_1, \dots, t_n) \in \mathcal{T}(\mathcal{F}_c)_{s_1} * \dots * \mathcal{T}(\mathcal{F}_c)_{s_n}$ there exists one and only one leaf θ of $\mathcal{A}$ and a ground constructor substitution ρ such that $\rho(C(\theta)) = f(t_1, \dots, t_n)$.

Fact 4.4. For every branch of $\mathcal{A}$ from the root to a leaf $(\theta_1, x_1), \dots, (\theta_{k-1}, x_{k-1})$, θ_k and for all $i \leq j \leq k$, there exists a constructor substitution $\sigma_{j,i}$ such that $\sigma_{j,i}(C(\theta_i)) = C(\theta_j)$.

Definition 4.5. The *recursive length* of a term t of sort s is defined by:

1. if t is a constant c, then $lg(c) = 0$,
2. if $t = C(t_1, \dots, t_n)$ with $C : s_1, \dots, s_n \to s \in \mathcal{F}_c$ then $lg(t) = 1 + \sum_{s_j = s} lg(t_j)$.

Definition 4.6. Let $\mathcal{E}$ be a specification of a function $f : s_1, \dots, s_n \to s$ such that there exists a distributing tree $\mathcal{A}$ for $\mathcal{E}$. The *R-measure* $\Omega_R : \mathcal{T}(\mathcal{F}_c)_{s_1} * \dots * \mathcal{T}(\mathcal{F}_c)_{s_n} \to \omega^\omega$, where ω is the least infinite ordinal, is defined as follows:
Let $t = (t_1, \dots, t_n)$ be an element of the domain and θ be the leaf of $\mathcal{A}$ such that there is a substitution ρ with $\rho(C(\theta)) = f(t)$ (Fact 4.3). Let $\mathcal{B}$ be the branch $(\theta_1, x_1), \dots, (\theta_{k-1}, x_{k-1}), \theta$ of $\mathcal{A}$ from the root to θ, let $\sigma_{r,s}$ be the substitutions of Fact 4.4. Then $\Omega_R(t)$ is defined as the following ordinal sum:

$$\Omega_R(t) = \sum_{i=1}^{k-1} \omega^{\mathcal{H}(\theta_i, \mathcal{A})} * lg(\rho(\sigma_{k,i}(x_i))) \ ,$$

We now need some definitions before giving Theorem 1.

Definition 4.7. A finite sequence of positive integers q will be called a position, ϵ will denote the empty sequence and $\cdot$ the concatenation operation on sequences.

For each position q and sort s, we will assume there is a new variable of sort s indexed by q distinct from those of $\mathcal{X}$. The following definition allows us to state Theorem 1 below.

Definition 4.8. Let be a term t and q be a position, the term $[\![t]\!]_q$ is defined as follows: $[\![c]\!]_q = c$ if c is a constant, $[\![x]\!]_q = x$ if x is a variable, $[\![C(t_1, \dots, t_n)]\!]_q = C([\![t_1]\!]_{q \cdot 1}, \dots, [\![t_n]\!]_{q \cdot n})$ if $C \in \mathcal{F}_c$, and $[\![f(t_1, \dots, t_n)]\!]_q = x_q$ if $f \in F_d$.

Theorem 1. *Let $\mathcal{E}$ be a specification of a function $f : s_1, \dots, s_n \to s$ and $\mathcal{A}$ be a distributing tree $\mathcal{A}$ for $\mathcal{E}$ having the right terminal state property. The associated measure Ω_R then satisfies the decreasing property. That is to say, for each recursive call $(f(t_1, \dots, t_n), f(u_1, \dots, u_n))$ of $\mathcal{E}$ and for every ground constructor substitution φ we have: $\Omega_R(\varphi(t_1), \dots, \varphi(t_n)) > \Omega_R(\varphi([\![u_1]\!]_1), \dots, \varphi([\![u_n]\!]_n))$*

Unfortunately, though Theorem 1 holds in the context of R-proofs (see [14]), examples show that it fails in the current context. Consider, for instance, the simple example of the specification of the addition function $add : nat, nat \to nat$, defined with an unusual way illustrating our purpose.

$$\begin{aligned} & add(s(x), s(y)) = add(s(s(x)), y) \\ & add(0, y) = y \\ & add(s(x), 0) = s(x) \end{aligned}$$

There exists a tree which enjoys the right terminal state property that leads to the following measure: $\Omega_R(u, v) = \omega * lg(u) + lg(v)$. Obviously the decreasing property does not hold.

In the remaining of the section, we introduce new measures that enable the theorem to be restored.

4.2 The New Ramified Measures

As already mentioned, an ordering relation $\sqsubset$ on term is introduced in the extended system. In contrast to the previous system, this relation can be checked outside of the formal proofs and so can be easily modified independently of the logical framework of the system. The ordering relation is related to a measure on terms in the following way.

Definition 4.9. Assume a measure m on the terms ranging over natural numbers. Let $u, v \in \mathcal{T}(\mathcal{F}_c, \mathcal{X})_s$ for a given sort s. We say that $u \sqsubset v$ iff:

1) $m(u) < m(v)$, 2) $\mathcal{V}ar(u) \subseteq \mathcal{V}ar(v)$, 3) u is linear

A special measure, the so called size measure lgi, is used in the system and is defined as follows:

Definition 4.10. The *size measure* of a term t of sort s is given by:

1. if t is a constant or a variable, then $lgi(t) = 1$,
2. if $t = C(t_1, \dots, t_n)$ with $C : s_1, \dots, s_n \to s \in \mathcal{F}_c$ then $lgi(t) = 1 + lgi(t_1) + \dots + lgi(t_n)$

Note that Definition 4.13 uses only the value on constructor ground terms for the measure m, but this one is also defined on constructor terms because it is needed for the termination proofs of the *ProPre* system.
In order to be able to prove the decreasing property of the new ordinal measures defined below, we will only need to assume a property on the measure m.

Property 4.11. Let $u, v \in \mathcal{T}(F, \mathcal{X})_s$ such that $u \sqsubset v$. Then for all constructor substitutions σ, we have $m(\sigma(u)) < m(\sigma(v))$.

Note that the lemma obviously holds for lgi. For that, it is enough to remark that $lgi(t) - 1 \geq 0$ and $lgi(\sigma(t)) = lgi(t) + \#(x,t) * \sum_{x \in \mathcal{V}ar(t)} (lgi(\sigma(x)) - 1)$ for any term t, where $\mathcal{V}ar(t)$ denotes the set of variables which occur in t and $\#(x,t)$ is the number of the occurrences of the variable x in t.

It is now necessary to distinguish the sequents coming respectively from an application of the *Struct*-rule and the *Ind*-rule. Therefore we introduce the following:

Definition 4.12. Let θ be a judgment in a distributing tree $\mathcal{A}$ and θ' an immediate children of θ. We say that θ is *decreasing* and θ' is an Ind-judgment if one comes from the other using the *Ind* rule. The *test* function ξ is defined on each node as follows: $\xi(\theta)$ is 1 if θ is a decreasing judgment and 0 if not.

Definition 4.13. Let $\mathcal{E}$ be a specification of a function $f : s_1, \dots, s_n \to s$ such that there exists a distributing tree $\mathcal{A}$ for $\mathcal{E}$. The new *ramified measure* $\Omega_I : \mathcal{T}(\mathcal{F}_c)_{s_1} * \dots * \mathcal{T}(\mathcal{F}_c)_{s_n} \to \omega^{\omega}$, is defined as follows:

Let $t = (t_1, \ldots, t_n)$ be an element of the domain and θ be the leaf of $\mathcal{A}$ such that there is a substitution ρ with $\rho(C(\theta)) = f(t)$ (Fact 4.3). Let $\mathcal{B}$ be the branch $(\theta_1, x_1), \ldots, (\theta_{k-1}, x_{k-1}), \theta$ of $\mathcal{A}$ from the root to θ, let $\sigma_{r,s}$ be the substitutions of Fact 4.4. Then

$$\Omega_I(t) = \sum_{i=1}^{k-1} \omega^{\mathcal{H}(\theta_i, \mathcal{A})} * \xi(\theta_i) * m(\rho(\sigma_{k,i}(x_i))) .$$

The intuition would suggest to substitute only the measure m instead of the recursive lg in Definition 4.6. But once again, examples show that Theorem 1 fails in that case. It is now far from obvious that the new ordinal measures enjoy the decreasing property. However Theorem 1 now holds with the new measures. whose version is given below with Theorem 2

Theorem 2. *Let $\mathcal{E}$ be a specification of a function $f : s_1, \ldots, s_n \to s$ and $\mathcal{A}$ be a distributing tree $\mathcal{A}$ for $\mathcal{E}$ having the right terminal state property. The associated measure Ω_I then satisfies the decreasing property. That is to say, for each recursive call $(f(t_1, \ldots, t_n), f(u_1, \ldots, u_n))$ of $\mathcal{E}$ and for every ground constructor substitution φ we have: $\Omega_I(\varphi(t_1), \ldots, \varphi(t_n)) > \Omega_I(\varphi([\![u_1]\!]_1), \ldots, \varphi([\![u_n]\!]_n))$*

Proof: The proof is long but it can be derived from the main Proposition 5.25 below. The reader is referred to [8] for a detailed proof of Theorem 2. □

Now that we have Theorem 2, we can extract from an automated termination proof of the *flatten* function defined at Section 3 the following ordinal measure which has the decreasing property:

$$\Omega_I(le) = \omega \qquad \Omega_I(br(le, a)) = \omega * (1 + lgi(a))$$
$$\Omega_I(br(br(a, b), c) = \omega * (2 + lgi(a) + lgi(b) + lgi(c)) + 1 + lgi(a) + lgi(b).$$

5 The Analysis of the I-formulas

This section is devoted to the analysis of the I-formulas. Due to the shape of the distributing trees and the I-formula that appear in the branches, we need to introduce some definitions and to establish several lemmas which will is used for the proof of Theorem 2 and Proposition 5.25 .

Definition 5.1. For a term t and a subterm u of t that has only one occurrence in t, $u \triangleright t$ will denote the position of u in t.

Definition 5.2. $\mathcal{RH}(F)$ denotes the set of the restrictive hypotheses of an I-formula F and for $P = \forall z(Dz_{\prec s} \to F')$ with F' an I-formula, we define $\mathcal{RH}(P) = \mathcal{RH}(F')$. For P_i and P_j in $\mathcal{RH}(F)$ we say that P_i *is before* P_j if F can be written $P_1, \ldots, P_k \to D(t)$ with $1 \leq j < i \leq k$. Moreover, for a restrictive hypothesis P of F, then $\#(P, F) = 1 + card\{P' \in \mathcal{R}(F), P'\ before\ P\}$.

One can easily see that, if θ' is an immediate antecedent of θ in a distributing tree, then each restrictive hypothesis of θ corresponds to a restrictive hypothesis in θ'. A new restrictive hypothesis is also in θ' if the rule is *Ind.* Formally we have the following definition.

Definition 5.3. Let θ be a judgment in a distributing tree and θ' an immediate antecedent of θ. We define an injective application $\mathcal{R}es_{\theta',\theta} : \mathcal{R}(\theta) \hookrightarrow \mathcal{R}(\theta')$ with $\mathcal{R}es_{\theta',\theta}(P)$ the restrictive hypothesis P' in $\mathcal{R}(\theta')$ such that $\#(P',\theta') = \#(P,\theta)$.

$\mathcal{R}es_{\theta',\theta}(P)$ can be seen as the residual of P in θ' and therefore the application can be generalized to any antecedent θ' of θ using composition of applications.

Definition 5.4. For an Ind-judgment θ' in a distributing tree, the restrictive hypothesis P in θ such that $\#(P,\theta') = card(\mathcal{R}(\theta'))$ is called the *new hypothesis*, denoted by $\mathcal{N}(\theta')$. In particular, it is such that all restrictive hypotheses in θ' are before P.

Remark 5.5. We can remark that if θ is a decreasing judgment with x the induction variable and θ' an immediate antecedent then $x \triangleright C(\theta) = z \triangleright C(\mathcal{N}(\theta))$ where the new hypothesis $\mathcal{N}(\theta)$ is of the form $\forall z(Dz_{\prec s} \to H)$. This will be used for the proof of Proposition 5.25.

If θ' is an immediate antecedent of a decreasing judgment θ, we know that θ' is of the form: $\forall x_1 D_1(x_1), \ldots, \forall x_k D_k(x_k), \mathcal{N}(\theta') \to \theta_{-D(x)}[w/x]$, with $\mathcal{N}(\theta') = z(Dz_{\prec w} \to \theta_{-D(x)}[z/x])$. So, for a Ind-judgment θ', we can easily define the application $\mathcal{D}_{\theta'} : \mathcal{R}(\mathcal{N}(\theta')) \hookrightarrow \mathcal{R}(\theta')$ where $\mathcal{D}_{\theta'}(Q)$ is the restrictive hypothesis Q' of $\theta_{-D(x)}[w/x]$ with $\#(Q', \theta_{-D(x)}[w/x]) = \#(Q, \theta_{-D(x)}[z/x])$. We can say that $\mathcal{D}$ is a *duplication* of restrictive hypotheses.

Lemma 5.6. Let $P = \forall z(Dz_{\prec s}, H_1, \ldots, H_k \to D(t))$ be a restrictive hypothesis θ of a judgment in a distributing tree then
1) the variables of s are free in P and have no other occurrences in P,
2) the variables in P distinct of those in s are bounded in P.
3) s is a subterm of $C(\theta)$ and $s \triangleright C(\theta) = z \triangleright C(P)$.

Proof: See [12]. □

Definition 5.7. Let G and F be two restrictive hypotheses. We define a congruence relation as follows: F and G are said similar, denoted by $F \approx G$ if they are respectively of the form $\forall z(D(z)_{\prec s} \to H)$ and $\forall z(D(z)_{\prec t} \to H)$.

Lemma 5.8. Given an Ind-judgment θ in a distributing tree and P a restrictive hypothesis of $\mathcal{N}(\theta)$. Then $\mathcal{D}_\theta(P) \approx P$.

Proof: According to the form of $\mathcal{N}(\theta)$ (see the definition of $\mathcal{D}_{\theta'}$), we know that P and $\mathcal{D}_\theta(P)$ are of the form $\forall y(D'(y)_{\prec s'} \to H')[z/x]$ and $\forall y(D'(y)_{\prec s'} \to H')[w/x]$. Lemma 5.6 says that x does not occur in H (and may not possibly occur in s'). Therefore $P = \forall y(D'(y)_{\prec s'[z/x]} \to H')$ and $\mathcal{D}_\theta(P) = \forall y(D'(y)_{\prec s'[w/x]} \to H')$, thus $P \approx \mathcal{D}_\theta(P)$. □

Lemma 5.9. Let P be a restrictive hypothesis of θ in a distributing tree, and θ' an antecedent of θ. Then $\mathcal{R}es_{\theta',\theta}(P) \approx P$.

Proof: By induction on the branch between θ and θ'. □

Corollary 5.10. If θ is a judgment in a distributing tree, θ' an immediate antecedent of θ, and P a restrictive hypothesis of θ, then $\mathcal{R}(\mathcal{R}es_{\theta',\theta}(P)) = \mathcal{R}(P)$.

Proof: By Lemma 5.9, we have $P = \forall z(D(z)_{\prec s_1} \rightarrow F)$ and $\mathcal{R}es_{\theta',\theta}(P) = \forall z(D(z)_{\prec s_2} \rightarrow F)$. Thus $\mathcal{R}(P) = F = \mathcal{R}(\mathcal{R}es_{\theta',\theta}(P))$. □

Lemma 5.11. For all judgments θ in a distributing tree, then there does not exist two restrictive hypotheses similar in θ.

Proof: See [8] □

Definition 5.12. Let θ be a judgment in a distributing tree and $\theta_1, \ldots,$ $\theta_n = \theta$ the consecutive judgments from the root θ_1 to θ. Let P be a restrictive hypothesis of θ. We note $\mathcal{J}(P)$ the first integer j such that there is $Q \in \mathcal{R}(\theta_j)$ with $P = \mathcal{R}es_{\theta,\theta_j}(Q)$, which is correct since $\mathcal{R}_{\theta,\theta}(P) = P$.

Since every application $\mathcal{R}es_{\theta',\theta}$ is injective, $\mathcal{R}es^{-1}_{\theta',\theta}(P)$ will denote the antecedent of P with the assumption that P is in the image of the application.

Lemma 5.13. In the context of the previous definition, the rule between $\theta_{\mathcal{J}(P)}$ and $\theta_{\mathcal{J}(P)-1}$ is the *Ind*-rule, and $\mathcal{R}es^{-1}_{\theta,\theta_{\mathcal{J}(P)}}(P) = \mathcal{N}(\theta_{\mathcal{J}(P)})$.

Proof: The opposite leads to a contradiction with the definition of $\mathcal{J}(P)$. □

Corollary 5.14. Let P be a restrictive hypothesis of a judgment θ in a distributing tree. Then, using also Corollary 5.10, we have

$$\mathcal{R}(P) = \mathcal{R}(\mathcal{R}es^{-1}_{\theta,\theta_{\mathcal{J}(P)}}(P)) = \mathcal{R}(\mathcal{N}(\theta_{\mathcal{J}(P)})).$$

Definition 5.15. Let θ be a judgment in a distributing tree and P be a restrictive hypothesis of θ. Then we can now etasblish the following diagram and thereby define the application $\Upsilon_{P,\theta} : \mathcal{R}(P) \hookrightarrow \mathcal{R}(\theta)$, with $\Upsilon_{P,\theta} = \mathcal{R}es_{\theta,\theta_{\mathcal{J}(P)}} \circ \mathcal{D}_{\theta_{\mathcal{J}(P)}}$.

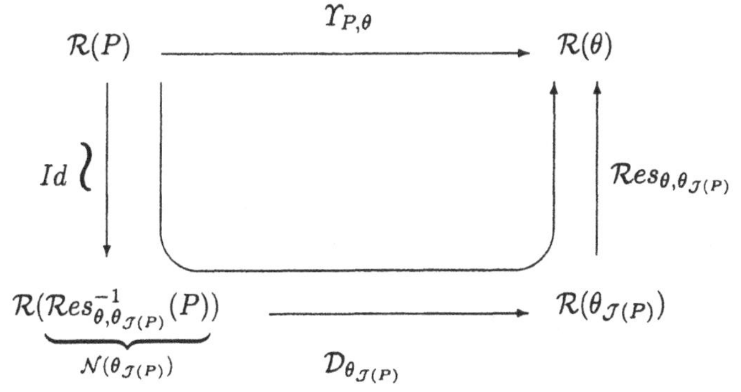

In the case where θ is an Ind-judgment and $P = \mathcal{N}(\theta)$, then $\theta_{\mathcal{J}(P)} = \theta$ and $\Upsilon_{P,\theta} = \mathcal{D}_\theta$. So, Υ can be seen as a generalization of $\mathcal{D}$ for all restrictive hypotheses of any θ.

Fact 5.16. We remark that $\Upsilon_{P,\theta}$ is injective by composition of injective applications. Moreover, according to Lemmas 5.8 and 5.9, $\Upsilon_{P,\theta}(Q) \approx Q$ for all $Q \in \mathcal{R}(P)$.

Lemma 5.17. For a restrictive hypothesis P of a judgment θ in a distributing tree and Q a restrictive hypothesis of P, we have $\mathcal{J}(P) > \mathcal{J}(\Upsilon_{P,\theta}(Q))$.

Proof: See [8] □

Lemma 5.18. Let $\mathcal{A}$ be a distributing tree for a specification of a function, having the right terminal state property. Let θ be a leaf of $\mathcal{A}$ and (t, v) be a recursive call of $C(\theta)$. In this context, if P is the restrictive hypothesis of θ holding Definition 3.8 of the r.t.s.p of $\mathcal{A}$ and H and H_0 holding the point 2) of Definition 3.8 with the same notations, then $\Upsilon_{P,\theta}(H) = H_0$ and $\mathcal{J}(P) > \mathcal{J}(H_0)$.

Proof: According to the point 2) of Definition 3.8, we have $H \approx H_0$. Furthermore, by Fact 5.16, $\Upsilon_{P,\theta}(H) \approx H$. Hence Lemma 5.11 gives us that $\Upsilon_{P,\theta}(Q) = H_0$ and then $\mathcal{J}(P) > \mathcal{J}(H_0)$ with Lemma 5.17. □

Definition 5.19. For any θ in a distributing tree and an antecedent θ' of θ, then $[\theta, \theta']_D$ (respectively $[\theta, \theta'[_I$) will denote the set of the decreasing judgments (respectively Ind-judgments) between θ and θ' (respectively without θ').

Fact 5.20. Let $\mathcal{E}$ be a specification of a function f and $\mathcal{A}$ be a distributing tree for $\mathcal{E}$. If θ_1 is the root of $\mathcal{A}$, that is to say the termination statement of f, and if θ is an Ind-judgment in $\mathcal{A}$, then $card(\mathcal{R}(\mathcal{N}(\theta))) = card([\theta_1, \theta[_R)$.

Proof: Since $card(\mathcal{R}(\theta)) = card(\mathcal{R}(\mathcal{N}(\theta)))+1$, it is actually enough to show that $card(\mathcal{R}(\theta)) = card([\theta_1, \theta]_R)$ which is then straightforward by induction on the number of judgments $\theta_1, \dots, \theta$. □

Fact 5.21. Let P and P' be two distinct restrictive hypotheses of a judgment θ, then $\mathcal{J}(P) \neq \mathcal{J}(P')$.

Proof: The opposite leads to a contradiction thanks to Lemma 5.13. □

Lemma 5.22. Let $\mathcal{A}$ be a distributing tree having the r.t.s.p. with the root θ_1. Let P be the restrictive hypothesis of a leaf θ_k in the definition of the r.s.t.p., then for all $\theta \in [\theta_1, \theta_{\mathcal{J}(P)}[_I$, there is one and only one $H \in \mathcal{R}(P)$ such that $\theta = \theta_{\mathcal{J}(\Upsilon_{P,\theta_k}(H))}$.

Proof: By Lemma 5.13, for all $H \in \mathcal{R}(P)$, $\theta_{\mathcal{J}(\Upsilon_{P,\theta_k}(H))}$ is an Ind-judgment. Furthermore Lemma 5.18 says that $\mathcal{J}(P) > \mathcal{J}(\Upsilon_{P,\theta_k}(H))$ and so $\theta_{\mathcal{J}(\Upsilon_{P,\theta_k}(H))}$

$\in [\theta_1, \theta_{\mathcal{J}(P)}[_I$. Let $U = \bigcup_{H \in \mathcal{R}(P)} \{\theta_{\mathcal{J}(\Upsilon_{P,\theta_k}(H))}\}$ included in $[\theta_1, \theta_{\mathcal{J}(P)}[_I$. As Υ_{P,θ_k} is injective, then, using Fact 5.21, we get $card(U) = card(\mathcal{R}(P))$. Now

$$\begin{aligned} Card([\theta_1, \theta_{\mathcal{J}(P)}[_I) &= card(\mathcal{R}(\mathcal{N}(\theta_{\mathcal{J}(P)}))) && \text{(Fact 5.20)} \\ &= card(\mathcal{R}(\mathcal{R}es^{-1}_{\theta,k\theta_{\mathcal{J}(P)}}(P))) && \text{(Lemma 5.13)} \\ &= card(\mathcal{R}(P)) && \text{(Corollary 5.14)} \end{aligned}$$

Hence $U = [\theta_1, \theta_{\mathcal{J}(P)}[_I$. □

Lemma 5.23. Let θ and θ' be two judgments in a distributing tree of a specification then $C(\theta)$ and $C(\theta')$ match the same term iff θ and θ' are in the same branch.

Proof: Fact 4.4 gives one sense, the other one is made assuming the opposite and using the fact that if a judgment does not match a term, then its antecedent do not neither. □

Lemma 5.24. Let θ be a judgment in a distributing tree of a specification and θ' an antecedent of θ. If P is a restrictive hypothesis of θ' such that $\theta_{\mathcal{J}(P)-1} \in [\theta, \theta'[_R$ then $C(\theta)$ matches $C(P)$.

Proof: by the previous lemma $C(\theta)$ matches $C(\theta_{\mathcal{J}(P)-1})$. Furthermore, let Q' denotes $\mathcal{R}es_{\theta',\theta_{\mathcal{J}(P)}}(P)$, then $Q \approx P$ with Lemma 5.9 and so $C(Q) = C(P)$. Now, since Q is the new hypothesis of $\theta_{\mathcal{J}(P)}$, it is easy to see that $C(\theta_{\mathcal{J}(P)-1})$ matches $C(Q)$. Hence $C(\theta)$ matches $C(P)$. □

We now state the main Proposition below that enables Theorem 2 to hold.

Proposition 5.25. Let $\mathcal{A}$ be a distributing tree of a specification $\mathcal{E}$ with the right terminal state property and (t, u) be an inductive call of $\mathcal{E}$. Let also $\mathcal{B} = (\theta_1, x_1), \ldots, (\theta_{k-1}, x_{k-1}), \theta_k$ be a branch of $\mathcal{A}$ with $C(\theta_k) = t$. Let P be a restrictive hypothesis of θ_k and σ^u be the substitution such that $\sigma^u(C(P)) = u$ with respect the r.t.s.p.. Then for each decreasing judgment θ_i in $\mathcal{B}$ which is a strict descendent of $\theta_{\mathcal{J}(P)-1}$ (i.e. $i < \mathcal{J}(P) - 1$), $C(\theta_i)$ (respectively $C(\theta_{\mathcal{J}(P)-1})$) matches u according to a substitution σ_i^u (respectively $\sigma^u_{\mathcal{J}(P)-1}$) and

$$m(\varphi \circ \sigma_i^u(x_i)) \leq m(\varphi \circ \sigma_{k,i}(x_i)),$$
$$m(\varphi \circ \sigma^u_{\mathcal{J}(P)-1}(x_{\mathcal{J}(P)-1})) < m(\varphi \circ \sigma_{k,\mathcal{J}(P)-1}(x_{\mathcal{J}(P)-1}))$$

for all ground constructor substitution φ (where $\sigma_{k,j}$ are given in Fact 4.4).

Proof: Let θ_i be a decreasing judgment with $i < \mathcal{J}(P) - 1$. By Fact 4.4, we know that $C(\theta_i)$ matches $C(\theta_{\mathcal{J}(P)-1})$ which matches also $C(P)$ according to Lemma 5.24 (with $\theta = \theta_{\mathcal{J}(P)-1}, \theta' = \theta_k$), and so $C(\theta_i)$ matches u.
Now, we are going to show the first inequality. Since θ_{i+1} is an Ind-judgment, by Lemma 5.22, there is a restrictive Q of P such that $\mathcal{J}_{\Upsilon_{P,\theta_k}(Q)} = i + 1$. Let $\mathcal{N}(\theta_{i+1}) = \forall z(Dz_{\prec s} \rightarrow G)$ be the new hypothesis of θ_{i+1} and let Q_0 be $\Upsilon_{P,\theta_k}(Q)$. We know that $Q \approx Q_0$, likewise $Q_0 \approx \mathcal{R}es^{-1}_{\theta_k,\theta_{\mathcal{J}(Q_0)}}(Q_0) = \mathcal{N}(\theta_{\mathcal{J}(Q_0)})$. Hence $Q \approx \mathcal{N}(\theta_{i+1})$ and we can write $Q = \forall z(Dz_{\prec s'} \rightarrow G)$ and $Q_0 = \forall z(Dz_{\prec s_0} \rightarrow G)$.

Now
$x_i \rhd C(\theta_i) = z \rhd C(\mathcal{N}(\theta_{i+1}))$ (Remark 5.5)
$= z \rhd C(Q)$ $(Q \approx \mathcal{N}(\theta_{i+1}))$
$= s' \rhd C(P)$ (Lemma 5.6).
Moreover $C(\theta_i)$ matches $C(P)$ which matches u. Then, with the previous equalities, we have $\sigma_i^u(x_i) = \sigma^u(s')$.
Furthermore:
$z \rhd C(Q) = z \rhd C(\Upsilon_{P,\theta_k}(Q))$ $(Q \approx \Upsilon_{P,\theta_k}(Q))$
$= s_0 \rhd C(\theta_k)$ (Lemma 5.6)
$= s_0 \rhd t$ $(C(\theta_k) = t)$.

With the inequalities we have $x_i \rhd C(\theta_i) = s_0 \rhd t$. Hence, since $C(\theta_i)$ matches $C(\theta_k) = t$, we get $\sigma_{k,i}(x_i) = s_0$.
Finally, point 2) of the right terminal state property says that $\sigma^u(s') \sqsubseteq s_0$, and so, by Property 4.11, $m(\varphi \circ \sigma^u(s')) \leq m(\varphi(s_0))$. That is to say $m(\varphi \circ \sigma_i^u(x_i)) \leq m(\varphi \circ \sigma_{k,i}(x_i))$

It remains to show the second inequality. We recall that $\theta_{\mathcal{J}(P)}$ is an Ind-judgment whose new hypothesis is $\mathcal{N}(\theta_{\mathcal{J}(P)}) = \mathcal{R}es^{-1}_{\theta_{\mathcal{J}(P)},\theta_k}(P) \approx P$. Then
$x_{\mathcal{J}(P)-1} \rhd C(\theta_{\mathcal{J}(P)-1}) = z \rhd C(\mathcal{N}(\theta_{\mathcal{J}(P)}))$ (Remark 5.5)
$= z \rhd C(P)$ $(C(\mathcal{N}(\theta_{\mathcal{J}(P)})) = C(P))$
$= s \rhd C(\theta_k)$ (Lemma 5.6)
$= s \rhd t$ $(C(\theta_k) = t)$.

Thus $\sigma_{k,\mathcal{J}(P)-1}(x_{\mathcal{J}(P)-1}) = s$.
Furthermore, we have seen for the first inequality that $C(\theta_{\mathcal{J}(P)-1})$ matches P which matches u, then by a previous equality, $\sigma^u_{\mathcal{J}(P)-1}(x_{\mathcal{J}(P)-1}) = \sigma^u(z)$. Now using point 1) of the right terminal state property, we have $\sigma^u(z) \sqsubset s$ which gives, by Property 4.11, $m(\varphi \circ \sigma^u(z)) < m(\varphi(s))$. Therefore $m(\varphi \circ \sigma^u_{\mathcal{J}(P)-1}(x_{\mathcal{J}(P)-1})) < m(\varphi \circ \sigma_{k,\mathcal{J}(P)-1}(x_{\mathcal{J}(P)-1}))$. □

6 Conclusion

While the measures found from the termination proofs of the recursive definition command of Coq were shown in [14] to be suitable for other systems such as the NQTHM of [2,3], they cannot be defined in the extended termination system without losing the decreasing property. We have solved the problem by showing the existence of other decreasing measures in the extended termination system in question (the new *ProPre* of [12]). Moreover, the new measures we found in this paper, enlarge the class of suitable measures in the sense that each recursive algorithm proven to terminate in the previous system *ProPre* [11] is also proven to terminate in the extended *ProPre* system [12].
The orders characterised by the measures differ from the lexicographic combinations of one fixed ordering [18,15,19]. We can also mention the work of [7] which supports the use of term orderings coming from the rewriting systems area especially those methods of [5,17] which aim at automatically synthesising suitable polynomial orderings for termination of functional programs.

There is now no more obstacle to provide the measures to other systems that require such measures. The investigations of formal proofs in this paper highlight new measures and advocate as in [14] a termination method based on ordinal measures.

References

1. A. Ben Cherifa and P. Lescanne. *Termination of rewriting systems by polynomial interpretations and its implementation.* Science of Computer Programming 9(2), 137-159, 1987.
2. R.S. Boyer and J S. Moore. *A computational logic*, Academic Press, New York, 1979.
3. R.S. Boyer and J S. Moore. *A computational logic handbook*, Academic Press, 1988.
4. C. Cornes *et al.*. The Coq proof assistant reference manual version 5.10. *Technical Report 077*, INRIA, 1995.
5. J. Giesl. *Generating polynomial orderings for termination proofs.* Proceedings of the 6th International Conference on Rewriting Techniques and Application, Kaiserlautern, volume 914 of LNCS, 1995.
6. J. Giesl. *Automated termination proofs with measure functions.* Proceedings of the 19th Annual German Conference on Artificial Intelligence, Bielefeld, volume 981 of LNAI, 1995.
7. J. Giesl. *Termination analysis for functional programs using term orderings.* Proceedings of the Second International Static Analysis Symposium, Glasgow, volume 983 of LNCS, 1995.
8. F.D. Kamareddine and F. Monin. *On Formalised Proofs of Termination of Recursive Function.* http://www.cee.hw.ac.uk/ fairouz/papers/research-reports/ppdp99full.ps.
9. J.L. Krivine and M. Parigot. Programming with proofs. *J. Inf. Process Cybern.*, EIK 26(3):149-167, 1990.
10. D.S. Lankford. On proving term rewriting systems are Noetherian. *Technical Report Memo MTP-3*, Louisiana Technology University, 1979.
11. P. Manoury. *A User's friendly syntax to define recursive functions as typed lambda-terms.* Proceedings of Type for Proofs and Programs TYPES'94, volume 996 of LNCS 996, 1994.
12. P. Manoury and M. Simonot. *Des preuves de totalité de fonctions comme synthèse de programmes.* PhD thesis, University Paris 7, 1992.
13. P. Manoury and M. Simonot. Automatizing termination proofs of recursively defined functions. *Theoretical Computer Science* 135(2): 319-343, 1994.
14. F. Monin and M. Simonot. An ordinal measure based procedure for termination of functions. To appear in *Theoretical Computer Science.*
15. F. Nielson and H.R. Nielson. Operational semantics of termination types. *Nordic Journal of Computing*, 3(2):144-187, 1996.
16. M. Parigot. Recursive programming with proofs. *Theoretical Computer Science* 94(2): 335-356, 1992.
17. J. Steinbach. Generating polynomial orderings. *Information Processing Letters*, 49:85-93, 1994.

18. C. Walther. Argument-bounded algorithms as a basis for automated termination proofs. *Proceedings of 9th International Conference on Automated Deduction*, Argonne, Illinois, volume 310 of LNCS, 1988.
19. C. Walther. On proving the termination of algorithms by machine. *Artificial Intelligence*, 71(1):101-157, 1994.

Argument Filtering Transformation

Keiichirou Kusakari, Masaki Nakamura, and Yoshihito Toyama

School of Information Science, JAIST
Tatsunokuchi, Ishikawa 923-1292, Japan
{kusakari,masaki-n,toyama}@jaist.ac.jp

Abstract. To simplify the task of proving termination of term rewriting systems, several elimination methods, such as the dummy elimination, the distribution elimination, the general dummy elimination and the improved general dummy elimination, have been proposed. In this paper, we show that the argument filtering method combining with the dependency pair technique is essential in all the above elimination methods. We present remarkable simple proofs for the soundness of these elimination methods based on this observation. Moreover, we propose a new elimination method, called the argument filtering transformation, which is not only more powerful than all the other elimination methods but also especially useful to make clear the essential relation hidden behind these methods.

Keywords: Term Rewriting System, Termination, Elimination Method, Dependency Pair, Argument Filtering

1 Introduction

Term Rewriting Systems (TRSs) can be regarded as a model for computation in which terms are reduced, using a set of directed equations. They are used to represent abstract interpreters of functional programming languages and to model formal manipulating systems used in various applications, such as program optimization, program verification and automatic theorem proving [5,9].

Termination is one of the most fundamental properties of term rewriting systems. While in general termination of TRSs is an undecidable property, several methods for proving termination have been developed. To simplify the task of proving termination of TRSs to which these methods cannot be directly applied, several elimination methods have been proposed. Elimination methods try to transform a given TRS into a TRS whose termination is easier to prove than the original one. The dummy elimination [6], the distribution elimination [13,16], the general dummy elimination [7] and the improved general dummy elimination [15] are examples of elimination methods.

Recently, Arts and Giesl proposed the notion of the dependency pair, which can offer an effective method for analyzing an infinite reduction sequence [1,2,3]. Using dependency pairs, we can easily show the termination property of TRSs to which traditional techniques cannot be applied. Since this method compares

G. Nadathur (Ed.): PPDP'99, LNCS 1702, pp. 47–61, 1999.

rewrite rules and dependency pairs by a weak reduction pair instead of a reduction order, to find an appropriate weak reduction pair for a given TRS is necessary. The argument filtering method introduced [4,8] allows us to make a weak reduction pair from an arbitrary reduction order.

In this paper, we first extend the argument filtering method by combining subterm relation. Next, we study the relation between the argument filtering method and various elimination methods. The key of our result is the observation that the argument filtering method combining with the dependency pair technique is essential in all the above elimination methods. Indeed, we present remarkable simple proofs for the soundness of these elimination methods based on this observation, though the original proofs presented in the literatures [6,7,13,15,16] are complicated and treated as rather different methods respectively. This observation also leads us to a new powerful elimination method, called the argument filtering transformation, which is not only more powerful than all the other elimination methods but also especially useful to make clear the essential relation hidden behind these methods. The main contributions of this paper are as follows:

(1) We show that the argument filtering method combining with the dependency pair technique can clearly explain in a uniform framework why various elimination methods work well.
(2) A new powerful elimination method, called the argument filtering transformation, is proposed. Since the transformation is carefully designed by removing all unnecessary rewrite rules generated by other elimination methods, it is the most powerful among these elimination methods.
(3) We make the relation clear among various elimination methods through comparing them with corresponding restricted argument filtering transformation. For example, the dummy elimination method can be seen as a restricted argument filtering transformation in which each argument filtering always removes all arguments, and the distribution elimination method restricts each argument filtering into collapsing one.

The remainder of this paper is organized as follows. The next section gives the definition of term rewriting systems. In section 3, we explain the dependency pair technique and introduce a new argument filtering method. Using these results, we show a general and essential property for elimination methods to be sound with respect to termination. In section 4, we propose the argument filtering transformation and show the soundness of this transformation. In section 5, we compare various elimination methods with the argument filtering transformation, and give simple proofs for the soundness of these elimination methods.

2 Preliminaries

We assume that the reader is familiar with notions of term rewriting systems [5].

A signature Σ is a finite set of function symbols, where each $f \in \Sigma$ is associated with a non-negative integer n, written by $arity(f)$. A set $\mathcal{V}$ is an enumerable set of variables with $\Sigma \cap \mathcal{V} = \emptyset$. The set of terms constructed from Σ and $\mathcal{V}$ is written by $\mathcal{T}(\Sigma, \mathcal{V})$. $Var(t)$ is the set of variables in t. We define $root(f(t_1, \ldots, t_n)) = f$. Identity of terms is denoted by $\equiv$. A substitution $\theta : \mathcal{V} \to \mathcal{T}(\Sigma, \mathcal{V})$ is a mapping. A substitution over terms is defined as a homomorphic extension. We write $t\theta$ instead of $\theta(t)$. A context is a term which has a special constant $\Box$, called a hole. A term $C[t]$ denotes the result of replacing t in the hole of C.

A rewrite rule is a pair of terms, written by $l \to r$, with $l \notin \mathcal{V}$ and $Var(l) \supseteq Var(r)$. A term rewriting system (TRS) is a set of rules. The set of defined symbols in a TRS R is denoted by $DF(R) = \{root(l) \mid l \to r \in R\}$. A reduction relation $\underset{R}{\to}$ is defined as follows: $s \underset{R}{\to} t \overset{\text{def}}{\iff} \exists\, l \to r \in R, \exists C[\;], \exists\theta\; (s \equiv C[l\theta] \wedge t \equiv C[r\theta])$. We often omit the subscript R whenever no confusion arises. A TRS R is terminating if there is no infinite sequence such that $t_0 \underset{R}{\to} t_1 \underset{R}{\to} t_2 \underset{R}{\to} \cdots$. The transitive-reflexive closure and the transitive closure of $\to$ are denoted by $\overset{*}{\to}$ and $\overset{+}{\to}$, respectively.

A strict order $>$ is a reduction order if $>$ is well-founded, monotonic ($s > t \Rightarrow C[s] > C[t]$) and stable ($s > t \Rightarrow s\theta > t\theta$). Note that a TRS R is terminating iff there exists a reduction order $>$ that satisfies $l > r$ for all $l \to r \in R$. A reduction order $>$ is a simplification order if $C[t] > t$ for all t and C ($\not\equiv \Box$). A TRS R is simply terminating if there exists a simplification order $>$ that satisfies $l > r$ for all $l \to r \in R$.

3 Soundness Condition for Transformation

In this section, we first explain the dependency pair and the argument filtering method, whose notions greatly extend the provable class of termination. Using these notions, we show a theorem, which makes a general and essential property clear for transformations of TRSs to be sound with respect to termination.

Definition 31. *[1,2,3] $\Sigma^\# = \{f^\# \mid f \in \Sigma\}$ is the set of marked symbols disjoint from $\Sigma \cup \mathcal{V}$. We define the root-marked terms by $(f(t_1, \ldots, t_n))^\# = f^\#(t_1, \ldots, t_n)$. The set of the dependency pairs of R, written by $DP^\#(R)$, is $\{\langle u^\#, v^\# \rangle \mid u \to C[v] \in R,\ root(v) \in DF(R)\}$. The set of the unmarked dependency pairs of R, written by $DP(R)$, is obtained by erasing marks of symbols in $DP^\#(R)$.*

Example 32. *Let $R = \{add(x, 0) \to x,\ add(x, s(y)) \to s(add(x, y))\}$. Then, $DP^\#(R) = \{\langle add^\#(x, s(y)), add^\#(x, y) \rangle\}$. and $DP(R) = \{\langle add(x, s(y)), add(x, y) \rangle\}$*

Definition 33. *A pair $(\gtrsim, >)$ of binary relations on terms is a weak reduction pair if it satisfies the following three conditions:*

- $\gtrsim$ is monotonic and stable
- $>$ is stable and well-founded
- $\gtrsim \cdot > \;\subseteq\; >$ or $> \cdot \gtrsim \;\subseteq\; >$

In the above definition, we do not assume that $\gtrsim$ is a quasi-order (reflexive and transitive) or $>$ is a strict order (irreflexive and transitive). This simplifies the design of a weak reduction pair. We should mention that this simplification does not lose the generality of our definition, because for a given weak reduction pair $(\gtrsim, >)$ we can make the weak reduction pair $(\gtrsim^*, >^+)$ in which $\gtrsim^*$ is a quasi-order and $>^+$ is a strict order. Note that $>$ is a reduction order if and only if $(>, >)$ is a weak reduction pair.

Theorem 34. *For any TRS R, the following three properties are equivalent.*

1. TRS R is terminating.
2. There exists a weak reduction pair $(\gtrsim, >)$ such that $\forall l \to r \in R.\ l \gtrsim r$ and $\forall \langle u, v\rangle \in DP(R).\ u > v$.
3. There exists a weak reduction pair $(\gtrsim, >)$ such that $\forall l \to r \in R.\ l \gtrsim r$ and $\forall \langle u^\#, v^\#\rangle \in DP^\#(R).\ u^\# > v^\#$.

Proof. $(1 \Rightarrow 2)$ We define $s \gtrsim t$ by $s \xrightarrow[R]{*} t$, and $s > t$ by $s \xrightarrow[R]{+} C[t]$ for some C. Then, it is trivial that $(\gtrsim, >)$ is a weak reduction pair such that $\forall l \to r \in R.\ l \gtrsim r$ and $\forall \langle u, v\rangle \in DP(R).\ u > v$. $(2 \Rightarrow 3)$ It is easily shown by identifying $f^\#$ with f. $(3 \Rightarrow 1)$ This case has already been shown in [1,2,3,4,8]. □

Note that the proofs for $(2 \Rightarrow 1)$ and for $(1 \Rightarrow 3)$ have already been shown in [10,14] and [4] [1], respectively.

The above theorem shows that the weak reduction pair plays an important role. To design a weak reduction pair, the argument filtering method introduced in [4,8] is very useful, which is defined as recursive program schemata [9]. In the next definition, we introduce a new argument filtering method by combining the subterm relation, which is more effective in our framework than original one.

Definition 35. *An argument filtering function is a function π such that for any $f \in \Sigma$, $\pi(f)$ is either an integer i or a list of integers $[i_1, \ldots, i_m]$ $(m \geq 0)$ where those integers $i, i_1, \ldots, i_m$ are positive and not more than arity(f). We can naturally extend π over terms as follows:*

$$\begin{cases} \pi(x) = x & \\ \pi(f(t_1, \ldots, t_n)) = \pi(t_i) & \text{if } \pi(f) = i \\ \pi(f(t_1, \ldots, t_n)) = f(\pi(t_{i_1}), \ldots, \pi(t_{i_m})) & \text{if } \pi(f) = [i_1, \ldots, i_m] \end{cases}$$

For any argument filtering function π and any reduction order $>$, we define the pair $(\gtrsim_\pi, >_\pi)$ as follows:

$$s \gtrsim_\pi t \overset{\text{def}}{\iff} \pi(s) > \pi(t) \ \ or \ \ \pi(s) \equiv \pi(t)$$

$$s >_\pi t \overset{\text{def}}{\iff} \exists C.\ \pi(s) > C[\pi(t)] \ \ or \ \ \exists C \not\equiv \Box.\ \pi(s) \equiv C[\pi(t)]$$

[1] The proof for $(1 \Rightarrow 3)$ in [4] is based on the claim that if R is terminating then so is $R \cup DP^\#(R)$. However, the same proof method can not work well for $(1 \Rightarrow 2)$, because the termination of R does not ensure that of $R \cup DP(R)$ [11].

We hereafter assume that if $\pi(f)$ is not defined explicitly then it is intended to be $[1, \ldots, arity(f)]$.

Example 36. *Let* $t \equiv f(e(e'(0,1),2), e''(3,4,5))$, $\pi(e) = 1$, $\pi(e') = []$ *and* $\pi(e'') = [1,3]$. *Then,* $\pi(t) = f(e', e''(3,5))$.

Theorem 37. *Let* $>$ *be a reduction order and* π *an argument filtering function. Then, the pair* $(\gtrsim_\pi, >_\pi)$ *is a weak reduction pair.*

Proof. We define the substitution $\pi(\theta)$ as $\pi(\theta)(x) = \pi(\theta(x))$. Then, the claim $\pi(t\theta) \equiv \pi(t)\pi(\theta)$ is easily proved by induction on t. Using this claim, the stability of $\gtrsim_\pi$ and $>_\pi$ is easily proved. The other conditions are routine. □

Definition 38. *We define the including relation* $\sqsubseteq$ *as follows:*

$$R_1 \sqsubseteq R_2 \stackrel{\text{def}}{\iff} \forall l \to r \in R_1 . \exists C.\ l \to C[r] \in R_2$$

Theorem 39. *Let* R *be a TRS,* R' *a terminating TRS and* π *an argument filtering function. If* $\pi(R) \subseteq R'$ *and* $\pi(DP(R)) \sqsubseteq R'$ *then* R *is terminating.*

Proof. We define $>$ by $\overset{+}{\underset{R'}{\to}}$. The termination of R' ensure that $>$ is a reduction order. Using the argument filtering method, we design the weak reduction pair $(\gtrsim_\pi, >_\pi)$. It is obvious that $\forall l \to r \in R.\ l \gtrsim_\pi r$ and $\forall \langle u, v\rangle \in DP(R).\ u >_\pi v$. From theorem 34, R is terminating. □

Taking R and R' as a given TRS and a transformed TRS in elimination methods respectively, the above simple theorem can uniformly explain why elimination methods work well. This fact is very interesting because in the original literatures the soundness of these elimination methods were proved by complicated different methods. In the following sections, we will explain how theorem 39 simplifies the requirement conditions in elimination methods into acceptable one.

Corollary 310. *Let* R *be a TRS,* R' *a simply terminating TRS and* π *an argument filtering function. If* $\pi(R \cup DP(R)) \sqsubseteq R'$ *then* R *is terminating.*

Proof. As similar to theorem 39 by defining $>$ as $\overset{+}{\underset{R' \cup Emb}{\to}}$. □

4 Argument Filtering Transformation

In this section, we design a new elimination method, called the argument filtering transformation. This transformation is designed based on theorem 39, which is essential for elimination methods.

Definition 41. *(Argument Filtering Transformation) Let* π *be an argument filtering function. The argument filtering transformation* (AFT_π) *is defined as follows:*

$$- \begin{cases} dec_\pi(x) = \emptyset \\ dec_\pi(f(t_1,\ldots,t_n)) = \bigcup_{i\neq\pi(f)}\{t_i\} \;\cup\; \bigcup_{i=1}^{n} dec_\pi(t_i) & \textit{if } \pi(f) = i \\ dec_\pi(f(t_1,\ldots,t_n)) = \bigcup_{i\notin\pi(f)}\{t_i\} \;\cup\; \bigcup_{i=1}^{n} dec_\pi(t_i) & \textit{otherwise} \end{cases}$$

– $pick_\pi(T) = \{t \in T \mid \overline{\pi}(t)$ *includes some defined symbols of* $R\}$

$$\textit{where} \quad \overline{\pi}(f) = \begin{cases} [i] & \textit{if } \pi(f) = i \\ \pi(f) & \textit{otherwise} \end{cases}$$

– $AFT_\pi(R) = \pi(R) \cup \{\pi(l) \to \pi(r') \mid l \to r \in R,\ r' \in pick_\pi(dec_\pi(r))\}$

Example 42. *Let*

$$R = \{f(x, f(x,x)) \to f(e(e'(0,1,2),3), e''(f(4,5),6)),\ 4 \to 1,\ 5 \to 1\}.$$

Here, $DF(R) = \{f,4,5\}$. *Let* $\pi(e) = []$, $\pi(e') = [1,3]$, $\pi(e'') = 2$ *and* $r \equiv f(e(e'(0,1,2),3), e''(f(4,5),6))$. *Then, we obtain* $AFT_\pi(R)$ *as follows (Fig.1):*

$$\begin{aligned} \pi(r) &= f(e,6) \\ dec_\pi(r) &= \{e'(0,1,2),\ 1,\ 3,\ f(4,5)\} \\ pick(dec_\pi(r)) &= \{f(4,5)\} \\ \pi(R) &= \{f(x,f(x,x)) \to f(e,6),\ 4 \to 1,\ 5 \to 1\} \\ AFT_\pi(R) &= \pi(R) \cup \{\, f(x,f(x,x)) \to f(4,5)\,\} \end{aligned}$$

The termination of $AFT_\pi(R)$ *is easily proved by recursive path order [5]. Thus,* R *is terminating, if the argument filtering transformation is sound. The soundness is showed in this section. Note that the termination of* R *is not easily proved, because* R *is not simply terminating.*

Lemma 43. *Let* C *be a context and* t *a term. Then, there exists a context* D *such that* $D[\pi(t)] \in \pi(dec_\pi(C[t]))$ *or* $D[\pi(t)] \equiv \pi(C[t])$.

Proof. We prove the claim by induction on the structure of C. In the case $C \equiv \Box$, it is trivial. Suppose that $C \equiv f(t_1,\ldots,t_{i-1},C',t_{i+1},\ldots,t_n)$. From induction hypothesis, there exists a context D' such that $D'[\pi(t)] \in \pi(dec_\pi(C'[t]))$ or $D'[\pi(t)] \equiv \pi(C'[t])$. In the former case, it follows that $D'[\pi(t)] \in \pi(dec_\pi(C'[t])) \subseteq \pi(dec_\pi(C[t]))$. In the latter case, if $i = \pi(f)$ or $i \in \pi(f)$ then trivial. Otherwise, $D'[\pi(t)] \equiv \pi(C'[t]) \in \pi(dec_\pi(C[t]))$ from the definition of dec_π. □

Theorem 44. *If* $AFT_\pi(R)$ *is terminating then* R *is terminating.*

Proof. From the definition, $\pi(R) \subseteq AFT_\pi(R)$. Let $\langle u,v\rangle \in DP(R)$. From the definition of DP, there exists a rule $u \to C[v] \in R$. From lemma 43, there exists a context D such that $D[\pi(v)] \in \pi(dec_\pi(C[v]))$ or $D[\pi(v)] \equiv \pi(C[v])$. In the former case, from the definition of DP and $\overline{\pi}$, $root(\overline{\pi}(v))$ is a defined symbol. Thus, $D[\pi(v)] \in \pi(pick_\pi(dec_\pi(C[v])))$. Therefore, it follows that $\pi(u) \to D[\pi(v)] \in AFT_\pi(R)$. In the latter case, it follows that $\pi(u) \to D[\pi(v)] \in \pi(R) \subseteq AFT_\pi(R)$.

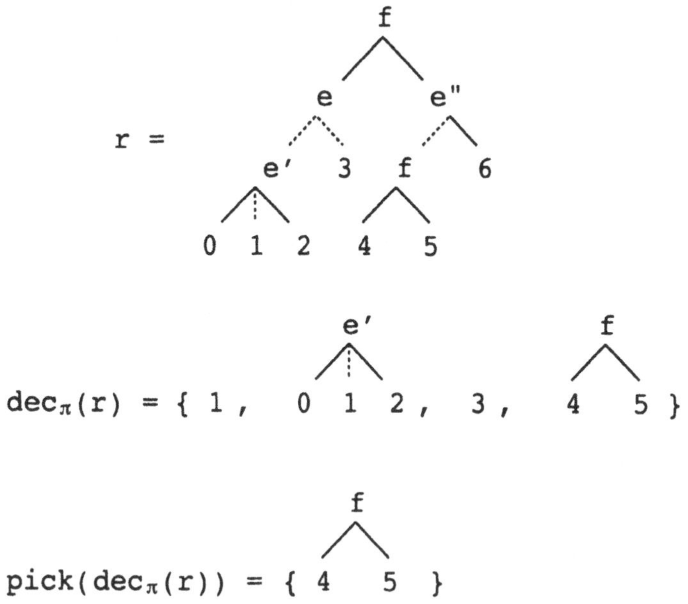

Fig. 1. Argument Filtering Transformation

From theorem 39, R is terminating. □

From the proof of the above theorem, it is obvious that the second argument $\{\pi(l) \to \pi(r') \mid l \to r \in R,\ r' \in pick_\pi(dec_\pi(r))\}$ of the definition of the argument filtering transformation AFT_π is used only to keep information of dependency pairs. Thus, introducing redundancy context does not destroy the soundness of argument filtering transformation. Therefore, we can define another argument filtering transformation $AFT_\pi^{\boldsymbol{C}_i}(R)$ as

$$AFT_\pi^{\boldsymbol{C}_i}(R) = \pi(R) \cup \{l_1 \to C_1[r_1], \ldots, l_n \to C_n[r_n]\}$$

where $\{l_1 \to r_1, \ldots, l_n \to r_n\} = \{\pi(l) \to \pi(r') \mid l \to r \in R,\ r' \in pick_\pi(dec_\pi(r))\}$ and $\boldsymbol{C}_i$ denotes the list of contexts $C_1, C_2, \ldots, C_n$.

Corollary 45. *If $AFT_\pi^{\boldsymbol{C}_i}(R)$ is terminating then R is terminating.*

5 Comparison with Other Eliminations

For proving termination, several transformation methods, which simplify that task, have been proposed. As examples of such transformations the dummy elimination [6], the distribution elimination [13,16], the general dummy elimination [7] and the improved general dummy elimination [15], were proposed. In this section, we compare these elimination methods to the argument filtering transformation. As a result, we conclude that the argument filtering transformation is a generalization of these elimination methods.

5.1 Dummy Elimination

Definition 51. *(Dummy Elimination)[6] Let e be a function symbol, called an eliminated symbol. The dummy elimination (DE_e) is defined as follows:*

– $$\begin{cases} cap_e(x) = x \\ cap_e(e(t_1, \ldots, t_n)) = \diamond \\ cap_e(f(t_1, \ldots, t_n)) = f(cap_e(t_1), \ldots, cap_e(t_n)) \quad \text{if } f \neq e \end{cases}$$

– $$\begin{cases} dec_e(x) = \emptyset \\ dec_e(e(t_1, \ldots, t_n)) = \bigcup_{i=1}^{n}(\{cap_e(t_i)\} \cup dec_e(t_i)) \\ dec_e(f(t_1, \ldots, t_n)) = \bigcup_{i=1}^{n} dec_e(t_i) \quad \text{if } f \neq e \end{cases}$$

– $DE_e(R) = \{cap_e(l) \to r' \mid l \to r \in R,\ r' \in \{cap_e(r)\} \cup dec_e(r)\}$

Example 52. *Let* $t \equiv f(e(0, g(1, e(2,3))), 4)$. *Then,* $cap_e(t) = f(\diamond, 4)$ *and* $dec_e(t) = \{0,\ 2,\ 3,\ g(1, \diamond)\}$ *(Fig.2).*

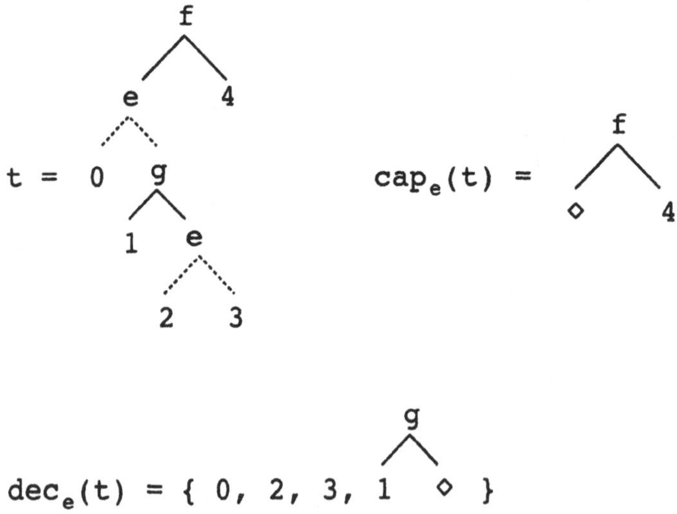

Fig. 2. Dummy Elimination

Proposition 53. *[6] If $DE_e(R)$ is terminating then R is terminating.*

For $\pi(e) = []$, we can treat the constant $\pi(e(\cdots))$ as $\diamond$.

Theorem 54. *For $\pi(e) = []$, $AFT_\pi(R) \subseteq DE_e(R)$.*

Proof. It suffices to show that $\pi(dec_\pi(t)) = dec_e(t)$ by induction on t. In the case $t \in \mathcal{V}$, it is trivial. Suppose that $t \equiv f(t_1, \ldots, t_n)$. In the case $f \not\equiv e$, $\pi(dec_\pi(f(t_1, \ldots, t_n))) = \bigcup_{i=1}^n \pi(dec_\pi(t_i)) = \bigcup_{i=1}^n dec_e(t_i) = dec_e(f(t_1, \ldots, t_n))$. In the case $f = e$, $\pi(dec_\pi(e(t_1, \ldots, t_n))) = \bigcup_{i=1}^n (\{\pi(t_i)\} \cup \pi(dec_\pi(t_i))) = \bigcup_{i=1}^n (\{cap_e(t_i)\} \cup dec_e(t_i)) = dec_e(e(t_1, \ldots, t_n))$. □

This theorem means that the argument filtering transformation is a proper extension of the dummy elimination, because $AFT_\pi(R)$ is terminating whenever $DE_e(R)$ is terminating.

5.2 Distribution Elimination

Definition 55. *(Distribution Elimination)[16]*
A rule $l \to r$ is a distribution rule for e if $l \equiv C[e(x_1, \ldots, x_n)]$ and $r \equiv e(C[x_1], \ldots, C[x_n])$ for some non-empty context C in which e does not occur and pairwise different variables $x_1, \ldots, x_n$. Let e be an eliminated symbol. The distribution elimination (DIS_e) is defined as follows:

- $E_e(t) = \begin{cases} \{t\} & \text{if } t \in \mathcal{V} \\ \bigcup_{i=1}^n E_e(t_i) & \text{if } t \equiv e(t_1, \ldots, t_n) \\ \{f(s_1, \ldots, s_n) \mid s_i \in E_e(t_i)\} & \text{if } t \equiv f(t_1, \ldots, t_n) \text{ with } f \not\equiv e \end{cases}$
- $DIS_e(R) = \{l \to r' \mid l \to r \in R \text{ is not a distribution rule for } e,\ r' \in E_e(r)\}$

Example 56. *Let $t \equiv f(e(0, g(1, e(2, 3))), 4)$.*
Then, $E_e(t) = \{f(0, 4),\ f(g(1, 2), 4),\ f(g(1, 3), 4)\}$ (Fig.3).

In general, the distribution elimination is not sound with respect to termination, i.e., termination of $DIS_e(R)$ does not ensure termination of R. Thus, the distribution elimination requires suitable restrictions to ensure the soundness.

Proposition 57. *[13,16]*

(a) *If $DIS_e(R)$ is terminating and right-linear then R is terminating.*
(b) *If $DIS_e(R)$ is terminating and non-constant symbol e does not occur in the left-hand sides of R then R is terminating.*

Lemma 58. *Let $\pi(e) = 1$. Under the condition (b), for any $l \to r \in AFT_\pi(R)$, there exists a context C such that $l \to C[r] \in DIS_e(R)$.*

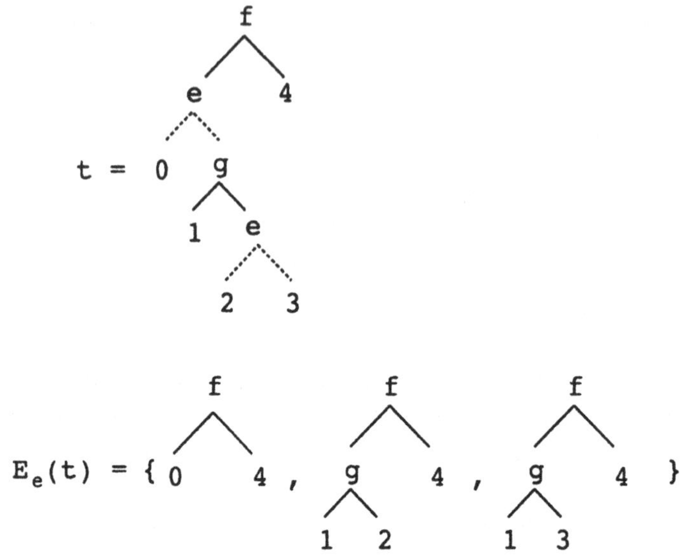

Fig. 3. Distribution Elimination

Proof. From the definition of AFT_π, for any $l \to r \in AFT_\pi(R)$ there exists a rule $l' \to C'[r'] \in R$ with $l \equiv \pi(l')$ and $r \equiv \pi(r')$. Thus, it suffices to show that for any t and C', there exists a context C such that $C[\pi(t)] \in E_e(C'[t])$. It is easily proved by induction on C'. □

Theorem 59. *Let $\pi(e) = 1$. Under the condition (b), the following properties hold.*

(i) $AFT_\pi^{C_i}(R) \subseteq DIS_e(R)$ for some C_i.
(ii) If $DIS_e(R)$ is simply terminating then $AFT_\pi(R)$ is simply terminating.

Proof. (i) It is trivial from lemma 58.
(ii) From the assumption and (i), $AFT_\pi^{C_i}(R)$ is simply terminating. Thus $AFT_\pi(R)$ is simply terminating since $AFT_\pi(R) \sqsubseteq AFT_\pi^{C_i}(R)$. □

5.3 General Dummy Elimination

For any $e \in \Sigma$, an e-status τ satisfy $\tau(e) = (\emptyset, 0)$ or (I, i) with $i \in I$.

Definition 510. *(General Dummy Elimination)[7]*
Let e be an eliminated symbol and $\tau(e) = (I, i)$. The general dummy elimination (GDE_e) is defined as follows:

– $$cap_i(t) = \begin{cases} t & \text{if } t \in \mathcal{V} \\ f(cap_i(t_1), \ldots, cap_i(t_n)) & \text{if } t \equiv f(t_1, \ldots, t_n) \wedge f \neq e \\ cap_i(t_i) & \text{if } t \equiv e(t_1, \ldots, t_n) \wedge i \neq 0 \\ \diamond & \text{if } t \equiv e(t_1, \ldots, t_n) \wedge i = 0 \end{cases}$$

– $$E_i(t) = \begin{cases} \{t\} & \text{if } t \in \mathcal{V} \\ \{f(s_1, \ldots, s_n) \mid s_j \in E_i(t_j)\} & \text{if } t \equiv f(t_1, \ldots, t_n) \wedge f \neq e \\ E(t_i) & \text{if } t \equiv e(t_1, \ldots, t_n) \end{cases}$$

– $$E(t) = \begin{cases} \{t\} & \text{if } t \in \mathcal{V} \\ \{cap_0(t)\} & \text{if } I = \emptyset \\ \bigcup_{j \in I} E_j(t) & \text{if } I \neq \emptyset \end{cases}$$

– $$dec(t) = \begin{cases} \emptyset & \text{if } t \in \mathcal{V} \\ \bigcup_{j=1}^{n} dec(t_j) & \text{if } t \equiv f(t_1, \ldots, t_n) \wedge f \neq e \\ \bigcup_{j=1}^{n} dec(t_j) \cup \bigcup_{j \notin I} E(t_j) & \text{if } t \equiv e(t_1, \ldots, t_n) \end{cases}$$

– $GDE_e(R) = \{cap_i(l) \to r' \mid l \to r \in R,\ r' \in E(r) \cup dec(r)\}$

Example 511. *Let $t \equiv f(0, e(f(1, e(2,3,4)), 5, 6))$ and $\tau(e) = (\{1,3\}, 1)$. Then, $E(t) = \{f(0,6),\ f(0, f(1,2)),\ f(0, f(1,4))\}$ and $dec(t) = \{5,\ 3\}$ (Fig.4).*

Proposition 512. *[7] If $GDE_e(R)$ is terminating then R is terminating.*

Theorem 513. *Let $\tau(e) = (I, i)$. In the case $\tau(e) = (\emptyset, 0)$, we define $\pi(e) = []$. In the case $\tau(e) = (I, i)$ with $i \in I$, we define $\pi(e) = i$. Then, the following properties hold.*

(i) $AFT_\pi^{C_i}(R) \subseteq GDE_e(R)$ for some C_i.
(ii) If $GDE_e(R)$ is simply terminating then $AFT_\pi(R)$ is simply terminating.

Proof. (i) In the case $\tau(e) = (\emptyset, 0)$, it is trivial that $DE_e(R) = GDE_e(R)$. Thus, $AFT_\pi(R) \subseteq GDE_e(R)$. In the case $\tau(e) = (I, i)$ with $i \in I$, as similar to theorem 59 (i) by replacing $E_e(r)$ with $dec(r) \cup E(r)$. (ii) As similar to theorem 59 (ii). □

We give the two following examples that the argument filtering transformation can be applied to, but the general dummy elimination can not be; the former is for showing that removing the unnecessary rules is effective and the latter is for showing that we can take well a defined function symbol as an eliminated symbol.

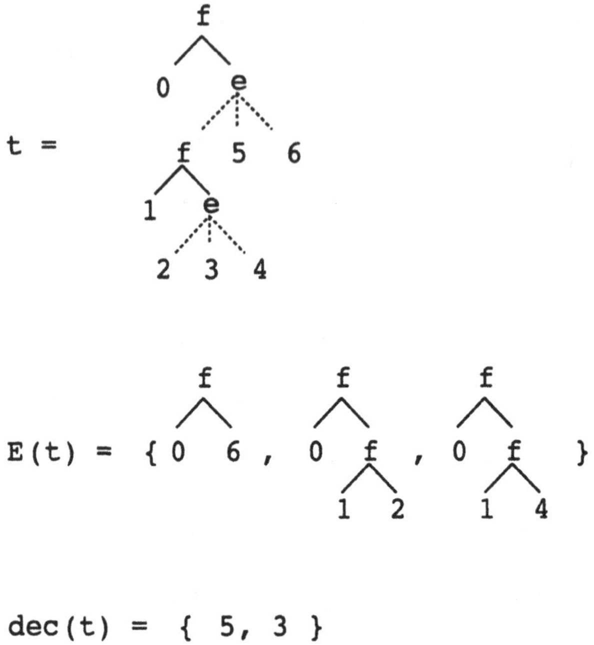

Fig. 4. General Dummy Elimination

Example 514. *Consider TRS*

$$R = \begin{cases} f(a) \to f(b) \\ \quad\;\; b \to g(a) \end{cases}$$

Let $\pi(g) = []$. *Then,*

$$AFT_\pi(R) = \begin{cases} f(a) \to f(b) \\ \quad\;\; b \to \diamond \end{cases}$$

The termination of $AFT_\pi(R)$ *is easily proved by recursive path order [5]. We easily observe that the dummy elimination, the distribution elimination and the general dummy elimination can not be applied. Indeed, the following systems are clearly not terminating.*

$\tau(g)$	$GDE_g(R)$	
$(\emptyset, 0)$	$f(a) \to f(b)$ $b \to \diamond$ $b \to a$	$(= DE_g(R))$
$(\{1\}, 1)$	$f(a) \to f(b)$ $b \to a$	$(= DIS_g(R))$

Note that termination of R *is not easily proved since* R *is not simply terminating.*

Example 515. *Consider TRS*

$$R = \begin{cases} f(f(x)) \to f(g(f(x), x)) \\ g(x, y) \to y \end{cases}$$

Let $\pi(g) = [2]$. *Then,*

$$AFT_\pi(R) = \begin{cases} f(f(x)) \to f(g(x)) \\ f(f(x)) \to f(x) \\ g(y) \to y \end{cases}$$

The termination of $AFT_\pi(R)$ *is easily proved by recursive path order. We easily observe that the general dummy elimination can not be applied. Indeed, the following systems are clearly not terminating.*

$\tau(g)$	$GDE_g(R)$
$(\emptyset, 0)$	$f(f(x)) \to f(\diamond)$ $f(f(x)) \to f(x)$ $f(f(x)) \to x$ $\diamond \to y$
$(\{1\}, 1)$	$f(f(x)) \to f(x)$ $f(f(x)) \to x$ $x \to y$
$(\{2\}, 2)$	$f(f(x)) \to f(x)$ $y \to y$
$(\{1,2\}, 1)$	$f(f(x)) \to f(f(x))$ $f(f(x)) \to f(x)$ $x \to y$
$(\{1,2\}, 2)$	$f(f(x)) \to f(f(x))$ $f(f(x)) \to f(x)$ $y \to y$

The dummy elimination and the distribution elimination cannot be applied, too. Note that termination of R is not easily proved since R is not simply terminating.

5.4 Improved General Dummy Elimination

Definition 516. *(Improved General Dummy Elimination)[15]*
The functions cap_i, E *and dec are the same as that of the general dummy elimination. In the case* $e \in DF(R)$, *we take* $IGDE_e(R) = GDE_e(R)$. *Otherwise,*

- $E'(t) = \{s \in E(t) \mid s \text{ includes some defined symbols of } R\}$
- $dec'(t) = \{s \in dec(t) \mid s \text{ includes some defined symbols of } R\}$
- $IGDE_e(R) = \{cap_i(l) \to r' \mid l \to r \in R,\ r' \in \{cap_i(r)\} \cup E'(r) \cup dec'(r)\}$

Proposition 517. *[15] If $IGDE_e(R)$ is terminating then R is terminating.*

Theorem 518. *Let $\tau(e) = (I, i)$. In the case $\tau(e) = (\emptyset, 0)$, we define $\pi(e) = []$. In the case $\tau(e) = (I, i)$ with $i \in I$, we define $\pi(e) = i$. Then, the following properties hold.*

(i) $AFT_\pi^{C_i}(R) \subseteq IGDE_e(R)$ for some C_i.
(ii) If $IGDE_e(R)$ is simply terminating then $AFT_\pi(R)$ is simply terminating.

Proof. As similar to theorem 513 □

At the end, we give an example that the argument filtering transformation can be applied to, but other elimination methods discussed here can not be.

Example 519. *Consider TRS*

$$R = \begin{cases} f(f(x)) \to f(g(f(x), x)) \\ f(g(x, y)) \to f(y) \end{cases}$$

Let $\pi(g) = [2]$. Then,

$$AFT_\pi(R) = \{f(f(x)) \to f(g(x)),\ f(f(x)) \to f(x),\ f(g(y)) \to f(y)\}.$$

The termination of $AFT_\pi(R)$ is easily proved by recursive path order. We easily observe that the improved general dummy elimination can not be applied. Indeed, the following systems are clearly not terminating.

$\tau(g)$	$IGDE_g(R)$
$(\emptyset, 0)$	$f(f(x)) \to f(\diamond)$ $f(f(x)) \to f(x)$ $f(\diamond) \to f(y)$
$(\{1\}, 1)$	$f(f(x)) \to f(x)$ $f(x) \to f(y)$
$(\{2\}, 2)$	$f(f(x)) \to f(x)$ $f(y) \to f(y)$
$(\{1,2\}, 1)$	$f(f(x)) \to f(f(x))$ $f(f(x)) \to f(x)$ $f(x) \to f(y)$
$(\{1,2\}, 2)$	$f(f(x)) \to f(f(x))$ $f(f(x)) \to f(x)$ $f(y) \to f(y)$

The dummy elimination, the distribution elimination and the general dummy elimination cannot be applied, too. Note that termination of R is not easily proved since R is not simply terminating.

Acknowledgments

We would like to thank Jürgen Giesl for introducing us the papers [4,8] and discussion on this work, Masahiko Sakai and the referees for their useful comments.

This work is partially supported by Grants from Ministry of Education, Science and Culture of Japan, #10139214 and #10680346.

References

1. T.Arts, Automatically Proving Termination and Innermost Normalization of Term Rewriting Systems, PhD thesis, Utrecht University, 1997.
2. T.Arts, J.Giesl, Automatically Proving Termination where Simplification Orderings Fail, LNCS 1214 (TAPSOFT 97), 261-272, 1997.
3. T.Arts, J.Giesl, Proving Innermost Normalization Automatically, LNCS 1232 (RTA 97), 157-171, 1997.
4. T.Arts, J.Giesl, Termination of Term Rewriting Using Dependency Pairs, *to appear in Theoretical Computer Science.*
5. F.Baader, T.Nipkow, Term Rewriting and All That, Cambridge University Press, 1998.
6. M.Ferreira, H.Zantema, Dummy Elimination: Making Termination Easier, LNCS 965 (FCT 95), 243-252, 1995.
7. M.Ferreira, Termination of Term Rewriting, Well-foundedness, Totality and Transformations, PhD thesis, Utrecht University, 1995.
8. J.Giesl, E.Ohlebusch, Pushing the Frontiers of Combining Rewrite Systems Farther Outwards, In Proceedings of the Second International Workshop on Frontiers of Combining Systems, FroCos '98, Applied Logic Series, Amsterdam, The Netherlands, October 1998.
9. J.W.Klop, Term Rewriting Systems, Handbook of Logic in Computer Science II, 1-112, Oxford University Press, 1992.
10. K.Kusakari, Y.Toyama, On Proving AC-Termination by AC-Dependency Pairs, Research Report IS-RR-98-0026F, School of Information Science, JAIST, 1998.
11. K.Kusakari, Y.Toyama, The Hierarchy of Dependency Pairs, Research Report IS-RR-99-0007F, School of Information Science, JAIST, 1999.
12. K.Kusakari, M.Nakamura, Y.Toyama, Argument Filtering Transformation, Research Report IS-RR-99-0008F, School of Information Science, JAIST, 1999.
13. A.Middeldorp, H.Ohsaki, H.Zantema, Transforming Termination by Self-Labelling, LNCS 1104 (CADE-13), 373-387, 1996.
14. C.Marche, X.Urbain, Termination of Associative-Commutative Rewriting by Dependency Pairs, LNCS 1379 (RTA 98), 241-255, 1998.
15. M.Nakamura, K.Kusakari, Y.Toyama, On Proving Termination by General Dummy Elimination, to appear in Trans. of IEICE (in Japanese).
16. H.Zantema, Termination of Term Rewriting: Interpretation and Type Elimination, Journal of Symbolic Computation 17, 23-50, 1994.

A Primitive Calculus for Module Systems*

Davide Ancona** and Elena Zucca

Dipartimento di Informatica e Scienze dell'Informazione
Via Dodecaneso, 35,16146 Genova (Italy)
{davide,zucca}@disi.unige.it

Abstract. We present a simple and powerful calculus of modules supporting mutual recursion and higher order features.
The calculus allows to encode a large variety of existing mechanisms for combining software components, including parameterized modules, extension with overriding of object-oriented programming, mixin modules and extra-linguistic mechanisms like those provided by a linker.
As usual, we first present an untyped version of our calculus and then a type system which is proved sound w.r.t. the reduction semantics; moreover we give a translation of other primitive calculi.

Introduction

Considerable effort has been recently invested in studying theoretical foundations and developing new forms of module systems; let us mention the wide literature about foundations and improvements of Standard ML's module system [18] (see e.g. [16,14]), the notions of *mixins* (see e.g. [7,11,13] and our previous work [5]) and *units* [12], the type-theoretical analysis of recursion between modules proposed in [10].

Two principles which seem to emerge as common ideas of all these approaches are the following.

First, a module system should have two linguistic levels, a *module language* providing operators for combining software components, constructed on top of a *core language* (following the terminology introduced with Standard ML) for defining module components. The module language should have its own typing rules and be as independent as possible from the core language; even more, it could be in principle instantiated over different core languages (see [17] for an effective demonstration).

Second, the modules should actually correspond to compilation units, and typing rules of the module language should formalize the *inter-check phase* described in [8]. Note that, indeed, operators of the module language could also correspond, in practice, to an extra-linguistic tool like a linker.

* Partially supported by Murst - Tecniche formali per la specifica, l'analisi, la verifica, la sintesi e la trasformazione di sistemi software and CNR - Formalismi per la specifica e la descrizione di sistemi ad oggetti.

** The final version of this paper was produced while visiting Oregon Graduate Institute, Portland, OR, USA.

G. Nadathur (Ed.): PPDP'99, LNCS 1702, pp. 62–79, 1999.

In this paper, we define a primitive module calculus based on these two principles and suitable for encoding various existing mechanisms for composing modules, in the same way as λ-calculus provides a theoretical basis for functional languages; in particular it supports mutually recursive modules and higher-level features (modules with module components), and it is parametric in the underlying core language.

A basic module of this calculus is written, using some syntactic sugar and considering here for simplicity the untyped version, as follows:

```
import X1 as x1, .., Xm as xm
export E1 as Y1, .., En as Yn
z1 = E'1, .., zp = E'p
```

We write in upper-case names of the components the module either *imports* from (*input* components X_1, .., X_m) or *exports* to (*output* components Y_1, .., Y_n) the outside. We write in lower-case variables used in definitions inside the module (the expressions E_1, .., E_n, E'_1, .., E'_p, which can be expressions of the core language or in turn module expressions if the module has module components). These variables can be either *deferred* (x_1, .., x_m), i.e. associated with some input component, or locally defined (z_1, .., z_p). This distinction between component names and variables is essential for keeping the module independent from the core level, as will be explained in more detail later.

Now, as example of a typical operator which can be easily encoded in our calculus, consider an operator *link* used for merging two or more modules. This operator can be thought as either an operation provided by a module language in order to define structured module expressions or an extra-linguistic mechanism to combine object files provided by a tool for modular software development. Independently from the view we take, we can informally define this operator as follows. For any pair of modules M_1 and M_2, *link*(M_1, M_2) is well-defined if (a) the set of the input components of M_1 (resp. M_2) is included in the set of the output components of M_2 (resp. M_1); (b) the sets of the output components of M_1 and M_2 are disjoint.

If the conditions (a) and (b) hold then *link*(M_1, M_2) corresponds to a module with no input components (called a *concrete module*) where each input component of one module has been bound to the definition of the corresponding output component of the other module.

For instance, let the modules BOOL and INT define the evaluation of some boolean and integer expressions in a mutually recursive way:

```
module BOOL is
 import IntEv as ext_ev
 export ev    as BoolEv
 fun ev(be)=if kind(be)==EQ then ext_ev(lhs(be))==ext_ev(rhs(be))
            else if ...
 fun lhs(be)= ...; fun rhs(be)= ...
 fun kind(be)= ...
end BOOL;
```

```
module INT is
 import BoolEv as ext_ev
 export ev     as IntEv
 fun ev(ie)=if kind(ie)==IF then
              if ext_ev(cond(ie)) then ev(ifBr(ie)) else ev(elseBr(ie))
             else if ...
 fun cond(ie)= ...; fun ifBr(ie)= ...; fun elseBr(ie)= ...
 fun kind(ie)= ...
end INT;
```

then *link*(BOOL, INT) intuitively corresponds to the module

```
module BOOL_INT is
 export iev as IntEv
 export bev as BoolEv
 fun bev(be)=if bkind(be)==EQ then iev(lhs(be))==iev(rhs(be))
              else if ...
 fun lhs(be)= ...;  fun rhs(be)= ...;
 fun bkind(be)= ...
 fun iev(ie)=if ikind(ie)==IF then
              if bev(cond(ie)) then iev(ifBr(ie)) else iev(elseBr(ie))
            else if ...
 fun cond(ie)= ...; fun ifBr(ie)= ...; fun elseBr(ie)= ...;
 fun ikind(ie)= ...
end BOOL_INT;
```

Note that the separation between component names and variables allows one to use the same identifier `ev` for the evaluation function in the two modules.

In the following, we define a simple language where module expressions are either basic modules which are, apart from syntactic sugar, those described above, or constructed by three operators (sum, reduct and freeze); moreover, a selection operator allows one to extract a module component (Sect.1.1). In Sect.1.2 we define a reduction semantics for the language. In Sect.2 we define a typed version of the calculus. In Sect.3 we illustrate how various existing constructs for composing modules can be encoded in the calculus, analyzing in particular the *link* operator shown in this introduction (Sect.3.1), parameterized modules (Sect.3.2) and object-oriented features (Sect.3.3). Finally, in the Conclusion we summarize the contribution of the paper and outline further work.

1 An Untyped Calculus

1.1 Syntax

The abstract syntax of the untyped calculus is given in Fig.1.

Lower case meta-variable x ranges over an infinite numerable set *Var* of *variables*, whereas upper case meta-variables X and Y range over an infinite numerable set *Name* of *component names*. This distinction at the level of the calculus reflects, at more practical level, the separation that a linker makes between *internal names* (what we call variables) and *external names* (what we call component names).

$E ::= K \mid M$	
$K ::= C$	| (plain core expressions)
$C[x_i \overset{i\in I}{\mapsto} E_i]$	(enriched core expressions)
$M ::= [\iota;\ o;\ \rho]$	| (basic module)
$E_1 + E_2$	| (sum)
${}_{\sigma^\iota}\vert E\vert_{\sigma^o}$	| (reduct)
$\mathit{freeze}_{\sigma^f}(E)$	| (freeze)
$E.X$	(selection)
$\iota ::= x_i \overset{i\in I}{\mapsto} X_i$	(ι-assignment)
$o ::= X_i \overset{i\in I}{\mapsto} E_i$	(o-assignment)
$\rho ::= x_i \overset{i\in I}{\mapsto} E_i$	(ρ-assignment)
$\sigma ::= X_i \overset{i\in I}{\mapsto} Y_i, Y_j{}^{j\in J}$	(renaming)

Fig. 1. Abstract syntax of the untyped calculus.

The meta-variable E ranges over the set of all expressions (denoted by $\mathcal{E}_E$) containing both the set of module expressions (denoted by $\mathcal{E}_M$) and of core language expressions possibly having module sub-terms (denoted by $\mathcal{E}_K$).

The meta-variable C ranges over the set of pure core expressions (denoted by $\mathcal{E}_C$). The syntax is parametric in $\mathcal{E}_C$; we assume that $\mathit{Var} \subseteq \mathcal{E}_C$.

In the production $K ::= C[x_i \overset{i\in I}{\mapsto} E_i]$ the substitution symbol is used at the meta-level, i.e. $C[x_i \overset{i\in I}{\mapsto} E_i]$ denotes the expression obtained from the core expression C by the usual capture-avoiding substitution of expressions E_i for free variables x_i ($i \in I$), enjoying all the standard properties. Expressions of this kind are needed for the (selection) reduction rule (see Fig.2) which otherwise would not be well-defined. We require that this production can be applied only under the conditions $C \notin \mathit{Var}$, $I \neq \emptyset$ and $x_i \in FV(C)$ for all $i \in I$, in order to rule out some trivial and redundant case.

The independence of the calculus from the core language is *effective*, in the sense that reduction and typing rules we will provide are constructed on top of those of the core language, so that a type-checker or an interpreter for the module language could be constructed in a modular way enriching one for the core level, as done in [17]. The prototype we have developed for the calculus is actually built following this idea (see the Conclusion).

A *basic module* corresponds to the ability of building a module by collecting a set of components. A basic module is made up of an assignment of *input names* to *deferred variables* (also called ι-assignment), of *expressions* to *output names* (also called o-assignment) and of *expressions* to *local variables* (also called ρ-assignment or substitution); all these assignments have a scope that is indicated by the square brackets delimiters. The notation $x_i \overset{i\in I}{\mapsto} X_i$ is used for representing the unique surjective and finite map ι s.t. $\mathit{dom}(\iota) = \{x_i \mid i \in I\}$, $\mathit{cod}(\iota) = \{X_i \mid i \in I\}$ and $\iota(x_i) = X_i$ for all $i \in I$. Notice that in opposition to the meta-substitution used for defining K, here the finite set of indexes I can be empty. We assume that for any i_1 and i_2 in I, if $i_1 \neq i_2$ then $x_{i_1} \neq x_{i_2}$. A similar notation is used also for the other kinds of assignments. Finally, we assume that the set of deferred and local variables are disjoint ($dom(\iota) \cap dom(\rho)$). On the contrary, the sets of input and output components can have a non empty intersection. Finally, note that the calculus supports higher order modules.

For instance, the basic module:

$$[ext\_ev \mapsto IntEv;\ BoolEv \mapsto ev;\ ev \mapsto e, lhs \mapsto ..., rhs \mapsto ..., kind \mapsto ...]$$

with

$$e = \lambda be.\text{if } kind(be) == EQ \text{ then } ext\_ev(lhs(be)) == ext\_ev(rhs(be)) \text{ else if...}$$

corresponds to the module BOOL defined in the Introduction.

As already mentioned, there exist several (both technical and methodological) motivations for keeping component names separated from variables.

Technically speaking, variables can be α-converted, in the sense that we can rename (in an appropriate way) the variables of an expression e without changing the observable semantics of e. The same cannot be done for component names (see Sect.1.2). Furthermore, if we want the module calculus to be independent from the core level, then component names have to be necessarily independent from the variables of the core language.

Methodologically speaking, this separation is a way of abstracting from the particular programming language a module comes from, even allowing composition of heterogeneous software components; variables correspond to the particular dialect spoken inside each module, whereas names represent a sort of lingua franca which allows modules to talk each other.

Analogous distinctions are those between program variables and labels that connects fragments in [14], those between variables and field/method names in the Abadi and Cardelli's object calculus [1] and those between names and identifiers in [16]; also in MzScheme's *units* [12] imported and exported variables have separate internal (binding) and external (linking) names, and the internal names within a unit can be α-renamed.

Modules can be merged together by means of the sum operator.

The reduct operator is a powerful form of renaming of the component names; input and output components are separately renamed via two renamings (see below) σ^ι and σ^o, respectively, which are two finite maps over *Name*.

The freeze operator allows the binding between input and output names; this binding is specified by the renaming σ^f.

Finally, it is possible to access an output component from the outside via the selection operator.

The meta-variable σ ranges over the set of renamings (finite maps over *Name*). The notation $X_i \overset{i \in I}{\mapsto} Y_i, Y_j{}^{j \in J}$ is used for representing the unique map σ s.t. $dom(\sigma) = \{X_i \mid i \in I\}$, $cod(\sigma) = \{Y_i \mid i \in I \cup J\}$ and $\sigma(X_i) = Y_i$, for all $i \in I$. We assume that for any i_1 and i_2 in I, if $i_1 \neq i_2$ then $X_{i_1} \neq X_{i_2}$ and, similarly, for any j_1 and j_2 in J, if $j_1 \neq j_2$ then $Y_{j_1} \neq Y_{j_2}$. Furthermore, $\{Y_i \mid i \in I\}$ and $\{Y_j \mid j \in J\}$ are assumed to be disjoint sets.

We introduce the following abbreviations for the reduct: if σ^ι is an inclusion, i.e. of the form $X_i \overset{i \in I}{\mapsto} X_i, X_j{}^{j \in J}$, then ${}_{\sigma^\iota|}E_{|\sigma^o}$ is written ${}_{cod(\sigma^\iota)|}E_{|\sigma^o}$; if in particular $J = \emptyset$, i.e. σ^ι is the identity, then we simply write $E_{|\sigma^o}$. Symmetrically, if σ^o is of the form $X_I \overset{i \in I}{\mapsto} X_i, X_j{}^{j \in J}$, then ${}_{\sigma^\iota|}E_{|\sigma^o}$ is written ${}_{\sigma^\iota|}E_{|dom(\sigma^o)}$ and, if σ^o is the identity, then we simply write ${}_{\sigma^\iota|}E$.

Notations and Definitions: for any module expression E, let $FV(E)$ denotes the set of free variables of E inductively defined by:

$FV(C)$ is core language dependent
$FV(C[x_i \overset{i\in I}{\mapsto} E_i] = (FV(C) \setminus \{x_i \mid i \in I\}) \cup \bigcup_{i\in I} FV(E_i)$
$FV([\iota;\ o;\ \rho]) = (\bigcup_{E\in cod(o)} FV(E) \cup \bigcup_{E\in cod(\rho)} FV(E)) \setminus (dom(\iota) \cup dom(\rho))$
$FV(E_1 + E_2) = FV(E_1) \cup FV(E_2)$ $\qquad FV({}_{\sigma^\iota|}E_{|\sigma^o}) = FV(E)$
$FV(\mathit{freeze}_{\sigma^f}(E)) = FV(E)$ $\qquad FV(E.X) = FV(E)$

As expected, at the module level the only binding construct is for basic modules. If $E = [\iota;\ o;\ \rho]$ then we denote by $BV(E)$ the set $dom(\iota) \cup dom(\rho)$ of its binding variables; finally, we define $V(E)$ to be $BV(E) \cup FV(E)$ and $AV(E)$ to be the set of all variables in E.

We extend the notation for substitution to ρ-assignment, i.e. $E[\rho]$ denotes the expression obtained by capture-avoiding simultaneous substitution of E_i for the free occurrences of x_i in E, for all $i \in I$. Finally, if ρ' is another ρ-assignment, then $\rho[\rho']$ denotes the ρ-assignment $x_i \overset{i\in I}{\mapsto} E_i[\rho']$; an analogous notation is used for o-assignments.

1.2 Reduction Rules

The reduction rules for the untyped calculus are defined in Fig.2.

$$\text{(core)}\quad \frac{C \overset{C}{\to} C'}{C \to C'} \qquad \text{(sub)}\quad \frac{M_i \to E_i}{C[x_i \overset{i\in I}{\mapsto} M_i] \to C[x_i \overset{i\in I}{\mapsto} E_i]} \quad i \in I$$

$$(\alpha 1)\quad \frac{}{[x \mapsto X, \iota;\ o;\ \rho] \to [x' \mapsto X, \iota;\ o[x \mapsto x'];\ \rho[x \mapsto x']]} \quad x' \notin AV(E)$$

$$(\alpha 2)\quad \frac{}{[\iota;\ o;\ x \mapsto E, \rho] \to [\iota;\ o[x \mapsto x'];\ x' \mapsto E[x \mapsto x'], \rho[x \mapsto x']]} \quad x' \notin AV(E)$$

$$\text{(sum)}\quad \frac{}{E_1 + E_2 \to [\iota_1, \iota_2;\ o_1, o_2;\ \rho_1, \rho_2]} \quad \begin{array}{l} E_i = [\iota_i;\ o_i;\ \rho_i],\ i = 1, 2 \\ BV(E_1) \cap V(E_2) = \emptyset \\ BV(E_2) \cap V(E_1) = \emptyset \\ dom(o_1) \cap dom(o_2) = \emptyset \end{array}$$

$$\text{(reduct)}\quad \frac{}{{}_{\sigma^\iota|}[\iota;\ o;\ \rho]_{|\sigma^o} \to [\sigma^\iota \circ \iota;\ o \circ \sigma^o;\ \rho]} \quad \begin{array}{l} cod(\iota) \subseteq dom(\sigma^\iota) \\ cod(\sigma^o) \subseteq dom(o) \end{array}$$

$$\text{(freeze)}\quad \frac{}{\mathit{freeze}_{\sigma^f}([\iota_1, \iota_2;\ o;\ \rho]) \to [\iota_2;\ o;\ \rho, o \circ \sigma^f \circ \iota_1]} \quad \begin{array}{l} cod(\iota_1) \cap cod(\iota_2) = \emptyset \\ dom(\sigma^f) = cod(\iota_1) \\ cod(\sigma^f) \subseteq dom(o) \end{array}$$

$$\text{(selection)}\quad \frac{}{[;\ o;\ \rho].X \to o(X)[x_i \overset{i\in I}{\mapsto} E_i.Y]} \quad \begin{array}{l} \forall i \in I\ E_i = [; Y \mapsto \rho(x_i); \rho] \\ dom(\rho) = \{x_i \mid i \in I\} \\ X \in dom(o) \end{array}$$

Fig. 2. Reduction rules for the untyped calculus.

Values are all basic module expressions together with all core values. As usual, besides the rules of Fig.2, it is implicitly defined also the rule for contexts closure. The following definition of context determines the reduction strategy we refer to in this paper:

$$\mathcal{C}[\,]::=[\,] \mid \mathcal{C}[\,]+E \mid E+\mathcal{C}[\,] \mid {}_{\sigma^\iota|}\mathcal{C}[\,]_{|\sigma^o} \mid \mathit{freeze}_{\sigma^f}(\mathcal{C}[\,]) \mid \mathcal{C}[\,].X$$

Core: the definition of the reduction relation for the module calculus is parametric in the core reduction relation $\xrightarrow{c}$; the meaning of the (core) rule is obvious.

Substitution: the (sub) rule is needed for reducing enriched core terms to plain core terms, so that eventually the core reduction relation can be applied. The use of meta-variable M rules out all non interesting cases; this simplifies the proof of subject reduction (Theorem 1). Finally, because of our assumptions over the syntax, recall that $C \notin \mathit{Var}$, $I \neq \emptyset$ and $x_i \in FV(C)$ for all $i \in I$.

α-conversion: for simplicity, the α-rule for the binding construct of basic modules has been split into two rules which separately deal with deferred and local variables renaming, respectively.

Note that, as mentioned before, the separation between variables and components is essential for having a correct α-rule; indeed, the α-conversion makes sense for variables but not for names. For instance, the term $E = [;\ Y = 0;\ ]$ is not observationally equivalent to $E' = [;\ X = 0;\ ]$ since these two terms clearly behave differently w.r.t. the context $\mathcal{C}[\,].Y$ (or, equivalently, $\mathcal{C}[\,].X$): $E.Y$ reduces to 0, whereas the reduction for $E'.Y$ gets stuck. It should be clear from this example that the crucial point stands in recognizing which are the entities which can be correctly α-converted rather than in the separation between *Var* and *Name*: technically, these two sets could be equal, however it is better to keep them separated since, conceptually, variables and components are different entities.

Sum: the reduction rule for sum is straightforward; this operation has simply the effect of gluing together two modules. However, a particular attention is needed for correctly applying this rule. The binding variables of one module must be disjoint from those of the other, otherwise the result of the sum would not be syntactically correct (recall the assumptions for basic modules in Sect.1.1). Furthermore, we have to pay attention that the free variables of one module are not captured by the binding variables of the other. As a result, the set of binding variables of one module must be disjoint from the set of (either binding or free) variables of the other. If this does not happen, then the (sum) rule can be applied only after an appropriate α-conversion of (possibly) both the modules.

The output components of the two modules must be disjoint for the same reason explained for binding variables; however, in opposition to what happens for binding variables, if this condition does not hold for output components then the reduction gets stuck since this conflict cannot be resolved by an α-conversion. The only way to solve this problem is to explicitly rename the output components in an appropriate way by means of the reduct operator, thus changing the term. The sets of the input components of the two modules can have a non empty intersection and the resulting set of the input components of the sum is simply the union of them; this means that the input components having the same name in the two modules are shared in the resulting sum.

Finally, note that sum represents a very primitive way of assembling together two modules, since it provides no way for inter-connecting their components (apart from the fact that input components are shared[1]). This can be done only at a second stage, after sum has been performed, by means of the freeze operator (see below). In other words, sum corresponds to the ability of collecting pieces of unrelated code.

Reduct: the reduct operator performs only a renaming of component names and does not change the ρ-assignment and the variables of a module; its effect is simply a composition of maps. However this form of renaming is rather powerful. Input and output names are renamed in a separate way, by specifying two renamings σ^ι and σ^o, respectively[2]. The two renamings are contravariant for the same reason that a function from A to B can be converted into a function from A' to B' whenever two conversion functions from A' to A and from B to B' are provided. Note that the two renamings can be non-injective and non-surjective. A non-injective map σ^ι allows sharing of input components, whereas a non-surjective one is used for adding dummy input components (in the sense that no variable is associated with them); a non-injective map σ^o allows duplication of definitions, a non-surjective one is used for hiding output components.

Finally, note that the syntactic representation chosen for ι-assignments is not suitable for expressing non-surjective maps, although composition of such assignments with non-surjective renamings may produce non-surjective assignments. Hence, we represent a non-surjective assignment by associating a fresh variable with each input component which is not reached in ι. For instance, the term ${}_{\{X,W\}|}[x \mapsto X;\ Y \mapsto x+1, Z \mapsto 1;\ ]_{|\{Y\}}$ reduces to $[x \mapsto X, w \mapsto W;\ Y \mapsto x+1;\ ]$, where w is a fresh variable.

Freeze: as already stated, the freeze operator is essential for binding input with output components in order to accomplish inter-connection between components. In other words, freeze corresponds to the phase, typical of any linker, of external names resolution which immediately follows the merge of the object files. However in this case the resolution is neither implicit nor exhaustive. A renaming σ^f explicitly specifies how the resolution has to be performed, associating output to input components; furthermore, the domain of σ^f can be a proper subset of all input components of the module so that the resolution is partial.

The effect of applying the freeze operator is that all input components that are resolved (represented by the set $dom(\sigma^f)$) disappear and the deferred variables mapped into them (represented by the set $dom(\iota_1)$) become local. These variables are associated with the definition of the output component to which they are bound by σ^f (i.e., $o(\sigma^f(\iota_1(x)))$, for all $x \in dom(\iota_1)$).

[1] We could avoid implicit sharing of input components in the (sum) rule by requiring $dom(\iota_1) \cap dom(\iota_2) = \emptyset$, thus forcing the user to make this sharing explicit by means of the reduct operator.

[2] Indeed in the primitive calculus there exists no relationship between the names of the input and output components and the fact that these two sets of names may not be disjoint has no semantic consequence; we will consider later (Sect.3.3) how to encode in the calculus module systems with *virtual*, i.e. both input and output, components.

The deferred variables and the input components which are not resolved (represented by $dom(\iota_2)$ and $cod(\iota_2)$, respectively) and the o-assignment are not affected.

As an example, the module expression

$$freeze_{F\mapsto G}([f\mapsto F, k\mapsto K;\ G\mapsto \lambda x.\text{if } x=0 \text{ then } 1 \text{ else } k * f(x-1);\ ])$$

reduces to

$$[k\mapsto K;\ G\mapsto e;\ f\mapsto e]$$

with e denoting the expression $\lambda x.\text{if } x=0 \text{ then } 1 \text{ else } k * f(x-1)$.

Selection: finally, output components can be accessed from the outside by means of the selection operator. Selection is legal only for modules where all input components have been resolved (called *concrete* modules), hence, for all modules having an empty ι-assignment. Furthermore, the selected name must be in $dom(o)$ (i.e., it must be an output component of the module).

Since definitions in modules can be mutually dependent, the expression corresponding to the selected component (determined by $o(X)$) may contain some (necessarily local) variables $\{x_i \mid i \in I\}$ which have to be replaced with their corresponding definition. Therefore, for each $i \in I$, the variable x_i is replaced with the term $E_i.Y$, where $E_i = [;\ Y\mapsto \rho(x_i);\ \rho]$ is equal to the module E upon which selection is performed, with the exception that only the x_i variable is made visible via the component name Y (since we are interested in selecting only the expression assigned to x_i); this variable must be visible even though it is local in E, since the definition of an output component has free access to the local variables of its module. Note that recursion is obtained by propagating the ρ-assignment of E in the resulting term by means of the substitution $x_i \overset{i\in I}{\mapsto} E_i.Y$.

As an example, the module expression

$$[;\ G\mapsto g;\ k\mapsto 2, g\mapsto \lambda x.\text{if } x=0 \text{ then } 1 \text{ else } k * g(x-1)].G$$

reduces to

$$\lambda x.\text{if } x=0 \text{ then } 1 \text{ else } E_1.Z * E_2.Z(x-1)$$

where E_1, E_2 and e denote $[;\ Z\mapsto 2;\ k\mapsto 2, g\mapsto e]$, $[;\ Z\mapsto e;\ k\mapsto 2, g\mapsto e]$ and $\lambda x.\text{if } x=0 \text{ then } 1 \text{ else } k * g(x-1)$, respectively.

2 A Typed Calculus

In this section we address the problem of defining a sound type system for the calculus presented in Sect.1. As usual, soundness means that the reduction of each closed and well-typed term never gets stuck, so that it is possible to statically detect errors like clashes of output components while summing modules, binding of deferred variables to expressions of the wrong type, selection of output components not present in a module and so on.

Since here we are mainly interested in type checking rather than in type inference algorithms, the terms of the typed calculus are decorated with types so that they are slightly different from those of the untyped calculus.

The type system we define turns out to satisfy the subject reduction property (see [6] for technical details); we conjecture that a proof of the soundness of the type system can be obtained by adapting the proof for subject reduction.

The types of the calculus are defined by $\tau ::= c\tau \mid [X_i{:}\tau_i{}^{i\in I};\ X_j{:}\tau_j{}^{j\in J}]$.

A type is either a core type $c\tau$ (i.e., a type of the core language) or a module type $[X_i{:}\tau_i{}^{i\in I};\ X_j{:}\tau_j{}^{j\in J}]$ (abbreviated by $[\Sigma^\iota;\ \Sigma^o]$). For sake of simplicity we do not introduce recursive types. Notice that according to the definition above core types cannot be built on top of module types, hence we are forcing the core and module language to be stratified so that modules are not first-class values. See the Conclusion for a discussion about this restriction.

A module type is well-formed if it contains well-formed types and input (resp. output) components are not overloaded. This is formalized by the judgment $\vdash [\Sigma^\iota;\ \Sigma^o]$ defined by the following rules:

$$\frac{\Vdash \Sigma^\iota,\ \Vdash \Sigma^o}{\vdash [\Sigma^\iota;\ \Sigma^o]} \qquad \frac{\vdash \tau_i\ \ \forall i \in I}{\Vdash X_i{:}\tau_i{}^{i\in I}} \quad X_i{}^{i\in I} \text{ distinct}$$

Intuitively, if a module M has type $[X_i{:}\tau_i{}^{i\in I};\ X_j{:}\tau_j{}^{j\in J}]$ then $\{X_i \mid i \in I\}$ and $\{X_j \mid j \in J\}$ represent its sets of input and output components, respectively.

The type annotation $X_i{:}\tau_i$ says that the input component X_i can be correctly bound only to expressions of type τ_i, whereas $X_j{:}\tau_j$ says that the output component X_j is associated with an expression of type τ_j.

The syntax of the typed calculus is the same as that of the untyped version, apart from basic modules where deferred and local variables are decorated with types: $[x_i{:}\tau_i \overset{i\in I}{\mapsto} X_i;\ X_j \overset{j\in J}{\mapsto} E_j;\ x_k{:}\tau_k \overset{k\in K}{\mapsto} E_k]$.

The type decoration must be coherent in the sense that if $x_{i_1}{:}\tau_{i_1}$, $x_{i_2}{:}\tau_{i_2}$ and $\iota(x_{i_1}) = \iota(x_{i_2})$ then $\tau_{i_1} = \tau_{i_2}$ for any pair of deferred variables x_{i_1}, x_{i_2}, so that the type of the module is well-formed.

For instance, the module

$$[f{:}int \to int \mapsto F, k{:}int \mapsto K;\ G \mapsto \lambda x{:}int.\text{if } x = 0 \text{ then } 1 \text{ else } k * f(x-1);\ ]$$

has type $[F{:}int \to int, K{:}int;\ G{:}int \to int]$.

The typing rules for the typed calculus are defined in Fig.3.

A context Γ is a finite (possibly empty) sequence of assignments of types to variables where variable repetition is allowed. The predicate $\Gamma(x) = \tau$ is inductively defined as follows:

- $\emptyset(x) = \tau$ is false for any variable x and type τ;
- $(\Gamma, x{:}\tau)(x') = \tau'$ iff $(x = x'$ and $\tau = \tau')$ or $(x \neq x'$ and $\Gamma(x') = \tau')$.

The predicates $x \in \Gamma$ and $\Gamma \subseteq \Gamma'$ are defined as follows: $x \in \Gamma$ iff there exists τ s.t. $\Gamma(x) = \tau$; $\Gamma \subseteq \Gamma'$ iff for any variable x and any type τ, $\Gamma(x) = \tau$ implies $\Gamma'(x) = \tau$.

The (core) typing rule expresses the dependence from the core type system; core typing judgments have form $\Gamma \overset{c}{\vdash} C{:}c\tau$, where Γ is a context containing only core types, C is a (plain) core expression and $c\tau$ a core type. The side condition $\Gamma \subseteq \Gamma'$ is essential for eliminating the part of the context which is not well-formed at the core level. For instance, when trying to prove

$$\emptyset \vdash [x \mapsto X;\ V \mapsto x.Y + 1;\ ]{:}[X{:}[;\ Y{:}int];\ V{:}int],$$

we end up with proving $x{:}[;\ Y{:}int],\ y{:}int \vdash y + 1{:}int$, which can be derived at the core level only if we get rid of the assumption $x{:}[;\ Y{:}int]$.

$$\text{(core)}\quad \frac{\Gamma \overset{C}{\vdash} C{:}c\tau}{\Gamma' \vdash C{:}c\tau} \quad \Gamma \subseteq \Gamma'$$

$$\text{(sub)}\quad \frac{\Gamma, x_i{:}\tau_i{}^{i\in I} \vdash C{:}c\tau,\ \Gamma \vdash E_i{:}\tau_i\ \forall i \in I}{\Gamma \vdash C[x_i \overset{i\in I}{\mapsto} E_i] : c\tau} \quad \forall i \in I.x_i \notin \Gamma$$

$$\text{(basic)}\quad \frac{\begin{array}{c}\vdash [\Sigma^\iota;\ \Sigma^o] \\ \Gamma, x_i{:}\tau_i{}^{i\in I}, x_k{:}\tau_k{}^{k\in K} \vdash E_j{:}\tau_j\ \forall j \in J \\ \Gamma, x_i{:}\tau_i{}^{i\in I}, x_k{:}\tau_k{}^{k\in K} \vdash E_k{:}\tau_k\ \forall k \in K\end{array}}{\Gamma \vdash [x_i{:}\tau_i \overset{i\in I}{\mapsto} X_i;\ X_j \overset{j\in J}{\mapsto} E_j;\ x_k{:}\tau_k \overset{k\in K}{\mapsto} E_k]{:}[\Sigma^\iota;\ \Sigma^o]} \quad \begin{array}{l}\{\Sigma^\iota\} = \{X_i{:}\tau_i{}^{i\in I}\} \\ \Sigma^o = X_j{:}\tau_j{}^{j\in J}\end{array}$$

$$\text{(sum)}\quad \frac{\vdash [\Sigma^\iota, \Sigma^\iota_1, \Sigma^\iota_2;\ \Sigma^o_1, \Sigma^o_2],\ \Gamma \vdash E_1{:}[\Sigma^\iota, \Sigma^\iota_1;\ \Sigma^o_1],\ \Gamma \vdash E_2{:}[\Sigma^\iota, \Sigma^\iota_2;\ \Sigma^o_2]}{\Gamma \vdash E_1 + E_2{:}[\Sigma^\iota, \Sigma^\iota_1, \Sigma^\iota_2;\ \Sigma^o_1, \Sigma^o_2]}$$

$$\text{(reduct)}\quad \frac{\Gamma \vdash E{:}[\Sigma^\iota;\ \Sigma^o]}{\Gamma \vdash {}_{\sigma^\iota|}E_{|\sigma^o}{:}[\Sigma'^\iota;\ \Sigma'^o]} \quad \begin{array}{l}\sigma^\iota{:}\, \Sigma^\iota \rightarrow \Sigma'^\iota \\ \sigma^o{:}\, \Sigma'^o \rightarrow \Sigma^o\end{array}$$

$$\text{(freeze)}\quad \frac{\Gamma \vdash E{:}[\Sigma^f, \Sigma^\iota;\ \Sigma^o]}{\Gamma \vdash \mathit{freeze}_{\sigma^f}(E){:}[\Sigma^\iota;\ \Sigma^o]} \quad \sigma^f{:}\, \Sigma^f \rightarrow \Sigma^o$$

$$\text{(selection)}\quad \frac{\Gamma \vdash E{:}[;\ X_j{:}\tau_j{}^{j\in J}]}{\Gamma \vdash E.X_k{:}\tau_k} \quad k \in J$$

Fig. 3. Typing rules for the typed calculus.

The (sub) typing rule corresponds to a substitution lemma for enriched core expressions. Recall that $C \notin \mathit{Var}$, $I \neq \emptyset$ and $x_i \in FV(C)$ for all $i \in I$; the side-condition says that no type assumptions are needed for the variable we substitute for.

In the (basic) typing rule the side condition $\{\Sigma^\iota\} = \{X_i{:}\tau_i{}^{i\in I}\}$ means that for any $i \in I$, $X_i{:}\tau_i \in \Sigma^\iota$ and for any $X{:}\tau \in \Sigma^\iota$, $X{:}\tau \in X_i{:}\tau_i{}^{i\in I}$ (recall that there might be repetitions in $\{X_i{:}\tau_i{}^{i\in I}\}$).

The (sum) typing rule allows sharing of input components having the same name and type (represented by Σ^ι), whereas output components cannot be shared. The notation Σ_1, Σ_2 denotes the concatenation of Σ_1 with Σ_2.

The side conditions having form $\sigma{:}\, X_i{:}\tau_i{}^{i\in I} \rightarrow X_j{:}\tau_j{}^{j\in J}$ ensure that the renaming σ preserves types (see typing rules (reduct) and (freeze)); formally, this means that $\sigma{:}\, \{X_i \mid i \in I\} \rightarrow \{X_j \mid j \in J\}$ and $\sigma(X_i) = X_j \Rightarrow \tau_i = \tau_j$ for all $i \in I$, $j \in J$.

The reduction rules for the typed calculus are simply the rules of Fig.2 annotated with types.

In order to prove subject reduction, we need some assumptions over the core language on top of which the module language is defined.

1. **(No Interference)** $\mathcal{E}_M \cap \mathcal{E}_K = \emptyset$ and if $x_i \in FV(C)$ for all $i \in I$, then $C[x_i \overset{i\in I}{\mapsto} E_i] \in \mathcal{E}_C \iff \forall i \in I,\ E_i \in \mathcal{E}_C$.
2. **(Weakening)** If $\Gamma \overset{C}{\vdash} C{:}c\tau$ and $\Gamma \subseteq \Gamma'$ (Γ' core contex) then $\Gamma' \overset{C}{\vdash} C{:}c\tau$.

3. **(Substitution)** If $\Gamma, x_i{:}c\tau_i{}^{i\in I} \overset{c}{\vdash} C{:}c\tau$ and $\Gamma \overset{c}{\vdash} C_i{:}c\tau_i$ for all $i \in I$, then $\Gamma \overset{c}{\vdash} C[x_i \overset{i\in I}{\mapsto} C_i]{:}c\tau$.
4. **(Subject Reduction)** If $C \overset{c}{\to} C'$ and $\Gamma \overset{c}{\vdash} C{:}c\tau$ then $\Gamma \overset{c}{\vdash} C'{:}c\tau$.

Assumption 1 avoids ambiguous expressions that may have a different semantics at the core and the module level. For instance, we cannot use the usual arithmetic symbol $+$ at the core level as long as this symbol is used for module sum since expressions like $x + y$ result to be ambiguous. For the same reason, we do not want all terms obtained as $C[x_i \overset{i\in I}{\mapsto} M_i]$ (with $i \neq \emptyset$, $C \notin \mathit{Var}$ and $x_i \in FV(C)$ for all $i \in I$) to belong to the set $\mathcal{E}_C$ of core expressions. The other direction of implication could be removed since closure of the core language w.r.t. substitution can be considered a standard (and therefore implicit) assumption.

The following lemmas hold for any core calculus verifying the four assumptions above. For reason of space we have omitted all proofs (see [6]).

Lemma 1 (Coherence). *If $C \to C'$ then $C \overset{c}{\to} C'$. Furthermore, if $\Gamma \vdash C{:}\tau$ then $\Gamma' \overset{c}{\vdash} C{:}\tau$ for a certain core context $\Gamma' \subseteq \Gamma$.*

The coherence lemma states that the module calculus is a conservative extension of the core calculus. In particular, coherence of the type system (second part) is needed for proving subject reduction; we conjecture that coherence of the reduction semantics (first part) is needed for proving soundness. The remaining two lemmas express standard properties.

Lemma 2 (Weakening). *If $\Gamma \vdash E{:}\tau$, then $\Gamma' \vdash E{:}\tau$ for any well-formed context Γ' s.t. $\Gamma \subseteq \Gamma'$.*

Lemma 3 (Substitution). *If $\Gamma, x_i{:}\tau_i{}^{i\in I} \vdash E{:}\tau$ and $\Gamma \vdash E_i{:}\tau_i$ for all $i \in I$, then $\Gamma \vdash E[x_i \overset{i\in I}{\mapsto} E_i]{:}\tau$.*

Theorem 1 (Subject Reduction). *For any pair of terms E, E', if $E \to E'$ and $\Gamma \vdash E{:}\tau$, then $\Gamma \vdash E'{:}\tau$.*

3 Expressive Power of the Calculus

In this section we show how various composition operators can be encoded in the calculus; we analyze in particular the *link* operator shown in the Introduction (3.1), parameterized modules (3.2) and object-oriented features (3.3).

3.1 Linking Modules

The *link* operator informally described in the Introduction has the following typing rule

$$\text{(link)} \quad \frac{\Gamma \vdash E_1{:}[\Sigma^\iota, \Sigma^\iota_1, \Sigma^b_1;\ \Sigma^o_1],\ \Gamma \vdash E_2{:}[\Sigma^\iota, \Sigma^\iota_2, \Sigma^b_2;\ \Sigma^o_2] \quad \Vdash \Sigma^\iota_1, \Sigma^B_1, \Sigma^\iota_2, \Sigma^B_2,\ \Vdash \Sigma^o_1, \Sigma^o_2}{\Gamma \vdash \mathit{link}_{\sigma_1,\sigma_2}(E_1, E_2){:}[\Sigma^\iota, \Sigma^\iota_1, \Sigma^\iota_2;\ \Sigma^o_1, \Sigma^o_2]} \quad \begin{array}{l} \sigma_1{:}\, \Sigma^b_1 \rightarrow \Sigma^o_2 \\ \sigma_2{:}\, \Sigma^b_2 \rightarrow \Sigma^o_1 \end{array}$$

(where Σ^b_1 denotes the input components of E_1 which have to be bound to some output components of E_2 as indicated by σ_1, and conversely), and can be easily defined in terms of the basic operators as follows

$$\mathit{link}_{\sigma_1,\sigma_2}(E_1, E_2) = \mathit{freeze}_{\sigma_2}(\mathit{freeze}_{\sigma_1}(E_1 + E_2)).$$

Alternatively, σ_1 and σ_2 could be implicitly specified by equality of component names, as we have assumed for *link*(BOOL, INT) in the Introduction, i.e. defining $\mathit{link}(E_1, E_2) = \mathit{link}_{\iota_1,\iota_2}(E_1, E_2)$ with ι_i, $i = 1, 2$, the obvious inclusions.

Note that this operator returns a concrete module only if each input component of M_1 is mapped into an output component of M_2 and conversely.

Even if the link operator looks very natural as way of assembling modules, there are few concrete examples of module languages which support this operator, allowing in practice mutually recursive definitions of modules. The proposal which more directly uses an analogous operator is that of *units* [12]. Basic units are very close to basic modules of our calculus, since they are, in their graphical representation, boxes with an import, an export and an internal section (however, differently from our modules units are run-time entities with an initialization part). Many units can be composed by a linking process which is graphically described by putting all the boxes inside a collecting box and connecting some input to export ports by arrows. This corresponds in our formalism to a composition of *link* operators plus a reduct operation which performs the connections from/to ports of the collecting box. Indeed, there is a natural graphical representation of all our operators over modules, omitted here for reasons of space, which very strictly resembles that given in [12] for units; the interested reader can refer to [5].

Other proposals for recursive modules are those in [11] for adding this feature to Standard ML[3] and the theoretical analysis in [10]; some comparison with them is provided in the Conclusion.

3.2 Parameterized Modules and a Translation for the λ-Calculus

Module systems as those of Standard ML [18] or Objective Caml [17] are based on the idea of designing the module language as a small applicative language of its own. Hence, modules are of two kinds: constant modules (*structures* in ML terminology), which can be seen in our calculus as basic modules without input components, and functions from modules into modules (*functors* in ML terminology), which can be seen in our calculus as basic modules whose input components are the expected components of the structure which is the parameter of the functor and output components are those defined by the functor itself.

[3] The authors use the name *mixins* for their mutually recursive modules; we prefer to reserve this name to modules which support both mutual recursion and overriding with dynamic binding as in the object-oriented approach (see 3.3).

In these module systems, the only significant operation for composing modules is function application, which can be encoded following the schema illustrated in Fig.4, where we show a translation of the λ-calculus into the module calculus (both in the untyped version).

(var) $\ll x \gg = x$ (lambda) $\ll \lambda x.e \gg = [x \mapsto \mathit{Arg};\ \mathit{Res} \mapsto \ll e \gg;\ ]$

(app) $\ll (e_1 e_2) \gg = (\mathit{freeze}_{\mathit{Arg} \mapsto \mathit{Arg}}(\ll e_1 \gg + [;\ \mathit{Arg} \mapsto \ll e_2 \gg;\ ])).\mathit{Res}$

Fig. 4. Translation of the λ-calculus into the module calculus.

Interestingly enough, this translation can be defined by using the instantiation of the module calculus over the simplest core language we could choose: the language of variables (recall that the only syntactic assumption over the core language is that it must contain the set *Var*). This shows that the module language is a powerful language of its own, regardless the expressive power of the underlying core language.

We can verify that the α- and β-rules are valid under the translation.

For the α-rule we have that the term $\lambda x.e$ can be α-converted into $\lambda y.e[x \mapsto y]$ (with $y \notin AV(\lambda x.e)$) and then translated into

$E_1 = [y \mapsto \mathit{Arg};\ \mathit{Res} \mapsto \ll e[x \mapsto y] \gg;\ ]$.

On the other hand $\lambda x.e$ can be translated into $[x \mapsto \mathit{Arg};\ \mathit{Res} \mapsto \ll e \gg;\ ]$ and then α-converted into

$E_2 = [y \mapsto \mathit{Arg};\ \mathit{Res} \mapsto \ll e \gg [x \mapsto y];\ ]$ (with $y \notin AV(\ll \lambda x.e \gg)$).

Now, by induction over the structure of λ-terms, trivially $AV(e) = AV(\ll e \gg)$ and $\ll e[x \mapsto y] \gg = \ll e \gg [x \mapsto y]$ for any $y \notin AV(e)$, hence $E_1 = E_2$.

For the β-rule we have that the term $(\lambda x.e_1\ e_2)$ can be β-converted into $e_1[x \mapsto e_2]$ (assuming that $AV(\lambda x.e_1) \cap FV(e_2) = \emptyset$) and then translated into $E_1 = \ll e_1[x \mapsto e_2] \gg$. Then, trivially by induction over the structure of λ-terms, $E_1 = \ll e_1 \gg [x \mapsto \ll e_2 \gg]$. On the other hand $(\lambda x.e_1\ e_2)$ can be translated into

$(\mathit{freeze}_{\mathit{Arg} \mapsto \mathit{Arg}}(([x \mapsto \mathit{Arg};\ \mathit{Res} \mapsto \ll e_1 \gg;\ ] + [;\ \mathit{Arg} \mapsto \ll e_2 \gg;\ ]))).\mathit{Res}$

and then reduced to $E_2 = \ll e_1 \gg [x \mapsto [;\ Z \mapsto \ll e_2 \gg;\ x \mapsto \ll e_2 \gg].Z]$. Now, since trivially $FV(e_2) = FV(\ll e_2 \gg)$ and by hypothesis $x \notin FV(e_2)$, we have that the term $[;\ Z \mapsto \ll e_2 \gg;\ x \mapsto \ll e_2 \gg].Z$ reduces to $\ll e_2 \gg$, hence E_1 and E_2 are observationally equivalent.

3.3 Object-Oriented Features

In the examples considered until now, modules are essentially of two kinds: modules with no input components (concrete modules), which can be effectively used, and modules with some input components, which need to be combined with other modules before to be used. Indeed the selection rule can be applied only to concrete modules.

The key idea of the object-oriented approach w.r.t. modularity features can be considered the possibility it offers to write modules (classes) which combine the two features, i.e. where components (methods) are simultaneously ready to be used via selection, i.e. are output components, and can be modified by overriding in a way that changes the behavior of the components referring to them, i.e. are input components (this is sometimes called the *open-closed* property of the object-oriented approach). Components like these are called *virtual*.

In other words, a module with virtual components has, intuitively, two different semantics: an *open* semantics as a function, which is needed when the module is extended via overriding, and a *closed* semantics (the fixed point of the function), which is needed when the module is used via selection of a component (following the idea originally due to [9,19]).

Virtual components can be encoded in our calculus in an indirect way, by defining a *(generalized) selection* operator which, differently from the basic operators of the calculus, takes into account the fact that a component name appears both in the input and output assignment.

Formally, this operation has the following typing rule

$$\text{(generalized selection)} \qquad \frac{\Gamma \vdash E{:}[X_i{:}\tau_i{}^{i\in I};\ X_j{:}\tau_j{}^{j\in J}]}{\Gamma \vdash E \bullet X_k{:}\tau_k} \qquad k \in J,\ I \subseteq J$$

and can be expressed by $E \bullet X = (\mathit{freeze}_\iota(E)).X$ with ι the inclusion from $\{Y_i \mid i \in I\}$ into $\{Y_j \mid j \in J\}$.

A simple overriding operator has the following typing rule:

$$\text{(overriding)} \qquad \frac{\vdash [\Sigma^\iota, \Sigma_1^\iota, \Sigma_2^\iota;\ \Sigma^o, \Sigma_1^o, \Sigma_2^o] \quad \Gamma \vdash E_1{:}[\Sigma^\iota, \Sigma_1^\iota;\ \Sigma^o, \Sigma_1^o],\ \Gamma \vdash E_2{:}[\Sigma^\iota, \Sigma_2^\iota;\ \Sigma^o, \Sigma_2^o]}{\Gamma \vdash E_1 \leftarrow E_2{:}[\Sigma^\iota, \Sigma_1^\iota, \Sigma_2^\iota;\ \Sigma^o, \Sigma_1^o, \Sigma_2^o]}$$

(where Σ^o denotes the output components in E_1 which are overridden by those in E_2) and can be expressed by $E_1 \leftarrow E_2 = E_{1|\Sigma_1^o} + E_2$

An extended presentation of how to translate various overriding operators, including the *super* mechanism, in a module language supporting the three basic operators of sum, reduct and freeze can be found in [4]. We will say that a module language supports *mixin modules* (or simply *mixins*) if it provides both mutual recursion (operators like *sum* or *link*) and overriding with dynamic binding, like the calculus defined in this paper.

Note that, although methods of a parent and an heir class can refer to each other, traditional object-oriented languages do not support mixins since an heir class cannot be used as a real module in the sense of the two principles mentioned in the Introduction, since it relies on a fixed parent class. Extensions of object-oriented languages with mixins (also called *mixin classes* or *parametric heir classes* in this case) are proposed in [7,13].

As further illustration of how to encode object-oriented features, we show an example of translation from the Abadi and Cardelli's object calculus [1] into our calculus (both in the untyped version). The example shows in particular how to encode the self-reference mechanism (for a more general encoding see [6]).

Consider the object defined by $\mathit{Cnt} = [\mathit{val} = 0, \mathit{inc} = \varsigma(s)s.\mathit{val} := s.\mathit{val} + 1]$. The method *val* returns the current value of the counter, whereas *inc* returns the counter itself where its value has been incremented by one.

The encoding of *Cnt* is given by the term C defined by

$$C = [v \mapsto Val;\ Val \mapsto 0, Inc \mapsto (s \leftarrow [;\ Val \mapsto v+1;\ ]);\ s \mapsto E],$$
$$E = [v \mapsto Val;\ Val \mapsto 0, Inc \mapsto (s \leftarrow [;\ Val \mapsto v+1;\ ])].$$

The variable s corresponds to the *self* object. The term $s \leftarrow [;\ Val \mapsto v+1;\ ]$ is the translation of $s.val := s.val + 1$.

Since *val* is a virtual component of the object[4], *Val* is both an input and an output component, so that every redefinition of *val* must change the behavior of methods depending on it. Indeed, this is the case for the method *inc* whose definition in the encoding depends on the deferred variable v.

Since C is an open module, because of the input component *Val*, before selecting an output component C must be closed with the freeze operator; in other words we have to use the generalized selection defined above. Therefore, the method invocation *Cnt.inc.val* is encoded in the term $(C \bullet Inc) \bullet Val$, i.e., $freeze_{Val \mapsto Val}(freeze_{Val \mapsto Val}(C).Inc).Val$ which reduces, as expected, to 1.

4 Conclusion

We have presented a simple and powerful calculus for module systems equipped with a reduction semantics and a sound type system. Moreover, we have illustrated that it can be actually used as a primitive kernel in which to encode various existing mechanisms for combining software components. We have also implemented a prototype interpreter for the calculus[5].

An extended version of this paper, including proofs and the definition of a subtyping relation, is [6]. We have already discussed relations with some recent proposals for advanced module systems in Sect.3. Some further consideration is needed for comparing our calculus with work which more specifically deals with the problem of recursive type definitions spanning module boundaries, like the type-theoretical analysis in [10] in the context of the phase distinction formalism [15], or the ad-hoc proposal for Standard ML in [11].

From the point of view of our calculus, adding the possibility of type definitions in modules requires an ad-hoc treatment. The basic problem is that mutually recursive definitions of types cannot be left open to redefinition (i.e., type components cannot be virtual, following the terminology used in this paper), since the static correctness of other components may rely on their current implementation. Hence, module operators must be refined in order to handle type components in a special way: for instance, when summing two modules the binding of deferred types of one module with corresponding defined types of the other must be always implicitly performed, whereas other components are implicitly bound by means of the freeze operator.

In this paper we have not considered type components since here we are mainly interested in defining a set of both powerful and simple primitive module operators. We have already developed a categorical approach to the denotational semantics of modules dealing with types in [5] and a concrete module language built on top of a simple functional language in [2] (Chapter 5). Hence, defining an enriched calculus with type components will be the more important and

[4] For sake of simplicity we assume the method *inc* to be non-virtual.

[5] See `http://www.disi.unige.it/person/AnconaD/Java/UPCMS.html`.

immediate subject of further work; we expect that more additional ingredients than those required in this paper will be needed at the core level, e.g. a syntax for type definitions, or for *type constraints* (see [3]) if we want to take into account a more flexible approach allowing types to be "partially" specified.

Other interesting research directions are a further study of the properties of the calculus, like soundness, and a more accurate comparison with other basic calculi as outlined in Sect.3.

Acknowledgments

We warmly thank Xavier Leroy and Eugenio Moggi for many useful suggestions on a preliminary version of this calculus. In particular, Xavier provided interesting hints for the encoding of λ-calculus. Many thanks also to Zino Benaissa, Mark Jones and Walid Taha.

References

1. M. Abadi and L. Cardelli. *A Theory of Objects*. Monographs in Computer Science. Springer Verlag, New York, 1996.
2. D. Ancona. *Modular Formal Frameworks for Module Systems*. PhD thesis, Dipartimento di Informatica, Università di Pisa, 1998.
3. D. Ancona. An algebraic framework for separate type-checking. In J. Fiadeiro, editor, *WADT'98 (13th Workshop on Algebraic Development Techniques)*, Lecture Notes in Computer Science. Springer Verlag, 1999. To appear.
4. D. Ancona and E. Zucca. Overriding operators in a mixin-based framework. In H. Glaser, P. Hartel, and H. Kuchen, editors, *PLILP '97 - 9th Intl. Symp. on Programming Languages, Implementations, Logics and Programs*, number 1292 in Lecture Notes in Computer Science, pages 47–61, Berlin, 1997. Springer Verlag.
5. D. Ancona and E. Zucca. A theory of mixin modules: Basic and derived operators. *Mathematical Structures in Computer Science*, 8(4):401–446, August 1998.
6. D. Ancona and E. Zucca. A modular calculus for module systems. Technical report, Dipartimento di Informatica e Scienze dell'Informazione, Università di Genova, June 1999.
7. G. Bracha. *The Programming Language JIGSAW: Mixins, Modularity and Multiple Inheritance*. PhD thesis, Department of Comp. Sci., Univ. of Utah, 1992.
8. L. Cardelli. Program fragments, linking, and modularization. In *ACM Symp. on Principles of Programming Languages 1997*, pages 266–277. ACM Press, January 1997.
9. W. Cook. *A Denotational Semantics of Inheritance*. PhD thesis, Dept. Comp. Sci., Brown University, 1989.
10. K. Crary, R. Harper, and S. Puri. What is a recursive module? In *PLDI'99 - ACM Conf. on Programming Language Design and Implementation*, 1999. To appear.
11. D. Duggan and C. Sourelis. Mixin modules. In *Intl. Conf. on Functional Programming*, pages 262–273, Philadelphia, June 1996. ACM Press. SIGPLAN Notices, volume 31, number 6.
12. M. Flatt and M. Felleisen. Units: Cool modules for HOT languages. In *PLDI'98 - ACM Conf. on Programming Language Design and Implementation*, pages 236–248, 1998.
13. M. Flatt, S. Krishnamurthi, and M. Felleisen. Classes and mixins. In *ACM Symp. on Principles of Programming Languages 1998*, pages 171–183, January 1998.

14. R. Harper and M. Lillibridge. A type theoretic approach to higher-order modules with sharing. In *ACM Symp. on Principles of Programming Languages 1994*, pages 127–137. ACM Press, 1994.
15. R. Harper, M. Lillibridge, and E. Moggi. Higher-order modules and the phase distinction. In *ACM Symp. on Principles of Programming Languages 1990*, pages 341–354, S. Francisco, CA, January 1990. ACM Press.
16. X. Leroy. Manifest types, modules and separate compilation. In *ACM Symp. on Principles of Programming Languages 1994*, pages 109–122. ACM Press, 1994.
17. X. Leroy. A modular module system. Technical Report 2866, Institute National de Recherche en Informatique et Automatique, April 1996.
18. R. Milner, M. Tofte, and R. Harper. *The Definition of Standard ML*. The MIT Press, Cambridge, Massachussetts, 1990.
19. U. S. Reddy. Objects as closures: Abstract semantics of object-oriented languages. In *Proc. ACM Conf. on Lisp and Functional Programming*, pages 289–297, 1988.

Non-dependent Types for Standard ML Modules*

Claudio V. Russo

LFCS, Division of Informatics, University of Edinburgh,
JCMB, KB, Mayfield Road, Edinburgh EH9 3JZ
cvr@dcs.ed.ac.uk
http://www.dcs.ed.ac.uk/~cvr

Abstract. Two of the distinguishing features of the Standard ML modules language are its term dependent type syntax and the use of type generativity in its static semantics. From a type-theoretic perspective, the former suggests that the language involves first-order dependent types, while the latter has been regarded as an extra-logical device that bears no direct relation to type-theoretic constructs. We reformulate the existing semantics of Standard ML modules to reveal a purely second-order type theory. In particular, we show that generativity corresponds precisely to existential quantification over types and that the remainder of the modules type structure is based exclusively on the second-order notions of type parameterisation, universal type quantification and subtyping. Our account is more direct than others and has been shown to scale naturally to both higher-order and first-class modules.

1 Introduction

Standard ML [14] comprises two programming languages: the *Core* language expresses details of algorithms and data structures; the *Modules* language expresses the modular architecture of a software system. In Modules, Core language definitions of type and term identifiers can be packaged together into possibly nested terms called *structures*. Access to structure components is by the dot notation and provides good control of the name space in a large program.

The use of the dot notation to project types from terms suggests that the type structure of Standard ML is based on first-order dependent types. In this interpretation, proposed in [11] and refined in [3], nested structures are modelled as dependent pairs whose types are first-order existentially quantified types. Standard ML functors, that define functions mapping structures to structures, are modelled using dependent functions whose types are first-order universally quantified types. Adopting standard first-order dependent types in a programming language is problematic as it rules out the consistent extension to first-class modules [3] without introducing undecidable type checking. In [4], the authors observe that standard dependent types also violate the phase distinction between

* This research has been partially supported by EPSRC grant GR/K63795

G. Nadathur (Ed.): PPDP'99, LNCS 1702, pp. 80–97, 1999.

Core Types	$\mathrm{u} ::= \mathrm{t}$		type identifier
	$\mid \mathrm{u} \rightarrow \mathrm{u}'$		function type
	$\mid$ **int**		integers
	$\mid \mathrm{sp.t}$		type projection
Signature Bodies	$\mathrm{B} ::=$ **type** $\mathrm{t} = \mathrm{u}; \mathrm{B}$		transparent type specification
	$\mid$ **type** $\mathrm{t}; \mathrm{B}$		opaque type specification
	$\mid$ **val** $\mathrm{x} : \mathrm{u}; \mathrm{B}$		value specification
	$\mid$ **structure** $\mathrm{X} : \mathrm{S}; \mathrm{B}$		structure specification
	$\mid \epsilon_{\mathrm{B}}$		empty body
Signature Expressions	$\mathrm{S} ::=$ **sig** B **end**		encapsulated body

Fig. 1. Type Syntax of Mini-SML

compile-time type checking and run-time evaluation and propose a non-standard interpretation of dependent types that preserves the phase distinction and has decidable typing, but fails to account for other significant features of Modules, namely: type generativity, named structure components and subtyping on structures. More recently proposed module calculi [2,5,7,8,9,10] that capture most, but not all, of the features of Standard ML, and significantly generalise them, also resort to non-standard formulations of dependent types. Though enjoying a phase distinction, these calculi have other undesirable properties (undecidable subtyping in the presence of first-class modules [2,10]; no principal types in the presence of higher-order functors [2,5,7,8,10]).

In this paper, we take a second look at the type structure of Standard ML Modules by studying a representative toy language, Mini-SML. The static semantics of Mini-SML is based directly on that of Standard ML, but our choice of notation reveals an underlying type structure that, despite the term dependent type syntax, is based entirely on the simpler, second-order notions of type parameterisation, universal type quantification and subtyping. What remains to be explained is the role of type generativity in the semantics, that lends it a procedural, non type-theoretic flavour by requiring a global state of generated types to be maintained and updated during type checking. We explain and eliminate generativity by presenting an alternative, but equivalent, static semantics based on the introduction and elimination of second-order existential types [13], thus accounting for all of Mini-SML's type structure in a purely second-order type theory.

2 Syntax

Mini-SML includes the essential features of Standard ML Modules but, for presentation reasons, is constructed on top of a simple Core language of explicitly typed, monomorphic functions. The author's thesis [15], on which this paper is based, presents similar results for a generic Core language that may be instantiated to Standard ML's Core (which supports the definition of parameterised types, is implicitly typed, and polymorphic). The *type* and *term* syntax of Mini-SML is defined by the grammar in Figures 1 and 2, where $\mathrm{t} \in \mathrm{TypId}$, $\mathrm{x} \in \mathrm{ValId}$,

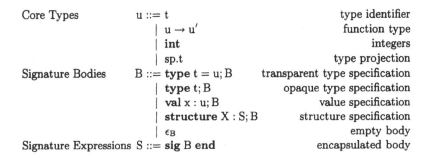

Core Expressions	$\mathrm{e} ::=$	x	value identifier
	$\mid$	$\lambda \mathrm{x} : \mathrm{u}.\mathrm{e}$	function
	$\mid$	$\mathrm{e}\ \mathrm{e}'$	application
	$\mid$	i	integer constant
	$\mid$	$\mathrm{sp}.\mathrm{x}$	value projection
Structure Paths	$\mathrm{sp} ::=$	X	structure identifier
	$\mid$	$\mathrm{sp}.\mathrm{X}$	structure projection
Structure Bodies	$\mathrm{b} ::=$	**type** t = u; b	type definition
	$\mid$	**datatype** t = u **with** x, x′; b	datatype definition
	$\mid$	**val** x = e; b	value definition
	$\mid$	**structure** X = s; b	structure definition
	$\mid$	**local** X = s **in** b	local structure definition
	$\mid$	**functor** F (X : S) = s **in** b	functor definition
	$\mid$	ϵ_b	empty body
Structure Expressions	$\mathrm{s} ::=$	sp	structure path
	$\mid$	**struct** b **end**	structure body
	$\mid$	F(s)	functor application
	$\mid$	s : S	transparent constraint
	$\mid$	s :> S	opaque constraint

Fig. 2. Term Syntax of Mini-SML

$\mathrm{X} \in \mathrm{StrId}$, and $\mathrm{F} \in \mathrm{FunId}$ range over disjoint sets of type, value, structure and functor identifiers.

A *core type* u may be used to define a type identifier or to specify the type of a Core value. These are just the types of a simple functional language, extended with the projection sp.t of a type component from a structure path. A *signature body* B is a sequential specification of a structure's components. A type component may be specified *transparently*, by equating it with a type, or *opaquely*, permitting a variety of implementations. Value and structure components are specified by their type and signature. The specifications in a body are dependent in that subsequent specifications may refer to previous ones. A *signature expression* S merely encapsulates a body. A structure *matches* a signature expression if it provides an implementation for all of the specified components, and possibly more.

Core expressions e describe a simple functional language extended with the projection of a value identifier from a structure path. A *structure path* sp is a reference to a bound structure identifier or the projection of one of its substructures. A *structure body* b is a sequence of definitions: subsequent definitions in the body may refer to previous ones. A type definition abbreviates a type. A datatype definition generates a new (recursive) type with value *constructor* x and value *destructor* x′. Value, structure and local definitions bind term identifiers to the values of expressions. A functor definition introduces a named function on structures: X is the functor's formal argument, S specifies the argument's type, and s is the functor's body that may refer to X. The functor may be applied to any argument that matches S. A *structure expression* s evaluates to a struc-

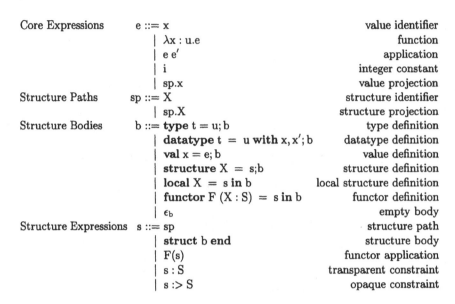

$$
\begin{array}{rll}
\alpha \in \mathit{Var} & \stackrel{\text{def}}{=} \{\alpha, \beta, \delta, \gamma, \ldots\} & \text{type variables} \\
M,N,P,Q \in \mathit{VarSet} & \stackrel{\text{def}}{=} \mathrm{Fin}(\mathit{Var}) & \text{sets of type variables} \\
u \in \mathit{Type} & ::= \alpha & \text{type variable} \\
& \mid\ u \rightarrow u' & \text{function space} \\
& \mid\ \mathrm{int} & \text{integers} \\
\varphi \in \mathit{Real} & \stackrel{\text{def}}{=} \mathit{Var} \stackrel{\text{fin}}{\rightarrow} \mathit{Type} & \text{realisations} \\
\mathcal{S} \in \mathit{Str} & \stackrel{\text{def}}{=} \left\{ \begin{array}{l|l} \mathcal{S}_{\mathrm{t}} \cup & \mathcal{S}_{\mathrm{t}} \in \mathrm{TypId} \stackrel{\text{fin}}{\rightarrow} \mathit{Type}, \\ \mathcal{S}_{\mathrm{x}} \cup & \mathcal{S}_{\mathrm{x}} \in \mathrm{ValId} \stackrel{\text{fin}}{\rightarrow} \mathit{Type}, \\ \mathcal{S}_{\mathrm{X}} & \mathcal{S}_{\mathrm{X}} \in \mathrm{StrId} \stackrel{\text{fin}}{\rightarrow} \mathit{Str} \end{array} \right\} & \text{semantic structures} \\
\mathcal{L} \in \mathit{Sig} & ::= \Lambda P.\mathcal{S} & \text{semantic signatures} \\
\mathcal{X} \in \mathit{ExStr} & ::= \exists P.\mathcal{S} & \text{existential structures} \\
\mathcal{F} \in \mathit{Fun} & ::= \forall P.\mathcal{S} \rightarrow \mathcal{X} & \text{semantic functors} \\
\mathcal{C} \in \mathit{Context} & \stackrel{\text{def}}{=} \left\{ \begin{array}{l|l} \mathcal{C}_{\mathrm{t}} \cup & \mathcal{C}_{\mathrm{t}} \in \mathrm{TypId} \stackrel{\text{fin}}{\rightarrow} \mathit{Type}, \\ \mathcal{C}_{\mathrm{x}} \cup & \mathcal{C}_{\mathrm{x}} \in \mathrm{ValId} \stackrel{\text{fin}}{\rightarrow} \mathit{Type}, \\ \mathcal{C}_{\mathrm{X}} \cup & \mathcal{C}_{\mathrm{X}} \in \mathrm{StrId} \stackrel{\text{fin}}{\rightarrow} \mathit{Str}, \\ \mathcal{C}_{\mathrm{F}} & \mathcal{C}_{\mathrm{F}} \in \mathrm{FunId} \stackrel{\text{fin}}{\rightarrow} \mathit{Fun} \end{array} \right\} & \text{semantic contexts}
\end{array}
$$

Fig. 3. Semantic Objects of Mini-SML

ture. It may be a path or an encapsulated structure body, whose type, value and structure definitions become the components of the structure. The application of a functor evaluates its body with respect to the value of the actual argument, generating any new types created by the body. A transparent constraint restricts the visibility of the structure's components to those specified in the signature, which the structure must match, but preserves the actual implementations of type components with opaque specifications. An opaque constraint is similar, but generates new, and thus *abstract*, types for type components with opaque specifications.

Standard ML only permits functor definitions in the top-level syntax. Mini-SML allows local functor definitions in structure bodies, which can now serve as the top-level: this generalisation avoids the need for a separate top-level syntax.

3 Semantic Objects

Following Standard ML [14], the static semantics of Mini-SML distinguishes between the syntactic types of the language and their semantic counterparts called *semantic objects*. Semantic objects play the role of types in the static semantics. Figure 3 defines the semantic objects of Mini-SML. We let $\mathcal{O}$ range over all semantic objects.

Notation: For sets A and B, $\mathrm{Fin}(A)$ denotes the set of *finite subsets* of A, and $A \stackrel{\text{fin}}{\rightarrow} B$ denotes the set of *finite maps* from A to B. Let f and g be finite maps. $\mathcal{D}(f)$ denotes the *domain of definition* of f. The finite map $f + g$ has domain $\mathcal{D}(f) \cup \mathcal{D}(g)$ and values $(f+g)(a) \stackrel{\text{def}}{=}$ if $a \in \mathcal{D}(g)$ then $g(a)$ else $f(a)$.

Type variables $\alpha \in \mathit{Var}$ range over *semantic types* $u \in \mathit{Type}$. The latter are the semantic counterparts of syntactic Core types and are used to record the denotations of type identifiers and the types of value identifiers.

A *realisation* $\varphi \in \mathit{Real}$ maps type variables to semantic types and defines a *substitution* on type variables in the usual way. The operation of applying a realisation φ to an object $\mathcal{O}$ is written $\varphi(\mathcal{O})$.

Semantic structures $\mathcal{S} \in \mathit{Str}$ are used as the types of structure identifiers and paths. A semantic structure maps type components to the types they denote, and value and structure components to the types they inhabit. For clarity, we define the extension functions $\mathrm{t} \triangleright u, \mathcal{S} \stackrel{\text{def}}{=} \{\mathrm{t} \mapsto u\} + \mathcal{S}$, $\mathrm{x} : u, \mathcal{S} \stackrel{\text{def}}{=} \{\mathrm{x} \mapsto u\} + \mathcal{S}$, and $\mathrm{X} : \mathcal{S}, \mathcal{S}' \stackrel{\text{def}}{=} \{\mathrm{X} \mapsto \mathcal{S}\} + \mathcal{S}'$, and let $\epsilon_{\mathcal{S}}$ denote the empty structure $\emptyset$.

Note that Λ, $\exists$ and $\forall$ bind finite sets of type variables.

A *semantic signature* $\Lambda P.\mathcal{S}$ is a parameterised type: it describes the family of structures $\varphi(\mathcal{S})$, for φ a realisation of the parameters in P.

The *existential structure* $\exists P.\mathcal{S}$, on the other hand, is a quantified type: variables in P are existentially quantified in $\mathcal{S}$ and thus abstract.

A *semantic functor* $\forall P.\mathcal{S} \to \mathcal{X}$ describes the type of a functor identifier: the universally quantified variables in P are bound simultaneously in the functor's domain, $\mathcal{S}$, and its range, $\mathcal{X}$. These variables capture the type components of the domain on which the functor behaves polymorphically; their possible occurrence in the range caters for the propagation of type identities from the functor's actual argument: functors are polymorphic functions on structures. The range $\mathcal{X}$ of a functor is an existential structure $\mathcal{X} \equiv \exists Q.\mathcal{S}'$. Q is the functor's set of generative type variables, as described in the Definition of Standard ML [14]. When a functor with this range is applied, the type of the result is a variant of $\mathcal{S}'$, obtained by replacing variables in Q with new, generative variables.

The Definition of Standard ML [14] is decidedly non-committal in its choice of binding operators, using the uniform notation of parenthesised variable sets to indicate binding in semantic objects. We prefer to differentiate binders with the more suggestive notation Λ, $\forall$ and $\exists$.

A *context* $\mathcal{C}$ is a finite map mapping type identifiers to the semantic types they denote, and value, structure and functor identifiers to the types they inhabit. For clarity, we define the extension functions $\mathcal{C}, \mathrm{t} \triangleright u \stackrel{\text{def}}{=} \mathcal{C} + \{\mathrm{t} \mapsto u\}$, $\mathcal{C}, \mathrm{x} : u \stackrel{\text{def}}{=} \mathcal{C} + \{\mathrm{x} \mapsto u\}$, $\mathcal{C}, \mathrm{X} : \mathcal{S} \stackrel{\text{def}}{=} \mathcal{C} + \{\mathrm{x} \mapsto \mathcal{S}\}$, and $\mathcal{C}, \mathrm{F} : \mathcal{F} \stackrel{\text{def}}{=} \mathcal{C} + \{\mathrm{F} \mapsto \mathcal{F}\}$.

We let $\mathcal{V}(\mathcal{O})$ denote the set of variables occurring *free* in $\mathcal{O}$, where the notions of free and bound variable are defined as usual. Furthermore, we *identify* semantic objects that differ only in a renaming of bound type variables (α-conversion).

The operation of applying a realisation to a type (substitution) is extended to all semantic objects in the usual way, taking care to avoid the capture of free variables by bound variables.

Definition 1 (Enrichment Relation) *Given two structures $\mathcal{S}$ and $\mathcal{S}'$, $\mathcal{S}$ enriches $\mathcal{S}'$, written $\mathcal{S} \succeq \mathcal{S}'$, if and only if $\mathcal{D}(\mathcal{S}) \supseteq \mathcal{D}(\mathcal{S}')$, and*

$$\boxed{\mathcal{C} \vdash \mathrm{u} \rhd u} \qquad \frac{\mathrm{t} \in \mathcal{D}(\mathcal{C})}{\mathcal{C} \vdash \mathrm{t} \rhd \mathcal{C}(\mathrm{t})} \qquad \frac{\mathcal{C} \vdash \mathrm{u} \rhd u \quad \mathcal{C} \vdash \mathrm{u}' \rhd u'}{\mathcal{C} \vdash \mathrm{u} \to \mathrm{u}' \rhd u \to u'} \qquad \frac{}{\mathcal{C} \vdash \mathbf{int} \rhd \mathrm{int}}$$

$$\frac{\mathcal{C} \vdash \mathrm{sp} : \mathcal{S} \quad \mathrm{t} \in \mathcal{D}(\mathcal{S})}{\mathcal{C} \vdash \mathrm{sp.t} \rhd \mathcal{S}(\mathrm{t})} \ (1)$$

$$\boxed{\mathcal{C} \vdash \mathrm{B} \rhd \mathcal{L}} \qquad \frac{\mathcal{C} \vdash \mathrm{u} \rhd u \quad \mathcal{C}, \mathrm{t} \rhd u \vdash \mathrm{B} \rhd \Lambda P.\mathcal{S} \quad \mathrm{t} \notin \mathcal{D}(\mathcal{S}) \quad P \cap \mathcal{V}(u) = \emptyset}{\mathcal{C} \vdash (\mathbf{type}\ \mathrm{t} = \mathrm{u}; \mathrm{B}) \rhd \Lambda P.(\mathrm{t} \rhd u, \mathcal{S})}$$

$$\frac{\alpha \notin \mathcal{V}(\mathcal{C}) \quad \mathcal{C}, \mathrm{t} \rhd \alpha \vdash \mathrm{B} \rhd \Lambda P.\mathcal{S} \quad \mathrm{t} \notin \mathcal{D}(\mathcal{S}) \quad \alpha \notin P}{\mathcal{C} \vdash (\mathbf{type}\ \mathrm{t}; \mathrm{B}) \rhd \Lambda \{\alpha\} \cup P.(\mathrm{t} \rhd \alpha, \mathcal{S})} \ (2)$$

$$\frac{\mathcal{C} \vdash \mathrm{u} \rhd u \quad \mathcal{C}, \mathrm{x} : u \vdash \mathrm{B} \rhd \Lambda P.\mathcal{S} \quad \mathrm{x} \notin \mathcal{D}(\mathcal{S}) \quad P \cap \mathcal{V}(u) = \emptyset}{\mathcal{C} \vdash (\mathbf{val}\ \mathrm{x} : \mathrm{u}; \mathrm{B}) \rhd \Lambda P.(\mathrm{x} : u, \mathcal{S})}$$

$$\frac{\mathcal{C} \vdash \mathrm{S} \rhd \Lambda P.\mathcal{S} \quad P \cap \mathcal{V}(\mathcal{C}) = \emptyset \quad \mathcal{C}, \mathrm{X} : \mathcal{S} \vdash \mathrm{B} \rhd \Lambda Q.\mathcal{S}' \quad \mathrm{X} \notin \mathcal{D}(\mathcal{S}') \quad Q \cap (P \cup \mathcal{V}(\mathcal{S})) = \emptyset}{\mathcal{C} \vdash (\mathbf{structure}\ \mathrm{X} : \mathrm{S}; \mathrm{B}) \rhd \Lambda P \cup Q.(\mathrm{X} : \mathcal{S}, \mathcal{S}')}$$

$$\frac{}{\mathcal{C} \vdash \epsilon_{\mathrm{B}} \rhd \Lambda \emptyset.\epsilon_{\mathcal{S}}}$$

$$\boxed{\mathcal{C} \vdash \mathrm{S} \rhd \mathcal{L}} \qquad \frac{\mathcal{C} \vdash \mathrm{B} \rhd \mathcal{L}}{\mathcal{C} \vdash \mathbf{sig}\ \mathrm{B}\ \mathbf{end} \rhd \mathcal{L}}$$

$$\boxed{\mathcal{C} \vdash \mathrm{e} : u} \qquad \frac{\mathrm{x} \in \mathcal{D}(\mathcal{C})}{\mathcal{C} \vdash \mathrm{x} : \mathcal{C}(\mathrm{x})} \qquad \frac{\mathcal{C} \vdash \mathrm{u} \rhd u \quad \mathcal{C}, \mathrm{x} : u \vdash \mathrm{e} : u'}{\mathcal{C} \vdash \lambda \mathrm{x} : \mathrm{u.e} : u \to u'} \qquad \frac{\mathcal{C} \vdash \mathrm{e} : u' \to u \quad \mathcal{C} \vdash \mathrm{e}' : u'}{\mathcal{C} \vdash \mathrm{e\, e}' : u}$$

$$\frac{}{\mathcal{C} \vdash \mathrm{i} : \mathrm{int}} \qquad \frac{\mathcal{C} \vdash \mathrm{sp} : \mathcal{S} \quad \mathrm{x} \in \mathcal{D}(\mathcal{S})}{\mathcal{C} \vdash \mathrm{sp.x} : \mathcal{S}(\mathrm{x})}$$

$$\boxed{\mathcal{C} \vdash \mathrm{sp} : \mathcal{S}} \qquad \frac{\mathrm{X} \in \mathcal{D}(\mathcal{C})}{\mathcal{C} \vdash \mathrm{X} : \mathcal{C}(\mathrm{X})} \qquad \frac{\mathcal{C} \vdash \mathrm{sp} : \mathcal{S} \quad \mathrm{X} \in \mathcal{D}(\mathcal{S})}{\mathcal{C} \vdash \mathrm{sp.X} : \mathcal{S}(\mathrm{X})}$$

Fig. 4. Common Denotation and Classification Judgements

- *for all* $\mathrm{t} \in \mathcal{D}(\mathcal{S}')$, $\mathcal{S}(\mathrm{t}) = \mathcal{S}'(\mathrm{t})$,
- *for all* $\mathrm{x} \in \mathcal{D}(\mathcal{S}')$, $\mathcal{S}(\mathrm{x}) = \mathcal{S}'(\mathrm{x})$, *and*
- *for all* $\mathrm{X} \in \mathcal{D}(\mathcal{S}')$, $\mathcal{S}(\mathrm{X}) \succeq \mathcal{S}'(\mathrm{X})$.

Enrichment is a pre-order that defines a *subtyping* relation on semantic structures (i.e. $\mathcal{S}$ is a subtype of $\mathcal{S}'$ if and only if $\mathcal{S} \succeq \mathcal{S}'$).

Definition 2 (Functor Instantiation) *A semantic functor* $\forall P.\mathcal{S} \to \mathcal{X}$ *instantiates to a* functor instance $\mathcal{S}' \to \mathcal{X}'$, *written* $\forall P.\mathcal{S} \to \mathcal{X} > \mathcal{S}' \to \mathcal{X}'$, *if and only if* $\varphi(\mathcal{S}) = \mathcal{S}'$ *and* $\varphi(\mathcal{X}) = \mathcal{X}'$, *for some realisation* φ *with* $\mathcal{D}(\varphi) = P$.

Definition 3 (Signature Matching) *A semantic structure* $\mathcal{S}$ matches *a signature* $\Lambda P.\mathcal{S}'$ *if and only if there exists a realisation* φ *with* $\mathcal{D}(\varphi) = P$ *such that* $\mathcal{S} \succeq \varphi(\mathcal{S}')$.

$$\boxed{\mathcal{C}, N \vdash \mathrm{b} : \mathcal{S} \Rightarrow M} \qquad \frac{\mathcal{C} \vdash \mathrm{u} \triangleright u \quad (\mathcal{C}, \mathrm{t} \triangleright u), N \vdash \mathrm{b} : \mathcal{S} \Rightarrow M}{\mathcal{C}, N \vdash (\textbf{type}\ \mathrm{t} = \mathrm{u}; \mathrm{b}) : (\mathrm{t} \triangleright u, \mathcal{S}) \Rightarrow M}$$

$$\frac{\begin{array}{c}\alpha \notin N \qquad \mathcal{C}, \mathrm{t} \triangleright \alpha \vdash \mathrm{u} \triangleright u \\ (\mathcal{C}, \mathrm{t} \triangleright \alpha, \mathrm{x} : u \to \alpha, \mathrm{x}' : \alpha \to u), N \cup \{\alpha\} \vdash \mathrm{b} : \mathcal{S} \Rightarrow M\end{array}}{\mathcal{C}, N \vdash (\textbf{datatype}\ \mathrm{t}\ =\ u\ \textbf{with}\ \mathrm{x}, \mathrm{x}'; \mathrm{b}) : (\mathrm{t} \triangleright \alpha, \mathrm{x} : u \to \alpha, \mathrm{x}' : \alpha \to u, \mathcal{S}) \Rightarrow \{\alpha\} \cup M} \quad (3)$$

$$\frac{\mathcal{C} \vdash \mathrm{e} : u \quad (\mathcal{C}, \mathrm{x} : u), N \vdash \mathrm{b} : \mathcal{S} \Rightarrow M}{\mathcal{C}, N \vdash (\textbf{val}\ \mathrm{x} = \mathrm{e}; \mathrm{b}) : (\mathrm{x} : u, \mathcal{S}) \Rightarrow M}$$

$$\frac{\mathcal{C}, N \vdash \mathrm{s} : \mathcal{S} \Rightarrow P \quad (\mathcal{C}, \mathrm{X} : \mathcal{S}), N \cup P \vdash \mathrm{b} : \mathcal{S}' \Rightarrow Q}{\mathcal{C}, N \vdash (\textbf{structure}\ \mathrm{X}\ =\ \mathrm{s}; \mathrm{b}) : (\mathrm{X} : \mathcal{S}, \mathcal{S}') \Rightarrow P \cup Q} \quad (4)$$

$$\frac{\mathcal{C}, N \vdash \mathrm{s} : \mathcal{S} \Rightarrow P \quad (\mathcal{C}, \mathrm{X} : \mathcal{S}), N \cup P \vdash \mathrm{b} : \mathcal{S}' \Rightarrow Q}{\mathcal{C}, N \vdash (\textbf{local}\ \mathrm{X}\ =\ \mathrm{s}\ \textbf{in}\ \mathrm{b}) : \mathcal{S}' \Rightarrow P \cup Q}$$

$$\frac{\begin{array}{c}\mathcal{C} \vdash \mathrm{S} \triangleright \Lambda P.\mathcal{S} \qquad P \cap N = \emptyset \qquad (\mathcal{C}, \mathrm{X} : \mathcal{S}), N \cup P \vdash \mathrm{s} : \mathcal{S}' \Rightarrow Q \\ (\mathcal{C}, \mathrm{F} : \forall P.\mathcal{S} \to \exists Q.\mathcal{S}'), N \vdash \mathrm{b} : \mathcal{S}'' \Rightarrow M\end{array}}{\mathcal{C}, N \vdash (\textbf{functor}\ \mathrm{F}\ (\mathrm{X} : \mathrm{S})\ =\ \mathrm{s}\ \textbf{in}\ \mathrm{b}) : \mathcal{S}'' \Rightarrow M}$$

$$\frac{}{\mathcal{C}, N \vdash \epsilon_{\mathrm{b}} : \epsilon_{\mathcal{S}} \Rightarrow \emptyset}$$

$$\boxed{\mathcal{C}, M \vdash \mathrm{s} : \mathcal{S} \Rightarrow N} \qquad \frac{\mathcal{C} \vdash \mathrm{sp} : \mathcal{S}}{\mathcal{C}, N \vdash \mathrm{sp} : \mathcal{S} \Rightarrow \emptyset} \qquad \frac{\mathcal{C}, N \vdash \mathrm{b} : \mathcal{S} \Rightarrow M}{\mathcal{C}, N \vdash \textbf{struct}\ \mathrm{b}\ \textbf{end} : \mathcal{S} \Rightarrow M}$$

$$\frac{\mathcal{C}, N \vdash \mathrm{s} : \mathcal{S} \Rightarrow P \quad \mathcal{C}(\mathrm{F}) > \mathcal{S}' \to \exists Q.\mathcal{S}'' \quad \mathcal{S} \succeq \mathcal{S}' \quad Q \cap (N \cup P) = \emptyset}{\mathcal{C}, N \vdash \mathrm{F}(\mathrm{s}) : \mathcal{S}'' \Rightarrow P \cup Q} \quad (5)$$

$$\frac{\mathcal{C}, N \vdash \mathrm{s} : \mathcal{S} \Rightarrow P \quad \mathcal{C} \vdash \mathrm{S} \triangleright \Lambda Q.\mathcal{S}' \quad \mathcal{S} \succeq \varphi(\mathcal{S}') \quad \mathcal{D}(\varphi) = Q}{\mathcal{C}, N \vdash (\mathrm{s} : \mathrm{S}) : \varphi(\mathcal{S}') \Rightarrow P}$$

$$\frac{\mathcal{C}, N \vdash \mathrm{s} : \mathcal{S} \Rightarrow P \quad \mathcal{C} \vdash \mathrm{S} \triangleright \Lambda Q.\mathcal{S}' \quad \mathcal{S} \succeq \varphi(\mathcal{S}') \quad \mathcal{D}(\varphi) = Q \quad Q \cap N = \emptyset}{\mathcal{C}, N \vdash (\mathrm{s} :> \mathrm{S}) : \mathcal{S}' \Rightarrow Q} \quad (6)$$

Fig. 5. Generative Classification Judgements

4 Static Semantics

In this section we introduce two distinct static semantics for structure bodies and structure expressions. The systems rely on shared judgement forms relating Core types, signature bodies and signature expressions to their denotations, and Core expressions and structure paths to their types. The common judgements are shown in Figure 4. We can factor out these judgements because they do not generate any new *free* variables in their conclusions. Observe that the opaque type specifications in a signature expression give rise to the type parameters of the semantic signature it denotes (Rule 2).

4.1 Generative Semantics

Figure 5 presents a static semantics for structure bodies and expressions that employs *generative* classification judgements in the style of Standard ML [14].

Consider the form of the judgements $\mathcal{C}, N \vdash \mathrm{b} : \mathcal{S} \Rightarrow M$ and $\mathcal{C}, N \vdash \mathrm{s} : \mathcal{S} \Rightarrow M$. The set of type variables N is meant to capture a superset of the variables generated so far. Classification produces, besides the semantic object $\mathcal{S}$, the set of variables M generated *during* the classification of the phrase b or s. The variable sets are threaded through classification trees in a global, state-like manner. This avoids any unsafe confusion of existing variables with the fresh variables generated by datatype definitions (Rule 3), functor applications (Rule 5), and opaque constraints (Rule 6). The generative nature of classification is expressed by the following property:

Property 1 (Generativity) *If* $\mathcal{C}, N \vdash \mathrm{b}/\mathrm{s} : \mathcal{S} \Rightarrow M$ *then* $N \cap M = \emptyset$.[1]

Note that the sets of generated variables are *not* redundant. Suppose we deleted them from the classification judgements and replaced occurrences of N by $\mathcal{V}(\mathcal{C})$, so that variables are generated to be fresh with respect to just the current context instead of the state.

For a counterexample, consider the following phrase:

$$
\begin{array}{l}
\textbf{structure X} = \textbf{struct datatype t} \;=\; \textbf{int with c, d end;} \\
\textbf{structure Y} = \textbf{struct structure X} \;=\; \textbf{struct end;} \\
\qquad\qquad\qquad\qquad\quad \textbf{datatype u} \;=\; \textbf{int} \rightarrow \textbf{int with c, d} \\
\qquad\qquad\quad \textbf{end;} \\
\textbf{val x} = (\textbf{Y.d}\ (\textbf{X.c}\ 1))\ 2
\end{array}
$$

This phrase is unsound because the definition of **x** leads to the sad attempt of applying 1 to 2. The phrase should be rejected by a sound static semantics.

In the putatively simpler, state-less semantics, we only require that the type variables chosen for **t** and **u** are distinct from the variables free in the context of their respective definitions. The annotated phrase shows what can go wrong:

$$
\begin{array}{l}
\overset{\emptyset}{\lceil}\textbf{structure X} = \textbf{struct}\ \overset{\emptyset}{\lceil}\textbf{datatype t}_{\alpha} \;=\; \textbf{int with c, d end;} \\
\overset{\{\alpha\}}{\lceil}\textbf{structure Y} = \textbf{struct}\ \overset{\{\alpha\}}{\lceil}\textbf{structure X} \;=\; \textbf{struct end;} \\
\qquad\qquad\qquad\qquad\qquad\quad \overset{\emptyset}{\lceil}\textbf{datatype u}_{\alpha} \;=\; \textbf{int} \rightarrow \textbf{int with c, d} \\
\qquad\qquad\quad \textbf{end;} \\
\overset{\{\alpha\}}{\lceil}\textbf{val x} = (\textbf{Y.d}_{\alpha \rightarrow \textbf{int} \rightarrow \textbf{int}}(\textbf{X.c}_{\textbf{int} \rightarrow \alpha}\ 1)_{\alpha}\ )_{\textbf{int} \rightarrow \textbf{int}}\ 2
\end{array}
$$

Assuming an initially empty context, we have annotated the beginning of each structure body b with the set N of variables free in the local context, using the notation $\overset{N}{\lceil}\,\mathrm{b}$, the defining occurrences of **t** and **u** are decorated with their

[1] When P is a predicate, we use the abbreviation $P(\mathrm{b}/\mathrm{s})$ to mean $P(\mathrm{b})$ *and* $P(\mathrm{s})$.

denotations, and key subphrases with their types. The problem is that **t** and **u** are assigned the same type variable α, even though they must be distinguished. The problem arises because α, already set aside for **t**, no longer occurs free in the local context at the definition of **u**: the free occurrence is eclipsed by the shadow of the second definition of **X**. Thus the semantics may again choose α to represent **u**, and incorrectly accept the definition of **x**.

The generative semantics that uses a state maintains soundness as follows:

$$\begin{array}{llll}
\overset{\emptyset}{\downarrow} \textbf{structure X} = \textbf{struct} & \overset{\emptyset}{\downarrow} \textbf{datatype } \mathbf{t}_\alpha & = & \textbf{int with } \mathrm{c}, \mathbf{d}\overset{\{\alpha\}}{\uparrow} \textbf{ end}; \\
\overset{\{\alpha\}}{\downarrow} \textbf{structure Y} = \textbf{struct} & \overset{\{\alpha\}}{\downarrow} \textbf{structure X} & = & \textbf{struct end}; \\
 & \overset{\{\alpha\}}{\downarrow} \textbf{datatype } \mathbf{u}_\beta & = & \textbf{int} \rightarrow \textbf{int with } \mathrm{c}, \mathbf{d}\overset{\{\beta\}}{\uparrow} \overset{\{\beta\}}{\uparrow} \\
\qquad\qquad\quad \textbf{end}; & & & \\
\multicolumn{4}{l}{\overset{\{\alpha,\beta\}}{\downarrow} \textbf{val x} = \underline{(\mathbf{Y}.\mathbf{d}_{\beta \rightarrow \mathbf{int} \rightarrow \mathbf{int}}(\mathbf{X}.\mathbf{c}_{\mathbf{int} \rightarrow \alpha}\ 1)_\alpha\ )}\ 2}
\end{array}$$

Assuming an initially empty context and state, we have indicated, at the beginning of each structure body b, the state N of variables generated so far, and, at its end, the variables M generated during its classification. We use the notation $\overset{N}{\downarrow} \mathrm{b} \overset{M}{\uparrow}$, corresponding to a classification $\ldots, N \vdash \mathrm{b} : \ldots \Rightarrow M$. Observe that generated variables are accumulated in the state as we traverse the phrase. At the definition of **u**, α is recorded in the state, even though it no longer occurs free in the current context, forcing the choice of a distinct variable β. In turn, this leads to the detection of the type violation, which is underlined.

These observations motivate:

Definition 4 (Rigidity) *$\mathcal{C}$ is* rigid *w.r.t. N, written $\mathcal{C}, N$* **rigid**, *if and only if $\mathcal{V}(\mathcal{C}) \subseteq N$.*

As long as we start with $\mathcal{C}, N$ **rigid**, as a consequence of Property 1, those variables in M resulting from the classification of b and s will never be confused with variables visible in the context, even if these are temporarily hidden by bindings added to $\mathcal{C}$ during sub-classifications.

A similar example motivates the generativity of functor application. Consider this unsound phrase that applies 1 to 2 in the definition of **x**:

functor F(X: sig type t end) = struct datatype u = X.t with c, d end
in
structure Y = F(struct type t = int end);
structure Z = F(struct type t = int → int end);
val x = (Z.d (Y.c 1)) 2

In a naive semantics with applicative (non-generative) functors, we would simply add the generative variables returned by a functor's body to the state at the functor's definition, omitting the generation of fresh variables each time it is applied. Then each application of the functor would return equivalent abstract types. In our example, this means that the types **Y.u** and **Z.u** would be

$$\boxed{\mathcal{C} \vdash \mathrm{b} : \mathcal{X}} \qquad \frac{\mathcal{C} \vdash \mathrm{u} \triangleright u \quad \mathcal{C}, \mathrm{t} \triangleright u \vdash \mathrm{b} : \exists P.\mathcal{S} \quad P \cap \mathcal{V}(u) = \emptyset}{\mathcal{C} \vdash (\mathbf{type}\ \mathrm{t} = \mathrm{u}; \mathrm{b}) : \exists P.(\mathrm{t} \triangleright u, \mathcal{S})}$$

$$\frac{\begin{array}{ll} \alpha \notin \mathcal{V}(\mathcal{C}) & \mathcal{C}, \mathrm{t} \triangleright \alpha \vdash \mathrm{u} \triangleright u \\ \mathcal{C}, \mathrm{t} \triangleright \alpha, \mathrm{x} : u \to \alpha, \mathrm{x}' : \alpha \to u \vdash \mathrm{b} : \exists P.\mathcal{S}' & P \cap (\{\alpha\} \cup \mathcal{V}(u)) = \emptyset \end{array}}{\mathcal{C} \vdash (\mathbf{datatype}\ \mathrm{t} = u\ \mathbf{with}\ \mathrm{x}, \mathrm{x}'; \mathrm{b}) : \exists \{\alpha\} \cup P.(\mathrm{t} \triangleright \alpha, \mathrm{x} : u \to \alpha, \mathrm{x}' : \alpha \to u, \mathcal{S}')} \quad (7)$$

$$\frac{\mathcal{C} \vdash \mathrm{e} : u \quad \mathcal{C}, \mathrm{x} : u \vdash \mathrm{b} : \exists P.\mathcal{S} \quad P \cap \mathcal{V}(u) = \emptyset}{\mathcal{C} \vdash (\mathbf{val}\ \mathrm{x} = \mathrm{e}; \mathrm{b}) : \exists P.(\mathrm{x} : u, \mathcal{S})}$$

$$\frac{\mathcal{C} \vdash \mathrm{s} : \exists P.\mathcal{S} \quad P \cap \mathcal{V}(\mathcal{C}) = \emptyset \quad \mathcal{C}, \mathrm{X} : \mathcal{S} \vdash \mathrm{b} : \exists Q.\mathcal{S}' \quad Q \cap (P \cup \mathcal{V}(\mathcal{S})) = \emptyset}{\mathcal{C} \vdash (\mathbf{structure}\ \mathrm{X} = \mathrm{s}; \mathrm{b}) : \exists P \cup Q.(\mathrm{X} : \mathcal{S}, \mathcal{S}')} \quad (8)$$

$$\frac{\mathcal{C} \vdash \mathrm{s} : \exists P.\mathcal{S} \quad P \cap \mathcal{V}(\mathcal{C}) = \emptyset \quad \mathcal{C}, \mathrm{X} : \mathcal{S} \vdash \mathrm{b} : \exists Q.\mathcal{S}' \quad Q \cap P = \emptyset}{\mathcal{C} \vdash (\mathbf{local}\ \mathrm{X} = \mathrm{s}\ \mathbf{in}\ \mathrm{b}) : \exists P \cup Q.\mathcal{S}'} \quad (9)$$

$$\frac{\begin{array}{c} \mathcal{C} \vdash \mathrm{S} \triangleright \Lambda P.\mathcal{S} \qquad P \cap \mathcal{V}(\mathcal{C}) = \emptyset \qquad \mathcal{C}, \mathrm{X} : \mathcal{S} \vdash \mathrm{s} : \mathcal{X} \\ \mathcal{C}, \mathrm{F} : \forall P.\mathcal{S} \to \mathcal{X} \vdash \mathrm{b} : \mathcal{X}' \end{array}}{\mathcal{C} \vdash (\mathbf{functor}\ \mathrm{F}\ (\mathrm{X} : \mathrm{S}) = \mathrm{s}\ \mathbf{in}\ \mathrm{b}) : \mathcal{X}'} \quad (10)$$

$$\frac{}{\mathcal{C} \vdash \epsilon_{\mathrm{b}} : \exists \emptyset.\epsilon_{\mathcal{S}}}$$

$$\boxed{\mathcal{C} \vdash \mathrm{s} : \mathcal{X}} \qquad \frac{\mathcal{C} \vdash \mathrm{sp} : \mathcal{S}}{\mathcal{C} \vdash \mathrm{sp} : \exists \emptyset.\mathcal{S}} \qquad \frac{\mathcal{C} \vdash \mathrm{b} : \mathcal{X}}{\mathcal{C} \vdash \mathbf{struct}\ \mathrm{b}\ \mathbf{end} : \mathcal{X}}$$

$$\frac{\mathcal{C} \vdash \mathrm{s} : \exists P.\mathcal{S} \quad P \cap \mathcal{V}(\mathcal{C}(\mathrm{F})) = \emptyset \quad \mathcal{C}(\mathrm{F}) > \mathcal{S}' \to \exists Q.\mathcal{S}'' \quad \mathcal{S} \succeq \mathcal{S}' \quad Q \cap P = \emptyset}{\mathcal{C} \vdash \mathrm{F}(\mathrm{s}) : \exists P \cup Q.\mathcal{S}''}$$

$$\frac{\mathcal{C} \vdash \mathrm{s} : \exists P.\mathcal{S} \quad \mathcal{C} \vdash \mathrm{S} \triangleright \Lambda Q.\mathcal{S}' \quad P \cap \mathcal{V}(\Lambda Q.\mathcal{S}') = \emptyset \quad \mathcal{S} \succeq \varphi(\mathcal{S}') \quad \mathcal{D}(\varphi) = Q}{\mathcal{C} \vdash (\mathrm{s} : \mathrm{S}) : \exists P.\varphi(\mathcal{S}')}$$

$$\frac{\mathcal{C} \vdash \mathrm{s} : \exists P.\mathcal{S} \quad \mathcal{C} \vdash \mathrm{S} \triangleright \Lambda Q.\mathcal{S}' \quad P \cap \mathcal{V}(\Lambda Q.\mathcal{S}') = \emptyset \quad \mathcal{S} \succeq \varphi(\mathcal{S}') \quad \mathcal{D}(\varphi) = Q}{\mathcal{C} \vdash (\mathrm{s} :> \mathrm{S}) : \exists Q.\mathcal{S}'}$$

Fig. 6. Type-Theoretic Classification Judgements

identified, allowing the unsound definition of **x** to be accepted. In the generative semantics, each application of **F** returns new types, so that **Y.u** and **Z.u** are distinguished and the definition of **x** is correctly rejected. Observe that the definition of **u** depends on the functor argument's opaque type component **t**, whose realisation can vary with each application of **F**. The naive applicative semantics for functors is unsound because it does not take account of this dependency; the generative semantics does. (Note that the less naive semantics of applicative functors given in [8] is sound because the abstract types returned by a functor application are expressed as a function of the functor's actual term argument.)

4.2 Type-Theoretic Semantics

To a type theorist, the generative judgements appear odd. The intrusion of the state imposes a procedural ordering on the premises of the generative rules that is in contrast with the declarative, compositional formulation of typing rules in Type Theory. The fact that the type of the term may contain "new" free type variables, that do not occur free in the context, is peculiar (conventional type theories enjoy the free variable property: the type of a term is closed with respect to the variables occurring free in the context). Perhaps for this reason, generativity has developed its own mystique and its own terminology. In Standard ML [14], type variables are called "type names" to stress their persistent, generative nature. Generativity is often presented as an extra-logical device, useful for programming language type systems, but distinct from more traditional type-theoretic constructs. In this section, we show how to replace the generative judgements by more declarative, type-theoretic ones.

Figure 6 presents an alternative static semantics for structure bodies and expressions, defined by the judgements $\mathcal{C} \vdash \mathrm{b} : \mathcal{X}$ and $\mathcal{C} \vdash \mathrm{s} : \mathcal{X}$. Rather than maintaining a global state of variables threaded through classifications, we classify structure bodies and expressions using *existential structures.*

The key idea is to replace *global* generativity with the introduction and elimination of existential types — in essence: *local* generativity. In the rules, the side conditions on bound variables prevent capture of free variables in the usual way. Because they are bound, the variables can always be renamed to satisfy the side conditions. For intuition, we explain some of the rules:

(**datatype** t $=$ u **with** x, x′; b): The denotation of u is determined in the context extended with the recursive assumption that t denotes α, where α is a hypothetical type represented by a variable that is fresh for $\mathcal{C}$. This determines the types of the constructor x and the destructor x′ that are added to the context before classifying the body b. Provided b has existential structure $\exists P.\mathcal{S}$, which may contain occurrences of α, we conceptually eliminate the existential quantification over $\mathcal{S}$, introducing the hypothetical types P, extend the record of components t, x and x′ by $\mathcal{S}$ and then existentially quantify over both the hypothetical type α and the hypothetical types P we just introduced.

(**structure** X $=$ s;b): Provided s has existential structure $\exists P.\mathcal{S}$, we eliminate the existential, introducing the hypothetical types P, and classify b in the context extended with the assumption X : $\mathcal{S}$ to obtain the existential structure $\exists Q.\mathcal{S}'$ of b. Now $\exists Q.\mathcal{S}'$ may contain some of the hypothetical types in P that should not escape their scope. We eliminate this existential, extend the component X : $\mathcal{S}$ by $\mathcal{S}'$ and existentially quantify over the hypothetical types $P \cup Q$.

(**functor** F (X : S) $=$ s **in** b): The signature expression S denotes a family of semantic structures, $\Lambda P.\mathcal{S}$. For every φ with $\mathcal{D}(\varphi) = P$, F should be applicable at any enrichment, i.e. subtype, of $\varphi(\mathcal{S})$. To this end, we classify the body s of F in the context extended with the assumption X : $\mathcal{S}$. By requiring that P is a locally fresh choice of type variables, we ensure that $\mathcal{S}$ is a *generic* example of a structure matching $\Lambda P.\mathcal{S}$, and that variables in P act as formal type parameters during the classification of the body. Classifying s yields an existential structure $\mathcal{X}$ that may contain occurrences of the parameters P. If this succeeds for a generic choice of parameters, it will also succeed for any realisation of these parameters[2]. We discharge the type parameters by universal quantification over P and add the assumption that F has the polymorphic type $\forall P.\mathcal{S} \rightarrow \mathcal{X}$ to the context. The scope b of the functor definition determines the type $\mathcal{X}'$ of the entire phrase.

(F(s)): Provided s has existential structure $\exists P.\mathcal{S}$, we locally eliminate the quantifier and choose an appropriate instance $\mathcal{S}' \rightarrow \exists Q.\mathcal{S}''$ of the functor's type. This step corresponds to eliminating the functor's polymorphism by choosing a realisation φ of its type parameters. The functor may applied if the actual argument's type $\mathcal{S}$ enriches the instance's domain $\mathcal{S}'$, i.e. provided $\mathcal{S}$ is a subtype of $\mathcal{S}'$. The range $\exists Q.\mathcal{S}''$ of the instance determines the type of the application, and may propagate some of the hypothetical types in P via the implicit realisation φ. To prevent these from escaping their scope, we abstract them by extending the existential quantification over $\mathcal{S}''$ to cover both P and Q.

(s : S): Provided s has existential type $\exists P.\mathcal{S}$ and S denotes a semantic signature, we first eliminate the existential quantification and then check that $\mathcal{S}$ matches the denotation of S. The denotation $\Lambda Q.\mathcal{S}'$ describes a family of semantic structures and the requirement is that the type $\mathcal{S}$ of the structure expression is a subtype of some member $\varphi(\mathcal{S}')$ of this family. Since φ is applied to $\mathcal{S}'$ in the conclusion $\exists P.\varphi(\mathcal{S}')$, the actual denotations of type components that have opaque specifications in S are preserved: however, the visibility of some components of s may be curtailed. The realised structure $\varphi(\mathcal{S}')$ may mention hypothetical types in P. Existentially quantifying over P prevents them from escaping their scope.

(s :> S): We proceed as in the previous case, but the type of s :> S is $\exists Q.\mathcal{S}'$, not $\exists P.\varphi(\mathcal{S}')$. Introducing the existential quantification over Q hides the realisation, rendering type components specified opaquely in S abstract.

Before we can state our main result we shall need one last concept:

Definition 5 (Ground Functors and Contexts) *A semantic functor* $\mathcal{F} \equiv \forall P.\mathcal{S} \rightarrow \mathcal{X}$ *is* ground, *written* $\vdash \mathcal{F}$ **Gnd** *if and only if* $P \subseteq \mathcal{V}(\mathcal{S})$. *A context* $\mathcal{C}$ *is* ground, *written* $\vdash \mathcal{C}$ **Gnd**, *precisely when all the semantic functors in its range are ground.*

The ground property of a semantic functor $\mathcal{F}$ ensures that whenever we apply a functor of this type, the free variables of the range are either propagated from the actual argument, or were already free in $\mathcal{F}$. With this observation one can prove the following free variable lemma:

Lemma 1 (Free Vars) *If* $\vdash \mathcal{C}$ **Gnd** *then* $\mathcal{C} \vdash \mathrm{b}/\mathrm{s} : \mathcal{X}$ *implies* $\mathcal{V}(\mathcal{X}) \subseteq \mathcal{V}(\mathcal{C})$.

Note that the ground property of contexts is preserved as an invariant of the classification rules. We only need to impose it when reasoning about classifications derived with respect to an arbitrary context, which might be non-ground.

[2] (it can be shown that derivations are closed under realisation, hence for any φ with domain P, because $\mathcal{C}, \mathrm{X} : \mathcal{S} \vdash \mathrm{s} : \mathcal{X}$ we also know that $\varphi((\mathcal{C}, \mathrm{X} : \mathcal{S})) \vdash \mathrm{s} : \varphi(\mathcal{X})$ and this is equivalent to $\mathcal{C}, \mathrm{X} : \varphi(\mathcal{S}) \vdash \mathrm{s} : \varphi(\mathcal{X})$, since $P \cap \mathcal{V}(\mathcal{C}) = \emptyset$)

We can revisit the example of Section 4.1 to demonstrate how our alternative semantics maintains soundness, without relying on a global state of generated type variables:

$$
\begin{array}{l}
\mathbf{structure}\ \lfloor_{(\mathbf{t}\triangleright\alpha,\mathbf{c}:\mathbf{int}\to\alpha,\mathbf{d}:\alpha\to\mathbf{int})}\mathbf{X} = \lceil^{\exists\{\alpha\}.(\mathbf{t}\triangleright\alpha,\mathbf{c}:\mathbf{int}\to\alpha,\mathbf{d}:\alpha\to\mathbf{int})}\mathbf{struct\ datatype\ t}_{\alpha}\ =\ \mathbf{int\ with\ c,d\ end;} \\
\mathbf{structure}\ \lfloor_{(\mathbf{X}:\epsilon_{\mathcal{S}},\mathbf{u}\triangleright\beta,\mathbf{c}:(\mathbf{int}\to\mathbf{int})\to\beta,\mathbf{d}:\beta\to\mathbf{int}\to\mathbf{int})}\mathbf{Y} = \lceil^{\exists\{\alpha\}.(\mathbf{X}:\epsilon_{\mathcal{S}},\mathbf{u}\triangleright\alpha,\mathbf{c}:(\mathbf{int}\to\mathbf{int})\to\alpha,\mathbf{d}:\alpha\to\mathbf{int}\to\mathbf{int})}\mathbf{struct\ structure\ X}\ =\ \mathbf{struct\ \ end;} \\
\qquad\qquad\qquad\qquad\qquad\qquad \mathbf{datatype\ u}_{\alpha}\ =\ \mathbf{int}\to\mathbf{int\ with\ c,d} \\
\qquad\qquad\qquad \mathbf{end;} \\
\mathrm{val}\ \mathbf{x} = \underline{(\mathbf{Y.d}_{\beta\to\mathbf{int}\to\mathbf{int}}(\mathbf{X.c}_{\mathbf{int}\to\alpha}\ 1)_{\alpha}\ )}\ 2
\end{array}
$$

Assuming the initial context is empty, we have indicated the existential types of the defining structure expressions using the notation $\lceil^{\mathcal{X}}\mathrm{s}$, and the types of the identifiers **X** and **Y** in the context using the notation $\lfloor_{\mathcal{S}}\mathbf{X}$. We have also indicated the type variables chosen to represent **t** and **u** at their point of definition.

The existential type of the structure expression defining **X** is:

$$\exists\{\alpha\}.(\mathbf{t} \triangleright \alpha, \mathbf{c} : \mathbf{int} \to \alpha, \mathbf{d} : \alpha \to \mathbf{int}).$$

Since α is fresh for the empty context, we can eliminate this existential quantifier directly so that, after the definition of **X**, the context of **Y** contains a free occurrence of α. As in the unsound state-less semantics discussed in Section 4.1, we are free to re-use α to represent **u** at the definition of **u**, because α no longer occurs in the context after the second definition of **X**. However, inspecting the existential type,

$$\mathcal{X} \equiv \exists\{\alpha\}.(\mathbf{X} : \epsilon_{\mathcal{S}}, \mathbf{u} \triangleright \alpha, \mathbf{c} : (\mathbf{int} \to \mathbf{int}) \to \alpha, \mathbf{d} : \alpha \to \mathbf{int} \to \mathbf{int}),$$

of the structure expression defining **Y**, we can see that this variable is distinguished from the free occurrence of α in the context by the fact that it is existentially bound. Before we can extend the context with the type of **Y**, we need to eliminate this existential quantifier. The first side-condition of Rule 8 requires that we avoid capturing the free occurrence of α in the context of **Y**. To do this, it is necessary to choose a renaming of $\mathcal{X}$, in this case

$$\exists\{\beta\}.(\mathbf{X} : \epsilon_{\mathcal{S}}, \mathbf{u} \triangleright \beta, \mathbf{c} : (\mathbf{int} \to \mathbf{int}) \to \beta, \mathbf{d} : \beta \to \mathbf{int} \to \mathbf{int}),$$

for a variable β that is *locally* fresh for the context of **Y**, and, in particular, distinct from α. After eliminating the renamed quantifier and extending the context with the type of **Y**, the abstract types **X.t** and **Y.u** are correctly distinguished by α and β, catching the underlined type violation in the definition of **x**.

5 Main Result

Having defined our systems, we can now state the main result of the paper:

Theorem 1 (Main Result) *Provided* $\vdash \mathcal{C}$ **Gnd** *and* $\mathcal{C}, N$ **rigid**:

Completeness *If* $\mathcal{C}, N \vdash \mathrm{b}/\mathrm{s} : \mathcal{S} \Rightarrow M$ *then* $\mathcal{C} \vdash \mathrm{b}/\mathrm{s} : \exists M.\mathcal{S}$.
Soundness *If* $\mathcal{C} \vdash \mathrm{b}/\mathrm{s} : \mathcal{X}$ *then there exist* $\mathcal{S}$ *and* M *such that* $\mathcal{C}, N \vdash \mathrm{b}/\mathrm{s} : \mathcal{S} \Rightarrow M$ *with* $\mathcal{X} = \exists M.\mathcal{S}$.

An operational view of the systems in Figures 5 and 6 is that we have replaced the notion of *global* generativity by *local* generativity and the ability to rename bound variables when necessary. The proof of completeness is easy because a variable that is globally fresh will certainly be locally fresh, enabling a straightforward construction of a corresponding state-less derivation.

Proof (Completeness). By strong induction on the generative classification rules. We only describe the case for structure definitions, the others are similar:

Rule 4 Assume $\mathcal{C}, N \vdash \mathrm{s} : \mathcal{S} \Rightarrow P$ (i), $(\mathcal{C}, \mathrm{X} : \mathcal{S}), N \cup P \vdash \mathrm{b} : \mathcal{S}' \Rightarrow Q$ (ii) and induction hypotheses $\vdash \mathcal{C}$ **Gnd** $\supset \mathcal{C}, N$ **rigid** $\supset \mathcal{C} \vdash \mathrm{s} : \exists P.\mathcal{S}$ (iii) and $\vdash \mathcal{C}, \mathrm{X} : \mathcal{S}$ **Gnd** $\supset (\mathcal{C}, \mathrm{X} : \mathcal{S}), N \cup P$ **rigid** $\supset \mathcal{C}, \mathrm{X} : \mathcal{S} \vdash \mathrm{b} : \exists Q.\mathcal{S}'$ (iv). Suppose $\vdash \mathcal{C}$ **Gnd** (v) and $\mathcal{C}, N$ **rigid** (vi). Now by induction hypothesis (iii) on (v) and (vi) we obtain $\mathcal{C} \vdash \mathrm{s} : \exists P.\mathcal{S}$ (vii). Property 1 of (i), together with (vi), ensures that $P \cap \mathcal{V}(\mathcal{C}) = \emptyset$ (viii). Clearly (v) extends to $\vdash \mathcal{C}, \mathrm{X} : \mathcal{S}$ **Gnd** (ix). Lemma 1 on (v) and (vii) ensures $\mathcal{V}(\exists P.\mathcal{S}) \subseteq \mathcal{V}(\mathcal{C})$. It follows from (vi) that $\mathcal{V}(\mathcal{S}) \subseteq N \cup P$ (x) and consequently $(\mathcal{C}, \mathrm{X} : \mathcal{S}), N \cup P$ **rigid** (xi). Applying induction hypothesis (iv) to (ix) and (xi) yields $\mathcal{C}, \mathrm{X} : \mathcal{S} \vdash \mathrm{b} : \exists Q.\mathcal{S}'$ (xii). Property 1 of (ii) ensures $Q \cap (N \cup P) = \emptyset$ which, together with (x), entails $Q \cap (P \cup \mathcal{V}(\mathcal{S})) = \emptyset$ (xiii). Rule 8 on (vii), (viii), (xii) and (xiii) derives the desired result $\mathcal{C} \vdash$ (**structure** X = s;b) : $\exists P \cup Q.(\mathrm{X} : \mathcal{S}, \mathcal{S}')$.

In the complete proof, Property 1 and Lemma 1 conspire to ensure the side conditions on existentially bound variables and hence that implicit renamings of these variables are never required.

5.1 Soundness

Soundness is more difficult to prove, because the state-less rules in Figure 6 only requires subderivations to hold for *particular* choices of locally fresh variables. A variable may be locally fresh without being globally fresh, foiling naive attempts to construct a generative derivation from a state-less derivation.

To address this problem, we introduce a modified formulation of the state-less classification judgements with the judgement forms $\mathcal{C} \vdash' \mathrm{b} : \mathcal{X}$ and $\mathcal{C} \vdash' \mathrm{s} : \mathcal{X}$ that have similar rules but with stronger premises. Instead of requiring premises to hold for *particular* choices of fresh variables, the modified rules require them to hold for *every* choice of variables. To express these rules, we define the concept of a *renaming* $\pi \in \mathit{Var} \xrightarrow{\mathrm{fin}} \mathit{Type}$ that is similar to a realisation, but simply maps type variables to type variables. The operation of applying a renaming to a semantic object $\mathcal{O}$, written $\pi\langle\mathcal{O}\rangle$, is extended to all semantics objects in a way that avoids the capture of free variables by bound variables. For instance, the modified version of Rule 8 receives a stronger second premise that subsumes the second and third premises of the original rule:

$$\frac{\mathcal{C} \vdash' \mathrm{s} : \exists P.\mathcal{S} \quad \forall \pi.\mathcal{D}(\pi) = P \supset \mathcal{C}, \mathrm{X} : \pi\langle\mathcal{S}\rangle \vdash' \mathrm{b} : \pi\langle\exists Q.\mathcal{S}'\rangle \quad Q \cap (P \cup \mathcal{V}(\mathcal{S})) = \emptyset}{\mathcal{C} \vdash' (\mathbf{structure}\ \mathrm{X} = \mathrm{s;b}) : \exists P \cup Q.(\mathrm{X} : \mathcal{S}, \mathcal{S}')}$$

Similar changes are required to Rules 7, 9 and 10 that extend the context with objects containing locally fresh variables. The generalised premises make it easy to construct a generative derivation from the derivation of a generalised judgement. Although these rules are not finitely branching, the judgements are well-founded and amenable to inductive arguments. This technique is adapted from [12].

Our proof strategy is to first show that any derivation of a state-less judgement gives rise to a corresponding derivation of a generalised judgement:

Lemma 2 *If* $\vdash \mathcal{C}$ **Gnd** *and* $\mathcal{C} \vdash \mathrm{b/s} : \mathcal{X}$ *then* $\mathcal{C} \vdash' \mathrm{b/s} : \mathcal{X}$.

We then show that any derivation of a generalised judgement gives rise to a corresponding generative derivation:

Lemma 3 *If* $\vdash \mathcal{C}$ **Gnd** *and* $\mathcal{C} \vdash' \mathrm{b/s} : \mathcal{X}$ *then, for any* N *satisfying* $\mathcal{C}, N$ **rigid**, *there exist* $\mathcal{S}$ *and* M *such that* $\mathcal{C}, N \vdash \mathrm{b/s} : \mathcal{S} \Rightarrow M$, *with* $\mathcal{X} = \exists M.\mathcal{S}$.

The proofs require stronger induction hypotheses and are technically involved. Further details can be found in the author's thesis [15].

6 Contribution

Theorem 1 is an equivalence result, but we propose that the state-less semantics provides a better *conceptual* understanding of the type structure of Standard ML.

The core type phrase sp.t, which introduces a dependency of Mini-SML's type syntax on its term syntax, suggests that Mini-SML's type structure is based on first-order dependent types. However, arguing from our semantics, we can show that first-order dependent types play no role in the semantics.

Compare the syntactic types of Mini-SML with their semantics counterparts, the semantic objects that are used to classify Mini-SML terms. Where type phrases allow occurrences of type identifiers and term dependent projections sp.t, semantic types instead allow occurrences of *type variables* $\alpha \in Var$. Type variables range over semantic types and are thus *second-order* variables. While the component specifications of a signature expression are dependent, in that subsequent specifications can refer to term identifiers specified previously in the body, the body of a semantic signature is just an unordered finite map, with no dependency between its components: the identifiers in a semantic structure, like the field names of record types, do not have scope. Thus there is a clear distinction between syntactic types and semantics objects: where syntactic types have first-order dependencies on term identifiers, semantic types have second-order dependencies on type variables.

The reduction of first-order to second-order dependencies is achieved by Mini-SML's denotation judgements. In particular, the denotation of the term dependent type sp.t is determined by the type, not the value, of the term sp. In conjunction with Rule 2, that assigns type variables to opaque type specifications, Rule 1 reduces the first-order dependencies of syntactic types on terms to second-order dependencies of semantic types on type variables.

We can illustrate this reduction by comparing the following signature expression with its denotation:

```
sig structure X : sig type t
                  end;
    structure Y : sig type u;
                      type v = X.t → u
                  end;
    val y: X.t → Y.v
end
```

$$\Lambda\{\alpha,\beta\}.\ (\mathbf{X} : (\mathbf{t} \triangleright \alpha),\ \mathbf{Y} : (\mathbf{u} \triangleright \beta,\ \mathbf{v} \triangleright \alpha \to \beta),\ \mathbf{y} : \alpha \to \alpha \to \beta)$$

The opaque types **t** and **u** are represented by type variables α and β; the dependency on the terms **X** and **Y** in the specifications of **v** and **y** have disappeared.

As another example, let S be the above signature expression and consider the following functor and its type:

```
functor F(Z : S) =
    struct type w = Z.X.t → Z.Y.v;
           val z = Z.y
    end
```

$$\forall\{\alpha,\beta\}.(\mathbf{X} : (\mathbf{t} \triangleright \alpha),\ \mathbf{Y} : (\mathbf{u} \triangleright \beta,\ \mathbf{v} \triangleright \alpha \to \beta),\ \mathbf{y} : \alpha \to \alpha \to \beta) \to \exists\emptyset.(\mathbf{w} \triangleright \alpha \to \alpha \to \beta,\ \mathbf{z} : \alpha \to \alpha \to \beta)$$

F returns the type **w** whose definition depends on the term argument **Z**. In the semantic object, this first-order dependency has been eliminated, in favour of a second-order dependency on the functor's type parameters α and β.

Our choice of binding notation and the reformulation of the generative classification rules further underline the fact that Mini-SML, and thus Standard ML, is based on a purely second-order type theory. In this interpretation, signatures are types parameterised on type variables, functor are polymorphic functions whose types have universally quantified type variables, and structure expressions have types with existentially quantified type variables. A universal quantifier is explicitly introduced when a functor is defined and silently eliminated when it is applied. An existential quantifier is explicitly introduced by a datatype definition or an opaque signature constraint, and silently eliminated and re-introduced at other points in the semantics. (The limited computation on modules means that, unlike the first-class existential types of [13], the witness of an existential type can depend at most on the static interpretation of type variables in the context, but never on the dynamic interpretation of term identifiers.) Allowing a functor's actual argument and a constraint's structure expression to have a richer type is an appeal to subtyping that can easily be factored into a separate subsumption rule as in traditional formalisations of subtyping in Type Theory. We have not done this to keep the classification rules syntax directed: this avoids admitting non-principal classifications and simplifies the statement and proof of soundness.

The style of semantics presented here scales naturally to both higher-order and first-class modules [15,16]. Both extensions are compatible with ML-style type inference for the Core. The higher-order extension is competive with, though subtly different from, the calculi of [2,7,8,10]. Where these caculi have the advantage of syntactic types, ours has the advantage of enjoying principal types. In [2,7,8,10], the application of a functor to an anonymous argument may not have a syntactic type unless one can promote the functor's range to a supertype that does not propagate any opaque types of the actual argument. This proviso leads to a loss of principal types, since there may be two or more unrelated types to which one may promote the range when it is a functor signature: one can narrow its domain or promote its range (Section 9.2.2 of [15]). Because the style of semantics presented here can represent anonymous opaque types using existential type variables, there is no need to promote the functor's range in an arbitrary manner, preserving principality. The extension to first-class modules, which requires just three new Core constructs to specify, introduce and eliminate first-class module types, has a decidable type checking problem. It avoids the undecidability of subtyping in the first-class module calculi of [2,10] by preserving the distinction between Modules and Core level types and disallowing subtyping between Core types that encapsulate modules.

Independent of this work: [6] uses type parameterisation and quantification to model a fragment of Standard ML Modules; [1] presents a declarative type system similar to ours to simplify the proof of correctness of a novel compilation scheme for Modules; [17] combines type parameterisation and quantification with non-standard first-order dependent types in an explicitly typed modules language, promising the advantages of both.

Acknowledgements

Many thanks to Don Sannella and Healfdene Goguen.

References

1. M. Elsman. Program Modules, Separate Compilation, and Intermodule Optimisation. PhD thesis. Dept. of Computer Science, University of Copenhagen. 1999.
2. R. Harper, M. Lillibridge. A type-theoretic approach to higher-order modules with sharing. In *21st ACM Symp. Principles of Prog. Lang.*, 1994.
3. R. Harper, J. C. Mitchell. On the type structure of Standard ML. In *ACM Trans. Prog. Lang. Syst.*, volume 15(2), pages 211–252, 1993.
4. R. Harper, J. C. Mitchell, E. Moggi. Higher-order modules and the phase distinction. T. R. ECS-LFCS-90-112, Dept. of Computer Science, University of Edinburgh, 1990.
5. R. Harper, C. Stone. An Interpretation of Standard ML in Type Theory. T. R. CMU-CS-97-147, School of Computer Science, Carnegie Mellon University, 1997.

6. M. P. Jones. Using parameterized signatures to express modular structure. In *Proc. 23rd Symp. Principles of Prog. Lang.* ACM Press, 1996.
7. X. Leroy. Manifest types, modules, and separate compilation. In *Proc. 21st Symp. Principles of Prog. Lang.*, pages 109–122. ACM Press, 1994.
8. X. Leroy. Applicative functors and fully transparent higher-order modules. In *Proc. 22nd Symp. Principles of Prog. Lang.*, pages 142–153. ACM Press, 1995.
9. X. Leroy. A syntactic theory of type generativity and sharing. *Journal of Functional Programming*, 6(5):1—32, 1996.
10. M. Lillibridge. Translucent Sums: A Foundation for Higher-Order Module Systems. PhD thesis, School of Computer Science, Carnegie Mellon University, 1997.
11. D. MacQueen. Using dependent types to express modular structure. In *13th ACM Symp. on Principles of Prog. Lang.*, 1986.
12. J. McKinna, R. Pollack. Pure Type Sytems formalized. In *Proc. Int'l Conf. on Typed Lambda Calculi and Applications, Utrecht*, pages 289–305, 1993.
13. J. C. Mitchell, G. D. Plotkin. Abstract types have existential type. *ACM Transactions on Programming Languages and Systems*, 10(3):470–502, July 1988.
14. R. Milner, M. Tofte, R. Harper, D. MacQueen. *The Definition of Standard ML (Revised).* MIT Press, 1997.
15. C. V. Russo. Types For Modules. PhD Thesis, Laboratory for Foundations of Computer Science, University of Edinburgh, 1998.
16. C. V. Russo. First-Class Structures for Standard ML. Unpublished manuscript, Laboratory for Foundations of Computer Science, University of Edinburgh, 1999.
17. Z. Shao. Parameterized Signatures and Higher-Order Modules. T. R. YALEU/DCS/TR-1161, Dept. of Computer Science, Yale University, August 1998.

Constraint Programming in OPL

P. Van Hentenryck[1], L. Michel[2], L. Perron[2], and J.-C. Régin[2]

[1] UCL, Place Sainte-Barbe, 2, B-1348 Louvain-La-Neuve, Belgium
[2] Ilog SA, 9 rue de Verdun, F-94253 Gentilly Cedex, France

Abstract. OPL is a modeling language for mathematical programming and combinatorial optimization problems. It is the first modeling language to combine high-level algebraic and set notations from modeling languages with a rich constraint language and the ability to specify search procedures and strategies that is the essence of constraint programming. In addition, OPL models can be controlled and composed using OPLSCRIPT, a script language that simplifies the development of applications that solve sequences of models, several instances of the same model, or a combination of both as in column-generation applications. This paper illustrates some of the functionalities of OPL for constraint programming using frequency allocation, sport-scheduling, and job-shop scheduling applications. It also illustrates how OPL models can be composed using OPLSCRIPT on a simple configuration example.

1 Introduction

Combinatorial optimization problems are ubiquitous in many practical applications, including scheduling, resource allocation, planning, and configuration problems. These problems are computationally difficult (i.e., they are NP-hard) and require considerable expertise in optimization, software engineering, and the application domain.

The last two decades have witnessed substantial development in tools to simplify the design and implementation of combinatorial optimization problems. Their goal is to decrease development time substantially while preserving most of the efficiency of specialized programs. Most tools can be classified in two categories: mathematical modeling languages and constraint programming languages. Mathematical modeling languages such as AMPL [4] and GAMS [1] provides very high-level algebraic and set notations to express concisely mathematical problems that can then be solved using state-of-the-art solvers. These modeling languages do not require specific programming skills and can be used by a wide audience. Constraint programming languages such as CHIP [3], PROLOG III and its successors [2], OZ [12], and ILOG SOLVER [11] have orthogonal strenghts. Their constraint languages, and their underlying solvers, go beyond traditional linear and nonlinear constraints and support logical, high-order, and global constraints. They also make it possible to program search procedures to specify how to explore the search space. However, these languages are mostly aimed at computer scientists and often have weaker abstractions for algebraic and set manipulation.

G. Nadathur (Ed.): PPDP'99, LNCS 1702, pp. 98–116, 1999.

The work described in this paper originated as an attempt to unify modeling and constraint programming languages and their underlying implementation technologies. It led to the development of the optimization programming language OPL [13], its associated script language OPLScript [14], and its development environment OPL Studio.

OPL is a modeling language sharing high-level algebraic and set notations with traditional modeling languages. It also contains some novel functionalities to exploit sparsity in large-scale applications, such as the ability to index arrays with arbitrary data structures. OPL shares with constraint programming languages their rich constraint languages, their support for scheduling and resource allocation problems, and the ability to specify search procedures and strategies. OPL also makes it easy to combine different solver technologies for the same application.

OPLScript is a script language for composing and controlling OPL models. Its motivation comes from the many applications that require solving several instances of the same problem (e.g., sensibility analysis), sequences of models, or a combination of both as in column-generation applications. OPLScript supports a variety of abstractions to simplify these applications, such as OPL models as first-class objects, extensible data structures, and linear programming bases to name only a few.

OPL Studio is the development environment of OPL and OPLScript. Beyond support for the traditional "edit, execute, and debug" cycle, it provides automatic visualizations of the results (e.g., Gantt charts for scheduling applications), visual tools for debugging and monitoring OPL models (e.g., visualizations of the search space), and C++ code generation to integrate an OPL model in a larger application. The code generation produces a class for each model objects and makes it possible to add/remove constraints dynamically and to overwrite the search procedure.

The purpose of this paper is to illustrate some of the constraint programming features of OPL through a number of models. Section 2 describes a model for a frequency allocation application that illustrates how to use high-level algebraic and set manipulation, how to exploit sparsity, and how to implement search procedures in OPL. Section 3 describes a model for a sport-scheduling applications that illustrates the use of global constraints in OPL. Section 4 describes an application that illustrates the support for scheduling applications and for search strategies in OPL. Section 5 shows how OPL models can be combined using OPLScript on a configuration application. All these applications can be run on ILOG OPL Studio 2.1.

2 Frequency Allocation

The frequency-allocation problem [11] illustrates a number of interesting features of OPL: the use of complex quantifiers, and the use of a multi-criterion ordering to choose which variable to assign next. It also features an interesting data representation that is useful in large-scale linear models.

The frequency-allocation problem consists of allocating frequencies to a number of transmitters so that there is no interference between transmitters and the number of allocated frequencies is minimized. The problem described here is an actual cellular phone problem where the network is divided into cells, each cell containing a number of transmitters whose locations are specified. The interference constraints are specified as follows:

- The distance between two transmitter frequencies within a cell must not be smaller than 16.
- The distances between two transmitter frequencies from different cells vary according to their geographical situation and are described in a matrix.

The problem of course consists of assigning frequencies to transmitters to avoid interference and, if possible, to minimize the number of frequencies. The rest of this section focuses on finding a solution using a heuristic to reduce the number of allocated frequencies.

```
int nbCells = ...;
int nbFreqs = ...;
range Cells 1..nbCells;
range Freqs 1..nbFreqs;
int nbTrans[Cells] = ...;
int distance[Cells,Cells] = ...;

struct TransmitterType { Cells c; int t; };
{TransmitterType} Transmits = { <c,t> | c in Cells & t in 1..nbTrans[c] };
var Freqs freq[Transmits];

solve {
   forall(c in Cells & ordered t1, t2 in 1..nbTrans[c])
      abs(freq[<c,t1>] - freq[<c,t2>]) >= 16;

   forall(ordered c1, c2 in Cells : distance[c1,c2] > 0)
      forall(t1 in 1..nbTrans[c1] & t2 in 1..nbTrans[c2])
         abs(freq[<c1,t1>] - freq[<c2,t2>]) >= distance[c1,c2];
};
search {
   forall(t in Transmits
         ordered by increasing <dsize(freq[t]),nbTrans[t.c]>)
      tryall(f in Freqs ordered by decreasing nbOccur(f,freq))
         freq[t] = f;
};
```

Fig. 1. The Frequency-Allocation Problem (`alloc.mod`).

Figure 1 shows an OPL statement for the frequency-allocation problem and Figure 2 describes the instance data. Note the separation between models and data which is an interesting feature of OPL. The model data first specifies the number of cells (25 in the instance), the number of available frequencies (256 in the instance), and their associated ranges. The next declarations specify the number of transmitters needed for each cell and the distance between cells. For example, in the instance, cell 1 requires eight transmitters while cell 3 requires six transmitters. The distance between cell 1 and cell 2 is 1.

The first interesting feature of the model is how variables are declared:

```
struct TransmitterType { Cells c; int t; };
{TransmitterType} Transmits = { <c,t> | c in Cells & t in 1..nbTrans[c] };
var Freqs freq[Transmits];
```

As is clear from the problem statement, transmitters are contained within cells. The above declarations preserve this structure, which will be useful when stating constraints. A transmitter is simply described as a record containing a cell number and a transmitter number inside the cell. The set of transmitters is computed automatically from the data using

```
{TransmitterType} Transmits = { <c,t> | c in Cells & t in 1..nbTrans[c] };
```

which considers each cell and each transmitter in the cell. OPL supports a rich language to compute with sets of data structures and this instruction illustrates some of this functionality. The model then declares an array of variables

```
var Freqs freq[Transmits];
```

indexed by the set of transmitters; the values of these variables are of course the frequencies associated with the transmitters. This declaration illlustrates a fundamental aspect of OPL: arrays can be indexed by arbitrary data. In this application, the arrays of variables `freq` is indexed by the elements of `transmitters` that are records. This functionality is of primary importance to exploit sparsity in large-scale models and to simplify the statement of many combinatorial optimization problems.

There are two main groups of constraints in this model. The first set of constraints handles the distance constraints between transmitters inside a cell. The instruction

```
forall(c in Cells & ordered t1, t2 in 1..nbTrans[c])
    abs(freq[<c,t1>] - freq[<c,t2>]) >= 16;
```

enforces the constraint that the distance between two transmitters inside a cell is at least 16. The instruction is compact mainly because we can quantify several variables in `forall` statements and because of the keyword `ordered` that makes sure that the statement considers triples `<c,t1,t2>` where `t1 < t2`. Of particular interest are the expressions `freq[<c,t1>]` and `freq[<c,t2>]` illustrating that the indices of array `freq` are records of the form `<c,t>`, where `c` is a cell and `t` is a transmitter. Note also that the distance is computed using the

```
nbCells = 25;
nbFreqs = 256;
nbTrans = [8 6 6 1 4 4 8 8 8 8 4 9 8 4 4 10 8 9 8 4 5 4 8 1 1];
distance = [
   [16 1 1 0 0 0 0 0 1 1 1 1 1 2 2 1 1 0 0 0 2 2 1 1 1]
   [1 16 2 0 0 0 0 0 2 2 1 1 1 2 2 1 1 0 0 0 0 0 0 0 0]
   [1 2 16 0 0 0 0 0 2 2 1 1 1 2 2 1 1 0 0 0 0 0 0 0 0]
   [0 0 0 16 2 2 0 0 0 0 0 0 0 0 0 0 0 1 1 1 0 0 0 1 1]
   [0 0 0 2 16 2 0 0 0 0 0 0 0 0 0 0 0 1 1 1 0 0 0 1 1]
   [0 0 0 2 2 16 0 0 0 0 0 0 0 0 0 0 0 1 1 1 0 0 0 1 1]
   [0 0 0 0 0 0 16 2 0 0 1 1 1 0 0 1 1 1 1 2 0 0 0 1 1]
   [0 0 0 0 0 0 2 16 0 0 1 1 1 0 0 1 1 1 1 2 0 0 0 1 1]
   [1 2 2 0 0 0 0 0 16 2 2 2 2 2 2 1 1 1 1 1 1 1 0 1 1]
   [1 2 2 0 0 0 0 0 2 16 2 2 2 2 2 1 1 1 1 1 1 1 0 1 1]
   [1 1 1 0 0 0 1 1 2 2 16 2 2 2 2 2 2 1 1 2 1 1 0 1 1]
   [1 1 1 0 0 0 1 1 2 2 2 16 2 2 2 2 2 1 1 2 1 1 0 1 1]
   [1 1 1 0 0 0 1 1 2 2 2 2 16 2 2 2 2 1 1 2 1 1 0 1 1]
   [2 2 2 0 0 0 0 0 2 2 2 2 2 16 2 1 1 1 1 1 1 1 1 1 1]
   [2 2 2 0 0 0 0 0 2 2 2 2 2 2 16 1 1 1 1 1 1 1 1 1 1]
   [1 1 1 0 0 0 1 1 1 1 2 2 2 1 1 16 2 2 2 1 2 2 1 2 2]
   [1 1 1 0 0 0 1 1 1 1 2 2 2 1 1 2 16 2 2 1 2 2 1 2 2]
   [0 0 0 1 1 1 1 1 1 1 1 1 1 1 1 2 2 16 2 2 1 1 0 2 2]
   [0 0 0 1 1 1 1 1 1 1 1 1 1 1 1 2 2 2 16 2 1 1 0 2 2]
   [0 0 0 1 1 1 2 2 1 1 2 2 2 1 1 1 1 2 2 16 1 1 0 1 1]
   [2 0 0 0 0 0 0 0 1 1 1 1 1 1 1 2 2 1 1 1 16 2 1 2 2]
   [2 0 0 0 0 0 0 0 1 1 1 1 1 1 1 2 2 1 1 1 2 16 1 2 2]
   [1 0 0 0 0 0 0 0 0 0 0 0 1 1 1 1 0 0 0 1 1 16 1 1]
   [1 0 0 1 1 1 1 1 1 1 1 1 1 1 1 2 2 2 2 1 2 2 1 16 2]
   [1 0 0 1 1 1 1 1 1 1 1 1 1 1 1 2 2 2 2 1 2 2 1 2 16]];
};
```

Fig. 2. Instance Data for the Frequency-Allocation Problem (`alloc.dat`).

function abs, which computes the absolute value of its argument (which may be an arbitrary integer expression).

The second set of constraints handles the distance constraints between transmitters from different cells. The instruction

```
forall(ordered c1, c2 in Cells : distance[c1,c2] > 0)
    forall(t1 in 1..nbTrans[c1] & t2 in 1..nbTrans[c2])
       abs(freq[<c1,t1>] - freq[<c2,t2>]) >= distance[c1,c2];
```

considers each pair of distinct cells whose distance must be greater than zero and each two transmitters in these cells, and states that the distance between the frequencies of these transmitters must be at least the distance specified in the matrix distance.

Another interesting part of this model is the search strategy. The basic structure is not surprising: OPL considers each transmitter and chooses a frequency nondeterministically. The interesting feature of the model is the heuristic. OPL chooses to generate a value for the transmitter with the smallest domain and, in case of ties, for the transmitter whose cell size is as small as possible. This multicriterion heuristic is expressed using a tuple `<dsize(freq[t]),nbTrans[t.c]>` to obtain

```
forall(t in Transmits ordered by increasing <dsize(freq[t]),nbTrans[t.c]>)
```

Each transmitter is associated with a tuple $< s, c >$, where s is the number of possible frequencies and c is the number of transmitters in the cell to which the transmitter belongs. A transmitter with tuple $< s_1, c_1 >$ is preferred over a transmitter with tuple $< s_2, c_2 >$ if $s_1 < s_2$ or if $s_1 = s_2$ and $c_1 < c_2$.

Once a transmitter has been selected, OPL generates a frequency for it in a nondeterministic manner. Once again, the model specifies a heuristic for the ordering in which the frequencies must be tried. To reduce the number of frequencies, the model says to try first those values that were used most often in previous assignments. This heuristic is implemented using a nondeterministic tryall instruction with the order specified using the nbOccur function (nbOccur(i,a) denotes the number of occurrences of i in array a at a given step of the execution):

```
forall(t in Transmits ordered by increasing <dsize(freq[t]),nbTrans[t.c]>)
    tryall(f in Freqs ordered by decreasing nbOccur(f,freq))
       freq[t] = f;
```

This search procedure is typical of many constraint satisfaction problems and consists of using a first heuristic to dynamically choose which variable to instantiate next (variable choice) and a second heuristic to choose which value to assign nondeterministically to the selected variable (value choice). The forall instruction is of course deterministic, while the tryall instruction is nondeterministic: potentially all possible values are chosen for the selected variable. Note that, on the instance depicted in Figure 2, OPL returns a solution with 95 frequencies in about 3 seconds.

3 Sport Scheduling

This section considers the sport-scheduling problem described in [7,10]. The problem consists of scheduling games between n teams over $n-1$ weeks. In addition, each week is divided into $n/2$ periods. The goal is to schedule a game for each period of every week so that the following constraints are satisfied:

1. Every team plays against every other team;
2. A team plays exactly once a week;
3. A team plays at most twice in the same period over the course of the season.

A solution to this problem for 8 teams is shown in Figure 3. In fact, the problem can be made more uniform by adding a "dummy" final week and requesting that all teams play exactly twice in each period. The rest of this section considers this equivalent problem for simplicity.

	Week 1	Week 2	Week 3	Week 4	Week 5	Week 6	Week 7
period 1	0 vs 1	0 vs 2	4 vs 7	3 vs 6	3 vs 7	1 vs 5	2 vs 4
period 2	2 vs 3	1 vs 7	0 vs 3	5 vs 7	1 vs 4	0 vs 6	5 vs 6
period 3	4 vs 5	3 vs 5	1 vs 6	0 vs 4	2 vs 6	2 vs 7	0 vs 7
period 4	6 vs 7	4 vs 6	2 vs 5	1 vs 2	0 vs 5	3 vs 4	1 vs 3

Fig. 3. A Solution to the Sport-Scheduling Application with 8 Teams

The sport-scheduling problem is an interesting application for constraint programming. On the one hand, it is a standard benchmark (submitted by Bob Daniel) to the well-known MIP library and it is claimed in [7] that state-of-the-art MIP solvers cannot find a solution for 14 teams. The OPL models presented in this section are computationally much more efficient. On the other hand, the sport-scheduling application demonstrates fundamental features of constraint programming including global and symbolic constraints. In particular, the model makes heavy use of arc-consistency [6], a fundamental constraint satisfaction techniques from artificial intelligence.

The rest of this section is organized as follows. Section 3.1 presents an OPL model that solves the 14-teams problem in about 44 seconds. Section 3.2 show how to specialize it further to find a solution for 14 to 30 teams quickly. Both models are based on the constraint programs presented in [10].

3.1 A Simple OPL Model

The simple model is depicted in Figure 4. Its input is the number of teams `nbTeams`. Several ranges are defined from the input: the teams `Teams`, the weeks `Weeks`, and the extended weeks `EWeeks`, i.e., the weeks plus the dummy week. The model also declares an enumerated type `slot` to specify the team position in a game (`home` or `away`). The declarations

```
int nbTeams = ...;
range Teams 1..nbTeams;
range Weeks 1..nbTeams-1;
range EWeeks 1..nbTeams;
range Periods 1..nbTeams/2;
range Games 1..nbTeams*nbTeams;
enum Slots = { home, away };

int occur[t in Teams] = 2;
int values[t in Teams] = t;

var Teams team[Periods,EWeeks,Slots];
var Games game[Periods,Weeks];

struct Play { int f; int s; int g; };
{Play} Plays = { <i,j,(i-1)*nbTeams+j> | ordered i, j in Teams };
predicate link(int f,int s,int g) in Plays;

solve {
   forall(w in EWeeks)
      alldifferent( all(p in Periods & s in Slots) team[p,w,s]) onDomain;
   alldifferent(game) onDomain;
   forall(p in Periods)
      distribute(occur,values,all(w in EWeeks & s in Slots) team[p,w,s])
         extendedPropagation;
   forall(p in Periods & w in Weeks)
      link(team[p,w,home],team[p,w,away],game[p,w]);
};

search {
   generate(game);
};
```

Fig. 4. A Simple Model for the Sport-Scheduling Model.

```
int occur[t in Teams] = 2;
int values[t in Teams] = t;
```

specifies two arrays that are initialized generically and are used to state constraints later on. The array `occur` can be viewed as a constant function always returning 2, while the array `values` can be tought of as the identify function over teams.

The main modeling idea in this model is to use two classes of variables: team variables that specify the team playing on a given week, period, and slot and the game variables specifying which game is played on a given week and period. The use of game variables makes it simple to state the constraint that every team must play against each other team. Games are uniquely identified by their two teams. More precisely, a game consisting of home team `h` and away team `a` is uniquely identified by the integer `(h-1)*nbTeams + a`. The instruction

```
var Teams team[Periods,EWeeks,Slots];
var Games game[Periods,Weeks];
```

declares the variables. These two sets of variables must be linked together to make sure that the game and team variables for a given period and a given week are consistent. The instructions

```
struct Play { int f; int s; int g; };
{Play} Plays = { <i,j,(i-1)*nbTeams+j> | ordered i, j in Teams };
```

specify the set of legal games `Plays` for this application. For 8 teams, this set consists of tuples of the form

```
<1,2,2>
<1,3,3>
...
<7,8,56>
```

Note that this definition eliminates some symmetries in the problem statement since the home team is always smaller than the away team. The instruction

```
predicate link(int f,int s,int g) in Plays;
```

defines a symbolic constraint by specifying its set of tuples. In other words, `link(h,a,g)` holds if the tuple `<h,a,g>` is in the set `Plays` of legal games. This symbolic constraint is used in the constraint statement to enforce the relation between the game and the team variables.

The constraint declarations in the model follow almost directly the problem description. The constraint

```
alldifferent( all(p in Periods & s in Slots) team[p,w,s]) onDomain;
```

specifies that all the teams scheduled to play on week `w` must be different. It uses an aggregate operator `all` to collect the appropriate team variables by iterating over the periods and the slots and an annotation `onDomain` to enforce arc consitency. See [8] for a description on how to enforce arc consistency on this global constraint. The constraint

```
distribute(occur,values,all(w in EWeeks & s in Slots) team[p,w,s])
    extendedPropagation
```

specifies that a team plays exactly twice over the course of the "extended" season. Its first argument specifies the number of occurrences of the values specified by the second argument in the set of variables specified by the third argument that collects all variables playing in period p. The annotation **extendedPropagation** specifies to enforce arc consistency on this constraint. See [9] for a description on how to enforce arc consistency on this global constraint. The constraint

```
alldifferent(game) onDomain;
```

specifies that all games are different, i.e., that all teams play against each other team. These constraints illustrate some of the global constraints of OPL. Other global constraints in the current version include a sequencing constraint, a circuit constraint, and a variety of scheduling constraints. Finally, the constraint

```
link(team[p,w,home],team[p,w,away],game[p,w]);
```

is most interesting. It specifies that the game **game[p,w]** consists of the teams **team[p,w,home]** and **team[p,w,away]**. OPL enforces arc-consitency on this symbolic constraint.

The search procedure in this statement is extremely simple and consists of generating values for the games using the first-fail principle. Note also that generating values for the games automatically assigns values to the team by constraint propagation. As mentioned, this model finds a solution for 14 teams in about 44 seconds on a modern PC (400mhz).

3.2 A Round-Robin Model

The simple model has many symmetries that enlarge the search space considerably. In this section, we describe a model that uses a round-robin schedule to determine which games are played in a given week. As a consequence, once the round-robin schedule is selected, it is only necessary to determine the period of each game, not its schedule week. In addition, it turns out that a simple round-robin schedule makes it possible to find solutions for large numbers of teams. The model is depicted in Figures 5 and 6.

The main novelty in the statement is the array **roundRobin** that specifies the games for every week. Assuming that n denotes the number of teams, the basic idea is to fix the set of games of the first week as

$$< 1,2 > \cup \{< p+1, n-p+2 > \mid p > 1\}$$

where p is a period identifier. Games of the subsequent weeks are computed by transforming a tuple $< f, s >$ into a tuple $< f', s' >$ where

$$f' = \begin{cases} 1 & \text{if } f = 1 \\ 2 & \text{if } f = n \\ f+1 & \text{otherwise} \end{cases}$$

```
int nbTeams = ...;
range Teams 1..nbTeams;
range Weeks 1..nbTeams-1;
range EWeeks 1..nbTeams;
range Periods 1..nbTeams/2;
range Games 1..nbTeams*nbTeams;
enum Slots = { home, away };

int occur[t in Teams] = 2;
int values[t in Teams] = t;

var Teams team[Periods,EWeeks,Slots];
var Games game[Periods,Weeks];

struct Play { int f; int s; int g; };
{Play} Plays = { <i,j,(i-1)*nbTeams+j> | ordered i, j in Teams };
predicate link(int f,int s,int g) in Plays;

Play roundRobin[Weeks,Periods];
initialize {
   roundRobin[1,1].f = 1;
   roundRobin[1,1].s = 2;
   forall(p in Periods : p > 1) {
      roundRobin[1,p].f = p+1;
      roundRobin[1,p].s = nbTeams - (p-2);
   };
   forall(w in Weeks: w > 1) {
      forall(p in Periods) {
         if roundRobin[w-1,p].f <> 1 then
            if roundRobin[w-1,p].f = nbTeams then roundRobin[w,p].f = 2
            else roundRobin[w,p].f = roundRobin[w-1,p].f + 1 endif
         else
            roundRobin[w,p].f = roundRobin[w-1,p].f;
         endif;
         if roundRobin[w-1,p].s = nbTeams then roundRobin[w,p].s = 2
         else roundRobin[w,p].s = roundRobin[w-1,p].s + 1 endif;
      }
   };
   forall(w in Weeks, p in Periods)
      if roundRobin[w,p].f < roundRobin[w,p].s then
         roundRobin[w,p].g = nbTeams*(roundRobin[w,p].f-1) + roundRobin[w,p].s
      else
         roundRobin[w,p].g = nbTeams*(roundRobin[w,p].s-1) + roundRobin[w,p].f
      endif;
};
{int} domain[w in Weeks] = { roundRobin[w,p].g | p in Periods };
```

Fig. 5. A Round-Robin Model for the Sport-Scheduling Model (Part I).

```
solve {
   forall(p in Periods & w in Weeks)
      game[p,w] in domain[w];
   forall(w in EWeeks)
      alldifferent( all(p in Periods & s in Slots) team[p,w,s]) onDomain;
   alldifferent(game) onDomain;
   forall(p in Periods)
      distribute(occur,values,all(w in EWeeks & s in Slots) team[p,w,s])
         extendedPropagation;
   forall(p in Periods & w in Weeks)
      link(team[p,w,home],team[p,w,away],game[p,w]);
};

search {
   forall(p in Periods) {
      generateSeq(game[p]);
      forall(po in Periods : po > 1)
         generate(game[po,p]);
   };
};
```

Fig. 6. A Round-Robin Model for the Sport-Scheduling Model (Part II).

and

$$s' = \begin{cases} 2 & \text{if } s = n \\ s+1 & \text{otherwise} \end{cases}$$

This round-robin schedule is computed in the `initialize` instruction and the last instruction computes the game associated with the teams. The instruction

```
{int} domain[w in Weeks] = { roundRobin[w,p].g | p in Periods };
```

defines the games played in a given week. This array is used in the constraint

```
game[p,w] in domain[w];
```

which forces the game variables of period p and of week w to take a game allocated to that week.

The model also contains a novel search procedure that consists of generating values for the games in the first period and in the first week, then in the second period and the second week, and so on. Table 7 depicts the experimental results for various numbers of teams. It is possible to improve the model further by exploiting even more symmetries: see [10] for complete details.

4 Job-Shop Scheduling

One of the other significant features of OPL is its support for scheduling applications. OPL has a variety of domain-specific concepts for these applications that

nb. of teams	14	16	18	20	22	24	26	28	30
CPU Time (sec.)	3.91	4.97	1.00	6.41	10.36	11.81	45.66	36.2	42.38

Fig. 7. Experimental Results for the Sport-Scheduling Model

are translated into state-of-the-art algorithms. To name only a few, they include the concepts of activities, unary, discrete, and state resources, reservoirs, and breaks as well as the global constraints linking them.

Figure 8 describes a simple job-shop scheduling model. The problem is to schedule a number of jobs on a set of machines to minimize completion time, often called the *makespan*. Each job is a sequence of tasks and each task requires a machine. Figure 8 first declares the number of machines, the number of jobs, and the number of tasks in the jobs. The main data of the problem, i.e., the duration of all the tasks and the resources they require, are then given. The next set of instructions

```
ScheduleHorizon = totalDuration;
Activity task[j in Jobs, t in Tasks](duration[j,t]);
Activity makespan(0);
UnaryResource tool[Machines];
```

is most interesting. The first instruction describes the schedule horizon, i.e., the date by which the schedule should be completed at the lastest. In this application, the schedule horizon is given as the summation of all durations, which is clearly an upper bound on the duration of the schedule. The next instruction declares the activities of the problem. Activities are first-class objects in OPL and can be viewed (in a first approximation) as consisting of variables representing the starting date, the duration, and the end date of a task, as well as the constraints linking them. The variables of an activity are accessed as fields of records. In our application, there is an activity associated with each task of each job. The instruction

```
UnaryResource tool[Machines];
```

declares an array of unary resources. Unary resources are, once again, first-class objects of OPL; they represent resources that can be used by at most one activity at anyone time. In other words, two activities using the same unary resource cannot overlap in time. Note that the makespan is modeled for simplicity as an activity of duration zero.

Consider now the problem constraints. The first set of constraints specifies that the activities associated with the problem tasks precede the makespan activity. The next two sets specify the precedence and resource constraints. The resource constraints specify which activities require which resource. Finally, the search procedure

```
int nbMachines = ...;
range Machines 1..nbMachines;
int nbJobs = ...;
range Jobs 1..nbJobs;
int nbTasks = ...;
range Tasks 1..nbTasks;
Machines resource[Jobs,Tasks] = ...;
int+ duration[Jobs,Tasks] = ...;
int totalDuration = sum(j in Jobs, t in Tasks) duration[j,t];

ScheduleHorizon = totalDuration;
Activity task[j in Jobs, t in Tasks](duration[j,t]);
Activity makespan(0);
UnaryResource tool[Machines];

minimize
   makespan.end
subject to {
   forall(j in Jobs)
      task[j,nbTasks] precedes makespan;
   forall(j in Jobs & t in 1..nbTasks-1)
      task[j,t] precedes task[j,t+1];
   forall(j in Jobs & t in Tasks)
      task[j,t] requires tool[resource[j,t]];
};

search {
   LDSearch() {
      forall(r in Machines ordered by increasing localSlack(tool[r]))
         rank(tool[r]);
   }
}
```

Fig. 8. A Job-Shop Scheduling Model (`jobshop.mod`).

```
search {
   LDSearch() {
      forall(r in Machines ordered by increasing localSlack(tool[r]))
         rank(tool[r]);
   }
}
```

illustrates a typical search procedure for job-shop scheduling and the use of limited discrepancy search (LDS) [5] as a search strategy. The search procedure

```
forall(r in Machines ordered by increasing localSlack(tool[r]))
   rank(u[r]);
```

consists of ranking the unary resources, i.e., choosing in which order the activities execute on the resources. Once the resources are ranked, it is easy to find a solution. The procedure ranks first the resource with the smallest local slack (i.e., the machine that seems to be the most difficult to schedule) and then considers the remaining resource using a similar heuristic. The instruction `LDSearch()` specifies that the search space specified by the search procedure defined above must be explored using limited discrepancy search. This strategy, which is effective for many scheduling problems, assumes the existence of a good heuristic. Its basic intuition is that the heuristic, when it fails, probably would have found a solution if it had made a small number of different decisions during the search. The choices where the search procedure does not follow the heuristic are called *discrepancies.* As a consequence, LDS systematically explores the search tree by increasing the number of allowed discrepancies. Initially, a small number of discrepancies is allowed. If the search is not successful or if an optimal solution is desired, the number of discrepancies is increased and the process is iterated until a solution is found or the whole search space has been explored. Note that, besides the default depth-first search and LDS, OPL also supports best-first search, interleaved depth-first search, and depth-bounded limited discrepancy search. It is interesting to mention that this simple model solves MT10 in about 40 seconds and MT20 in about 0.4 seconds.

5 A Configuration Problem

This section illustrates OPLSCRIPT, a script language for controlling and composing OPL models. It shows how to solve an application consisting of a sequence of two models: a constraint programming model and an integer program. The application is a configuration problem, known as Vellino's problem, which is a small but good representive of many similar applications. For instance, complex sport scheduling applications can be solved in a similar fashion.

Given a supply of components and bins of various types, Vellino's problem consists of assigning the components to the bins so that the bin constraints are satisfied and the smallest possible number of bins is used. There are five types of components, i.e., glass, plastic, steel, wood, and copper, and three types of bins, i.e., red, blue, green. The bins must obey a variety of configuration constraints. Containment constraints specify which components can go into which bins: red bins cannot contain plastic or steel, blue bins cannot contain wood or plastic, and green bins cannot contain steel or glass. Capacity constraints specify a limit for certain component types for some bins: red bins contain at most one wooden component and green bins contain at most two wooden components. Finally, requirement constraints specify some compatibility constraints between the components: wood requires plastic, glass excludes copper and copper excludes plastic. In addition, we are given an initial capacity for each bin, i.e., red bins have a capacity of 3 components, blue bins of 1 and green bins of 4 and a demand for each component, i.e., 1 glass, 2 plastic, 1 steel, 3 wood, and 2 copper components.

```
Model bin("genBin.mod","genBin.dat");
import enum Colors bin.Colors;
import enum Components bin.Components;
struct Bin { Colors c; int n[Components]; };
int nbBin := 0;
Open Bin bins[1..nbBin];
while bin.nextSolution() do {
   nbBin := nbBin + 1;
   bins.addh();
   bins[nbBin].c := bin.c;
   forall(c in Components)
      bins[nbBin].n[c] := bin.n[c];
}
Model pro("chooseBin.mod","chooseBin.dat");
if pro.solve() then
   cout << "Solution at cost: " << pro.objectiveValue() << endl;
```

Fig. 9. A Script to Solve Vellino's Problem (`vellino.osc`) .

The strategy to solve this problem consists of generating all the possible bin configurations and then to choose the smallest number of them that meet the demand. This strategy is implemented using the script depicted in Figure 9 and two models `genBin.mod` and `chooseBin.mod` depicted in Figures 10 and 11. It is interesting to study the script in detail at this point. The instruction

```
Model bin("genBin.mod","genBin.dat");
```

declare the first model. Models are, of course, a fundamental concept of OPLSCRIPT: they support a variety of methods (e.g., `solve` and `nextSolution`), their data can be accessed as fields of records, and they can be passed as parameters to procedures. The instructions

```
enum Colors ...;
enum Components ...;
int capacity[Colors] = ...;
int maxCapacity = max(c in Colors) capacity[c];
var Colors c;
var int n[Components] in 0..maxCapacity;
solve {
   0 < sum(c in Components) n[c] <= capacity[c];
   c = red => n[plastic] = 0 & n[steel] = 0 & n[wood] <= 1;
   c = blue => n[plastic] = 0 & n[wood] = 0;
   c = green => n[glass] = 0 & n[steel] = 0 & n[wood] <= 2;
   n[wood] >= 1 => n[plastic] >= 1;
   n[glass] = 0 \/ n[copper] = 0;
   n[copper] = 0 \/ n[plastic] = 0;
};
```

Fig. 10. Generating the Bins in Vellino's Problem (genBin.mod) .

```
import enum Colors;
import enum Components;
struct Bin { Colors c; int n[Components]; };
import int nbBin;
import Bin bins[1..nbBin];
range R 1..nbBin;
int demand[Components] = ...;
int maxDemand = max(c in Components) demand[c];
var int produce[R] in 0..maxDemand;
minimize
   sum(b in R) produce[b]
subject to
   forall(c in Components)
      sum(b in R) bins[b].n[c] * produce[b] = demand[c];
```

Fig. 11. Choosing the Bins in Vellino's Problem (chooseBin.mod) .

```
import enum Colors bin.Colors;
import enum Components bin.Components;
```

import the enumerated types from the model to the script; these enumerated types will be imported by the second model as well. The instructions

```
struct Bin { Colors c; int n[Components]; };
int nbBin := 0;
Open Bin bins[1..nbBin];
```

declare a variable to store the number of bin configurations and an open array to store the bin configurations themselves. Open arrays are arrays that can grow and shrink dynamically during the execution. The instructions

```
while bin.nextSolution() do {
    nbBin := nbBin + 1;
    bins.addh();
    bins[nbBin].c := bin.c;
    forall(c in Components)
       bins[nbBin].n[c] := bin.n[c];
}
```

enumerate all the bin configurations and store them in the `bin` array in model `pro`. Instruction `bin.nextSolution()` returns the next solution (if any) of the model `bin`. Instruction `bins.addh` increases the size of the open array (`addh` stands for "add high"). The subsequent instructions access the model data and store them in the open array. Once this step is completed, the second model is executed and produces a solution at cost 8.

Model `genBin.mod` specifies how to generate the bin configurations: It is a typical constraint program using logical combinations of constraints that should not raise any difficulty. Model `chooseBin.mod` is an integer program that chooses and minimizes the number of bins. This model imports the enumerated types as mentioned previously. It also imports the bin configurations using the instructions

```
import int nbBin;
import Bin bins[1..nbBin];
```

It is important to stress to both models can be developed and tested independently since import declarations can be initialized in a data file when a model is run in isolation (i.e., not from a script). This makes the overall design compositional.

6 Conclusion

The purpose of this paper was to review, through four applications, a number of constraint programming features of OPL to give a basic understanding of the expressiveness of the language. These features include very high-level algebraic notations and data structures, a rich constraint programming language supporting logical, higher-level, and global constraints, support for scheduling and resource allocation problems, and search procedures and strategies. The paper also introduced briefly OPLSCRIPT, a script language to control and compose OPL models. The four applications presented in this paper should give a preliminary, although very incomplete, understanding of how OPL can decrease development time significantly.

Acknowledgments

Pascal Van Hentenryck is supported in part by the *Actions de recherche concertées (ARC/95/00-187)* of the Direction générale de la Recherche Scientifique (Communauté Française de Belgique).

References

1. J. Bisschop and A. Meeraus. On the Development of a General Algebraic Modeling System in a Strategic Planning Environment. *Mathematical Programming Study*, 20:1–29, 1982.
2. A. Colmerauer. An Introduction to Prolog III. *Commun. ACM*, 28(4):412–418, 1990.
3. M. Dincbas, P. Van Hentenryck, H. Simonis, A. Aggoun, T. Graf, and F. Berthier. The Constraint Logic Programming Language CHIP. In *Proceedings of the International Conference on Fifth Generation Computer Systems*, Tokyo, Japan, December 1988.
4. R. Fourer, D. Gay, and B.W. Kernighan. *AMPL: A Modeling Language for Mathematical Programming*. The Scientific Press, San Francisco, CA, 1993.
5. W.D. Harvey and M.L. Ginsberg. Limited Discrepancy Search. In *Proceedings of the 14th International Joint Conference on Artificial Intelligence*, Montreal, Canada, August 1995.
6. A.K. Mackworth. Consistency in Networks of Relations. *Artificial Intelligence*, 8(1):99–118, 1977.
7. K. McAloon, C. Tretkoff, and G. Wetzel. Sport League Scheduling. In *Proceedings of the 3th Ilog International Users Meeting*, Paris, France, 1997.
8. J-C. Régin. A filtering algorithm for constraints of difference in CSPs. In *AAAI-94, proceedings of the Twelth National Conference on Artificial Intelligence*, pages 362–367, Seattle, Washington, 1994.
9. J-C. Régin. Generalized arc consistency for global cardinality constraint. In *AAAI-96, proceedings of the Thirteenth National Conference on Artificial Intelligence*, pages 209–215, Portland, Oregon, 1996.
10. J-C. Régin. Sport league scheduling. In *INFORMS*, Montreal, Canada, 1998.
11. Ilog SA. Ilog Solver 4.31 Reference Manual, 1998.
12. G. Smolka. The Oz Programming Model. In Jan van Leeuwen, editor, *Computer Science Today*. LNCS, No. 1000, Springer Verlag, 1995.
13. P. Van Hentenryck. *The OPL Optimization Programming Language*. The MIT Press, Cambridge, Mass., 1999.
14. P. Van Hentenryck. *OPL Script: Composing and Controlling Models*. Research Report 99-05, Department of Computing Science and Engineering, UCL, Louvain-La-Neuve, April 1999.

Compiling Constraint Handling Rules into Prolog with Attributed Variables

Christian Holzbaur[1*] and Thom Frühwirth[2]

[1] University of Vienna
Department of Medical Cybernetics and Artificial Intelligence
Freyung 6, A-1010 Vienna, Austria
christian@ai.univie.ac.at
[2] Ludwig-Maximilians-University
Department of Computer Science
Oettingenstrasse 67, D-80538 Munich, Germany
fruehwir@informatik.uni-muenchen.de

Abstract. We introduce the most recent and advanced implementation of constraint handling rules (CHR) in a logic programming language, which improves both on previous implementations (in terms of completeness, flexibility and efficiency) and on the principles that should guide such a Prolog implementation consisting of a runtime system and a compiler. The runtime system utilizes attributed variables for the realization of the constraint store with efficient retrieval and update mechanisms. Rules describing the interactions between constraints are compiled into Prolog clauses by a multi-phase compiler, the core of which comprises a small number of compact code generating templates in the form of definite clause grammar rules.

Keywords: Logic and constraint programming, Implementation and compilation methods.

1 Introduction

In the beginning of constraint logic programming (CLP), constraint solving was "hard-wired" in a built-in constraint solver written in a low-level language. While efficient, this so-called "black-box" approach makes it hard to modify a solver or build a solver over a new domain, let alone debug, reason about and analyze it. This is a problem, since one lesson learned from practical applications is that constraints are often heterogeneous and application-specific. Consequently, several proposals have been made to allow more for flexibility and customization of constraint systems ("glass-box" or even "no-box" approaches):

- Demons, forward rules and conditionals in CHIP [6] allow the definition of propagation of constraints in a limited way.

* Part of this work was performed while visiting CWG at LMU with financial support from DFG.

G. Nadathur (Ed.): PPDP'99, LNCS 1702, pp. 117–133, 1999.

- Constraint combinators in cc(FD) [13] allow to build more complex constraints from simpler constraints.
- Constraints connected to a Boolean variable in BNR-Prolog [2] and "nested constraints" [31] allow to express any logical formula over primitive constraints.
- Indexicals in clp(FD) [5] allow to implement constraints over finite domains at a medium level of abstraction.
- Meta- and attributed variables [26], [21], [15] allow to attach constraints to variables at a low level of abstraction.

It should be noted that all the approaches but the last can only extend a solver over a given, specific constraint domain, typically finite domains. The expressive power to realize other (application-specific) constraint domains is only provided by the last approach.

Attributed variables provide direct access storage locations for properties associated with variables. When such variables are unified, their attributes have to be manipulated. Thus attributed variables make unification user-definable [15], [16], [17]. Attributed variables require roughly the same implementation effort as hard-wired delay (suspension) and coroutining mechanisms found in earlier Prolog implementations, while being more general. And indeed, attributed variables nowadays serve as the primary low-level construct for implementing suspension (delay) mechanisms and constraint solver extensions in many constraint logic programming languages, e.g. SICStus [4] and ECL^{i}PS^e [3] Prolog. However writing constraints this way is tedious, a kind of "constraint assembler" programming.

If there already is a powerful constraint assembler, one may wonder what an associated high-level language could look like. Our proposal is a declarative language extension especially designed for writing constraint solvers, called constraint handling rules (CHR) [10], [12], [18], [11]. With CHR, one can introduce user-defined constraints into a given high level host language, be it Prolog or Lisp. As language extension, CHR themselves are only concerned with constraints, all auxiliary computations are performed in the host language. CHR have been used in dozens of projects worldwide to encode dozens of constraint handlers (solvers), including new domains such as terminological and temporal reasoning. If comparable hard-wired constraint solvers are available, the price to pay for the flexibility of CHR is often within an order of magnitude in runtime. The performance gap can in many cases be eliminated by tailoring the CHR constraints to the specifics of the class of applications at hand.

CHR is essentially a committed-choice language consisting of guarded rules that rewrite constraints into simpler ones until they are solved. CHR can define both simplification of and propagation over user-defined constraints. Simplification replaces constraints by simpler constraints while preserving logical equivalence. Propagation adds new constraints which are logically redundant but may cause further simplification. CHR can be seen as a generalization of the various CHIP [6] constructs for user-defined constraints.

In contrast to the family of the general-purpose concurrent logic programming languages [29], concurrent constraint languages [28] and the ALPS [23] framework, CHR are a special-purpose language concerned with defining declarative objects, constraints, not procedures in their generality. In another sense, CHR are more general, since they allow for *multiple heads*, i.e. conjunctions of constraints in the head of a rule. Multiple heads are a feature that is essential in solving conjunctions of constraints. With single-headed CHR alone, unsatisfiability of constraints could not always be detected (e.g `X<Y,Y<X`) and global constraint satisfaction could not be achieved. The probably most distinguishing functionality of CHR is that they act as a powerful iteration, retrieval, and upadte mechanism over the constraint store, a data structure holding constraints.

The first implementation of CHR in 1991 was an interpreter written in ECL^{i}PS^e Prolog. Then, the CHR language has been implemented in 1993 in Common LISP at the German Research Institute for Artificial Intelligence [14] and in 1994 as a library of ECL^{i}PS^e [9], [10]. A CHR interpreter was written in the concurrent logical object-oriented constraint language OZ [32] in 1996. Independent of our work, a new experimental prototype of CHR has been implemented recently in ECL^{i}PS^e 4.0 [30].

CHR are typically realized as a library containing a compiler, runtime system and solvers written in CHR. With Prolog as the host language, the idea is to realize the CHR constraint store through attributed variables. Rule application compiles into Prolog clauses which inspect and update the constraint store at runtime. Thus CHR can also be understood as a powerful means to manipulate the attributes of variables in a declarative high-level fashion. In this paper we introduce the most recent and advanced implementation of CHR in SICStus Prolog [18], which improves both on the previous implementation [10] in terms of completeness, flexibility and efficiency and on the principles that should guide such an implementation [9]. The new release also includes about 30 constraint solvers written in CHR.

For the user, the new release of CHR improves over older versions in the following aspects:

- The number of heads in a rule is no longer limited to two.
- Guards now with Ask and Tell as in concurrent constraint languages.
- Code runs generally about twice as fast as in older versions.
- For more control, rules are compiled in textual order.
- Compilation is now transparent to the user, on-the-fly when loading.
- Improved set of built-in predicates for advanced CHR users.
- Constant time access to constraints of one type for elevated performance.
- New options and pragmas for powerful compiler optimizations.
- Runtime system includes a stepper for Prolog-like debugging.

Similar issues, i.e. compilation of committed-choice languages into Prolog, have been investigated before, be it translating GHC [33], implementations of delay declarations [25] or the efficient implementation of QD-Janus [8]. Today, we benefit from more powerful programming constructs, in particular customizable suspension mechanisms provided by attributed variables. CHR specific topics are multiple heads and propagation rules.

Overview of this Paper We quickly recapture syntax and semantics for CHR. Then we describe the three phases of the new compilation scheme and the runtime system for CHR. We conclude with a comparison with the previous implementation. This paper is a revised version of [19].

An example will guide us through the paper. Even though it does not define a typical constraint, we chose it for didactic reasons. It is small but can still illustrate the various stages of our compilation scheme. We use Prolog syntax in this paper.

Example 1 (Primes). We implement the sieve of Eratosthenes to compute primes in a way reminiscent of the "chemical abstract machine" [1]: The constraint `candidates(N)` generates candidates for prime numbers, `prime(M)`, where `M` is between `1` and `N`. The candidates react with each other such that each number absorbs multiples of itself. In the end, only prime numbers remain.

```
candidates(1) <=> true.
generate @ candidates(N) <=> N>1 | M is N-1, prime(N), candidates(M).

sieve @ prime(I) \ prime(J) <=> J mod I =:= 0 | true.
```

The first rule says that the number `1` is not a good candidate for a prime, `candidates(1)` is thus rewritten into `true`, a constraint that is always satisfied and therefore it has no effect. Note that head *matching* is used in CHR so the first rule will only apply to `candidates(1)`. A constraint for `candidates` with a free variable, like `candidates(X)`, will suspend (delay).

The `generate` rule generates a candidate `prime(N)` and proceeds recursively with the next smaller number, provided the guard (precondition, test) `N>1` is satisfied.

The third, multi-headed rule named `sieve` reads as follows: If there is a constraint `prime(I)` and some other constraint `prime(J)` such that `J mod I =:= 0` holds, i.e. `J` is a multiple of `I`, then keep `prime(I)` but remove `prime(J)` and execute the body of the rule, `true`.

2 Syntax and Semantics

We assume some familiarity with (concurrent) constraint (logic) programming, e.g. [29], [13], [28], [22], [24]. As a special purpose language, CHR extend a host language with (more) constraint solving capabilities. Auxiliary computations in CHR programs are executed as host language statements. Here the host language is (SICStus) Prolog. For more formal and detailed syntax and semantics of constraint handling rules see [12], [11].

2.1 Syntax

Definition 1. *There are three kinds of CHR. A* simplification CHR *is of the form*[1]

[1] For simplicity, we omit syntactic extensions like pragmas which are not relevant for this paper.

```
[Name '@'] Head1,...,HeadN '<=>' [Guard '|'] Body.
```

where the rule has an optional `Name`*, which is a Prolog term, and the multi-head* `Head1,...,HeadN` *is a conjunction of CHR constraints, which are Prolog atoms. The guard is optional; if present,* `Guard` *is a Prolog goal excluding CHR constraints; if not present, it has the same meaning as the guard* `'true |'`*. The body* `Body` *is a Prolog goal including CHR constraints.*

A propagation CHR *is of the form*

```
[Name '@'] Head1,...,HeadN '==>' [Guard '|'] Body.
```

A simpagation CHR *is a combination of the above two kinds of rule, it is of the form*

```
[Name '@'] Head1,...'\'...,HeadN '<=>' [Guard '|'] Body.
```

where the symbol `'\'` *separates the head constraints into two nonempty parts.*

A simpagation rule combines simplification and propagation in one rule. The rule `HeadsK \ HeadsR <=> Body` is equivalent to the simplification rule `HeadsK, HeadsR <=> HeadsK, Body`, i.e. `HeadsK` is kept while `HeadsR` is removed. However, the simpagation rule is more compact to write, more efficient to execute and has better termination behaviour than the corresponding simplification rule.

2.2 Semantics

Declaratively[2], a rule relates heads and body provided the guard is true. A simplification rule means that the heads are true if and only if the body is satisfied. A propagation rule means that the body is true if the heads are true.

In this paper, we are interested in the operational semantics of CHR in actual implementations. A CHR constraint is implemented as both *code* (a Prolog predicate) and *data* (a Prolog term) in the constraint store, which is a data structure holding constraints. Every time a CHR constraint is posted (executed) or woken (reconsidered), it triggers checks to determine the applicability of the rules it appears in. Such a constraint is called *(currently) active*, while the other constraints in the constraint store that are not executed at the moment are called *(currently) passive*.

Heads. For each CHR, one of its heads is matched against the constraint. Matching succeeds if the constraint is an instance of the head, i.e. the head serves as a pattern. If a CHR has more than one head, the constraint store is searched for *partner* constraints that match the other heads. If the matching succeeds, the guard is executed. Otherwise the next rule is tried.

Guard. A guard is a precondition on the applicability of a rule. The guard either succeeds or fails. A guard succeeds if the execution succeeds without

[2] Unlike general committed-choice programs, CHR programs can be given a declarative semantics since they are only concerned with defining constraints, not procedures in their generality.

causing an instantiation error[3] and without *touching* a variable from the heads. A variable is *touched* if it takes part in a unification or gets more constrained by a built-in constraint. If the guard succeeds, the rule applies. Otherwise it fails and the next rule is tried.

Body. If the firing CHR is a simplification rule, the matched constraints are removed from the store and the body of the CHR is executed. Similarly for a firing simpagation rule, except that the constraints that matched the heads preceding '\' are kept. If the firing CHR is a propagation rule the body of the CHR is executed without removing any constraints. It is remembered that the propagation rule fired, so it will not fire again (and again) with the same constraints. Since the currently active constraint has not been removed, the next rule is tried.

Suspension. If all rules have been tried and the active constraint has not been removed, it suspends (delays) until a variable occurring in the constraint is touched. Here suspension means that the constraint is inserted into the constraint store as data.

3 The Compiler

The compiler is written in (SICStus) Prolog [18] and translates CHR into Prolog on-the-fly, while the file is loaded (consulted). Its kernel consists of a definite clause grammar that generates the target instructions (clauses) driven by templates. We will use example 1 to explain the three phases of the compiler: (1) Parsing, (2) translating CHR into clauses using templates and (3) partial evaluation using macros. Of course, phase (2) is the essential one that encodes the algorithm.

3.1 Parsing Phase

Using the appropriate operator declarations, a CHR can be read and written as a Prolog term. Hence parsing basically reduces to computing information from the parse tree and to producing a canonical form of the rules. Information needed from the parse tree includes:

- The set of global variables, i.e. those that appear in the heads of a rule.
- The set of variables shared between the heads.

In the canonical form of the rules,

- each rule is associated with a unique identifier,
- rule heads are collected into two lists (named `Keep` and `Remove`), and
- guard and body are made explicit with defaults applied.

[3] A built-in predicate of Prolog complains about free variables where it needs instantiated ones.

One list, called Keep, contains all head constraints that are kept when the rule is applied, the other list, called Remove, contains all head constraints that are removed. Lists may be empty. As a result of this representation, simplification, propagation and simpagation rules can be treated uniformly.

Example 2 (Primes, contd.). The canonical form of the rules for the prime number example is given below.

```
% rule(Id,Keep,        Remove,           Guard,           Body)

  rule( 1,[],          [candidates(1)], true,            true).
  rule( 2,[],          [candidates(A)], A>1,            (B is A-1,prime(A),
                                                          candidates(B))).
  rule( 3,[prime(A)],[prime(B)],        B mod A =:= 0, true).
```

3.2 Translation Phase

Each CHR constraint compiles into Prolog clauses that try the constraint with all rules in whose heads it occurs. The resulting compilation process is nonlocal in the sense that a CHR constraint may appear in various head positions in various rules. Each occurrence of a CHR constraint in the head of a rule gives rise to one clause for that constraint. The clause head contains the active constraint, while the clause body does the following:

- match formal parameters to actual arguments of head constraint
- find and match partner constraints
- check the guard
- commit via cut
- remove matched constraints if required
- execute body of rule

We first illustrate the compilation with a simple example, a single-headed simplification CHR, then we consider general cases of arbitrary multi-headed rules.

Example 3 (Primes, contd.). For the constraint **candidates/1** the compiler generates the following intermediate code (edited for readability).

```
% in rule candidates(1) <=> true
candidates(A) :-                       % 1
        match([1], [A]),               % 2
        check_guard([], true),         % 3
        !,                             % 4
        true.                          % 5

% in rule candidates(N) <=> N>1 | M is N-1, prime(N), candidates(M)
candidates(A) :-                       % 6
        match([C], [A]),               % 7
```

```
        check_guard([C], C>1),          % 8
        !,                              % 9
        D is C-1,                       % 10
        prime(C),                       % 11
        candidates(D).                  % 12

% if no rule applied, suspend the constraint on its variables
candidates(A) :-                        % 13
        suspend(candidates(A)).         % 14
```

The predicate `match(L1,L2)` matches the actual arguments `L2` against the formal parameters `L1`. The predicate `check_guard(VL,G)` checks the guard `G`. `check_guard/2` fails as soon as the global variables (list `VL`) are touched[4].

When no rule applied, the last clause inserts the constraint into the constraint store using a suspension mechanism. It allocates the suspension data structure and associates it with each variable occurring in the constraint. Touching any such variable will wake the constraint.

The real challenge left is to implement *multi-headed* CHR. In a naive implementation of a rule, the constraint store is queried for the cross-product of matching constraints. For each tuple in the cross-product the guard is checked in the corresponding environment. If the guard is satisfied, constraints that matched heads in the `Remove` list are removed from the store and the instance of the rule's body is executed. Note that the removal of constraints removes tuples from the cross-product.

Our implementation computes only those tuples in the cross-product that are really needed (as in [9]). Moreover, nondeterministic enumeration of the constraints is preferred over deterministic iteration whenever possible, because Prolog is good at backtracking [20].

For each head constraint in a rule the compiler does the following: It is deleted from the `Keep` or `Remove` list, respectively, and it is rendered as the *active* one. Whether the active constraint is removed when the rule applies, and whether any other head constraints are removed, leads to the following three prototypical cases, each covered by a code generating template in the compiler:

1. Case Active constraint from `Remove` list
2. Case Active constraint from `Keep` list, `Remove` list nonempty
3. Case Active constraint from `Keep` list, `Remove` list empty

Interestingly, the three cases do not directly correspond to the three kinds of CHR.

Case 1. Active constraint from `Remove` list The active head constraint is to be removed if the rule applies, so the rule under consideration is either a simplification or simpagation rule. It can be applied at most once with the

[4] In most Prolog implementations, it is more efficient to re-execute head matching and guards instead of suspending all of them and executing them incrementally.

current active constraint. The search for the partner constraints in this case can be done through nondeterministic enumeration. Here is the template as DCG grammar rule, slightly abridged. The predicate ndmpc generates the code to nondeterministically enumerate and match the partners, one by one.

```
compile(remove(Active), Remove, Keep, Guard, Body, ...) -->
        % compiler code
        {
          Active =.. [_|Args],
          same_length(Args, Actual),
          ...
          ndmpc(Remove, RemoveCode, RemCs, ...),
          ndmpc(Keep, KeepCode, ...)
        },
        % generated code
        [(constraint(head(F/A,R-N), args(Actual)) :-
                  match(Args, Actual),
                  RemoveCode,                    % Identify Remove partners
                  KeepCode,                      % Identify Keep partners
                  check_guard(Vars, Guard),
                  !,
                  remove_constraints(RemCs),
                  Body
        )].
```

The variables F,A,R and N stand for functor, arity of the constraint, rule identifier and number of head in rule, respectively.

Example 4 (Primes, contd.). The second occurrence of prime/1 in rule 3 of Example 1 matches this template, and here is its instantiation:

```
% prime(I) \ prime(J) <=> J mod I =:= 0 | true.
constraint(head(prime/1,3-2), args([A])) :-
        match([C], [A]),
    % RemoveCode (for one partner constraint)
        get_constr_via([], Constraints),
        nd_init_iteration(Constraints, prime/1, Candidate),
        get_args(Candidate, [F]),
        match([C]-[G], [C]-[F]),
    % KeepCode (no partner constraints to be kept in this case)
        true,
    % Guard
        check_guard([G,C], (C mod G =:= 0)),
        !,
        remove_constraints([]),  % no constraints to remove here
    % Body
        true.
```

The predicate `get_constr_via(VL,Cs)` returns a handle `Cs` to the constraints suspended on a free variable occurring in the list `VL`. If there is no variable in `VL`, it returns a handle to all the constraints in the store. `nd_init_iteration(Cs, F/A, Candidate)` nondeterministically returns a candidate constraint with functor `F` and arity `A` through the handle `Cs`.

Case 2. Active constraint from `Keep` list, `Remove` list nonempty This case applies only if there is at least one constraint to be removed, but the active constraint will be kept. It can only originate from a simpagation rule. Since the active constraint is kept, one has to continue looking for applicable rules, even after the rule applied. However, since at least one partner constraint will have been removed, the same rule will only be applicable again with another constraint from the store in place of the removed one. Therefore, we can deterministically iterate over the constraints that are candidates for matching the corresponding head from `Remove`, while the remaining partners can be found via nondeterministic enumeration as before. At the end of the iteration, we have to continue with the remaining rules for the active constraint.

Example 5 (Primes, contd.). For space reasons, we just present a simple instance of the template, originating from the first occurrence of prime/1 in rule 3 (for readability with the predicate already flattened, as described in Section 3.3):

```
% rule prime(I) \ prime(J) <=> J mod I =:= 0 | true.
prime(A, B) :-
        get_constr_via([], C),            % get constraints from store
        init_iteration(C, prime/1, D),    % get partner candidates
        !,
        prime(D, B, A).                   % try to apply the rule

prime(A, B, C) :-
        iteration_last(A),                % no more partner candidate
        prime_1(C, B).                    % try next rule head
prime(A, B, C) :-
        iteration_next(A, D, E),          % try next partner candidate
        (  get_args(D, [F]),
           match([C]-[G], [C]-[F]),
           check_guard([C,G], (G mod C =:= 0))
        ->                                % rule applies
           remove_constraints([D]),       % remove the partner from store
        ;
           true                           % rule did not apply
        ),                                % in any case, try same rule
        prime(E, B, C).                   % with another partner candidate
prime_1(C, B) :- ...                      % code to try next rule head
```

Case 3. Active constraint from `Keep` list, `Remove` list empty This case originates from propagation rules. Since no constraint will be removed, all possible combinations of matching constraints have to be tried. The rule under consideration may apply with each combination. Therefore, all the partners (not just one as in the previous case) have to be searched through nested deterministic iteration. No matter if and how often the rule was applicable, at the end we have to continue with the remaining rules for the active constraint as in Case 2.

Example 6. This propagation rule is part of an interval solver. `X::Min:Max` constrains `X` to be within lower and upper bounds `Min` and `Max`.

```
X le Y, X::MinX:MaxX, Y::MinY:MaxY ==> X::MinX:MaxY, Y::MinX:MaxY.
```

The propagation rule produces roughly the following code for `X le Y`.

```
X le Y :- le_1(X, Y).

le_1(X, Y) :-                          % active constraint (X le Y)
    get_constr_via([X], CXs),          % get constraints on X
    init_iteration(CXs, ::/2, PCXs),   % get partner candidates
    !,
    le_1_0(PCXs, X, Y).                % try to apply the rule
le_1(X, Y) :-                          % rule was not applicable at all
    le_2(X, Y).                        % continue with next rule

le_2(X, Y) :-                          % no next rule
    suspend(X le Y).                   % done, suspend the constraint

le_1_0(PCXs, X, Y) :-                  % outer loop for X::MinX:MaxX
    iteration_last(PCXs),              % no more partner candidate
    le_2(X, Y).                        % continue with next rule
le_1_0(PCXs, X, Y) :-
    iteration_next(PCXs, CX, PCXs1),   % try next partner candidate for X
    (   get_args(CX,...), match(...),% match arguments
        get_constr_via([Y], CYs),      % constraints on Y for next head
        init_iteration(CYs, ::/2, PCYs)
    ->
          le_1_1(PCYs, PCXs1, X, Y)    % try to apply the rule
    ;
          le_1_0(PCXs1, X, Y)          % try next partner candidate for X
    ).

le_1_1(PCYs, PCXs, X, Y) :-            % inner loop for Y::MinY:MaxY
    iteration_last(PCYs),              % no more partner candidate for Y
    le_1_0(PCXs, X, Y).                % continue with outer loop for X
le_1_1(PCYs, PCXs, X, Y) :-
    iteration_next(PCYs, CY, PCYs1),   % try next partner candidate for Y
    (   get_args(CY,...), match(...),% match arguments
    ->                                 % rule applies finally
          X::MinX:MaxY, Y::MinX:MaxY,% rule body
          le_1_1(PCYs1, PCXs, X, Y)    % continue, find another Y partner
    ;                                  % rule did not apply
          le_1_1(PCYs1, PCXs, X, Y)    % continue, find another Y partner
    ).
```

3.3 Partial Evaluation Phase

The translation granularity was chosen so that the generated code would roughly run as is, with little emphasis on efficiency coming from local optimizations and specializations. These are performed in the final, third phase of the compiler using a simple instance of partial evaluation (PE). It is performed by using macros as they are available in most Prolog systems, e.g. [4]. In contrast to approaches that address all aspects of a language in a partial evaluator such as Mixtus [27], our restricted form of PE can be realized with an efficiency that meets the requirements of a production compiler.

The functionalities of the main compiler macros:

- The generic predicates steering the iteration over partner constraints are specialized with respect to a particular representation of these multi sets.
- Recursions (typically iterations over lists) that are definite at compile time are unfolded at compile time.
- As in [33], head matching is specialized into unification instructions guarded by `nonvar/1` tests.
- The intermediate code uses redundant function symbols for the convenience of the compiler writers, e.g. to keep object, compiler and runtime-system variables visually apart. The redundant function symbols also help in type-checking the compiler. Redundant function symbols are absent in the target code. In particular, clause heads are flattened to facilitate clause indexing. For example, `constraint(head(prime/1,3-2), args([A]))` will be transformed into something like `prime1_3_2(A)`.

Example 7 (Primes, contd.). The macro expansion phase results in the following code for our example 3. The code for matching and guard checking has been inlined. The resulting trivial matchings (line 7), guards (line 3) and bodies (line 5) have been removed by PE.

```
% rule candidates(1) <=> true.
candidates(A) :-                    % 1
        A==1,                       % 2
        !.                          % 4
% rule candidates(N) <=> N>1 | M is N-1, prime(N), candidates(M).
candidates(A) :-                    % 6
        nonvar(A),                  % 8
        A>1,                        % 8
        !,                          % 9
        B is A-1,                   % 10
        prime(A),                   % 11
        candidates(B).              % 12
candidates(A) :-                    % 13
        suspend(candidates(A)).     % 14
```

4 The Runtime System

The code generated by the compiler utilizes Prolog since CHR compile into clauses. Thus e.g. memory management is already taken care of. There are however functionalities that are not provided directly by most Prolog implementations:

- We need means to suspend, wake and re-suspend constraint predicates.
- We need efficient access to suspended constraints in the store through different access paths.

The vanilla suspension mechanisms used by earlier CHR implementations addressed the first issue above, but did not optimize re-suspension. The second issue was partially ignored in that plain linear search in (parts of) the constraint store was used.

4.1 Suspensions

Typically, the attributes of variables are goals that suspend on that variable. They are re-executed (woken) each time one of their variables is touched. Via the attributed variables interface as found in SICStus or ECL^iPS^e Prolog the behaviour of attributed variables under unification is specified with a user-defined predicate. In the CHR implementation, suspended goals are our means to store constraints.

In more detail, the components of the CHR suspension data structure are:

- Constraint goal
- State of constraint
- Unique identifier
- Propagation history
- Re-use counter

The state indicates if the constraint is active or passive.[5] The unique identifier is used, together with the propagation history, to ensure termination for propagation rules. Each propagation rule fires at most once for each tuple formed by the set of matched head constraints. The re-use counter is incremented with every re-use of the suspension. It is used for profiling and some more subtle aspects of controlling rule termination outside the scope of this paper.

To optimize re-suspensions, we made the suspension itself an argument of the re-executed goal. Internally, each constraint has an additional argument. When first executed, the argument is a free variable. When the constraint suspends, this extra argument is bound to the suspension itself. When it runs again, the suspension mechanism now has a handle to the suspension and can update its state. Traces of this mechanism were removed from the listed code samples in this paper to avoid confusion.

[5] In actuality the granularity of states and transitions is more copious. The additional mechanics mainly address lazy constraint removal to anticipate the possibility of subsequent constraint re-introduction.

4.2 Access Paths

When a CHR searches for a partner constraint, a variable common to two heads of a rule considerably restricts the number of candidate constraints to be checked, because both partners must be suspended on this variable. Thus we usually access the constraint store by looking at only those constraints (cf. `get_constr_via/2`). We also know functor and arity of the partner. Consequently, we want direct access to the set of constraints of given functor/arity. Earlier implementations performed this selection by linear search over a part of the suspended constraints.

Access to data through a variable, and then functor/arity, is exactly the functionality provided efficiently by attributed variables. In our runtime system we map every functor/arity pair to a fixed attribute slot of a variable at compile time yielding *constant time* access to the constraints of one type. Only the arguments need to be matched at runtime.

5 Preliminary Empirics

Benchmarks are difficult, because the new implementation is in SICStus Prolog, while the previous one was in ECL^{i}PS^e Prolog. Attributed variables are implemented differently in these Prologs. That said, our inchoate measurements indicate that the new compiler produces code that is roughly twice as fast. Specifically, we compared our new SICStus 3#7 CHR implementation with the one in distribution with ECL^{i}PS^e 3.5.2, measuring the variation between the two Prolog implementations together with the actual CHR implementation differences. Times are given in seconds. ECL^{i}PS^e and SICStus were run on the same machine (a Sun workstation). In ECL^{i}PS^e, the solvers were compiled without debugger hooks[6]. We have two columns for SICStus: one for native code, one for emulated code. The last column relates *emulated* SICStus and ECL^{i}PS^e.

Benchmark	SICStus native	a) SICStus emulated	b) ECL^{i}PS^e	ratio a/b
solver bool				
deussen1 ulm027r1, all solutions	0.370	0.470	0.900	0.52
schur(10,_), all solutions	1.020	1.300	2.584	0.50
schur(13,_), 1st solution	0.230	0.290	1.233	0.24
schur(13,_), all solutions	2.040	2.520	7.483	0.34
bnqueens(8,L), 1st solution	1.240	1.500	9.817	0.15
testbl(5,L), all solutions	0.750	0.900	1.467	0.61
solver lists				
word problem, 1st solution	0.380	0.460	0.633	0.73
word problem, 2nd solution	2.940	3.660	4.717	0.78

The new CHR version was faster on all examples, the ratio new vs. old ranging from 0.15 to 0.78, averaging 0.5 with a standard deviation of 0.2. The boolean

[6] Option `nodbgcomp`.

constraint solver features several different kinds of constraints and consequently benefits more from the new data structures than the solver for lists (that basically allows for equality between concatenations of lists).

Most problems are well-known from the literature: The Deussen problem ulm027r1 was originally provided by Mark Wallace, Schur's lemma and Boolean n-queens by Daniel Diaz. The final one is a puzzle of unknown origin posted by Bart Demoen in the newsgroup comp.lang.prolog. The word problem was provided by Klaus Schulz.

6 Conclusions

With the CHR system outlined in this paper we aimed at improvements in terms of completeness, flexibility and efficiency.

With regard to completeness some former limitations were removed:

- The number of heads in a rule is no longer limited to two. The restriction was motivated originally by efficiency considerations since more heads need more search time. One can encode rules with more than two heads using additional auxiliary intermediate constraints. But then, the resulting rules are not only hard to understand, they are also less efficient than a true multi-headed implementation. In addition, rules apply now in textual order, which gives the programmer more control.
- Guards now support *Ask* and *Tell* [28]. In this way, CHR can also be used as a general-purpose concurrent constraint language. (In this paper we only considered *Ask* parts of guards.)
- Due to space limitations we also have not discussed *options* and *pragmas* in this paper - these are annotations to programs, rules or constraints that enable the compiler to perform powerful optimizations, that can sometimes make programs terminate or reduce their complexity class.

The gain in flexibility of the implementation proper can be attributed to the following facts:

- The CHR compiler has been "orthogonalized" by introducing three clearly defined compilation phases. Compilation is now on-the-fly, while loading. The template-based translation with subsequent macro-based partial evaluation allows for easy experimentation with different translation schemata. It created the elbow room for a rather quick implementation of various compiler options and pragmas. The system was implemented in four man-months. The compiler is 1100 lines of Prolog, the runtime system around 600, which together is less than half of the ECL^iPS^e implementation.
- CHR specific demands, such as access paths and suspension recycling, are taken care of explicitly through customized versions of the suspension mechanism.
- Attributed variables let us efficiently implement the generalized suspension mechanism needed for CHR at the *source level*. In particular, constant time

access to constraints of one type can now be provided, instead of the linear time access in previous implementations.

Plans for the future development of the CHR implementation are the introduction of a priority scheme, realized through a scheduler [33] that makes the order in which simultaneously applicable rules are executed explicit, and the factorization of common matching instructions [7].

More information about CHR is available at the CHR homepage
`http://www.informatik.uni-muenchen.de/~fruehwir/chr-intro.html`

References

1. Banatre J.-P., Coutant A., Le Metayer D., A Parallel Machine for Multiset Transformation and its Programming Style, Future Generation Computer Systems 4:133-144, 1988.
2. Benhamou F., Older W.J., Bell Northern Research, June 1992, Applying interval arithmetic to Integer and Boolean constraints, Technical Report.
3. Brisset P. et al., ECL^{i}PS^e 4.0 User Manual, IC-Parc at Imperial College, London, July 1998.
4. Carlsson M., Widen J., Sicstus Prolog Users Manual, Release 3#0, Swedish Institute of Computer Science, SICS/R-88/88007C, 1995.
5. Diaz D., Codognet P., A Minimal Extension of the WAM for clp(FD), in Warren D.S.(Ed.), Proceedings of the Tenth International Conference on Logic Programming, The MIT Press, Budapest, Hungary, pp.774-790, 1993.
6. Dincbas M. et al., The Constraint Logic Programming Language CHIP, Fifth Generation Computer Systems, Tokyo, Japan, December 1988.
7. Debray S., Kannan S., Paithane M., Weighted Decision Trees, in Apt K.R.(Ed.), Logic Programming - Proceedings of the Joint International Conference and Symposium on Logic Programming, MIT Press, Cambridge, MA, pp.654-668, 1992.
8. Debray S.K., QD-Janus : A Sequential Implementation of Janus in Prolog, Software—Practice and Experience, Volume 23, Number 12, December 1993, pp. 1337-1360.
9. Frühwirth T., Brisset P., High-Level Implementations of Constraint Handling Rules, Technical Report ECRC-95-20, ECRC Munich, Germany, June 1995.
10. Frühwirth T., and Brisset P., Chapter on Constraint Handling Rules, in ECL^{i}PS^e 3.5.1 Extensions User Manual, ECRC Munich, Germany, December 1995.
11. Frühwirth T., Abdennadher S., Meuss H., Confluence and Semantics of Constraint Simplification Rules, Constraint Journal, Kluwer Academic Publishers, to appear.
12. Frühwirth T., Theory and Practice of Constraint Handling Rules, Special Issue on Constraint Logic Programming (P. Stuckey and K. Marriot, Eds.), Journal of Logic Programming, Vol 37(1-3), pp 95-138, October 1998.
13. Hentenryck P.van, Simonis H., Dincbas M., Constraint Satisfaction Using Constraint Logic Programming, Artificial Intelligence, 58(1-3):113–159, December 1992.
14. Herbig B., Eine homogene Implementierungsebene für einen hybriden Wissensrepräsentationsformalismus, Master Thesis, in German, University of Kaiserslautern, Germany, April 1993.

15. Holzbaur C., Specification of Constraint Based Inference Mechanisms through Extended Unification, Department of Medical Cybernetics and Artificial Intelligence, University of Vienna, Dissertation, 1990.
16. Holzbaur C., Metastructures vs. Attributed Variables in the Context of Extensible Unification, In 1992 International Symposium on Programming Language Implementation and Logic Programming, pages 260–268. LNCS631, Springer Verlag, August 1992.
17. Holzbaur C., Extensible Unification as Basis for the Implementation of CLP Languages, in Baader F., et al., *Proceedings of the Sixth International Workshop on Unification*, Boston University, MA, TR-93-004, pp.56-60, 1993.
18. Holzbaur C., Frühwirth T., Constraint Handling Rules Reference Manual, for SICStus Prolog, Österreichisches Forschungsinstitut für Artificial Intelligence, Vienna, Austria, TR-98-01, March 1998.
19. Holzbaur C., Frühwirth T., Compiling Constraint Handling Rules (CHR), Third ERCIM/Compulog Network Workshop on Constraints, CWI Amsterdam, The Netherlands, September 1998.
20. Holzbaur C., Frühwirth T., Join Evaluation Schemata for Constraint Handling Rules, 13th Workshop Logische Programmierung WLP'98, TU Vienna, Austria, September 1998.
21. Huitouze S.le, A new data structure for implementing extensions to Prolog, in Deransart P. and Maluszunski J.(Eds.), Programming Language Implementation and Logic Programming, Springer, Heidelberg, 136-150, 1990.
22. Jaffar J., Maher M.J., Constraint Logic Programming: A Survey, Journal of Logic Programming, 1994:19,20:503-581.
23. Maher M.J., Logic Semantics for a Class of Committed-Choice Programs, Fourth Intl Conf on Logic Programming, Melbourne, Australia, MIT Press, pp 858-876.
24. Marriott K., Stuckey J.P, Programming with Constraints, MIT Press, USA, March 1998.
25. Naish L., Prolog control rules, Proceedings of the Ninth International Joint Conference on Artificial Intelligence, Los Angeles, California, September 1985, pp. 720-722.
26. Neumerkel U., Extensible unification by metastructures, In Proc. of Metaprogramming in Logic (META'90), Leuven, Belgium, 1990.
27. Sahlin D., An Automatic Partial Evaluator for Full Prolog, Swedish Institute of Computer Science, 1991.
28. Saraswat V.A., Concurrent Constraint Programming, MIT Press, Cambridge, 1993.
29. Shapiro E., The Family of Concurrent Logic Programming Languages, ACM Computing Surveys, 21(3):413-510, September 1989.
30. Shen K., The Extended CHR Implementation, chapter in ECL^{i}PS^e 4.0 Library Manual, IC-Parc at Imperial College, London, July 1998.
31. Sidebottom G.A., A Language for Optimizing Constraint Propagation, 1993, Simon Fraser University, Canada.
32. Smolka G, Treinen R.(Ed.), DFKI Oz Documentation Series, DFKI, Saarbrücken, Germany, 1994.
33. Ueda K., Chikayama T., Concurrent Prolog Compiler on Top of Prolog, in Symposium on Logic Programming, The Computer Society Press, pp.119-127, 1985.

Parallel Execution Models for Constraint Programming over Finite Domains *

Alvaro Ruiz-Andino, Lourdes Araujo, Fernando Sáenz, and José Ruz

Department of Computer Science
University Complutense of Madrid

Abstract. Many problems from artificial intelligence can be described as constraint satisfaction problems over finite domains (CSP(FD)), that is, a solution is an assignment of a value from a finite domain to each problem variable such that a set of constraints is satisfied. Arc-consistency algorithms remove inconsistent values from the set of values that can be assigned to a variable (its domain), thus reducing the search space. We have developed two parallelisation models of arc-consistency to be run on MIMD multiprocessors. Two different policies, static and dynamic, to schedule the execution of constraints have been tested. In the static scheduling policy, the set of constraints is divided into N partitions, which are executed in parallel on N processors. We discuss an important factor affecting performance, the criterion to establish the partition in order to balance the run-time workload. In the dynamic scheduling policy, any processor can execute any constraint, improving the workload balance. However, a coordination mechanism is required to ensure a sound order in the execution of constraints. Both parallelisation models have been implemented on a CRAY T3E multiprocessor with up to thirty four processors. Empirical results on speedup and behaviour of both models are reported and discussed.

1 Introduction

Constraint Programming over finite domains (CP(FD)) [5,7] has been used for specifying and solving complex constraint satisfaction and optimisation problems, as resource allocation, scheduling and hardware design [6,17]. Finite domain Constraint Satisfaction Problems (CSP) usually describe NP-complete search problems, but it has been shown that by working locally on constraints and their related variables it is possible to dynamically prune the search space in an efficient way. Techniques following this approach, called arc-consistency algorithms, eliminate inconsistent values from the solution space. They can be used to reduce the size of the search space both before and while searching. Waltz [18] proposed the first arc-consistency algorithm, and several improved versions are described in the literature: AC-3 [10], AC-4 [11], AC-5 [15], and AC-6 [1].

AC-3, AC-4 and AC-6 deal with extensional constraints, that is, constraints are expressed as the set of tuples that satisfies it, whereas AC-5 can be specialised

* Supported by project TIC98-0445-C03-02.

G. Nadathur (Ed.): PPDP'99, LNCS 1702, pp. 134–151, 1999.

for functional, anti-functional and monotonic constraints. This specialisation provides an efficient decision procedure for the basic constraints of constraint programming languages.

We have developed and tested two parallelisation models of arc-consistency for MIMD distributed shared memory multiprocessors. These models arise from two policies of *scheduling* the constraints to be processed, static and dynamic. In the static model, the set of constraints is partitioned into N partitions, which are processed in parallel on N processors. We discuss the two main issues affecting the performance of this model: the criterion to distribute constraints among processors, and the frequency of updating shared variables. In the dynamic model any processor can process any constraint, improving the workload balance. However, a coordination mechanism is required to ensure a sound processing order of constraints.

Several parallel processing methods for solving CSPs have been proposed. In [20], a parallel constraint solving technique for a special class of CSP, acyclic constraint networks, is developed. It also presents some results on parallel complexity, generalising results in [8]. In [9], it is concluded that parallel complexity of constraint networks is critically dependent on subtle properties of the network which do not influence its sequential complexity. They propose massively parallel processing of arc-consistency with also very simple processing elements.

In [2,12] Nguyen, Deville and Baudot proposed distributed versions for AC-3, AC-4, and AC-6 for binary CSPs, based on a static scheduling. Our work considers both static and dynamic scheduling policies, and it is focused on the AC-5 specialisation for functional, anti-functional and monotonic n-ary constraints. More precisely, it is a parallelisation of the *indexical* scheme [4,3,16]. We have integrated the parallel execution of arc-consistency within a labelling process that searches for solutions to the constraint satisfaction problem, embedded in a constraint logic programming language. Labelling is performed sequentially, that is, parallel arc-consistency phases are interleaved with variable-value assignment phases, synchronous and identically performed by every processing element, in contrast with other distributed constraint satisfaction techniques as [19].

The rest of the paper is organised as follows. Next section describes basic concepts of constraint programming over finite domains of integers. Section 3 discusses the parallelism presented by the arc-consistency algorithm and introduces two models to exploit it. Section 4 describes the static scheduling execution model, whereas Section 5 is devoted to the dynamic one. Section 6 reports and discusses the experimental results. Finally, conclusions are drawn in section 7.

2 Constraint Programming

A constraint satisfaction problem over finite domains may be stated as follows. Given a tuple $\langle \mathcal{V}, \mathcal{D}, \mathcal{C} \rangle$, where

- $\mathcal{V} \equiv \{v_1, \cdots, v_n\}$, is a set of domain variables,
- $\mathcal{D} \equiv \{d_1, \cdots, d_n\}$, is the set of an initial *finite domain* (finite set of values) for each variable,

- $\mathcal{C} \equiv \{c_1, \cdots, c_m\}$, is a set of constraints among the variables in $\mathcal{V}$. A constraint $c \equiv (V_c, R_c)$ is defined by a subset of variables $V_c \subseteq \mathcal{V}$, and a subset of allowed tuples of values $R_c \subseteq \bigotimes_{i \in \{j/v_j \in V_c\}} d_i$, where $\bigotimes$ denotes Cartesian product.

The goal is to find an assignment for each variable $v_i \in \mathcal{V}$ of a value from each $d_i \in \mathcal{D}$ which satisfies every constraint $c_i \in \mathcal{C}$.

A constraint $c \equiv (V_c, R_c) \in \mathcal{C}$, $V_c \equiv \{v_1, \cdots, v_k\}$, is arc-consistent with respect to domains $\{d_1, \cdots, d_k\}$ iff for all $v_i \in V_c$, for all $a \in d_i$, there exists a tuple $(b_1, \cdots, b_{i-1}, a, b_{i+1}, \cdots, b_k) \in R_c$, where $b_j \in d_j$. A CSP is called arc-consistent iff all $c_i \in C$ are arc-consistent with respect to $\mathcal{D}$.

The starting point of this work is a sequential constraint solver which implements consistency using the *indexical scheme* [4,3,16]. In this scheme, a constraint is translated into a set of reactive functional expressions, called *indexicals*, which maintain consistency. An indexical has the form "v in $E(V)$", where $v \in \mathcal{V}$, $V \subseteq \mathcal{V}$, and $E(V)$ is a monotonic functional expression which returns a finite set of values. Given an indexical $I \equiv v$ in $E(V)$, we call V its *set of arguments*, and we say that, for all $v_i \in V$, I *depends on* v_i, and I *writes* the domain variable v. A constraint $c \equiv (V_c, R_c)$ relating the set of domain variables $V_c \equiv \{v_1, \cdots, v_k\}$, is translated into a set of k indexicals $\{I_i \equiv v_i \text{ in } E_i(V_c - \{v_i\})\}$. Each indexical I_i writes variable v_i and depends on the remaining $k-1$ variables. Functional expressions $E_i(V_c - \{v_i\})$ are properly defined for arc-consistency to be achieved (removal of inconsistent values) with respect to constraint c. Most common high level constraints, such as arithmetic, symbolic and relational ones can be easily translated to indexicals.

The set of finite domains that keeps the current domain of each variable in $\mathcal{V}$ is called the *store*. The initial value of the store is defined by $\mathcal{D}$. The execution of an indexical v in $E(V)$, is triggered by changes in the domains of its set of arguments V in a data driven way. When an indexical is executed, the domain of v in the store is updated with $d_v \cap Eval(E(V))$, where d_v denotes the current value of the domain of v in the store, and $Eval(E(V))$ denotes the evaluation of $E(V)$ with the current domains of the set of variables V in the store.

Figures 1 and 2 show the sequential arc-consistency algorithm. Its input argument is the CSP $\langle \mathcal{V}, \mathcal{D}, \mathcal{C} \rangle$ whose arc-consistency is to be achieved. The set of constraints $\mathcal{C}$ is expressed as a set of indexicals. The algorithm returns either a store where the domain for each variable has been pruned achieving arc-consistency, or `FAILURE` if inconsistency is detected (the domain of a variable was pruned to an empty domain).

A sequential arc-consistency algorithm executes indexicals until either the fixed point is reached, or inconsistency is detected. The fixed point is reached iff the store is arc-consistent. A propagation queue is used to schedule the execution of indexicals (`PropagationQueue`, figure 1). As the result of the execution of an indexical (`Arc_Consistent()`), the domain of a variable may be pruned, and in such a case the variable is queued (`Update()`). Initially, all indexicals are executed, initialising the `PropagationQueue` (line 1). The main loop (lines 2 to 9) iterates until either the propagation queue is empty, or inconsistency is

```
   function Arc-Consistent-CSP(⟨VarSet, DomSet, ConstrSet⟩): Store
   begin
1     Queue_Init(PropagationQueue, ··· );
2     while NOT Empty(PropagationQueue) do
3        Queue_Pop(PropagationQueue, vᵢ);
4        for each indexical Iⱼ which depends on vᵢ do
5           if NOT Arc_Consistent(Iⱼ,Store,PropagationQueue) then
6              return FAILURE;
7           end-if;
8        end-for;
9     end-while;
10    return Store;
   end;
```

Fig. 1. Arc consistency algorithm.

detected. In each iteration, a variable is dequeued and those indexicals that depend on it are executed.

```
   function Arc_Consistent( 'vᵢ in E()',
                            Var Store, Var PropQueue ) : Boolean
   begin
      NewDomain := Eval(E(), Store);
      return (Update(NewDomain,vᵢ,Store,PropQueue) <> EMPTY);
   end;

   function Update( NewDomain, vᵢ, Var Store,
                            Var PropQueue): RESULT
   begin
      NewDomain := NewDomain ∩ Store[vᵢ];
      if Empty(NewDomain) then return EMPTY; end-if;
      if (NewDomain ⊂ Store[vᵢ]) then
         Store[vᵢ] := NewDomain;
         Queue_Push(vᵢ, PropQueue);
         return PRUNED;
      end-if;
      return NOT_PRUNED;
   end;
```

Fig. 2. Store and propagation queue updating.

Termination, correctness, complexity, and properties of the algorithm have been studied extensively in the literature [15,14,3]. Correctness is independent of the order of reexecution of indexicals, which constitutes the basis for the correctness of the parallel version of the algorithm.

3 Parallel Arc-Consistency

The arc-consistency algorithm presents inherent parallelism. Each indexical behaves as a concurrent process which updates the store, triggered by changes in the store. There is an inherent sequentiality, as well, since an indexical must be executed only as the consequence of a previous execution of another indexical. This sequentiality defines a partial order among (re)execution of indexicals. An indexical is *ready* if any of its arguments has changed after its last execution. At any time during the execution of the arc-consistency algorithm there will be a set of ready indexicals, called the *ready set.* In a sequential version of a consistency algorithm the ready set is stored in a *propagation queue* (updated whenever a variable is modified), ensuring a sound execution order of indexicals, that is, that an indexical is executed after the pruned variable has been updated. Parallel consistency algorithms simultaneously execute the indexicals in the ready set, providing mechanisms to maintain a sound order.

We have investigated the feasibility of both static and dynamic scheduling policies for execution of indexicals.

In the static scheduling model, the set of indexicals is divided into N partitions, which are executed in parallel on N processors. A static scheduling ensures a sound execution order of indexicals, since the parallel algorithm is basically the sequential one, but applied to a subset of the indexicals. The only coordination mechanism needed by this model comes from the detection of termination, which can be carried out by one of the processors, called the *distinguished* one. The mapping of indexicals to processors is generated previously to the execution of arc-consistency. An important factor for the efficiency of this model is the criterion for the distribution of indexicals among processors, therefore different criteria have been investigated.

A dynamic scheduling policy requires a coordination mechanism to guarantee a sound execution order. Section 5 discusses the dynamic scheduling model where a sound execution order is achieved by means of synchronisation points.

Parallelisation of the consistency algorithm requires every processor to have access to a common store. Since the considered parallelisation models are focused on distributed shared memory architecture, each processor has a (partial) local copy of the store. Changes in the variables' domains must be communicated to concerned processors in order to maintain coherency among local copies of the store.

4 Static Scheduling of Indexicals

The set of indexicals $\mathcal{C}$ is partitioned into n disjoint subsets, $\mathcal{C} = \mathcal{C}_1 \cup \cdots \cup \mathcal{C}_n$. This partitioning induces a distribution of the set of domain variables $\mathcal{V}$ in n not necessarily disjoint subsets $V_1, \cdots, V_n$ ($\mathcal{V} = V_1 \cup \cdots \cup V_n$). For all indexicals $I_j \in C_i$, the variable written by I_j, and those variables on which I_j depends on, constitute V_i ($\forall I_j \in C_i, I_j \equiv v$ in $E(V_j), V_i = \{v\} \cup V_j$.) Figure 3 sketches the partitioning process of the CSP.

Partitions $\langle V_i, D_i, C_i \rangle$ are mapped one-to-one to processing elements P_i. Each processing element P_i performs sequential arc-consistency, executing those indexicals in C_i, and consequently updating local copies of variables in V_i. Since the distribution of the set of variables $\mathcal{V}$ is non-disjoint, some variables will be located at several processing elements. Therefore, each processing element P_i must broadcast the pruning of the domain of variable v to every processing element P_j which had been assigned any of those indexicals which depend on v. Upon receiving the notification, processing elements P_j intersect their local copies of the domain with the incoming domain, probably triggering further propagation. Communication among processors is also needed in order to detect termination of the algorithm, either because of reaching the global fixed point, or because of inconsistency detection.

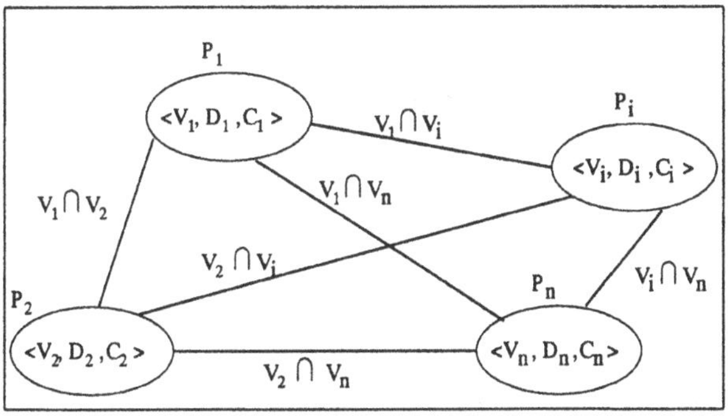

Fig. 3. Partitioning the CSP. Sub-CSP $\langle V_i, D_i, C_i \rangle$ is assigned to processing element (PE) P_i. An edge between two PE's is labelled with the set of variables located at both PE's ($V_i \cap V_j$). Communication is needed to maintain the same domain for some of the variables in $V_i \cap V_j$.

4.1 Parallel Algorithm

Figures 4 and 5 show the parallel execution algorithm. As in the sequential one, initially every indexical assigned to the processor is executed, initialising the local propagation queue (line 3). The main loop (lines 4 to 23) is executed until either global fixed point (`GlobalFixedPoint`) or inconsistency (`Failure`) is detected. The latter can be caused either by:

- an empty domain results from the execution of a local indexical (`Local_Arc_Consistent()`).
- an empty domain results from the intersection of the local domain of a variable with the domain received from another processor (`Remote_Arc_Consistent()`).
- inconsistency is detected at (and broadcasted from) another processor (`RemoteFailure`).

Each processor maintains a private propagation queue (`LocalPropQueue`). The inner loop (lines 6 to 14) performs local propagation until either the queue is empty or inconsistency is detected, like the main loop of the sequential algorithm. Once a local fixed point is reached, the processor notifies it to the *distinguished* processor of this status (`Notify_Local_Fixed_Point()`), and it waits (lines 17 to 21) until either:

- global fixed point is detected (`Check_Global_Fixed_Point()`).
- some other processor communicates inconsistency (`RemoteFailure`).
- the processor receives a message which updates its local propagation queue. In this case, the processor notifies it (`Notify_Active()`) to the distinguished one and continues executing indexicals.

```
    function Parallel-Consistency(
                      ⟨VarSubSet, DomSubSet, ConstrSubSet⟩ ) : Store
    begin
1      Parallel_State_Reset();
2      Synchronisation;
3      Queue_Init(LocalPropQueue, ··· );
4      while NOT Failure AND NOT GlobalFixedPoint do
5         Notify_Active();
6         while NOT Failure AND NOT Empty(LocalPropQueue)) do
7            Queue_Pop (LocalPropQueue, v_i);
8            for each indexical I_i which depends on v_i do
9               Failure := RemoteFailure OR
10                 NOT Local_Arc_Consistent(I_i,Store,LocalPropQueue) OR
11                 NOT Remote_Arc_Consistent(Store,LocalPropQueue);
12              if Failure then break; end-if;
13           end-for;
14        end-while;
15        if NOT Failure then
16           Notify_Local_Fixed_Point(···);
17           repeat
18              Failure := RemoteFailure OR
19                      NOT Consistency_Msg(Store,LocalPropQueue);
20              GlobalFixedPoint := Check_Global_Fixed_Point();
21           until Failure OR GlobalFixedPoint OR Message_Received();
22        end-if;
23     end-while;
24     if Failure then
25        Synchronisation(); return FAILURE;
26     end-if
27     return Store;
    end-function;
```

Fig. 4. Static Parallel Consistency Algorithm.

When the local execution of an indexical (`Local_Arc_Consistent()`, figure 5) results in the modification of the domain of a variable v (`Update()`, figure 5), the processor broadcasts a message (`Broadcast_Update()`, line 7) to the set of processors that have been assigned any of those indexicals which depends on variable v. Upon receiving the message (`Remote_Arc_Consistent()`, figure 5), these processors either detect inconsistency or properly update their local propagation queue and their local copy of variable v. Whenever a processor detects inconsistency, it broadcasts the failure to the rest of processors (`Broadcast_Failure()`).

```
  function Local_Arc_Consistent( 'vi in E()',
                                  Var Store, Var PropQueue ): Boolean
  begin
1   NewDomain := Eval(E(), Store);
2   switch (Update (NewDomain, vi, Store, PropQueue))
3      case EMPTY :
4         Broadcast_Failure(RemoteFailure);
5         return FALSE;
6      case PRUNED:
7         Broadcast_Update(vi, Store[vi]);
8   end-switch;
9   return TRUE;
  end-function;

  function Remote_Arc_Consistent( Var Store,
                                  Var PropQueue ) : Boolean
  begin
1   while NOT Empty(MsgQueue) do
2      Pop_Message(MsgQueue, vi, NewDomain);
3      if (Update(NewDomain,vi,Store, PropQueue) = EMPTY) then
4         Broadcast_Failure(RemoteFailure);
5         return FALSE;
6      end-if;
7   end-while;
8   return TRUE;
  end-function;
```

Fig. 5. Parallel consistency functions.

The algorithm terminates when every processor reaches a local fixed point and there are no pending messages. The distinguished processor is the only one responsible for the detection of termination. However, it performs local propagation as any other processor. In order to be able to detect the global fixed point, processors must notify to the distinguished one whenever they reach a local fixed point –along with the number of messages they have sent and received– (`Notify_Local_Fixed_Point()`), and whenever they leave it due to an incoming message (`Notify_Active()`). The distinguished processor keeps record of which processors are at a local fixed point, and the number of messages sent and received by all processors. When termination is detected, the distinguished processor notifies it to the rest of processors (`GlobalFixedPoint`).

Since this parallel algorithm is part of a labelling procedure where variable-value assignment is performed synchronously, a synchronisation point among all processing elements is needed at the beginning of the algorithm, just after the initialisation of the communication status variables (`Parallel_State_Reset()`, line 2, figure 4). Another synchronisation (line 25) is needed if the algorithm finishes with failure; otherwise, the global fixed point detection implies a synchronisation among processors. Synchronisation points guarantee that every processing element waits until the last processing element has finished the current arc-consistency cycle before it starts working on the next one.

4.2 Partition of the CSP

The way the set of indexicals is partitioned has shown to be an essential factor for the efficiency of the parallel algorithm. A CSP $\langle \mathcal{V}, \mathcal{D}, \mathcal{C} \rangle$ can be represented as a hyper-graph where the set of nodes is the set of domain variables $\mathcal{V}$ and the set of hyper-edges is the set of indexicals defined by $\mathcal{C}$. Therefore, partitioning the CSP among processors means partitioning the set of hyper-edges in disjoints subsets, inducing a not necessarily disjoint partitioning of the set of nodes. We have tested two different graph partition criteria:

- Strength of connection among partitions.
- Static estimation of run-time ready set distribution.

Strength of connection among partitions The graph topology can be considered in order to partition the graph in *strongly connected subgraphs*, or *highly disconnected subgraphs.*

In the former case, communications are minimised, but the ready set will be badly balanced, in general. A strongly connected partitioning induces an almost disjoint partitioning of the set of variables $\mathcal{V}$, thus avoiding communications. However, it is very likely that most of those indexicals which depend on a variable v are assigned to the same processing element P. Whenever variable v is pruned, the ready set is enlarged with those indexicals which depend on v, but almost all of them will be sequentially executed by P, thus loosing the potential parallelism exploitation.

In the latter case, the ready set is better balanced, but it is likely that almost every variable will be located at almost every processing element, increasing communications.

Experimental results show the benefit of a better balanced ready set versus a communications reduction. Moreover, partitioning the CSP in strongly connected subgraphs is a hard problem, whereas a highly disconnected CSP partitioning is easily achieved with a shuffle distribution of indexicals.

Static estimation of run-time ready set distribution A partition of the set of indexicals that balances the run-time ready set is expected to improve the performance, providing that communications do not increase. Since this model is based on a static partitioning of the CSP among processors, balancing run-time ready set requires some kind of compile-time static estimation.

The idea is to partition the set of indexicals in such a way that updating any variable causes a similar number of indexicals to be executed by each processor [13]. We have defined an objective function to be minimised, which considers the peak workload for each processor and variable. Experimental measures of run-time workload have confirmed the accuracy of our static estimation. Since we are dealing with n-ary constraints, finding the optimal solution is a NP problem. Therefore, we recourse to an algorithm which assigns indexicals one by one, in a decreasing arity order, greedily choosing the processor which minimises the objective function. Solutions found with this greedy algorithm have shown to be quite close to the optimal one when the CSP is constituted by a large number of low-arity constraints. Taking into account that this is just an estimation of the actual run-time ready set distribution, the greedy approach is fully justified.

5 Dynamic Scheduling of Indexicals

A dynamic scheduling policy dispatches the *ready set* of indexicals every *execution cycle*, in order to balance workload. However, these models require mechanisms to ensure that the indexicals depending on a variable are executed after the change in the domain of the variable have been updated in the store of the processor executing the indexical. The alternatives to achieve a sound execution order are either to introduce synchronisation points during the execution (distributed control) or to include a master processor (centralised control) to perform the dispatching of indexicals. The latter model leads to tasks of small granularity, inappropriate for a distributed memory architecture. Therefore, we concentrate on the distributed control alternative.

The dynamic parallelisation model is based on dividing the execution in synchronised *execution cycles*. An execution cycle consists of generating of the ready set, distributed selection and execution of the ready set, and a synchronisation point. In order to distribute the queued indexicals, every processor must generate identical propagation queues of indexicals. In this way, each processor independently selects and executes, according to a fixed rule, a different subset of indexicals of those present in the propagation queue. Synchronisation points between execution cycles are introduced in order to generate identical propagation queues. Besides, the store must be replicated in every processor.

The consistency algorithm for this model initially queues every indexical. Then, execution cycles are performed until either there are no indexicals to execute or inconsistency is detected. An execution cycle comprises the following actions:

- Each indexical in the queue is executed by a particular processor, until the queue is empty. The coordination criterion ensures that every queued index-

ical is selected by only one processor, and that the workload is well balanced in each execution cycle.
- Modified variables are recorded and broadcasted, but indexicals are not queued in the current propagation queue.
- Changes in domains of variables received from remote processors are updated and queued.
- Once the propagation queue is empty, and after a synchronisation, which ensures that all processors have the same value of the domains of the variables, a new propagation queue is generated, queuing all indexicals depending on modified variables.

Two criteria to select indexicals from the queue have been investigated in order to tune the model:

- Assigning the same number of indexicals to each processor. This criterion can lead to unbalanced workload since each indexical involves a different amount of work.
- Dynamic distribution, in which each processor selects, in mutual exclusion, the next pending indexical.

First criterion has yielded better results, showing that workload balance is good enough, while second criterion increases communication overhead.

6 Experimental Results

The presented parallel algorithms have been written in C, and developed and tested on a CRAY T3E multiprocessor with thirty four 400-MHz DEC Alpha processors, 128 Mb of memory per processor, under UNICOS (UNIX) operating system. Notification of failure, global and local fixed point detection, activity status, and number of messages sent and received, have been implemented using the remote memory write feature of the CRAY T3E multiprocessor. Queues of messages are used for receiving domain updates. Messages are broadcasted to queues also using the fast remote memory write feature.

Reported results correspond to the time required to reach the first or all solutions, depending on the benchmark, performing a first fail sequential labelling. Therefore, reported speedup is lower than speedup achieved in a single call to the arc-consistency algorithm, since the search for a solution usually comprises a large number of calls to the arc-consistency algorithm, executed in parallel, interleaved with the selection and assignment of a value to a variable, executed sequentially.

6.1 Benchmarks

We have tested the parallelisation models on a set of benchmarks:

1. *Arithmetic* is a synthetic benchmark. It is formed by sixteen blocks of arithmetic relations, $\{B_1, \cdots, B_{16}\}$. Each block contains fifteen equations and inequations among six variables. Blocks B_i, B_{i+1} are connected by an additional equation between a pair of variables, one from B_i and the other one from B_{i+1}. Coefficients were randomly generated. The goal is to find an integer solution vector.
2. *Suudoku* is a crypto-arithmetic Japanese problem. Given a grid of 25x25 squares, where 317 of them are filled with a number between 1 and 25, fill the rest of squares such that each row and column is a permutation of numbers 1 to 25. Furthermore, each of the twenty-five 5x5 squares starting in columns (rows) 1, 6, 11, 16, 21 must also be a permutation of numbers 1 to 25.
3. *N-Queens* problem consists in placing N queens in an N×N chess board in such a way that no queen attacks each other. The instance presented corresponds to N = 111, size which leads to a significant execution time.
4. *Parametrizable Binary Constraint Satisfaction Problem* (PBCSP). Synthetic PBCSPs allow studying the performance of arc-consistency algorithms as some significant problem parameters vary. Instances of this problem are randomly generated given four parameters: number of variables, the size of the initial domains, density, and tightness. All constraints are binary, that is, they involve only two variables. A constraint is defined as the set of pairs of values that satisfies it. Density and tightness are defined as follows:

$$Density = \frac{nc}{nv - 1} \qquad Tightness = 1 - \frac{np}{ds^2}$$

where nv is the number of variables, nc is the number of constraints involving one variable (it is the same for all variables), np is the number of pairs that satisfies the constraint, and ds is the size of the initial domains. Figure 6 reports results obtained for an instance of this problem where $nv = 100$, $ds = 20$, $Density = 0.75$, and $Tightness = 0.85$.

Table 1. Benchmarks characteristics.

	Arithmetic	*Suudoku*	*N-Queens*	*PBCSP*
Search for	first sol.	first sol.	first sol.	all sol.
No. of Variables	126	308	111	100
No. of Constraints	254	13,942	6,105	3,713
No. of Indexicals	1,468	27,884	12,210	7,426
No. of Calls to Consistency	15,969	72,196	8,660	65
Seq. Exec. Time (s.)	15.05	132.98	12.62	5.25
No. of ind. executed	1,953,660	9,764,960	246,262	318,552
Avg. time per call (ms.)	0.9	1.8	1.5	80.8

Table 1 summarises relevant data about the four benchmarks. The three first benchmarks are executed searching for the first solution, whereas the fourth one keeps searching until all solutions (40) are found. The table shows the number of variables, number of constrains and number of indexicals for all benchmarks, as well as the number of calls to the arc-consistency algorithm. It also reports the sequential execution time, and the total number of indexicals executed in the sequential version. Finally, the table reports the average execution time per call to the arc-consistency algorithm, which indicates the granularity of the process to be parallelised.

6.2 Speedup

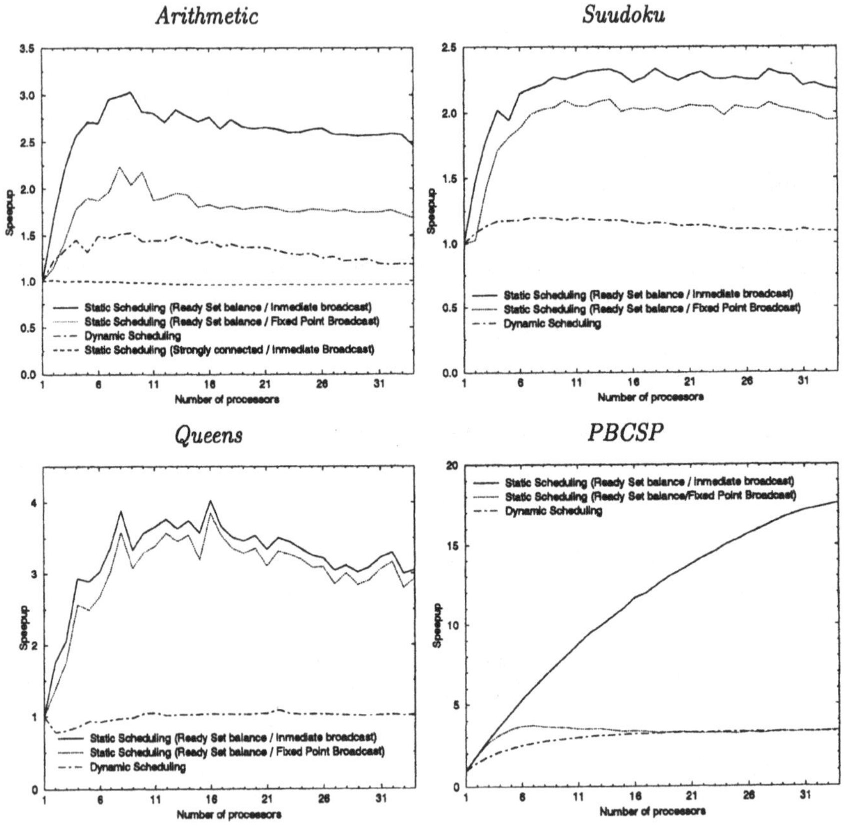

Fig. 6. Speedup curves for selected benchmarks.

Charts in figure 6 show, for each benchmark, the speedup vs. the number of processors. For the static scheduling policy the ready set balance estimation was used, comparing broadcast frequency: immediate (solid line) vs. fixed point (dotted line). Chart for the *Arithmetic* benchmark also shows the speedup obtained with a strongly connected graph partitioning (dashed line). This criterion has not been considered for the other benchmark, since it clearly provides worse results than ready set balance, and because it is too computationally expensive to apply. The speedup obtained with the dynamic scheduling policy (dot-dashed line) is worse than the best one of the static policy, mainly because the overhead due to the synchronisation points introduced in the dynamic model is too large versus the granularity of indexicals in the considered problems. However, this model could be more efficient using large granularity indexicals or propagators, as those arising from global constraints.

It can also be observed that whereas the *PBCSP* problem presents a nearly linear speedup for the best static scheduling policy, the speedup for the rest of benchmarks stops increasing from a certain number of processors. The main factor for this different behaviour is that in the *PBCSP* benchmark calls to the arc-consistency algorithm have a larger execution time, and indexicals executions have larger granularity (see Table 1). Besides, *PBCSP* has a constraint graph with a more uniform topology, leading to a better workload balance. In order to study this factor we have measured the workload distribution among the processing elements.

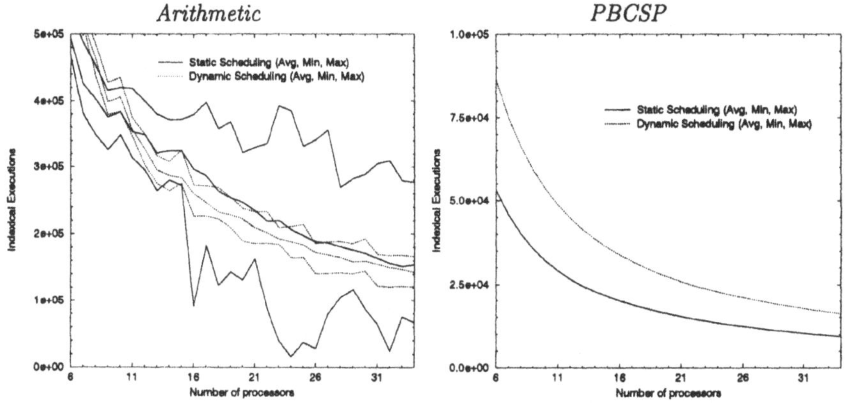

Fig. 7. Average, minimum and maximum number of executions of indexicals per processor.

Figure 7 shows the average, the minimum, and the maximum number of indexicals executed per processor, for the dynamic scheduling policy and the static scheduling policy with immediate broadcast. The difference between minimum and maximum indicates workload balance quality. It can be observed that, in the *Arithmetic* problem, the larger number of processors, the worse workload balance is. This fact limits the performance, since the execution time corresponds to the slower processor, because of serialisation between consecutive call to arc-consistency. The dynamic scheduling policy exhibits a better workload balance. Nevertheless, the speedup for this model is limited by the need of synchronisation points. For the *PBCSP* benchmark, the minimum and maximum curves do not differ in the static neither in the dynamic policy, indicating a high quality workload balance. Nevertheless, it can be expected that *PBCSP* benchmark will also reach a saturation point for a larger number of processors.

6.3 Scaleup

It is important to know how the performance of the parallel system depends on the characteristics of the problem. The *PBCSP* benchmark, as a generic parametrizable constraint satisfaction problem, offers the opportunity to study what characteristics are desirable in a problem in order to achieve a high performance when executed in parallel.

Table 2. Benchmarks characteristics of figure 8(a), scaleup vs. number of variables.

No. of variables	**25**	**50**	**100**	**200**
No. of Constraints	228	910	3,713	14,932
No. of Indexicals	456	1,820	7,426	29,864
No. of Calls to Consistency	63	61	65	66
Seq. Exec. Time (s.)	0.29	1.19	5.25	22.46
No. of ind. exec.	18,192	71,218	318,552	1,311,061
Avg. time per call (ms.)	4.6	19.5	80.8	340.3

Table 3. Benchmarks characteristics of figure 8(b), scaleup vs. density.

Density	**0.25**	**0.50**	**0.75**	**1.00**
No. of Constraints	1,216	2,464	3,713	4,950
No. of Indexicals	2,432	4,928	7,426	9,900
No. of Calls to Consistency	64	64	65	62
Seq. Exec. Time (s.)	1.78	3.40	5.25	6.59
No. of ind. exec.	105,542	205,400	318,552	400,430
Avg. time per call (ms.)	27.8	53.1	80.8	106.3

The size of a *PBCSP* mainly depends on the number of variables and the density of the constraint graph. Figure 8(a) shows the speedup versus the number of processors, for four different numbers of variables, fixing density to 0.75, tightness to 0.85, and domain size to 20. Figure 8(b) shows the speedup versus the number of processors, for different densities, fixing the number of variables to 100, tightness to 0.85, and domain size to 20. Tables 2 and 3 summarises relevant data about the problem instances used to plot the curves. All instances were run searching for all solutions (40). Both charts indicate that the larger the problem is, the higher speedup is obtained. This fact indicates the suitability of the system for large problems, provided a uniform constraint graph, which is a much desirable property in order to solve the real scale combinatorial problems which constraint programming aims to tackle.

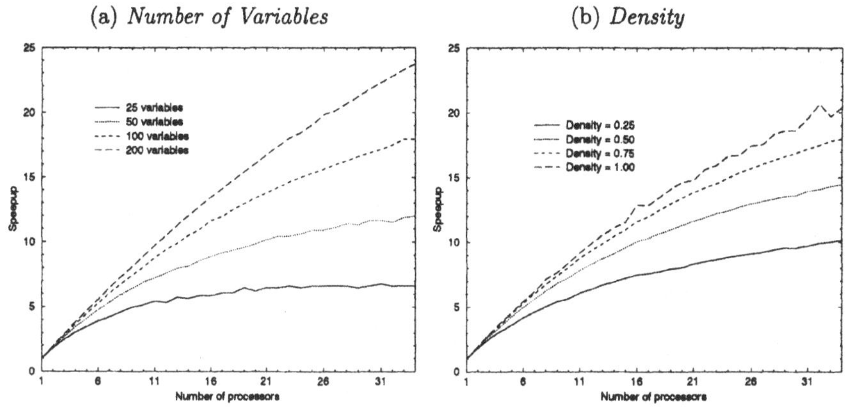

Fig. 8. Scaleup with the number of variables and the density of the problem.

7 Conclusions

We have developed and evaluated parallelisation models of an arc-consistency algorithm for constraint satisfaction problems over finite domains. These models have been implemented on a CRAY T3E, a distributed shared memory MIMD multiprocessor, and empirical data is reported for several benchmarks.

Two different techniques for scheduling the execution of constraints, dynamic and static, have been tested. The dynamic model has shown poor speedups, particularly when compared with those obtained with the static model, therefore we have focused our work on the static scheduling policy.

A number of topics affecting performance have been investigated in order to tune the static scheduling model. The way constraints are distributed among processors, and the frequency of updating shared variables, are determining factors for the performance of the model. The study of the distribution of constraints among processors has shown that a strongly connected partitioning (high number of shared variables) is worse than a partition based on an estimation of the run-time workload balance. Tests on broadcast frequency revealed the convenience of an immediate broadcast.

The speedup obtained is nearly linear for *PBCSP* benchmark, whereas for the rest of them it stops increasing from a problem dependent number of processors. This difference is mainly due to the more uniform constraint graph and larger granularity of the *PBCSP* benchmark, which leads to a better workload balance.

Anyway, the *PBCSP* benchmark would also reach a saturation point for a larger number of processors.

In order to study how the performance of the parallel system depends on the characteristics of the constraint satisfaction problem to solve, the parametrizable synthetic benchmark has been tested for different sets of parameters. Results show that the system is better suited for large scale problems with a dense constraint graph.

References

1. Bessiere, D.: Arc-consistency and arc-consistency again. Artificial Intelligence Journal 65 (1994) 179-190.
2. Baudot, B., Deville, Y.: Analysis of Distributed Arc-Consistency Algorithms. Tech. Rep. 97-07. Uni. of Louvain, Belgium (1997).
3. Carlson, B.: Compiling and Executing Finite Domain Constraints. PhD Thesis, Computer Science Department, Uppsala Univ. (1995).
4. Codognet, P., Diaz, D.: A Simple and Efficient Boolean Constraint Solver for Constraint Logic Programming. Journal of Automated Reasoning. 17,1 (1996) 97-128.
5. Dincbas, M., Van Henteryck, P., Simmons H., Aggoun, A.: The Constraint Programming Language CHIP Proceedings of the 2nd International Conference on Fifth Generation Computer Systems. (1988), 249-264.
6. Dincbas, M., Simonis, H., Van Hentenryck, P.: Solving Large Combinatorial Problems in Logic Programming. Journal of Logic Programming 8 (1990).
7. ILOG: ILOG Solver 3.2 User's Manual (1996).
8. Kasif, S.: On the parallel complexity of discrete relaxation in constraint satisfaction networks. Artificial Intelligence 45 (1990) 275-286.
9. Kasif, S., Delcher, A.L.: Local Consistency in Parallel Constraint-Satisfaction Networks. Artificial Intelligence 69 (1994) 307-327.
10. Mackworth, A.K.: Consistency in networks of relations. Artificial Intelligence 28 (1977) 225-233.
11. Mohr, R., Henderson, T.C.: Arc and path consistency revisited. Artificial Intelligence 28 (1996) 225-233.
12. Nguyen, T., Deville, Y.: A Distributed Arc-Consistency Algorithm. Science of Computer Programming, 30 (1998) 227-250.
13. Ruiz-Andino, A., Araujo, L., Ruz, J.: Parallel constraint satisfaction and optimisation. The PCSO system. Technical Report 71.98. Department of Computer Science. Universidad Complutense de Madrid (1998).
14. Saraswat, V.A.: Concurrent Constraint Programming Languages. MIT Press (1993).
15. Van Hentenryck P., Deville, Y., Teng C.M.: A generic Arc-consistency Algorithm and its Specialisations. Artificial Intelligence 57 (1992) 291-321.
16. Hentenryck, P.V., Saraswat, V.A., Deville, Y.: Constraint Logic Programming over Finite Domains: the Design, Implementation and Applications of cc(FD). Tech. Rep., Computer Science Dept., Brown University (1992).
17. Wallace, M.: Constraints in Planing, Scheduling and Placement Problems. Constraint Programming, Springer-Verlag (1994).
18. Waltz, D.: Generating semantic descriptions for drawings of scenes with shadows. Technical Report AI271, MIT, Cambridge, MA. (1972).

19. Yokoo, M.: Asynchronous weak-commitment search for solving distributed constraint satisfaction problems. Principles and Practice of Constraint Programming (1995) 88-102.
20. Zhang, Y., Mackworth, A.K.: Parallel and Distributed Finite Constraint Satisfaction: Complexity, Algorithms and Experiments. Parallel Processing for Artificial Intelligence. Elsevier Science. (1993).

Functional Plus Logic Programming with Built-In and Symbolic Constraints*

P. Arenas-Sánchez, F.J. López-Fraguas, and M. Rodríguez-Artalejo

Dpto. Sistemas Informáticos y Programación, UCM, Madrid
{puri,fraguas,mario}@sip.ucm.es

Abstract. In this paper we propose a lazy functional logic language, named SETA, which allows to handle *multisets*, *built-in arithmetic constraints* over the domain of real numbers, as well as various *symbolic constraints* over datatypes. As main theoretical results, we have proved the existence of free term models for all SETA programs and we have developed a correct and complete goal solving mechanism.

1 Introduction

Functional logic programming (FLP, in short) aims to combine into a single paradigm the nicest properties of both functional and logic programming. In many approaches to FLP (see [11] as a survey) programs are seen as constructor-based conditional rewrite systems. One of such approaches is the CRWL-framework of [9] where classical equational logic is replaced by a suitable constructor-based rewriting logic which expresses properly the behaviour of reduction for lazy, partial and possibly non-deterministic functions.

Most approaches to FLP, including CRWL, are based on *free* constructors. However, for some applications it is more convenient to represent data by means of non-free constructors, for which some equational specification is given. An extension of [9] along this line has been presented in [4,5], where a general framework for FLP with polymorphic algebraic types is investigated. One particular interesting case is that of *multisets*, which are known to be useful to model a variety of scenarios, like the Gamma programming model [6] or action and change problems [18]. On the other hand, many problems involve computations over specific domains –like real numbers, boolean functions or finite domains– for which the constructor-based approach is not adequate at all. A crucial contribution to this issue within the field of logic programming has been the *constraint logic programming* paradigm [14] and its different instances, such as the language $CLP(\mathcal{R})$ [15] which is known to have a wide and growing range of applications.

Our aim in this work is to merge the expressive power of polymorphic algebraic types and constraints into a single language (named SETA[1]) which can be understood as an *extended instance* of the framework in [4,5]. It is an instance

* This research has been partially supported by the Spanish National Project TIC98-0445-C03-02 "TREND" and the Esprit BRA Working Group EP-22457 "CCLII".

[1] SETA is not an acronym, but simply the spanish word for *mushroom*.

G. Nadathur (Ed.): PPDP'99, LNCS 1702, pp. 152–169, 1999.

in the sense that the *multiset constructor* is the unique non-free constructor we consider, but it is extended since it incorporates primitive "built-in" data (the real numbers), constraints over them and also "symbolic" constraints over constructor terms (in particular, over multisets), including *equality*, *disequality*, *membership* and *non-membership*. Following a line similar to that of [9,4,5], we develop proof-theoretic and model-theoretic semantics (including the existence of free term models) of SETA programs, and then propose an operational semantics by means of a sound and complete goal solving calculus which combines lazy narrowing, unification modulo the equational axiom of multisets and constraint solving. The combination of lazy functions, multisets, arithmetic constraints and symbolic constraints is not found in other related declarative languages, as e.g. [8,7,13]. Moreover, the range of potential applications of SETA is very large. To those which make use in isolation of either multisets or real constraints, we must add others which can take profit of the combination of both. One of such application fields is the parsing of visual languages [12,17], where symbolic and arithmetic constraints can be naturally combined to specify the construction of complex graphic figures from (a multiset of) components.

The rest of the paper is organized as follows. Next section introduces the language SETA , includes a small example illustrating the capabilities of SETA and develops a proof theory in the form of a constrained, goal-oriented, constructor-based rewriting calculus. Section 3 presents the model theory for SETA programs, whereas Section 4 contains a sketch of the goal solving calculus for SETA and the corresponding soundness and completeness results. Last section summarizes some conclusions. Due to space limitations, proofs and many other technical details have been left out, but they can be found in [2].

2 The Language SETA

Due to the fact that language SETA handles real numbers, the presentation of the language is based on two levels: The *primitive level* (containing everything related to real numbers) and the *symbolic level* (containing multisets, free datatypes, and constraints over them).

2.1 The Primitive Level

Σ_p denotes the *primitive signature* defined as the triple $\langle PT, PO, PP\rangle$, where PT has *Real* as unique *Primitive Type*, $PO = \{0, 1 :\to Real, +, * : (Real, Real) \to Real\}$ is a set of type declarations for *Primitive Operations*, and $PP = \{==, \not=, \leq : (Real, Real)\}$ is a set of type declarations for *Primitive Predicates.*

Given a denumerable set $x, y, \ldots \in DV$ of data variables, the set $T_p(DV)$ of *primitive terms* $t^p, s^p, \ldots$ is built from DV and PO. The set $R_p(DV)$ of *primitive constraints* φ^p is defined as $\varphi^p ::= True \mid t_1^p \Diamond t_2^p \mid \varphi_1^p \wedge \varphi_2^p \mid \exists x \varphi^p$, where[2] $x \in DV$, $\Diamond \in \{==, \not=, \leq\}$, $t_i^p \in T_p(DV)$, $\varphi_i^p \in R_p(DV)$, $1 \leq i \leq 2$.

[2] Note that the constraints $\geq$, $<$ and $>$ may be easily defined from $\not=$ and $\leq$.

In the following, we will use $\mathcal{R}$ to denote the field of real numbers $(\mathbb{R}, 0^{\mathbb{R}}, 1^{\mathbb{R}}, +^{\mathbb{R}}, *^{\mathbb{R}})$. η^p will denote a primitive valuation (i.e., a mapping from DV to $\mathbb{R}$), and $(\mathcal{R}, \eta^p) \models_{\mathcal{R}} \varphi^p$ will express the validity of the primitive constraint $\varphi^p \in R_p(DV)$ in $\mathcal{R}$ under η^p. Finally, given a set Γ_p of primitive constraints and a constraint $\varphi^p \in R_p(DV)$, the notation $\Gamma_p \models_{\mathcal{R}} \varphi^p$ will mean that φ^p is a logical consequence of Γ_p when both are interpreted over $\mathcal{R}$.

2.2 The Symbolic Level

Let TV be a countable set of *type variables* $\alpha, \beta, \ldots$, and $TC = \bigcup_{n\geq 0} TC^n$ a countable alphabet of *type constructors* $K, K', \ldots$ including the multiset type constructor $Mset \in TC^1$. *Polymorphic types* $\tau, \tau', \ldots \in Type_{TC}(TV)$ are built from TV and TC. The set of type variables occurring in τ is written $tvar(\tau)$.

We define a *polymorphic signature* Σ over TC as $\Sigma = \Sigma_p \cup \langle TC, DC, FS, PS\rangle$, where:

- ▷ DC is a set of type declarations for *data constructors*, of the form $c : (\tau_1, \ldots, \tau_n) \to \tau$ with $\bigcup_{i=1}^{n} tvar(\tau_i) \subseteq tvar(\tau)$ and $\tau \notin TV \cup PT$. We assume that DC contains the type declarations $\{\!\!\{\ \}\!\!\} :\to Mset(\alpha)$ (representing the *empty multiset*) and $\{\!\!\{\cdot|\cdot\}\!\!\} : (\alpha, Mset(\alpha)) \to Mset(\alpha)$ (representing the *multiset constructor*[3]). The multiset constructor is governed by the equation $(\textsc{mset}) : \{\!\!\{x, y|xs\}\!\!\} \approx \{\!\!\{y, x|xs\}\!\!\}$. Here, we have used $\{\!\!\{x, y|xs\}\!\!\}$ as abbreviation for $\{\!\!\{x|\{\!\!\{y|xs\}\!\!\}\}\!\!\}$. In the sequel we will continue using such notation.
- ▷ FS is a set of type declarations for *defined function symbols*, of the form $f : (\tau_1, \ldots, \tau_n) \to \tau$.
- ▷ $PS = \{==, /=: (\alpha, \alpha), \in, \notin: (\alpha, Mset(\alpha))\}$ is a set of type declarations for *predicate symbols*. $==$ and $/=$ stand for *strict equality* and *disequality* respectively, whereas $\in$, $\notin$ represent *membership* and *non-membership* respectively.

We require that $DC \cup FS$ does not include multiple type declarations for the same symbol. We will write $h \in DC^n \cup FS^n$ to indicate the arity of a symbol according to its type declaration. In the following, $DC_\perp$ will denote DC extended by a new declaration $\perp :\to \alpha$. The bottom constant constructor $\perp$ is intended to represent an undefined value. Analogously, $\Sigma_\perp$ will denote the result of replacing DC by $DC_\perp$ in Σ.

Total expressions $e, es, r, \ldots \in E_\Sigma(DV)$ are built from DV, PO, DC and FS. The set $E_{\Sigma_\perp}(DV)$ of *partial expressions* is defined in the same way, but using $DC_\perp$ in place of DC. *Total data terms* $T_\Sigma(DV) \subseteq E_\Sigma(DV)$ and *partial data terms* $T_{\Sigma_\perp}(DV) \subseteq E_{\Sigma_\perp}(DV)$ are built by using variables, primitive operations and data constructors only. In the sequel, we reserve t, ts, s, l, ls, m, ms, to denote possibly partial data terms, and we write $dvar(e)$ for the set of all data variables occurring in an expression e.

The set $\varphi, \varphi', \ldots \in R_{\Sigma_\perp}(DV)$ of *partial constraints* is defined as $\varphi ::= True \mid e_1 \diamondsuit e_2 \mid \varphi_1 \wedge \varphi_2 \mid \exists x \varphi$, where $\diamondsuit \in \{==, /=, \leq, \in, \notin\}$, $x \in DV$, $e_i \in E_{\Sigma_\perp}(DV)$,

[3] The intended meaning of $\{\!\!\{x|xs\}\!\!\}$ is to add a new copy of the element x to the multiset xs.

$\varphi_i, \varphi \in R_{\Sigma_\perp}(DV)$, $1 \leq i \leq 2$. We say that $\varphi \in R_{\Sigma_\perp}(DV)$ is a *total constraint* if $\perp$ does not occur in φ. The set of all *total constraints* is denoted by $R_\Sigma(DV)$.

The rewriting calculus in Subsection 2.3 will deal with an *extended* notion of expressions and constraints, for which all real numbers are available as new constants. Formally, the set $E^*_{\Sigma_\perp}(DV)$ of *extended partial expressions* is defined as $e ::= \perp \mid x \mid 0 \mid 1 \mid d \mid e_1 \Diamond e_2 \mid h(e_1, \ldots, e_n)$, where $h \in DC^n \cup FS^n$, $e_i \in E^*_{\Sigma_\perp}(DV)$, $1 \leq i \leq n$, $d \in \mathbb{R}$, $\Diamond \in \{+, *\}$, $x \in DV$. If we eliminate $\perp$ in the definition above, we obtain the set $E^*_\Sigma(DV)$ of *extended total expressions.* Analogously, by ignoring *FS* we can define the sets $T^*_{\Sigma_\perp}(DV)$ and $T^*_\Sigma(DV)$ of *extended partial* and *total data terms*, respectively. The sets $R^*_{\Sigma_\perp}(DV)$ and $R^*_\Sigma(DV)$ of *extended partial constraints* and *extended total constraints* are defined similarly to the sets $R_{\Sigma_\perp}(DV)$ and $R_\Sigma(DV)$ respectively, but now all considered expressions must be extended. An *extended primitive term* $T^*_p(DV)$ will be an extended total data term not containing symbols in DC. Similarly, the set $R^*_p(DV) \subseteq R^*_\Sigma(DV)$ of *extended primitive constraints* is composed of all those extended total constraints containing only primitive symbols and variables.

We define possibly *partial data substitutions* δ as mappings from DV to $T^*_{\Sigma_\perp}(DV)$. In the rest of the paper, $DSub(A)$, where A is a subset of $T^*_{\Sigma_\perp}(DV)$, will denote the set of all data substitutions mapping DV to A.

An *environment* is defined as any set V of type-annotated data variables $x : \tau$, such that V does not include two different annotations for the same variable. By considering that any $d \in \mathbb{R}$ has an associated type declaration $d :\to Real$, it is possible to determine when an extended partial expression $e \in E^*_{\Sigma_\perp}(DV)$ has type τ in an environment V. The set $E^{*^\tau}_{\Sigma_\perp}(V)$ (resp. $E^{*^\tau}_\Sigma(V)$) of all extended partial expressions (resp. extended total expressions) that admit type τ w.r.t. V is defined in the usual way; see e.g. [4]. Note that $E^{*^\tau}_{\Sigma_\perp}(V)$ has $T^{*^\tau}_{\Sigma_\perp}(V)$ and $T^{*^\tau}_\Sigma(V)$ as subsets. We can talk also about the sets $E^\tau_{\Sigma_\perp}(V)$ and $T^\tau_{\Sigma_\perp}(V)$ (resp. $E^\tau_\Sigma(V)$ and $T^\tau_\Sigma(V)$) of partial expressions and terms (resp. total expressions and terms) which admit type τ in V.

A constraint $\varphi \in R^*_{\Sigma_\perp}(DV)$ is well-typed w.r.t. an environment V iff one of the following items hold:

- ▷ $\varphi \equiv True$ or $\varphi \equiv e_1 \leq e_2$ and $e_i \in E^{*^{Real}}_{\Sigma_\perp}(V)$, $1 \leq i \leq 2$.
- ▷ $\varphi \equiv e_1 \Diamond e_2$, $\Diamond \in \{==, /=\}$ and $e_i \in E^{*^\tau}_{\Sigma_\perp}(V)$, $1 \leq i \leq 2$, for some $\tau \in Type_{TC}(TV)$. Or $\varphi \equiv e_1 \Diamond e_2$, $\Diamond \in \{\in, \notin\}$ and $e_1 \in E^{*^\tau}_{\Sigma_\perp}(V)$, $e_2 \in E^{*^{Mset(\tau)}}_{\Sigma_\perp}(V)$, for some $\tau \in Type_{TC}(TV)$.
- ▷ $\varphi \equiv \varphi_1 \wedge \varphi_2$ and φ_i are well-typed w.r.t. V, $1 \leq i \leq 2$.
- ▷ $\varphi \equiv \exists x \varphi'$ and there exists $\tau \in Type_{TC}(TV)$ such that $\varphi'[x/y]$ is well-typed w.r.t. $V[y : \tau]$, where y is a fresh variable and $V[y : \tau]$ denotes the environment resulting of adding to V the type-annotation $y : \tau$.

Assuming a type declaration $f : (\tau_1, \ldots, \tau_n) \to \tau \in FS$, a *defining rule* for f has the form $f(t_1, \ldots, t_n) \to r \Leftarrow \varphi$, where the left-hand side is linear, $t_i \in T_\Sigma(DV)$ does not contain any primitive symbol in PO, $1 \leq i \leq n$, $r \in E_\Sigma(DV)$, $\varphi \in R_\Sigma(DV)$ and $dvar(r) \subseteq \bigcup_{i=1}^n dvar(t_i)$. A program rule is *well-typed* iff there exists an environment V such that $t_i \in T_\Sigma^{\tau_i}(V)$, $1 \leq i \leq n$, $r \in E_\Sigma^{\tau}(V)$ and φ is well-typed w.r.t. V.

We define *programs* as pairs $\mathcal{P} = \langle \Sigma, \mathrm{R} \rangle$, where Σ is a polymorphic signature and R is a finite set of defining rules for defined functions symbols in Σ. We say that a program $\mathcal{P}$ is *well-typed* iff all program rules in R are well-typed. Note that primitive operations are not allowed in the left-hand sides of program rules. This implies no loss of expressiveness, due the availability of equality constraints.

As argued in [4,5,3], the expressive power of the multiset constructor can be used to tackle any kind of problem which is related to the widely applicable idea of *multiset rewriting*; see e.g. [6,18,17]. We present here a small example which shows the advantages of combining multisets, real numbers and constraints to generate and recognize graphic figures, which is very related to the issue of parsing visual languages [12,17].

Example 1. Consider the problem of building quadrilaterals from given points in the plane, in such a way that the resulting figures have no common vertices. Points and quadrilaterals can be respectively represented by means of the data constructors:

$$P : (\mathit{Real}, \mathit{Real}) \rightarrow \mathit{Point}, \quad Q : (\mathit{Point}, \mathit{Point}, \mathit{Point}, \mathit{Point}, \mathit{Point}) \rightarrow \mathit{Quadrilateral}.$$

The intended meaning of two consecutive points P, P' in a term of the form $Q(P1, P2, P3, P4, P1)$ is that there exists a line from P to P'. Figures will be multisets of quadrilaterals. In order to solve the problem, we define the functions:

$$\begin{array}{l}
\mathsf{figure} : \mathit{Mset}(\mathit{Point}) \rightarrow \mathit{Mset}(\mathit{Quadrilateral}) \\
\quad \mathit{figure}(\{\!\!\{\ \}\!\!\}) \rightarrow \{\!\!\{\ \}\!\!\} \\
\quad \mathit{figure}(\{\!\!\{ p1, p2, p3, p4 | ps \}\!\!\}) \rightarrow \{\!\!\{ Q(p1, p2, p3, p4, p1) | \mathit{figure}(ps) \}\!\!\} \\
\quad\quad \Leftarrow p1 \notin ps \wedge p2 \notin ps \wedge p3 \notin ps \wedge p4 \notin ps \wedge \mathit{quadrilateral}(p1, p2, p3, p4) == \mathit{True}
\end{array}$$

where the function quadrilateral checks if four points generate a quadrilateral by using the following result: "The four midpoints of the lines composing a quadrilateral form a parallelogram". The code for this function is the following:

$$\begin{array}{l}
\mathsf{quadrilateral} : (\mathit{Point}, \mathit{Point}, \mathit{Point}, \mathit{Point}) \rightarrow \mathit{Bool} \\
\quad \mathit{quadrilateral}(p1, p2, p3, p4) \rightarrow \mathit{True} \Leftarrow \\
\quad\quad \mathit{midpoint}(p1, p2, m1) == \mathit{True} \ \wedge \ \mathit{midpoint}(p2, p3, m2) == \mathit{True} \wedge \\
\quad\quad \mathit{midpoint}(p3, p4, m3) == \mathit{True} \ \wedge \ \mathit{midpoint}(p4, p1, m4) == \mathit{True} \wedge \\
\quad\quad \mathit{parallelogram}(m1, m2, m3, m4) == \mathit{True}
\end{array}$$

Of course, *True* is a boolean constant. Functions midpoint and parallelogram are defined as:

$$\begin{array}{l}
\mathsf{midpoint} : (\mathit{Point}, \mathit{Point}, \mathit{Point}) \rightarrow \mathit{Bool} \\
\quad \mathit{midpoint}(P(x1, y1), P(x2, y2), P(x3, y3)) \rightarrow \mathit{True} \\
\quad\quad \Leftarrow 2 * x3 == x1 + x2 \wedge 2 * y3 == y1 + y2
\end{array}$$

$$\begin{array}{l}
\mathsf{parallelogram} : (\mathit{Point}, \mathit{Point}, \mathit{Point}, \mathit{Point}) \rightarrow \mathit{Bool} \\
\quad \mathit{parallelogram}(P(x1, y1), P(x2, y2), P(x3, y3), P(x4, y4)) \rightarrow \mathit{True} \\
\quad\quad \Leftarrow x1 - x4 == x2 - x3 \wedge y1 - y4 == y2 - y3
\end{array}$$

Considering the goal:

$$\begin{array}{l}
G \equiv \mathit{figure}(\{\!\!\{ P(-3,0), P(3,0), P(4,3), P(5,-4), \\
\quad\quad P(8,0), P(12,3), P(14,-2), P(11,-6) \}\!\!\}) == l
\end{array}$$

and using the lazy narrowing calculus presented in Sect. 4, we can obtain various computed answers, as e.g.

$l = \{\!\!\{ Q(P(-3,0), P(4,3), P(3,0), P(5,-4), P(-3,0)),$
$\quad Q(P(8,0), P(12,3), P(14,-2), P(11,-6), P(8,0)) \}\!\!\}$

2.3 A Constrained Goal-Oriented Rewriting Calculus

In the rest of this section we present a *Constrained Goal-Oriented constructor-based Rewriting Calculus* (named *CGORC*) which is intended as a proof theoretical specification of program's semantics.

A constraint $\varphi \in R^*_{\Sigma_\perp}(DV)$ is in *solved form* iff $\varphi \in R^*_p(DV)$ or $\varphi \equiv x /\!= t$ or $\varphi \equiv s \notin xs$, where $x, xs \in DV$, $t, s \in T^*_{\Sigma_\perp}(DV)$, $x \not\equiv t$. Given a finite set Γ of constraints in *solved form*, the rewriting calculus *CGORC* allows to derive statements of the form $e \rightarrow t$ (named *approximation statements*) and constraints φ, where $e \in E^*_{\Sigma_\perp}(DV)$, $t \in T^*_{\Sigma_\perp}(DV)$, $\varphi \in R^*_{\Sigma_\perp}(DV)$ and $\Gamma \subseteq R^*_{\Sigma_\perp}(DV)$.

The intended meaning of an approximation statement $e \rightarrow t$ is that the possibly partial data term t approximates e's value. As notation, $\Gamma \vdash_{\mathcal{P}} \chi$, where χ is either an approximation statement or a constraint, and $\Gamma \subseteq R^*_{\Sigma_\perp}(DV)$ is in solved form, will denote the derivability of χ from Γ in *CGORC* .

The constraint symbols $==$ and $/\!=$ are overloaded and they must be treated differently depending on the level they belong to. For this reason, we need the notion of *the primitive part* of a finite set $\Gamma \subseteq R^*_{\Sigma_\perp}(DV)$ in solved form. Intuitively, this is the part $PP(\Gamma)$ of Γ depending on those variables forced (by Γ) to take primitive (i.e., numeric) values. Formally, we define the set $primvar(\Gamma)$ of *primitive variables* in Γ as the least set of variables verifying:

▷ If $\varphi^p \in R^*_p(DV) \cap \Gamma$ and $\varphi^p \not\equiv x /\!= y$, then $lib(\varphi^p) \subseteq primvar(\Gamma)$, where $lib(\varphi^p)$ denotes the set of free variables of φ^p.

▷ If $x /\!= y \in \Gamma$ or $y /\!= x \in \Gamma$ and $x \in primvar(\Gamma)$ then $y \in primvar(\Gamma)$.

and we define the *primitive part* of Γ as the set

$$PP(\Gamma) = \{\varphi^p \mid \varphi^p \in R^*_p(DV) \cap \Gamma, \varphi^p \not\equiv x /\!= y, x, y \in DV\} \cup \{x /\!= y \mid x /\!= y \in \Gamma, x, y \in primvar(\Gamma)\}.$$

For instance, if $\Gamma = \{x \leq 2, x /\!= y, y /\!= z, y \notin xs\}$ then $primvar(\Gamma) = \{x, y, z\}$, and $PP(\Gamma) = \{x \leq 2, x /\!= y, y /\!= z\}$.

Rules of the *CGORC* Calculus: Now we are ready to define the rewriting calculus *CGORC*. In the following, the notation $h(\bar{e}_n)$ is a shorthand for $h(e_1, \ldots, e_n)$, where $h \in DC^n \cup FS^n$. The calculus *CGORC* is composed of the following inference rules:

- *CGORC*-rules for $\rightarrow$

$$(\mathsf{PR})^1_{\rightarrow}\ \frac{PP(\Gamma) \models_{\mathcal{R}} t^p == s^p}{\Gamma \vdash_{\mathcal{P}} t^p \rightarrow s^p} \qquad (\mathsf{PR})^2_{\rightarrow}\ \frac{\Gamma \vdash_{\mathcal{P}} e_1 \rightarrow t^p_1, \Gamma \vdash_{\mathcal{P}} e_2 \rightarrow t^p_2, \Gamma \vdash_{\mathcal{P}} t^p_1 \Diamond t^p_2 \rightarrow t^p_3}{\Gamma \vdash_{\mathcal{P}} e_1 \Diamond e_2 \rightarrow t^p_3}$$

$dvar(t^p \rightarrow s^p) \subseteq primvar(\Gamma)$, $\Diamond \in \{+, *\}$, $e_1 \Diamond e_2 \in E^*_{\Sigma_\perp}(DV) - T^*_{\Sigma_\perp}(DV)$.

$$(\mathsf{B})\ \frac{}{\Gamma \vdash_{\mathcal{P}} e \rightarrow \perp} \qquad (\mathsf{RR})\ \frac{}{\Gamma \vdash_{\mathcal{P}} x \rightarrow x} \qquad (\mathsf{DC})\ \frac{\Gamma \vdash_{\mathcal{P}} e_1 \rightarrow t_1, \ldots, \Gamma \vdash_{\mathcal{P}} e_n \rightarrow t_n}{\Gamma \vdash_{\mathcal{P}} c(\bar{e}_n) \rightarrow c(\bar{t}_n)}$$

$x \in DV, x \notin primvar(\Gamma)$ and $c \in DC^n$, $n \geq 0$.

$$\text{(OMUT)}\ \frac{\Gamma \vdash_{\mathcal{P}} e \to t_1, \Gamma \vdash_{\mathcal{P}} es \to \{\!\{ t_2|ts \}\!\}, \Gamma \vdash_{\mathcal{P}} \{\!\{ t_2, t_1|ts \}\!\} \to ts'}{\Gamma \vdash_{\mathcal{P}} \{\!\{ e|es \}\!\} \to ts'} \quad ts' \not\equiv \perp$$

$$\text{(OR)}\ \frac{\Gamma \vdash_{\mathcal{P}} e_1 \to s_1\delta, \ldots, \Gamma \vdash_{\mathcal{P}} e_n \to s_n\delta, \Gamma \vdash_{\mathcal{P}} r\delta \to t, \Gamma \vdash_{\mathcal{P}} \varphi\delta}{\Gamma \vdash_{\mathcal{P}} f(\bar{e}_n) \to t}$$

$t \not\equiv \perp$, $f(\bar{s}_n) \to r \Leftarrow \varphi \in \text{R}$ and $\delta \in DSub(T^*_{\Sigma_\perp}(DV))$.

- *CGORC*-**rules for** $R^*_{\Sigma_\perp}(DV)$

$$\text{(PR)}_\varphi\ \frac{PP(\Gamma) \models_{\mathcal{R}} \varphi^p}{\Gamma \vdash_{\mathcal{P}} \varphi^p} \quad \varphi^p \in R^*_p(DV),\ lib(\varphi^p) \subseteq primvar(\Gamma)$$

If rule (PR)_φ is not applicable, then we can use the following rules, in which the superscript S means that a symmetric rule is implicitly assumed.

$$\text{(HIP)}\ \frac{}{\Gamma \vdash_{\mathcal{P}} \varphi} \quad \varphi \in \Gamma \qquad \text{(CONJ)}\ \frac{\Gamma \vdash_{\mathcal{P}} \varphi_1, \Gamma \vdash_{\mathcal{P}} \varphi_2}{\Gamma \vdash_{\mathcal{P}} \varphi_1 \wedge \varphi_2} \qquad \text{(EX)}\ \frac{\Gamma \vdash_{\mathcal{P}} \varphi'[x/t]}{\Gamma \vdash_{\mathcal{P}} \exists x \varphi'}$$

$$\text{(C)}\ \frac{\Gamma \vdash_{\mathcal{P}} e \to t, \Gamma \vdash_{\mathcal{P}} r \to t}{\Gamma \vdash_{\mathcal{P}} e == r} \quad t \in T^*_\Sigma(DV)$$

$$\text{(LEQ)}\ \frac{\Gamma \vdash_{\mathcal{P}} e \to t^p, \Gamma \vdash_{\mathcal{P}} r \to s^p, \Gamma \vdash_{\mathcal{P}} t^p \leq s^p}{\Gamma \vdash_{\mathcal{P}} e \leq r}$$

$$\text{(MEMB)}_\to\ \frac{\Gamma \vdash_{\mathcal{P}} es \to \{\!\{ t|ts \}\!\}, \Gamma \vdash_{\mathcal{P}} e \in \{\!\{ t|ts \}\!\}}{\Gamma \vdash_{\mathcal{P}} e \in es} \quad es \in E^*_{\Sigma_\perp}(DV) - T^*_{\Sigma_\perp}(DV)$$

$$\text{(NMEMB)}_\to\ \frac{\Gamma \vdash_{\mathcal{P}} es \to ts, \Gamma \vdash_{\mathcal{P}} e \notin ts}{\Gamma \vdash_{\mathcal{P}} e \notin es} \quad es \in E^*_{\Sigma_\perp}(DV) - T^*_{\Sigma_\perp}(DV)$$

$$\text{(MEMB)}_1\ \frac{\Gamma \vdash_{\mathcal{P}} e == t}{\Gamma \vdash_{\mathcal{P}} e \in \{\!\{ t|ts \}\!\}} \qquad \text{(NMEMB)}_1\ \frac{}{\Gamma \vdash_{\mathcal{P}} e \notin \{\!\{\ \}\!\}}$$

$$\text{(MEMB)}_2\ \frac{\Gamma \vdash_{\mathcal{P}} e \in ts}{\Gamma \vdash_{\mathcal{P}} e \in \{\!\{ t|ts \}\!\}} \qquad \text{(NMEMB)}_2\ \frac{\Gamma \vdash_{\mathcal{P}} e \not\models t, \Gamma \vdash_{\mathcal{P}} e \notin ts}{\Gamma \vdash_{\mathcal{P}} e \notin \{\!\{ t|ts \}\!\}}$$

$$\text{(NEQ)}_\to\ \frac{\Gamma \vdash_{\mathcal{P}} e \to t, \Gamma \vdash_{\mathcal{P}} r \to s, \Gamma \vdash_{\mathcal{P}} t \not\models s}{\Gamma \vdash_{\mathcal{P}} e \not\models r}$$

If $e \not\equiv \{\!\{\ \}\!\}$, $r \not\equiv \{\!\{\ \}\!\}$ and $e \not\models r$ contains some symbol $f \in FS$, or e (resp. r) has the multiset constructor as outermost symbol.

$$\text{(NEQ)}_1\ \frac{}{\Gamma \vdash_{\mathcal{P}} c(\bar{t}_n) \not\models d(\bar{s}_m)} \quad c \in DC^n,\ d \in DC^m,\ c \not\equiv d,\ c, d \not\equiv \{\!\{ \cdot|\cdot \}\!\}$$

$$\text{(NEQ)}_2\ \frac{\Gamma \vdash_{\mathcal{P}} t_i \not\models s_i}{\Gamma \vdash_{\mathcal{P}} c(\bar{t}_n) \not\models c(\bar{s}_n)} \quad c \in DC^n,\ c \not\equiv \{\!\{ \cdot|\cdot \}\!\},\ \text{one rule for each } 1 \leq i \leq n$$

$$\text{(NEQ)}_3^S\ \frac{\Gamma \vdash_{\mathcal{P}} t \notin ms}{\Gamma \vdash_{\mathcal{P}} \{\!\{ t|ts \}\!\} \not\models ms} \qquad \text{(NEQ)}_4\ \frac{\Gamma \vdash_{\mathcal{P}} t == l, \Gamma \vdash_{\mathcal{P}} ts \not\models ls}{\Gamma \vdash_{\mathcal{P}} \{\!\{ t|ts \}\!\} \not\models \{\!\{ l|ls \}\!\}}$$

Some comments are needed in order to clarify the rules above. Firstly, remark that all *CGORC*-rules associated to $\to$ and $==$ are similar to those presented in

[4], except for rules $(\mathsf{PR})^i_{\rightarrow}$, $1 \le i \le 2$. Rule $(\mathsf{PR})^1_{\rightarrow}$ refers to approximation statements between primitive terms. In this case, we remit ourselves to the primitive level. On the other hand, $(\mathsf{PR})^2_{\rightarrow}$ deals with approximation statements whose left-hand side has $+$ or $*$ as the outermost operation, but contains some symbol in FS. In this case, it is enough to look for approximations t_i^p for e_i, $1 \le i \le 2$, which must be primitive terms, and finally prove the approximation statement $t_1^p \Diamond t_2^p \rightarrow t_3^p$ (this will be done by means of rule $(\mathsf{PR})^1_{\rightarrow}$).

With respect to the $CGORC$-rules associated to $R^*_{\Sigma_\perp}(DV)$, note that the rules (HIP), (CONJ) and (EX) represent general forms of inference, accepted as valid in the intuitionistic fragment of predicate logic; see e.g. [19]. Rule $(\mathsf{PR})_\varphi$ establishes that a primitive constraint φ^p which involves only primitive variables ($lib(\varphi^p) \subseteq primvar(\Gamma)$) must be handled at the primitive level.

The $CGORC$-rules for $\in$ and $\notin$ are really very intuitive. Let us see now how to prove a disequality between two expressions e and r. Rule $(\mathsf{NEQ})_{\rightarrow}$ has two tasks: To get approximations to the values represented by e and r (removing all function symbols) and, in presence of multisets, to reorder the elements by applying the $CGORC$-rule (OMUT). Disequality between terms not containing the multiset constructor at head can be checked by detecting disagreement of constructor symbols at head (rule $(\mathsf{NEQ})_1$) or by proving the disequality between some of the arguments (rule $(\mathsf{NEQ})_2$). In order to prove a disequality between two multisets ms and ms' we proceed as done in [3].

To conclude the discussion, note that a constraint of the form $e \le r$, where $e \le r \notin R^*_p(DV)$, must be proved by using the $CGORC$-rule (LEQ), which "evaluates" e and r in order to get primitive terms, and then proving the corresponding constraint between such primitive terms.

Semi-extended Data Terms and restricted *CGORC* Derivations: The calculus $CGORC$ that we have just defined will be used in Section 4 to prove soundness of a goal solving mechanism. Completeness of goal solving will rely on a *restricted use* of $CGORC$-provability. In order to introduce this idea, we define the set $T^*_{DC_\perp}(DV)$ of *semi-extended partial data terms* as the subset of $T^*_{\Sigma_\perp}(DV)$ composed of all those extended partial data terms not containing the symbols $+$, $*$, 0 and 1. Similarly, the set $T^*_{DC}(DV) \subseteq T^*_{DC_\perp}(DV)$ of *semi-extended total data terms* is composed of those semi-extended partial data terms not containing the constant symbol $\perp$. Note that a semi-extended primitive term is either a variable or an element from $\mathbb{R}$.

We will use the notation $\Vdash_{\mathcal{P}} \chi$ to indicate that χ can be proved (from $\Gamma = \emptyset$) using a *restricted CGORC* derivation. By definition, this means a $CGORC$ derivation built according to the following limitations:

- ▷ Substitutions used in rule (OR) must map DV to $T^*_{DC_\perp}(DV)$.
- ▷ Rules $(\mathsf{PR})^2_{\rightarrow}$, (OMUT), (C), $(\mathsf{NEQ})_{\rightarrow}$, $(\mathsf{MEMB})_{\rightarrow}$, $(\mathsf{NMEMB})_{\rightarrow}$ and (LEQ) must use approximation statements $e \rightarrow t$ with $t \in T^*_{DC_\perp}(DV)$.

Trivially, $\Vdash_{\mathcal{P}} \chi$ implies $\vdash_{\mathcal{P}} \chi$. As a consequence of Theorem 3 below, the converse implication will also hold. Semi-extended data terms will be useful also for the construction of free term models in Section 3.

3 Model-Theoretic Semantics

In this section we present a model-theoretic semantics, showing also its relation to the rewriting calculus *CGORC* and its restricted use. We will make use of several basic notions from the theory of semantic domains A *poset* with bottom $\perp$ is any set S partially ordered by $\sqsubseteq$, with least element $\perp$. $\mathsf{Def}(S)$ denotes the set of all maximal elements $u \in S$, also called *totally defined.* $X \subseteq S$ is a *directed set* iff for all $u, v \in X$ there exists $w \in X$ s.t. $u, v \sqsubseteq w$. X is a *cone* iff $\perp \in X$ and X is downward closed w.r.t. $\sqsubseteq$. X is and *ideal* iff X is a directed cone. We write $\mathcal{C}(S)$ and $\mathcal{I}(S)$ for the sets of cones and ideals of S, respectively. $\mathcal{I}(S)$ ordered by set inclusion $\subseteq$ is a poset with bottom $\{\perp\}$, called the *ideal completion* of S. Mapping each $u \in S$ into the principal ideal $\langle u \rangle = \{v \in S | v \sqsubseteq u\}$ gives an order preserving embedding. It is known that $\mathcal{I}(S)$ is the least cpo D s.t. S can be embedded into D. Due to these results, our semantic constructions below could be reformulated in terms of Scott domains. In particular, totally defined elements $u \in \mathsf{Def}(S)$ correspond to finite and maximal elements $\langle u \rangle$ in the ideal completion.

As in [9,4], to represent non-deterministic lazy functions we use models with posets as carriers, interpreting function symbols as monotonic mappings from elements to cones. The elements of the poset are viewed as finite approximations of possibly infinite values. For given posets D and E, we define the set of all *non-deterministic* and *deterministic* functions from D to E, respectively as follows:

$$[D \rightarrow_{nd} E] = \{f : D \rightarrow \mathcal{C}(E) \mid \forall u, u' \in D : (u \sqsubseteq_D u' \Rightarrow f(u) \subseteq f(u'))\}$$
$$[D \rightarrow_{d} E] = \{f \in [D \rightarrow_{nd} E] \mid \forall u \in D : f(u) \in \mathcal{I}(E)\}$$

Note that any non-deterministic function f can be extended to a monotonic mapping $f^* : \mathcal{C}(D) \rightarrow \mathcal{C}(E)$ defined as $f^*(C) = \bigcup_{c \in C} f(c)$. Abusing of notation, we will identify f with its extension f^*.

3.1 Specification of $\not\models$, $\in$ and $\notin$ by Horn Clauses

Let us now define the behaviour of predicate symbols in *PS* (except for $==$) by means of Horn clauses. Note that all Horn clauses below have a direct correspondence with the rewriting calculus *CGORC*, and they will determine the class of models of a program $\mathcal{P}$. The Horn clauses are the following:

$H^1_{\in} : x \in \{\!\!\{ y|ys \}\!\!\} \Leftarrow x == y$ $\qquad$ $H^1_{\notin} : x \notin \{\!\!\{\ \}\!\!\} \Leftarrow$

$H^2_{\in} : x \in \{\!\!\{ y|ys \}\!\!\} \Leftarrow x \in ys$ $\qquad$ $H^2_{\notin} : x \notin \{\!\!\{ y|ys \}\!\!\} \Leftarrow x \not\models y, x \notin ys$

$H^1_{\neq} : c(\bar{x}_n) \not\models d(\bar{y}_m) \Leftarrow$ $\qquad$ % $c \not\equiv d$, $c, d \not\equiv \{\!\!\{ \cdot|\cdot \}\!\!\}$

$H^2_{\neq} : c(\bar{x}_n) \not\models c(\bar{y}_n) \Leftarrow x_i \neq y_i$ $\qquad$ % $c \not\equiv \{\!\!\{ \cdot|\cdot \}\!\!\}$, one clause for each $1 \leq i \leq n$

$H^3_{\neq} : \{\!\!\{ x|xs \}\!\!\} \not\models ys \Leftarrow x \notin ys$ $\qquad$ $H^4_{\neq} : xs \not\models \{\!\!\{ y|ys \}\!\!\} \Leftarrow y \notin xs$

$H^5_{\neq} : \{\!\!\{ x|xs \}\!\!\} \not\models \{\!\!\{ y|ys \}\!\!\} \Leftarrow x == y, xs \not\models ys$

$H^6_{\neq} : \{\!\!\{ x|xs \}\!\!\} \not\models \{\!\!\{ y|ys \}\!\!\} \Leftarrow \{\!\!\{ x|xs \}\!\!\} \rightarrow \{\!\!\{ x'|xs' \}\!\!\}, \{\!\!\{ y|ys \}\!\!\} \rightarrow \{\!\!\{ y'|ys' \}\!\!\},$
$\qquad \{\!\!\{ x'|xs' \}\!\!\} \not\models \{\!\!\{ y'|ys' \}\!\!\}$

3.2 Algebras and Models

We are now prepared to introduce our algebras, extending those from [4]. Formally, a *polymorphic Σ-algebra* has the following structure:
$\langle D^{\mathcal{A}}, T^{\mathcal{A}}, :^{\mathcal{A}}, \{K^{\mathcal{A}}\}_{K\in\{Real\}\cup TC}, \{\Diamond^{\mathcal{A}}\}_{\Diamond\in PO\cup DC}, \{\Diamond^{\mathcal{A}}\}_{\Diamond\in PP\cup PS}, \{f^{\mathcal{A}}\}_{f\in FS}\rangle$
where:

(1) $D^{\mathcal{A}}$ (data universe) is a poset with partial order $\sqsubseteq^{\mathcal{A}}$ and bottom element $\perp^{\mathcal{A}}$. Furthermore, $D^{\mathcal{A}}$ contains a copy $D^{\mathcal{A}_p}$ of $\mathbb{R}$ given by a bijective mapping h_p from $D^{\mathcal{A}_p}$ to $\mathbb{R}$, and verifies that: If $d \sqsubseteq^{\mathcal{A}} d'$ and $d' \in D^{\mathcal{A}_p}$ (resp. $d \in D^{\mathcal{A}_p}$), then $d \equiv \perp^{\mathcal{A}}$ or $d \equiv d'$ (resp. $d' \equiv d$)
(2) $T^{\mathcal{A}}$ (type universe) is any non-empty set.
(3) $:^{\mathcal{A}} \subseteq D^{\mathcal{A}} \times T^{\mathcal{A}}$ is a binary relation such that for all $\ell \in T^{\mathcal{A}}$, it holds that $\mathcal{E}^{\mathcal{A}}(\ell) = \{d \in D^{\mathcal{A}} \mid d :^{\mathcal{A}} \ell\} \in \mathcal{C}(D^{\mathcal{A}})$ and $\mathcal{E}^{\mathcal{A}}(Real^{\mathcal{A}}) = D^{\mathcal{A}_p} \cup \{\perp^{\mathcal{A}}\}$.
(4) For each $K \in TC^n$, $K^{\mathcal{A}} : (T^{\mathcal{A}})^n \to T^{\mathcal{A}}$ is a function.
(5) $0^{\mathcal{A}} = \{h_p^{-1}(0^{\mathcal{R}}), \perp^{\mathcal{A}}\} = \langle h_p^{-1}(0^{\mathcal{R}})\rangle$ and $1^{\mathcal{A}} = \{h_p^{-1}(1^{\mathcal{R}}), \perp^{\mathcal{A}}\} = \langle h_p^{-1}(1^{\mathcal{R}})\rangle$.
(6) For any $d_1, d_2 \in D^{\mathcal{A}}$, $\Diamond \in \{+, *\}$: $d_1 \Diamond^{\mathcal{A}} d_2 = \{h_p^{-1}(h_p(d_1) + h_p(d_2)), \perp^{\mathcal{A}}\} = \langle h_p^{-1}(h_p(d_1) + h_p(d_2))\rangle$, if $d_1, d_2 \in D^{\mathcal{A}_p}$ and $d_1 \Diamond^{\mathcal{A}} d_2 = \langle \perp^{\mathcal{A}}\rangle$, otherwise.
(7) For each $c \in DC^n$, $c^{\mathcal{A}} \in [(D^{\mathcal{A}})^n \to_d (D^{\mathcal{A}} - D^{\mathcal{A}_p})]$ and satisfies: For all $d_i \in D^{\mathcal{A}}$, $1 \le i \le n$, there exists $d \in (D^{\mathcal{A}} - D^{\mathcal{A}_p})$ such that $c^{\mathcal{A}}(d_1, \ldots, d_n) = \langle d\rangle$. Furthermore, if d_i are totally defined, $1 \le i \le n$, then d is totally defined.
(8) For all $d_1, d_2 \in D^{\mathcal{A}}$: $(d_1, d_2) \in \le^{\mathcal{A}}$ iff $d_1, d_2 \in D^{\mathcal{A}_p}$ and $h_p(d_1) \le h_p(d_2)$.
(9) For all $d_1, d_2 \in D^{\mathcal{A}}$: $(d_1, d_2) \in ==^{\mathcal{A}}$ iff d_1, d_2 are totally defined and $d_1 \equiv d_2$.
(10) For all $\Diamond \in \{\not=, \in, \notin\}$, $\Diamond^{\mathcal{A}} \subseteq (D^{\mathcal{A}})^2$ and it is monotonic. Moreover:
- If $d_1, d_2 \in D^{\mathcal{A}_p}$ and $h_p(d_1) \not\equiv h_p(d_2)$ then $(d_1, d_2) \in \not=^{\mathcal{A}}$.
- If $(d_1, d_2) \in \not=^{\mathcal{A}}$ and $d_2 \in D^{\mathcal{A}_p}$ (resp. $d_1 \in D^{\mathcal{A}_p}$), then $d_1 \in D^{\mathcal{A}_p}$ (resp. $d_2 \in D^{\mathcal{A}_p}$) and $h_p(d_1) \not\equiv h_p(d_2)$.

(11) For all $f \in FS^n$, $f^{\mathcal{A}} \in [(D^{\mathcal{A}})^n \to_{nd} D^{\mathcal{A}}]$.

In the following, $Alg(\Sigma)$ will denote the class of polymorphic Σ-algebras. Note that item (7) ensures that constructors are interpreted as deterministic mappings that preserve finite and maximal elements. Furthermore, note also that all primitive symbols in Σ_p are interpreted in any algebra $\mathcal{A}$ according to their standard meaning in $\mathcal{R}$.

A *valuation* in $\mathcal{A}$ has the form $\xi = (\mu, \eta)$, where $\mu : TV \to T^{\mathcal{A}}$ is a *type valuation* and $\eta : DV \to D^{\mathcal{A}}$ is a *data valuation*. η is called *totally defined* iff $\eta(x)$ is totally defined, for all $x \in DV$. $Val(\mathcal{A})$ denotes the set of all valuations over $\mathcal{A}$.

For a given $\xi = (\mu, \eta) \in Val(\mathcal{A})$, *type denotations* $[\![\tau]\!]^{\mathcal{A}}\xi = [\![\tau]\!]^{\mathcal{A}}\mu \in T^{\mathcal{A}}$ and *extended partial expression denotations* $[\![e]\!]^{\mathcal{A}}\xi = [\![e]\!]^{\mathcal{A}}\eta \in \mathcal{C}(D^{\mathcal{A}})$ are defined as usual, by considering that all $d \in \mathbb{R}$ is interpreted in $\mathcal{A}$ as $\langle h_p^{-1}(d)\rangle = \{h_p^{-1}(d), \perp^{\mathcal{A}}\}$.

We are particularly interested in those algebras that are well-behaved w.r.t. types. We say that $\mathcal{A} \in Alg(\Sigma)$ is *well-typed* iff for all $h : (\tau_1, \ldots, \tau_n) \to \tau_0 \in DC_\perp \cup FS \cup PO$, we have that $h^{\mathcal{A}}(\mathcal{E}^{\mathcal{A}}([\![\tau_1]\!]^{\mathcal{A}}\mu), \ldots, \mathcal{E}^{\mathcal{A}}([\![\tau_1]\!]^{\mathcal{A}}\mu)) \subseteq \mathcal{E}^{\mathcal{A}}([\![\tau_0]\!]^{\mathcal{A}}\mu)$, for every type valuation μ. Also, for given $\xi = (\mu, \eta) \in Val(\mathcal{A})$, we say that ξ

is *well-typed* w.r.t an environment V iff $\eta(x) \in \mathcal{E}^{\mathcal{A}}([\![\tau]\!]^{\mathcal{A}}\mu)$ for every $x : \tau \in V$. Reasoning by structural induction, we can prove that expression denotations behave as expected w.r.t. well-typed algebras and valuations:

Theorem 1. *Let V be an environment. Let $\mathcal{A} \in Alg(\Sigma)$ be well-typed and $\xi = (\mu, \eta) \in Val(\mathcal{A})$ well-typed w.r.t. V. For all $e \in E^{*\tau}_{\Sigma_\perp}(V)$, $[\![e]\!]^{\mathcal{A}}\eta \subseteq \mathcal{E}^{\mathcal{A}}([\![\tau]\!]^{\mathcal{A}}\mu)$.*

Next we define the notion of *model*. Consider $\mathcal{A} \in Alg(\Sigma)$. Let η be a data valuation over $\mathcal{A}$. Then:

- ▹ $(\mathcal{A}, \eta) \models e_1 \Diamond e_2$, $\Diamond \in PP \cup PS$, iff there exist $d_i \in [\![e_i]\!]^{\mathcal{A}}\eta$, $1 \leq i \leq 2$, such that $(d_1, d_2) \in \Diamond^{\mathcal{A}}$.
- ▹ $(\mathcal{A}, \eta) \models \varphi_1 \wedge \varphi_2$ iff $(\mathcal{A}, \eta) \models \varphi_i$, $1 \leq i \leq 2$.
- ▹ $(\mathcal{A}, \eta) \models \exists x \varphi$ iff there exists $d \in D^{\mathcal{A}}$ such that $(\mathcal{A}, \eta[x \leftarrow d]) \models \varphi$.
- ▹ $(\mathcal{A}, \eta) \models e \rightarrow e'$ iff $[\![e']\!]^{\mathcal{A}}\eta \subseteq [\![e]\!]^{\mathcal{A}}\eta$.
- ▹ $\mathcal{A} \models \{\!\!\{x, y|xs\}\!\!\} \approx \{\!\!\{y, x|xs\}\!\!\}$ iff for any η, it holds that $[\![\{\!\!\{x, y|xs\}\!\!\}]\!]^{\mathcal{A}}\eta = [\![\{\!\!\{y, x|xs\}\!\!\}]\!]^{\mathcal{A}}\eta$.
- ▹ $\mathcal{A}$ satisfies a Horn clause of the form $A \Leftarrow B_1, \ldots, B_m$ iff for any data valuation η such that $(\mathcal{A}, \eta) \models B_i$, $1 \leq i \leq m$, it holds that $(\mathcal{A}, \eta) \models A$.
- ▹ $\mathcal{A}$ satisfies a defining rule $e \rightarrow r \Leftarrow \varphi$ iff every data valuation η such that $(\mathcal{A}, \eta) \models \varphi$ verifies that $(\mathcal{A}, \eta) \models e \rightarrow r$.
- ▹ Let $\mathcal{P} = \langle \Sigma, \mathrm{R} \rangle$ be a program. $\mathcal{A} \models \mathcal{P}$ iff $\mathcal{A}$ satisfies every defining rule in R and (MSET).

The class $\mathcal{M} \subseteq Alg(\Sigma)$ of polymorphic algebras is composed of those $\mathcal{A} \in Alg(\Sigma)$ such that $\mathcal{A}$ satisfies (MSET) and all Horn clauses in Subsection 3.1, whereas $\mathcal{M}(\mathcal{P}) =_{Def} \{\mathcal{A} \in \mathcal{M} \mid \mathcal{A} \models \mathcal{P}\}$.

Definition 1. ***(Logical consequence)*** *Consider $\Gamma \subseteq R^*_{\Sigma_\perp}(DV)$ in solved form and $\chi \equiv e \rightarrow t$ or $\chi \in R^*_{\Sigma_\perp}(DV)$, where $e \in E^*_{\Sigma_\perp}(DV)$, $t \in T^*_{\Sigma_\perp}(DV)$. It holds that $\Gamma \models \chi$ iff for all $\mathcal{A} \in \mathcal{M}(\mathcal{P})$, and for all $\eta \in Val(\mathcal{A})$ totally defined, if $(\mathcal{A}, \eta) \models \Gamma$ then $(\mathcal{A}, \eta) \models \chi$.*

The following theorem establishes the soundness of the rewriting calculus *CGORC*. It can be proved by induction on *CGORC* derivations.

Theorem 2. ***(Soundness of** CGORC**)*** *Consider $\Gamma \subseteq R^*_{\Sigma_\perp}(DV)$ in solved form, and $\chi \in R^*_{\Sigma_\perp}(DV)$ or $\chi \equiv e \rightarrow t$, where $e \in E^*_{\Sigma_\perp}(DV)$, $t \in T^*_{\Sigma_\perp}(DV)$. If $\Gamma \vdash_{\mathcal{P}} \chi$ then $\Gamma \models \chi$.*

3.3 Free Term Models

Given a program $\mathcal{P} = \langle \Sigma, \mathrm{R} \rangle$ and an environment V, we define the term algebra $MT(V, \mathcal{P})$ as follows:

• Let X be the set of data variables occurring in V. The set $T^*_{DC_\perp}(X)/{\approx_{Mset}}$ is the data universe, where $T^*_{DC_\perp}(X)/{\approx_{Mset}} =_{Def} \{[t] \mid t \in T^*_{DC_\perp}(X)\}$. $[t]$ is defined as the set $\{t' \in T^*_{DC_\perp}(X) \mid t \approx_{Mset} t'\}$, where $t \approx_{Mset} t'$ iff $\Vdash_{\mathcal{P}} t \rightarrow t'$ and $\Vdash_{\mathcal{P}} t' \rightarrow t$.

The bottom element is $[\perp] = \{\perp\}$, and the partial order $\sqsubseteq^{MT(V,\mathcal{P})}$ is defined as: For any $[t], [t'] \in T^*_{DC_\perp}(X)/{\approx_{Mset}}$, $[t] \sqsupseteq^{MT(V,\mathcal{P})} [t']$ iff $\Vdash_{\mathcal{P}} t \rightarrow t'$.

Note that $T^*_{DC_\perp}(X)/\!\approx_{Mset}$ contains $\{[d] \mid d \in \mathbb{R}\}$ as copy of $\mathbb{R}$ given by the bijective mapping $h_p([d]) = d$, for all $d \in \mathbb{R}$.

- Let A be the set of type variables occurring in V. The type universe is $Type(A) = \{\tau \in Type_{TC}(TV) \mid tvar(\tau) \subseteq A\}$.
- For all $[t] \in T^*_{DC_\perp}(X)/\!\approx_{Mset}$, $\tau \in Type(A)$, $[t] :^{MT(V,\mathcal{P})} \tau$ iff $t \in T^{*\tau}_{DC_\perp}(V)$.
- For all $K \in TC^n \cup \{Real\}$, $\tau_i \in Type(A)$: $K^{MT(V,\mathcal{P})}(\tau_1, \ldots, \tau_n) = K(\tau_1, \ldots, \tau_n)$.
- $0^{MT(V,\mathcal{P})} = \langle [0^{\mathcal{R}}] \rangle$ and $1^{MT(V,\mathcal{P})} = \langle [1^{\mathcal{R}}] \rangle$.
- For all $[t], [t'] \in T^*_{DC_\perp}(X)/\!\approx_{Mset}$, $\diamondsuit \in \{+, *\}$: $[t]\diamondsuit^{MT(V,\mathcal{P})}[t'] = \langle [t\diamondsuit t'] \rangle$, if $t, t' \in \mathbb{R}$ and $[t]\diamondsuit^{MT(V,\mathcal{P})}[t'] = \langle [\perp] \rangle$ otherwise.
- For all $c \in DC^n$, $[t_i] \in T^*_{DC_\perp}(X)/\!\approx_{Mset}$: $c^{MT(V,\mathcal{P})}([t_1], \ldots, [t_n]) = \langle [c(t_1, \ldots, t_n)] \rangle$.
- For all $[t_i] \in T^*_{DC_\perp}(X)/\!\approx_{Mset}$: $([t_1], [t_2]) \in \leq^{MT(V,\mathcal{P})}$ iff $t_1, t_2 \in \mathbb{R}$ and $t_1 \leq t_2$.
- For all $[t_i] \in T^*_{DC_\perp}(X)/\!\approx_{Mset}$: $([t_1], [t_2]) \in ==^{MT(V,\mathcal{P})}$ iff $[t_1] = [t_2]$ and $t_1 \in T^*_{DC}(X)$.
- For all $[t_i] \in T^*_{DC_\perp}(X)/\!\approx_{Mset}$, $\diamondsuit \in \{\not=, \in, \not\in\}$: $([t_1], [t_2]) \in \diamondsuit^{MT(V,\mathcal{P})}$ iff $\Vdash_{\mathcal{P}} t_1 \diamondsuit t_2$.
- For all $[t_i] \in T^*_{DC_\perp}(X)/\!\approx_{Mset}$, $1 \leq i \leq n$, $f \in FS^n$: $f^{MT(V,\mathcal{P})}([t_1], \ldots, [t_n]) = \{[t] \in T^*_{DC_\perp}(X)/\!\approx_{Mset} \mid \Vdash_{\mathcal{P}} f(t_1, \ldots, t_n) \to t\}$.

Next result ensures that $MT(V, \mathcal{P})$ belongs to the class of algebras $\mathcal{M}(\mathcal{P})$, and that restricted $CGORC$-derivability is sound and complete with respect to our notion of model.

Theorem 3. *(Adequateness of $MT(V, \mathcal{P})$) Let $\mathcal{P} = \langle \Sigma, \mathrm{R} \rangle$ be a program and V an environment. It holds:*

(1) $MT(V, \mathcal{P}) \in \mathcal{M}(\mathcal{P})$ and if $\mathcal{P}$ is well-typed then $MT(V, \mathcal{P})$ is well-typed.

(2) Consider $\chi \equiv e \to t$ or $\chi \in R^*_{\Sigma_\perp}(X)$, where $e \in E^*_{\Sigma_\perp}(X)$, $t \in T^*_{DC_\perp}(X)$. Then the following statements are equivalent:

(2.1) $\Vdash_{\mathcal{P}} \chi$.

(2.2) $(\mathcal{A}, \eta) \models \chi$, for all $\mathcal{A} \in \mathcal{M}(\mathcal{P})$ and for all η totally defined.

(2.3) $(MT(V, \mathcal{P}), [id]) \models \chi$, where id is the identity substitution over X.

Due to Theorem 2, *unrestricted* $CGORC$-derivability is sound w.r.t. models in the class $\mathcal{M}(\mathcal{P})$. Nevertheless, completeness in the sense of Theorem 3 holds only for *restricted* $CGORC$-derivability. For instance, it is true that $(MT(V, \mathcal{P}), [id]) \models x + 1 \to x + 1$, but there is no $CGORC$ proof for $\vdash_{\mathcal{P}} x + 1 \to x + 1$. The point is that $x + 1$ *is not a semi-extended data term.*

We can also give a characterization of $MT(V, \mathcal{P})$ as a *free object* in the category of all models of $\mathcal{P}$. This relies on a notion of morphism similar to that from [4], extended to deal with constraints in a natural way. See [2] for details.

4 Operational Semantics

This section presents a *Lazy Narrowing Calculus* (*LNC* for short), which is a goal solving procedure that combines lazy narrowing with unification modulo (MSET) and constraint solving. In order to ensure the completeness of *LNC* (Theorem 4), the process of solving a goal is divided in two main phases, as done in [10,5]. A *derivation* for a goal G (composed of constraints) is a finite sequence of $\hookrightarrow_{\mathcal{P}}$-steps (named $\hookrightarrow_{\mathcal{P}}$-derivation) followed by a finite sequence of $\hookrightarrow_{DV}$-steps (named a $\hookrightarrow_{DV}$-derivation). The $\hookrightarrow_{\mathcal{P}}$-derivation transforms G into a quasi-solved goal G' containing only approximation statements of the form $t \to x$ and constraints in solved form, while the $\hookrightarrow_{DV}$-derivation processes variables, thereby transforming G' into a solved goal which represents a solution for G. The whole process preserves well-typing.

Formally, an *admissible goal* G for a program $\mathcal{P}$ has the structure $G \equiv \exists \bar{u} \cdot S \Box P \Box R$, where:

- ▷ $S \equiv x_1 = t_1, \ldots, x_n = t_n$ is a system of equations in *solved form*, i.e., x_i occurs exactly once in G. Note that S represents the substitution $\delta_S \in DSub(T_\Sigma(DV))$ defined as $\delta_S(x_i) = t_i$, $1 \leq i \leq n$ and $\delta_S(z) = z$ otherwise.
- ▷ $P \equiv e_1 \to s_1, \ldots, e_k \to s_k$ is a multiset of approximation statements.
- ▷ $R \subseteq R_\Sigma(DV)$ is a multiset of constraints, and must fulfill several technical requirements similar to those presented in [9,5] in order to achieve soundness and completeness, along with the new condition:

  (PR) For all $e \Diamond t \in S \cup P$, $\Diamond \in \{=, \to\}$, t does not contain to 0, 1, + and $*$.

$G \equiv \exists \bar{u} \cdot S \Box P \Box R$ is *well-typed* iff there exists an environment V such that for all $e \Diamond e' \in S \cup P$, $\Diamond \in \{\to, =\}$, there exists $\tau \in \mathit{Type}_{TC}(TV)$ such that $e, e' \in E^\tau_\Sigma(V)$, and for all $\varphi \in R$, φ is well-typed w.r.t. V.

4.1 Demanded and Pending Variables

Similarly to [9,5], *LNC* uses a notion of *demanded variable* to deal with lazy evaluation. Intuitively, approximation statements $e \to x$ in G, where e contains some function symbol, do not propagate the binding x/e. Instead, evaluation of e must be triggered, *provided that x is demanded.* The result will be shared by all the occurrences of x.

A variable x of $G \equiv \exists \bar{u} \cdot S \Box P \Box R$ is *demanded* iff P contains a sequence of approximation statements of the form: $t_0 \to x_1, t_1 \to x_2, \ldots, t_n \to x_{n+1}$, where $t_i \in T_\Sigma(DV)$, $0 \leq i \leq n$, $x \in dvar(t_0)$, $x_i \in DV$, $1 \leq i \leq n+1$, $x_i \in dvar(t_i)$, $1 \leq i \leq n$, and one of the following conditions holds:

- ▷ $x_{n+1} \Diamond e \in R$ or $e \Diamond x_{n+1} \in R$, where $\Diamond \in \{==, \not=, \in\}$.
- ▷ $e \notin x_{n+1} \in R$ or $x_{n+1} \notin \{\!\!\{ e|es \}\!\!\} \in R$.
- ▷ $x_{n+1} \in lib(\varphi^p)$, where $\varphi^p \in R_p(DV) \cap R$.

Demanded variables x are forced by solutions to take values different from $\perp$. This justifies why x is not considered as demanded in constraints $x \notin es$, where es has not the form $\{\!\!\{ r|rs \}\!\!\}$.

We also need a notion of *pending variable* to detect situations where goal solving must proceed by trying different imitation bindings. Formally, given a goal $G \equiv \exists \bar{u} \cdot S \Box P \Box R$, we say that x_n is pending in G iff P contains a sequence of the form $e \to x_0, t_1 \to x_1, t_2 \to x_2, \ldots, t_n \to x_n$, where $e \in E_\Sigma(DV) - T_\Sigma(DV)$, $t_i \in T_\Sigma(DV)$, $1 \leq i \leq n$, $x_i \in DV$, $0 \leq i \leq n$ and $x_i \in dvar(t_{i+1})$, $0 \leq i \leq n-1$. The set of pending variables of G will be noted as $\mathsf{pend}(G)$ in the sequel.

As an example, consider a goal of the form $\exists \bar{u} \cdot S \Box e \to x \Box x \notin xs$, where e contains defined function symbols and possibly denotes an infinite value. Variable x is not demanded and the constraint $x \notin xs$ is solved, but the whole goal is not solved. Since x is pending, the *LNC* calculus will allow goal solving to progress by trying two possible imitation bindings for xs: binding xs to $\{\!\{\ \}\!\}$ will lead immediately to a solved goal, while binding xs to $\{\!\{y|ys\}\!\}$ will produce a new goal including a constraint $x \notin \{\!\{y|ys\}\!\}$, which can be further processed.

4.2 Goals in Solved Form, Answers and Solutions

An admissible goal G is *quasi-solved* iff G has the form $\exists\bar{u} \cdot S \square P \square R$, where R contains only constraints in solved form or equalities $x == y$, $x, y \in DV$, and P contains only approximation statements of the form $t \to x$, where $t \in T_\Sigma(DV) - DV$ and x is not a demanded variable, or $t \in DV$. Note that it is important to require x to be not demanded in such approximation statements. This is needed in order to preserve quasi-solved goals when applying variable elimination rules. For instance, if we allow the goal $G \equiv \square A \to x \square x \not\models A$, where A is a constant symbol (note that x is demanded), then when propagating the binding x/A, the resulting goal $G' \equiv \square\square A \not\models A$ would not be quasi-solved.

An admissible goal G is in *solved form* iff G has the form $\exists\bar{u} \cdot S \square\square R$, where R contains only constraints in solved form, and for all $x == y \in R$, $x, y \in DV$, it holds that $x == y \in PP(G)$, where $PP(G)$ is defined similarly to $PP(\Gamma)$ but now considering that also equality constraints $x == y$ contribute to $PP(G)$.

W. r. t. primitive constraints, *LNC* is not going to perform any explicit transformation. Without loss of generality, we can suppose that all *LNC*-irreducible goals suffer a process of simplification similar to that in $CLP(\mathcal{R})$. This is possible because all the primitive constraints within a goal G in solved form will be isolated in the primitive part $PP(G)$.

A *correct answer* for $G \equiv \exists\bar{u} \cdot S \square P \square R$ is a pair (δ, Γ) such that $\delta \in DSub(T^*_{DC}(DV))$, $\Gamma \subseteq R_{\Sigma_\perp}(DV)$ is finite and in solved form and there exists $\bar{t} \in T^*_{DC_\perp}(DV)$ such that $\delta' = \delta[\bar{u}/\bar{t}]$ (called an *existential extension* of δ in the sequel) verifies that:

- ▷ There exists a primitive valuation η^p over $\mathcal{R}$ such that $(\mathcal{R}, \eta^p) \models_\mathcal{R} PP(\Gamma)$.
- ▷ For every equation $x = s \in S$: $x\delta' \equiv s\delta' \in T^*_{DC}(DV)$.
- ▷ For all $\chi \in P \cup R$, it holds that $\Gamma \vdash_\mathcal{P} \chi\delta'$. Any multiset containing *CGORC*-proofs for all the elements in $(P \cup R)\delta'$ is named a *witness* $\mathcal{M}$ for G and (δ, Γ).

A *solution* for G is a correct answer (δ, Γ) for G such that $\Gamma \equiv \emptyset$. Note that the condition (PR) in admissible goals ensures that every $e \to t \in G$ verifies that t does not contain the symbols $+$, $*$, 0 and 1. But Theorems 2 and 3 ensure that $\vdash_\mathcal{P}$ and $\Vdash_\mathcal{P}$ are equivalent in presence of approximation statements of the form $e \to t$, where $e \in E^*_{\Sigma_\perp}(DV)$, $t \in T^*_{DC_\perp}(DV)$ and constraints $\varphi \in R^*_{\Sigma_\perp}(DV)$. Thus, given any solution $\delta \in DSub(T^*_{DC}(DV))$ for G and $\chi \in P \cup R$, to prove $\vdash_\mathcal{P} \chi\delta'$ is equivalent to prove that $\Vdash_\mathcal{P} \chi\delta'$, where δ' is an existential extension of δ. This means that the notion of solution for a goal can be established in terms of *restricted* *CGORC*-derivations.

On the contrary, the notion of correct answer needs the full power of *unrestricted* *CGORC*-derivations. For instance, $(\{\ \}, \{x == y\})$ happens to be a *LNC* computed answer for the goal $G \equiv c(x+1) == c(y+1)$. According to the Soundness Theorem 4 below, this computed answer must be correct, and there must be some *unrestricted* $CGORC$-derivation proving $\{x == y\} \vdash_{\mathcal{P}} c(x+1) == c(y+1)$.

4.3 *LNC* Transformation Rules. Soundness and Completeness

Due to the lack of space, we will not present completely all the transformation rules for *LNC* but we will give the main ideas behind the transformation rules. A complete description of *LNC* can be found in [2].

All transformation rules in *LNC* have been designed in order to get a completeness result (Theorem 4) whose proof is based on the following idea: Given an admissible goal G different from $FAIL$ and not solved, and a solution δ for G, it is possible to find a transformation rule T such that when we apply T to G, "something decreases" while preserving (possibly modulo (MSET)) the solution δ. Here, $FAIL$ represents an irreducible and inconsistent goal.

In the case of non quasi-solved goals, "something" refers to a witness, and δ is totally preserved. By "decreasing" we refer to the following multiset ordering: Let $\mathcal{M} = \{\!\{ \Pi_1, \ldots, \Pi_n \}\!\}$ and $\mathcal{M}' = \{\!\{ \Pi'_1, \ldots, \Pi'_m \}\!\}$ be multisets of $\Vdash_{\mathcal{P}}$-proofs, then $\mathcal{M}$ is smaller than $\mathcal{M}'$ iff $\{\!\{ |\Pi_1|, \ldots, |\Pi_n| \}\!\} \prec \{\!\{ |\Pi'_1|, \ldots, |\Pi'_m| \}\!\}$, where $|\Pi|$ is the size (i.e., the number of inference steps without considering the applications of the rule $(\mathsf{PR})_\varphi$) of Π, and $\prec$ is the multiset extension of the usual ordering over the natural numbers.

In the case of quasi-solved goals, "something" refers to G, and δ is preserved modulo (MSET). Now, by "decreasing" we refer to the following lexicographic ordering: Given any two quasi-solved goals $G \equiv \exists \bar{u} \cdot S \Box P \Box R$ and $G' \equiv \exists \bar{u}' \cdot S' \Box P' \Box R'$, we say that G is smaller than G' iff $(n_1, m_1) < (n_2, m_2)$, where n_1 (resp. n_2) is the number of approximation statements in G (resp. in G'), whereas m_1 (resp. m_2) is the number of constraints of the form $x == y$, such that $x == y \notin PP(G)$ (resp. $x == y \notin PP(G')$).

Now, in order to design *LNC*, it is enough to analyze the different kinds of approximation statements and constraints in a not yet solved admissible goal G, looking for some transformation which allows to ensure what we have commented above. This is done by analyzing the possible structure of a goal G. In the analysis below, δ will denote a solution for G and δ' will be an existential extension of δ. With respect to approximation statements, let us analyze some of the possibilities. If G is of the form:

▷ $G \equiv \exists \bar{u} \cdot S \Box c(\bar{e}_n) \to d(\bar{t}_m), P \Box R$, where $c \in DC^n$, $d \in DC^m$. The definition of solution establishes that $c(\bar{e}_n)\delta' \to d(\bar{t}_m)\delta'$ must be $\Vdash_{\mathcal{P}}$-provable. Such a proof must use as first inference rule (DC) or (OMUT). According to these two $CGORC$-rules, we have, respectively, the following two $\hookrightarrow_{\mathcal{P}}$-rules:

$\mathsf{Dec}_{\to}$: $\exists \bar{u} \cdot S \Box c(\bar{e}_n) \to c(\bar{t}_n), P \Box R \hookrightarrow_{\mathcal{P}} \exists \bar{u} \cdot S \Box e_1 \to t_1, \ldots, e_n \to t_n, P \Box R$

$\mathsf{Mut}_{\to}$: $\exists \bar{u} \cdot S \Box \{\!\{ e | es \}\!\} \to s, P \Box R \hookrightarrow_{\mathcal{P}}$

$\quad \exists \bar{u}, x, y, xs \cdot S \Box e \to x, es \to \{\!\{ y | xs \}\!\}, \{\!\{ y, x | xs \}\!\} \to s, P \Box R$

where x, y, xs are fresh variables.

$\triangleright$ $G \equiv \exists\bar{u} \cdot S\Box f(\bar{e}_n) \to t, P\Box R$, where $f \in FS^n$. Now, the only possibility of proving $\Vdash_{\mathcal{P}} f(\bar{e}_n)\delta' \to t\delta'$ is using as last inference rule (OR) but ensuring that $t\delta' \not\equiv \perp$. Hence, the $\hookrightarrow_{\mathcal{P}}$-transformation rule will be:

Rule$_\to$: $\exists\bar{u} \cdot S\Box f(\bar{e}_n) \to t, P\Box R \hookrightarrow_{\mathcal{P}} \exists\bar{u},\bar{x} \cdot S\Box e_1 \to t_1, \ldots, e_n \to t_n, r \to t, P\Box\varphi, R$

If $t \notin DV$ or t is a demanded variable (which ensures that $t\delta' \not\equiv \perp$), where $f(\bar{t}_n) \to r \Leftarrow \varphi$ is a fresh variant of a rule in R with variables $\bar{x}$.

The rest of cases can be reasoned similarly; see [2]. With respect to constraints, let us analyze several cases:

$\triangleright$ $G \equiv \exists\bar{u}S\Box P\Box e \in es, R$, where $es \notin DV$. Then, if es contains a function symbol, according to $(\mathsf{MEMB})_\to$, we will have the rule:

Memb$_\to$: $\exists\bar{u} \cdot S\Box P\Box e \in es, R \hookrightarrow_{\mathcal{P}} \exists\bar{u}, x, xs \cdot S\Box es \to \{\!|\, x|xs \,|\!\}, P\Box e \in \{\!|\, x|xs \,|\!\}, R$

where x, xs are fresh variables.

Otherwise (es have the form $\{\!|\, t|ts \,|\!\}$), then we will have two new rules, according to the $CGORC$-rules $(\mathsf{MEMB})_1$ and $(\mathsf{MEMB})_2$ respectively, that can be designed similarly to Memb$_\to$.

$\triangleright$ $G \equiv \exists\bar{u} \cdot S\Box P\Box e \notin xs, R$, where $xs \in DV$. If e contains some function symbol in FS or $e \in T_\Sigma(DV)$ but e contains some variable of the set $\mathsf{pend}(G)$, then let us analyze all possible forms of the proof $\Vdash_{\mathcal{P}} e\delta' \notin xs\delta'$. If such a proof has used $(\mathsf{NMEMB})_1$, then we have the following LNC-transformation rule:

Nmemb III: $\exists\bar{u} \cdot S\Box P\Box e \notin xs, R \hookrightarrow_{\mathcal{P}} \exists\bar{u} \cdot xs = \{\!|\;\;|\!\}(S\Box P\Box R)[xs/\{\!|\;\;|\!\}]$

Otherwise, the proof $\Vdash_{\mathcal{P}} e\delta' \notin xs\delta'$ has used $(\mathsf{NMEMB})_2$, and the corresponding LNC-rule will be defined.

The rest of the rules for solving constraints can be designed similarly. Something similar happens with $\hookrightarrow_{DV}$-rules. In presence of approximation statements of the form $t \to x$, where t is either a non-variable primitive term or a variable belonging to $primvar(G)$, we generate a new goal transforming $t \to x$ into $t == x$. Otherwise, $t \to x$ disappear, propagating the binding x/t.

The soundness and completeness theorem for LNC, whose proof can be found in [2], is stated below. As notation, $\delta' =_{Mset} \delta$ means that $\delta'(x) \approx_{Mset} \delta(x)$, for all $x \in DV$.

Theorem 4. ***(Soundness and completeness)***
Soundness: Let G be an initial goal, G' a quasi-solved goal and $G'' \equiv \exists\bar{u} \cdot S\Box\Box RR$ a goal in solved form such that $G \hookrightarrow^*_{\mathcal{P}} G' \hookrightarrow^*_{DV} G''$. Then (δ_S, RR) is a correct answer for G.
Completeness: Let $\mathcal{P} = \langle\Sigma, \mathrm{R}\rangle$ be a program, G an initial goal and δ a solution for G. Then there exist a quasi-solved goal G' and a goal G'' in solved form such that $G \hookrightarrow^*_{\mathcal{P}} G' \hookrightarrow^*_{DV} G'' \equiv \exists\bar{u} \cdot S\Box\Box RR$, and G'' has a solution σ verifying that $\sigma =_{Mset} \delta$. Furthermore, if $\mathcal{P}$ and G are well-typed then $G\delta_S$ is well-typed.

Note that our completeness result is restricted to solutions instead to correct answers. For instance, consider the program rules $f \to Zero$ and $g(y, ys) \to True \Leftarrow y \notin ys$, and the initial goal $G \equiv \Box\Box g(Suc(f), zs) == True$. It is easy to check that $(\{\,\}, \underbrace{\{Suc(Zero) \notin zs\}}_{\Gamma})$ is a correct answer for G. However,

LNC can not compute the correct answer $(\{\ \}, \{Suc(Zero) \notin zs\})$. Instead, *LNC* enumerates infinite solutions $zs = \{\!\!\{\ \}\!\!\}$, $zs = \{\!\!\{ Zero \}\!\!\}$, ..., i.e., the correct answer is covered by an infinite number of solutions.

5 Conclusions

Starting from the framework of [4,5], limited to the case where all the data constructors except the multiset constructor are free, we have proposed the language SETA, which differs from other related languages (as e.g. [8,7,13]) in its rich combination of lazy functions, datatypes and arithmetic constraints. SETA has a firm mathematical foundation, with proof-theoretic and model-theoretic semantics, as well as a sound and complete goal solving mechanism. Moreover, SETA seems to have a potential wide range of applications, including parsing of visual languages, which are worth of further investigation.

Our narrowing calculus is not intended to serve, "as it is", as a concrete computational model. An actual implementation should avoid an indiscriminate use of the multiset equation (MSET), which can obviously lead to useless infinite computations. A first attempt to build such an implementation has been presented in our previous paper [3], where neither mathematical foundations nor built-in arithmetic constraints were considered. More work on implementation methods is still needed, also in regard to efficient narrowing strategies such as *demand driven*, also called *needed* narrowing [16,1], whose generalization to the case of *non-free* data constructors does not seem obvious.

References

1. Antoy, R., Echahed, R., Hanus, M.: *A Needed Narrowing Strategy.* Proc. POPL'94, ACM Press, pages 268–279.
2. Arenas-Sánchez P., López-Fraguas F.J., Rodríguez-Artalejo M.: *Functional plus Logic Programming with Built-in and Symbolic Constraints.* Technical Report SIP-85/98, UCM. Available at ftp://147.96.25.167/pub/seta.ps.gz
3. Arenas-Sánchez P., López-Fraguas F.J., Rodríguez-Artalejo M.: *Embedding Multiset Constraints into a Lazy Functional Logic Language.* Proc. PLILP'98, Springer LNCS 1490, pages 429–444, 1998.
4. Arenas-Sánchez P., Rodríguez-Artalejo M.: *A Semantic Framework for Functional Logic Programming with Algebraic Polymorphic Types.* Proc. TAPSOFT'97, Springer LNCS 1214, pages 453–464, 1997.
5. Arenas-Sánchez P., Rodríguez-Artalejo M.: *A Lazy Narrowing Calculus for Functional Logic Programming with Algebraic Polymorphic Types.* Proc. ILPS'97, the MIT Press, pages 53–69, 1997.
6. Banâtre, J.P. and Le Métayer, D.: *The Gamma model and its discipline of programming.* Science of Computer Programming, Vol. 15, pages 55–77, 1990.
7. Dovier, A., Omodeo, E., Pontelli, E. and Rossi, G.: *{log}: A language for programming in logic with finite sets.* Journal of Logic Programming, Vol. 28, No. 1, pages 1–44, 1996.
8. Dovier, A. and Rossi, G.: *Embedding extensional finite sets in CLP.* Proc. ICLP'93, the MIT Press, pages 540–556, 1993.

9. González-Moreno J.C., Hortalá-González T., López-Fraguas F.J, Rodríguez-Artalejo M.: *An Approach to Declarative Programming Based on a Rewriting Logic.* Journal of Logic Programming, Vol. 40, No. 1, pages 47–87, 1999.
10. Hanus, M.: *Lazy Narrowing with Simplification.* Journal of Computer Languages, Vol. 23, No. 2–4, pages 61–85, 1997.
11. Hanus M.: *The Integration of Functions into Logic Programming. A Survey.* Journal of Logic Programming Special issue "Ten Years of Logic Programming", Vol. 19 & 20, pages 583–628, 1994.
12. Helm R., Marriot K.: *Declarative Specification and Semantics for Visual Languages.* Journal of Visual Languages and Computing, Vol. 2, pages 211–331, 1991.
13. Jayaraman, B. and Devashis, J.: *Set constructors, finite sets and logical semantics.* Journal of Logic Programming, Vol. 38, No. 1, pages 55–77 1999.
14. Jaffar J., Maher M.J.: *Constraint Logic Programming: A Survey.* Journal of Logic Programming, Vol. 19–20, pages 503–582, 1994.
15. Jaffar J., Michaylov S., Stuckey P.J., Yap R.H.C.: *The CLP($\mathcal{R}$) Language and System.* ACM Transactions on Programming Languages and Systems, Vol. 14, No. 3, pages 339–395, July 1992.
16. Loogen R., López-Fraguas F.J., Rodríguez-Artalejo M.: *A Demand Driven Computation Strategy for Lazy Narrowing.* Proc. PLILP'93, Springer LNCS 714, pages 184–200, 1993.
17. Marriott, K.: *Constraint multiset grammars.* In Proc. IEEE Symposium on Visual Languages, IEEE Computer Society Press, pages 118–125, 1994.
18. Martí-Oliet N., Meseguer J.: *Action and Change in Rewriting Logic.* In R. Pareschi & B. Fronhöfer (eds.). Theoretical Approaches to Dynamic Worlds in Computer Science and Artificial Intelligence. Cambridge M.P., 1995.
19. Van Dalen D.: *Logic and Structure.* Berlin, Heidelberg, New York. Springer Verlag, 1980.

A Calculus for Interaction Nets

Maribel Fernández[1] and Ian Mackie[2]

[1] LIENS (CNRS UMR 8548), École Normale Supérieure
45 Rue d'Ulm, 75005 Paris, France
maribel@dmi.ens.fr
[2] CNRS-LIX (UMR 7650), École Polytechnique
91128 Palaiseau Cedex, France
mackie@lix.polytechnique.fr

Abstract. Interaction nets are graphical rewriting systems which can be used as either a high-level programming paradigm or a low-level implementation language. However, an operational semantics together with notions of strategy and normal form which are essential to reason about implementations, are not easy to formalize in this graphical framework. The purpose of this paper is to study a textual calculus for interaction nets, with a formal operational semantics, which provides a foundation for implementation. In addition, we are able to specify in this calculus various strategies, and a type system which formalizes the notion of partition used to define semi-simple nets. The resulting system can be seen as a kernel for a programming language, analogous to the λ-calculus.

1 Introduction

Interaction nets, introduced by Lafont [12], offer a graphical paradigm of computation based on net rewriting. They have proven themselves successful for application in computer science, most notably with the coding of the λ-calculus, where optimal reduction (specifically Lamping's algorithm [13]) has been achieved [9].

Although the graphical representation of interaction nets is very intuitive, graphical interfaces (editors) have not been forthcoming; a textual language is therefore necessary. Such a language would require ways of representing the interaction nets and rules, together with a reduction system to express how a rule should be applied. Lafont suggested in [12] a rather beautiful textual notation for interaction rules, but a general study of it has not emerged.

In this paper we define a calculus of interaction nets based on this notation. We provide the coding of interaction nets and rules, and a reduction system which can be seen as a decomposed system of interaction. Various notions of normal form and strategies for reduction can be formalized in this calculus, which provides the starting point for a more general treatment of abstract machines for implementing interaction nets. To enforce a discipline of programming, a type assignment system with user-defined types is introduced, which incorporates the notion of partition used by Danos and Regnier to generalize the multiplicative connectives of linear logic [5], and by Lafont to define semi-simple nets [12].

G. Nadathur (Ed.): PPDP'99, LNCS 1702, pp. 170–187, 1999.

Apart from the fact that it simplifies the actual writing of programs, a formal, textual, operational account of interaction nets has many advantages. Static properties of nets, such as types, can be defined in a more concise and formal way (compare the definition of the type system given in Sect. 3 and the definitions given in e.g. [6,12]). By giving a formal account of the rewriting process, the calculus provides the basis of an implementation of interaction nets. Interaction nets are strongly confluent, but like in all rewriting systems, there exist different notions of strategies and normal forms (for instance, irreducible nets, or weak normal forms associated to lazy reduction strategies). These are hard to formalize in a graphical framework, but we will see that they can be precisely defined in the calculus. Such strategies have applications for encodings of the λ-calculus, where interaction nets have had the greatest impact, and where a notion of a strategy is required to avoid non-termination of disconnected nets (see [16]).

Reduction algorithms and strategies also play a crucial rôle in the study of the operational semantics of interaction nets, in particular, operational equivalences of nets. Applications of this include [7] where the definition of a strategy was essential to show the correspondence between bisimilarity and contextual equivalence. In [7] an informal textual notation was used throughout the paper to help writing nets, but the formal definitions of strategy of evaluation and operational equivalence had to be given in the graphical framework. The calculus defined in this paper provides a formal and uniform notation for writing nets and defining their properties.

Related Work. Banach [3] showed that interaction nets are closely related to connection graphs of Bawden [4] and gave a formal account of these formalisms via hypergraph rewriting, using a categorical approach. Honda and Yoshida [10,18,19] studied various graphical and textual process calculi that generalize interaction nets; their emphasis is in the study of concurrent computations. The Interaction Systems of Laneve [14] are a class of combinatory reduction systems closely related to interaction nets (the intuitionistic nets). Strategies have been well studied in this framework, in particular for optimal reduction. Related to this work is also the encoding of interaction nets as combinatory reduction systems given in [8]. The notations that we introduce in the present work are inspired by formalisms for cyclic rewriting [2], and proof expressions for linear logic [1].

Overview. The rest of this paper is structured as follows: In the next section we recall some basic preliminaries on interaction nets and present several textual languages for interaction nets. Section 3 gives a thorough study of the calculus and presents the type system. Section 4 shows how strategies and reduction algorithms can be easily expressed in this framework. Finally, we conclude the paper in Section 5.

2 Background

An interaction net system is specified by a set Σ of symbols, and a set $\mathcal{R}$ of interaction rules. Each symbol $\alpha \in \Sigma$ has an associated (fixed) *arity*. An occurrence of a symbol $\alpha \in \Sigma$ will be called an *agent*. If the arity of α is n, then the agent has $n+1$ *ports*: a distinguished one called the *principal port* depicted by an arrow, and n *auxiliary ports* corresponding to the arity of the symbol. We will say that the agent has $n+1$ *free* ports.

A *net* N built on Σ is a graph (not necessarily connected) with agents at the vertices. The edges of the net connect agents together at the ports such that there is only one edge at every port (edges may connect two ports of the same agent). A net may also have edges with free extremes, called *wires*, and their extremes are called ports by analogy. The *interface* of a net is the set of free ports it has. There are two special instances of a net: a wiring (no agents), and the empty net. A pair of agents $(\alpha, \beta) \in \Sigma^2$ connected together on their principal ports is called an *active pair*; the interaction net analogue of a redex. An *interaction rule* $((\alpha, \beta) \Longrightarrow N) \in \mathcal{R}$ replaces an occurrence of the active pair (α, β) by the net N. Rules have to satisfy two very strong conditions: the interface must be preserved, and there is at most one rule for each pair of agents. The following diagram illustrates the idea, where N is any net built from Σ.

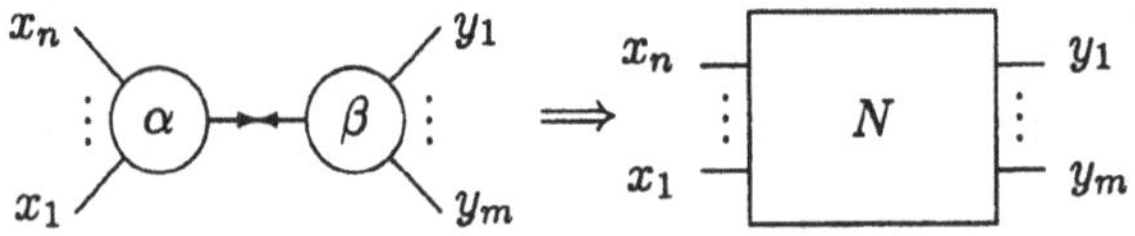

As a running example, we use the system of interaction for proof nets of multiplicative linear logic, which consists of two agents, ⅋ and ⊗ of arity 2, and one interaction rule. The following diagram indicates the interaction rule and an example net.

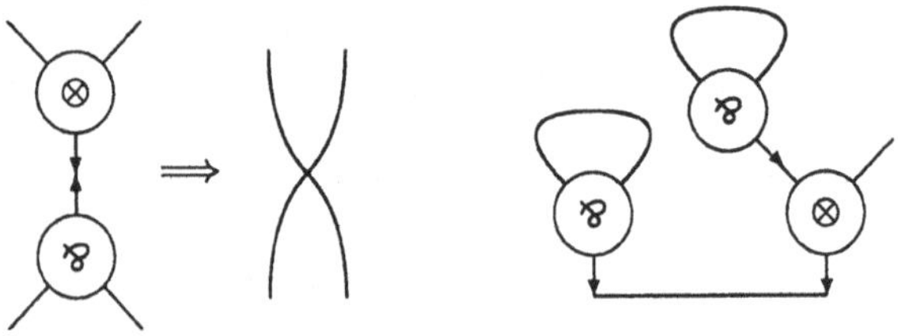

Three textual languages for interaction nets have been proposed in the literature. Inspired by Combinatory Reduction Systems [11], a net can be "flattened" by replacing ports of agents by names, and representing edges by two occurrences of a name. The expression $\otimes(a,b,c), ⅋(a,d,d), ⅋(b,e,e)$ represents the example net above, where the first argument of each agent is the principal port. The interaction rule is written: $\otimes(a,b,c), ⅋(a,d,e) \Longrightarrow I(c,e), I(b,d)$ where $I(a,b)$ is a wire with extremes a, b. This language has been used as a notation for interaction nets in [7,8], and is quite straightforward to relate to the graphical notation.

A second textual notation [15] eliminates the variables. The ports of each agent are indexed $\alpha.i$, with the principal port given by $\alpha.0$. A wiring relation is used to express the connectivity of the ports of agents in a net: $\alpha.i \equiv \beta.j$ indicates that there is a link between port i of agent α and port j of agent β. For example,

$(\wp_i, \otimes_j) \longrightarrow (\emptyset, \{\wp_i.1 \equiv \otimes_j.1, \wp_i.2 \equiv \otimes_j.2\})$ represents the interaction rule for proof nets. The left-hand side denotes an active pair and the right-hand side is a set of agents (empty in this example) together with a wiring.

Lafont [12] proposed a textual notation for interaction rules, where the example rule is written as $\otimes(x, y) \bowtie \wp(x, y)$. This notation is much lighter syntactically, but more esoteric. It seems the most useful as a formal language for interaction nets, although some practice is needed to become acquainted with it. This notation inspired the calculus that we develop in the rest of the paper.

3 The Calculus

We begin by introducing a number of syntactic categories.

Agents: Let Σ be a set of symbols, ranged over by $\alpha, \beta, \ldots$, each with a given *arity* $\mathsf{ar} : \Sigma \to \mathbb{N}$. An occurrence of a symbol will be called an *agent*. The arity of a symbol corresponds precisely to the number of auxiliary ports.

Names: Let N be a set of names, ranged over by x, y, z, etc. N and Σ are assumed disjoint.

Terms: A term is built on Σ and N by the grammar: $t ::= x \mid \alpha(t_1, \ldots, t_n)$, where $x \in N$, $\alpha \in \Sigma$, $\mathsf{ar}(\alpha) = n$ and $t_1, \ldots, t_n$ are terms, with the restriction that each name can appear at most twice. If $n = 0$, then we omit the parentheses. If a name occurs twice in a term, we say that it is *bound*, otherwise it is *free*. Since free names occur exactly once, we say that terms are *linear*. We write $\vec{t}$ for a list of terms $t_1, \ldots, t_n$. A term of the form $\alpha(\vec{t})$ can be seen as a tree with the principal port of α at the root, and where the terms $t_1, \ldots, t_n$ are the subtrees connected to the auxiliary ports of α.

Equations: If t and u are terms, then the (unordered) pair $t = u$ is an *equation*. Δ, $\Theta, \ldots$ will be used to range over multisets of equations. Examples of equations include: $x = \alpha(\vec{t})$, $x = y$, $\alpha(\vec{t}) = \beta(\vec{u})$.

Rules: Rules are pairs of terms written as $\alpha(\vec{t}) \bowtie \beta(\vec{u})$, where $(\alpha, \beta) \in \Sigma^2$ is the active pair of the rule. All names occur exactly twice in a rule, and there is at most one rule for each pair of agents.

Definition 1 (Names in terms). *The set $\mathcal{N}(t)$ of names of a term t is defined in the following way, which extends to multisets of equations and rules in the obvious way.*

$$\begin{aligned} \mathcal{N}(x) &= \{x\} \\ \mathcal{N}(\alpha(t_1, \ldots, t_n)) &= \mathcal{N}(t_1) \cup \cdots \cup \mathcal{N}(t_n) \end{aligned}$$

Given a term, we can replace its free names by new names, provided the linearity restriction is preserved.

Definition 2 (Renaming). *The notation $t[y/x]$ denotes a renaming that replaces the free occurrence of x in t by a new name y. Remark that since the name x occurs exactly once in the term, this operation can be implemented directly as an assignment, as is standard in the linear case. This notion extends to equations, and multisets of equations in the obvious way.*

More generally, we consider substitutions that replace free names in a term by other terms, always assuming that the linearity restriction is preserved.

Definition 3 (Substitution). *The notation $t[u/x]$ denotes a substitution that replaces the free occurrence of x by the term u in t. We only consider substitutions that preserve the linearity of the terms. Note that renaming is a particular case of substitution.*

Lemma 1. *Assume that $x \notin \mathcal{N}(v)$. If $y \in \mathcal{N}(u)$ then $t[u/x][v/y] = t[u[v/y]/x]$, otherwise $t[u/x][v/y] = t[v/y][u/x]$.*

Definition 4 (Instance of a rule). *If r is a rule $\alpha(t_1, \ldots, t_n) \bowtie \beta(u_1, \ldots, u_m)$, then $\hat{r} = \alpha(\widehat{t_1}, \ldots, \widehat{t_n}) \bowtie \beta(\widehat{u_1}, \ldots, \widehat{u_m})$ denotes a new generic* instance *of r, that is, a copy of r where we introduce a new set of names.*

We now have all the machinery that we need to define interaction nets.

Definition 5 (Configurations). *A* configuration *is a pair: $c = (\mathcal{R}, \langle \mathbf{t} \mid \Delta \rangle)$, where $\mathcal{R}$ is a set of rules, $\mathbf{t}$ a multiset $\{t_1, \ldots, t_n\}$ of terms, and Δ a multiset of equations. Each variable occurs at most twice in c. If a name occurs once in c then it is* free, *otherwise it is* bound. *For simplicity we sometimes omit $\mathcal{R}$ when there is no ambiguity. We use c, c' to range over configurations. We call $\mathbf{t}$ the* head *and Δ the* body *of a configuration.*

Intuitively, $\langle \mathbf{t} \mid \Delta \rangle$ represents a net that we evaluate using $\mathcal{R}$; Δ gives the set of active pairs and the renamings of the net. The roots of the terms in the head of the configuration and the free names correspond to ports in the interface of the net. We work modulo α-equivalence for bound names as usual, but also for free names. Configurations that differ only on the names of the free variables are equivalent, since they represent the same net.

Example 1 (Configurations). The empty net is represented by $\langle \mid \rangle$, and the configuration $\langle \mid \parr(a,a) = \otimes(b,b) \rangle$ represents a net without an interface, containing an active pair. A configuration $\langle \mathbf{t} \mid \rangle$ represents a net without active pairs and without cycles of principal ports.

There is an obvious (although not unique) translation between the graphical representation of interaction nets, and the configurations that we are using. Briefly, to translate a net into a configuration, we first orient the net as a collection of trees, with all principal ports facing in the same direction. Each pair of trees connected at their principal ports is translated as an equation, and any tree whose root is free or any free port of the net goes in the head of the configuration. We give a simple example to explain this translation. The usual encoding of the addition of natural numbers uses the agents $\Sigma = \{Z, S, Add\}$, $\mathsf{ar}(Z) = 0$, $\mathsf{ar}(S) = 1$, $\mathsf{ar}(Add) = 2$. The diagrams below illustrate the net representing the addition $1 + 0$ in the "usual" orientation, and also with all the principal ports facing up.

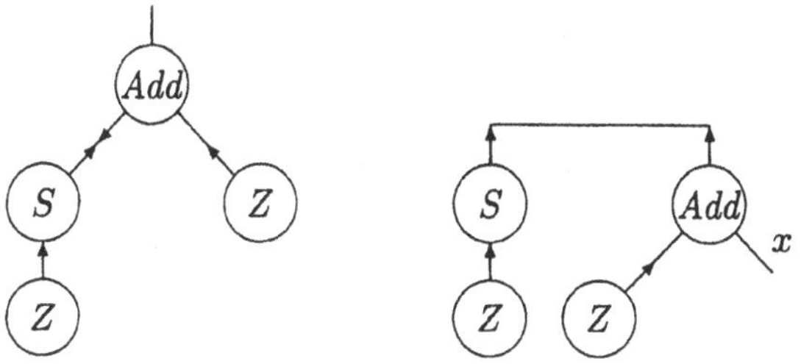

We then obtain the configuration $\langle x \mid S(Z) = Add(x, Z)\rangle$ where the only port in the interface is x, which we put in the head of the configuration.

The reverse translation simply requires that we draw the trees for the terms, connect the common variables together, and connect the trees corresponding to the members of an equation together on their principal ports.

Remark 1. The multiset $\mathbf{t}$ is the *interface of the configuration*, and this can be all, or just part of, the interface of the net represented by $\langle \mathbf{t} \mid \Delta\rangle$. For example, the net consisting of the agents *Succ* and *True* can be represented by $\langle True \mid y = Succ(x)\rangle$, $\langle True, Succ(x) \mid \rangle$, or $\langle \mid x = True, y = Succ(z)\rangle$. In other words, we can select a part of the interface of the net to be displayed as "observable" interface; the same net can be represented by several different configurations. See [7] for an example of use of observable interface.

Definition 6 (Computation Rules). *The operational behaviour of the system is given by a set of four computation rules.*

Indirection: *If* $x \in \mathcal{N}(u)$, *then* $x = t, u = v \longrightarrow u[t/x] = v$.
Interaction: *If* $\alpha(t'_1, \ldots, t'_n) \bowtie \beta(u'_1, \ldots, u'_m) \in \mathcal{R}$, *then*

$$\alpha(t_1, \ldots, t_n) = \beta(u_1, \ldots, u_m) \longrightarrow \\ t_1 = \widehat{t'_1}, \ldots, t_n = \widehat{t'_n}, u_1 = \widehat{u'_1}, \ldots, u_m = \widehat{u'_m}$$

Context: *If* $\Delta \longrightarrow \Delta'$, *then* $\langle \mathbf{t} \mid \Gamma, \Delta, \Gamma'\rangle \longrightarrow \langle \mathbf{t} \mid \Gamma, \Delta', \Gamma'\rangle$.
Collect: *If* $x \in \mathcal{N}(\mathbf{t})$, *then* $\langle \mathbf{t} \mid x = u, \Delta\rangle \longrightarrow \langle \mathbf{t}[u/x] \mid \Delta\rangle$.

The calculus puts in evidence the real cost of implementing an interaction step, which involves generating an instance, i.e. a new copy, of the right-hand side of the rule, plus renamings (rewirings). Of course this also has to be done when working in the graphical framework, even though it is often seen as an atomic step. The calculus therefore shows explicitly how an interaction step is performed.

Example 2 (Natural Numbers). We show two different encodings of natural numbers. The first is the standard one, the second is a more efficient version which offers a constant time addition operation.

1. Let $\Sigma = \{Z, S, Add\}$ with $\mathsf{ar}(Z) = 0$, $\mathsf{ar}(S) = 1$, $\mathsf{ar}(Add) = 2$, and $\mathcal{R}$:

$$\begin{array}{ll} Add(S(x), y) & \bowtie S(Add(x, y)) \\ Add(x, x) & \bowtie Z \end{array}$$

   As shown previously, the net for 1+0 is given by the configuration $(\mathcal{R}, \langle a \mid Add(a, Z) = S(Z)\rangle)$. One possible sequence of rewrites for this net is the following:

$$\begin{array}{l} \langle a \mid Add(a, Z) = S(Z)\rangle \\ \quad \longrightarrow \langle a \mid a = S(x'), y' = Z, Z = Add(x', y')\rangle \\ \quad \longrightarrow^* \langle S(x') \mid Z = Add(x', Z)\rangle \\ \quad \longrightarrow \langle S(x') \mid x'' = x', x'' = Z\rangle \\ \quad \longrightarrow^* \langle S(Z) \mid \rangle \end{array}$$

2. Let $\Sigma = \{S, N, N^*\}$, $\mathsf{ar}(S) = 1$, $\mathsf{ar}(N) = \mathsf{ar}(N^*) = 2$. Numbers are represented as a list of S agents, where N is the constructor holding a pointer to the head and tail of the list. 0 is defined by $N(x, x)$, and n by $N(S^n(x), x)$. The operation of addition can then be encoded by the configuration

$$\langle N(b, c), N^*(a, b), N^*(c, a) \mid \rangle$$

   which simply appends two numbers. There is only one rule that we need: $N(a, b) \bowtie N^*(b, a)$, which is clearly a constant time operation. To show how this works, we give an example of the addition of 1+1:

$$\begin{array}{l} \langle N(b, c) \mid N(S(x), x) = N^*(a, b), N(S(y), y) = N^*(c, a)\rangle \\ \quad \longrightarrow^* \langle N(b, c) \mid b = S(a), a = S(c)\rangle \\ \quad \longrightarrow^* \langle N(S(S(c)), c) \mid \rangle \end{array}$$

Example 3 (Proof Nets for Multiplicative Linear Logic). The usual encoding of proof nets in interaction nets uses $\Sigma = \{\otimes, \parr\}$, $\mathsf{ar}(\otimes) = \mathsf{ar}(\parr) = 2$, and the interaction rule: $\otimes(x, y) \bowtie \parr(x, y)$. We show a configuration representing the net used as a running example in the previous section, and a reduction sequence:

$$\begin{array}{l} \langle c \mid \parr(a, a) = \otimes(\parr(b, b), c)\rangle \\ \quad \longrightarrow \langle c \mid x_1 = a, y_1 = a, x_1 = \parr(b, b), y_1 = c\rangle \\ \quad \longrightarrow^* \langle c \mid c = \parr(b, b)\rangle \\ \quad \longrightarrow \langle \parr(b, b) \mid \rangle \end{array}$$

The next example shows how we can capture semi-simple nets [12], where vicious circles of principal ports cannot be created during computation. The notion of partition was used in [12] with the purpose of defining this class of nets. For each agent $\alpha \in \Sigma$ the (possibly empty) set of auxiliary ports is divided into one or several classes, each of them called *a partition.* A *partition mapping* establishes, for each agent in Σ, the way its auxiliary ports are grouped into partitions. We recall the graphical definition of semi-simple nets and at the same time show the translation to configurations.

Example 4 (Semi-simple Nets). Semi-simple nets are inductively defined as:

1. The empty net is semi-simple, and is represented by the configuration $\langle\ \mid\ \rangle$.
2. A wire is a semi-simple net, and is represented by a configuration of the form $\langle y, y \mid\ \rangle$.
3. If N_1, N_2 are semi-simple nets, their juxtaposition (called Mix) gives a new semi-simple net which is represented by the configuration $\langle \mathbf{s}, \mathbf{t} \mid \Delta, \Theta\rangle$, where $\langle \mathbf{t} \mid \Delta\rangle$ and $\langle \mathbf{s} \mid \Theta\rangle$ are the configurations representing N_1 and N_2 respectively (without loss of generality we assume that these configurations do not share variables, since we work modulo α-conversion).
4. If N_1, N_2 are semi-simple nets, a Cut between ports i and j builds a semi-simple net represented by the configuration $\langle \mathbf{s} - s_i, \mathbf{t} - t_j \mid \Delta, \Theta, s_i = t_j\rangle$, where $N_1 = \langle \mathbf{s} \mid \Delta\rangle$ and $N_2 = \langle \mathbf{t} \mid \Theta\rangle$, $\mathbf{s} - s_i$ is the multiset $\mathbf{s}$ without the element s_i, and $\mathbf{t} - t_j$ is the multiset $\mathbf{t}$ without the element t_j.
5. If $N_1, \ldots, N_n$ are semi-simple nets, the Graft of an agent α to the nets $N_1, \ldots, N_n$ according to its partitions builds a semi-simple net represented by $\langle \alpha(\vec{s_1}, \ldots, \vec{s_n}), \mathbf{t}_1, \ldots, \mathbf{t}_n \mid \Delta_1, \ldots, \Delta_n\rangle$, where $N_i = \langle \mathbf{s}_i, \mathbf{t}_i \mid \Delta_i\rangle$, $1 \leq i \leq n$, and we assume without loss of generality that these configurations do not share variables.

Example 5 (Non-termination). Consider the net $\langle x, y \mid \alpha(x) = \beta(\alpha(y))\rangle$ and the rule $\alpha(a) \bowtie \beta(\beta(\alpha(a)))$. The the following non-terminating reduction sequence is possible: $\langle x, y \mid \alpha(x) = \beta(\alpha(y))\rangle \longrightarrow \langle x, y \mid x = a, \beta(\alpha(a)) = \alpha(y)\rangle \longrightarrow \langle a, y \mid \beta(\alpha(a)) = \alpha(y)\rangle \longrightarrow \cdots$.

There is an obvious question to ask about this language with respect to the graphical formalism: can we write all interaction rules? Under some assumptions, the answer is yes. There are in fact two restrictions. The first one is that there is no way of writing a rule with an active pair in the right-hand side. This is not a problem since interaction nets can be assumed to satisfy the optimization condition [12], which requires no active pairs in right-hand sides. The second problem is the representation of interaction rules for active pairs without interface. In the calculus, an active pair without interface can only rewrite to the empty net. In other words, it will be erased, and so can be ignored. This coincides with the operational semantics defined in [7].

3.1 A Type Discipline

We now define a typed version of the calculus using type variables $\varphi_1, \varphi_2, \ldots$, and type constructors with fixed arities (such as **int**, **bool**, ... of arity 0; list,... of arity 1; $\times$, $\otimes$, $⅋$, ... of arity 2; ...). The terms built on this signature (τ = $\mathsf{list}(\mathbf{int}), \mathsf{list}(\mathsf{list}(\mathbf{bool})), \otimes(\varphi_1, \varphi_2), \ldots$) are the types of the system, and they are used-defined in the same way as the set Σ of agents is. Note that we may have type constructors with the same names as agents, as in the case of $\otimes$ which is traditionally used as a type constructor and as an agent in proof nets.

Types may be decorated with *signs*: τ^+ will be called an *output type*, and τ^- an *input type*. The *dual* of an atomic type σ^+ (resp. σ^-) is σ^- (resp. σ^+), and in general we will denote by $\sigma^\perp$ the dual of the type σ, which is defined by a set of type equations of the form $C(\sigma_1,\ldots,\sigma_n)^\perp = C^\perp(\sigma_1^\perp,\ldots,\sigma_n^\perp)$ such that $(\sigma^\perp)^\perp = \sigma$. For example

$$\begin{aligned}
(\mathsf{list}^-(\sigma))^\perp &= \mathsf{list}^+(\sigma^\perp)\\
(\mathsf{list}^+(\sigma))^\perp &= \mathsf{list}^-(\sigma^\perp)\\
(\otimes(\sigma,\tau))^\perp &= \parr(\sigma^\perp,\tau^\perp)\\
(\parr(\sigma,\tau))^\perp &= \otimes(\sigma^\perp,\tau^\perp)
\end{aligned}$$

Moreover, we might have other equations defining equalities between types, such as: $(\sigma\times\tau)\times\rho = \sigma\times(\tau\times\rho)$.

Types will be assigned to the terms of the calculus by using the following inference rules, which are a form of one-sided sequents.

Identity Group. The Axiom allows variables of dual types to be introduced to the system, and the Cut rule says that an equation is typeable (denoted $t{=}u{:}\diamond$) if both sides are typeable with dual types.

$$\frac{}{x{:}\,\sigma, x{:}\,\sigma^\perp}\,(\mathsf{Ax}) \qquad \frac{\Gamma, t{:}\,\sigma \quad \Delta, u{:}\,\sigma^\perp}{\Gamma,\Delta, t = u{:}\diamond}\,(\mathsf{Cut})$$

Structural Group. The Exchange rule allows permutations on the order of the sequent, and the Mix rule allows the combination of two sequents:

$$\frac{\Gamma, t{:}\,\sigma, u{:}\,\tau, \Delta}{\Gamma, u{:}\,\tau, t{:}\,\sigma, \Delta}\,(\mathsf{Exchange}) \qquad \frac{\Gamma \quad \Delta}{\Gamma,\Delta}\,(\mathsf{Mix})$$

User-defined Group. For each agent $\alpha\in\Sigma$, there is a rule that specifies the way types are assigned to terms rooted by α. The general format is:

$$\frac{\Gamma_1, t_1{:}\,\sigma_1,\ldots,t_{i_1}{:}\,\sigma_{i_1} \quad \ldots \quad \Gamma_k, t_k{:}\,\sigma_k,\ldots,t_{i_k}{:}\,\sigma_{i_k}}{\Gamma_1,\ldots,\Gamma_k, \alpha(t_1,\ldots,t_n){:}\,\sigma}\,(\mathsf{Graft})$$

The Graft rule for α specifies its partitions, that is, the way the subterms $t_1,\ldots,t_n$ are distributed in the premises. For example, a set of Graft rules for the system defined in Example 2, Part 1 (arithmetic), together with a polymorphic erasing agent ϵ defined by rules of the form $\epsilon \bowtie \alpha(\epsilon,\ldots,\epsilon)$, can be defined as follows:

$$\frac{\Gamma, t{:}\,\mathbf{int}^+}{\Gamma, S(t){:}\,\mathbf{int}^+}\,(S) \qquad \frac{\Gamma}{\Gamma, Z{:}\,\mathbf{int}^+}\,(Z) \qquad \frac{\Gamma, t_1{:}\,\mathbf{int}^- \quad \Delta, t_2{:}\,\mathbf{int}^+}{\Gamma,\Delta, \mathit{Add}(t_1,t_2){:}\,\mathbf{int}^-}\,(\mathit{Add}) \qquad \frac{\Gamma}{\Gamma, \epsilon{:}\,\sigma}\,(\epsilon)$$

Definition 7 (Typeable Configurations). *Let $\{x_1,\ldots,x_m\}$ be the set of free names of t, then t is a term of type σ if there is a derivation ending in*

$x_1{:}\,\tau_1,\ldots,x_m{:}\,\tau_m, t{:}\,\sigma$. *Equations are typed in a similar way: if* $t = u$ *is an equation with free names* $\{x_1,\ldots,x_m\}$, *then it is typeable if there is a derivation for* $x_1{:}\,\tau_1,\ldots,x_m{:}\,\tau_m, t = u{:}\,\diamond$. *This notion can be extended to multisets of equations in a straightforward way. A configuration* $\langle \mathrm{t} \mid s_1 = u_1,\ldots,s_m = u_m\rangle$ *with free names* $x_1,\ldots,x_p$ *is typeable by* $\sigma_1,\ldots,\sigma_n$, *if there is a derivation for* $x_1{:}\,\rho_1,\ldots,x_p{:}\,\rho_p, t_1{:}\,\sigma_1,\ldots,t_n{:}\,\sigma_n, s_1 = u_1{:}\,\diamond,\ldots,s_m = u_m{:}\,\diamond$.

Example 6. The following is a type derivation for the net $\langle a \mid Add(a,Z) = S(Z)\rangle$ in Example 2, Part 1, using the set of Graft rules defined above.

$$\dfrac{\dfrac{\dfrac{}{a{:}\,\mathbf{int}^+, a{:}\,\mathbf{int}^-}(\mathsf{Ax}) \quad \dfrac{}{Z{:}\,\mathbf{int}^+}(Z)}{a{:}\,\mathbf{int}^+, Add(a,Z){:}\,\mathbf{int}^-}(Add) \quad \dfrac{\dfrac{}{Z{:}\,\mathbf{int}^+}(Z)}{S(Z){:}\,\mathbf{int}^+}(S)}{a{:}\,\mathbf{int}^+, Add(a,Z) = S(Z){:}\,\diamond}(\mathsf{Cut})$$

The typing of rules is more delicate, since we have to ensure that both sides are consistent with respect to types so that the application of the Interaction Rule preserves types (Subject Reduction). We do this in two steps: first we find a type derivation for the active pair (using arbitrary names for the free variables), and then use this derivation as a template to build a derivation for the right-hand side.

Definition 8 (Typeable Rules). *Let* Σ *be a given set of agents, with a corresponding set of Graft rules. We say that a rule* $\alpha(t_1,\ldots,t_n) \bowtie \beta(s_1,\ldots,s_m)$ *is typeable if*

1. *there is a derivation* D *with conclusion* $\alpha(x_1,\ldots,x_n) = \beta(y_1,\ldots,y_m){:}\,\diamond$ *and leaves containing assumptions for* $x_1,\ldots,x_n,y_1,\ldots,y_m$, *built by application of the Cut rule and the Graft rules for* α, β,
2. *there is a type derivation with the same assumptions leading to the conclusion* $x_1 = t_1{:}\,\diamond,\ldots,x_n = t_n{:}\,\diamond, y_1 = s_1{:}\,\diamond,\ldots,y_m = s_m{:}\,\diamond$,
3. *and whenever an equation* $\alpha(t'_1,\ldots,t'_n) = \beta(s'_1,\ldots,s'_m)$ *is typeable, its type derivation is obtained by using the Cut rule and instances of the Graft rules for* α, β *applied in* D.

Example 7. The interaction rules for addition given in Example 2, Part 1, are typeable. We show the type derivation for $Add(S(x),y) \bowtie S(Add(x,y))$. First we build the most general derivation for the active pair (to ensure that condition 3 in Definition 8 holds):

$$\dfrac{\dfrac{x_1{:}\,\mathbf{int}^- \quad x_2{:}\,\mathbf{int}^+}{Add(x_1,x_2){:}\,\mathbf{int}^-}(Add) \quad \dfrac{x_3{:}\,\mathbf{int}^+}{S(x_3){:}\,\mathbf{int}^+}(S)}{Add(x_1,x_2) = S(x_3){:}\,\diamond}(\mathsf{Cut})$$

Then we use this template to build a second derivation:

$$\dfrac{x_1\colon \mathbf{int}^- \qquad \dfrac{x_2\colon \mathbf{int}^+ \qquad \dfrac{x_3\colon \mathbf{int}^+ \qquad \dfrac{\dfrac{\dfrac{}{x\colon \mathbf{int}^-, x\colon \mathbf{int}^+}\,(\mathsf{Ax})}{x\colon \mathbf{int}^-, S(x)\colon \mathbf{int}^+}\,(S) \qquad \dfrac{}{y\colon \mathbf{int}^-, y\colon \mathbf{int}^+}\,(\mathsf{Ax})}{y\colon \mathbf{int}^-, S(x)\colon \mathbf{int}^+, Add(x,y)\colon \mathbf{int}^-}\,(Add)}{y\colon \mathbf{int}^-, S(x)\colon \mathbf{int}^+, x_3 = Add(x,y)\colon \diamond}\,(\mathsf{Cut})}{S(x)\colon \mathbf{int}^+, x_2 = y\colon \diamond, x_3 = Add(x,y)\colon \diamond}\,(\mathsf{Cut})}{x_1 = S(x)\colon \diamond, x_2 = y\colon \diamond, x_3 = Add(x,y)\colon \diamond}\,(\mathsf{Cut})$$

Consider now the encoding of proof nets (Example 3), with the interaction rule $\otimes(a,b) \bowtie \invamp(a,b)$. We will show that a cut-elimination step in linear logic proof nets is typeable. Here is the most general derivation for the active pair:

$$\dfrac{\dfrac{x_1\colon \sigma_1 \quad x_2\colon \sigma_2}{\otimes(x_1,x_2)\colon \otimes(\sigma_1,\sigma_2)}\,(\otimes) \qquad \dfrac{x_3\colon \sigma_1^\perp, x_4\colon \sigma_2^\perp}{\invamp(x_3,x_4)\colon \invamp(\sigma_1^\perp,\sigma_2^\perp)}\,(\invamp)}{\otimes(x_1,x_2) = \invamp(x_3,x_4)\colon \diamond}\,(\mathsf{Cut})$$

We build now the second derivation using this template:

$$\dfrac{x_1\colon \sigma_1 \qquad \dfrac{x_2\colon \sigma_2 \qquad \dfrac{\dfrac{}{a\colon \sigma_1^\perp, a\colon \sigma_1}\,(\mathsf{Ax}) \qquad \dfrac{\dfrac{}{b\colon \sigma_2^\perp, b\colon \sigma_2}\,(\mathsf{Ax}) \qquad x_3\colon \sigma_1^\perp, x_4\colon \sigma_2^\perp}{b\colon \sigma_2^\perp, x_3\colon \sigma_1^\perp, x_4 = b\colon \diamond}\,(\mathsf{Cut})}{a\colon \sigma_1^\perp, b\colon \sigma_2^\perp, x_3 = a\colon \diamond, x_4 = b\colon \diamond}\,(\mathsf{Cut})}{a\colon \sigma_1^\perp, x_2 = b\colon \diamond, x_3 = a\colon \diamond, x_4 = b\colon \diamond}\,(\mathsf{Cut})}{x_1 = a\colon \diamond, x_2 = b\colon \diamond, x_3 = a\colon \diamond, x_4 = b\colon \diamond}\,(\mathsf{Cut})$$

The last condition in Definition 8 is crucial for Subject Reduction, as the following example shows.

Example 8 (Untypeable Rule). Let $\Sigma = \{\alpha, S\}$ where $\mathsf{ar}(\alpha) = \mathsf{ar}(S) = 1$, together with the interaction rule $\alpha(x) \bowtie S(x)$. The agents are typed with the Graft rules:

$$\dfrac{\Gamma, t\colon \mathbf{int}^+}{\Gamma, S(t)\colon \mathbf{int}^+}\,(S) \qquad \dfrac{\Gamma, t\colon \sigma}{\Gamma, \alpha(t)\colon \mathbf{int}^-}\,(\alpha)$$

We first build a type derivation for the active pair:

$$\dfrac{\dfrac{x_1\colon \mathbf{int}^-}{\alpha(x_1)\colon \mathbf{int}^-}\,(\alpha) \qquad \dfrac{y_1\colon \mathbf{int}^+}{S(y_1)\colon \mathbf{int}^+}\,(S)}{\alpha(x_1) = S(y_1)\colon \diamond}\,(\mathsf{Cut})$$

With this template we can build a type derivation for the right-hand side:

$$\dfrac{x_1 \colon \mathbf{int}^- \qquad \dfrac{\dfrac{}{x \colon \mathbf{int}^+, x \colon \mathbf{int}^-}\,(\mathsf{Ax}) \qquad y_1 \colon \mathbf{int}^+}{x \colon \mathbf{int}^+, y_1 = x \colon \diamond}\,(\mathsf{Cut})}{x_1 = x \colon \diamond, y_1 = x \colon \diamond}\,(\mathsf{Cut})$$

But the equation $\alpha(x') = S(y')$ is also typeable by:

$$\dfrac{\dfrac{x' \colon \mathbf{bool}^-}{\alpha(x') \colon \mathbf{int}^-}\,(\alpha) \qquad \dfrac{y' \colon \mathbf{int}^+}{S(y') \colon \mathbf{int}^+}\,(S)}{\alpha(x') = S(y') \colon \diamond}\,(\mathsf{Cut})$$

which is not an instance of the first derivation. This means that condition 3 in Definition 8 is not satisfied, therefore the rule is not typeable. If we accept this rule, we obtain a system that is not sound with respect to types: the net $\langle \mid \alpha(\mathit{True}) = S(Z)\rangle$ where *True* has type **bool** and Z **int**, is typeable, but reduces to $\langle \mid \mathit{True} = Z\rangle$ which is not typeable.

Theorem 1 (Subject Reduction). *The computation rules Indirection, Interaction, Context and Collect, preserve typeability and types: For any set $\mathcal{R}$ of typeable rules and configuration c on Σ, if $c \to^* c'$ then c' can be assigned the same types as c.*

Proof. The cases of Indirection with Context and Collect are straightforward, we show the case of Interaction. Let

$$c = \langle \mathsf{t} \mid \Gamma, \alpha(\vec{u}) = \beta(\vec{v}), \Gamma'\rangle \to c' = \langle \mathsf{t} \mid \Gamma, u = \overrightarrow{\widehat{u}'}, v = \overrightarrow{\widehat{v}'}, \Gamma'\rangle$$

using the interaction rule $\alpha(\vec{u'}) \bowtie \beta(\vec{v'})$. Assume that c is typeable (more precisely, there is a derivation for the sequent $\Delta, \alpha(\vec{u}) = \beta(\vec{v}) \colon \diamond$ corresponding to c), and that the rule $\alpha(\vec{u'}) \bowtie \beta(\vec{v'})$ is typeable. We show that the sequent $\Delta, u = \overrightarrow{\widehat{u}'} \colon \diamond, v = \overrightarrow{\widehat{v}'} \colon \diamond$ corresponding to c' is derivable. By Definition 8 (part 2), there is a proof tree for $x = \overrightarrow{\widehat{u}'} \colon \diamond, y = \overrightarrow{\widehat{v}'} \colon \diamond$ using as template the proof tree of $\alpha(\vec{x}) = \beta(\vec{y}) \colon \diamond$. By Definition 8 (part 3), the (α) and (β) typing rules used in the proof of c are instances (say with a substitution S) of the ones used in the proof of $\alpha(\vec{x}) = \beta(\vec{y}) \colon \diamond$. Hence, we can build the derivation tree for the sequent associated to c' by using the instance (by substitution S) of the proof tree of $x = \overrightarrow{\widehat{u}'} \colon \diamond, y = \overrightarrow{\widehat{v}'} \colon \diamond$, replacing x_i, y_i by u_i, v_i, and replacing the leaves containing assumptions for x_i, y_i by the corresponding proofs of u_i, v_i (subtrees of the proof of c). □

We remark that the notion of partition is built-in in our type system: the partitions of an agent correspond to the hypotheses in its Graft rule. This means that our type system can be used to check semi-simplicity of nets.

Proposition 1. *Typeable configurations are semi-simple (without vicious circles of principal ports).*

Proof. Induction on the type derivation. Note that the names given to the type rules of our system coincide with the names given to the operations that build semi-simple nets (cf. Example 4). □

Related systems. Danos and Regnier [5] generalized the multiplicative connectives of linear logic, showing the general format of the introduction rule (for a connective and its dual), and the cut-elimination step. Each connective corresponds to an agent and a type constructor in our system, and their rules coincide with our Graft rules. The cut-elimination steps are defined through interaction rules in our system (and are not necessarily rewirings, as in the case of multiplicatives).

Lafont [12] introduced a basic type discipline for the graphical framework of interaction nets, using a set of constant types ($\tau \in \{\mathsf{atom}, \mathsf{nat}, \mathsf{list}, \ldots\}$). For each agent, ports are classified between *input* and *output*: input ports have types of the form τ^-, whereas output ports have types τ^+. A net is *well-typed* in Lafont's system if each agent is used with the correct type and input ports are connected to output ports of the same type. Our system is a generalization of Lafont's system (since we introduce polymorphism and a more general notion of duality) integrating the notion of partition. It is easy to see that the typed nets of Lafont are represented by configurations which are typeable in our calculus (the proof is by a straightforward induction on the structure of the configuration).

In [6] another type system for interaction nets is discussed, using type variables and intersection types. The intersection free part of this system is also a subsystem of ours, but we consider also polymorphic type constructors and build-in the notion of partition.

3.2 Properties of the Calculus

This section is devoted to showing various properties of the rewriting system defined by the rules Indirection, Interaction, Context, and Collect. These results are known for the graphical formalism of interaction nets, but here we show that the calculus, which is a decomposed system of interaction, also preserves these properties.

Proposition 2 (Confluence). $\longrightarrow$ *is strongly confluent.*

Proof. All the critical pairs are joinable in one step, using Lemma 1. □

We write $c \Downarrow c'$ iff $c \twoheadrightarrow c' \not\rightarrow$. As an immediate consequence of the previous property we obtain:

Proposition 3 (Determinacy). $c \Downarrow c'$ *and* $c \Downarrow c''$ *implies* $c' = c''$.

It is a rather interesting phenomenon that interaction nets representing infinite loops (infinite computations) can terminate. This is analogous to "black hole" detection, which is well-known in graph reduction for functional languages. Two examples of this are the following configurations: $\langle y \mid x = \delta(x, y)\rangle$, where δ is the duplicator agent, and $\langle \ \mid x = x\rangle$, which both can be thought of as representing the cyclic term $\alpha = \alpha$ in cyclic term rewriting [2]. Both of these configurations are irreducible. The latter is a net without an interface, and the first is the same thing with an interface. Hence our interaction net configurations allow us to distinguish these two cases.

Proposition 4. *The rules Indirection and Collect are terminating.*

Proof. Both rules decrease the number of equations in a configuration. □

Non-termination arises because of the Interaction rule (cf. Example 5). There are several criteria for termination of nets, which were defined for the graphical framework, see for example [3] and [8]. These can be recast in the textual language in a much cleaner, concise way.

4 Normal Forms and Strategies

Although we have stressed the fact that systems of interaction are strongly confluent, there are clearly many ways of obtaining the normal form (if one exists), and moreover there is scope for alternative kinds of normal form, for instance those induced by weak reduction.

In this section we study several different notions of normal form and strategies for evaluation of interaction nets. The calculus provides a simple way of expressing these concepts which are quite hard to formalize in the graphical framework. In addition, we define some extra rules that can optimize the computations.

There are essentially two standard notions of normal form for rewriting systems: full normal form and weak normal form (also known as root stable, weak head normal form, etc). In the λ-calculus one also has notions such as head normal form, which allows reduction under the top constructor.

These notions can be recast in our calculus, providing in this way a theory for the implementation of interaction nets. One of the most fruitful applications of this would be the implementation of nets containing disconnected non-terminating computations, which are crucial for the coding of the λ-calculus, and functional programming languages for instance.

We begin with the weakest form of reduction that we will introduce.

Definition 9 (Interface Normal Form). *A configuration $(\mathcal{R}, \langle \mathbf{t} \mid \Delta\rangle)$ is in* interface normal form *(INF) if each t_i in* $\mathbf{t}$ *is of one of the following forms:*

- $\alpha(\vec{s})$. *E.g.* $\langle S(x) \mid x = Z, \Delta\rangle$.
- x *where* $x \in \mathcal{N}(t_j)$, $i \neq j$. *This is called an* open path. *E.g.* $\langle x, x \mid \Delta\rangle$
- x *where x occurs in a* cycle *in* Δ. *E.g.* $\langle x \mid y = \alpha(\beta(y), x), \Delta\rangle$.

Clearly any net with no interface $\langle \mid \Delta\rangle$ *is in interface normal form.*

Intuitively, an interaction net is in interface normal form when there are agents with principal ports on all of the observable interface, or, if there are ports in the interface that are not principal, then they will never become principal by reduction (since they are in an open path or a cycle). This idea can also be adapted to the typed framework, where we may require that only terms with positive types appear in the head of the configuration in interface normal form. This corresponds exactly to the Canonical Forms defined in [7], where negative ports are not observable. Additionally, this notion of normal form can be generalized to deal with a user defined set of values in the interface (Value Normal Form), which can allow some reduction under the top constructor.

The second notion of normal form that we introduce is the strongest one in that all reductions possible have been done, and corresponds to the usual notion of normal form for interaction nets.

Definition 10 (Full Normal Form). *A configuration* $(\mathcal{R}, \langle \mathbf{t} \mid \Delta\rangle)$ *is in* full normal form *if either* Δ *is empty, or all equations in* Δ *are of the form* $x = t$ *where* $x \in t$ *or* x *is free in* $\langle \mathbf{t} \mid \Delta\rangle$.

Having defined the notions of normal form, we now give the corresponding algorithms to compute them. We suggest different ways of evaluating a net to normal form, each of which could be useful for various applications.

Full Reduction. To obtain the full normal form of a net, we apply the computation rules until we obtain an irreducible configuration. Since interaction nets are strongly confluent, there is clearly no need to impose a strategy, since all reductions will eventually be done. However, there are additional factors, involving the size of the net and non-termination, that suggest that different strategies can be imposed:

Priority Reduction. As many of the examples that we have already given indicate, there are interaction rules which reduce the size of the net, keep the size constant, and increase the size of the net. More formally, we define the size of a term:

$$\begin{aligned} |x| &= 0 \\ |\alpha(t_1, \ldots, t_n)| &= 1 + |t_1| + \cdots + |t_n| \end{aligned}$$

The size of an equation is given by $|t = u| = |t| + |u|$. For an interaction rule $r = \alpha(\vec{t}) \bowtie \beta(\vec{u})$, let $s = |\vec{t}| + |\vec{u}|$. Then r is said to be expansive if $s > 2$, reducing if $s < 2$, otherwise it is stable. We can then define an ordering on the rules, and give priority to the ones which are reducing.

Connected reduction. Using this strategy, an application of Interaction to $t = u$ in $\langle \mathbf{t} \mid t = u, \Delta\rangle$ would only be allowed if $\mathcal{N}(\mathbf{t}) \cap \mathcal{N}(t = u) \neq \emptyset$. Thus subnets that are not connected to the observable interface will not be evaluated. As a direct application of this strategy we can define an *accelerated garbage collection.*

Interaction nets are very good at capturing the explicit dynamics of garbage collection. However, nets have to be in normal form before they can be erased. Therefore, non-terminating nets can never be erased. With this strategy, we can ignore isolated nets since they will never contribute to the interface of the net. It is therefore useful to add an additional rule, called **Cleanup**, which explicitly removes these components, without reducing to normal form first. If there are no free names in the equation $t = u$, then

$$\langle \mathbf{t} \mid t = u, \Delta \rangle \longrightarrow \langle \mathbf{t} \mid \Delta \rangle$$

Weak Reduction. Computing interface normal forms suggests that we do the minimum work required to bring principal ports to the interface; computing value normal form requires that each agent in the observable interface is a value. Both of these can be described by placing conditions on the rewrite system. Here we just focus on interface normal form. The following conditional version of the computation rules is enough to obtain this. Given a configuration of the form: $\langle t_1, \ldots, x, \ldots, t_n \mid t = u, \Delta \rangle$, where $x \in \mathcal{N}(t = u)$, then any of the computation rules can be applied to $t = u$. This process is repeated until the Collect rule has brought agents to the interface, or the configuration is irreducible. We can formalize this as a set of evaluation rules, for instance one such way is:

Axiom:

$$\frac{c \in INF}{c \Downarrow c}$$

Collect:

$$\frac{\langle t_1, \ldots, t, \ldots, t_n \mid \Delta \rangle \Downarrow c}{\langle t_1, \ldots, x, \ldots, t_n \mid x = t, \Delta \rangle \Downarrow c}$$

Indirection: if $x \in \mathcal{N}(u)$ and $y \in \mathcal{N}(t, u = v)$

$$\frac{\langle t_1, \ldots, y, \ldots, t_n \mid u[t/x] = v, \Delta \rangle \Downarrow c}{\langle t_1, \ldots, y, \ldots, t_n \mid x = t, u = v, \Delta \rangle \Downarrow c}$$

Interaction: if $x \in \mathcal{N}(\alpha(\vec{t}) = \beta(\vec{u})), \alpha(\vec{t'}) = \beta(\vec{u'}) \in \mathcal{R}$

$$\frac{\langle s_1, \ldots, x, \ldots, s_n \mid \overrightarrow{t = \widehat{t'}}, \overrightarrow{u = \widehat{u'}}, \Delta \rangle \Downarrow c}{\langle s_1, \ldots, x, \ldots, s_n \mid \alpha(\vec{t}) = \beta(\vec{u}), \Delta \rangle \Downarrow c}$$

Note the simplicity of this definition, compared with the definitions given in the graphical framework.

5 Conclusions

We have given a calculus for interaction nets, together with a type system, and its operational theory. This calculus provides a solid foundation for an implementation of interaction nets. In particular, we can express strategies, and define notions of weak reduction which are essential for actual implementations of interaction nets for realistic computations.

The language has also been extended to attach a value to an agent, and allow interaction rules to use this value in the right-hand side of the rule. Such a system is analogous to the extension of the λ-calculus with δ rules, as done for instance with the language **PCF**.

There are various directions for further study. The operational account has lead to the development of an Abstract Machine for interaction nets [17]. This could be used as a basis for formalizing an implementation and could also serve as the basis for the development of a parallel abstract machine.

References

1. S. Abramsky. Computational Interpretations of Linear Logic. *Theoretical Computer Science*, 111:3–57, 1993.
2. Z. M. Ariola and J. W. Klop. Lambda calculus with explicit recursion. *Information and Computation*, 139(2):154–233, 1997.
3. R. Banach. The algebraic theory of interaction nets. Technical Report UMCS-95-7-2, University of Manchester, 1995.
4. A. Bawden. Connection graphs. In *Proceedings of ACM Conference on Lisp and Functional Programming*, pages 258–265, 1986.
5. V. Danos and L. Regnier. The structure of multiplicatives. *Archive for Mathematical Logic*, 28:181–203, 1989.
6. M. Fernández. Type assignment and termination of interaction nets. *Mathematical Structures in Computer Science*, 8(6):593–636, 1998.
7. M. Fernández and I. Mackie. Coinductive techniques for operational equivalence of interaction nets. In *Proceedings of the 13th Annual IEEE Symposium on Logic in Computer Science (LICS'98)*, pages 321–332. IEEE Computer Society Press, 1998.
8. M. Fernández and I. Mackie. Interaction nets and term rewriting systems. *Theoretical Computer Science*, 190(1):3–39, 1998.
9. G. Gonthier, M. Abadi, and J.-J. Lévy. The geometry of optimal lambda reduction. In *Proceedings of the 19th ACM Symposium on Principles of Programming Languages (POPL'92)*, pages 15–26. ACM Press, 1992.
10. K. Honda. Types for dyadic interaction. In *CONCUR 93*, Lecture Notes in Computer Science. Springer-Verlag, 1993.
11. J.-W. Klop, V. van Oostrom, and F. van Raamsdonk. Combinatory reduction systems, introduction and survey. *Theoretical Computer Science*, 121:279–308, 1993.
12. Y. Lafont. Interaction nets. In *Proceedings of the 17th ACM Symposium on Principles of Programming Languages (POPL'90)*, pages 95–108. ACM Press, 1990.
13. J. Lamping. An algorithm for optimal lambda calculus reduction. In *Proceedings of the 17th ACM Symposium on Principles of Programming Languages (POPL'90)*, pages 16–30. ACM Press, 1990.
14. C. Laneve. *Optimality and Concurrency in Interaction Systems*. PhD thesis, Dipartmento di Informatica, Università degli Studi di Pisa, 1993.
15. I. Mackie. Static analysis of interaction nets for distributed implementations. In P. van Hentenryck, editor, *Proceedings of the 4th International Static Analysis*

Symposium (SAS'97), number 1302 in Lecture Notes in Computer Science, pages 217–231. Springer-Verlag, 1997.

16. I. Mackie. YALE: Yet another lambda evaluator based on interaction nets. In *Proceedings of the 3rd ACM SIGPLAN International Conference on Functional Programming (ICFP'98)*, pages 117–128. ACM Press, 1998.
17. J. S. Pinto. An abstract machine for interaction nets, 1999. École Polytechnique.
18. N. Yoshida. Graph notation for concurrent combinators. In *Proceedings of TPPP'94*, number 907 in Lecture Notes in Computer Science, pages 364–397. Springer-Verlag, 1995.
19. N. Yoshida. Minimality and separation results on asynchronous mobile processes: Representability theorems by concurrent combinators. In *Proceedings of CONCUR'98*, number 1466 in Lecture Notes in Computer Science, pages 131–146. Springer-Verlag, 1998.

Distributed Programming in a Multi-Paradigm Declarative Language*

Michael Hanus

Informatik II, RWTH Aachen, D-52056 Aachen, Germany
hanus@informatik.rwth-aachen.de

Abstract. Curry is a multi-paradigm declarative language covering functional, logic, and concurrent programming paradigms. Curry's operational semantics is based on lazy reduction of expressions extended by a possibly non-deterministic binding of free variables occurring in expressions. Moreover, constraints can be executed concurrently which provides for concurrent computation threads that are synchronized on logical variables. In this paper, we extend Curry's basic computational model by a few primitives to support distributed applications where a dynamically changing number of different program units must be coordinated. We develop these primitives as a special case of the existing basic model so that the new primitives interact smoothly with the existing features for search and concurrent computations. Moreover, programs with local concurrency can be easily transformed into distributed applications. This supports a simple development of distributed systems that are executable on local networks as well as on the Internet. In particular, sending partially instantiated messages containing logical variables is quite useful to implement reply messages. We demonstrate the power of these primitives by various programming examples.

1 Introduction

Curry [9,13] is a multi-paradigm declarative language which integrates functional, logic, and concurrent programming paradigms. Curry combines in a seamless way features from functional programming (nested expressions, lazy evaluation, higher-order functions), logic programming (logical variables, partial data structures, built-in search), and concurrent programming (concurrent evaluation of expressions with synchronization on logical variables). Moreover, Curry provides additional features in comparison to the pure paradigms (compared to functional programming: search, computing with partial information; compared to logic programming: more efficient evaluation due to the deterministic and demand-driven evaluation of functions) and amalgamates the most important operational principles developed in the area of integrated functional logic languages: "residuation" and "narrowing" (see [7] for a survey on functional logic programming).

* This research has been partially supported by the German Research Council (DFG) under grant Ha 2457/1-1 and by the DAAD under the PROCOPE programme.

G. Nadathur (Ed.): PPDP'99, LNCS 1702, pp. 188–205, 1999.

Curry's operational semantics is based on a single computation model, firstly described in [9], which combines lazy reduction of expressions with a possibly non-deterministic binding of free variables occurring in expressions. Thus, purely functional programming and purely logic programming are obtained as particular restrictions of this model. Moreover, impure features of Prolog (e.g., arithmetic, cut, I/O) are avoided and don't know non-deterministic computations can be encapsulated and controlled by the programmer [12]. For concurrent computations, the evaluation of functions can be suspended depending on the instantiation of arguments, and constraints can be executed concurrently. This provides an easy modeling of concurrent objects as functions synchronizing on a stream of messages. Based on this computation model, we propose to add a new kind of constraint to relate a multiset of incoming messages with a list containing these messages. Such port constraints have been proposed in the context of concurrent logic programming [16] for the local communication between objects. We generalize and embed them into the functional logic language Curry to obtain a simple but powerful mechanism to implement distributed applications that are executable on a network with an unknown number of communication partners.

The paper is structured as follows. In the next section, we review the basics of the operational model of Curry. We introduce and discuss the necessary extensions of this model to support distributed applications in Section 3. We demonstrate the use of these features by several examples in Section 4. Section 5 discusses some implementation issues and Section 6 relates our approach to other existing proposals before we conclude in Section 7.

2 Operational Semantics of Curry

In this section, we sketch the basic computation model of Curry. More details and a formal definition can be found in [9,13].

From a syntactic point of view, a Curry program is a functional program[1] extended by the possible inclusion of free (logical) variables in conditions and right-hand sides of defining rules. Thus, the basic computational domain of Curry consists of *data terms*, constructed from constants and data constructors, whose structure is specified by a set of *data type declarations* like

```
data Bool = True | False
data List a = [] | a : List a
```

`True` and `False` are the Boolean constants and `[]` (empty list) and : (non-empty list) are the constructors for polymorphic lists (`a` is a type variable and the type `List a` is usually written as `[a]` for conformity with Haskell). Then, a *data term* is a well-formed expression containing variables, constants, and data constructors, e.g., `True:[]` or `[x,y]` (the latter stands for `x:(y:[])`).

[1] Curry has a Haskell-like syntax [20], i.e., (type) variables and function names start with lowercase letters and the names of type and data constructors start with an uppercase letter. Moreover, the application of f to e is denoted by juxtaposition ("$f\ e$").

Functions are operations on data terms whose meaning is specified by (*conditional*) *rules* of the general form "l | c = r `where` vs `free`" where l has the form $f\, t_1 \ldots t_n$ with f being a function, $t_1, \ldots, t_n$ data terms and each variable occurs only once, the *condition* c is a constraint, r is a well-formed *expression* which may also contain function calls, and vs is the list of *free variables* that occur in c and r but not in l (the condition and the `where` parts can be omitted if c and vs are empty, respectively). A *constraint* is any expression of the built-in type `Constraint` where primitive constraints are equations of the form e_1 =:= e_2. A conditional rule can be applied if its condition is satisfiable. A *Curry program* is a set of data type declarations and rules.

Example 1. Assume that the above data type declarations are given. Then the following rules define the concatenation of lists, the last element of a list, and a constraint which is satisfied if the first list argument is a prefix of the second list argument:

```
conc [] ys = ys
conc (x:xs) ys = x : conc xs ys

last xs | conc ys [x] =:= xs = x where x,ys free

prefix ps xs = let ys free in conc ps ys =:= xs
```

If the equation "`conc ys [x] =:= xs`" is solvable, then `x` is the last element of the list `xs`. Similarly, `ps` is a prefix of `xs` if the equation "`conc ps ys =:= xs`" is solvable for some value `ys` (note that existentially quantified variables vs can be introduced in a constraint c by `let` vs `free in` c).

Functional programming: In functional languages, the interest is in computing *values* of expressions, where a value does not contain function symbols (i.e., it is a data term) and should be equivalent (w.r.t. the program rules) to the initial expression. The value can be computed by applying rules from left to right. For instance, we compute the value of "`conc [1] [2]`" by applying the rules for concatenation to this expression:

```
conc [1] [2] → 1 : (conc [] [2]) → [1,2]
```

To support computations with infinite data structures and a modular programming style by separating control aspects [14], Curry is based on a lazy (outermost) strategy, i.e., the selected function call in each reduction step is an outermost one among all reducible function calls. This strategy yields an optimal evaluation strategy [1] and a demand-driven search method [10] for the logic programming part that will be discussed next.

Logic programming: In logic languages, expressions (or constraints) may contain free variables. A logic programming system should compute solutions, i.e., find values for these variables such that the expression (or constraint) is reducible to some value (or satisfiable). Fortunately, it requires only a slight extension of the lazy reduction strategy to cover non-ground expressions and variable instantiation: if the value of a free variable is demanded by the left-hand sides of program rules in order to proceed the computation (i.e., no program rule is applicable if the variable remains unbound), the variable is non-deterministically bound to the different demanded values. For instance, if the function `f` is defined by the rules

```
f 0 = 2
f 1 = 3
```

(the integer numbers are considered as an infinite set of constants), then the expression "`f x`" with the free variable `x` is evaluated to `2` by binding `x` to `0`, or it is evaluated to `3` by binding `x` to `1`. Thus, a single computation step may yield a single new expression (*deterministic step*) or a disjunction of new expressions together with the corresponding bindings (*non-deterministic step*). For inductively sequential programs (these are, roughly speaking, function definitions without overlapping left-hand sides), this strategy, called *needed narrowing* [1], computes the shortest possible successful derivations (if common subterms are shared, as usual in implementations of lazy languages) and a minimal set of solutions, and it is fully deterministic if free variables do not occur.

Encapsulated search: Since functions in Curry have no side effects, the strategy to handle non-deterministic computations is not fixed in Curry (in contrast to Prolog which fixes a backtracking strategy). To provide flexible application-oriented search strategies and to avoid global backtracking like in Prolog which causes problems when integrated with I/O and concurrent computations, don't know non-deterministic computations can be encapsulated and controlled by the programmer [12]. For this purpose, a *search goal* is a lambda abstraction \\x->c where c is the constraint to be solved and x is the search variable occurring in c for which solutions should be computed. Based on a single language primitive to control non-deterministic computation steps, various search strategies can be defined (see [12] for details). For instance, **`findall`** computes the list of all solutions for a search goal with a depth-first strategy, i.e., the expression "**`findall \ps->prefix ps`** `[1,2]`" reduces to the list `[[],[1],[1,2]]` (w.r.t. the program in Example 1).

An important point in the treatment of encapsulated search is that (i) the search has only local effects and (ii) non-deterministic steps are only performed if they are unavoidable. To satisfy requirement (i), "global" variables (i.e., variables that are visible outside the search goal) are never bound in local search steps. To satisfy requirement (ii), a possible non-deterministic step in a search goal is suspended if the search goal contains a global variable (since binding this variable outside the search goal might make this step deterministic) or another deterministic step is possible. This corresponds to the *stability* requirement in AKL [15]. In the context of this paper, the important point is that non-deterministic steps are not performed if the search goal has a reference to some global variable. Since we shall model the coordination of distributed activities by partially instantiated global variables, non-deterministic steps are automatically avoided if they refer to global communication channels.

Constraints: In functional logic programs, it is necessary to solve equations between expressions containing defined functions (see Example 1). In general, an *equation* or *equational constraint* e_1`=:=`e_2 is satisfied if both sides e_1 and e_2 are reducible to the same value (data term). As a consequence, if both sides are undefined (non-terminating), then the equality does not hold (*strict equality* [5]). Operationally, an equational constraint e_1`=:=`e_2 is solved by evaluating e_1 and e_2 to unifiable data terms where the lazy evaluation of the expressions is interleaved with the binding of variables to constructor terms. Thus, an equational constraint e_1`=:=`e_2 without occurrences of defined functions has the same meaning (unification) as in Prolog. The basic kernel of Curry only provides equational constraints. Since it is conceptually fairly easy to add other constraint structures, extensions of Curry can provide richer constraint systems to support constraint logic programming applications. In this paper, we add one special kind of constraint ("port constraint", see Section 3) to enable the efficient sending of messages from different clients to a server.

Concurrent computations: To support flexible computation rules and avoid an uncontrolled instantiation of free argument variables, Curry provides the *suspension of a function call* if a demanded argument is not instantiated. Such functions are called *rigid* in contrast to *flexible* functions which instantiate their arguments if it is necessary to proceed their evaluation. As a default in Curry (which can be easily changed), constraints (i.e., functions with result type `Constraint`) are flexible and non-constraint functions are rigid. Thus, purely logic programs (where predicates correspond to constraints) behave as in Prolog, and purely functional programs are executed as in lazy functional languages like Haskell.

To continue computations in the presence of suspended function calls, constraints can be combined with the *concurrent conjunction* operator `&`, i.e., c_1 `&` c_2 is a constraint which is evaluated by solving c_1 and c_2 concurrently. There is also a *sequential conjunction* operator `&>`, i.e., the expression c_1 `&>` c_2 is evaluated by first evaluating c_1 and then c_2.

A design principle of Curry is the clear separation of sequential and concurrent activities. Sequential computations, which form the basic units of a program, can be expressed as usual functional (logic) programs, and they are composed to concurrent computation units via concurrent conjunctions of constraints. This separation supports the use of efficient and optimal evaluation strategies for the sequential parts, where similar techniques for the concurrent parts are not available. This is in contrast to other, more fine-grained concurrent computation models like AKL [15], CCP [22], or Oz [25]. In this paper, we extend the basic concurrent computation model to support distributed applications where different (external) clients interact.

Monadic I/O: Since the communication with external programs require some knowledge about performing I/O declaratively, we assume familiarity with the monadic I/O concept of Haskell [20,27] which is also used in Curry. Due to lack of space, we cannot describe it here in detail but it is sufficient to remember that I/O actions are sequentially composed by the operators `>>=` and `>>`, `putStrLn` is an action that prints its string argument to the output stream, and `done` is the empty action. Since disjunctive I/O actions as a result of a program are not reasonable, all possible search must be encapsulated between I/O operations, otherwise the entire program suspends.

3 From Concurrent to Distributed Computations

This section motivates the primitives which we add to Curry to support distributed applications. Since these primitives should smoothly interact with the basic computation model, in particular encapsulated search and local concurrent computations, we introduce them as a specialization of the existing features for concurrent object-oriented programming.

It is well known from concurrent logic programming [24] that (concurrent) objects can be easily implemented as predicates processing a stream of incoming messages. The internal state of the object is a parameter which may change in recursive calls when a message is processed. For instance, a counter object which understands the messages `Set` v, `Inc`, and `Get` v can be implemented in Curry as follows (the predefined type `Int` denotes the type of all integer values and `success` denotes the always satisfiable constraint):

```
data CounterMessage = Set Int | Inc | Get Int

counter eval rigid
counter _ (Set v : ms) = counter v ms
counter n (Inc : ms) = counter (n+1) ms
counter n (Get v : ms) = v=:=n & counter n ms
counter _ [] = success
```

The *evaluation annotation* "`counter eval rigid`" marks `counter` as a rigid function, i.e., an expression "`counter` n s" can reduce only if s is a bound variable. The first argument of `counter` is the current value of the counter and the second argument is the stream of messages. Thus, the evaluation of the constraint "`counter 0 s`" creates a new counter object with initial value 0 where messages are sent by instantiating the variable `s`. The final rule terminates the object if the stream of incoming messages is finished. For instance, the constraint

```
let s free in counter 0 s & s=:=[Set 41, Inc, Get x]
```

is successfully evaluated by binding `x` to the value 42. Although the stream variable `s` is instantiated at once to all messages in this simple example, it should be clear that messages can be individually sent by incrementally instantiating `s`.

If there is more than one process sending messages to the same counter object, it is necessary to merge the message streams from the different processes into a single message stream (otherwise, the processes must coordinate themselves for message sending). Since the processes work concurrently, the stream merger must be fair. A fair merger can be implemented in Curry as follows:

```
merge eval choice
merge (x:xs) ys = x : merge xs ys
merge xs (y:ys) = y : merge xs ys
merge [] ys = ys
merge xs [] = xs
```

The evaluation annotation `choice` has the effect that at most one rule is applied to a call to `merge` even if there is another applicable rule (where all alternatives are evaluated in a fair manner), i.e., this corresponds to a committed choice in concurrent logic languages. Although a committed choice restricts the declarative reading of programs and destroys the completeness results for the basic operational semantics [9], such or a similar construct is usually introduced to program reactive systems. Using the indeterministic `merge` function, we can create a counter that accepts messages from different clients:

```
counter 0 (merge s1 s2) & client1 s1 & client2 s2
```

If we want to access the counter object from n different clients, it is immediate to use $n-1$ mergers to combine the different message streams into a single one. It has been argued [16] that this causes a significant overhead due to the forwarding of incoming messages through the mergers. Moreover, this solution causes difficulties if the number of clients can change dynamically as in many distributed applications. Therefore, Janson et al. [16] proposed the use of ports to solve these problems. Ports provide a constant time message merging w.r.t. an arbitrary number of senders and a convenient way to dynamically extend the number of senders. Therefore, we also propose an extension of the base language by ports but embed this concept into concurrent functional logic programming (where Janson et al. proposed ports for the concurrent logic language AKL) and extend it to communication with external partners.

In principle, a *port* is a constraint between a multiset and a list that is satisfied if all elements in the multiset occur in the list and vice versa. A port is created by evaluating the constraint "`openPort p s`" where `p` and `s` are uninstantiated free variables. `p` and `s` will later be constrained to the multiset and list of elements, respectively. Since sending messages is done through `p`, `p` is often identified with the port and `s` is the stream of incoming messages. "`Port a`" denotes the type of a port to which messages of type `a` can be sent, i.e., `openPort` has the type definition

```
openPort :: Port a -> [a] -> Constraint
```

A message is sent to the port by evaluating the constraint "`send m p`" which constrains (in constant time) `p` and the corresponding stream `s` to hold the element `m`. From a logic programming point of view, the stream `s` has always an uninstantiated variable `s_tail` at the end and evaluating the `send` constraint means evaluating the constraint

```
let s_tail1 free in s_tail =:= (m : s_tail1)
```

Thus, the new message is appended at the end of the stream by instantiating the current open end of the stream. Since the instantiation is done by solving

a strict equation (compare Section 2), it is also evident that the message `m` is evaluated before sending it ("strict communication", like in Eden [3]). If the communication were lazy, the lazy evaluation of messages at the receiver's side would cause a communication overhead.
Using ports, we can rewrite our counter example with two clients as

```
openPort p s &> counter 0 s & client1 p & client2 p
```

Thus, the code for the object remains unchanged but we have to replace the instantiation of the streams in the clients by calls to the **send** constraint.

This approach to communication between different processes has remarkable consequences:

- It has a logical reading, i.e., communication is not done by predicates or functions with side effects (like, e.g., the socket library of Sicstus-Prolog) but can be described as instantiation of logical variables and constraint solving. Thus, the operational semantics of our communication primitives is a simple extension of the operational semantics of the base language.
- It interacts smoothly with the operational principles of the base language. For instance, local search and non-deterministic computations are only possible if the search goal contains no reference to global variables (compare Section 2). Thus, it is impossible to send messages to global ports inside local search computations or to split a server object into two non-deterministic computation threads. This is perfectly intended, since backtracking on network-oriented applications or copying server processes to interact with non-deterministic clients is difficult to implement.
- It provides an efficient implementation since message sending can be implemented without forwarding through several mergers and the senders have no reference to old messages, i.e., the multiset of the port must not be explicitly stored.
- Partially instantiated messages containing free variables (e.g., message "`Get x`") provide an elegant approach to return values to the sender without explicitly creating reply channels.
- The number of senders can be dynamically extended—every process which gets access to the port reference (the multiset variable) can send messages to the port. This property can be exploited in many distributed applications (see below).

Up to now, we can use ports only inside one program (similarly to [16]) but for many distributed applications (like Internet servers) it is necessary to communicate between different programs. Therefore, we introduce two operations to create and connect to *external ports*, i.e., ports that are accessible from outside. Since the connections of ports to the outside world changes the environment of the program, these operations are introduced as I/O actions (see Section 2).

The I/O action "`openNamedPort` n" creates a new external port with name n and returns the stream of incoming messages. If this action is executed on machine m (where m is a symbolic Internet name), the port (but not the stream of incoming messages) is now globally accessible as "n`@`m" by other applications.

On the client side, the I/O action "`connectPort` *pn*" returns the external port which has the symbolic name *pn* so that clients can send messages to this port. For instance, to create a globally accessible "counter server", we add the following definitions to our counter:

```
main = openNamedPort "counter" >>= counter_server
counter_server s | counter 0 s = done
```

If we execute `main` on the machine `medoc.cs.rwth.de`, we can implement a client by

```
client port_name msg = connectPort port_name >>= sendPort msg
sendPort msg p | send msg p = done
```

and increment the global counter by evaluating

```
client "counter@medoc.cs.rwth.de" Inc
```

Before we present some more interesting examples, we introduce a final primitive which has no declarative meaning but is useful in real distributed applications. Since the communication over networks is unsafe and a selected server could be down or may not respond in a given period of time, one want to take another action (for instance, choosing a different server or inform the user) if this happens. Therefore, we introduce a temporal constraint "`after` t" which is satisfied t milliseconds after the constraint has been checked for the first time, i.e., "`after 0`" is immediately satisfied. Typically, this temporal constraint is used as an alternative in a committed choice like in

```
getAnswer eval choice
getAnswer (msg:_) = msg
getAnswer _ | after 5000 = <take an alternative action>
```

For instance, if `getAnswer` is called with a stream of a port as an argument, it returns the first message if it is received within five seconds, otherwise an alternative action is taken.

The following type definitions summarizes the proposed new primitives to support the development of distributed applications:

```
-- open an internal port for messages of type "a":
openPort :: Port a -> [a] -> Constraint

send :: a -> Port a -> Constraint -- send message to port

-- open a new external port, return stream of messages:
openNamedPort :: String -> IO [a]

-- connect to external port, return port for sending messages:
connectPort :: String -> IO (Port a)

after :: Int -> Constraint -- timeout
```

4 Examples

In this section, we demonstrate the use of the primitives for distributed applications introduced in the previous section. In order to avoid presenting all the tedious details of such applications, we have simplified the examples so that we concentrate on the communication structures.

4.1 A Name Server

The first example represents a class of client/server applications where the server holds some database which is requested by the clients. For the sake of simplicity, we consider a simple name server which stores an assignment from symbolic names to numbers. It understands the messages "`PutName` n i" to store the name n with number i and "`GetName` n i" to retrieve the number i associated to the name n. The name server is implemented as a function which has the assignment from names to numbers as the first argument (function `n2i` below) and the incoming messages as the second argument (initially, `0` is assigned to all names by the lambda abstraction `\_->0`):

```
nameserver = openNamedPort "nameserver" >>= ns_loop \_->0

ns_loop n2i (GetName n i : ms) | i=:=(n2i n) = ns_loop n2i ms
ns_loop n2i (PutName n i : ms) = ns_loop new_n2i ms
where new_n2i m = if m==n then i else n2i m
```

In the first rule of `ns_loop`, the (usually uninstantiated) variable `i` is instantiated with the number assigned to the name `n` by solving the equational constraint in the condition. In the second rule, a modified assignment map `new_n2i` is passed to the recursive call. If we evaluate `nameserver` on the machine `medoc.cs.rwth.de`, then we can add the assignment of the name `talk` to the number 42 by evaluating

```
client "nameserver@medoc.cs.rwth.de" (PutName "talk" 42)
```

on some machine connected to the Internet (where `client` was defined in Section 3). After this assignment, the evaluation of

```
client "nameserver@medoc.cs.rwth.de" (GetName "talk" x)
```

binds the free variable `x` to the value 42.

Note that the sending of messages containing free variables is an elegant way to return values to the sender. Here we exploit the fact that the base language is an integrated functional logic language which can deal with logical variables. Functional languages extended for distributed programming like Eden [3], Erlang [2], or Goffin [4] require the explicit creation or sending of reply channels.

An extension of our name server should demonstrate the advantages of using logical variables in messages. Consider a hierarchical name server organization: if the local name server has no entry for the requested name (i.e., the assigned number is the initial value `0`), it forwards this request to another name server. This can be easily expressed by changing the first rule of `ns_loop` to

```
ns_loop n2i (GetName n i : ms)
| if (n2i n)==0 then send (GetName n i) master else i=:=(n2i n)
= ns_loop n2i ms
```

It is assumed that **master** is the port of the other name server to which the request is forwarded. Note that the local name server can immediately proceed its service after forwarding the request to the master server and need not to wait for the answer from the master since the master becomes responsible for binding the free variable in the **GetName** message.

If the requested name server is down so that no answer is returned, one would like to inform the user about this fact instead of an infinite waiting. This can be easily implemented with a temporal constraint by the following function:

```
showAnswer eval choice
showAnswer ans | ans==ans = show ans
showAnswer _  | after 10000 = "No answer from name server"
```

"$t_1 == t_2$" denotes strict equality on ground data terms like in Haskell, i.e., if t_1 or t_2 reduces to a data term containing an uninstantiated variable, the evaluation of this equality is suspended until the variable has been bound to some ground data term. Thus, "`showAnswer` x" yields a string representation of the value of x if it evaluates to a ground data term or it yields the string `"No answer from name server"` if x has not been bound to a ground term within ten seconds. Thus, the evaluation of

```
client "nameserver@medoc.cs.rwth.de" (GetName "talk" x)
>> putStrLn (showAnswer x)
```

prints the value assigned to `talk` or the required timeout message.

4.2 Talk

The next example shows a distributed application between two partners where both of them act as a server as well as a client. The application is a simplification of the well known Unix "talk" program. Here we consider only the main talk activity (and not the calling of the partner via the talk daemon) where each partner program must do the following (we assume that each partner has an external *talk port* with symbolic name `talk` to receive the messages from the partner):

- If the user inputs a line on the keyboard (which is transmitted through the port with symbolic name `stdin`), this line is sent to the talk port of the partner.
- If the program receives a line from the partner through its own talk port, this line (preceded by '`*`') is shown at the screen by the I/O action `putStrLn`.

Since the sequence of both events is not known in advance, the standard input port as well as the talk port must be examined in parallel. For this purpose, we use a committed choice. Thus, the talk program consists of a loop function `tloop`

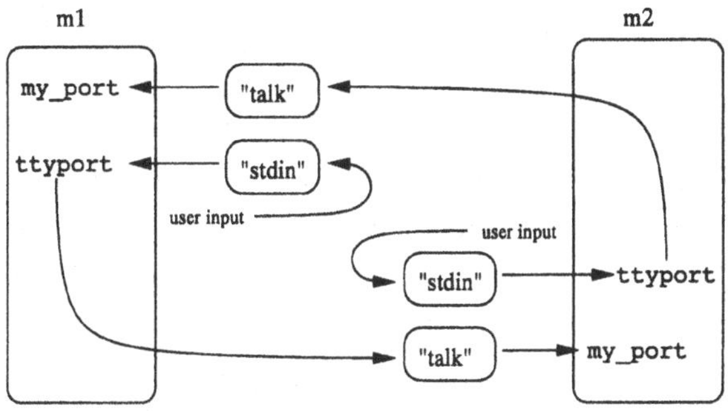

Fig. 1. Communication structure of the talk program

which has three arguments: the talk port of the partner, the stream connected to the own standard input, and the stream connected to the own talk port:

```
tloop eval choice
tloop your tty (m:ms) = putStrLn ('*':m) >> tloop your tty ms
tloop your (m:ms) my = sendPort m your >> tloop your ms my
```

The `tloop` is activated by the following main program:[2]

```
talk your_portname = do my_port <- openNamedPort "talk"
tty_port <- openNamedPort "stdin"
your_port <- connectPort your_portname
tloop your_port tty_port my_port
```

If a user on machine `m1` wants to talk with the user on machine `m2`, they must evaluate

on machine `m1`: `talk "talk@m2"`
on machine `m2`: `talk "talk@m1"`

The communication structure created by these calls is shown in Fig. 1.

4.3 A Computation Server

Since our communication through ports is strict, i.e., messages are evaluated before sending them (cf. Section 3), there is no direct way to distribute computational work like remote procedure calls (RPCs) where procedures are evaluated at some other node in the network. Although port communication corresponds to message passing, we can easily implement RPCs using the higher-order features of the base language. For instance, a computation server, i.e., a process running on some node in the network offering to execute some work by evaluating functions, can be implemented as a function accepting messages containing triples (f, x, y) where f is a function to be applied to the actual argument x

[2] Here we make use of Haskell's `do` notation [20] where "`do` p_1`<-`e_1`;`...`,`p_n`<-`e_n`;`e" is syntactic sugar for "e_1 `>>=` `\`p_1`->`...e_n `>>=` `\`p_n`->`e".

and y is a free variable which is instantiated with the result of $f\,x$. Thus, the entire computation server can be implemented as follows:

```
start_compserver = openNamedPort "compserver" >>= compserver
compserver ((f,x,y) : ms) | y=:=(f x) = compserver ms
```

If `prime` is a function to compute the n-th prime number, we can use this computation server to compute prime numbers, e.g., the execution of

```
client "compserver@cs" (prime,1000,p)
```

binds the free variable p to the 1000th prime number where the computation is performed on the node `cs` where the server has been started. This remarkable simple implementation needs some comments.

1. In Section 2, we introduced the constraint `=:=` as equality on data terms and, thus, it might be unclear how we can send functional objects in messages. For this purpose, we consider partially applied functions, i.e., functions where the number of actual arguments is less than their arity, as data terms since they are not evaluable. This is conform with standard methods to add higher-order features to logic programming [28] and theoretically justified for lazy functional logic languages in [6]. As a consequence, an equation like "`x=:=prime`" is solved by binding the variable x to the function name `prime`. Since partially applied function calls are considered as data terms, the code implementing the function is not immediately sent in the above message but it will be transferred from the client to the server when the server evaluates it (dynamic code fetching).
2. The RPC is asynchronously performed since the client sends its request without explicitly waiting for the answer. The client can proceed with other computations as long as it does not need the result of this call which is passed back through the third argument of the message. Thus, the free result variable is similar to a "promise" which has been proposed by Liskov and Shrira [17] to overcome the disadvantages of synchronous RPCs. A promise is a special place holder for a future return value from an RPC. Since we can use the logic part of the base language for this purpose, no linguistic extension is necessary to implement asynchronous RPCs.
3. The attentive reader might raise the question what happens if the execution of the transmitted function causes a non-deterministic computation step. Does the server split into two disjunctive branches? This does not happen since, as mentioned at the end of Section 2, non-deterministic steps between I/O actions are suspended. One method to avoid this suspension is to return only the first solution to the sender. This can be done by encapsulating the search, i.e., we could replace the constraint "`y=:=(f x)`" by the expression

```
y =:= head (findall \z -> z=:=(f x))
```

A disadvantage of the above computation server is the fact that the complete server is blocked if the evaluation of a single RPC is suspended or takes a long time. Fortunately, it is very simple to provide a concurrent version of this server using the concurrency features of the base language. For this purpose, we turn the server function into a constraint and evaluate the RPC in parallel to the main server process:

```
start_compserver = openNamedPort "compserver" >>= serve
where serve ms | compserver ms = done

compserver eval rigid³
compserver ((f,x,y) : ms)  =  y=:=(f x) & compserver ms
```

4.4 Encrypting Messages

To support more security during message sending, messages should be encrypted before sending. For this purpose, public key methods are often used. The idea of public key methods is to encode a message with a key before sending and to decode the message with another key after receiving. Both keys must be chosen in a way so that decoding the encoded message gives the original message back. Since the coding algorithm as well as one key are publicly known, it is essential for the security of the method to choose keys that are large enough.

In the following, we use a similar idea but functions instead of keys, i.e., the encoding algorithm as well as the key is put into a single function. Thus, one has to choose a public encrypt function e and a private decrypt function d so that $d(e(m)) = m$ for all messages m (the additional property $e(d(m)) = m$ would be necessary for authentication).

As a simple example, we show a server which processes requests and returns the answers encrypted. The public encrypt function is sent together with the message. This has the advantage that for each message and client, another encryption can be used. Since there are a huge number of encrypt/decrypt function pairs, the functions could be relatively simple without sacrificing security. Similarly to the computation server, this server receives triples (*e*,*rq*,*rs*) where *e* is the public encrypt function, *rq* is the request to the server and *rs* will be instantiated to the encrypted result (the unspecified function `computeanswer` determines the main activity of the server):

```
start_crypticserver = openNamedPort "cryptserver" >>= cserver

cserver ((encode,rq,rs) : ms) | rs =:= encode(computeanswer rq)
   = cserver ms
```

For strings, i.e., lists of characters, the pair `rev/rev` (list reversing) is a simple encrypt/decrypt pair. Thus, we can send a request to the server and decode the answer by

```
client "cryptserver@cs" (rev,"Question...",y) >> show (rev y)
```

Although this example is simplified, it should be obvious that further features like authentication can be easily added.

[3] The rigid annotation is necessary since constraints are flexible by default in Curry.

5 Implementation

The full implementation of the presented concepts is ongoing. We have tested the examples in this paper with a prototypical implementation of Curry based on Sicstus-Prolog. In this implementation, we used the socket library of Sicstus-Prolog to implement the port communication via sockets. Free variables sent in messages are implemented by dynamic reply channels on which the receiver sends the value back if the variable is instantiated.

Currently, we are working on a more efficient implementation based on the compiler from Curry into Java described in [11]. In this implementation, we use the distribution facilities of Java to implement our communication model. In particular, we use Java's RMI model to implement ports. Sending a message amounts to binding a free variable (the stream connected to the port) by a method call on the remote machine. Free variables sent in messages reside in the sender's computation space and if the receiver binds this variable, he calls a remote method on the sender's machine to bind this variable. The implementation of functional objects sent in messages is more advanced. It could be implemented by sending a reference to the code that implements this function. If the function is applied and evaluated by the receiver, the function code is dynamically loaded from the sender to the receiver (dynamic code fetching).

6 Related Work

Since features for concurrent and distributed programming become important for many applications, there are a various approaches to extend functional or logic programming languages with such features. In the following, we relate our proposal to some of the existing ones.

Initiated by Japan's fifth generation project, various approaches to add concurrency features to logic programming [23] have been proposed culminating in Saraswat's framework for concurrent constraint programming [22]. Usually, these approaches consider only concurrency inside an application but provide no features for connecting different programs to a distributed system. The concurrent logic language AKL [15] also supports only concurrency inside a program but proposed ports [16] for the efficient communication between objects. Ports have been also adapted to Oz [25] where it has been also embedded into a framework for distributing the computational activities over a network [26]. In contrast to our approach, ports are not a primitive constraint but are implemented by the stateful features of Oz. All these languages are strict (and untyped) while our proposal combines optimal lazy reduction for the sequential computation parts with strict communication between the distributed and concurrent entities.

Concurrent Haskell [21] extends the lazy functional language Haskell by methods to start processes inside an application and synchronize them with mutable variables, but facilities for distribution are not provided. Closest to our approach w.r.t. the communication features are Erlang [2] and an extension of Goffin [4]. Erlang is a concurrent functional language developed for telecommunication applications. Processes in Erlang can communicate over a network via symbolic names which provides for communication between different applications. In contrast to our proposal, Erlang is a strict and untyped language and provides no features for logic programming. Thus, partial messages can not be sent so that explicit reply channels (process identifiers) must be included in messages where answers should be sent back. The extension of Goffin described in [4] extends a lazy typed concurrent functional language by a port model for internal and external communication. Although it uses logical variables for synchronization, it does not provide typical logic programming features like search for solutions. Differently to our proposal for communication, partial messages including logical variables are not supported, the creation of connections to external ports is not integrated in the I/O monad (and, hence, I/O operations like reading/writing files can not be used in a distributed program) and, once a port is made public on the network, every node can not only send messages to this port but can also read all messages incoming at this port. The latter property may cause security problems for many distributed applications. This is avoided in our proposal by allowing only one server process to read the incoming messages at an external port.

7 Conclusions

We have proposed an extension of the concurrent functional logic language Curry that supports a simple implementation of distributed applications. This extension is based on communication via ports. The important point is that the meaning of port communication can be described in terms of computation with constraints. This has the consequence that (i) the communication mechanism interacts smoothly with the existing language features for search and concurrency so that all these features can be used to program server applications, and (ii) existing programs can be fairly easy integrated into a distributed environment. Moreover, the use of logical variables in partially instantiated messages is quite useful to avoid complicated communication structures with reply channels. Nevertheless, external communication ports can be given a symbolic name so that they can be passed in messages as in the π-calculus [18]. We have demonstrated the appropriateness and feasibility of our language extensions by implementing several distributed applications. As far as we know, this is the first approach which combines functional logic programming based on a lazy (optimal) evaluation strategy with features for concurrent and distributed programming.

For future work, we will investigate the application of program analysis techniques to ensure the safe execution of distributed applications. For instance, deadlock exclusion can be approximated by checking groundness of relevant variables [8] or the non-conflicting use of free variables transmitted in messages could be ensured by proving that they are instantiated by at most one receiver.

Acknowledgements.

The author is grateful to Frank Steiner and Philipp Niederau for many discussions and comments on this paper and for providing the implementation of the talk program.

References

1. S. Antoy, R. Echahed, and M. Hanus. A Needed Narrowing Strategy. In *Proc. 21st ACM Symp. on Principles of Programming Languages*, pp. 268–279, 1994.
2. J. Armstrong, M. Williams, C. Wikstrom, and R. Virding. *Concurrent Programming in Erlang*. Prentice Hall, 1996.
3. S. Breitinger, R. Loogen, and Y. Ortega-Mallen. Concurrency in Functional and Logic Programming. In *Fuji International Workshop on Functional and Logic Programming*. World Scientific Publ., 1995.
4. M.M.T. Chakravarty, Y. Guo, and M. Köhler. Distributed Haskell: Goffin on the Internet. In *Proc. of the Third Fuji International Symposium on Functional and Logic Programming*. World Scientific, 1998.
5. E. Giovannetti, G. Levi, C. Moiso, and C. Palamidessi. Kernel LEAF: A Logic plus Functional Language. *Journal of Computer and System Sciences*, Vol. 42, No. 2, pp. 139–185, 1991.
6. J.C. González-Moreno, M.T. Hortalá-González, and M. Rodríguez-Artalejo. A Higher Order Rewriting Logic for Functional Logic Programming. In *Proc. Int. Conference on Logic Programming (ICLP'97)*, pp. 153–167. MIT Press, 1997.
7. M. Hanus. The Integration of Functions into Logic Programming: From Theory to Practice. *Journal of Logic Programming*, Vol. 19&20, pp. 583–628, 1994.
8. M. Hanus. Analysis of Residuating Logic Programs. *Journal of Logic Programming*, Vol. 24, No. 3, pp. 161–199, 1995.
9. M. Hanus. A Unified Computation Model for Functional and Logic Programming. In *Proc. 24th ACM Symp. Principles of Programming Languages*, pp. 80–93, 1997.
10. M. Hanus and P. Réty. Demand-driven Search in Functional Logic Programs. Research Report RR-LIFO-98-08, Univ. Orléans, 1998.
11. M. Hanus and R. Sadre. An Abstract Machine for Curry and its Concurrent Implementation in Java. *Journal of Functional and Logic Programming*, 1999(6).
12. M. Hanus and F. Steiner. Controlling Search in Declarative Programs. In *Principles of Declarative Programming*, pp. 374–390. Springer LNCS 1490, 1998.
13. M. Hanus (ed.). Curry: An Integrated Functional Logic Language (Vers. 0.5). Available at `http://www-i2.informatik.rwth-aachen.de/~hanus/curry`, 1999.
14. J. Hughes. Why Functional Programming Matters. In D.A. Turner, editor, *Research Topics in Functional Programming*, pp. 17–42. Addison Wesley, 1990.
15. S. Janson and S. Haridi. Programming Paradigms of the Andorra Kernel Language. In *Proc. 1991 Int. Logic Programming Symposium*, pp. 167–183. MIT Press, 1991.
16. S. Janson, J. Montelius, and S. Haridi. Ports for Objects in Concurrent Logic Programs. In *Research Directions in Concurrent Object-Oriented Programming*. MIT Press, 1993.
17. B. Liskov and L. Shrira. Promises: Linguistic Support for Efficient Asynchronous Procedure Calls in Distributed Systems. In *Proc. SIGPLAN'88 Conference on Programming Language Design and Implementation*, pp. 260–267, 1988.

18. R. Milner, J. Parrow, and D. Walker. A calculus of mobile processes, Parts I and II. *Information and Computation*, Vol. 100, pp. 1–77, 1992.
19. J.J. Moreno-Navarro and M. Rodríguez-Artalejo. Logic Programming with Functions and Predicates: The Language BABEL. *Journal of Logic Programming*, Vol. 12, pp. 191–223, 1992.
20. J. Peterson et al. Haskell: A Non-strict, Purely Functional Language (Version 1.4). Technical Report, Yale University, 1997.
21. S.L. Peyton Jones, A. Gordon, and S. Finne. Concurrent Haskell. In *Proc. 23rd ACM Symp. on Principles of Programming Languages*, pp. 295–308, 1996.
22. V.A. Saraswat. *Concurrent Constraint Programming.* MIT Press, 1993.
23. E. Shapiro. The family of concurrent logic programming languages. *ACM Computing Surveys*, Vol. 21, No. 3, pp. 412–510, 1989.
24. E. Shapiro and A. Takeuchi. Object Oriented Programming in Concurrent Prolog. In *Concurrent Prolog: Collected Papers*, volume 2, pp. 251–273. MIT Press, 1987.
25. G. Smolka. The Oz Programming Model. In *Computer Science Today: Recent Trends and Developments*, pp. 324–343. Springer LNCS 1000, 1995.
26. P. Van Roy, S. Haridi, P. Brand, G. Smolka, M. Mehl, and R. Scheidhauer. Mobile Objects in Distributed Oz. *ACM TOPLAS*, 19(5), pp. 804–851, 1997.
27. P. Wadler. How to Declare an Imperative. In *Proc. of the 1995 International Logic Programming Symposium*, pp. 18–32. MIT Press, 1995.
28. D.H.D. Warren. Higher-order extensions to PROLOG: are they needed? In *Machine Intelligence 10*, pp. 441–454, 1982.

Logical and Meta-Logical Frameworks
(Abstract)

Frank Pfenning

Carnegie Mellon University
School of Computer Science
fp@cs.cmu.edu

Logical frameworks have been designed as meta-languages in which deductive systems can be specified naturally and concisely. By providing direct support for common concepts of logics and programming languages, framework implementations such as Isabelle allow the rapid construction of theorem proving environments for specific logics. Logical frameworks have found significant applications in a variety of areas, including program and protocol verification and safe execution of mobile code.

Recently, researchers have exploited the directness of encodings of deductive systems in logical frameworks to reason not only *within* but *about* logics. At the core of these efforts lies the design and implementation of *meta-logical frameworks*—languages in which properties of logical systems can be expressed and proven.

In this tutorial talk we first provide a brief introduction to the central techniques of logical frameworks. We then analyze the requirements for meta-logical frameworks and sketch and compare three different approaches: inductive definitions [1], definitional reflection [2], and dependent pattern matching and recursion [3]. The last appears to be most amenable to automation and we discuss its design and implementation in the Twelf system in more detail. Recent successful experiments with this implementation include automatic proofs of cut-elimination for full first-order intuitionistic logic, the diamond property for parallel reduction in the untyped λ-calculus, and the soundness and completeness of uniform derivations for hereditary Harrop formulas.

References

1. David A. Basin and Robert L. Constable. Metalogical frameworks. In G. Huet and G. Plotkin, editors, *Logical Environments*, pages 1–29. Cambridge University Press, 1993.
2. Raymond McDowell and Dale Miller. A logic for reasoning with higher-order abstract syntax: An extended abstract. In Glynn Winskel, editor, *Proceedings of the Twelfth Annual Symposium on Logic in Computer Science*, pages 434–445, Warsaw, Poland, June 1997.
3. Carsten Schürmann and Frank Pfenning. Automated theorem proving in a simple meta-logic for LF. In Claude Kirchner and Hélène Kirchner, editors, *Proceedings of the 15th International Conference on Automated Deduction (CADE-15)*, pages 286–300, Lindau, Germany, July 1998. Springer-Verlag LNCS 1421.

G. Nadathur (Ed.): PPDP'99, LNCS 1702, pp. 206–206, 1999.

A Simple and General Method for Integrating Abstract Interpretation in SICStus

Dante Baldan*, Nicola Civran, Gilberto Filé **, and Francesco Pulvirenti

Department of Pure and Applied Mathematics, University of Padova
Via Belzoni 7, 35131 - Padova - Italy {dante,gilberto}@math.unipd.it

Abstract. We study the problem of producing a good compiler for Prolog that generates efficient code for its input programs on the basis of the information inferred by a static analysis of those programs.
The main contribution of our work is to show that in many cases such an optimizing compiler can be obtained by a simple modification of an already existing Prolog compiler.
Our general method is illustrated by describing how the SICStus compiler has been modified in such a way that it uses information about uninitialized variables in order to generate better code than that it would generate without that information. We give tables that measure the costs and advantages of producing that optimizing SICStus compiler. In order to show the generality of our approach, we present also the design of a simple modification of SICStus compiler incorporating recursively dereferenced variables.

Keywords: Abstract Interpretation, Logic Programming, WAM.

1 Introduction

Since the 60's some form of data flow or static analysis has been included in compilers in order to generate efficient code. However, those analyses were in general *ad hoc* and no general theory existed till the pioneering work of the Cousots [4]. The general theory introduced by the Cousots, called *abstract interpretation*, is fundamental both for facilitating the design of static analyses and for proving their correctness. Abstract interpretation has been applied to all programming paradigms. The language Prolog has been extensively studied in this respect because there is a number of interesting run-time properties of that language that can be captured by static analyses. Unfortunately, it has been produced a very limited number of optimizing Prolog compilers using those static analyses. We are aware of only two such compilers: the Aquarius of Van Roy [13] and the PARMA of Taylor [12]. These two compilers have been very valuable for showing the impact that static analysis could have in generating efficient code, however, they are "academic" compilers much less efficient than industrial Prolog compilers such as, for instance, the Quintus and SICStus compilers. Therefore, these

* Phone: + 39 049 827 58 99, Fax: + 39 049 875 85 96
** Phone: + 39 049 827 5989

G. Nadathur (Ed.): PPDP'99, LNCS 1702, pp. 207–223, 1999.

works have had a very limited impact on the people using Prolog for industrial applications.

We have followed a different approach: instead of constructing a new optimizing compiler from scratch, we have modified an already existing industrial compiler in such a way that it can cooperate with a static analyzer in order to generate better code.

The compiler that we have transformed in this way is the SICStus compiler and we have made it cooperate with several analyses that infer different run-time properties (uninitialized variables and variable safeness). The work presented in this paper is actually the final part of a broader project that includes also the formal design of those static analyses within the Cousots' abstract interpretation framework and the proof of their correctness. The complete account of this project can be found in [2].

For showing the generality of our approach, we describe in this paper how static analyzers inferring information about *uninitialized variables* and *recursively dereferenced variables* can be incorporated within SICStus. A variable is uninitialized if its store location (in the WAM architecture) needs not be initialized when that variable is first encountered, [13]. We give experimental evaluation for proving the effectiveness of our integration of *uninitialized variables* within SICStus. A variable is recursively dereferenced if the store location (in the WAM architecture) containing its value can be accessed directly, i.e., without indirect addressing [13]. Moreover, if the value of that variable is a compound term then also the arguments of that term have to be recursively dereferenced.

The method illustrated by these examples can be also followed in other cases (as we have done in [2]), but there are cases in which it becomes less convenient: it is convenient when the optimization supported by the information produced by a static analysis, does not require an important change in the abstract machine model underlying a compiler. For the SICStus compiler the underlying abstract machine is the Warren Abstract Machine (WAM), [1]. For instance, the optimization of SICStus supported by an uninitialized variable analysis requires, as described later, the introduction of some new operations (specializing the traditional WAM operations), with no change to the basic WAM architecture of the SICStus compiler.

An example of information whose use could not be integrated easily into SICStus is that concerning *uninitialized registers* that are used to store output values when returning from a procedure call, [13]. The use of these registers interferes with last call optimization and environment trimming, [3]. Thus, probably in this case the approach, followed by Van Roy, of defining a new abstract machine (called the BAM) and constructing a new compiler adopting that architecture, is the most appropriate.

We think that our work is a useful step towards two important goals:

1. The production of efficient optimizing compilers exploiting sophisticated static analyses that are formally defined and proven correct and that are also really competitive with the industrial compilers used in Prolog applications.

2. The definition of a general method (eventually supported by software tools) for integrating static analyzers within a (good) compiler. The ability of performing rapidly such integrations would be very important for testing quickly the practical value of new static analyses.

The rest of the paper is organized as follows. Section 2 contains an example illustrating how uninitialized variables are detected and used. Section 3 describes briefly the implementation of our analyzer for detecting uninitialized variables and gives the details of the integration of that analyzer into SICStus Compiler and Emulator. Section 4 presents some statistical evaluations of our version of SICStus. Sections 5 and 6 show that the method presented in Section 3 can be applied also for incorporating recursively dereferenced variables in SICStus. Finally Section 7 closes this paper.

2 Uninitialized Variable Analysis of `nreverse/2`

In a Prolog program a variable is *uninitialized* [13], when in all computations it just receive a non-variable value, i.e., a compound term or a constant. As usual in the WAM architecture, those variables are assigned a store cell, but clearly those cells need not be initialized because they will immediately later be assigned a value.

In what follows, by means of a simple example, we will show that the knowledge that a Prolog program contains uninitialized variables supports a significant optimization of the code we can generate for that program.

The example we consider is the program P that defines the (naïve) reverse of a list. The program P is given below in a convenient form in which every atom has distinct variables in its argument positions.

```
cl0 :  main :- V1 = [1,2,3,4,5,6,7,8,9,10,11,12,13,14,15,16,17,18,
                     19,20,21,22,23,24,25,26,27,28,29,30],
                     nreverse(V1,V2).
cl1 :  nreverse(V1,V2) :- V1 = [], V2 = [].
cl2 :  nreverse(V1,V2) :- V1 = [V3|V4], nreverse(V4,V5), V6 = [V3],
                          append(V5,V6,V2).
cl3 :  append(V1,V2,V3) :- V1 = [], V2 = V3.
cl4 :  append(V1,V2,V3) :- V1 = [V4|V5], V3 = [V4|V6],
                           append(V5,V2,V6).
```

Through a static analysis of this program one can detect that the second argument of `nreverse/2` and the third argument of append/3 are uninitialized variables. This result is found using the analyzer described in [2], the analyzer of [13] and that described in [7].

Let us explain intuitively why this result is correct. An analysis starts from predicate `main/0` and simulates the SLD resolution [8]. Predicate `nreverse/2` is called, in `cl0`, with its second argument V2 free and unaliased.

Clearly, `cl1` binds the second argument of `nreverse/2` to the empty list. For `cl2`, it is also immediate to see that in the recursive call of `nreverse/2` the second argument is again free and unaliased. However, some more thinking is needed for deriving that the second argument of the head of cl2 is bound to a non variable value by the call of append/3.

In order to see this fact, the analyzer must discover that append/3 is always called with the second argument bound to a non variable value and with the third argument free and unaliased. This fact, together with cl3 implies that the third argument of append/3 is uninitialized. Thus, the third argument of append/3 will be bound to a non variable value when returning from every call executed in P. This holds in particular for the call in the body of cl2 and hence the second argument of the head of cl2 gets assigned a non variable value.

From the definition of uninitialized variables given before, it follows directly that any static analysis aiming at inferring this information, has to infer also information about the variables that are bound to non variable values. In fact, all uninitialized variable analyses we know of, i.e., our analysis, [2], that of Van Roy [13] and that of Lindgren [7], compute also that information [1]. More precisely, our abstract domain is the set of 3-tuples (N, F, U) of sets of program variables such that:

- N is the set of variables having a non-variable value;
- F is the set of free and unaliased variables;
- U is the set of uninitialized variables;
- $N \cap F = \emptyset$;
- $U \subseteq N$.

We say that $(N_1, F_1, U_1) \leq (N_2, F_2, U_2)$ if $N_2 \subseteq N_1$, $F_2 \subseteq F_1$, $U_2 \subseteq U_1$, and, for having a complete lattice, we add a bottom element $\bot$ such that $\forall (N, F, U) : \bot \leq (N, F, U)$. The definition of a formal semantics and operations on our abstract domain can be found in [2].

In the following section we will describe how uninitialized variables support the generation of optimized code for the program P presented above.

2.1 Use of Uninitialized Variables

It is immediate from the definition of uninitialized variables that, when we know that some variable of a program is uninitialized, we can avoid to initialize that variable. This amounts to substituting the normal put instruction, that would be used to create a memory location for that variable, with a new specialized and more efficient put instruction that does not initialize the location assigned to that variable. As a matter of fact, the situation is a bit more complicated than this: as explained below, also specialized get instructions are needed. However, the point we want to stress is that new instructions are a completely straightforward specialization of the corresponding original WAM instructions.

Let us consider again program P given in Section 2. In a normal compilation of that program, the variable V2 of clause cl0 would be allocated

[1] The analysis of Van Roy computes also groundness information and the set of recursively dereferenced terms

through a "put_void A_2" (where A_2 is the second argument of **nreverse/2**). Using the knowledge that V2 is uninitialized, an optimized compiler would substitute "put_void A_2" with the more efficient "put_uninit_void A_2" whose definition is shown in the table below.

put_void A_2	put_uninit_void A_2
A_2 = *HEAP*[H] = (*REF*,H++);	A_2 = (*REF*,H++);
P += instruction_size(P);	P += instruction_size(P);

Clearly, having uninitialized arguments in a call requires to have also new specialized **get** instructions in the clauses that can be activated by that call. The specialized **get** instructions must simply avoid to dereference those arguments that are uninitialized. Notice, again, that new instructions are more efficient than the original WAM instructions.

In order to illustrate the global optimization that can be obtained for program P, in what follows we present the usual WAM code produced for it and then point out the optimizations that uninitialized variables allow to perform. Dots are used to replace the WAM code allocating the list of the first 30 natural numbers.

```
main/0 :
    put_list X29
    set_constant 30
    set_constant []
    put_list X28
    set_constant 29
    set_value X29
    ...
    put_list X1
    set_constant 2
    set_value X2
    put_list A1
    set_constant 1
    set_value X1
    put_void A2                                        (1)
    execute nreverse/2
nreverse/2 :
    switch_on_term V1, L1, C1, fail
C1: switch_on_constant 1, {([], N1)}
V1: try_me_else M1
N1: get_constant [], A1
    get_constant [], A2                                (2)
    proceed
M1: trust_me
L1: allocate
    get_list A1
    unify_variable Y2
    unify_variable X1
    get_variable Y3, A2
    put_value X1, A1
```

```
    put_variable Y1, A2                                  (3)
    call nreverse/2, 3
    put_unsafe_value Y1, A1
    put_list A2
    set_value Y2
    set_constant []
    put_value Y3, A3
    deallocate
    execute append/3
append/3 :
    switch_on_term V2, L2, C2, fail
C2: switch_on_constant 1, {([], N2)}
V2: try_me_else M2
    get_constant [], A1
    get_value A2, A3                                     (4)
    proceed
M1: trust_me
L1: get_list A1
    unify_variable X4
    unify_variable X1
    get_list A3                                          (5)
    unify_value X4
    unify_variable X3                                    (6)
    put_value X1 A1
    put_value X3 A3
    execute append/3
```

The optimized code is obtained by replacing:

- "put_void A2" with "put_uninit_void A2" at line (1);
- "get_constant [], A2" with "get_uninit_constant [], A2" at line (2);
- "put_variable Y1, A2" with "put_uninit_variable Y1, A2" at line (3);
- "get_value A2, A3" with "get_uninit_value A2, A3" at line (4);
- "get_list A3" with "get_uninit_list A3" at line (5);
- "unify_variable X3" with "unify_uninit_variable X3" at line (6).

where new specialized instructions are defined as follows:

put_uninit_void A_2 A_2 = (*REF*,H++); P += instruction_size(P);	put_uninit_variable Y_1, A_2 A_2 = (*REF*,&Y_1); P += instruction_size(P);
get_uninit_structure f/*n*, A_i (*REF*, *addrA*) = A_i; *HEAP*[H] = (*STR*,H+1); *HEAP*[H+1] = f/*n*; *STORE*[*addrA*] = (*STR*,H+1); H = H+2; *mode* = *write*; P += instruction_size(P);	get_uninit_list A_i (*REF*, *addrA*) = A_i; *HEAP*[H] = (*LIS*,H+1); *STORE*[*addrA*] = (*LIS*,H+1); H++; *mode* = *write*; P += instruction_size(P);
get_uninit_constant c, A_i (*REF*, *addrA*) = A_i; *STORE*[*addrA*] = (*CON*,c); P += instruction_size(P);	get_uninit_value V_n, A_i *addrV* = deref(V_n); (*REF*, *addrA*) = A_i; *STORE*[*addrA*] = *STORE*[*addrV*]; P += instruction_size(P);
unify_uninit_variable X_3 X_3 = (*REF*,H++); P += instruction_size(P);	

where "&Y_1" is the address of the stack location associated with Y_1. The whole list of Extended WAM instructions for handling uninitialized variables can be found in [2].

3 Implementation and Integration of Uninitialized Variable Analysis

We have implemented our uninitialized variable analysis using the Generic Abstract Interpretation Analyzer GAIA [6]. We modified the parsing phase of the original version of GAIA and we implemented our abstract domain and its associated operations [2]. The modification of the parsing phase of input programs has been realized because uninitialized variable analysis concerns only with the variables occurring in a term and not with its compound subterms. Thus, we simplified the parsing phase of original GAIA following the normal form of Prolog programs illustrated in `nreverse/2` (Section 2).

The output of our analyzer is a sequence of lists, one for each clause of the analyzed program, where the list associated to a clause specifies the WAM instructions that can be optimized for that clause. For example, the list associated with `cl0` in P is: `[main/0/1, [put_void(2)]]`.

In order to integrate our analyzer into SICStus, we modified the original system in two points:

- we modified the SICStus Compiler in such a way that, using the lists produced by our analyzer, it generates extended WAM code of the form shown in Section 2.1;
- we also modified the emulator associated with the SICStus compiler in such a way that it can execute the new instructions.

The modification of the SICStus Compiler is very simple. We inserted a procedure at the point where the SICStus compiler is about to generate the WAM code. That procedure, before generating any (potentially optimizable) WAM instruction for some clause, consults if that instruction is on the list produced by our analyzer for that clause. In this case, clearly, an optimized WAM instruction (cf. [2]) is generated in place of the original one.

Our strategy for integrating the SICStus compiler with our analyzer has two main advantages: its simplicity and its generality. Its simplicity is shown also by the fact that the described modification of the SICStus compiler consists in the addition of 277 lines of `Prolog` code to the original SICStus Compiler (precisely in file *plwam.p4*).

As far as the generality of our approach is concerned, it is important to stress again, cf. the discussion on this point contained in the Introduction, that our approach is based on the fact that the optimization supported by a static analysis must not cause important changes in the basic WAM model. Observe that this is surely true in the case of uninitialized variables where the optimizations are in fact local to each clause.

Clearly, our strategy is rather inefficient because any potentially optimizable instruction needs to be tested. However, we think that its simplicity and generality outweight this shortcoming.

Since new instructions are generated by the modified SICStus compiler described above, we had to define new bytecodes for those new instructions as well as to modify the Emulator in order to handle properly their bytecodes. Both these modifications were rather simple to carry out. The file containing the bytecodes of WAM instructions (*insdef.h*) increased by 21 lines of C code. The modification of the SICStus Emulator amounts to 302 lines of C code added to files *wam.c*, *wam.h*, *support.h*, *u2defs.h*, and *termdefs.h*.

4 Statistics

In what follows we present tables evaluating our uninitialized variable analyzer and the modified SICStus compiler. Section 4.1 evaluates the impact, in terms of execution time, of our uninitialized variable analyzer within the modified SICStus Compiler. Also, Section 4.1 illustrates and compares the performance of our uninitialized variable analyzer with respect to the dataflow analyzer included in Aquarius [13]. Section 4.2 presents the results about the quality and the benefit of our uninitialized variable analysis.

4.1 Performance of Uninitialized Variable Analysis

We consider the execution time of our uninitialized variable analyzer and the modified SICStus compiler for a set of benchmarks, taken from [13]. In this way we can compare our compiler and analyzer with those of Van Roy. A comparison of the execution time of our uninitialized variable analyzer with that of Lindgren was not possible because we didn't have any information about performance of his analyzer.

Table 1 contains the benchmarks used in our statistics with a brief description and their size measured in lines of code (not including comments), number of predicates, and clauses. The benchmarks in the first block are called small benchmarks whereas the other ones are large benchmarks.

Small Benchmarks	Lines	Preds	Clauses	Description
divide10	27	3	10	Symbolic differentiation
fast_mu	54	7	17	An optimized version of the mu-math prover
log10	27	3	10	Symbolic differentiation
mu	26	9	16	Prove a theorem of Hofstadter's "mu-math"
nreverse	10	4	5	Naïve-Reverse of 30-integers list
ops8	27	3	10	Symbolic differentiation
poly_10	86	12	32	Symbolic rise a polynomial to the tenth power
qsort	19	4	6	Quicksort of 50-integers list
queens_8	31	8	11	Solution of the 8 Queens Problem
query	68	6	54	Query a static database (with integer arithmetic)
serialise	29	8	13	Calculate serial numbers of a list
tak	15	2	3	Recursive integer arithmetic
times10	27	3	10	Symbolic differentiation
zebra	36	6	11	A logical puzzle based on constraints
Large Benchmarks	**Lines**	**Preds**	**Clauses**	**Description**
boyer	384	24	140	An extract from a Boyer-Moore theorem prover
browse	103	14	31	Build and query a database
chat_parser	1130	155	519	Parse a set of English sentences
flatten	158	28	58	Source transformation to remove disjunctions
meta_qsort	74	8	27	A meta-interpreter running qsort
nand	493	40	152	A logic synthesis program based on heuristic search
prover	81	10	32	A simple theorem prover
reducer	301	30	140	A graph reducer based on combinators
sdda	273	29	105	A dataflow analyzer that represents alias
simple_analyzer	443	67	135	A dataflow analyzer analyzing qsort
unify	125	28	55	A compiler code generator for unification

Table 1. Benchmarks

Each benchmark is run ten times and the arithmetic mean of the results is taken. Table 2 contains the execution time of our uninitialized variable analyzer alone and integrated within the SICStus Prolog Compiler. The fourth column indicates the impact of our uninitialized variable analysis on the compilation time and is obtained as the third column (multiplied by 100) over the second one. These experiments were performed on a SparcStation Classic 40Mb RAM powered by a MicroSparc Processor equipped with SunOS 4.1.3.

The geometric mean value of the ratio of the analysis on the compilation time (with analysis) is 34.2% and 37.0% for small and large programs, respectively. The fact that small and large programs have similar mean indicates that the analysis scales well.

Benchmarks	Compilation Time with Analysis (sec.)	Time of Analysis (sec.)	Ratio
divide10	0.84	0.29	34.5%
fast_mu	1.22	0.23	18.9%
log10	1.02	0.39	38.2%
mu	1.35	0.46	34.1%
nreverse	0.52	0.09	17.3%
ops8	0.98	0.34	34.7%
poly_10	2.43	0.75	30.9%
qsort	2.70	1.45	53.7%
queens_8	1.30	0.67	45.7%
query	1.86	0.74	39.8%
serialise	2.10	1.30	61.9%
tak	3.42	2.99	87.4%
times10	1.01	0.34	33.7%
zebra	0.75	0.08	10.7%
Mean	1.54	Geometric Mean	34.2%
boyer	7.75	2.61	33.7%
browse	2.55	1.16	45.5%
chat_parser	27.43	15.6	56.9%
flatten	3.65	0.92	25.2%
meta_qsort	1.82	0.47	25.8%
nand	18.07	6.29	34.8%
prover	2.67	0.97	36.3%
reducer	9.26	3.59	38.8%
sdda	8.05	3.60	44.7%
simple_analyzer	11.45	4.44	38.8%
unify	6.83	2.56	37.5%
Mean	9.05	Geometric Mean	37.0%

Table 2. Impact of our Analysis on Compilation Time

Table 3 contains the execution time of the uninitialized variable analysis performed by the Aquarius Dataflow Analyzer. The compilation and analysis times are obtained executing Aquarius 1.0 on the considered benchmarks. These experiments were performed on a SparcStation Classic 40Mb RAM powered by a MicroSparc Processor equipped with SunOS 4.1.3.

Benchmarks	Compilation Time with Analysis (sec.)	Time of Analysis (sec.)	Ratio
divide10	17.5	1.20	6.9%
fast_mu	72.3	3.4	4.7%
log10	17.4	1.3	7.5%
mu	22.4	1.3	5.8%
nreverse	3.7	1.0	27.0%
ops8	17.3	1.2	6.9%
poly_10	103.1	3.3	3.2%
qsort	8.2	1.2	14.6%
queens_8	15.2	1.7	11.2%
query	16.8	1.5	8.9%
serialise	15.3	1.4	9.2%
tak	6.4	1.1	17.2%
times10	17.4	1.2	6.9%
zebra	31.7	1.5	4.7%
Mean	26.1	Geometric Mean	8.2%
boyer	282.6	6.9	2.4%
browse	42.9	4.2	9.8%
chat_parser	1084.0	54.8	5.1%
flatten	71.9	6.3	8.8%
meta_qsort	45.8	2.5	5.5%
nand	699.7	39.8	5.7%
prover	50.3	2.8	5.6%
reducer	1496.9	11.4	0.8%
sdda	314.6	8.5	2.7%
simple_analyzer	349.6	16.2	4.6%
unify	130.3	11.7	9.0%
Mean	415.3	Geometric Mean	4.5%

Table 3. Impact of Van Roy's Analysis on Compilation Time

Tables 2 and 3 allow us to establish the following points:

- both our analysis and Van Roy's analysis scale well in all considered benchmarks;
- the impact of our analysis on compilation is greater than the one of the analysis by Van Roy, due to the fact that SICStus is an efficient compiler;

– in absolute terms, our compiler performs 40 times better than Van Roy's.

We argue that our compiler is worth of attention in that it increases the whole compilation time of only one third obtaining final acceptable compilation times.

4.2 Quality and Benefit of our Analysis

In terms of quality, on the considered benchmarks, our analysis computes exactly the same information as that of Lindgren and Van Roy. Also, we evaluated the benefit of optimized code in terms of execution time of the compiled code. Table 4 gives, for each benchmark, both the execution time of optimized and not optimized (or simply, WAM) code executed on a PC-i586 36Mb RAM CPU 300 MHz powered by an AuthenticAMD Processor equipped with Red Hat Linux 5.1[2]. Also, the fifth column is the difference (multiplied by 100) between the second and the third column, over the second column, i.e., Saving = 100 × (WAM Code - Optimized Code)/WAM Code.

The executions of each benchmark are grouped into *batches*. We added to every benchmark the following lines of Prolog code, where `main(Nexec,Nbatch)` indicates that `Nexec` executions of every benchmark are repeated `Nbatch` times. The execution time indicated in Table 4 is the arithmetic mean of the execution time of each batch. For uniformity reasons, we used `Nbatch = 10` whereas `Nexec` is indicated in the second column of Table 4.

```
main(Nexec,Nbatch) :- batch(Nexec,Nbatch,0,0,Tbatch,Ltime),
    write('Mean Among Batches:'), Mean is Tbatch/Nbatch, write(Mean),nl.

batch(_,Nbatch,Nbatch,Tbatch,Tbatch,[]).
batch(Nexec,Nbatch,Ndone,Tpart,Tbatch,[Tcurr|L]) :- Nleft > 0,
    statistics(runtime,_),
    batch(Nexec),
    statistics(runtime,[_|Tcurr]),
    Tpart1 is Tpart + Tcurr,
    Ndone1 is Ndone+1,
    write('Execution No.'), write(Ndone1),
    write('Time ='), write(Tcurr),nl,
    batch(Nexec,Nbatch,Ndone1,Tpart1,Tbatch,L).

batch(0).
batch(N) :- N > 0,
    main,
    N1 is N-1,
    batch(N1).

%[Prolog code of the benchmark]
```

[2] We ported SICStus 2.1 to Linux by adding option -G to `m4` preprocessor version GNU 1.4.

where main/0 is the entry procedure of the considered benchmark.

Table 4 shows that the geometric mean of saved execution time is better for small benchmarks rather than for the large ones. A reason for that is that large benchmarks heavily use built-ins whose execution time is not affected by our optimization. Also, we cannot compare the execution time of our optimized code with the corresponding optimized code of Van Roy because it is not possible, in the BAM, to perform only uninitialized variable optimization. The static analysis of the BAM performs also groundness and recursively dereferenced variable analyses together with uninitialized variable analysis. Thus, we cannot give a fair comparison with Aquarius.

Benchmarks	No. Executions (Nexec)	Execution Time (msec.)		
		WAM Code	Optimized Code	Saving
divide10	5000	226.7	215.6	4.9%
fast_mu	250	278.4	264.2	5.1%
log10	15000	252.4	240.3	4.8&
mu	250	209.4	198.0	5.4&
nreverse	500	200.7	191.1	4.8%
ops8	5000	137.5	131.0	4.7%
poly_10	3	145.6	138.0	5.2%
qsort	250	149.6	142.7	4.6%
queens_8	50	178.5	168.9	5.4%
query	50	226.5	214.5	5.3%
serialise	300	144.5	137.1	5.1%
tak	1	183.5	174.4	5.0%
zebra	3	147.6	140.5	4.8%
			Geometric Mean	5.0%
boyer	1	603.5	584.8	3.1%
browse	1	816.6	789.7	3.3%
chat_parser	1	166.5	160.2	3.8%
flatten	100	152.4	147.7	3.1%
meta_qsort	50	319.6	306.8	4.0%
nand	10	270.6	259.2	4.2%
prover	200	212.7	202.9	4.6%
reducer	10	406.4	386.5	4.2%
sdda	100	313.4	303.4	3.2%
simple_analyzer	10	205.6	198.8	3.3%
unify	100	298.6	286.1	4.2%
			Geometric Mean	3.7%

Table 4. Benefits of our Analysis

5 Recursively Dereferenced Variables

The method presented in Section 3 for integrating a static analyzer detecting uninitialized variables within SICStus can be applied also for extending SICStus with recursively dereferenced variables. The next Section presents the set of instructions that extend the SICStus Compiler for handling recursively dereferenced variables. We implemented the static analyzer described in [5] for detecting recursively dereferenced variables and we are currently implementing the extension of SICStus using that static analyzer.

In what follows, by means of the program `P` given in Section 2, we will show how recursively dereferenced variables can be detected using the analyses given both in [5] and [13]. Both analyses start from predicate `main/0` and simulate the SLD resolution [8]. Predicate `nreverse/2` is called, in `cl0`, with both its arguments recursively dereferenced. This is true because `V1` is directly bound to a list and `V2` is free and unaliased.

Clearly, `cl1` binds both arguments of `nreverse/2` to the empty list and thus, they remain recursively dereferenced. For `cl2`, it is also immediate to see that both arguments of the recursive call of `nreverse/2` are recursively dereferenced. However, some more thinking is needed for deriving that both arguments remain recursively dereferenced through the call of `append/3`.

In order to see this fact, the analyzer must discover that `append/3` is always called and exited with recursively dereferenced arguments. This can be achieved by adding the information that, at any call of `append/3`, the first argument of `append/3` is recursively dereferenced and ground, the second argument of `append/3` is recursively dereferenced and bound to a non variable value, and that the third argument of `append/3` is free and unaliased. Let us explain how that information is used to conclude that `append/3` is always called and exited with recursively dereferenced arguments. As regards `cl3`, `V2 = V3` leaves `V2` and `V3` recursively dereferenced because `V3` is free and unaliased whereas `V2` is bound to a recursively dereferenced non variable value. As far as `cl4` is concerned, `V1 = [V4|V5], V3 = [V4|V6]` leave `V3` recursively dereferenced because `V6` is initially free and unaliased and `V4` is ground and recursively dereferenced (because `V1` is ground and recursively dereferenced, and `V3` is initially free and unaliased).

From the definition of recursively dereferenced variables given before, it follows directly that any static analysis aiming at inferring this information, has to infer also information about the variables that are free and unaliased and the variables that are bound to ground values and non variable values. In fact, both analyses of recursively dereferenced variables we know of, i.e., our analysis, [5] and that of Van Roy [13] compute also this information.

6 Use of Recursively Dereferenced Variables

The information that a variable is recursively dereferenced can be exploited, for example, for optimizing WAM unification. The WAM instructions performing a unification would dereference all program variables involved in that unification whereas we can avoid to dereference all variables that are recursively dereferenced.

The instructions we added to the WAM are a simplification of some existing WAM instructions. For example, "`get_rderef_value Vn, Ai`" is derived from "`get_value Vn, Ai`" by replacing the call to the WAM generic unification procedure "`unify`" with "`rderef_unify`" described in Figure 1, where PDL is a stack of addresses, *pop* and *push* are the usual stack operations, and "`bind`" is given in [2].

```
get_value Vn, Ai
unify(Vn,Ai);
if(fail) backtrack;
else
 P += instruction_size(P);
```

```
get_rderef_value Vn, Ai
rderef_unify(Vn,Ai);
if(fail) backtrack;
else
 P += instruction_size(P);
```

```
unify(a1, a2:address){
push(a1,PDL);
push(a2,PDL);
fail = FALSE;
do{
  d1 = deref(pop(PDL));
  d2 = deref(pop(PDL));
  if(d1!=d2){
    (t1,v1) = STORE[d1];
    (t2,v2) = STORE[d2];
    if(t1==REF) bind(d1,d2);
    else switch t2
      case REF : bind(d1,d2);
        break;
      case CON :
        fail = (t1!=CON) || (v1!=v2);
        break;
      case LIS :
        if(t1!=LIS) fail = TRUE;
        else
        {push(v1,PDL);
        push(v2,PDL);}
        break;
      case STR :
        if(t1!=STR) fail = TRUE;
        else {f1/n1 = STORE[v1];
          f2/n2 = STORE[v2];
          if(f1!=f2) || (n1!=n2)
            fail = TRUE;
          else
            for(i = 1; i <= n1; i++){
              push(v1 + i, PDL);
              push(v2 + i, PDL);}
            }
        break;
  }
  while !(empty(PDL) || fail) }
```

```
rderf_unify(a1, a2:address){
push(a1,PDL);
push(a2,PDL);
fail = FALSE;
do{
  d1 = pop(PDL);
  d2 = pop(PDL);
  if(d1!=d2){
    (t1,v1) = STORE[d1];
    (t2,v2) = STORE[d2];
    if(t1==REF) bind(d1,d2);
    else switch t2
      case REF : bind(d1,d2);
        break;
      case CON :
        fail = (t1!=CON) || (v1!=v2);
        break;
      case LIS :
        if(t1!=LIS) fail = TRUE;
        else
        {push(v1,PDL);
        push(v2,PDL);}
        break;
      case STR :
        if(t1!=STR) fail = TRUE;
        else {f1/n1 = STORE[v1];
          f2/n2 = STORE[v2];
          if(f1!=f2) || (n1!=n2)
            fail = TRUE;
          else
            for(i = 1; i <= n1; i++){
              push(v1 + i, PDL);
              push(v2 + i, PDL);}
            }
        break;
  }
  while !(empty(PDL) || fail) }
```

Fig. 1. Unification

The complete list of optimized instructions can be found in [2]. We remark that our extension of the WAM is fairly simple. The corresponding extension of SICStus Compiler and Emulator can be carried out using an analyzer that produces, for each clause of an input Prolog program, the list of WAM instructions that can be optimized. Following the guidelines given in Section 3, we can then insert a procedure at the point where the SICStus compiler is about to generate the WAM code. This procedure, before generating any (potentially optimizable) WAM instruction for some clause, consults if this instruction is on the list produced by our analyzer for that clause. In this case, clearly, an optimized WAM instruction (cf. [2]) is generated in place of the original one. This shows that our method for incorporating uninitialized variables within SICStus can be applied also for introducing recursively dereferenced variables.

7 Conclusion

We presented a general and simple method for integrating static analyses within Prolog compilers based on the WAM. Our method has been illustrated showing the integration of uninitialized variable analysis in the SICStus Compiler and Emulator. The experimental evaluation shows that our approach is rather promising: the modified SICStus compiler obtained is still reasonably efficient and the execution time of the optimized code is, on the average, 4,4% less than that of non optimized code. In order to show that this approach can be applied to other static analyses, we outlined also the integration of recursively dereferenced variable analysis in the SICStus Compiler and Emulator.

Currently, we are finishing the integration of the recursively dereferenced variables analysis within SICStus[3]. For the future, we plan to integrate into SICStus other analyses such as the indexing analysis and the pointer chain analysis, i.e., the analysis estimating the length of the pointer chains that have to be dereferenced in order to reach the value of a variable [11]. We will also investigate the application of our method to the logic language Mercury [10]. In this context it would be interesting to consider analyses such as variable liveness [9].

References

1. H. Ait-Kaci. *Warren's Abstract Machine.* The MIT Press, Cambridge, MA, 1991. Prepared with LaTeX.
2. D. Baldan. *An Abstract Interpretation Framework for WAM Level Properties.* PhD thesis, Department of Pure and Applied Mathematics, University of Padova, Italy, 1999.
3. P. A. Bigot, D. Gudeman, and S. K. Debray. Output value placement in moded logic programs. In Pascal van Hentenryck, editor, *Logic Programming - Proceedings of the Eleventh International Conference on Logic Programming*, pages 175–189, Massachusetts Institute of Technology, 1994. The MIT Press.
4. P. Cousot and R. Cousot. Abstract interpretation: a unified lattice model for static analysis of programs by construction or approximation of fixpoints. In *Fourth ACM Symposium on Principles of Programming Languages*, pages 238–252, Los Angeles, California, January 1977. ACM Press, New York.

[3] Garbage collection can be integrated within our optimized SICStus Compiler through a liveness analysis that informs garbage collector about dead memory locations.

5. A. Grassi. *L'individuazione dei Termini Ricorsivamente Dereferenziati nei Programmi Prolog*. PhD thesis, Università degli Studi di Padova, March 1998.
6. B. Le Charlier and P. Van Hentenryck. Experimental evaluation of a generic abstract interpretation algorithm for PROLOG. *ACM Transactions on Programming Languages and Systems*, 16(1):35–101, January 1994.
7. T. Lindgren. Polyvariant detection of uninitialized arguments of prolog predicates. *Journal of Logic Programming*, 28(3):217–229, September 1996.
8. J. W. Lloyd. *Foundation of Logic Programming*. Springer-Verlag, 2 edition, 1988.
9. Anne Mulkers. Live data structures in logic programs: Derivation by means of abstract interpretation. *Lecture Notes in Computer Science*, 675:1–??, 1993.
10. Zoltan Somogyi, Fergus Henderson, Thomas Conway, and David Jeffery. *The Mercury Language Reference Manual*, 1997.
11. A. Taylor. Removal of dereferencing and trailing in prolog compilation. In Levi, Giorgio; Martelli, Maurizio, editor, *Proceedings of the 6th International Conference on Logic Programming (ICLP '89)*, pages 48–62, Lisbon, Portugal, June 1989. MIT Press.
12. A. Taylor. *High Performance Prolog Implementation*. PhD thesis, Basser Department of Computer Science, University of Sydney, June 1991.
13. P. L. Van Roy. *Can Logic Programming Execute as Fast as Imperative Programming*. PhD thesis, Computer Science Division, University of California Berkeley, December 1990.

Run Time Type Information in Mercury

Tyson Dowd, Zoltan Somogyi, Fergus Henderson,
Thomas Conway, and David Jeffery

Department of Computer Science and Software Engineering,
University of Melbourne, Parkville, 3052 Victoria, Australia
Phone: +61 3 9344 9100, Fax: +61 3 9348 1184
{trd,zs,fjh,conway,dgj}@cs.mu.OZ.AU

Abstract. The logic/functional language Mercury uses a strong, mostly static type system based on polymorphic many-sorted logic. For efficiency, the Mercury compiler uses type specific representations of terms, and implements polymorphic operations such as unifications via generic code invoked with descriptions of the actual types of the operands. These descriptions, which consist of automatically generated data and code, are the main components of the Mercury runtime type information (RTTI) system. We have used this system to implement several extensions of the Mercury system, including an escape mechanism from static type checking, generic input and output facilities, a debugger, and automatic memoization, and we are in the process of using it for an accurate, native garbage collector. We give detailed information on the implementation and uses of the Mercury RTTI system as well as measurements of the space costs of the system.

1 Introduction

Many modern functional and logic programming languages have a strong static type system and support parametric polymorphism. For efficiency, since the types of almost all values are known at compile-time, it is desirable to specialize the representation of data for each type, rather than using a single representation for data of any type (as is typically done with dynamically typed languages). When the type is known statically, the compiler is able to emit the proper type-specific code to manipulate those values. In some cases, however, the compiler does not know the exact type of a value. For example, in a polymorphic predicate or function, the compiler may know that type of a variable is `list(T)`, but may not know what type the type variable `T` is bound to, since that can vary from call to call. Nevertheless, for some operations it may still be necessary to examine the representation.

In such circumstances, implementors have two main choices. One alternative is to create separate copies of the implementation for each possible type `T` can be bound to, thus restoring the compiler's full knowledge of the types of variables. This is the approach taken for the implementation of generics in most imperative languages. Its advantage is execution speed, due to the exclusive use of type-specific operations; the corresponding disadvantage is the cost in code space and

G. Nadathur (Ed.): PPDP'99, LNCS 1702, pp. 224–243, 1999.

locality of the multiple copies, many of which will typically be used quite rarely. Another significant disadvantage with this approach is that it makes separate compilation much more difficult.

The other alternative is to have only one implementation, but make this one able to handle all the calls. This obviously requires callers to make available runtime type information (RTTI) about the actual type bound to T that can then be interpreted by a single implementation. The advantages of this alternative are its small space cost, and ease of separate compilation, while its disadvantage is the time costs of lookup and interpretation.

In this paper we describe the RTTI system of Mercury, a purely declarative logic/functional language. Since most Mercury programs use polymorphism much more frequently than imperative language programs use generics, we believe that the space cost of the first approach would be prohibitive. However, we also want the implementation to be fast, so we have settled on a hybrid of the approaches. This hybrid uses RTTI to allow us to get away with only one implementation of each polymorphic predicate, but the most frequently used operations (unification and comparison) do not require interpretation. Other, less frequently used operations do, since for them this is the proper space-time tradeoff.

Since the system has RTTI, we make it available to users who may wish to perform type specific operations (e.g. pretty-printing) on terms of polymorphic types, as well as to system programmers working to implement new language features. In the last two years, we have extended the Mercury implementation with several features that require access to RTTI, some of which required us to extend the RTTI system. Automatic memoization requires detailed knowledge of the data representations of types to construct efficient indexes. The debugger needs similar knowledge in order to be able to print out the values of variables on demand, and our (as yet incomplete) native garbage collector needs it to be able to trace through and to copy terms. (The Mercury runtime system currently relies upon the Boehm conservative garbage collector for C [5].)

The rest of this paper is organized as follows. Section 2 introduces the relevant aspects of the Mercury language and describes how the Mercury implementation represents terms. Section 3 describes, at a significantly deeper level of detail than most other papers on RTTI, the data structures we use to store RTTI and how the information in these data structures is made available both to relevant parts of the implementation and to programmers. Section 4 evaluates the space impact of our RTTI implementation. Section 5 presents comparisons with related work.

2 Background

2.1 Mercury

Mercury is a pure logic/functional programming language intended for general purpose large-scale programming. We will describe in detail the data representation used by the Mercury implementation, but for an overview of Mercury we refer the reader to the Mercury language reference manual [10] which is available from the Mercury home page `http://www.cs.mu.oz.au/mercury/`.

2.2 Data Representation

The Mercury implementation uses a different, specialized representation for the terms of each type. This is possible because the Mercury compiler knows the types of almost all terms at compile time, and the few exceptions do not present insoluble problems; we will discuss the solutions of some of these problems later. The advantage of specializing term representations is that it reduces storage requirements somewhat and improves time efficiency considerably. The disadvantage is that you cannot tell the value represented by a bit pattern without knowing what type it is.

```
:- type dir ---> north ; south ; east ; west.
:- type example ---> a ; b(int, dir) ; c(example).
```

Types such as `dir`, in which every alternative is a constant, correspond to enumerated types in other languages. Mercury implements them as if they were enumerated types, representing the alternatives by consecutive small integers starting with zero. These integers are stored directly in machine words, as are values of builtin types that fit in a word, such as integers. Values of builtin types that do not fit in a word, e.g. strings and (on some machines) double precision floating point numbers, are stored in memory and represented by a pointer to that memory, to allow us to establish the invariant that all values fit into a word. Polymorphic code depends on this invariant; without it, the compiler could not generate a single piece of code that can pass around values of a type that is unknown at compile time.

Types such as `example`, in which some alternatives have arguments, obviously need a different representation. One possible representation would be as a pointer to a memory block, in which the first word specifies the function symbol, and the later words contain its arguments, with the block being just big enough to contain these arguments. The size of the memory block may therefore depend on the identity of the function symbol.

The Mercury implementation uses a more sophisticated and efficient variant of this representation. This implementation exploits the fact that virtually all modern machines, and all those we are interested in, address memory in bytes but access it in words. Many of these machines require words to be aligned on natural boundaries, and even the ones that don't usually suffer a performance penalty when accessing unaligned words. The Mercury implementation therefore stores all data in aligned words on all machines. This means that the address of any Mercury data item will have zeros in its low-order 2 bits on 32-bit machines or low-order 3 bits on 64-bit machines. We can therefore use these bits, which we call *primary tags*, to distinguish between function symbols. (Mercury works on both 32-bit and 64-bit machines, but for simplicity of exposition, we will assume 32-bit machines for the rest of this paper.)

In the case of type `example`, we assign the primary tag value 0 to `a`, the primary tag value 1 to `b`, and the primary tag value 2 to `c`. Using primary tags in this way allows us to reduce the size of the memory blocks we use, since these no longer have to identify the function symbol, It also allows us to avoid using a memory block at all for constant function symbols such as `a`, whose representation therefore does not need a pointer at all, and in which we therefore set the non-primary-tag bits of the word to zero.

Of course, some types have more function symbols than a primary tag can distinguish. In such cases, some function symbols have to share the same primary tag value. If all functors sharing the same primary tag value are constants, we distinguish them via the non-primary-tag bits of the word; we call this a *local secondary tag.* If at least one of them is not a constant, we distinguish them by storing an extra word at the start of the argument block; we call this a *remote secondary tag.* Both local and remote secondary tags are integers allocated consecutively from zero among the function symbols sharing the relevant primary tag. The compiler has a fairly simple algorithm that decides, for each function symbol, what primary tag value its representation has, and if that primary tag value is shared, whether the secondary tag is local or remote and what its value is. To save both space and time, this algorithm will share a primary tag value only between several constants or several non-constants, and will not share between a constant and a non-constant.

Following pointers that have primary tags on their low order bits does not actually cost us anything in execution time. To make sense of the word retrieved through the pointer, the code must have already tested the primary tag on the pointer. (It does not make sense to look up an argument in a memory block without knowing what function symbol it is an argument of, and it does not make sense to look at a remote secondary tag without knowing what function symbols it selects among.) When following the tagged pointer, the implementation must subtract the (known) value of the primary tag and add the (known) offset in the pointed-to memory block of the argument or remote secondary tag being accessed. (Actually, remote secondary tags always have an offset of zero.) The two operations can be trivially combined into one, which means adding a possibly negative, but small constant to the pointer. On most machines, this is the most basic memory addressing mode; one cannot access memory faster any other way.

3 Run-Time Type Information

One important design principle of the Mercury implementation, which we followed during our design of the RTTI system, is the avoidance of "distributed fat", which are implementation artifacts required by one language feature that impose efficiency costs even when that feature is not used. In other words, we don't want the RTTI system to slow down any parts of the program that do not use RTTI. Of course, we also want the RTTI system to have good efficiency for the parts of the program that do use RTTI. The aspect of efficiency that most concerns us is time efficiency; we are usually willing to trade modest and bounded amounts of space for speed.

3.1 Describing Type Constructors

The Mercury data representation scheme is compositional, i.e. the representation of a list does not depend on the type of the elements of the list. Therefore the run-time representation of a composite type such as `tree(string, list(int))` can be described by writing down the representation rules of the type constructors occurring in the type and showing how these type constructors fit together. Since a given type constructor will usually occur in many types, storing the information about the type constructor just once and referring to it from the descriptions of many types is obviously sensible. We call the data structure that holds all the runtime type information about a type constructor a `type_ctor_info`. When compiling a module, the Mercury compiler automatically generates a static data structure containing a `type_ctor_info` for every `:- type` declaration in the module. This data structure has a unique but predictable name derived from the name of the type constructor, which makes it simple to include references to it in other modules.

The `type_ctor_info` is a pointer to a vector of words containing the following fields:

- the arity of the type constructor,
- the address of the constructor-specific unification procedure,
- the address of the constructor-specific index procedure,
- the address of the constructor-specific comparison procedure,
- a pointer to the constructor's `type_ctor_layout` structure,
- a pointer to the constructor's `type_ctor_functors` structure, and
- the module qualified name of the type constructor.

Like the `type_ctor_info`, the constructor-specific unification, index and comparison procedures and `type_ctor_layout` and `type_ctor_functors` structures are also automatically generated by the compiler for each type declaration. We will provide details on these fields later.

3.2 Describing Types

A type is a type constructor applied to zero or more arguments, which are themselves types. Due to the compositionality of data representation in Mercury, the data structure that holds all the runtime type information about a type, which we call a `type_info`, is a pointer to a vector of words containing

- a `type_ctor_info` pointer, and
- zero or more `type_info` pointers describing the argument types.

The number of other `type_info` pointers is given by the arity of the type constructor, which can be looked up in the `type_ctor_info`. If the arity is zero, this representation is somewhat wasteful, since it requires an extra cell and

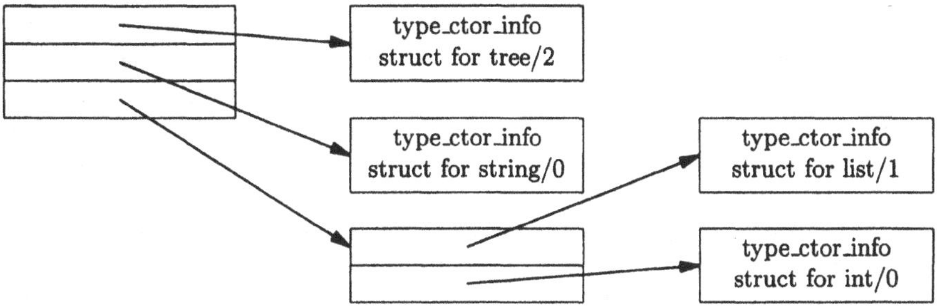

Fig. 1. The `type_info` structure for `tree(string, list(int))`

imposes an extra level of indirection. The Mercury system therefore has an optimization which allows the `type_ctor_info` for a zero-arity type constructor to also function as a `type_info` for the type named by the type constructor. Code that inspects a `type_info` now needs to check whether the `type_info` has the structure just above or whether it is the `type_ctor_info` for a zero-arity type constructor. Fortunately, the check is simple; whereas the first word of a real `type_info` structure is a pointer and can never be null, the first word of the `type_ctor_info` structure contains the arity of the constructor, and therefore for a zero-arity constructor will always be null. This can be a worthwhile optimization, because zero-arity types occur often; the leaves of every type tree are type constructors of arity zero.[1] Figure 1 shows the `type_info` structure of the type `tree(string, list(int))` with this optimization.

3.3 Implementing Polymorphism

In the presence of polymorphism, the compiler cannot always know the actual type of the terms bound to a given variable in a given predicate. If an argument of a polymorphic predicate is e.g. of type `T`, then for some calls the argument will be a term of type `int`, for others a term of type `list(string)`, and so on. The question then is: how can the compiler arrange the correct functioning of operations (such as unification) that depend on the actual type of the term bound to the variable?

The answer is that the compiler can make available to those operations the `type_info` for the actual type. An early phase of the compiler inspects every predicate, and for each type variable such as `T` in the type declaration of the predicate, it adds an extra argument to the predicate; this argument will contain a `type_info` for the actual type bound to `T`. The same phase also transforms the bodies of predicates so that calls to polymorphic predicates set these arguments to the right values.

[1] On some modern architectures, mispredicted branches can be more expensive than memory lookups, which often hit in the cache. For these architectures, the Mercury compiler has a switch that turns off this optimization.

As an example, consider a predicate p1 that passes an argument of type tree(string, list(int)) to a predicate p2 that expects an argument of type tree(T1, T2). Since T1 and T2 are type variables in the signature of p2, the compiler will add two extra arguments to p2, one each for T1 and T2. As the value of the first of these extra arguments, p1 must pass the type_info for string; as the value of the second of these extra arguments, p1 must pass the type_info for list(int). If p1 does not already have pointers to the required type_info structures, it must construct them. This means that while there can be only one type_ctor_info structure for each type constructor, there may be more than one type_info structure and therefore more than one type_info pointer for each type.

If p2 wants to pass a value of type list(T1) to a predicate p3 that expects a value of type U, p2 can construct the type_info structure expected by p3 even though the type bound to T1 is not known at compile time. To create this type_info structure, the compiler simply emits code that creates a two-word cell on the heap, and copies the pointer to the globally known type_ctor_info for list/1 to the first word and the pointer it has to the type_info for T1 to the second word.

3.4 Implementing Unification and Comparison

One operation that polymorphic predicates frequently perform on their polymorphic arguments is unification (consider member/2). To unify two values whose type it does not know, the compiler calls unify/2, the generic unification procedure in the Mercury runtime system. Since unify/2 is declared to take two arguments of type T, the polymorphism transformation will transform calls to it by adding an extra argument containing the type_info describing the common type of the two original arguments.

The implementation of unify/2 consists of looking up the address of the unification procedure in the top-level type_ctor_info of the type_info, and calling it with the right arguments. For builtin type constructors, the unification procedures are in the runtime system; for user-defined type constructors, they are automatically generated by the compiler. The technique the compiler uses for this is quite simple; it generates one clause for each alternative functor in the type constructor's type declaration, and in each clause, it generates one unification for each argument of that functor. Here is one example of a type and its automatically generated unification predicate:

```
:- type tree(K, V) ---> leaf ; node(tree(K, V), K, V, tree(K, V)).

unify_tree(leaf, leaf).
unify_tree(node(L1, K1, V1, R1), node(L2, K2, V2, R2)) :-
        unify(L1, L2),
        unify(K1, K2),
        unify(V1, V2),
        unify(R1, R2).
```

After creating the unification predicate, the compiler optimizes it by recognizing that for the first and last calls to **unify**, the top-level constructor of the type is known, and that those calls can thus be replaced by calls to **unify_tree** itself. Later still, the optimized predicate will go through the polymorphism transformation, which yields the following code:

```
unify_tree(TI_K, TI_V, leaf, leaf).
unify_tree(TI_K, TI_V, node(L1, K1, V1, R1),
                node(L2, K2, V2, R2)) :-
        unify_tree(TI_K, TI_V, L1, L2),
        unify(TI_K, K1, K2),
        unify(TI_V, V1, V2),
        unify_tree(TI_K, TI_V, R1, R2).
```

This shows that when the generic unification predicate **unify** is called upon to unify two trees, e.g. two terms of type **tree(string, list(int))**, two of the arguments it must call **unify_tree** with are the **type_info**s of the types **string** and **list(int)**. It can do so easily, since the required **type_info**s are exactly the ones following the **type_ctor_info** of **tree/2** in the **type_info** structure of **tree(string, list(int))**, a pointer to which was passed to **unify** as its extra argument. (**unify** of course got the address of **unify_tree** from the **type_ctor_info** of **tree/2**.)

Automatically generated comparison predicates call automatically generated index predicates which return the position of the top-level functor of a term in the list of alternative functors of the type. This allows for comparisons to be made for less than, equal to or greater than without comparing each functor to every other functor. After the initial comparison the comparison code has a similar recursive structure to the code generated for unification, and the polymorphism transformation is analogous.

3.5 Interpreting Type-Specialized Term Representations

Some polymorphic predicates wish to perform operations on polymorphic values for which there is no compiler-generated type-representation-specific code the way there is for unifications and comparisons. Copying terms and printing terms are examples of such operations. In such cases, the implementation of the operation must itself decode the meaning of a term in a type-specific data representation. Since it is the compiler that decides how values of each type are represented, this requires cooperation from the compiler. This cooperation takes the form of a compiler-generated **type_ctor_layout** structure for each type constructor, pointed to from the **type_ctor_info** structure of the constructor. Like the **type_ctor_info**, the **type_ctor_layout** structure is static, and there is only ever one **type_ctor_layout** for a given type constructor.

Since most values in Mercury programs belong to types which are discriminated unions, we chose to optimize **type_ctor_layout** structures so that given a word containing a value belonging to such a type, it is as efficient as possible to find out what the term represented by that word is. The `type_ctor_layout` is therefore a vector of descriptors indexed by the primary tag value of the data word, which thus contain four descriptors on 32-bit machines and eight on 64-bit machines. Each word says how to interpret data words with the corresponding primary tag. For types which are not discriminated unions (such as `int`), and thus do not use primary tags, all the descriptors in the vector will be identical; since there are few such types, and the vectors are small, this is not a problem.

To make the `type_ctor_layout` as small as possible, each descriptor is a single tagged word; here we use a 2-bit descriptor tag regardless of machine architecture. The value of this descriptor tag, which can be unshared, shared_remote, shared_local or equivalence, tells us how to interpret the rest of the word.

If the value of the descriptor tag is unshared, then this value has a discriminated union type and the primary tag of the data word uniquely identifies the functor. The rest of the descriptor word is then a pointer to a *functor descriptor* which contains

- the arity of the functor (n),
- n `pseudo_type_infos` for the functor arguments,
- a pointer to a string containing the functor name, and
- information on the primary tag of this functor, and its secondary tag, if any.

The last field is redundant when the functor descriptor is accessed via the `type_ctor_layout` structure; it is used only when it is accessed via the `type_ctor_functors` structure which is discussed below in section 3.6.

Many type declarations contain functors whose arguments are of polymorphic type; for example, all the arguments of the functor `node` in our example above contain a type variable in their type. For such an argument, the `type_ctor_layout` structure, being static, cannot possibly contain the actual `type_info` of the argument. Instead, it contains a `pseudo_type_info`, which is a generalization of a typeinfo. Whereas a `type_info` is always a pointer to a `type_info` structure, a `pseudo_type_info` is either a small integer that refers to a type variable, or a pointer to a `pseudo_type_info` structure, which is exactly like a `type_info` structure except that the fields after the `type_ctor_info` are `pseudo_type_infos` rather than `type_infos`.

The functor descriptor for the functor `node` will contain the small integers 1 and 2 as its second and third `pseudo_type_infos`, standing for the type variables K and V respectively, which are first and second type variables in the polymorphic type `tree(K, V)`. The first and fourth `pseudo_type_infos` will be pointers to `pseudo_type_info` structures in which the `type_ctor_info` slot points to the the `type_ctor_info` structure for `tree/2` and the following two `pseudo_type_infos` are the small integers 1 and 2. When a piece of code that has a `type_info` for the type `tree(string, list(int))` looks up the arguments of the `node` functor, it will construct `type_infos` for the arguments by substituting any `pseudo_type_infos` in the arguments (or in arguments of the arguments, and so on), with their corresponding parameters, i.e. the `type_infos` for `string` and for `list(int)`, which are at offsets 1 and 2 in the `type_info` structure for `tree(string, list(int))`. Note the exact correspondence between the offsets and the values of the `pseudo_type_infos` representing the type variables.

We can distinguish between small integers and pointers by imposing an arbitrary boundary between them. If the integer value of a word is smaller than a given limit, currently 1024, then the word contains a small integer; if it is greater than or equal to the limit, it is a pointer. This works because we can ensure that all small integers are below this limit, in this case by imposing an upper bound on the arities of type constructors, and because we can ensure that all pointers to data are bigger than the limit. (The text segment comes before the data segment, and the size of the text segment of the compulsory part of the Mercury runtime system is above the limit; in any case, most operating systems make the first page of the address space inaccessible in order to catch null pointer errors.)

If the value of the descriptor tag is shared_remote, then this value has a discriminated union type and the primary tag of the data word is shared between several functors, which are distinguished by a remote secondary tag. The rest of the descriptor word is then a pointer to a vector of words which contains

- the number of functors that share this tag (f), and
- f pointers to *functor descriptors.*

To find the information for the functor in the data word, we must use the secondary tag pointed to by the data word to index into the vector of functor descriptors.

If the value of the descriptor tag is shared_local, then there are three possibilities: (a) this value has a discriminated union type and the primary tag of the data word is shared between several functors, which must all be constants because which are distinguished by a local secondary tag; (b) this value has an enumerated type, such as type `example` from 2.2; or (c) this value has a builtin type such as `int` or `string`. For alternative (c), the rest of the descriptor word is a small integer that directly identifies the builtin type. For alternatives (a) and (b), the rest of the descriptor word is a pointer to an *enumeration vector*, which contains

- a boolean that says whether this is an enumeration type or not, and thus selects between (a) and (b),
- s, the number of constants that share this tag (for (a)) or the number of constants in the entire enumeration type (for (b)), and
- s pointers to strings containing the names of the constants.

To find the name of the functor in the data word, we must use the local secondary tag in the data word (for alternative (a)) or the entire data word (for alternative (b)) to index into the vector of names.

If the value of the descriptor tag is equivalence, then the value is either of a type that was declared as an equivalence type by the programmer, or it is of a *no_tag* type, a discriminated union type with one functor of one argument, which the compiler considers to be an equivalence type for purposes of internal although not external representation. Here is one example of each.

```
:- type equiv(T1, T2) == foo(int, T2, T1).
:- type notag(T1, T2) ---> wrapper(foo(int, T2, T1)).
```

In the latter case, the compiler uses the same internal representation for values of the types `notag(T1, T2)` and `foo(int, T2, T1)`, just as it does for the true equivalence.

The rest of the descriptor tag is a pointer to an *equivalence vector*, which contains

- a flag saying whether this type is a no_tag type or a user-defined equivalence type,
- a `pseudo_type_info` giving the equivalent type, and
- for no_tag types, a pointer to a string giving the name of the wrapper functor involved.

3.6 Creating Type-Specialized Term Representations

A `type_ctor_layout` structure has complete information about how types with a given type constructor are represented. While the organization of this structure is excellent for operations that want to interpret the representation of an already existing term, the organization is not at all suitable for operations that want to build new terms, such as parsing a term from an input stream. The `type_ctor_functors` table is an alternate organization of the same information that is designed to optimize the operation of searching for the information about a given functor. Like the `type_ctor_info` that points to it, the `type_ctor_functors` structure is static, and there is only ever one `type_ctor_functors` structure for a given type constructor.

The first word of the `type_ctor_functors` structure is an indicator saying whether this type is a discriminated union, an enumeration type, a no_tag type, an equivalence, or a builtin. The contents of the rest of the structure vary depending on the indicator. For discriminated unions, the structure contains the number of functors in the type, and a vector of pointers to the *functor descriptor* for each functor. For enumerations, it contains a pointer to the *enumeration vector*. For no_tag types, it has a pointer to the *functor descriptor* for its single functor. For true equivalence types, it contains the `pseudo_type_info` for the equivalent type. For builtin types, it contains the small integer that identifies the builtin type.

3.7 Accessing RTTI from User Level Code

A natural application of RTTI is dynamic typing [1]. The Mercury standard library provides an abstract data type called `univ` which encapsulates a value of any type, together with its `type_info`. The library provides a predicate `type_to_univ` for converting a value of any type to type `univ`.

```
:- pred type_to_univ(T, univ).
:- mode type_to_univ(in, out) is det.
:- mode type_to_univ(out, in) is semidet.
```

Note that type_to_univ has two modes. The second (reverse) mode lets you try to convert a value of type univ to any type; this conversion will fail if the value stored in the univ does not have the right type. The reverse mode implementation compares the type_info for T, which the compiler passes as an extra argument, with the type_info stored in the univ.

In addition to this implicit use of RTTI, Mercury allows user programs to make explicit use of RTTI, by providing some RTTI types and operations on those types as part of the Mercury standard library.

We provide abstract data types to represent runtime type information such as type_infos and type_ctor_infos. The operations on them include:

```
:- func type_of(T) = type_info.
:- func type_name(type_info) = string.
:- pred type_ctor_and_args(type_info::in, type_ctor_info::out,
          list(type_info)::out) is det.
:- pred functor(T::in, string::out, int::out) is det.
:- func argument(T::in, int::in) = (univ::out) is semidet.
```

The type_of function returns a type_info describing its argument. Its implementation is trivial: the compiler will pass the type_info for the type T as an extra argument to this function, and type_of can just return this extra argument.

Once you have a type_info, you can find out the name of the type it represents; this is useful e.g. in giving good error messages in code manipulating values of polymorphic types. You can also special-case operations on some types, for purposes such as pretty-printing. You can also use type_ctor_and_args to decompose type_infos into their constituent parts, This is mostly useful in conjunction with operations that decompose terms, such as functor and arg. Still other operations are designed to allow programs to construct types (that is, type_infos at runtime) by combining existing type constructors in new ways, and to construct terms of possibly dynamically created types.

3.8 Representing Type Information about Sets of Live Variables

When a program calls io:print to pretty-print a term or io:read to read one in, the polymorphism transformation passes the required type_info(s) to the predicate involved. This is possible because the predicate deals with a fixed number of polymorphic arguments and because the number of type variables in the types of those arguments is also known statically.

However, in some cases we want one piece of code to be able to deal with arbitrary numbers of terms, which have an unknown number of type variables in their types. Two examples are the Mercury debugger and the Mercury native garbage collector. They both need to be able to interpret the representations of all live variables at particular points in the program, in the case of the debugger so that it can print out the values of those variables if the user so requests, and in the case of the garbage collector so that it can copy the values of those variables from *from-space* to *to-space*. To handle this, at each program point that may be of interest to the debugger or to the native collector, the compiler generates a data structure describing the set of live variables, and lets the debugger and the native collector interpret this description. Of course, if the compilation options do not request debugging information and if they request the conservative, rather than the native collector, there will be no such programs points, and the data structures we discuss in this subsection will not be generated.

The debugger and the native collector both need to know how to walk the stacks (for printing the values of variables in ancestors for the debugger and because all live values in all stack frames are part of the root set for the native collector). For the nondet stack this is not a problem, since nondet stack frames store the pointer to the previous stack frame and the saved return address in fixed slots. However, frames on the det stack have no fixed slots, and they are of variable size. To be able to perform a step in a stack walk starting from a det stack frame, one must know how big the frame is and where within it the saved return address is. The compiler therefore generates a *proc layout* structure for each procedure, which includes

- the address of the entry to this procedure
- the determinism of this procedure (this controls which stack it uses)
- the size of the stack frame
- the location of the return address in the stack frame

The stack frame size and saved return address location are redundant for procedures on the nondet stack, but it is simpler to include this information for all procedures.

The debugger and the native collector both have their own methods for getting hold of the proc layout structure for the active procedure, and can thus find out what address the active procedure will return to. However, without knowing what procedure this return address is in, they won't be able to take the next step in the stack walk. Therefore when debugging or the native collector is enabled, the compiler will generate a *label layout* table for every label that represents the return address of a call. Label layout tables contain:

- a pointer to the proc layout structure for this procedure,
- n, the number of live and "interesting" variables at the label,
- a pointer to two consecutive n-element vectors, one containing `pseudo_type_info`s for the types of the live variables, and one containing the descriptors of the locations of live variables,
- a pointer to a vector of type parameter locations, the first element of which gives the number of type parameters and hence the size of the rest of the vector; as an optimization, the pointer will be null if the count is zero, and
- a pointer to a vector of n offsets into a module-wide string table giving the variables' names (this field is present only when debugging).

The Mercury runtime has a table which can take the address of a label (such as a return address) and return a pointer to the label layout structure for that label. That table, the proc layout structures and the first fields of label layout structures together contain all the information required for walking the stacks.

The other fields in a label layout structure describe the "interesting" variables that are live at that label. Here the debugger and the native collector have related but slightly different requirements. The collector needs the type of all variables (including compiler introduced temporaries) but not their names, whereas the debugger needs names but does not need information about temporaries. If both are enabled, the label layout structure will contain the union of the information the two systems need.

The debugger and native collector are also interested in somewhat different sets of labels. While both are interested in return labels, the debugger is also interested in labels representing entry to and exit from the procedure, and labels at program points that record decisions about the path execution, e.g. the entry points into the then parts and else parts of if-then-elses; these are irrelevant for the native collector.

Each live, interesting variable at the label has an entry in two consecutive vectors pointed to by the label's layout structure. The entry in one of the vectors gives the location of the variable. Some bits in this entry say whether the variable is in an abstract machine register, in a slot on the det stack, or in a slot on the nondet stack, while the other bits give the number of the register or the offset of the slot. The entry in the other vector is the `pseudo_type_info` for the type of the variable. Before this `pseudo_type_info` can be used to interpret the value of the variable, it must be converted into a `type_info` by substituting, for every type variable in the `pseudo_type_info`, the `type_info` of the actual type bound to the type variable.

Consider a polymorphic predicate, one of whose argument is of type `list(T)`. Its caller will pass an extra argument giving the `type_info` of the actual type bound to `T`; this is the `type_info` that must be substituted into the `pseudo_type_info` of the `list(T)` argument. Since the signature of the procedure may include more than one type variable, each of which will have the actual type bound to it specified by an extra `type_info` argument, the compiler assigns consecutive integers, starting at 1, to all the type variables that occur in the types of any of the arguments (actually, to all the type variables that occur in the types of any of the variables of the procedure, which includes the arguments), and makes the `pseudo_type_info`s in the vector of pairs refer to each type variable by its assigned number. For every label that has a label layout structure, the compiler takes the set of live, interesting variables, and finds the set of type variables that occur in their types. The compiler then includes a description of the location of the `type_info` structure for the actual type bound to the type parameter in the type parameter location vector of the label layout structure, at the index given by the number assigned to the type variable.

That may sound complex, but to look up the type of a variable, one need only (a) convert the vector of type parameter locations in the label layout structure into an equal sized vector of `type_info`s, by decoding each location descriptor and looking up the value stored at the indicated location, which will be a `type_info`, and (b) using the resulting vector of `type_info`s to convert the `pseudo_type_info` for the variable into the `type_info` describing its type, exactly as we did in section 3.5 (except that the source of the `type_info` vector that identifies the types bound to the various type variables is now different).

One consequence of including information about the locations of variables that hold `type_info`s in label layout structures is that the compiler must ensure that a variable that holds the `type_info` describing the actual type bound to a given type variable must be live at a label that has a layout structure if any variable whose type includes that type variable is live at that label. Normally, the compiler considers every variable dead after its last use. However, when the options call for the generation of label layouts, the compiler, as a conservative approximation, considers a variable that holds the `type_info` to be live whenever any variable whose type includes that corresponding type variable is live. This rule of *typeinfo liveness* often extends the life of variables containing `type_info`s, and sometimes prevents such variables from being optimized away.

4 Evaluation

Hard numbers on RTTI systems are rare: there are few papers on RTTI, and many of these papers do not have performance evaluations of the RTTI system itself (although they often evaluate some feature enabled by RTTI). In this section we therefore provide some such numbers.

The Mercury implementation depends on RTTI in very basic ways. We cannot just turn off RTTI and measure the speed of the resulting system, because without RTTI, polymorphic predicates do not know how to perform unification and comparison. We would have to remove all polymorphism from the program first. This would require a significant amount of development effort, particularly since many language primitives implemented in C cannot be specialized automatically.

We therefore cannot report results on the exact time cost of the RTTI system. We can report two kinds of numbers though. First, a visual inspection of the C code generated by the Mercury compiler leads us to estimate that the fraction of the time that a Mercury program spends constructing `type_info`s and moving them around (all the other RTTI data structures are defined statically) is usually between 0 to 8%, probably averaging 1 to 3%. In earlier work [12], we measured this cost as being less than 2% for a selection of small benchmarks. One reason why these numbers are small is that the Mercury compiler includes an optimization that removes unused arguments; most of the arguments thus removed are `type_info` structures. Second, the researchers working on HAL, a constraint logic programming language, have run experiments showing the speed impact of type-specialized term representations. They took some Prolog benchmark programs, and translated them to HAL in two different ways: once with every variable being a member of its natural type, once with every variable being a member of a universal type that contained all the function symbols mentioned in the program. The HAL implementation, which compiles HAL programs into

Mercury, compiles each HAL type into its own Mercury type, so this distinction is preserved in the resulting Mercury programs too. The experimental results [6] show that the versions using natural types, and therefore type-specific term representations, are on average about 1.4 times the speed of the versions using the universal type and thus a generic term representation. Since an implementation using a generic term representation can be made to work without RTTI but one using type-specific term representations cannot, one could read these results as indicating a roughly 40% speed advantage enabled by the use of RTTI. Due to the small number and size of the benchmarks involved in the experiments and the differences between native Mercury code and Mercury code produced by the HAL compiler, this number should be treated with caution. However, it seems clear that the time costs of RTTI are outweighed by the benefits it brings in enabling type-specific term representations.

The parts of RTTI that are essential for polymorphism (and which also suffice to support dynamic casts, i.e. the `univ` type) are the `type_info` structures and the parts of `type_ctor_info` structures containing the type constructor arity and the addresses of the unification and comparison procedures, i.e. the structures discussed up to but not including section 3.5. The structures discussed from that point forward, including the `type_ctor_layout` and `type_ctor_functors` structures, are needed only for other aspects of the system, including generic term I/O, debugging, native garbage collection, and user-level access to type-specialized representations. Since all these structures are defined statically, they do not impact the runtimes of programs except through cache effects.

To get an appreciation for space costs, we have measured the sizes of object files generated for the Mercury compiler and standard library, which are written in Mercury itself, compiled with various subsets of runtime type information. The compiler and library together consist of 225 modules and define about 950 types and about 7650 predicates; they total about 206,000 lines of code. Our measurement platform was an x86 PC running Linux 2.0.36.

Without any of the static data structures or automatically generated predicates described in this paper, the object files contain a total of 3666 Kb of code and 311 Kb of data. This version of the system cannot do anything that depends on RTTI. The automatically generated unification and comparison predicates add 462 Kb of code and 12 Kb of data to this; the static `type_ctor_info` structures add another 120 Kb of code and 47 Kb of data on top of that. (`type_ctor_info`s contain the addresses of unification and comparison procedures, which prevents the compiler from optimizing those procedures away even if they are otherwise unused; this is where the code size increase comes from.) This version of the system supports polymorphic unifications and comparisons, dynamic typing (with the `univ` type) and the `type_name/1` function.

To support other RTTI-dependent operations, e.g. generic I/O, the system needs the `type_ctor_layout` and `type_ctor_functors` structures as well. Adding the `type_ctor_layout` structures alone adds 81 Kb of data, while adding the `type_ctor_functors` structures alone adds 78 Kb of data. However, since these two kinds of structures share many of their components (e.g. functor descriptors), adding both adds only 99 Kb of data.

If we wish to do something using stack layouts, the compiler must follow the rule of typeinfo liveness. This rule by itself adds 14 Kb of code and 17 Kb of data. This increase comes from the requirement to save type variables on the stack and to load them into registers more often (this must cause a slight slowdown, but this slowdown is so small that we cannot measure it). This brings us up to 4247 Kb of code and 469 Kb of data, for a total size of 4747 Kb. We will use this as the baseline for the percentage figures below.

Adding the stack layouts themselves has a much more substantial cost. Switching from conservative gc to native gc increases code size by 822 Kb and data size by 2229 Kb; total system size increases by 64% to 7798 Kb. The increase in code size is due to the native collector's requirement that certain optimizations which usually reduce code size be turned off; the increase in data size is due to the label layout structures. Sticking with conservative gc but adding full debugging support, increases code size by 6438 Kb and data size by 5248 Kb; total system size increases by 246% to 16433 Kb. The code size increase is much bigger because debugging inserts into the code many calls to the debugger entry point[9] (it also turns off optimizations that could confuse the user). The data size increase is much bigger because debugging needs label layout structures at more program points (e.g. the entry point of the then part of an if-then-else), and because it needs the names of variables.

We already use several techniques for reducing the size of the static structures generated by the Mercury compiler, most of which are related to RTTI. The most important such technique we have not covered earlier in the paper is looking for identical static structures in each module and merging them into a single structure. Merging identical static structures in different modules would yield a further benefit, but since we want to retain separate compilation, it would require significant extensions to our compilation environment. Another potential optimization we could implement is merging two structures whenever one is a prefix of the other.

5 Related Work

We expect that techniques and data structures at least somewhat similar to the ones we have described have been and/or are being used in the implementations of other mostly-statically typed languages (e.g. SML, Haskell and Algol 68; see the references cited in [8]). However, it is difficult to be sure, since papers that discuss RTTI implementations at any significant level of detail are few and far between. The exceptions we know of all deal with garbage collection of strongly typed languages, using the (obvious) model of walking the stack, finding out what the types of the live variables are in each frame and then recursively marking their values.

Goldberg [8] describes a system, apparently never implemented, that associates garbage collection information with each return point; this information takes the form of a compiler-generated function for tracing all the live variables of the stack frame being returned to. To handle polymorphism, it has these functions pass among themselves the addresses of other functions that trace single values (e.g. a function for tracing a list would take as an argument a function for tracing the list elements). This is a less general solution than our `pseudo_type_infos`. The garbage collection and tracing functions are single-purpose and are likely to be much bigger than our layout structures.

Tolmach [14] describes how, by using explicit lazily computed type parameters that describe the type environment (set of type bindings) of a function, one can simplify the reconstruction of types.

The TIL compiler for SML [13] uses a similar scheme but eagerly evaluates type parameters, making it quite similar to the combination of tables and type-info parameters used by the Mercury compiler, except for TIL's use of type tags on heap-allocated data. Unfortunately the paper lacks a detailed description of the data representations and runtime behaviour of the type information generated by the TIL compiler, and is unclear about whether this information can be used for purposes other than garbage collection.

Aditya et al [3,2] describe a garbage collector and debugger for Id that has an approach to RTTI that is similar to ours, the main difference being that in their system, callers of polymorphic functions do not pass type information to the callee; instead, the garbage collector or debugger searches ancestor stack frames for type information when necessary. Although this scheme avoids the cost of passing type information around, we have not found this cost to be significant. On the other hand, the numbers in [3] show that propagating type information in the stack is quite expensive for polymorphic code. This is probably not the right tradeoff for Mercury, since we want to encourage programmers to write polymorphic code.

In the logic programming field, Kwon et al [11] and Beierle et al [4] both describe schemes for implementing polymorphically typed logic programming languages with dynamic type tests. Their schemes both extend the WAM; both annotate the representations of unbound variable with type information and add additional WAM instructions for handling typed unification. But we believe that an approach which is based on a high-level program transformation, like our handling of `type_infos`, is simpler than one which requires significant modifications to the underlying virtual machine. Neither scheme makes use of type-specific term representations.

None of these papers cited above give measurements of the storage costs of their schemes. Future comparisons of space usage and type reconstruction performance between Mercury and the systems described in those papers may yield interesting results.

Elsman [7] uses a transformation very similar to the one we use to introduce `type_infos`, for a very similar purpose: to enable type-specific data representations; the performance benefits he reports broadly match our experience. However, his system, whose purpose is the efficient handling of polymorphic equality types in ML, only passes around the addresses of equality functions, not comparison functions, type names, or layout information. As such, his system constitutes a very limited form of RTTI that is useful only for polymorphic equality, not for dynamic types, garbage collection, debugging, etc.

6 Conclusion

Our results show that a run time type information system can be added to Mercury without compromising the speed of the basic execution mechanism, and with relatively small space overheads in most cases. The RTTI system allows many useful extensions both to the language and to the implementation.

In future work, we would like to explore the tradeoffs between table-driven generic operations and specialized code. Trends in microprocessor design, in particular the increasing relative costs of mispredicted branches and cache misses, mean that it is quite possible that a generic unification routine using `type_ctor_info` structures may now be faster than the automatically generated procedures we now use. However, executing code is inherently more flexible than interpreting fixed-format tables. At the moment, we take advantage of this in our implementation of types with user-defined equality theories, for which we simply override the pointer to the automatically generated unification procedure with a pointer to the one provided by the user. Such a facility would still need to be provided even in a system that used table-driven unification.

To make table-driven generic operations more competitive, we are in the process of simplifying our data structures. At the moment, the information about what kind of type the type constructor represents (a discriminated union type, an equivalence type, a no_tag type, an enumeration type or a builtin type) is scattered in several different parts of the `type_ctor_layout` structure and its components (e.g. functor descriptors), even though this information is available directly in the `type_ctor_functors` structure. The reason for this is that initially, the Mercury RTTI system only had `type_ctor_layouts`; `type_ctor_functors` were added later. The design we are moving towards puts the type kind directly into the `type_ctor_info`, and specializes the rest of the `type_ctor_info` according to the type kind (e.g. `type_ctor_layout` and `type_ctor_functors` structures will be present only if the type is a discriminated union type).

We would like to thank the Australian Research Council for their support.

References

1. M. Abadi, L. Cardelli, B. Pierce, and G. Plotkin. Dynamic typing in a statically typed language. *ACM Transactions on Programming Languages and Systems*, 13(2):237–268, April 1991.
2. Shail Aditya and Alejandro Caro. Compiler-directed type reconstruction for polymorphic languages. In *Proceedings of the 1993 ACM Conference on Functional Programming Languages and Computer Architecture*, Copenhagen, Denmark, June 1993.

3. Shail Aditya, Christine Flood, and James Hicks. Garbage collection for strongly-typed languages using run-time type reconstruction. In *Proceedings of the 1994 ACM Conference on Lisp and Functional Programming*, pages 12–23, June 1994.
4. C. Beierle, G. Meyer, and H. Semle. Extending the warren abstract machine to polymorphic order-sorted resolution. In *Proceedings of the International Logic Programming Symposium*, pages 272–286, 1991.
5. Hans Boehm and Mark Weiser. Garbage collection in an uncooperative environment. *Software - Practice and Experience*, 18:807–820, 1988.
6. Bart Demoen, Maria Garcia de la Banda, Warwick Harvey, Kim Marriott, and Peter Stuckey. Herbrand constraint solving in HAL. Technical Report 99/18, Department of Software Engineering and Computer Science, University of Melbourne, Melbourne, Australia, 1998.
7. Martin Elsman. Polymorphic equality — no tags required. In *Second International Workshop on Types in Compilation*, volume 1473 of *Lecture Notes in Computer Science*. Springer Verlag, 1998.
8. Benjamin Goldberg. Tag-free garbage collection for strongly typed programming languages. In *Proceedings of the SIGPLAN '91 Conference on Programming Languages Design and Implementation*, pages 165–176, Toronto, Ontario, June 1991.
9. D.R. Hanson and M. Raghavachari. A machine-independent debugger. *Software - Practice and Experience*, 26:1277–1299, 1996.
10. Fergus Henderson, Thomas Conway, Zoltan Somogyi, and David Jeffery. The Mercury language reference manual. Technical Report 96/10, Department of Computer Science, University of Melbourne, Melbourne, Australia, 1996.
11. K. Kwon, G. Nadathur, and D.S. Wilson. Implementing polymorphic typing in a logic programming language. In *Computer Languages*, volume 20(1), pages 25–42, 1994.
12. Zoltan Somogyi, Fergus Henderson, and Thomas Conway. The execution algorithm of Mercury, an efficient purely declarative logic programming language. *Journal of Logic Programming*, 26(1-3):17–64, October-December 1996.
13. D. Tarditi, G. Morrisett, P. Cheng, C. Stone, R. Harper, and P. Lee. TIL : A type-directed optimizing compiler for ML. In *Proceedings of the SIGPLAN '96 Conference on Programming Language Design and Implemantation*, pages 181–192, New York, May 21–24 1996.
14. Andrew Tolmach. Tag-free garbage collection using explicit type parameters. In *Proceedings of the SIGPLAN '94 Conference on Programming Languages Design and Implementation*, pages 1–11, Orlando, Florida, June 1994.

A Virtual Machine for a Process Calculus

Luís Lopes[1], Fernando Silva[1], and Vasco T. Vasconcelos[2]

[1] DCC-FC & LIACC, Universidade do Porto,
Rua do Campo Alegre, 823, 4150 Porto, Portugal
{lblopes,fds}@ncc.up.pt
[2] DI-FC, Universidade de Lisboa,
Campo Grande, 1700 Lisboa, Portugal
vv@di.fc.ul.pt

Abstract. Despite extensive theoretical work on process-calculi, virtual machine specifications and implementations of actual computational models are still scarce.
This paper presents a virtual machine for a strongly typed, polymorphic, concurrent, object-oriented programming language based on the TyCO process calculus. The system runs byte-code files, assembled from an intermediate assembly language representation, which is in turn generated by a compiler. Code optimizations are provided by the compiler coupled with a type-inference system. The design and implementation of the virtual machine focuses on performance, compactness, and architecture independence with a view to mobile computing. The assembly code emphasizes readability and efficient byte code generation. The byte code has a simple layout and is a compromise between size and performance. We present some performance results and compare them to other languages such as Pict, Oz, and JoCaml.

Keywords: Process-Calculus, Concurrency, Abstract-Machine, Implementation.

1 Introduction

In recent years researchers have devoted a great effort in providing semantics for pure concurrent programming languages within the realm of process-calculi. Milner, Parrow and Walker's π-calculus or an equivalent asynchronous formulation due to Honda and Tokoro has been the starting point for most of these attempts [9,17].

In this paper we use Vasconcelos' Typed Concurrent Objects to define TyCO, a strongly typed, polymorphic, concurrent, object-oriented language [23,25]. Typed Concurrent Objects is a form of the asynchronous π-calculus featuring first class objects, asynchronous messages, and template definitions. The calculus formally describes the concurrent interaction of ephemeral objects through asynchronous communication. Synchronous communication can be implemented with continuations. Templates are specifications of processes abstracted on a sequence of variables allowing, for example, for classes to be modeled. Unbounded

G. Nadathur (Ed.): PPDP'99, LNCS 1702, pp. 244–260, 1999.

behavior is modeled through explicit instantiation of recursive templates. A type system assigns monomorphic types to variables and polymorphic types to template variables [25]. Other type systems have been proposed that support non-uniform object interfaces [20]. The calculus is reminiscent of the Abadi and Cardelli's ς-calculus in the sense that objects are sums of labeled methods attached to names, the *self* parameters, and messages can be seen as asynchronous method invocations [3].

TyCO is a very low-level programming language with a few derived constructs and constitutes a building block for higher level idioms. We are interested in using TyCO to study the issues involved in the design and implementation of languages with run-time support for distribution and code mobility. In this paper we focus on the architecture and implementation of a sequential run-time system for TyCO. Introducing distribution and mobility is the focus of a cooperating project [24]. Our long term objectives led us to the following design principles:

1. the system should have a compact implementation and be self-contained;
2. it should be efficient, running close to languages such as Pict [19], Oz [16] or JoCaml [2];
3. the executable programs must to have a compact, architecture independent, format.

The architecture of the run-time system is a compact byte-code emulator with a heap for dynamic data-structures, a run-queue for fair scheduling of byte-code and two stacks for keeping local variable bindings and for evaluating expressions. Our previous experience in parallel computing makes us believe that more compact designs are better suited for concurrent object-oriented languages, whether we want to explore local and typically very fine grained parallelism or concurrency, or evolve to mobile computations over fast heterogeneous networks where the latencies must be kept to the lowest possible.

The remainder of the paper is organized as follows: section 2 introduces the TyCO language; sections 3 describes the design and some implementation details of the run-time system; section 4 describes the optimizations implemented in the current implementation; section 5 presents some performance figures obtained with the current implementation, and finally; sections 6 and 7, respectively overview some related work, present some conclusions and future research issues.

2 Introducing TyCO

TyCO is a strongly, implicitly typed concurrent object-oriented programming language based on a predicative polymorphic calculus of objects [23,25]. TyCO is a kernel language for the calculus, and grows from it by adding primitive types with a set of basic operations, and a rudimentary I/O system.

In the sequel we introduce the syntax and semantics of TyCO. The discussion is much abbreviated due to space constraints. For a fully detailed description the reader may refer to the language definition [23].

Syntax Overview The basic syntactic categories are: *constants* (booleans and integers), ranged over by $c, c', \ldots$; *value variables*, ranged over by $x, y, \ldots$; *expressions*, ranged over by $e, e', \ldots$; *labels*, ranged over by $l, l', \ldots$, and; *template variables*, ranged over by $X, Y, \ldots$. Let $\tilde{x}$ denote the sequence $x_1 \cdots x_k$, with $k \geq 0$, of pairwise distinct variables (and similarly for $\tilde{e}$ where the expressions need not be distinct). Then the set of processes, ranged by $P, Q, \ldots$ is given by the following grammar.

P	$::=$	$\texttt{inaction}$	terminated process
	$\mid$	$P \mid P$	concurrent composition
	$\mid$	$\texttt{new}\ \tilde{x}\ P$	channel declaration
	$\mid$	$x\ !\ l[\tilde{e}]$	message
	$\mid$	$x\ ?\ M$	object
	$\mid$	$X[\tilde{e}]$	instance
	$\mid$	$\texttt{def}\ D\ \texttt{in}\ P$	recursion
	$\mid$	$\texttt{if}\ e\ \texttt{then}\ P\ \texttt{else}\ P$	conditional
	$\mid$	(P)	grouping
D	$::=$	$X_1(\tilde{x}_1) = P_1\ \texttt{and} \ldots \texttt{and}\ X_k(\tilde{x}_k) = P_k$	template declaration
M	$::=$	$\{l_1(\tilde{x}_1) = P_1 , \ldots , l_k(\tilde{x}_k) = P_k\}$	methods
e	$::=$	$e_1\ op\ e_2 \mid op\ e \mid x \mid c \mid (e)$	expressions

Some restrictions apply to the above grammar, namely: a) no collection of methods may contain the same label twice; b) no sequence of variables in a template declaration or collection of methods may contain the same variable twice, and; c) no declaration may contain the same template variable twice.

A method labeled l_i in an object $x?\{l_1(\tilde{x}_1) = P_1, \ldots, l_k(\tilde{x}_k) = P_k\}$ is selected by a message of the form $x!l_i[\tilde{e}]$; the result is the process P_i where the variables in $\tilde{x}_i$ are replaced by the values of the expressions in $\tilde{e}$. This form of reduction is called *communication*. Similarly, an instance $X_i[\tilde{e}]$ selects the template X_i in a template declaration $X_1(\tilde{x}_1) = P_1\ \texttt{and} \ldots \texttt{and}\ X_k(\tilde{x}_k) = P_k$; the result is the process P_i where the variables in $\tilde{x}_i$ are replaced by the values of the expressions in $\tilde{e}$. This form of reduction is called *instantiation*.

We let the scope of variables, introduced with `new`, extend as far to the right as possible, i.e., up to the end of the current composition of processes. We single out a label — `val` — to be used in objects with a single method. This allows us to abbreviate the syntax of messages and objects. Single branch conditionals are also defined from common conditionals with an `inaction` in the else branch.

$$x![\tilde{e}] \equiv x!\texttt{val}[\tilde{e}]$$
$$x?(\tilde{y}) = P \equiv x?\{\texttt{val}(\tilde{y}) = P\}$$
$$\texttt{if}\ e\ \texttt{then}\ P \equiv \texttt{if}\ e\ \texttt{then}\ P\ \texttt{else inaction}$$

To illustrate the programming style and syntax of the language we sketch a simple example: a single element polymorphic cell. We define a template object with two attributes: the `self` channel and the value u itself. The object has two methods one for reading the current cell value and another to change it. The recursion keeps the cell alive.

```
def Cell( self, u ) =
self ? {
    read( r ) = r![u] | Cell[self, u],
    write( v ) = Cell[self, v]
}
in  new x Cell[x,9] | new y Cell[y,true]
```

The continuation of the definition instantiates an integer cell and a boolean cell at the channels x and y, respectively.

3 The Virtual Machine

The implementation of the virtual machine is supported by a formal specification of an abstract machine for TyCO[15]. This abstract machine grows from Turner's abstract machine for Pict [22], but modifies it in the following major ways:

1. objects are first class entities and substitute input processes. Objects are more efficient than Pict's encoding in π [26] both in reduction and heap usage;
2. we use recursion instead of replication for persistence. This allows a cleaner design of the abstract machine – no need for distinct ? and ?* rules, and allows a more rational heap usage;
3. we introduce a new syntactic category – the *thread* – that represents the basic schedulable and runnable block in the abstract machine. Threads are identified as bodies of template definitions or method implementations;
4. threads cannot be suspended. With this property, our objects are very akin to actors and provide a good model for object oriented concurrent languages [4,5]. This choice, along with the previous item, also simplifies the treatment of local bindings, introduced with `new` statements, and the management of environments.

The abstract machine is sound, i.e., every state transition in the abstract machine can be viewed as a reduction or a congruence between their process encodings in the base calculus [15]. It also features important run-time properties such as: a) at any time during a computation the queues associated with names are either empty or either have communications or method-closures [22]; b) for well-typed programs the abstract machine does not deadlock. This property is linked intimately to the ability of the type system to guarantee that no run-time protocol errors will occur, and; c) the machine is fair, in the sense that every runnable thread will be executed in a constant time after its creation.

The virtual machine closely maps the formal specification and executes TyCO programs quite efficiently.

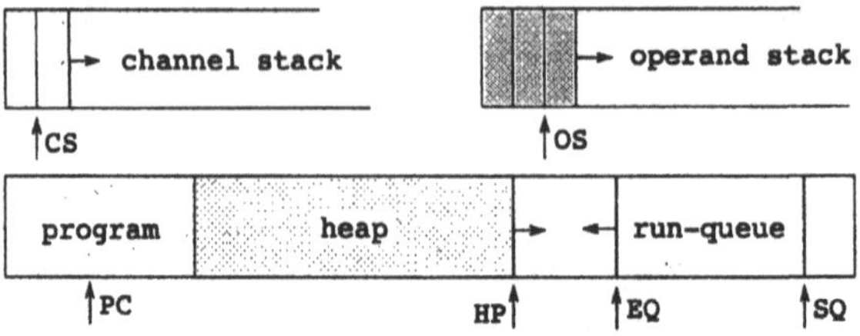

Fig. 1. Memory Layout of the Virtual Machine

The Memory Layout The virtual machine uses five logically distinct memory areas (figure.1) to compute.

The *program* area keeps the byte-code instructions to be executed. The byte-code is composed of instruction blocks and method tables (sequences of pointers to byte-code blocks).

Dynamic data-structures such as objects, messages, channels and builtin values are allocated in the *heap*. The basic building block of the heap is a machine *word*. The basic allocation unit in the heap is the *frame* and consists of one or more contiguous heap words with a descriptor for garbage collection.

When a reduction (either communication or instantiation) occurs, a new virtual machine thread (*vm_thread*) is created. The new vm_thread is simply a frame with a pointer to the byte-code and a set of bindings, and is allocated in the *run-queue* where it waits to be scheduled for execution. Using a run-queue to store vm_threads ready for execution provides fairness. The heap and the run-queue are allocated in the bottommost and topmost areas, respectively, of a single memory block. They grow in opposite directions and garbage collection is triggered when a collision is predicted.

Local variables, introduced with new statements, are bound to fresh channels allocated in the heap and the bindings (pointers) are kept in the *channel stack*. These bindings are discarded after a vm_thread finishes but the channels, in the heap, may remain active outside the scope of the current vm_thread through scope extrusion.

Finally, expressions with builtin data-types are evaluated in the *operand stack*. Simple values do not require evaluation and are copied directly in the heap. Using an operand stack to perform built-in operations enables the generation of more compact byte-codes since many otherwise explicit arguments (e.g., registers for the arguments and result of an operation) are implicitly located at the top of the stack.

Heap Representation of Processes and Channels TyCO manipulates three basic kinds of processes at runtime: messages, objects and instantiations (figure 2). Messages and objects are located in shared communication channels. Internally, the virtual machine sees all these abstractions as simple frames, although their internal structure is distinct. A message frame holds the label of the method it is invoking plus a variable number of arguments. An object frame, on the other hand, holds a pointer to the byte-code (the location of its method table) plus a variable number of bindings for variables occurring free in its methods. An instance frame has a pointer to the byte-code for the template and a variable number of arguments.

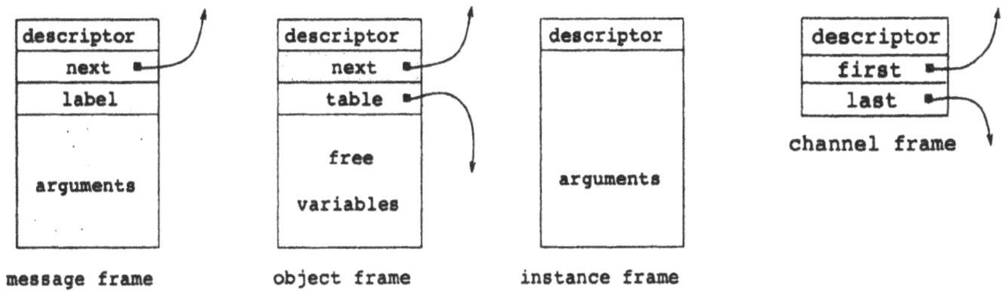

Fig. 2. Message, object, instance and channel frames.

Channel frames hold communication queues which at run-time have either only objects or only messages or are empty. The first word of the three that compose a channel is the descriptor for the frame which in this case also carries the state of the channel. This state indicates the internal configuration and composition of the queue. The other two words hold pointers to, respectively, the first and last message (object) frame in the queue.

The Machine Registers The virtual machine uses a small set of global registers to control the program flow and to manipulate machine and user data-structures. Register PC (Program Counter) points to the next instruction to be executed. Register HP (Heap Pointer) points to the next available position in the heap. Registers SQ (Start Queue) and EQ (End Queue) point to the limits of the run-queue. Finally, registers OS (Operand Stack) and CS (Channel Stack) point to the last used position in each area.

When a program starts, register PC is loaded with the address of the first instruction. Register CC (Current Channel) points to the channel which is currently being used to try a reduction. Register CF (Current Frame) holds frames temporarily until they are either enqueued or used in a reduction. If a reduction takes place, the frame for the other redex's component is kept in the register OF (Other Frame). Registers FV (Free Variable bindings) and PM (ParaMeter bindings) are used to hold the free variable and parameter bindings, respectively.

The Instruction Set The virtual machine instruction set was intentionally designed to be minimal in size and to have a very simple layout. Instructions are identified by an unique opcode held in the word pointed to by the program counter PC. For most instructions the opcode of an instruction determines the number of arguments that follow in contiguous words. Alternatively, the first argument indicates the number of remaining arguments as in `switch`. In the sequel we let n,k range over the natural numbers, l over code labels and w over machine words (representing constants or heap references).

The first set of instructions is used to allocate heap space for dynamic data-structures.

`msgf` n,k `objf` n,l `instf` n `newc` k

`msgf` n,k allocates a frame for a message with label k and with n words for the arguments. `objf` n,l does the same for an object with a method table at l and n words for free variable bindings. `instf` n allocates a frame for a template instance with n words for arguments. `newc` k allocates a channel in the heap and keeps a reference for it in the stack position k.

Next we have instructions that move data, one word at a time, within the heap and between the heap and the operand and channel stacks.

`put` k, w `push` w `pop` k

`put` k, w copies the word w directly to the position k in the frame currently being assembled. `push` w pushes the data in w to the top of the operand stack. `pop` k moves the result of evaluating an expression from the top of the operand stack to the position k in the frame currently being assembled.

We also need the following basic control flow instructions.

`if` l `switch` $n,l_1,,\ldots,l_n$ `jump` l `ret`

`if` l jumps to label l if the value at the top of the operand stack is (boolean) false. `switch` $n,l_1,,\ldots,l_n$ jumps to label l_k, where k is taken from the top of the operand stack. `jump` l jumps unconditionally to the code at label l. Finally, `ret` checks the halt condition and exits if it holds; otherwise it loads another vm_thread for execution from the run-queue.

For communication queues we need instructions to check and update their state and insert and remove items from the queues.

`state` w `update` k `reset` `enqueue` `dequeue`

`state` w takes the state of the channel in word w and places it at the top of the operand stack. `update` k changes the state of the current channel to k. In a unoptimized setting the state of a channel is 0 if it is empty, 1 if it has messages or 2 if it has objects. `reset` sets the state to 0 if the current channel is empty. `enqueue` enqueues the current frame (at `CF`) in the current channel (at `CC`) whereas `dequeue` dequeues a frame from the current channel (at `CC`) and prepares it for reduction (placing it at `OF`).

Finally, we require instructions that handle reductions: both communication and instantiation.

`redobj` w `redmsg` w `instof` l

`redobj` w reduces the current object frame with a message. `redmsg` w is similar, reducing the current message frame with an object. Finally, `instof` l creates a new vm_thread, an instance of the byte-code at label l, with the arguments in the current frame.

In addition to this basic set there is a set of operations on builtin datatypes and also specialized instructions that implement some optimizations. For example, in case a sequence of words is copied preserving its order, the `put` and `pop` operations may be replaced by optimized versions where the k argument is dropped.

The Emulator Before running a byte-code file, the emulator links the opcodes in the byte-code to the actual addresses of the instructions (C functions). It also translates integer offsets within the byte-code into absolute hardware addresses. This *link* operation avoids an extra indirection each time a new instruction is fetched and also avoids the computation of addresses on-the-fly. The emulator loop is a very small `while` loop adapted from the STG machine [11]. Each instruction is implemented as a parameterless C function that returns the address of the following instruction. The emulation loop starts with the first instruction in the byte-code and ends when a NULL pointer is returned. The emulator halts whenever a vm_thread ends and the run-queue is empty.

Garbage Collection A major concern of the implementation is to make the emulator run programs in as small a heap space as possible. Efficient garbage collection is essential for such a goal. The emulator triggers garbage collection whenever the gap between the top of the heap, pointed to by `HP`, and the end of the run-queue, pointed to by `EQ`, is smaller than the required number of words to execute a new vm_thread.

Making this test for every instruction that uses the heap before actually executing it would be very costly. Instead, when a byte-code file is assembled the maximum number of heap words required for the execution of each vm_thread is computed and placed in the word immediately preceding the first instruction of the vm_thread. At run-time, before starting executing a new vm_thread, the emulator checks whether there is enough space in the heap to safely run it. If not then garbage collection is triggered. The emulator aborts if the space reclaimed by the garbage collector is less than `required`.

If the space between the heap limit and `SQ` is enough, then the garbage collector just shifts the run-queue upwards and returns; if not, it must perform a full garbage collection. We use a *copying* garbage collection algorithm. The algorithm performs one pass through the run-queue to copy the active frames. Active frames are those that can still be accessed by taking each item in the run-queue as the root of a tree and recursively following the links in the heap frames. The garbage collector does not use any knowledge about the internal structure of the frames (e.g., if they represent objects or messages).

Compilation TyCO programs are compiled into the virtual machine instruction set by the language compiler. This instruction set maps almost one-to-one with the byte-code representation. The syntax of the intermediate representation reflects exactly the way the corresponding byte-code is structured. It is important that the compilation preserves the nested structure of the source program in the final byte-code. This provides a very efficient way of extracting byte-code blocks at run-time when considering code mobility in distributed computations [14,24]. To illustrate the compilation we present a skeletal version of the unoptimized, intermediate code for the Cell example presented in section 2. The run-time environment of a vm_thread is distributed into three distinct locations: the parameter and free variable bindings pointed to by registers PM and FV, respectively, and the bindings for local variables held in the channel stack CS. In the machine instructions the words PM[k], FV[k] and CS[k] are represented by pk, fk and ck, respectively.

```
main  = {
   def Cell = {
      objf     2                     % self located object with parameters
      put      p0                    % p0=self
      put      p1                    % p1=u
      trobj    p0 = {
         { read, write }
         read = {                    % the method 'read', p0=r,f0=self,f1=u
            msgf     1,0             % message r![u]
            put      f1
            trmsg    p0
            instof   2,Cell          % instantiation Cell[self,u]
            put      f0
            put      f1
         }
         write = {                   % the method 'write', p0=v,f0=self,f1=u
            instof   2,Cell          % instantiation Cell[self,v]
            put      f0
            put      p0
         }
      }
   }
   newc     c0                       % creation of x
   instof   2,Cell                   % instantiation Cell[x,9]
   put      c0
   put      9
   newc     c1                       % creation of y
   instof   2,Cell                   % instantiation Cell[y,true]
   put      c1
   put      true
}
```

4 Optimizations

This section describes a sequence of optimizations that we applied to the emulator with support from the compiler to improve performance. Some optimizations rely on type information, namely channel usage properties, gathered at compile time by the type inference system [6,12,13,23].

Compacted messages and objects This optimization is due to Turner [22]. Given that at any time a channel is very likely to hold at most a single object or message frame in its queue before a communication takes place, we optimize the channel layout for this case. The idea is to avoid the overhead of queuing and dequeuing frames and instead to access the frame contents directly.

Optimizing frame sizes We minimize the size of the frames required by each process frame. For example, messages or objects in a synchronization channel do not require a `next` field. This minimizes heap consumption and improves performance.

Single method objects These objects do not require a method table. The compiler generates the code for an object with an offset for the byte-code of the method, instead of an offset for a method table. This avoids one extra indirection before each method invocation.

Fast reduction This optimization can be performed in cases where we can assure that a given channel will have exactly one object. Two important cases are: uniform receptors [21] where a persistent object is placed in a channel and receives an arbitrary number of messages, and; linear synchronization channels [13] where an ephemeral object and a message meet once in a channel for synchronization and the arrival order is unknown. The main point of this optimization is that we never allocate the channel in the heap to hold the object (figure 3a). We just create a frame for the object in the heap and use its pointer directly as a binding (figure 3b).

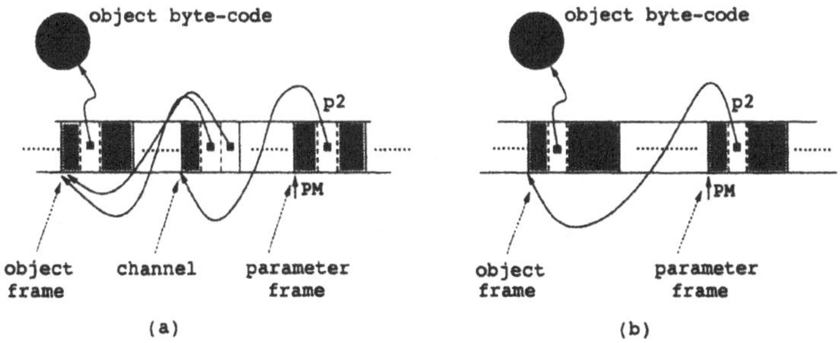

Fig. 3. Fast reduction

In the case of uniform receptors, when a message arrives for this binding (p2 in the figure) we can reduce at once since the binding already holds a pointer to the object frame. For linear channels, if we have, say, a message for p2, we first check the value at p2. If it is null we assign it the pointer for the message frame, otherwise the binding must point to an object frame and reduction is immediate. What distinguishes persistent from linear synchronization channels in our model is the fact that, since we use recursion to model persistence, a persistent object must always have a self referencing pointer in its closure when it goes to the run-queue. This preserves the frame if garbage collection is triggered. In the case of a linear channel this link cannot exist and so, the object frame only lasts until the resulting vm_thread ends.

Merging instructions Certain instructions occur in patterns that are very common, sometimes pervasive, in the intermediate assembly. Since an instruction-by-instruction execution is expensive (one unconditional jump per instruction) we create new instructions that merge a few basic ones to optimize for the common case. One such optimization is shown for macros `trobj` and `trmsg`, used to try to reduce objects and messages immediately. For example, `trobj` w checks the state of channel w. If it has messages then it dequeues a message frame and creates a new vm_thread in the run-queue from the reduction with the current object. If the channel state is either empty or already has objects the current frame is enqueued. The case for `trmsg` w is the dual.

```
trobj w:
        state     w
        switch    3,empty,msg,obj
empty:  enqueue
        update    2
        jump      end
msg:    dequeue
        redobj    w
        reset
        jump      end
obj:    enqueue
end:
```

```
trmsg w:
        state     w
        switch    3,empty,msg,obj
empty:  enqueue
        update    1
        jump      end
msg:    enqueue
        jump      end
obj:    dequeue
        redmsg    w
        reset
end:
```

Inline arguments in the run-queue Each time a template instantiation or a fast reduction occurs we copy the arguments directly to the run-queue. The advantage of the optimization is that the space used for vm_threads in the run-queue is reclaimed immediately after the vm_thread is selected for execution. This increases the number of *fast* (and decreases the number of *full*) garbage collections. Fast garbage collections are very light weight involving just a shift of the run-queue.

5 System Performance

Currently, we have an implementation of the TyCO programming language which includes a source to assembly compiler and a byte-code assembler. We have chosen to separate the intermediate assembly code generation from the byte-code generation to allow us more flexibility namely in programming directly in assembly. The emulator is a very compact implementation of the virtual machine with about 4000 lines of C code. Figure 4 illustrates the architecture of the TyCO system.

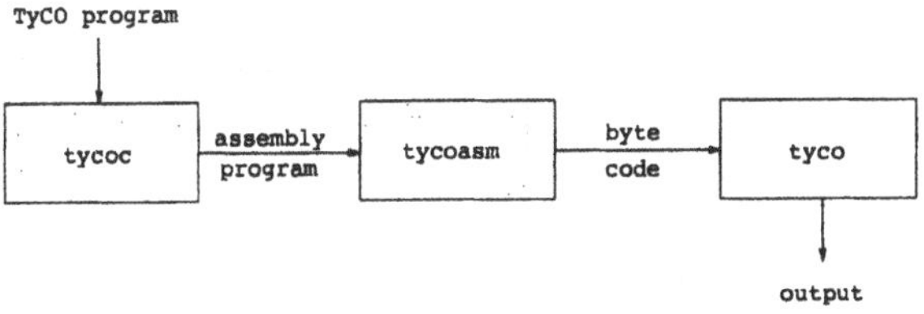

Fig. 4. The TyCO system

We used a set of small programs to measure the efficiency of the current implementation relative to the concurrent programming languages Pict [19], Oz [16] and the JoCaml implementation of the Join calculus [8]. Both JoCaml and Oz may use byte-codes whereas Pict generates binary files from intermediate C code.

The values presented in table 1 are just indicative of the system's performance in terms of speed. These helped us in fine-tuning the implementation. A full performance evaluation will have to address larger, *real world* applications [18].

The benchmark programs used include some standard programs such as `tak`, `sieve` and `queens`, and three other larger programs, `mirror`, `graph` and `fourier`, that best illustrate the potential of the language. `mirror` takes a tree with 10k nodes, leafs and buds, and builds another one which is its mirror image. It uses objects for pattern matching and is deeply recursive. `graph` takes a connected graph with 128 nodes and traverses it mapping a function on each node's attribute. Each node of the graph is an object with an integer attribute. The computation time for each node is exponential on the integer attribute. `fourier` takes a list of complex numbers (implemented as objects) and computes its Discrete Fourier Transform. We have implemented all programs in TyCO 0.2, Pict 4.1 [19], Oz 2.0.4 [16] and JoCaml [2] to compare the performance of these systems.

Table 1 shows, for each program, the smallest execution time of 10 consecutive runs in seconds. All the values observed were obtained with a default heap space of 256k words (when possible), in a 233MHz Pentium II machine with 128Mb RAM, running Linux. With Oz we used the switches `+optimize` and `-threadedqueries` to get full performance from the Oz code. Both Pict and the TyCO emulator were compiled with `-O3 -fommit-frame-pointer` optimization flags.

The initial results show that TyCO's speed is clearly in the same order of magnitude as Pict and Oz, and indeed compares favorably considering it is emulated code. TyCO is clearly faster than JoCaml as can be seen in the rightmost portion of the table. These results were obtained for distinct problem sizes, relative to the first set, since for some programs JoCaml ran into some problems

Program	Pict	Oz	TyCO	Program	JoCaml	TyCO
tak*10 22,16,8	4.40	11.7	24.31	tak 22,16,8	6.98	3.02
queens*10 10	17.0	33.1	58.09	queens 8	2.46	0.39
sieve*10 10k	9.90	19.2	20.92	lsieve 4k	62.37	8.33
mirror*10 10k	3.13	4.20	1.21	mirror 10k	2.51	0.24
graph*10 128	9.62	7.10	7.24	graph 128	—	—
fourier*10 64	2.30	2.60	0.91	fourier 64	0.95	0.21

Table 1. Execution times

either compiling (e.g., `graph`) or running them (e.g., `queens` 10). `lsieve` uses non-builtin lists to implement the sieve of primes while `sieve` uses a chain of objects. The performance gap is higher than average in the case of functional programs a fact that is explained by the optimized code generated by both Pict and Oz for functions. Further optimization, namely with information from the type system may allow this gap to be diminished. The performance ratio for applications that manipulate large numbers of objects (with more than one method), on the other hand, clearly favors TyCO. For example `mirror`, which uses objects to implement a large tree and to encode pattern matching, performs nearly three times faster than Pict and even more for Oz and JoCaml. Also notice that all the Oz programs required an increase in the heap size up to 3M words and once (`queens`) to 6M to terminate. Compare this with the very conservative 256k used by both in TyCO and Pict. The exception for Pict is `fourier` where there is a lot of parallelism and method invocations. Pict required 1.5M words to run the program, as opposed to 256k words in TyCO, and was about 2.3 times slower than TyCO. `fourier` shows that objects in both Pict and Oz are clearly less efficient than in TyCO. Pict showed lower performance on the object based benchmarks. This is due to the fact that the encoding of objects in the π-calculus is rather inefficient both in speed and heap usage.

	TyCO			**Pict**		
Program	Heap	shift-gc	full-gc	Heap	shift-gc	full-gc
tak 22,16,8	13487	406	18	11496	225	32
queens 10	12975	591	13	13933	390	55
sieve 10k	11110	218	31	11941	253	36
mirror 10k	505	4	0	1094	27	5
graph 128	3336	101	5	5769	139	25
fourier 64	538	18	1	4870	2	0

Table 2. Total heap usage and number of garbage collections.

Table 2 shows that TyCO uses more heap space than Pict in functional applications such as `tak`. The situation changes completely when we switch to programs with object based data-structures. TyCO performs more *shift* garbage collections since it uses the run-queue to store the arguments of instances and some messages directly and, on average, TyCO uses one extra word per heap frame. This increases the number of collisions with the top of the heap. On the other hand the number of *full* garbage collections performed is substantially smaller in TyCO. This is mostly due to the combined effect of the inlining of arguments in the run-queue and to the fact that TyCO does not produce run-time heap garbage in the form of unused channels or process closures. Pict produces significant amounts of heap garbage in applications where objects are pervasive since each object is modeled with: a) one channel for the object, one channel for each method and one process closure per method. Most of the times only a subset of these will actually be used. On the other hand an object in TyCO just requires a channel (*self*) and one closure for the method collection and the free variables. This effect is plainly visible in `mirror` for example.

We tried to measure the amount of overhead generated by our emulation strategy using a small test program that has a similar emulation cycle but always invokes the same function. An artificial addition was introduced in the body of the function as a way to simulate the overhead of adjusting the program counter for the next instruction, as is done in the actual machine. Running this small program with the optimizations `-O3 -fomit-frame-pointer`, we found that the emulation overhead accounts for 15 to 28% of the total execution time, with the higher limit observed for functional programs.

The run-time system for TyCO is very lightweight. It uses byte-codes to provide a small, architecture independent, representation of programs. The engine of the system is a compact (the binary occupies 39k) and efficient emulator with light system requirements, namely it features a rather conservative use of the heap.

This system architecture provides in our opinion the ideal starting point for the introduction of distribution and code mobility, which is the focus of an ongoing project.

6 Related Work

We briefly describe the main features of some concurrent process-based programming languages that relate to our work.

Pict is a pure concurrent programming language based on the asynchronous π-calculus [19]. The run-time system is based on Turner's abstract machine specification and the implementation borrows from the C and OCaml programming languages [22]. The basic programming abstractions are processes and names (channels). Objects in Pict are persistent with each method implemented as an input process held in a distinct channel. The execution of methods in concurrent objects by a client process is achieved by first interacting with a server process (that serves requests to the object and acts like a *lock* ensuring mutual exclusion), followed by the method invocation proper [26]. This protocol for method invocation involves two synchronizations as opposed to one in TyCO that uses branching structures. Moreover, this encoding of objects produces large amounts of computational garbage in the form of unused channels and process closures.

Also, Pict uses replication to model recursion whereas TyCO uses recursion. Recursion not only provides a more natural programming model but also allows replication only when it is strictly needed, avoiding the generation of unused process.

Oz is based on the γ-calculus and combines the functional, object-oriented and constraint logic programming paradigms in a single system [16]. The Oz abstract machine is fully self contained and its implementation is inspired in the AKL machine [10]. The basic abstractions are names, logical variables, procedural abstraction and cells. Constraints are built over logical variables by first-order logic equations, using a set of predefined predicates. Cells are primitive entities that maintain state and provide atomic read-write operations. Channels are modeled through first class entities called *ports*. They are explicitly manipulated queues that can be shared among threads and can be used for asynchronous communication. Oz procedures have encapsulated state so that objects can be defined directly as sets of methods (procedures) acting over their state (represented as a set of logical variables). This representation is close to objects in TyCO if we view the state held in logical variables as template parameter bindings.

Join implements the Join-calculus [7,8]. The JoCaml implementation integrates Join into the OCaml language. Join collapses the creation of new names, reception and replication into a single construct called a *join pattern*. Channels, both synchronous and asynchronous, expressions and processes are the basic abstractions. Programs are made of processes, communicating asynchronously and producing no values, and expressions evaluated synchronously and producing values. Processes communicate by sending messages on channels. Join patterns describe the way multiple processes (molecules) may interact with each other (the reactions) when receiving certain messages (molecules) producing other processes (molecules) plus eventual variable bindings. The JoCaml implementation has some fairly advanced tools for modular software development inherited from its development language OCaml and supports mobile computing [1].

7 Conclusions and Future Work

We presented a virtual machine for a programming language based on Typed Concurrent Objects, a process-calculus [25]. The virtual machine emulates byte-code programs generated by a compiler and an assembler. The performance of the byte-code is enhanced with optimizations based on type information gathered at compile-time. Preliminary results are promising and there is scope for plenty of optimizations. The current implementation performs close to Pict and Oz on average and clearly surpasses JoCaml. TyCO is faster in applications using objects and persistent data structures, despite being emulated. TyCO consistently runs in very small heap sizes, and performs significantly less garbage collection than either Pict or Oz.

Future work will focus on performance evaluation and fine tuning of the system using larger, *real world* applications [18]. Channel usage information from type systems such as those described can dramatically optimize the assembly and byte-code [13,12]. An ongoing project is introducing support for mobile computing in this framework as proposed in [24]. A multi-threaded/parallel implementation of the current virtual machine is also being considered since it will provide an interesting model for parallel data-flow computations.

The TyCO system, version 0.2 (*alpha* release) may be obtained from the web site: `http://www.ncc.up.pt/~lblopes/tyco.html`.

Acknowledgments

We would like to thank the anonymous referees for their valuable comments and suggestions. The authors are partially supported by projects Dolphin (contract PRAXIS/2/2.1/TIT/1577/95), and DiCoMo (contract PRAXIS/P/EEI/12059/98).

References

1. Objective CAML Home Page. `http://pauillac.inria.fr/ocaml`.
2. The JoCaml Home Page. `http://pauillac.inria.fr/jocaml`.
3. M. Abadi and L. Cardelli. *A Theory Of Objects*. Springer-Verlag, 1996.
4. G. Agha. *ACTORS: A Model of Concurrent Computation in Distributed Systems*. The MIT Press, 1986.
5. G. Agha and C. Hewitt. Actors: A Conceptual Foundation for Concurrent Object-Oriented Programming. *Research Directions on Object-Oriented Programming*, 1981. Shiver and Wegner, editors. MIT Press.
6. Roberto M. Amadio. An Asynchronous Model of Locality, Failure, and Process Mobility. In COORDINATION'97, volume 1282 of LNCS, pages 374–391. Springer-Verlag, 1997.
7. C. Fournet and G. Gonthier. The Reflexive Chemical Abstract Machine and the Join-Calculus. In *Proceedings of the 23rd ACM Symposium on Principles of Programming Languages*, pages 372–385. ACM, 1996.
8. C. Fournet and L. Maranget. *The Join-Calculus Language (release 1.02)*. Institute National de Recherche en Informatique et Automatique, June 1997.
9. K. Honda and M. Tokoro. An Object Calculus for Asynchronous Communication. In *5th European Conference on Object-Oriented Programming*, volume 512 of *LNCS, Springer-Verlag*, pages 141–162, 1991.
10. S. Janson. *AKL - A Multiparadigm Programming Language*. PhD thesis, SICS Swedish Institute of Computer Science, Uppsala University, 1994.
11. S. Jones. Implementing Lazy Functional Languages on Stock Hardware: the Spineless Tagless G-machine. *Journal of Functional Programming*, 2(2):127–202, July 92.
12. N. Kobayashi. Quasi-Linear Types. In *26th ACM SIGPLAN-SIGACT Symposium on Principles of Programming Languages*, pp. 29-42, January 1999.
13. N. Kobayashi, B. Pierce, and D. Turner. Linearity and the π-calculus. In *ACM Symposium on Principles of Programming Languages*, 1996.
14. L. Lopes, F. Silva, A. Figueira, and V. Vasconcelos. DiTyCO: An Experiment in Code Mobility from the Realm of Process Calculi. In *5th Mobile Object Systems Workshop*, 1999. part of ECOOP'99.

15. L. Lopes and V. Vasconcelos. An Abstract Machine for an Object-Calculus. Technical report, DCC-FC & LIACC, Universidade do Porto, May 1997.
16. M. Mehl, R. Scheidhauer, and C. Schulte. An Abstract Machine for Oz. Technical report, German Research Center for Artificial Intelligence (DFKI), June 1995.
17. R. Milner, J. Parrow, and D. Walker. A Calculus of Mobile Processes (parts I and II). *Information and Computation*, 100:1–77, 1992.
18. W. Partain. The nofib Benchmark Suite of Haskell Programs. In J. Launchbury and P.M. Sansom, editors, *Proceedings of Functional Programming Workshop*, Workshops in Computing, pages 195–202. Springer Verlag, 1992.
19. B. Pierce and D. Turner. Pict: A Programming Language Based on the Pi-Calculus. Technical Report CSCI 476, Computer Science Department, Indiana University, 1997. To appear in *Proof, Language and Interaction: Essays in H onour of Robin Milner*, Gordon Plotkin, Colin Stirling, and Mads Toft e, editors, MIT Press, 1999.
20. António Ravara and Vasco T. Vasconcelos. Behavioural types for a calculus of concurrent objects. In *Euro-Par'97*, volume 1300 of *LNCS*, pages 554–561. Springer Verlag, 1997.
21. D. Sangiorgi. The name discipline of receptiveness. In *24th ICALP*, volume 1256 of *Lecture Notes in Computer Science*. Springer Verlag, 1997.
22. D. Turner. *The Polymorphic Pi-calculus: Theory and Implementation*. PhD thesis, University of Edinburgh, 1995.
23. V. Vasconcelos and R. Bastos. Core-TyCO - The Language Definition. Technical Report TR-98-3, DI / FCUL, March 1998.
24. V. Vasconcelos, L. Lopes, and F. Silva. Distribution and mobility with lexical scoping in process calculi. In *3rd International Workshop on High-Level Concurrent Languages*, volume 16 of *Electronic Notes in Theoretical Computer Science*. Elsevier Science Publishers, 1998.
25. V. Vasconcelos and M. Tokoro. A Typing System for a Calculus of Objects. In *1st International Symposium on Object Technologies for Advanced Software, LNCS*, volume 742, pages 460–474. Springer-Verlag, November 1993.
26. D. Walker. Objects in the π-calculus. *Journal of Information and Computation*, 116(2):253–271, 1995.

Optimising Bytecode Emulation for Prolog

Vítor Santos Costa

LIACC and DCC-FCUP
Universidade do Porto
Porto, Portugal
vsc@ncc.up.pt

Abstract. Byte-code representation has been used to implement several programming languages such as Lisp, ML, Prolog, or Java. In this work, we discuss the impact of several emulator optimisations for the Prolog system YAP. YAP obtains performance comparable or exceeding well-known Prolog systems by applying several different styles of optimisations, such as improving the emulation mechanism, exploiting the characteristics of the underlying hardware, and improving the abstract machine itself. We give throughout a detailed performance analysis, demonstrating that low-level optimisations can have a very significant impact on the whole system and across a range of architectures.

1 Introduction

Byte-code representation [14,9,20] has been used to implement several programming languages including Lisp [25], ML [17], Prolog [24], and Java [2]. In this technique, the program is first compiled into a lower-level intermediate representation, known as the bytecode of a virtual machine or abstract machine. At run-time, an emulator interprets the virtual machine instructions. Emulation can be considered an intermediate case between pure compilation and pure interpretation. As in compilation, one can perform several optimisations to the program, benefitting from the lower-level nature of the abstract machine. As in interpretation, one avoids the full complexity of native code generation. Also, by writing the emulator itself in a portable language such as C, one can easily obtain portability between different platforms.

Prolog is an interesting example of the advantages and disadvantages of emulators. Most Prolog implementations are based on Warren's Abstract Machine (WAM) [30]. The WAM is a register-based abstract machine, that uses term copying to represent terms and environments to represent active clauses. In the last few years most research in the area has concentrated on obtaining fast performance through techniques such as native code generation and through global optimisations based on abstract interpretation [29]. Although such techniques do improve performance, the resulting systems are harder to maintain, and in fact most current Prolog systems are either emulator-based or do support emulators.

The fact that abstract machines will not go away easily leads to an interesting question: how fast can we make an abstract machine go? Our experience in implementing Prolog has shown that there are a few general issues that

G. Nadathur (Ed.): PPDP'99, LNCS 1702, pp. 261–277, 1999.

should be of interest to all abstract machine implementations. One always wants to use the best representation for the abstract machine. Moreover, one always wants to take the best advantage of the underlying hardware. Unfortunately, this means different things for different instruction set architectures (ISAs), different implementations of an ISA (pipelined versus super-scalar), and different implementation-language compilers.

How much do these individual factors affect performance, and how do they compare with other optimisations? In this work, we discuss the impact of several such optimisations for a Prolog implementation. Our work was performed for the WAM-based system YAP ("Yet Another Prolog"), a Prolog system developed at the University of Porto by Luís Damas and the author [8]. We evaluate the system with a well-known set of small benchmarks proposed by Van Roy [28]. This set is quite interesting in that it compares a large set of very different Prolog programs. We first compare the performance of YAP with SICStus Prolog, a well-known high-performance commercial Prolog system [1,6]. Next, we study three different styles of emulator optimisations: improving the emulation mechanism, exploiting the characteristics of the underlying hardware, and improving the abstract machine itself. We conclude with a general analysis and conclusions.

2 The YAP System

Work on YAP started at the Universidade do Porto by Luís Damas in 1984, and the author joined a year later. YAP originally consisted of a compiler written in C, of an emulator written in m68k assembly code, and a standard predicate library written in Prolog and C. Releases were externally available since 1986. The system has been widely used. It was commercially available, and is now freely available in source distribution [8].

The YAAM (Yet Another Abstract Machine) emulator is the core of YAP. As most other Prolog systems, YAP is based on David H. D. Warren's Abstract Machine for Prolog, usually known as the WAM [30]. As most other Prolog systems, YAP implements several extensions to the WAM, and YAP's full instruction set is called the YAAM [22]. The major differences are in the compilation of unification of compound terms, a different scheme for indexing, and in the `allocate` instruction. Whereas the WAM compiles unification in breadth-first fashion, Yap compiles unification in depth-first fashion since its original version [22]. A second contribution is that whereas in the WAM the `allocate` instruction is at the head of the call, the YAAM only performs the `allocate` just before calling the first goal. Last, YAP has a set of specialised instructions to avoid duplicate choice-points for the same goal, a problem of the original WAM, and indexes on the head of lists [22].

The YAAM emulator was initially implemented in m68k assembly. It was later ported to several other architectures namely the VAX, SPARC, HP-Prism and MIPS. Damas implemented a macro-processor to generate different instructions for each architecture. Experience showed that maintaining several architectures was cumbersome and ultimately inefficient, as it was quite hard to take the best advantage of different instruction sets (both ISAs and their implementations change quite significantly in time). Porting to the x86 architecture would also force a major redesign of the emulator. These considerations led to using `C` as the implementation language. The techniques we used to obtain high-performance in the new emulator are the main subject of this paper.

A first implementation of the emulator in `C` showed bad performance. In order to obtain maximum performance the emulator was completely rewritten in what we named **`assembly-C`**. The key idea was that each line in `C` should be easily translatable to very few lines in assembly. In other words, by looking at a line in `C` one should be able to understand the assembly code. This results in a very long emulator, but gives quite fine control over compilation quality. Similar goals but a different strategy have motivated Peyton Jones' `C--` [18] language.

The current emulator was specifically designed to take best advantage of the GNU `C` compiler (`GCC`) [23]. This compiler is widely available in a variety of platforms, tends to generate bug-free code of reasonable quality, and has support for threaded code [3,10]. Throughout the paper we will always use `GCC2.7.2` as the standard `C` compiler, in both platforms and for all systems.

The emulator is implemented as a single function, consisting of 8648 lines of `C` code. The compiled code takes about 42 KB on Linux/x86 and 45 KB on Solaris/SPARC. For the benchmark set we discuss next we would expect that interesting instructions should fit comfortably into most primary instruction caches. Larger Prolog applications may call external functions, so the working set should be analysed case by case (simulations tools such as SimOS [21] and SimICS [16] are available for this purpose).

Evaluating a compiler is very difficult. In the case of Prolog, performance depends on data-structure implementation for some applications, and in control for others. Performance issues are quite different for lists, trees, or integers. Some applications perform heavy search, others are fully deterministic and may never backtrack. On the other hand, applications may be deterministic, and still perform shallow backtracking. In this work we follow the set of benchmarks previously proposed by Van Roy [28]. These are small-to-medium size programs with few built-ins. They are quite interesting at stressing the different characteristics of the emulator.

The benchmark consists of 22 programs. The first applications are small benchmarks such as the popular naive list reversing benchmark (nreverse), the highly recursive Takeuchi function (tak), the quicksort algorithm (qsort), symbolic derivation (deriv), picking a serial number for an integer (serialise), the famous 8-queens problem (queens_8), deducing a formula in Hofstadter's Mu (mu and fast_mu), the zebra puzzle (zebra), and a cryptoarithmetic puzzle (crypt). More interesting examples are a meta-evaluation of Prolog for qsort (meta_qsort), a simple propositional theorem prover (prover), Gabriel's browse benchmark (browse) [11], a simple Prolog compiler processing unification (unify), disjunctions (flatten), and optimisation (sdda), and a graph-reducer for t-combinators (reducer). Further examples include Boyer's theorem prover benchmark, originally from Gabriel, (boyer), a simple abstract analysis system (simple_analyzer), circuit designer program (nand), and the parser part for the chat-80 natural language system. The latter programs may be considered medium-size Prolog programs.

2.1 YAP Performance

In order to validate our claim that Yap is a high-performance Prolog system, we next compare the performance of the optimised version of YAP4.1.10 with SICStus Prolog release 3 patch 6 [1], a widely available high-performance commercial Prolog system. SICStus Prolog supports emulated code through a C-based emulator, and native code on SPARC, m68k and MIPS platforms [12]. Both the SICStus Prolog native code compiler and the threaded-code emulator are considered to be high performance, versus other widely available Prolog systems. We perform the comparison with both native and threaded code on the SPARC platform, and only with threaded code on the x86 platform, as no native-code system is available.

Program	x86		SPARC		
	Yap	Sicstus	Yap	Sicstus	
				Native	Emulated
nreverse*50000	4.43	7.78 (76%)	15.5	3.23 (-383%)	18.6 (20%)
tak*20	1.41	1.77 (25%)	2.59	0.85 (-204%)	2.86 (10%)
qsort*20000	4.80	7.54 (57%)	11.7	4.06 (-188%)	12.8 (9%)
deriv*150000	8.44	12.1 (43%)	20.7	5.9 (-251%)	21.1 (2%)
serialise*50000	9.49	12.9 (36%)	20.5	7.77 (-164%)	21.4 (4%)
queens_8*5000	6.91	9.75 (41%)	15.6	4.93 (-216%)	16.0 (3%)
mu*6000	1.87	3.07 (64%)	4.65	2.14 (-117%)	5.55 (20%)
zebra*100	2.07	2.91 (41%)	3.42	2.88 (-19%)	4.24 (26%)
fast_mu*2000	1.09	1.71 (57%)	2.09	1.02 (-105%)	2.30 (10%)
crypt*1000	1.65	2.50 (55%)	3.51	2.34 (-105%)	4.05 (15%)
meta_qsort*500	1.36	1.79 (31%)	2.84	0.92 (-50%)	3.08 (8%)
prover*2000	1.10	1.54 (40%)	2.03	0.79 (-157%)	2.30 (13%)
browse*20	6.04	10.7 (77%)	15.0	7.15 (-109%)	18.1 (21%)
unify*1000	1.16	1.32 (14%)	2.13	0.67 (-217%)	2.07 (-3%)
flatten*10000	3.86	4.29 (11%)	6.34	3.52 (-80%)	6.45 (2%)
sdda*5000	1.17	1.44 (23%)	2.01	0.98 (-105%)	2.06 (3%)
reducer*100	1.71	2.42 (42%)	3.35	1.49 (-125%)	3.71 (11%)
boyer*5	1.57	1.91 (22%)	2.84	1.33 (-114%)	3.38 (19%)
simple_analyzer*100	1.03	1.31 (27%)	1.65	0.85 (-94%)	1.76 (7%)
nand*100	1.08	1.76 (63%)	1.95	0.99 (-97%)	2.58 (32%)
chat_parser*100	8.57	12.0 (40%)	14.7	7.51 (-96%)	15.7 (7%)
query*1000	1.44	2.41 (67%)	2.94	3.09 (5%)	4.14 (41%)
Average		43.3%		-135%	12.7%

Table 1. Application Performance

To obtain the full picture we use two platforms. A Linux Pentium-II 266MHz, 64MB memory Dell Latitude laptop, and a Sun Ultra-I workstation 167MHz, 64MB memory. Table 1 shows benchmark performance for both systems. The times are given in seconds. The number to the right of the * gives the number of times we ran the benchmark. Time variation in all cases was standard for Unix, up to a maximum of 3%. We always choose the best times from 7 runs. We compare with both the threaded-code based and native-code implementation in the SPARC machine, and only with the threaded-code version on the x86 machine. We also give in parenthesis a comparison of SICStus Prolog versus YAP performance as given by by:

$$(\frac{SICStus\ Prolog\ time}{YAP\ time} - 1) * 100\%$$

Table 1 shows that performance of YAP is somewhat better than emulated SICStus Prolog for the SPARC platform, but YAP benefits from more intensive optimisation in the x86 platform. In the case of Solaris, YAP performs particularly well in benchmarks that involve backtracking, whereas SICStus Prolog threaded performs better in benchmarks that perform heavy unification and also benefits from implementing shallow backtracking [5]. SICStus Prolog native is in average between two and three times faster than YAP, and performs particularly well in deterministic functional-style benchmarks. Surprisingly, YAP catches up in the query benchmark. The reason is that this benchmark is basically a search in the database followed by some arithmetic. The search component heavily depends on the hash-table searching in a *Index* instruction. SICStus Prolog native is five times faster for nreverse. This is a standard benchmark for Prolog, which is particularly simple and is usually the first target for any optimisation. These results with SICStus Prolog native are consistent with published results for the AQUARIUS [28] and Parma [27] systems, although both these system can improve performance by applying global analysis.

Note that there is no SICStus Prolog native for x86. SICStus Prolog was originally developed in m68k and then in SPARC or MIPS platforms, which are best supported. One would have to redesign most of the native code system to take full advantage of the x86 architecture [12]. Still, it is possible to implement native code systems for the x86: the `wamcc` generates `C`-code to be compiled by `GCC` [7], and Bin-Prolog is a non-WAM based system that generates native code for unification [26]. We have experimented with both the wamcc and Bin-Prolog on the x86 platform and found that YAP still obtained better performance for these benchmarks.

In general, both emulators are based on the same abstract machine, the WAM, and tend to perform comparably. This is quite clear on the SPARC machine. We can further conclude that YAP's emulator has good performance for a WAM-based emulator, and is usually between two to three times slower than a good Prolog native code system. YAP performs particularly well for x86 machines. To obtain this performance, several optimisation techniques were applied. They are the main subject of this work.

3 Optimising YAP

To optimise an emulator-based system, one can apply several different techniques:

1. One can improve the emulation mechanism. These techniques are quite interesting because they will improve every instruction, not just a few.
2. One can optimise access to underlying hardware. This includes writing code to optimise super-scalar execution, or taking best advantage of instructions. In general, such optimisations will impact most (but not all) instructions.
3. One can improve the abstract machine, say, by compacting several instructions into a single instruction, by generating special instructions for commonly found cases. Other examples include incorporating external functionality to the abstract machine.
   These techniques only apply to a subset of instructions and tend to increase emulator size. The previous discussion shows they should be applied with care.
4. One can improve compilation, say through improving YAAM register allocation or by applying results from global analysis. Note that to take best advantage of global analysis one may have to design new instructions, resulting in a larger and more complex emulator. In this regard, the consensus is that native code systems are best suited to this purpose, as they make it easier to specialise instructions.
   Global analysis is not currently being used in commercial Prolog systems, although robust systems are available available [4,15] and work is being done to improve their performance for large-scale applications [13].

In this work we concentrate on the first three styles of optimisation, as they are the ones that relate with emulator design. We would like to remark that improvements in other compilation techniques, namely differences in abstract machine register allocation between compilers, seem not be a major factor in performance, as for example SICStus Prolog implements a much more sophisticated abstract machine register allocator [6] than the simple one used in YAP.

Throughout this analysis we present the impact of each optimisation as the ratio between a fully optimised system with and without the optimisation. This form of analysis is more interesting to understand whether a specific optimisation is valuable in the final system. One should remember that most optimisations have a cost, if only in the effort one must put into the system. Whenever meaningful, we present the performance impact for both the x86 and SPARC implementations. Throughout, we always present speedups by the formula:

$$(\frac{Unoptimised\ time}{Optimised\ time} - 1) * 100\%$$

3.1 Improving the Emulation Mechanism

There are several techniques that can reduce the overheads for the basic emulation mechanism. The main techniques applied in YAP are threaded code emulation, abstract machine register access, and prefetching.

Threaded Code Emulation This is a very well-known optimisation. Fig. 1 shows the non-threaded and threaded code implementation of a WAM instruction `get_x_value A3,X4`. Note that differently from most abstract machines the WAM is register-based, not stack-based. This specific instruction unifies the contents of YAAM argument register 3 with the contents of argument register 4 (in the WAM `A` and `X` are aliases to the set of argument registers). Threaded code emulation only affects the opcode field.

(a) No threaded code **(b) Threaded code**

Fig. 1. Threaded Code

Without threaded-code emulation, the opcode field contains the number for the instruction. The number is traditionally a label associated with a switch statement. To execute an instruction one jumps to the beginning of the switch, executes the switch code (usually a direct array access), and jumps to the switch label. With threaded code, the instruction already contains the switch label. Executing an instruction is thus a question of fetching the opcode field and just jumping to it.

Unfortunately, threaded-code is not directly supported in standard `C`. One of the reasons for using `GCC` in emulator-based systems is that `GCC` allows labels as first order objects, thus greatly simplifying threaded code emulation. Table 2 shows the impact of this technique in YAP. The technique is quite effective, both in the x86 and SPARC architectures, and speedups are always more than 20%. The best results in SPARC were obtained for queens, unify, query and boyer, all with many simple `put` and `write` instructions. The x86 machine has a rather different and much wider variation. The problem here, as we shall see next, is that this optimisation also enables other important optimisations in the x86 machine.

Abstract Machine Register Access Fig. 2 shows the same principle at work for the abstract machine register access optimisation. Instead of adding the register offsets to a variable `X`, we can have abstract machine registers at fixed memory positions and store the address for each `X[i]`. Usually, each instruction will have at least one register access, and quite often two. In the SPARC architecture,

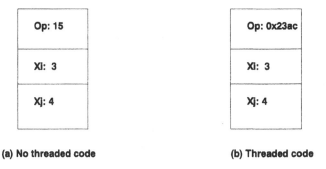

Program	x86			SPARC		
	Threaded	RegsAccess	Pref	Threaded	RegsAccess	Pref
nreverse*50000	193%	3%	10%	38%	6%	4%
tak*20	33%	4%	1%	21%	3%	0%
qsort*20000	76%	3%	8%	28%	5%	0%
deriv*150000	86%	3%	1%	36%	7%	0%
serialise*50000	57%	3%	3.5%	31%	-8%	4%
queens_8*5000	54%	3%	2%	54%	9%	0%
mu*6000	90%	3%	0%	28%	-8%	2%
zebra*100	35%	1.5%	0%	20%	-2%	2%
fast_mu*2000	39%	3%	0%	35%	-9%	11%
crypt*1000	41%	1%	2%	36%	7%	0%
meta_qsort*500	56%	1%	0%	30%	0%	0%
prover*2000	42%	3%	1%	35%	-8%	0%
browse*20	91%	5%	3%	31%	-3%	5%
unify*1000	28%	4%	2%	44%	3%	1%
flatten*10000	32%	3%	2%	25%	1%	0%
sdda*5000	47%	5%	1%	34%	0%	4%
reducer*100	56%	6%	2%	31%	-1%	0%
boyer*5	37%	7%	0%	39%	17%	0%
simple_analyzer*100	32%	0%	1%	33%	5%	2%
nand*100	45%	4%	4%	37%	7%	0%
chat_parser*100	27%	4%	1%	29%	-8%	0%
query*1000	39%	4%	0%	40%	0%	0%
Average	56%	3%	2%	33%	1%	2%

Table 2. Emulation Mechanism Speedups

we guarantee the emulator will have the base address for the abstract machine register in a physical register anyway, so we are saving an add and possibly an extra register. In an x86 machine, the optimisation allows using indirection, instead of having to use indexed addressing. The cost is that one needs a larger YAAM instruction: whereas we could store the register number in a 16-bit word, we now need to store a full address.

In both cases, the improvements are minor, as shown in Table 2. The simpler addressing mode results in constant improvements for the x86 implementation. Performance in the SPARC machine varies between an 8% speedup and a 17% slowdown, probably due to the larger instruction size. The effect for boyer is quite interesting. We have repeated this effect and believe it to be a cache effect, as this effect was not repeatable in an Ultra-II machine.

Hard-coding YAAM registers does have a second drawback that is not immediately obvious. Imagine one wants to implement a multi-threaded system. One would like to have several engines working concurrently. With this optimisation, the engines will have to share the same YAAM register set, meaning that context-switches between threads will be more expensive, as we need to save the `X` registers. Moreover, context-switching may only be performed at well defined points where we know how many YAAM registers are in use.

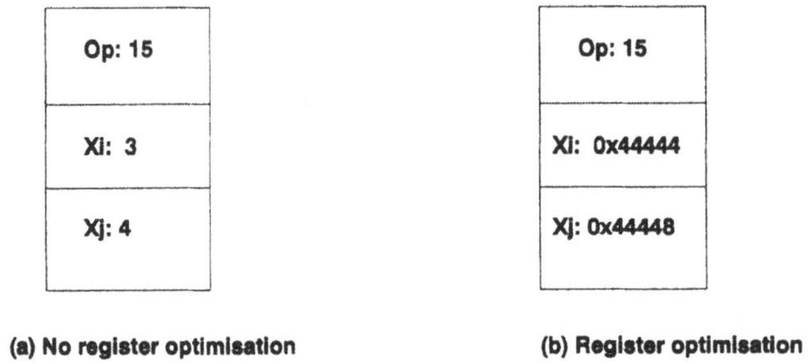

Fig. 2. Improving Register Access

Prefetching Using threaded code still generates a stall. One needs to increment the program counter, fetch the new opcode, and jump. The CPU will stall before jumping, as it needs to wait for the opcode. To avoid this problem, one can *prefetch* the new opcode, and guarantee that the CPU will know the jump address in advance.

Note that the technique requires for the new temporary variable to hold the prefetched value. This variable must be allocated in an extra machine register, otherwise execution may actually slowdown. The x86 lacks in registers, so we only applied the technique for instructions where we know the compiler will have sufficient registers. The SPARC architecture should have sufficient registers, and we apply the technique everywhere. Table 2 shows the results. In both cases they are quite disappointing (in fact the technique was originally designed for single-issue pipeline-based implementations, such as the 80486, where it did perform better). We believe the problem is that the CPUs are super-scalar and hence quite effective at prefetching arguments themselves. This removes some of the advantages from using software prefetching. Software prefetching further requires an extra register and thus adds extra pressure to the compiler.

We can apply a similar technique to argument access. Imagine the following sequence of instructions:

```
get_x_variable   X1,A2
get_list         X2
```

The observation is that in the WAM after instructions such as `get_x_variable` or `get_x_value` one most often will have a *Get* instruction (corresponding to the next argument). Moreover, the first argument to this instruction will access a YAAM register. The current instruction can therefore prefetch the next argument in the previous instruction, thus making it available to the next one. Unfortunately, this optimisation requires specialised instructions because in general we do not know whether the previous instruction did the prefetching or not.

The first argument is quite important in the WAM, as in entering a procedure the first instruction is likely to either be an indexing instruction or a `try` instruction. In both cases, that instruction will require the first argument. To optimise this case, instructions that call procedures must fetch the first argument in advance. We have implemented the optimisation for RISC architectures, where the prefetched YAAM register can be placed on an unused abstract machine register. The optimisation is not supported for x86 registers, because the instruction set does not have sufficient registers.

3.2 Taking Advantage of the Hardware

Ideally, given a fragment of code, the C-compiler should be able to take best advantage of the available hardware. In practice, C-compilers have several limitations and require a bit of help in order to achieve good performance. One major consideration concerns register allocation. Good register allocation is fundamental to obtain best performance, but is not always obtained by just giving the code to the compiler. A second consideration concerns scheduling within the CPU. We want to minimise stalls on memory and on branches. Ideally, the compiler should be able to reorder instructions for best performance. Unfortunately, C-compilers must worry about pointer aliasing. This is specifically a problem with emulators for high-level languages, as these languages heavily manipulate pointers.

To obtain maximum performance, YAP's emulator was written assuming a load-store mechanism. We also tried to maximise possible concurrency between instructions in the code. Unfortunately, it is very hard to measure the impact of these optimisations, as they are really embedded in the fabric of the emulator. In the next paragraphs we concentrate on two optimisations that are easier to measure: register allocation, and tag schemes.

Improving Register Allocation Machine register allocation is a totally different problem in the x86 and in the RISC architectures. This said, there is a simple rule of thumb we found of use in both cases: *reduce the scope of temporary variables to the very minimum.* Often one reuses a temporary variable, say `i`, with different purposes. For a very complex function as it is the emulator, this complicates register allocation, which is being stressed to the limit.

In the case of RISC architectures, the problem is how many abstract machine registers we are allowed to fit in the machine and still have the compiler doing decent allocation. In the specific case of the SPARC architecture, we found we could declare 7 registers to hold copies of WAM registers within the emulator. Moreover, in GCC we can declare 3 registers to be global variables storing YAAM registers. Adding extra registers will decrease code quality.

In the case of x86 architecture, we have 7 registers available, counting the frame pointer. We have used three techniques to improve performance:

1. all the abstract machine registers are stored in the emulator's activation frame. This means we can access them through the stack pointer. We can also guarantee they are very close to the top of the stack and use the corresponding x86 optimised instructions. This is not as effective for superscalar implementations as for older pipelined implementations.

2. We can explicitly copy an YAAM register to a temporary variable, if the instruction heavily depends on that register. This mechanism is particularly useful on the x86 architecture. Note that for RISC machines we can store quite a few YAAM registers as machine registers, so we must be careful lest this optimisation will confuse the compiler.
   We have found out experimentally that we can do always cache one abstract machine register, the global stack pointer `H`. The explanation is that, in order not to lose efficiency in SPARC machines we need that in RISC machines the compiler will alias the copy of `H` back to the original `H`. This works well for `H` because uses of `H` almost never cross uses of other pointers. For other three important abstract machine registers, the current environment pointer, `ENV`, the trail pointer, `TR`, and the latest choice-point pointer, `B`, we need to have conditional code for the x86, otherwise RISC code would suffer.
3. We can force YAAM registers to be x86 registers. In general, this is a bad idea because it dramatically decreases code quality. There is an important exception, though: the YAAM program counter is so important in program execution that there are large benefits in storing it as a x86 register.

It is very hard to study the impact of all these optimisations, as they are interspersed in the code. In the case of the x86, we next give performance data on x86-specific copying, and on using the abstract machine PC as an x86 register. In the case of the SPARC, we give performance data on copying the YAAM registers.

Table 3 shows the results. The x86 architecture is register starved and anything we can do to optimise register allocation is clearly welcome. Note that in theory, the C-compiler should be able to reuse copies of the abstract machine registers itself, and this optimisation should be unnecessary. The second optimisation again shows the limitations of the compiler. The YAAM program counter is by far the most often referred variable in the abstract machine. Storing it in a register is always highly beneficial, even if it worsens register allocation. We believe this optimisation to be the main improvement in YAP over the SICStus Prolog implementation.

The third column shows the advantage of copying the abstract-machine registers to registers for the SPARC machine (the exception is the YAAM PC that will always be in a register). Ideally, the compiler should do this copy itself. Surprisingly, this technique has a greater impact than actually using threaded-code.

4 Improving the Abstract Machine

The previous optimisations are designed to take best advantage of the instruction set and compiler. Their implementation decrease the YAAM's CPI (cycles per instruction). One can also consider optimisations that improve execution by changing the abstract machine specification itself. We found two optimisations to be most important: instruction merging and abstract machine extension.

For completeness sake, we would like to refer that YAP includes further, very WAM-specific optimisations. The major optimisation is on how to handle

Program	x86		SPARC
	Regs	P	Regs
nreverse*50000	24%	62%	65%
tak*20	6%	21%	112%
qsort*20000	28%	26%	61%
deriv*150000	29%	23%	47%
serialise*50000	21%	22%	53%
queens_8*5000	12%	41%	176%
mu*6000	33%	33%	61%
zebra*100	17%	14%	49%
fast_mu*2000	17%	23%	91%
crypt*1000	2%	30%	159%
meta_qsort*500	21%	21%	55%
prover*2000	19%	25%	63%
browse*20	25%	38%	64%
unify*1000	16%	22%	83%
flatten*10000	12%	22%	64%
sdda*5000	19%	18%	54%
reducer*100	18%	31%	55%
boyer*5	13%	31%	83%
simple_analyzer*100	9%	24%	64%
nand*100	15%	26%	64%
chat_parser*100	16%	26%	54%
query*1000	4%	22%	121%
Average	17%	27%	77%

Table 3. Register Allocation Speedups

reading or writing sub-arguments to compound terms. In the original WAM this is supported by an extra register, the `RWREG`, that is consulted at every unification instruction. In the YAAM this is implemented by having two opcode fields in each unify instruction. Instructions in write mode thus can use a different opcode from instructions in read mode. There are also possible optimisations not implemented in YAP. For instance, SICStus Prolog has specialised instructions for the WAM's `A1` register (the first argument in a call). The motivation is that this is the most commonly used, and if processed separately may be stored in a machine register. We do not implement this optimisation because it would significantly increase compilation times, and because the extra instructions would make the system harder to maintain.

Instruction Merging The idea of instruction merging is straightforward: to reduce the overheads of emulation by joining several instructions into a single instruction. The idea has shown to be quite effective [19]. Unfortunately, combining all pairs of instructions would square emulator size, whereas many combinations would never appear in practice. We therefore need to consider which combinations are more frequent. This clearly depends on our experience, and specifically *on the programs we want to optimise.* We next discuss the main optimisations as

Program	x86		SPARC	
	Merge s	Extension	Merge	Extension
nreverse*50000	21%	2%	24%	-3%
tak*20	0%	65%	-3%	74%
qsort*20000	9%	0%	13%	-3%
deriv*150000	-1%	4%	-2%	-2%
serialise*50000	20%	4%	7%	0%
queens_8*5000	4%	189%	4%	108%
mu*6000	7%	2%	17%	-3%
zebra*100	0%	-1%	-1%	-1%
fast_mu*2000	2%	48%	-4%	29%
crypt*1000	1%	136%	0%	99%
meta_qsort*500	0%	8%	2%	9%
prover*2000	2%	0%	3%	-1%
browse*20	7%	26%	8%	12%
unify*1000	1%	N/A	3%	N/A
flatten*10000	-2%	22%	1%	31%
sdda*5000	0%	16%	-5%	19%
reducer*100	2%	66%	1%	4%
boyer*5	0%	32%	2%	34%
simple_analyzer*100	-2%	14%	1%	21%
nand*100	8%	4%	14%	6%
chat_parser*100	1%	0%	1%	4%
query*1000	0%	89%	1%	73%
Average	4%	35%	4%	24%

Table 4. Abstract Machine Speedups

applied to YAP, note that this discussion is dependent on understanding WAM execution:

- It is common to have several void sub-arguments in a compound term. These sub-arguments can be joined into a single instruction with little overhead.
- A related common case is where we have two sub-arguments that are variables. There are four cases depending on whether it is a first access or not to each variable sub-argument.
- It is quite common in Prolog to access a list whose head is a variable. This means that `get_list` and `unify_variable` instructions can be merged.
- The last case optimises the recursive clause for the `member/2` predicate: we access a list where the first argument is void and the second is the first occurrence of a variable.

Performance analysis is given in the Merge columns for table 4. Notice that there are a negative results, which we believe, result from variations in timings. The results show the optimisation to be reasonably effective in the few cases where it applies, but only 6 out of 22 benchmarks have significant benefits. Moreover, in the larger programs only nand benefits. In general, Prolog programs tend to use a reasonably large number of instructions. Abstract instruction merging would need to be performed extensively or will hardly result in major speedups for most benchmarks.

Extending the Abstract Machine Most real Prolog applications depend on external functionality, such as:

- meta-predicates, such as `var/1` and friends;
- arithmetic builtins, such as arithmetic with the `is/2` built-in;
- explicit unification, through the `=/2` built-in;
- term manipulation or comparison, for instance, argument access with `arg/3`.

Yap implements most of the meta-predicates, integer arithmetic (although not comparison), unification, and the major term manipulations built-ins, `functor/3` and `arg/3` directly as abstract machine operations. Table 4 shows the impact in performance as compared to a version that does not improve arithmetic and uses the same code for meta-predicates, explicit unification and term manipulation, except that this code is now implemented outside the YAAM. Note that the N/A result is a bug in the non-optimised system.

Table 4 shows this optimisation to be effective for 11 out of 22 benchmarks. Also note that quite a few of the larger benchmarks benefit from this optimisation. In general, real Prolog programs depend heavily on features such as arithmetic or meta-predicates that are not available in the original WAM. This is particularly true for large programs. The best results were obtained for applications that require arithmetic. The impressive improvement in performance reflects effort in improving both compilation of arithmetic and its implementation as abstract machine instructions. Note that arithmetic comparisons are still performed outside the abstract machine, so performance could be further improved.

5 Conclusions and Future Work

We have discussed a set of optimisations for a Prolog emulator. Most of these techniques apply to any emulator. We have shown that substantial performance improvements can be obtained from improved register allocation, threaded code, and abstract machine extensions. We have found instruction merging not to be widely effective, and software prefetching to be of limited impact for modern superscalar machines.

One interesting advantage of the emulators is that they provide a perfect environment for experimenting with optimisation techniques. Ideally, the impact of an optimisation will be replicated in the many times the instruction will be executed. This makes it quite possible to do considerable hand-tuning, and in the best cases approach the performance of native-code systems. The major disadvantage is introduced by the granularity of abstract machine instructions. We have seen that it is not straightforward to optimise across instructions, and that instruction merging quickly increases instruction size for little benefit. In this regard, it will be interesting to see how new developments in VLIW style CPUs will impact the emulated versus native code ratios.

In general, the more complex the basic operations for the language are, the better will an emulator perform. In this regard, Prolog holds an intermediate position between languages such as Java and ML, on the one hand, and constraint or concurrent languages. Our general conclusion is that, at least for Prolog, emulation is still a valid technology for the implementation of high-level languages. Performance is acceptable and the general system is simpler and easier to adapt.

Further optimisations are possible. We mentioned using prefetching instructions from modern ISAs. We have also experimented with inline assembly for frequent WAM operations such as trailing, but we found out this makes life too hard for the compiler. We would also like to obtain a mathematical description of the relationship between each optimisation and benchmark performance. We have already worked in classifying instructions and deriving instruction frequency. Further work requires timing the execution of individual instructions.

Acknowledgments

The original YAP emulator was designed by Luís Damas, and this work ultimately results from our collaboration in this system. The author would like to thank Inês Dutra for her precious help in this paper. Fernando Silva and Ricardo Lopes have also collaborated in this work. We would like to thank the anonymous referees for their insightful comments. Our work has been partly supported by Fundação da Ciência e Tecnologia under the Melodia project (JNICT contract PBIC/C/TIT/2495/95) and by access to the computing facilities at COPPE/Sistemas, Universidade Federal do Rio de Janeiro, Brasil. The work presented here has been partially supported by funds granted to LIACC through the Programa de Financiamento Plurianual, Fundação para a Ciência e Tecnologia and Programa PRAXIS. Last, but not the least, the author wants to say thanks to all the YAP users whose demand for more and more performance has motivated this work.

References

1. J. Andersson, S. Andersson, K. Boortz, M. Carlsson, H. Nilsson, T. Sjoland, and J. Widén. SICStus Prolog User's Manual. Technical report, Swedish Institute of Computer Science, November 1997. SICS Technical Report T93-01.
2. K. Arnold and J. Gosling. *The Java Programming Language.* Addison Wesley, 1996.
3. J. R. Bell. Threaded code. *Communications of the ACM*, 16(6):370–372, 1973.
4. F. Bueno, M. G. d. l. Banda, and M. V. Hermenegildo. Effectiveness of Abstract Interpretation in Automatic Parallelization: A Case Study in Logic Programming. *ACM TOPLAS*, 1998.
5. M. Carlsson. On the efficiency of optimised shallow backtracking in Compiled Prolog. In *Proceedings of the Sixth International Conference on Logic Programming*, pages 3–15. MIT Press, June 1989.

6. M. Carlsson. *Design and Implementation of an OR-Parallel Prolog Engine.* SICS Dissertation Series 02, The Royal Institute of Technology, 1990.
7. P. Codognet and D. Diaz. wamcc: Compiling Prolog to C. In *12th International Conference on Logic Programming.* The MIT Press, 1995.
8. L. Damas, V. Santos Costa, R. Reis, and R. Azevedo. *YAP User's Guide and Reference Manual*, 1998. http://www.ncc.up.pt/~vsc/Yap.
9. E. H. Debaere and J. M. Van Campenhout. *Interpretation and Instruction Path Coprocessing.* The MIT Press, 1990.
10. M. A. Ertl. Stack caching for interpreters. In *SIGPLAN '95 Conference on Programming Language Design and Implementation*, pages 315–327, 1995.
11. R. P. Gabriel. *Performance and evaluation of Lisp systems.* MIT Press, 1985.
12. R. C. Haygood. Native code compilation in SICStus Prolog. In P. V. Hentenryck, editor, *Proceedings of the Eleventh International Conference on Logic Programming.* MIT Press, June 1994.
13. M. Hermenegildo, G. Puebla, K. Marriott, and P. Stuckey. Incremental Analysis of Logic Programs. In *International Conference on Logic Programming*, pages 797–811. MIT Press, June 1995.
14. P. Klint. Interpretation techniques. *Software Practice and Experience*, 11:963–973, 1981.
15. B. Le Charlier and P. Van Hentenryck. Experimental evaluation of a generic abstract interpretation algorithm for PROLOG. *ACM TOPLAS*, 16(1):35–101, January 1994.
16. P. S. Magnusson, F. Larsson, A. Moestedt, B. Werner, F. Dahlgren, M. Karlsson, F. Lundholm, J. Nilsson, P. Stenström, and H. Grahn. SimICS/sun4m: A virtual workstation. In *Proceedings of the USENIX 1998 Annual Technical Conference*, pages 119–130, Berkeley, USA, June 15–19 1998. USENIX Association.
17. R. Milner, M. Tofte, and R. Harper. *The Definition of Standard ML.* MIT Press, 1990.
18. Peyton Jones, Simon L. and Thomas Nordin and Dino Oliva. C--: A Portable Assembly Language. In *Proceedings of IFL'97*, 1997.
19. T. A. Proebsting. Optimizing an ANSI C interpreter with superoperators. In *Principles of Programming Languages (POPL '95)*, pages 322–332, 1995.
20. T. H. Romer, D. Lee, G. M. Voelker, A. Wolman, W. A. Wong, J.-L. Baer, B. N. Bershad, and H. M. Levy. The structure and performance of interpreters. In *Architectural Support for Programming Languages and Operating Systems (ASPLOS-VII)*, pages 150–159, 1996.
21. M. Rosenblum, S. A. Herrod, E. Witchel, and A. Gupta. Complete computer system simulation: The SimOS approach. *IEEE parallel and distributed technology: systems and applications*, 3(4):34–43, Winter 1995.
22. V. Santos Costa. Implementação de Prolog. Provas de aptidão pedagógica e capacidade científica, Universidade do Porto, Dezembro 1988.
23. R. M. Stallman. Using and porting gcc. Technical report, The Free Software Foundation, 1993.
24. L. Sterling and E. Shapiro. *The Art of Prolog.* MIT Press, 1994.
25. G. J. Sussman, G. L. Steele, Jr., and R. P. Gabriel. A brief introduction to Lisp. *ACM SIGPLAN Notices*, 28(3):361–362, Mar. 1993.
26. P. Tarau, K. De Bosschere, and B. Demoen. Partial Translation: Towards a Portable and Efficient Prolog Implementation Technology. *Journal of Logic Programming*, 29(1–3):65–83, Nov. 1996.
27. A. Taylor. Parma–bridging the performance gap between imperative and logic programming. *The Journal of Logic Programming*, 1-3, October 1996.

28. P. Van Roy. *Can Logic Programming Execute as Fast as Imperative Programming?* PhD thesis, University of California at Berkeley, November 1990.
29. P. Van Roy. 1983-1993: The Wonder Years of Sequential Prolog Implementation. *The Journal of Logic Programming*, 19/20, May/July 1994.
30. D. H. D. Warren. An Abstract Prolog Instruction Set. Technical Note 309, SRI International, 1983.

OPENLOG: A Logic Programming Language Based on Abduction

Jacinto A. Dávila

Centro de Simulación y Modelos (CESIMO)
Universidad de Los Andes. Mérida. Venezuela
FAX: +58 74 403873
jacinto@ing.ula.ve
http://cesimo.ing.ula.ve

Abstract. In this paper, we introduce a programming language for an abductive reasoner. We propose the syntax for an imperative language in the usual manner and its semantics as a mapping from the language statements to an abductive logic program. The design is such that any semantics for abductive logic programs could be taken as the basic semantics for the programming language that we propose. In this way, we build upon existing formalizations of abductive reasoning and abductive logic programming. One innovative aspect of this work is that the agent processing and executing OPENLOG programs will stay *open* to the environment and will allow for changes in its environment and assimilation of new information generated by these changes.

1 Introduction

Abduction is a non-valid form of reasoning in which one infers the premises of a rule given the consequent. This form of reasoning is not valid in classical first order logic since, for instance, one is not allow us to deduce the atom b from the clause $h \leftarrow b$ and the atom h. However, in general, in the presence of h and this clause, our intuition allows us to say that b could well be the case. That is, we are allowed to offer b as an explanation or a hypothesis for h in the context of that clause when we do not have more information. This is abduction. An abductive reasoner uses abduction as one of its inference rules. Abduction enables reasoning in the absence of full information about a particular problem or domain of knowledge.

In this paper, we introduce a programming language for an abductive reasoner. We propose the syntax for an imperative language in the usual manner (summarized in table 1) and its semantics is defined as a mapping from the language statements to an abductive logic program (shown in table 2). The design is such that any semantics for abductive logic programs could be taken as the basic semantics for the programming language that we propose. In this way, we build upon existing formalizations of abductive reasoning and abductive logic programming.

G. Nadathur (Ed.): PPDP'99, LNCS 1702, pp. 278–293, 1999.

A substantial effort has been made to formalize abductive reasoning. Poole's Theorist [27] was the first to incorporate the use of abduction for non-monotonic reasoning. Eshghi and Kowalski [10] have exploited the similarities between abduction and negation as failure and provided a proof procedure based on a transformation of logic programs with negation into logic programs with *abducible atoms.* de Kleer incorporates abduction into the so-called truth maintenance systems to obtain the ATMS [7]. Also, in [3], L. Console, D. Theiseider and P. Torasso analyse the relationships between abduction and deduction and define what they call an **abduction problem** as a pair $< \mathcal{T}, \phi >$ where:

1. $\mathcal{T}$ (the domain theory) is a hierarchical logic program[1] whose abducible atoms are the ones not occurring in the head of any clause.
2. ϕ (the observations to be explained) is a consistent conjunction of literals with no occurrence of abducible atoms.

A solution to the abduction problem is a set of abducible atoms that, together with $\mathcal{T}$, can be used to explain ϕ.

The purpose of imposing structures such as $< \mathcal{T}, \phi >$ upon a reasoning problem is to create **frameworks** in which the semantics of each component and its relationships with other components can be established in a declarative manner. A framework is a structure that distinguishes between types of elements in a formalization. For instance, the framework $< T, \phi, Ab >$ could be used to say that one has a theory T, a set of observations ϕ and that these observations can be explained by abducing predicates in T whose names appear in Ab (abducible predicates). These distinctions are then used to justify differential treatment of each type of component. In the cases considered here, for instance, abducible predicates and non-abducible predicates, so separated by the framework, are processed differently. The distinction captures the fact that the former, unlike the latter, denote uncertain or incomplete information.

The use of *frameworks* has been taken further by Kakas and Mancarella [17], Denecker and De Schreye [9], Toni [33], Fung [14] and more recently, Wetzel *et al* [36], [35] in the context of incorporating abduction into constraint logic programming. In [16] there is an overview of the first efforts to incorporate abduction into logic programs. In [13] there is a preliminary description of the abductive framework that we have used (in [6]) to formalize the reasoning mechanism of an agent. In this work, the agent is as an abductive reasoner that uses abduction to plan its actions to achieve its goals.

2 An Abductive Proof Procedure

In [13], Fung and Kowalski introduce an abductive proof procedure aimed at supporting abductive reasoning on predicate logic and, in particular, on *abductive logic programs.* The **iff** proof procedure, as they call it, (**iffPP** hereafter), is an aggregate of the following inference rules: unfolding, propagation, splitting,

[1] A hierarchical logic program is a logic program without recursive rules.

case analysis, factoring, logical simplifications and a set of rewriting rules to deal with equalities plus the *abductive rule* described above. Fung and Kowalski also produce soundness and completeness results in [13]. We describe an implementation of **iffPP** in [6] together with some examples of how it could be used.

A proof procedure can be seen as specifying an abstract machine that transforms formulae in other formulae. It could even be seen as "an implementation independent interpreter for" the language of those formulae [34]. That is, a proof procedure determines an operational semantics for logic programs (.ibid). Thus, **iffPP** specifies an operational semantics for *abductive logic programs*. By relating this operational semantics to a programming language, one can get to program the abductive reasoner for particular applications, such as hypothetical reasoning and problem solving (e.g. planning) in specific knowledge domains and for pre-determined tasks.

In this paper, we go a step further in the definition of a programming language for the abductive reasoner defined by **iffPP**. Instead of simply relying on the procedural interpretation of (abductive) logic programs, we introduce a more conventional imperative language and explain how this can be mapped onto abductive logic programs of a special sort. These abductive logic programs lend themselves to a form of default reasoning that extends the traditional use of programming languages, i.e., the new definition supposes a re-statement of what a program is.

In the context of this research, a program is seen as a scheme that an agent uses to generate plans to achieve some specified goal. These plans ought to lead that agent to display an effective, goal-oriented behaviour that, nevertheless, caters for changes in the environment due to other independent processes and agencies. This means that, although the agent would be following a well-defined program, it would stay *open* to the environment and allow for changes in its circumstances and the assimilation of new information generated by these changes.

So defined, a program is not a closed and strict set of instructions but a list of assertions that can be combined with assertions from other programs. One advantage of this definition is that the code being executed remains *open* to updates required by changes in the circumstances of execution. The other important advantage is that it allows the executor of the program to perform a form of default reasoning. By assuming certain set of circumstances, the agent will execute certain sequence of actions. If the circumstances change, perhaps another sequence will be offered for execution.

The paper is organized as follows: The next section shows an example to illustrate the principles of abductive programming. The following section introduces the syntax and semantics of a new logic programming language for abductive programming: OPENLOG. Then, the semantics of OPENLOG and its relationship with *background theories* based on the Event Calculus [20] is explained. A discussion of the characteristics and advantages of OPENLOG is also presented before concluding with some remarks about future research.

3 Toy Examples of Abductive Programming with OPENLOG

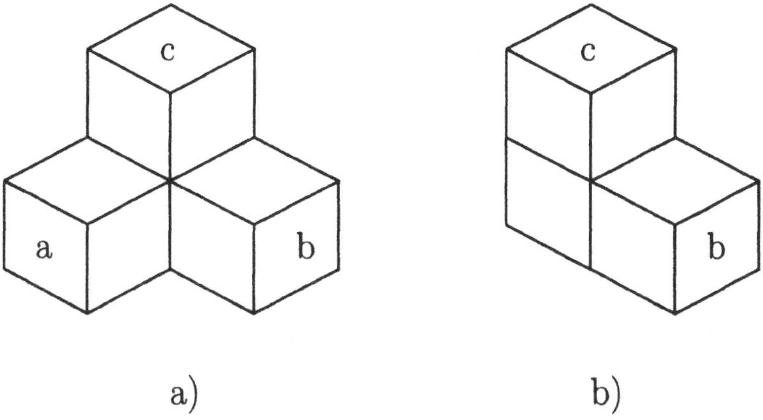

Fig. 1. Two Blocks-World scenarios for planning

In this section we illustrate with examples the relationship between abduction and planning based on pre-programmed routines. Consider the scenario in figure 1:

Example 1. An agent is presented with the challenge of climbing a mountain of blocks to get to the top. The agent can climb one block at a time provided, of course, that the block is there and at the same level (i.e. just in front). The planning problem is then to decide which blocks to climb onto and in which order. An OPENLOG procedure to guide this planning could be:

```
proc climb
  begin
    if infront( Block ) and currentlevel( Level )
       and  Block is_higher_than Level  then
         begin
           step_on( Block ) ; climb
         end
  end
```

Given the scenario in figure 1 a) and the OPENLOG code above, an abductive agent might generate the alternative plans:
$do(self, step\_on(a), t_1) \wedge t_1 < t_2 \wedge do(self, step\_on(c), t_2)$ and
$do(self, step\_on(b), t_1) \wedge t_1 < t_2 \wedge do(self, step\_on(c), t_2)$,

where $do(Agent, A, T)$ can be read as "Agent does action A at time T". This can be done by relating every OPENLOG program to an abductive logic program that refers to the predicates *do* and $<$, and declaring those predicates as *abducibles*. This *mapping* is provided by the definition of the predicate *done* as shown in section 6 and in section 7.

Still in this scenario, it might be the case that the agent interpreting this code learns that at some time t_i:

$t_1 < t_i < t_2 \ \wedge \ do(somebodyelse, remove(c), t_i)$,

i.e. an event happens that terminates the block *c* being where it is. The agent ought then to predict that its action *step_on*(*c*) will fail. This could be done, for instance, if the agent represented and, of course, processed an integrity constraint such as: $(do(Ag, Ac, T) \rightarrow preconds(Ac, T))$, where *preconds* verifies the preconditions of each action.

This type of reasoning that combines abduction with integrity constraints is the main feature of **iffPP**. The agent using **iffPP** as is reasoning procedure may predict that an action of type *Action* will fail and then either dismiss the corresponding plan (i.e. no longer consider it for execution) or repair the plan by abducing the (repairing) actions required to make $preconds(Action, T)$ hold at the right time. Transforming **iffPP** in a planner that allows replanning must be done with care, however, because, as we argue below, it may lead to "over-generation" of abducibles, i.e. to produce too many "repairing" alternatives (some of them with there own problems due to ramifications).

What we have done to tackle the original problem (transforming **iffPP** in the planner for an open agent) is to combine OPENLOG (with its solution for over-generation of abduction) with another programming language, this one based on integrity constraint, which we call ACTILOG [6]. We focus this paper on OPENLOG, due to space constraints and because integrity constraints equivalent to the one above (that involves the predicated *preconds*) can also be produced from OPENLOG code.

3.1 Over-Generation of Abducibles

As we said, one has to be careful with the generation of abducible predicates. Notice, for instance, that in figure 1 b) the only *feasible* plan is:

$do(self, step\_on(b), t_1) \wedge t_1 < t_2 \wedge do(self, step\_on(c), t_2)$,

because the block a is not there. The agent may know about actions that cause $infront(a)$ to be the case (such as, say, $put\_block\_in\_front(a)$). It could therefore schedule one of these actions to *repair* the plan. In (the more usual) case where the agent cannot actually perform the action, the only way to prevent the scheduling of the repairing action is to perform some (non-trivial) extra computation to establish, for instance, that the agent will not be able to "move the block a" in the current circumstances.

This type of behaviour is what one would get from a general purpose, abductive reasoner like **iffPP**. It will "generate" all the possible combinations of abducibles actions to satisfy its goals. And these may be too many, irrelevant or impossible. Observe that this general reasoner will generate the same sets of *step_on* actions for both situations a) and b) in figure 1. Moreover, it will add actions to repair the plans (all of them) in all the possible ways (e.g. moving blocks so that *infront* holds for all of them). The problem becomes even more complex if one considers other physical or spatial effects the agent should be taking care of (like how many blocks should be regarded as being in front of the agent).

We want to save the extra-computation forced on the agent by these repairing actions and other effects. We want to use the structures in the program (`climb` in this case) to decide when the agent should be testing the environment and when it should be *abducing* actions to achieve its goals. This is a form of interleaving testing and planning.

One of the advantages of our approach is that, as part of defining the mapping *procedural code* $\rightarrow$ *abductive logic programs*, we can inhibit that "over-generation" of abducible predicates. The strategy for this is simple: an expression C appearing in $if\ C\ then$ ... will not lead to the abduction of atoms. Any other statement in a program will. We have modified **iffPP** (and therefore the related operational semantics of abductive logic programs) to support a differential treatment of certain predicate definitions. When unfolding the expression C, in $if\ C\ then$ ..., the involved predicates are not allowed to contribute with more abducibles, but simply to test those previously collected in order to satisfy the definitions. Thus, the expression $if\ C\ then$ ... in OPENLOG is more than a mere shorthand to a set of clauses in an abductive logic program. It is a way for the OPENLOG programmer to state which part of the code must carry out tests (on the agent's knowledge) and which must lead to actions by the agent. This strategy adds expressiveness to the programming language and makes of abduction a practical approach for the planning module of an agent [6].

With the inhibited platform and the code in example 1 above we state that, at that stage, the agent is just interested in testing whether $infront(A)$ actually holds for some block A. If the programmer decides that the agent must also build the mountain to be climbed, then she will have to write for the "climber-builder" agent a program such as this:

Example 2. `proc climb`

```
begin
  if infront( Block ) and currentlevel( Level )
     and Block is_higher_than Level then
       begin
         step_on( Block ) ; climb
       end
  else
     if available( Block ) and not infront( Block ) then
        put_block_in_front( Block ) ; climb
end
```

In this second program, when the agent has no block in front (so that the first test fails) and there is some block available in the neighbourhood, then the agent will indeed schedule (abduce) the action $put\_block\_in\_front(A)$ for execution (provided that action is a primitive action).

Thus, with inhibited abduction the agent is interleaving the "testing" of properties with the "planning" of actions. This testing is program-driven, i.e. the programs and the goals establish when the system will be testing and when it will be planning (abducing). Moreover, notice that the "testing" is not restricted to the current state of the world. Earlier actions in a plan can be used to establish that some property holds at a certain time-point. For instance, the climbing agent above may be able to deduce that after $do(step\_on(a), t_1)$, $infront(c)$ will hold.

4 OPENLOG: From Structured to Logic Programming

In the following, a well-known programming language (STANDARD PASCAL) is used as the basis to create a language that supports the kind of *open* problem-solving and planning behaviour mentioned above. The semantics of the resulting language (OPENLOG) is based on a logic of actions and events that caters for input assimilation and reactivity. In combination with the reactive architecture described in [6], where the interleaving of planning and execution is clearly defined, this language can provide a solution to the problem of agent specification and programming.

OPENLOG is aimed at the same applications as the language GOLOG of Levesque *et al* [21] i.e. agent programming. Our approach differs from Levesque *et al*'s in that there is no commitment to a particular logical formalism. One can employ the Situation Calculus or the Event Calculus depending on the requirements of one's architecture. However, the Event Calculus has turned out to be more expressive and useful for the reactive architecture described in [6].

Like GOLOG, our approach also regards standard programming constructs as macros. However, here they are treated as special predicates or terms[2]. There is no problem with recursive or global procedures. Procedures are like predicates that can be referred to (globally and recursively or non-recursively) from within other procedures. Interpreting these macros is, in a sense, like translating traditional structured programs into normal logic programs.

The following section 5 describes the syntax of the language which is, basically, a subset of PASCAL extended with operators for parallel execution. Section 6 explains the semantics of OPENLOG by means of a logic program (defining the predicate *done*). In section 7, we introduce the *background theories*: the temporal reasoning platform on which OPENLOG semantics in based. In [6], we illustrate the use of OPENLOG and the background theories with a more elaborated example: The Elevator Controller.

[2] See [DN01] in table 2 below: **proc** can be regarded as a two-argument predicate, the following symbol is a term, and **begin** and **end** are bracketing a more complex term.

5 The Syntax of OPENLOG

The syntax of OPENLOG is described in BNF form[3] in table 1.

The syntax is left "open" to accommodate, in suitable syntactic categories, those symbols designated by the programmer to represent *fluents, primitive actions* and *complex actions.* In addition to the syntactic rules, the system must also provide translations between the "surface syntax", that the programmer will use to write each *Query*, and the underlining logical notation.

In this initial formalization, PASCAL syntax is *limited* to the least number of structures required for structured programming: (*";"*, *"if.. then.. else.."*, *"while"*). On the other hand, the syntax supports the representation of parallel actions through the compositional operators *par* [4] and + [5].

6 The Semantics of OPENLOG

The semantics of the language is stated in table[6] 2 by means of the predicate *done*[7]. The definition of *done* can also function as an interpreter for the language. Declaratively, $done(A, T_o, T_f)$ reads "an action of type A is started at T_o and completed at T_f". As the definition of *done* is a logic program, any semantics of normal logic programming can be used to give meaning to OPENLOG programs.

One of the innovations in OPENLOG is that between any two actions in a sequence it is always possible to "insert" a third event without disrupting the semantics of the programming language. Axiom [DN02] formalizes this possibility. This is what we mean by plans (derived from OPENLOG programs) as *being open to updates.*

The definition of semantics in table 2 needs to be completed with a "base case" clause for the predicate *done* and the definition of *holds*. These two elements are part of the semantics, but they are also the key elements of a *background theory* $\mathcal{B}$.

[3] In the table, S_j means an instance of S of sub-type j. $(A)^*$ indicates zero or more occurrences of category A within the brackets.

[4] Unlike those semantics of interleaving ([15], [24]) this is a form of real parallelism. Actions start simultaneously, although they may finish at different times. Notice that when all the actions have the same duration (or when they all are "instantaneous") this operator is equivalent to +. Also, observe that the agent architecture described in [18] only handle actions which last for one unit of time. We relax this limitation in [6].

[5] used as well to express real parallelism. Actions start and finish at the same time. This allows the programmer to represent actions that interact with each other so that the finishing time of one constraints the finishing time of the other. For instance, taking a bowl full of soup with both hands and avoiding spilling [32].

[6] PROLOG-like syntax is being used.

[7] The definitions of other predicates are also required but are not problematic.

Table 1 OPENLOG: Syntax		
Program	::= *Proc (Program)**	*A program*
Proc	::= ***proc*** $Func_{proc}$	
	begin *Commands* ***end***	*Procedure definition*
Block	::= ***begin*** *Commands* ***end***	*Block*
Commands	::= *Block*	*Block call*
	$\mid$ $Func_{proc}$	*Procedure call*
	$\mid$ $Func_{action}$	*Primitive action call*
	$\mid$ *Commands ; Commands*	*Sequential composition*
	$\mid$ *Commands* ***par*** *Commands*	*Parallel composition*
	$\mid$ *Commands + Commands*	*Strict parallel composition*
	$\mid$ ***if*** $Expr_{boolean}$ ***then*** *Commands*	*Test*
	$\mid$ ***if*** $Expr_{boolean}$ ***then*** *Commands*	
	else *Commands*	*Choice*
	$\mid$ ***while*** $Expr_{boolean}$ ***do*** *Block*	*Iteration*
Query	::= ...	*Logical expressions*
$Expr_j$	::= $Func_j$ *(Func, Func, ..., Func)*	*Expressions*
Func	::= $Func_{proc}$	
	$\mid$ $Func_{action}$	
	$\mid$ $Func_{fluent}$	
	$\mid$ $Func_{boolean}$	*Functors*
$Func_{proc}$	::= *serve(Term), build(Term), ...*	*User-defined names*
$Func_{action}$	::= ***nil***	*Null action*
	$\mid$ *up* $\mid$ *move(Term, Term)* $\mid$ ...	*User-defined primitive actions' names*
$Func_{fluent}$	::= *at(Term)* $\mid$ *on(Term,* $Func_{fluent}$ *)* $\mid$ ...	*User-defined fluents*
$Func_{boolean}$	::= ***and(*** $Func_{fluent}$, $Func_{boolean}$ *)*	
	$\mid$ ***or(*** $Func_{fluent}$, $Func_{boolean}$ *)*	
	$\mid$ ***not(*** $Func_{boolean}$ *)*	
	$\mid$ $Func_{fluent}$	*Boolean functions*
	$\mid$ *Query*	*Tests on "rigid" information*
Term	::= *Ind* $\mid$ *Var*	*Terms can be individuals or variables*
Ind	::= ...	*Individuals identified by the user*
Var	::= ...	*Sorted Variables*

Table 1. The Syntax of OPENLOG.

Table 2 OPENLOG : Semantics and interpreter		
$done(Pr, T_o, T_f)$	$\leftarrow$ **proc** Pr **begin** C **end** $\wedge\ done(C, T_o, T_f)$	**[DN01]**
$done((\ C_1\ ;\ C_2), T_o, T_f)$	$\leftarrow done(C_1, T_o, T_1) \wedge T_1 < T_2$ $\wedge\ done(C_2, T_2, T_f)$	**[DN02]**
$done((\ C_1$ **par** $C_2),$ $T_o, T_f)$	$\leftarrow done(C_1, T_o, T_1) \wedge done(C_2, T_o, T_f)$ $\wedge\ T_1 \leq T_f$ $\vee\ done(C_1, T_o, T_f) \wedge done(C_2, T_o, T_1)$ $\wedge\ T_1 < T_f$	**[DN03]**
$done((\ C_1 + C_2), T_o, T_f)$	$\leftarrow done(C_1, T_o, T_f) \wedge done(C_2, T_o, T_f)$	**[DN04]**
$done(($**if** E **then** $C_1),$ $T_o, T_f)$	$\leftarrow holdsAt(E, T_o) \wedge done(C_1, T_o, T_f)$ $\vee\ \neg holdsAt(E, T_o) \wedge T_o = T_f$	**[DN05]**
$done(($**if** E **then** C_1 **else** $C_2), T_o, T_f)$	$\leftarrow holdsAt(E, T_o) \wedge done(C_1, T_o, T_f)$ $\vee\ \neg holdsAt(E, T_o) \wedge done(C_2, T_o, T_f)$	**[DN06]**
$done(($**while** $\exists L\ (E_b(L)$ **do** $B(L))),$ $T_o, T_f)$	$\leftarrow (\neg\exists L\ holdsAt(E_b(L), T_o)$ $\wedge\ T_o = T_f)$ $\vee\ (holdsAt(E_b(L'), T_o)$ $\wedge\ done(B(L'), T_o, T_1)$ $\wedge\ T_o < T_1$ $\wedge\ done(($**while** $\exists L\ (E_b(L)$ **do** $B(L))\ ), T_1, T_f))$	**[DN07]**
$done(($**begin** C **end**$),$ $T_o, T_f)$	$\leftarrow done(C, T_o, T_f)$	**[DN08]**
$done($**nil**$, T_o, T_o)$		**[DN09]**
$holdsAt($**and**$(X, Y), T)$	$\leftarrow holdsAt(X, T) \wedge holdsAt(Y, T)$	**[DN10]**
$holdsAt($**or**$(X, Y), T)$	$\leftarrow holdsAt(X, T) \vee holdsAt(Y, T)$	**[DN11]**
$holdsAt($**not**$(X), T)$	$\leftarrow \neg holdsAt(X, T)$	**[DN12]**
$holdsAt(X, T)$	$\leftarrow nonrigid(X) \wedge holds(X, T)$	**[DN13]**
$holdsAt(Q, T)$	$\leftarrow rigid(Q) \wedge Q$	**[DN14]**
$nonrigid(X)$	$\leftarrow isfluent(X)$	**[DN15]**
$rigid(X)$	$\leftarrow \neg isfluent(X)$	**[DN16]**

Table 2. The Semantics of OPENLOG

7 Background Theories

Roughly, a *background theory* ($\mathcal{B}$) is a formal description of actions and properties and the relationships between action-types and property-types.

A background theory consists of two sub-theories: A set of *domain independent axioms* (DI$\mathcal{B}$) (notably the base case of *done* and the definition of *holds*) stating how actions and properties interact. These domain independent axioms also describe how persistence of properties is cared for in the formalism.

The other component of the background theory is a set of *domain dependent axioms* (DD$\mathcal{B}$), describing the particular properties, actions and interrelationships that characterize a domain of application (including the definitions of *initiates*, *terminates* and *isfluent*).

The semantics for OPENLOG can be isolated from the decision about what formalism to use to represent actions and to solve the frame problem (the problem of persistence of properties) in the background theory. Formulations based on the Event Calculus [20] and on the Situation Calculus [22][8] are equally well possible. The following one is based on the Event Calculus.

Probably, the most important element in a background theory is the definition of the *temporal projection predicate: holds.*

7.1 The Projection Predicate in the Event Calculus

$$\begin{array}{lll} holds(P,T) & \leftarrow do(A,T',T_1) \wedge initiates(A,T_1,P) & \\ & \quad \wedge T_1 < T \wedge \neg clipped(T_1,P,T) & \text{[EC1]} \end{array}$$

$$\begin{array}{lll} clipped(T_1,P,T_2) & \leftarrow do(A,T',T) \wedge terminates(A,T,P) & \\ & \quad \wedge T_1 < T \wedge T \leq T_2 & \text{[EC2]} \end{array}$$

These axioms are different from most formulations of the EC (in particular [19]) in that the well-known predicate $happens(Event, Time)$ is replaced by the predicate $do(Action, Starting\_Time, Finishing\_Time)$[9].

7.2 The Base-Case of *done* in the Event Calculus

As we said before, we use **iffPP** for interpreting OPENLOG programs and generating plans. The execution of those plans is interleaved with their generation and also with the assimilation of inputs from the environment([18], [6]). It is known ([11], [31], [25]) that to make an *abductive theorem prover* [33] behave as a planner, one has to define properly the set of abducibles, say *Ab*. In the

[8] in this case with certain sacrifice in expressiveness, however. The operators + and *par* would have to be excluded from the language as it is.

[9] The intention is to have the name of the agent also represented by a term in the predicate: $do(Agent, Action, Starting\_Time, Finishing\_Time)$. For the sake of simplicity, however, the term for agents is omitted here.

present context one can make $Ab = \{do, <, \leq, =\}$. The background theory can then be completed with the following definition (the base case of *done*):

$$done(A, T_o, T_f) \leftarrow primitive(A) \land do(A, T_o, T_f) \text{ [DNEC0]}$$

Notice that we do not include the predicate $preconds(A, To)$ in [DNEC0]. Strictly speaking, one should be "testing" the preconditions of action A at this point. We, however, leave to the programmer the job of testing preconditions within OPENLOG code (i.e. *if C then..* expressions).

7.3 How to Achieve the Inhibition of Abduction

As can be seen, the projection predicate *holds* is involved in the interpretation of every conditional expression in OPENLOG. Thus, to inhibit abduction, we simply establish that no *do* atom "derived" by unfolding a *holds* atom will be abduced. In this way, the *holds* predicate is used for "testing", whereas the base case of *done* is used for generation of plans, as we explained above.

8 Discussion

OPENLOG is a logic programming language that can be used to write procedural code which can be combined with a declarative specification of a problem domain (a background theory).

To define the language, logical characterization has been given to the traditional programming structures (**if then else**, **while**, ;, ...) in such a way that any program written with those structures can be translated into a set of logical sentences.

This mapping from procedural code to logical sentences is not only sought for the sake of clarity. The logic chosen to provide semantics for the procedural structures can also be used to specify a theory of actions that models dynamic universes[6]. This theory of actions can be based on Kowalski and Sergot's Event Calculus [20], a logical formalism with an ontology based on events and properties that can be initiated and terminated by events. The Event Calculus provides a solution to the Frame Problem and also permits the efficient representation of concurrent activities and continuous domains. This has permitted the extension of the capabilities of standard PASCAL to allow for the description of parallel actions in OPENLOG programs.

Thus, the designer/programmer is offered a specification-implementation language that can be used to model complex universes and also to write high-level algorithms to guide the activities of agents acting in a dynamic environment.

As in other logic programming languages, programs in OPENLOG are processed by a theorem prover. Unlike in other approaches, however, programs in OPENLOG are intended to be interpreted[10] rather than compiled[11]. The reason

[10] As in JAVA [23] and other commercial products, where code is pre-compiled to an intermediate form to be read by an interpreter/executive.

[11] As in Situated Agents [29] and GOLOG [21]

for this is crucial. The process of planning (the theorem prover transforming goals into plans) must be interleaved with the execution of those plans and the inputting and assimilation of observations. One has to expect many modifications and amendments of the plans. The system as a whole will process inputs as soon as it can, increasing its chances of an opportune response (normally by an minor adjustment to its plans as illustrated in [6]). The first practical consequence of this is that the system will generate and use *partial plans* which it will refine progressively as its knowledge of the environment increases. This is a crucial difference between OPENLOG's aims and those of a similar logic-based programming language: GOLOG [21]. We have explored the similarities and differences between GOLOG and a previous version of OPENLOG in [5].

Partial planning may seem atypical in the current context because theorem provers are normally backward-reasoning mechanisms. An interesting aspect of the representation here discussed is that it supports planning by searching the time line in a forward direction. This is called *progression*. The representational strategy that supports this form of planning is not new. It is at the core of a well known device to specify grammars and to program their parsers: Definite Clause Grammar or DCG [26]. OPENLOG programs are like DCG*s* in that they both are higher level macros that can be completely and unambiguously translated into logic programs. Unlike DCG however, OPENLOG provides for negative literals.

There is another critical difference between OPENLOG and DCG. In DCGs, the "state of the computation" (which in that case contains the sentence being parsed) is carried along through arguments as is common in stream logic programming. This has the inconvenience of requiring the explicit representation of all objects in the application domain and is, therefore, cumbersome and limiting (we tested the approach in the prototypical implementation of pathfinder reactive automatas that do forward planning, reported in [4]). Background theories are a flexible and powerful alternative to this approach.

9 Conclusions and Further Research

OPENLOG is a logic programming language. In OPENLOG one can write procedural code combined with a declarative specification of a dynamic domain (a background theory) to guide an agent at problem-solving in that domain.

The interpreter of OPENLOG is an abductive proof procedure which can be used to implement the planning module of an agent [6]. One innovative aspect of this work is that the agent processing and executing OPENLOG programs will stay *open* to the environment and will allow for changes in its environment and assimilation of new information generated by these changes.

Another novelty in this work is that we use a logic program (the definition of *done* and the other predicates) to specify the semantics of an imperative programming language. The semantics is provided as a mapping that links the semantics of the imperative code with any semantics for abductive logic programs. The definition of *done* has some other operational advantages. It can serve as an interpreter for OPENLOG, thus providing its operational semantics as well. And it can be used to "inhibit" the abductive proof procedure and prevent the over-generation of abducibles which would make of abduction an impractical approach for building the planning module of an agent.

We are exploring the relationship between OPENLOG and programming with integrity constraints [6]. Also in [6], "the Elevator example" is borrowed from [21] and is developed in with OPENLOG. We plan to use OPENLOG as the programming language for each agent in a platform to simulate multi-agents systems.

Acknowledgments

This research was supported by a grant from CONICIT-University of Los Andes, Venezuela. The author would like to thank Bob Kowalski, Fariba Sadri and Murray Shanahan for many interesting discussions and the referees for their useful comments.

References

1. James F. Allen. Temporal reasoning and planning. In J. F. Allen, H. Kautz, R. Pelavin, and J. Tenenberg, editors, *Reasoning About Plans*. Morgan Kauffmann Publishers, Inc., San Mateo, California, 1991. ISBN 1-55860-137-6.
2. E. Charniak and D. McDermott. *Introduction to Artificial Intelligence*. Addison-Wesley, Menlo Park, CA, 1985.
3. L. Console, T.. Dupre, and P. Torasso. On the relationship between abduction and deduction. *Journal of Logic and Computation*, 2(5):661–690, 1991.
4. Jacinto A. Dávila. Knowledge assimilation in multi-agents system. Master's thesis, Imperial College, London, September 1994.
5. Jacinto A. Dávila. A logic-based agent. Technical report, Imperial College, London, February 1996.
6. Jacinto A. Dávila. *Agents in Logic Programming*. PhD thesis, Imperial College, London, May 1997.
7. J. de Kleer. An assumption-based tms. *Artificial Intelligence*, 32, 1986.
8. Thomas Dean and Mark Boddy. An analysis of time-dependent planning. In *AAAI 88: The Seventh National Conference on AI*, volume 1, Saint Paul, Minnesota, August 1988.
9. M. Denecker and D. De Schreye. Sldnfa: an abductive procedure for abductive logic programs. The journal of logic programming. 1995.
10. K. Eshghi and R. Kowalski. Abduction compare with negation as failure. In G. Levi and M. Martelli, editors, *Proceedings of the International Conference on Logic Programming*, pages 234–255, Lisbon, Portugal, 1989. MIT Press.
11. Kave Eshghi. Abductive planning with event calculus. In *Proceedings 5th International Conference on Logic Programming*, 1988. pg. 562.
12. C.A. Evans. Negation as failure as an approach to the Hanks and McDermott problem. In F.J. Cantu-Ortiz, editor, *Proc. 2nd. International Symposium on Artificial Intelligence*, Monterrey, México, 1989. McGraw-Hill.

13. T Fung and R Kowalski. The iff proof procedure for abductive logic programming. The Journal of logic programming, 33(2): 151-178, 1997.
14. Tze Ho Fung. *Abduction by deduction.* PhD thesis, Imperial College, London, January 1996.
15. C.A.R. Hoare. *Communicating Sequential Processes.* Prentice-Hall, 1985.
16. A.C. Kakas, R. Kowalski, and F. Toni. Abductive logic programming. *Journal of Logic and Computation*, 2(6):719–770, 1993.
17. A.C. Kakas and P Mancarella. Abductive logic programming. In W. Marek, A. Nerode, D. Pedreschi, and V.S. Subrahmanian, editors, *Proc. NACLP Workshop on Non-monotonic Reasoning and Logic Programming*, Austin, Texas, 1990.
18. Robert Kowalski. Using metalogic to reconcile reactive with rational agents. In K. Apt and F. Turini, editors, *Meta-Logics and Logic Programming.* MIT Press, 1995. (Also at http://www-lp.doc.ic.ac.uk/UserPages/staff/rak/recon-abst.html).
19. Robert Kowalski and Fariba Sadri. The situation calculus and event calculus compared. In M. Bruynooghe, editor, *Proc. International Logic Programming Symposium*, pages 539–553. MIT Press, 1994. (Also at http://www-lp.doc.ic.ac.uk/UserPages/staff/fs/ilps94.html).
20. Robert Kowalski and Marek Sergot. A logic-based calculus of events. *New Generation Computing*, 4:67–95, 1986.
21. H. Levesque, R. Reiter, Y. Lespérance, L. Fangzhen, and R. B. Scherl. Golog: A logic programming language for dynamic domains. *The Journal of Logic Programming*, (31):59–84, 1997.
22. J. McCarthy and P. Hayes. Some philosophical problems from the standpoint of artificial intelligence. *Machine Intelligence*, 4:463–502, 1969.
23. Sun Microsystems. Hotjava home page. http://java.sun.com/.
24. Robin Milner. *Communication and Concurrency.* Prentice-Hall, 1989.
25. Lode Missiaen, Maurice Bruynooghe, and Marc Denecker. Chica, an abductive planning system based on event calculus. *Journal of Logic and Computation*, 5(5):579–602, October 1995.
26. F.C.N. Pereira and D.H.D. Warren. Definite clause grammars for language analysis-a survey of the formalism and a comparison with augmented transition networks. *Artificial Intelligence*, 13:231–278, 1980.
27. D. Poole. Explanation and prediction: an architecture for default and abductive reasoning. *Computational Intelligence Journal*, 5:97–110, 1989.
28. David Poole. Logic programming for robot control. In Chris S. Mellish, editor, *Proc. International Joint Conference on Artificial Intelligence*, pages 150–157, San Mateo, California, 1995. Morgan Kaufmann Publishers, Inc.
29. Stanley J. Rosenschein and Leslie Pack Kaelbling. A situated view of representation and control. *Artificial Intelligence*, 73:149–173, February 1995.
30. Stuart J. Russell and Peter Norvig. *Artificial Intelligence: A Modern Approach.* Prentice Hall, Englewood Cliffs - New Jersey, 1995.
31. Murray Shanahan. Prediction is deduction but explanation is abduction. In N.S. Sridharan, editor, *Proc. International Joint Conference on Artificial Intelligence*, pages 1055–1060. Morgan Kaufmann, Detroit. Mi, 1989.
32. Murray Shanahan. *Solving the Frame Problem: A Mathematical Investigation of the Common Sense Law of Inertia.* MIT Press, 1997.
33. Francesca Toni. *Abductive Logic Programming.* PhD thesis, Imperial College, London, July 1995.
34. M. van Emden and R. Kowalski. The semantics of predicate logic as a programming language. *Journal of the ACM*, 4(4):733–742, 1976.

35. Gerhard Wetzel. *Abductive and Constraint Logic Programming*. PhD thesis, Imperial College, London, March 1997.
36. Gerhard Wetzel, Robert Kowalski, and Francesca Toni. A theorem-proving approach to clp. In A. Krall and U. Geske, editors, *Workshop Logische Programmierung*, number 270, pages 63–72. GMD-Studien, September 1995.

An Operational Semantics of Starlog

Lunjin Lu and John G. Cleary

Department of Computer Science
University of Waikato
Hamilton, New Zealand
{lunjin,jcleary}@cs.waikato.ac.nz

Abstract. Starlog is a temporal logic programming language that supports declarative specification of reactive systems, input-output behaviour and destructive updates. This paper presents an operational semantics for Starlog. Its correctness and completeness with respect to a model semantics are proved.

Keywords: Operational Semantics; Constraint Logic Programs; Temporal Logic Programs; Stratification

1 Introduction

Starlog is a temporal logic programming (TLP for short) language. It evolved from such applications as simulation [9] and deductive databases [28]. These applications require temporal relationships between objects to be specified in a precise and direct manner. It is this requirement which dictates the design and implementation of Starlog.

While Starlog is similar in many ways to deductive databases it is intended as a full general programming language. This means in particular that two assumptions of deductive databases are untrue. The first is that the logic program can be finitely stratified on the predicate names. This is replaced by a more general ordering using integer timestamps and predicate names. The second assumption that is violated is the Datalog assumption that terms can only be of some finite depth. Starlog allows both unbounded terms and constraints. This paper is intended to provide a precise operational semantics for such a general bottom-up logic programming language.

Starlog uses the syntax of the constraint logic programs (CLP hereafter) [21]. Starlog is a CLP language with arithmetic constraints over integers and equality/disequality constraints over terms. This is different from other TLP languages that are based on a particular temporal logic [1,2,4,14,32,47]. Unlike other CLP languages such as CLP(R) [22] and BNR Prolog [33], Starlog programs are executed bottom-up. This is suitable for its intended applications which often use the specification of a real world system to construct a temporal model of the system.

Over the past decade, a working prototype implementation of Starlog has been developed and challenging applications have been written in Starlog. This

G. Nadathur (Ed.): PPDP'99, LNCS 1702, pp. 294–310, 1999.

paper provides Starlog with a formal operational semantics. Its purpose is two fold. Firstly, while the present implementation works experimentally, it is important that the implementation be verified with respect to a formal semantics. Secondly, the present implementation is rather inefficient. To improve its efficiency, it is necessary to perform various semantic based program analyses, for which a formal operational semantics is a necessity.

This paper presents an operational semantics for Starlog. Its correctness and completeness with respect to its model semantics are given. The operational semantics is a bottom-up execution mechanism which deals with negative literals in the same way as positive ones.

As programs in TLP languages such as Templog [1], Tokio [2], Temporal Prolog [14], Tempura [32] and Chronology [47] can be translated into CLP programs [7,34], our operational semantics offers a bottom-up execution mechanism for these TLP languages which use extensions of the SLD resolution as operational semantics.

Temporality is expressed in Starlog by explicitly timing truth. The operational semantics works on the class of Starlog programs that can be stratified in terms of time and predicate symbols. It generates in time order those facts whose ground instances are in the model semantics of the program. It repeatedly generates a fact using the program and transforms the program. Time-orderedness and stratification guarantee the correctness and the completeness of the operational semantics. Time-orderedness is essential in temporal applications such as simulation.

The rest of this paper is organised as follows. Section 2 introduces a subset of Starlog. The subset is the core of Starlog and is chosen to simplify the presentation of the paper. Section 3 introduces the notion of temporally stratified Starlog programs and defines its model semantics, and section 4 presents the operational semantics and gives its correctness and completeness. Section 5 concludes the paper and compares our operational semantics with related work. We assume that the reader is familiar with the terminology of constraint logic programming [21].

2 Starlog Language

Starlog was developed for specification and implementation of applications which require temporal reasoning. Starlog doesn't directly support temporal operators. However, most temporal operators can be programmed in Starlog as indicated in [7]. Moreover, Starlog allows more explicit temporal relationships to be expressed directly.

As a CLP language, Starlog can adopt any model semantics developed for the CLP scheme. This paper defines the model semantics of Starlog based on the stable model semantics [17]. Unlike other CLP languages such as [22,10,12,11,30,5,46], Starlog uses an explicit parameter for time. This can be thought of putting timestamps on truth values.

2.1 Syntax

Terms and constraints are formed as in other CLP(X) languages. Constraints are arithmetic constraints over integers and equality/disequality constraints over terms. We will use $\mathcal{D}$ to denote the underlying domain structure which interprets arithmetic constraints over integers and equality/disequality constraints over terms in the usual way [6,8]. There is no complete constraint solver for arbitrary integer arithmetic constraints. However, there are powerful decidable subsets of integer arithmetic constraints [27,31,19,39,20,44,41,18]. This paper focuses on decidable subsets of integer arithmetic constraints and assumes that $\mathcal{D}$ is satisfaction complete. The assumption, which can be relaxed, helps us to separate the issue of the completeness of the constraint solver from that of the completeness of the operational semantics itself. Substituting a decidable domain of integer arithmetic constraints for $\mathcal{D}$ will result in a particular instance of Starlog. An atom is defined to be of the form $p(s_1, \cdots, s_n)@t$ where t, called the timestamp, is a term consisting of variables, integers and arithmetic operators while each s_i is an arbitrary term. A literal is either an atom or negation of an atom. A clause is of the form $\mathbf{h} \leftarrow \delta, \mathbf{L}$ where δ is a constraint, $\mathbf{h}$ an atom and $\mathbf{L}$ a conjunction of literals. A Starlog program is a finite set of clauses. A clause without any body literal but possibly including constraints is called a fact while other clauses are called rules.

2.2 Causality

Causality is natural in temporal reasoning and is also a useful assumption which simplifies Starlog programming. Some other TLP languages also assume the causality of programs [4]. Causality means that no truth in the past is defined in terms of truth in the future. Thus, the following clause fails in Starlog.

```
retrospective_reasoning@T :-
        T=S-1000, current_finding@S.
```

Formally, a clause is causal if, in any $\mathcal{D}$-model of the clause, the timestamp of its head is no less than the timestamp of any literal in its body. Starlog implicitly adds causality constraints to program clauses.

2.3 Examples

Time in Starlog is discrete and positive. The following program defines a predicate even that is true at even time points and thus generates even numbers.

```
% even numbers program.

even@0.
even@T :-  T=S+1, not(even@S).
```

The following program generates prime numbers as a time sequence using the predicate prime. It also generates non-prime numbers by predicate mult. $T >= 2$, $T = J * K$, $K >= J$ and $J >= 2$ are constraints over integers.

```
% prime numbers program.

prime@T :-  T>=2, not(mult@T).
mult@T  :-  T=J*K, K>=J, J>=2, prime@J.
```

2.4 Normalised Programs

In the sequel, we shall only be concerned with normalised programs. A normalised program is a set of normalised clauses. A clause is normalised if its head and every atom occurring in its body are of the form $p(X_1, \cdots, X_n)@T$ where $X_1, \cdots, X_n$ and T are different variables. It is obvious that corresponding to each program, there is a semantically equivalent normalised program. The causality constraints implicit in a normalised Starlog program can be easily added.

2.5 Notations

Let $C = (h@T \leftarrow \delta, \mathbf{L})$, and t be an integer. Define $C^{\geq t} \stackrel{def}{=} (h@T \leftarrow (T \geq t), \delta, \mathbf{L})$ and $C^{<t} \stackrel{def}{=} (h@T \leftarrow (T < t), \delta, \mathbf{L})$. Let $\mathcal{P}$ be a program. $\mathcal{P}^f$ denotes the set of facts in $\mathcal{P}$ and $\mathcal{P}^r$ the set of rules in $\mathcal{P}$. $\mathcal{P} = \mathcal{P}^f \cup \mathcal{P}^r$. We sometimes write a clause as $h@T \leftarrow \delta, \wedge_{j \in J} a_j@S_j, \wedge_{k \in K} not(a_k@S_k)$ with J and K being disjoint sets of indices. $\mathcal{P}^-$ denotes the set of those rules in $\mathcal{P}^r$ which have only negative literals, and $\mathcal{P}^+$ denotes $\mathcal{P}^r \setminus \mathcal{P}^-$. Rules in $\mathcal{P}^-$ are called negative and those in $\mathcal{P}^+$ positive. Let δ be a constraint. Define $sat(\delta) \stackrel{def}{=} (\mathcal{D} \models \exists.\delta)$. $sat(\delta)$ is true iff δ is satisfiable with respect to $\mathcal{D}$. Let Q be a set of clauses. Define

$$[Q]_{\mathcal{D}} \stackrel{def}{=} \{\mu(\mathbf{h} \leftarrow \mathbf{L}) \mid (\mathbf{h} \leftarrow \delta, \mathbf{L}) \in Q \wedge (\mu \text{ is a valuation}) \wedge \mathcal{D} \models \mu(\delta)\}$$

We write $[\{S\}]_{\mathcal{D}}$ as $[S]_{\mathcal{D}}$ for simplicity.

3 Stratification and Model Semantics

This section defines the class of temporally stratified programs and their model semantics, and lays the technical ground for the operational semantics of temporally stratified programs including negation.

3.1 Temporally Stratified Programs

Stratification has been a useful notion in formulating the semantics of logic programs with negation [3,15,38,37]. The idea of stratification is to disallow recursion through negation. In other words, stratification makes it impossible for a predicate to recursively invoke itself through negation. This is guaranteed by requiring that any predicate symbol occurring negatively in the body of a clause belongs to a lower stratum than the head predicate symbol and any predicate symbol occurring positively in the body belongs to a stratum no higher than the head predicate symbol.

The timestamps in Starlog programs relax the above condition for stratification in that recursion through negation is allowed provided it is through decreasing timestamps. Let $\prod$ be the set of the predicate symbols in $\mathcal{P}$ and Nat be the set of natural numbers. Let *strat* be a function from $\prod$ to Nat. We extend *strat* as follows. $strat(p(\tilde{s})) \stackrel{def}{=} strat(p)$ and $strat((\mathbf{h} \leftarrow \delta, \mathbf{L})) \stackrel{def}{=} strat(\mathbf{h})$.

Definition 1. *A program $\mathcal{P}$ is temporally stratified if there is a function strat : $\prod \mapsto \mathsf{Nat}$ such that, for every rule $h@T \leftarrow \delta, \wedge_{j\in J}a_j@S_j, \wedge_{k\in K}not(a_k@S_k)$ in $\mathcal{P}$, for every $j \in J$, either $\mathcal{D} \models (\delta \rightarrow (T > S_j))$ or $strat(a_j) \leq strat(h)$, and for every $k \in K$, either $\mathcal{D} \models (\delta \rightarrow (T > S_k))$ or $strat(a_k) < strat(h)$.*

The above definition augments the traditional predicate stratification in the literature with time stratification. Procedure calls are primarily stratified on timestamps and secondarily on predicate symbols. It ensures that recursive calls through negation in a temporally stratified program involve time decrements. Under the assumption that $\mathcal{D}$ is satisfaction complete, temporal stratifiability is decidable. An algorithm for finding a predicate stratification function *strat* for a logic program in the literature, such as that in [45] (page 134), can be readily adapted for Starlog.

3.2 Model Semantics

We first recall the stable model semantics for logic programs [17] and then define model semantics of temporally stratified Starlog programs. Let $\mathcal{G}$ be a logic program consisting of a set of ground clauses and $\mathcal{M}$ be a set of ground atoms. Then the Gelfond-Lifschitz transformation is defined as follows.

$$GL(\mathcal{G}, \mathcal{M}) \stackrel{def}{=} \{H \leftarrow pos(\mathbf{L}) \mid (H \leftarrow \mathbf{L}) \in \mathcal{G} \wedge \mathcal{M} \models neg(\mathbf{L})\}$$

where $pos(\mathbf{L})$ is the conjunction of positive literals in $\mathbf{L}$ and $neg(\mathbf{L})$ is the conjunction of negative literals in $\mathbf{L}$. $GL(\mathcal{G}, \mathcal{M})$ is a definite logic program obtained by removing those clauses in $\mathcal{G}$ whose bodies contain the negation of an atom in $\mathcal{M}$ and deleting negative literals in other clauses in $\mathcal{G}$.

A set $\mathcal{M}$ of atoms is a stable model of $\mathcal{G}$ if $\mathcal{M}$ is the least model of $GL(\mathcal{G}, \mathcal{M})$. If $\mathcal{G}$ is locally stratified then $\mathcal{G}$ has a unique stable model which is also the least model of $\mathcal{G}$. For locally stratified programs, the stable model semantics coincides with the perfect model semantics [36,35] and the well-founded semantics [16].

Let $\mathcal{P}$ be a temporally stratified Starlog program. $[\mathcal{P}]_\mathcal{D}$ is a locally stratified logic program. Therefore, $[\mathcal{P}]_\mathcal{D}$ has one stable model which is also the least model of $[\mathcal{P}]_\mathcal{D}$. We take the unique stable model of $[\mathcal{P}]_\mathcal{D}$ as the canonical model semantics of $\mathcal{P}$, denoted as $CM(\mathcal{P})$. The operational semantics of temporally stratified Starlog programs computes a representation of $CM(\mathcal{P})$ in time order. A representation of $CM(\mathcal{P})$ is a set $\mathcal{F}$ of facts such that $[\mathcal{F}]_\mathcal{D} = CM(\mathcal{P})$.

Let $\mathbf{f}$ be a fact. Elements of $[\mathbf{f}]_{\mathcal{D}}$ are called ground instances of $\mathbf{f}$. Note that ground instances of $\mathbf{f}$ has an empty body and can be thought of as ground atoms. Let $\mathcal{M}$ be a set of ground atoms. We say that $\mathbf{f}$ is contained in $\mathcal{M}$ if all ground instances of $\mathbf{f}$ are in $\mathcal{M}$, i.e., $[\mathbf{f}]_{\mathcal{D}} \subseteq \mathcal{M}$.

3.3 Approximate Success Time

Let $\mathcal{P}$ be the current program. A key step in the operational semantics is to determine the minimum timestamp that an atom in $CM(\mathcal{P})$ has. Because of negation, the minimum timestamp can not be determined by the facts in $\mathcal{P}$ alone. Rules have to be taken into account. For example, the prime numbers program doesn't contain any fact and yet $\mathsf{prime@}T \leftarrow T \geq 2, T < 4$ is in its model semantics.

As we require the operational semantics to generate facts in time order, we naturally expect that such a fact be generated from a clause that has the smallest success time where the success time m_C of a clause C is defined as follows. Let C be $h@T \leftarrow \delta, \mathbf{L}$. Then

$$\mathsf{m}_C \stackrel{def}{=} \min\{t \mid \mathcal{D} \models \mu(\delta \wedge (T = t)) \wedge CM(\mathcal{P}) \models \mu(\mathbf{L}) \wedge (\mu \text{ is a valuation})\}$$

m_C is not computable but serves as a useful reference. The operational semantics uses a conservative approximation $\hat{\mathsf{m}}_C$ to m_C to choose a program clause from which the next fact is generated.

$$\hat{\mathsf{m}}_C \stackrel{def}{=} min\{t \mid sat(\delta \wedge (T = t))\}$$

$\hat{\mathsf{m}}_C$ is a conservative approximation to m_C in that $\hat{\mathsf{m}}_C$ never exceeds m_C. $\hat{\mathsf{m}}_C$ is determined by C alone. This is in contrast to m_C which also depends on other clauses in $\mathcal{P}$. $\hat{\mathsf{m}}_C$ is computable as $\mathcal{D}$ is satisfaction complete. If C is a fact then $\hat{\mathsf{m}}_C = \mathsf{m}_C$. We define approximate success time for a set of clauses as the minimum of the approximate success times of the clauses in the set.

3.4 Extracting Facts from Negative Rules

Time-orderedness requires that each time a fact is generated it has the smallest success time. If the smallest approximate success time of the program happens to be that of a fact in the program then the situation is simple. It is also the smallest success time of any fact in the model semantics of the program.

The situation becomes more complicated when the approximate success time of a rule is smaller than those of the facts in the program. In this case, there is a possibility that facts with success times smaller than those of the facts in the program can be generated by rules in the program, as shown later. We will develop a method to extract such facts from the program. The method is based on a few properties of temporally stratified programs that are detailed below. The following lemma states that if the success time of a fact in the model semantics of the program is smaller than those of the facts in the program then a negative rule in the program derives the fact.

Lemma 1. *Let $\mathcal{P}$ be a program and $a@t$ be a ground atom such that $a@t \in CM(\mathcal{P})$ and $t < \hat{m}_{\mathcal{P}^f}$. Then there are a valuation ν and a negative rule $C = (h@T \leftarrow \delta, \wedge_{k\in K} not(\mathbf{a}_k))$ such that $\mathcal{D} \models \nu(\delta)$, $\nu(\mathbf{a}_k) \notin CM(\mathcal{P})$ and $\nu(T) \leq t$.*

Proof. By contradiction. Assume there were no negative rule $C = (h@T \leftarrow \delta, \wedge_{k\in K} not(\mathbf{a}_k))$ and valuation ν such that $\mathcal{D} \models \nu(\delta)$, $\nu(\mathbf{a}_k) \notin CM(\mathcal{P})$ and $\nu(T) \leq t$. Then, $t' > t$ for each fact $h'@t'$ in $GL([\mathcal{P}]_{\mathcal{D}}, CM(\mathcal{P}))$. By the causality requirement, $a@t \notin CM(\mathcal{P})$ as $CM(\mathcal{P})$ is the least Herbrand model of $GL([\mathcal{P}]_{\mathcal{D}}, CM(\mathcal{P}))$. □

According to lemma 1, if all negative rules have an approximate time no less than $\hat{m}_{\mathcal{P}^f}$ then the success time of the next fact to generate is $\hat{m}_{\mathcal{P}^f}$.

When $\hat{m}_{\mathcal{P}^f} > \hat{m}_{\mathcal{P}^-}$, a fact can be extracted from a negative rule, as is stated in the following lemma.

Lemma 2. *Let $\mathcal{P}$ be a program such that $\hat{m}_{\mathcal{P}^f} > \hat{m}_{\mathcal{P}^-}$ and $C = (h@T \leftarrow \delta, \wedge_{k\in K} not(a_k@S_k))$ be a negative rule in $\mathcal{P}$ such that $\hat{m}_C = \hat{m}_{\mathcal{P}^-}$ and $strat(C) \leq strat(C')$ for any other negative rule C' in $\mathcal{P}$ with $\hat{m}_{C'} = \hat{m}_C$. Then $[h@T \leftarrow \delta \wedge (T = \hat{m}_{\mathcal{P}^-})]_{\mathcal{D}} \subseteq CM(\mathcal{P})$.*

Proof. First consider the simple case where C is the only one negative rule whose approximate success time is equal to $\hat{m}_{\mathcal{P}^-}$. Let ν be an arbitrary valuation such that $\mathcal{D} \models \nu(\delta \wedge (T = \hat{m}_{\mathcal{P}^-}))$. The temporal stratification and causality requirements ensure that for each $k \in K$, either (a) $\nu(S_k) < \hat{m}_{\mathcal{P}^-}$ or (b) $(\nu(S_k) = \hat{m}_{\mathcal{P}^-}) \wedge (strat(a_k) < strat(h))$. In the case (a), $\nu(a_k@S_k) \notin CM(\mathcal{P})$ by lemma 1. In the case (b), we also have $\nu(a_k@S_k) \notin CM(\mathcal{P})$ as shown in the following. We have $\mathsf{Pred}(a_k) \neq \mathsf{Pred}(h)$ where $\mathsf{Pred}(a)$ is the predicate symbol of the atom a. If $\mathsf{Pred}(a_k)$ is not defined by any positive rule then every clause for $\mathsf{Pred}(a_k)$ has an approximate success time greater than $\hat{m}_{\mathcal{P}^-}$ because C is the only negative rule whose approximate success time is equal to $\hat{m}_{\mathcal{P}^-}$. This implies $\nu(a_k@S_k) \notin CM(\mathcal{P})$. Now suppose that $\mathsf{Pred}(a_k)$ be defined by a positive rule $a_k@S \leftarrow \delta', \mathbf{L}$. Either $\mathbf{L}$ contains a positive call to a predicate q other than $\mathsf{Pred}(h)$, implying $\nu(a_k@S_k) \notin CM(\mathcal{P})$ because the approximate success time of any negative rule for q is greater than $\hat{m}_{\mathcal{P}^-}$, or every positive literal in $\mathbf{L}$ is a call to $\mathsf{Pred}(h)$, also implying $\nu(a_k@S_k) \notin CM(\mathcal{P})$ because such a call must involve a time decrement to satisfy the temporal stratification requirement. Thus,$\nu(a_k@S_k) \notin CM(\mathcal{P})$ in the case (b). So, $(\mathcal{D} \models \nu(\delta \wedge (T = \hat{m}_{\mathcal{P}^-}))) \rightarrow \nu(a_k@S_k) \notin CM(\mathcal{P})$ for any valuation ν, which implies $[h@T \leftarrow \delta \wedge (T = \hat{m}_{\mathcal{P}^-})]_{\mathcal{D}} \subseteq GL([\mathcal{P}]_{\mathcal{D}}, CM(\mathcal{P}))$.

Now suppose that there be more than one negative rules whose approximate success times equal $\hat{m}_{\mathcal{P}^-}$. Each such a clause defines a predicate in a stratum. Consider a negative rule $C = (h@T \leftarrow \delta, \wedge_{k\in K} not(a_k@S_k))$ that has the lowest stratum among these negative rules. The same reasoning as in the above paragraph leads to $[h@T \leftarrow \delta \wedge (T = \hat{m}_{\mathcal{P}^-})]_{\mathcal{D}} \subseteq GL([\mathcal{P}]_{\mathcal{D}}, CM(\mathcal{P}))$.

The lemma follows because $CM(\mathcal{P})$ is a model of $GL([\mathcal{P}]_{\mathcal{D}}, CM(\mathcal{P}))$. □

4 Operational Semantics

This section presents an operational semantics for temporally stratified programs.

Let $\mathcal{P}$ be the program. The operational semantics enumerates a representation of $CM(\mathcal{P})$ in time order. It repeatedly generates a fact $\mathbf{f}$ and then uses $\mathbf{f}$ to transform the current program $\mathcal{P}$ into a new program $\mathcal{P}'$. The transformation is done in such a way that any ground fact in $CM(\mathcal{P})$ is either a ground instance of $\mathbf{f}$ or in $CM(\mathcal{P}')$, and that any fact in $CM(\mathcal{P}')$ is also in $CM(\mathcal{P})$. The operational semantics keeps track of a timer. The timer records the minimum timestamp that the next fact to generate could have. The operational semantics ensures that all the facts with a timestamp smaller than the timer and in the model semantics of the original program has been generated and that all other facts in the model semantics of the original program are in the model semantics of the current program.

As the operational semantics discards generated facts, a newly generated fact must be propagated through each rule that matches the fact. The propagation results in several clauses which replace the rule through which the fact is propagated. Let $C = (h@T \leftarrow \delta, \wedge_{j \in J} a_j@S_j, \wedge_{k \in K} not(a_k@S_k))$ be a rule in $\mathcal{P}^r$, $\mathbf{f} = (\mathbf{h}' \leftarrow \delta')$ be the generated fact, and t be the value of the timer when $\mathbf{f}$ is generated. Then C is replaced by a set of clauses obtained by (1) replacing each $a_l@S_l$ in the body of C with $(a_l@S_l \wedge (S_l \geq t) \vee (a_l@S_l = \rho_l(\mathbf{h}') \wedge \rho_l(\delta')))$ where ρ_l is a renaming substitution, (2) converting the resulting body into its disjunctive normal form and throwing away conjuncts with unsatisfiable constraints, and (3) for each remaining conjunct, producing a clause with $h@T$ as its head and the conjunct as its body. Formally,

$$prop((h@T \leftarrow \delta, \wedge_{j \in J} a_j@S_j, \wedge_{k \in K} not(a_k@S_k)), (\mathbf{h}' \leftarrow \delta'), t)$$
$$\stackrel{def}{=} \{h@T \leftarrow \gamma, \mathbf{L} \mid (\gamma, \mathbf{L}) \in KK \wedge sat(\gamma)\}$$

with $KK = DNF\begin{pmatrix} \delta, \bigwedge_{j \in J}(S_j \geq t \wedge a_j@S_j \vee (a_j@S_j = \rho_j(\mathbf{h}')) \wedge \rho_j(\delta')), \\ \bigwedge_{k \in K} not(S_k \geq t \wedge a_k@S_k \vee (a_k@S_k = \rho_k(\mathbf{h}')) \wedge \rho_k(\delta')) \end{pmatrix}$
where $DNF(F)$ is the disjunctive normal form of F.

The definition of $prop(C, \mathbf{f}, t)$ doesn't distinguish atoms that match with the generated fact from those that do not. If $a_l@S_l$ doesn't match with $\mathbf{h}'$ then $(a_l@S_l \wedge (S_l \geq t) \vee (a_l@S_l = \rho_l(\mathbf{h}')) \wedge \rho_l(\delta')$ is equivalent to $a_l@S_l \wedge (S_l \geq t)$ and the effect is to strengthen the constraint part of C.

Let a be an atom. We define $\tau_{a,\mathcal{P}}$ as the minimum of the approximate success times of the clauses in $\mathcal{P}$ whose heads have the same predicate symbol as a.

Algorithm 1 *Given a temporally stratified program $\mathcal{P}$ and its predicate stratification function strat, the algorithm enumerates in time order a representation of $CM(\mathcal{P})$.*

- *Initialisation.*

$$t := 0$$
$$\mathcal{P} := \{\mathbf{h} \leftarrow \delta, \mathbf{L} \mid (\mathbf{h} \leftarrow \delta, \mathbf{L}) \in \mathcal{P} \wedge sat(\delta)\}$$

– *While* $(\mathcal{P}^- \cup \mathcal{P}^f) \neq \emptyset$ *do*

(Ia) $t := \hat{\mathfrak{m}}_{(\mathcal{P}^f \cup \mathcal{P}^-)}$

(Ib) $\mathcal{P} := \mathcal{P}^f \cup \mathcal{P}^+ \cup \bigcup_{C \in \mathcal{P}^-} extr\_t(C, \mathcal{P})$ *where,*

$$extr\_t((h@T \leftarrow \delta, \wedge_{k \in K} not(a_k@S_k)), \mathcal{P}) \stackrel{def}{=} \{h@T \leftarrow \gamma, \mathbf{L} \mid (\gamma, \mathbf{L}) \in KK \wedge sat(\gamma)\}$$

with $KK = DNF(\delta, \bigwedge_{k \in K}((S_k < \tau_{a_k,\mathcal{P}}) \vee ((S_k \geq \tau_{a_k,\mathcal{P}}) \wedge not(a_k@S_k))))$.

(Ic) If $t \neq \hat{\mathfrak{m}}_{\mathcal{P}^f}$ *then* $\mathcal{P} := \mathcal{P} \cup \{h@T \leftarrow \delta, (T = t)\}$, *assuming that* $C = (h@T \leftarrow \delta, \mathbf{L})$ *is a negative rule in* $\mathcal{P}$ *such that* $\hat{\mathfrak{m}}_C = t$ *and* $strat(C) \leq strat(C')$ *for any other negative rule* C' *in* $\mathcal{P}$ *with* $\hat{\mathfrak{m}}_{C'} = t$.

(II) Choose a fact $\mathbf{f} = (h'@T' \leftarrow \delta')$ *from* $\mathcal{P}^f$ *such that* $sat((T' = t) \wedge \delta')$.

(III) $\mathcal{P} := \mathcal{P}^f \setminus \{\mathbf{f}\} \cup \bigcup_{C \in \mathcal{P}^r} prop(C, \mathbf{f}, t)$

□

We sometimes write step (Ib) as $\mathcal{P} := extr\_t(\mathcal{P})$ with $extr\_t(\mathcal{P}) \stackrel{def}{=} \mathcal{P}^f \cup \mathcal{P}^+ \cup \bigcup_{C \in \mathcal{P}^-} extr\_t(C, \mathcal{P})$. We also write step (Ic) as $\mathcal{P} := extr\_p(\mathcal{P}, t)$. Define $extr(\mathcal{P}, t) \stackrel{def}{=} extr\_p(extr\_t(\mathcal{P}), t)$.

Given a program $\mathcal{P}$ and a predicate stratification function *strat* that can be obtained by a stratification algorithm [45] (page 134), the operational semantics first initialises the timer to 0 and removes the clauses with unsatisfiable body constraints and then repeatedly generates a fact and transforming the current program into a new program as follows.

Step (Ia) sets the timer to the minimum time at which the body constraint of any fact contained in $CM(\mathcal{P})$ can be satisfied. The minimum time is determined by $\mathcal{P}^f$ and $\mathcal{P}^-$ according to lemmas 1 and 2 and is no less than the previous value of the timer. Step (Ib) extracts positive information from negative rules in $\mathcal{P}^-$ using time stratification as follows. Each negative literal $not(a@S)$ in a negative rule is replaced by

$$S < \tau_{a,\mathcal{P}} \vee (S \geq \tau_{a,\mathcal{P}}) \wedge not(a@S)$$

Each such rule is then normalised, resulting in a set of clauses which replace the original negative rule. Step (Ic) extracts a fact from a negative rule using predicate symbol stratification. It ensures that there is always a fact to choose in step (II). Step (II) generates a fact $\mathbf{f}$. Through invocation of $prop(C, \mathbf{f}, t)$, step (III) replaces an atom $a_l@S_l$ with $(a_l@S_l \wedge (S_l \geq t) \vee [a_l@S_l = \rho_l(\mathbf{h}') \wedge \rho_l(\delta')])$. The first disjunct allows the further solution to $a_l@S_l$ to be considered while the second propagates its solution provided by $\mathbf{f}$.

The operational semantics is indeterministic. There might be several facts that can be extracted from negative rules in the current program at step (Ic). There might also a number of facts whose success time is equal to the current value of the timer. The operational semantics indeterministically chooses one at these steps.

Example 1. This example illustrates the operational semantics using the even numbers program. The following is the normalised even numbers program completed with causality constraints.

```
% even numbers program.

even@T :-  T=0.
even@T :-  T=S+1,S>=0, not(even@S).
```

The program is temporally stratified. The configuration after initialisation is illustrated in Figure 1(a).

As there is no positive literal in the body of either clause. $\mathcal{P}^r = \mathcal{P}^-$ throughout the execution of the program. The first iteration is as follows. The approximate success time of $\mathcal{P}^- \cup \mathcal{P}^f$ is 0. So, $t = 0$ after step (Ia). In step (Ib), the goal $not(even@S)$ in the only rule in $\mathcal{P}^-$ is replaced by $(S < 0) \vee (S >= 0) \wedge not(even@S)$. Normalising the resulting clause gives rise to two clauses: (a)

```
even@T :- T=S+1,S>=0,S<0.
```

and (b)

```
even@T :- T=S+1,S>=0, not(even@S).
```

(a) is thrown away as it has an unsatisfiable constraint part while (b) is a rule and replaces the original rule. Thus, after step (Ib), $\mathcal{P}^-$ contains one rule (b) and $\mathcal{P}^f$ contains one fact: (c)

```
even@T :- T=0.
```

Step (Ic) doesn't change the configuration. Step (II) selects (c) from $\mathcal{P}^f$. Step (III) removes (c) and propagates it through (b), resulting in the following rules

```
even@T :- T=S+1,S>=0,S<>0, S<0.
even@T :- T=S+1,S>=0,S<>0, S>=0, not(even@S).
```

The first clause is discarded as its body constraint is unsatisfiable. The configuration after the first iteration is illustrated in figure 1(b).

Now consider the second iteration. $\mathcal{P}^f$ is empty while $\mathcal{P}^-$ contains one rule. 2 is the approximate success time of $\mathcal{P}^-$. So, $t = 2$ after step (Ia). Step (Ib) extracts from the rule the following two clauses: (d)

```
 even@T :- T=S+1,S>=0,S<>0,S<2.
```

and (e)

```
 even@T :- T=S+1,S>=2,not(even@S).
```

(d) and (e) replace the original rule. Step (Ic) doesn't change the configuration. Step (II) generates (d). In step (III), (d) is removed and propagated through (e), giving rise to the following clauses

```
even@T :- T=S+1,S>=2,S<>2,S<2.
even@T :- T=S+1,S>=2,S<>2,S>=2, not(even@S).
```

(a) Intial Configuration:

```
Timer:    Current Program:                     Generated Facts:
t = 0
          even@T :-  T=0.
          even@T :-  T=S+1,S>=0,
                     not(even@S).
```

(b) Configuration after 1st iteration:

```
Timer:    Current Program:                     Generated Facts:
t = 0
          even@T :-  T=S+1,S>=0,S<>0,          even@T :-  T=0.
                     not(even@S).
```

(c) Configuration after 2nd iteration:

```
Timer:    Current Program:                     Generated Facts:
t = 2
          even@T :-  T=S+1,S>=2,S<>2,          even@T :- T=0.
                     not(even@S).              even@T :- T=2.
```

Fig. 1. The first three configurations for even number program

The first clause is discarded and the second replaces (e). The configuration after the second iteration is illustrated in figure 1(c).

□

We now present the correctness and the completeness of the operational semantics. It is obvious that the timestamps of generated facts are in ascending order. In the sequel, we will denote the original program by $\mathcal{P}$, the current context after the ith iteration by $(t_i, \mathcal{P}_i)$ and the generated fact during the ith iteration by $\mathbf{f}_i$. Thus, the sequence of configurations obtained during the execution of $\mathcal{P}$ is $(t_0, \mathcal{P}_0), \cdots, (t_i, \mathcal{P}_i), \cdots$ where $(t_0, \mathcal{P}_0)$ is the initial configuration and the sequence of generated facts are $\mathbf{f}_1, \cdots, \mathbf{f}_i, \cdots$. Note that t_{i+1} and $\mathbf{f}_{i+1}$ are determined by $(t_i, \mathcal{P}_i)$.

The following lemma shows that the model semantics of the current program can only contain ground facts whose timestamps are no less than the minimum time at which the body constraint of a clause is satisfiable.

Lemma 3. *Let a@t be a ground atom. If* $a@t \in CM(\mathcal{P}_i)$ *then* $t \geq \tau_{a,\mathcal{P}_i}$.

Proof. Let $a = p(\tilde{s})$ *and the set of the clauses for p in* $\mathcal{P}_i$ *be* $\{p(\tilde{x})@T \leftarrow \delta_o, \mathbf{L}_o \mid 1 \leq o \leq m\}$. *Let* $\mu = \{\tilde{x} \mapsto \tilde{s}, T \mapsto t\}$. *Since* $p(\tilde{s})@t \in CM(\mathcal{P}_i)$, *we have* $\mathcal{D} \models \mu(\delta_o)$ *and* $CM(\mathcal{P}_i) \models \mu(\mathbf{L}_o)$ *for some* $1 \leq o \leq m$. $t \geq \tau_{a,\mathcal{P}_i}$ *since* $\mathcal{D} \models (\mu(\delta_o) \rightarrow (\mu(T) \geq \tau_{a,\mathcal{P}_i}))$. □

The following lemma shows that steps (Ib) and (Ic) preserve the meaning of the program.

Lemma 4. $CM(\mathcal{P}_i) = CM(extr(\mathcal{P}_i, t_{i+1}))$.

Proof. Let $Q = extr\_t(\mathcal{P}_i)$ and $R = extr\_p(Q, t_{i+1})$. We first prove $CM(\mathcal{P}_i) = CM(Q)$ by showing $GL([extr\_t(C, \mathcal{P}_i)]_{\mathcal{D}}, CM(\mathcal{P}_i)) = GL([C]_{\mathcal{D}}, CM(\mathcal{P}_i))$ for each $C \in \mathcal{P}_i^-$. Let $C = (h@T \leftarrow \delta, \wedge_{k\in K} not(a_k@S_k))$.

($\subseteq$) Let $\mu(h@T \leftarrow) \in GL([extr\_t(C, \mathcal{P}_i)]_{\mathcal{D}}, CM(\mathcal{P}_i))$. Then $extr\_t(C, \mathcal{P}_i)$ contains a $C' = (h@T \leftarrow \delta, \wedge_{k\in K} \mathbf{b}_k)$ such that $\mathcal{D} \models \mu(\delta)$ and $CM(\mathcal{P}_i) \models_{\mathcal{D}} \mathbf{b}_k$. $\mathbf{b}_k$ is either $S_k < \tau_{a_k, \mathcal{P}_i}$ or $(S_k \geq \tau_{a_k, \mathcal{P}_i}) \wedge not(a_k@S_k)$. It can be shown that $\mu(a_k@S_k) \notin CM(\mathcal{P}_i)$ in both cases, implying $\mu(h@T \leftarrow) \in GL([C]_{\mathcal{D}}, CM(\mathcal{P}_i))$.

($\supseteq$) Let $\mu(h@T \leftarrow) \in GL([C]_{\mathcal{D}}, CM(\mathcal{P}_i))$. Then $\mathcal{D} \models \mu(\delta)$ and $\mu(a_k@S_k) \notin CM(\mathcal{P}_i)$ for each $k \in K$. Let $C' = (h@T \leftarrow \delta, \wedge_{k\in K} not(\mathbf{b}_k))$ with $\mathbf{b}_k$ being $S_k < \tau_{a_k, \mathcal{P}_i}$ if $\mathcal{D} \models \mu(S_k < \tau_{a_k, \mathcal{P}_i})$ or being $(S_k \geq \tau_{a_k, \mathcal{P}_i}) \wedge not(a_k@S_k)$ otherwise. Then we have $\mu(h@T \leftarrow) \in GL([C']_{\mathcal{D}}, CM(\mathcal{P}_i))$ implying $\mu(h@T \leftarrow) \in GL([extr\_t(C, \mathcal{P}_i)]_{\mathcal{D}}, CM(\mathcal{P}_i))$.

It remains to prove $CM(Q) = CM(R))$. $t_{i+1} = \hat{m}_{(Q^f \cup Q^-)}$ because, for any $C = (h@T \leftarrow \delta, \wedge_{k\in K} not(a_k@S_k))$ in $\mathcal{P}_i$, there is C' in Q such that $\hat{m}_{C'} = \hat{m}_C$ where $C' = (h@T \leftarrow \delta, \wedge_{k\in K} \mathbf{b}_k)$ with $\mathbf{b}_k$ being $S_k < \tau_{a_k, \mathcal{P}_i}$ if $\mathcal{D} \models (\delta, (S_k < \tau_{a_k; \mathcal{P}_i}))$ and $\mathbf{b}_k$ being $(S_k \geq \tau_{a_k, \mathcal{P}_i}) \wedge not(a_k@S_k)$ otherwise. If $t_{i+1} = \hat{m}_{Q^f}$ then $R = Q$ and hence $CM(Q) = CM(R)$. Otherwise, Q contains a $C = (h@T \leftarrow \delta, \wedge_{k\in K} not(a_k@S_k))$ such that $\hat{m}_C = t_{i+1}$, $strat(C) \leq strat(C'')$ for any other negative rule C'' in Q with $\hat{m}_{C''} = t_{i+1}$, and $R = Q \cup \{h@T \leftarrow \delta \wedge (T = t_{i+1})\}$. By lemma 2, we have $[h@T \leftarrow \delta \wedge (T = t_{i+1})]_{\mathcal{D}} \subseteq CM(Q)$ and $(\mathcal{D} \models \mu(\delta \wedge (T = t_{i+1}))) \rightarrow \mu(a_k@S_k) \notin CM(Q)$ for any valuation μ. So, $GL([R]_{\mathcal{D}}, CM(Q)) = GL([Q]_{\mathcal{D}}, CM(Q))$ implying that $CM(Q)$ is the least Herbrand model of $GL([R]_{\mathcal{D}}, CM(Q))$. Therefore, $CM(Q) = CM(R)$. □

The following lemma states that each cycle of iteration is correct and complete with respect to the model semantics.

Lemma 5. $CM(\mathcal{P}_i) = [\mathbf{f}_{i+1}]_{\mathcal{D}} \cup CM(\mathcal{P}_{i+1})$.

Proof. Let $R = extr(\mathcal{P}_i, t_{i+1})$. By lemma 4, it suffices to prove $CM(R) = [\mathbf{f}_{i+1}]_{\mathcal{D}} \cup CM(\mathcal{P}_{i+1})$ by proving (1) $CM(R) \supseteq [\mathbf{f}_{i+1}]_{\mathcal{D}} \cup CM(\mathcal{P}_{i+1})$ and (2) $CM(R) \subseteq [\mathbf{f}_{i+1}]_{\mathcal{D}} \cup CM(\mathcal{P}_{i+1})$.

(1). $CM(R) \supseteq [\mathbf{f}_{i+1}]_{\mathcal{D}}$ since $\mathbf{f}_{i+1} \in R$. So, it suffices to show $CM(R) \supseteq CM(\mathcal{P}_{i+1})$. $[\mathcal{P}_{i+1}]_{\mathcal{D}}$ is locally stratified and hence $CM(\mathcal{P}_{i+1})$ is the least Herbrand model of $[\mathcal{P}_{i+1}]_{\mathcal{D}}$. Therefore, it reduces to prove that $CM(R)$ is a model of $[\mathcal{P}_{i+1}]_{\mathcal{D}}$. $CM(R)$ is a model of $[\mathcal{P}_i^f \setminus \{\mathbf{f}_{i+1}\}]_{\mathcal{D}}$. So, it remains to prove that $CM(R)$ is a model of $[prop(C, \mathbf{f}_{i+1}, t_{i+1})]_{\mathcal{D}}$ for each $C \in R^r$. Let C be $h@T \leftarrow \delta, \wedge_{j\in J} a_j@S_j, \wedge_{k\in K} not(a_k@S_k)$ and $\mathbf{f}_{i+1}$ be $\mathbf{h}' \leftarrow \delta'$. Then $prop(C, \mathbf{f}_{i+1}, t_{i+1})$ is $h@T \leftarrow \delta, \wedge_{j\in J} \mathbf{b}_j, \wedge_{k\in K} not(\mathbf{b}_k)$ where $\mathbf{b}_l$ is $a_l@S_l \wedge (S_l \geq t_{i+1}) \vee (a_l@S_l = \rho_l(\mathbf{h}')) \wedge \rho_l(\delta')$. Let ν be an arbitrary valuation such that $\mathcal{D} \models \nu(\delta)$, (i) $CM(R) \models_{\mathcal{D}} \nu(\mathbf{b}_j)$ for $j \in J$, and (ii) $CM(R) \not\models_{\mathcal{D}} \nu(\mathbf{b}_k)$ for $k \in K$. (i) implies $\nu(a_j@S_j) \in CM(R)$ because $[\mathbf{f}_{i+1}]_{\mathcal{D}} \subseteq CM(R)$ and (ii) implies

$\nu(a_k@S_k) \notin CM(R)$. So, $\nu(h@T) \in CM(R)$ because $CM(R)$ is a model of $[C]_{\mathcal{D}}$. This completes the proof of (1).

(2). Let $W = [\mathbf{f}_{i+1}]_{\mathcal{D}} \cup CM(\mathcal{P}_{i+1})$. It reduces to proving that W is a model of $[R]_{\mathcal{D}}$ because R is locally stratified and $CM(R)$ is the least Herbrand model of $[R]_{\mathcal{D}}$. As $R^f \subseteq \mathcal{P}^f_{i+1} \cup \{\mathbf{f}_{i+1}\}$, it suffices to prove W is a model of $[C]_{\mathcal{D}}$ for every $C \in R^r$. Let C be $h@T \leftarrow \delta, \wedge_{j\in J} a_j@S_j, \wedge_{k\in K} not(a_k@S_k)$ and $\mathbf{f}_{i+1}$ be $\mathbf{h}' \leftarrow \delta'$. Then $prop(C, \mathbf{f}_{i+1}, t_{i+1})$ is $h@T \leftarrow \delta, \wedge_{j\in J}\mathbf{b}_j, \wedge_{k\in K} not(\mathbf{b}_k)$ where $\mathbf{b}_l = a_l@S_l \wedge (S_l \geq t_{i+1}) \vee ((a_l@S_l = \rho_l(\mathbf{h}')) \wedge \rho_l(\delta'))$. Let ν be any valuation such that $\mathcal{D} \models \nu(\delta)$, (iii) $W \models \nu(a_j@S_j)$ for $j \in J$ and (iv) $W \not\models \nu(a_k@S_k)$ for $k \in K$. (iii) implies $CM(\mathcal{P}_{i+1}) \models_{\mathcal{D}} \nu(\mathbf{b}_j)$ for otherwise, $\nu(a_j@S_j) \notin CM(\mathcal{P}_{i+1})$, $\nu(a_j@S_j) \notin [\mathbf{f}_{i+1}]_{\mathcal{D}}$ and hence $\nu(a_j@S_j) \notin W$. (iv) implies $CM(\mathcal{P}_{i+1}) \not\models_{\mathcal{D}} \nu(\mathbf{b}_k)$ for otherwise, either $CM(\mathcal{P}_{i+1}) \models_{\mathcal{D}} \nu(a_k@S_k \wedge (S_k \geq t_{i+1}))$ or $\nu(a_k@S_k) \in [\mathbf{f}_{i+1}]_{\mathcal{D}}$, contradicting $\nu(a_k@S_k) \notin W$. So, $\nu(h@T) \in CM(\mathcal{P}_{i+1}) \subseteq W$ as $CM(\mathcal{P}_{i+1}) \models [prop(C, \mathbf{f}_{i+1}, t_{i+1})]_{\mathcal{D}}$ and hence $W \models [C]_{\mathcal{D}}$. This completes the proof of (2). □

The following theorem establishes the correctness of the operational semantics, that is, every generated fact is contained in the model semantics of the program.

Theorem 2. *$[\mathbf{f}_i]_{\mathcal{D}} \subseteq CM(\mathcal{P})$ for each $i > 0$.*

Proof. We have $CM(\mathcal{P}) = [\{\mathbf{f}_1, \cdots, \mathbf{f}_i\}]_{\mathcal{D}} \cup CM(\mathcal{P}_{i+1})$ by repeatedly applying lemma 5. So, $[\mathbf{f}_i]_{\mathcal{D}} \subseteq CM(\mathcal{P})$ for each $i > 0$. □

The following theorem states that the operational semantics is complete in the sense that any ground atom in the model semantics of the original program is a ground instance of a generated fact or in the model semantics of the current program and that any ground atom in the model semantics of the original program with a timestamp smaller than the current value of the timer is a ground instance of a generated fact.

Theorem 3. *Let $\mathbf{f}$ be a fact. If $[\mathbf{f}]_{\mathcal{D}} \subseteq CM(\mathcal{P})$ then*

(a) $[\mathbf{f}]_{\mathcal{D}} \subseteq [\{\mathbf{f}_1, \cdots, \mathbf{f}_i\}]_{\mathcal{D}} \cup CM(\mathcal{P}_i)$; *and*
(b) $[\mathbf{f}^{<t_i}]_{\mathcal{D}} \subseteq [\{\mathbf{f}_1, \cdots, \mathbf{f}_{i-1}\}]_{\mathcal{D}}$.

Proof. (a) is a corollary of lemma 5. (b) follows lemmata 5 and 3. □

5 Conclusion and Discussion

We have presented a bottom-up operational semantics for temporally stratified Starlog programs. Its correctness and completeness with respect to its model semantics are given. For simplicity, we have assumed that every atom is timestamped. The operational semantics can be easily modified to cope with untimestamped literals by applying only predicate symbol stratification to untimestamped literals.

The operational semantics strictly generalises the previous work on bottom-up execution of CLP programs. There has been little effort on bottom-up execution of CLP programs and bottom-up execution of CLP programs has only been proposed for constraint deductive databases [25,23]. These proposals do not deal with negation. Upon generating a fact, our operational semantics propagates it through rules in the current program resulting in a new program. This removes the need for maintaining a list of generated facts and the need for garbage collecting useless facts in the list.

Bottom-up execution has been proposed for general logic programs. Among others, Fages [13], Teusink [43], Kemp etc. [24], and Sacca and Zaniolo [40] proposed fixpoint operators for computing stable and well-founded models of general logic programs. A major problem with applying these operator to Starlog programs is that none of these operators ensure the time-orderedness of generated facts which is essential in temporal applications such as simulation. Furthermore, a fact in a stable model of a general logic program can be generated by operators in [13,43,40] only after the model has been fully constructed. This is because a fact added to a model under construction may have to be withdrawn from the model later in order to resolve an inconsistency in the model. A second major problem is that these operators do not deal with constraints. Though our model semantics is based on the stable semantics of ground general logic programs, our operational semantics deals with Starlog programs directly instead of the corresponding ground general logic program. This is necessary because the ground general logic program corresponding to a Starlog program is usually infinite. This is in contrast with deductive databases for which the operators in [40] and [24] are formulated where the ground general logic program is finite.

TLP languages such as Templog [1], Tokio [2], Temporal Prolog [14], Tempura [32], Chronology [47] use top-down operational semantics that extend SLD resolution. Brzoska shows that Templog programs can be translated into CLP programs [7], and Orgun et. al suggest that programs in other TLP languages can also be translated into CLP programs [34]. Thus, our operational semantics offers a bottom-up execution mechanism for these TLP languages.

Xiao et. al propose a bottom-up algorithm for executing Starlog programs without rigorous proof of its correctness and completeness [49]. Xiao's algorithm also generates facts in time order and uses causality to deal with negation. However, its correctness and completeness with respect to a model semantics are not addressed. Our operational semantics works on constraint programs while Xiao's doesn't.

The operational semantics of Starlog presented in this paper is abstract. We have so far not considered the issue of termination for a number of reasons. Termination is undecidable, and there is no operational semantics which will terminate on all programs. Also, we observe that techniques for improving the termination of bottom-up evaluation of logic programs can be easily incorporated into our operational semantics without affecting its correctness and completeness.

The following example illustrates the need for subsumption tests [25,23,42,29]. Consider the following program.

```
p(X)@T :- T=0, X=a.
p(X)@T :- T>=0, p(X)@T.
```

It is obvious that the meaning of this program is the singleton set consisting of the fact

```
p(X)@T :- T=0, X=a.
```

It is easy to verify that each iteration of the operational semantics will generate the above fact and leave the program unchanged. That is, the program does not terminate. Simple checking for duplicate solutions will solve this case but in general more powerful subsumption tests are necessary [29]. This raises complex issues of the tradeoff between computational efficiency and the set of programs on which the operational semantics will terminate.

References

1. M Abadi and Z. Manna. Temporal logic programming. In *Proceedings of the 1987 Symposium on Logic Programming*, pages 4–16. The IEEE Computer Society Press, 1987.
2. T. Aoyagi, M. Fujita, and T. Moto-oka. Temporal logic programming language Tokio. *Lecture Notes in Computer Science*, 221:139–147, 1986.
3. K.R. Apt, H. Blair, and A. Walker. Towards a theory of declarative knowledge. In J. Minker, editor, *Foundations of Declarative Databases and Logic Programming*, pages 89–142. Morgan Kaufmann, 1988.
4. H Barringer, M fisher, D Gabbay, G Gough, and R Owens. METATEM: An introduction. *Formal Aspects of Computing*, 7(5):533–549, 1995.
5. F. Benhamou, D. McAllester, and P. Van Hentenryck. CLP(Intervals) revisited. In M. Bruynooghe, editor, *Logic Programming - Proceedings of the 1994 International Symposium*, pages 124–138. The MIT Press, 1994.
6. F. Benhamou and W. Older. Applying Interval Arithmetic to Real, Integer and Boolean Constraints. *Journal of Logic Programming*, 32(1):1–24, 1997.
7. C. Brzoska. Temporal logic programming and its relation to constraint logic programming. In *Proceedings of the 1991 International Symposium on Logic Programming*, pages 661–677. The MIT Press, 1991.
8. J.G. Cleary. Logical arithmetic. *Future Computing Systems*, 2(2):125–149, 1987.
9. J.G. Cleary. Colliding pucks solved in a temporal logic. In *Proceedings of 1990 Distributed Simulation Conference*, January, 1990.
10. A. Colmerauer. An introduction to Prolog III. *Communications of the ACM*, 33:69–90, 1990.
11. D. Diaz and P. Codognet. A minimal extension of the WAM for clp(FD). In Warren [48], pages 774–790.
12. M. Dincbas, P. Van Hentenryck, H. Simonis, A. Aggoun, T. Graf, and F. Berthier. The constraint logic programming language CHIP. In *Proceedings Intl. Conf. on Fifth Generation Computer Systems*, pages 693–702. Ohmsha Publishers, 1988.

13. F. Fages. A new fixpoint semantics for general logic programs compared with the well-founded and the stable model semantics. *New Generation Computing*, 9(3&4):425–444, 1991.
14. D.M. Gabbay. Modal and temporal logic programming. In A. Galton, editor, *Temporal Logics and Their Application*, pages 197–237. Academic Press, 1987.
15. A. Van Gelder. Negation as failure using tight derivations for general logic programs. *Journal of Logic Programming*, 6(1):109–133, 1987.
16. A. Van Gelder, K. Ross, and J. Schlipf. The well-founded semantics for general logic programs. *Journal of the ACM*, 38(3):620–650, 1991.
17. M. Gelfond and V. Lifschitz. The stable model semantics for logic programming. In Kowalski and Bowen [26], pages 1070–1080.
18. S. Grumbach and J. Su. Queries with arithmetical constraints. *Journal of Theoretical Computer Science*, 173(1):151–181, 1997.
19. P. Van Hentenryck, Y. Deville, and C.-M. Teng. A generic arc-consistency algorithm and its specializations. *Artificial Intelligence*, 57(2-3):291–321, 1992.
20. J. Jaffar, M. J. Maher, P. J. Stuckey, and R. H. C. Yap. Beyond finite domains. *Lecture Notes in Computer Science*, 874:86–94, 1994.
21. J. Jaffar and M.J. Maher. Constraint logic programming: A survey. *Journal of Logic Programming*, 19 & 20:503–582, 1994.
22. J. Jaffar, S. Michayov, P. Stuckey, and R. Yap. The CLP($\mathcal{R}$) language and system. *ACM Transactions on Programming Languages and Systems*, 14(3):339–395, 1992.
23. P.C. Kanellakis, G.M. Kuper, and P.Z. Revesz. Constraint query languages. *Journal of Computer and System Sciences*, 51(1):26–52, 1995.
24. D.B. Kemp, D. Srivastava, and P.J. Stuckey. Bottom-up evaluation and query optimization of well-founded models. *Journal of Theoretical Computer Science*, 146(1&2):145–184, 1995.
25. A. Klug. On conjunctive queries containing inequalities. *Journal of the ACM*, 35(1):146–160, 1988.
26. R. A. Kowalski and K. A. Bowen, editors. *Proceedings of the Fifth International Conference and Symposium on Logic Programming*. The MIT Press, 1988.
27. J. C. Lagarias. The computational complexity of simultaneous Diophantine approximation problems. *SIAM Journal on Computing*, 14(1):196–209, 1985.
28. M. Liu and J.G. Cleary. Deductive databases: Where to now? In *Proceedings of 1990 Far-East Workshop on Deductive Databases*, April, 1990.
29. M. Maher. A logic programming view of CLP. In Warren [48], pages 737–753.
30. A. Mantsivoda. Flang and its implementation. *Lecture Notes in Computer Science*, 714:151–165, 1993.
31. A. Monfroglio. Integer programs for logic constraint satisfaction. *Journal of Theoretical Computer Science*, 97(1):105–130, 1992.
32. B. Moszkowski. *Executing Temporal Logic Programs*. Cambridge University Press, 1986.
33. W. Older and F. Benhamou. Programming in CLP(BNR). In *The Proceedings of the First Workshop on Principles and Practice of Constraint Programming*, pages 239–249, Newport, RI, USA, 1993.
34. M. A. Orgun and W. Ma. An overview of temporal and modal logic programming. In D. M. Gabbay and H. J. Ohlbach, editors, *Proceedings of the First International Conference on Temporal Logic*, pages 445–479. Springer-Verlag, 1994.
35. T. C. Przymusinski. On the declarative semantics of deductive databases and logic programs. In J. Minker, editor, *Foundations of Deductive Databases and Logic Programming*, pages 193–216. Morgan Kaufmann, Los Altos, CA., 1988.

36. T. C. Przymusinski. Perfect model semantics. In Kowalski and Bowen [26], pages 1081–1096.
37. T. C. Przymusinski. Every logic program has a natural stratification and an iterated fixed point model. In *Proceedings of the Eighth Symposium on Principles of Database Systems*, pages 11–21. ACM SIGACT-SIGMOD, 1989.
38. T. C. Przymusinski. On the declarative and procedural semantics of logic programs. *Journal of Automated Reasoning*, 5(2):167–205, 1989.
39. P. Z. Revesz. A closed-form evaluation for Datalog queries with integer (gap)-order constraints. *Journal of Theoretical Computer Science*, 116(1):117–149, 1993.
40. D. Sacca and C. Zaniolo. Deterministic and non-deterministic stable models. *Journal of Logic and Computation*, 7(5):555–579, 1997.
41. B. Smith, S. Brailsford, P. Hubbard, and H. P. Williams. The Progressive Party Problem: Integer Linear Programming and Constraint Programming Compared. In *Proceedings of the first International Conference on Principles and Practice of Constraint Programming*, Marseilles, September 1995.
42. D. Srivastava. Subsumption and indexing in constraint query languages with linear arithmetic constraints. *Annals of Mathematics and Artificial Intelligence*, 8:315–343, 1993.
43. F. Teusink. A characterization of stable models using a non-monotonic operator. In L.M. Pereira and A. Nerod, editors, *Proceedings of the second International workshop Logic Programming and Non-Monotonic Reasoning*, pages 206–222. The MIT Press, 1993.
44. D. Toman, J. Chomicki, and D. S. Rogers. Datalog with integer periodicity constraints. In M. Bruynooghe, editor, *Logic Programming - Proceedings of the 1994 International Symposium*, pages 189–203. The MIT Press, 1994.
45. J.D. Ullman. *Principles of Database and Knowledge-Base Systems: Volume I.* Computer Science Press, 1988.
46. P. Van Hentenryck, V. Saraswat, and Y. Deville. Design, implementation, and evaluation of the constraint language cc(FD). *Lecture Notes in Computer Science*, 910:293–307, 1995.
47. W.W. Wadge. Tense logic programming: a respectable alternative. In *Proceedings of the 1988 International Symposium on Lucid and Intensional Programming*, pages 26–32, Sidney, B.C., April 7-8 1988.
48. D.S. Warren, editor. *Proceedings of the Tenth International Conference on Logic Programming.* The MIT Press, 1993.
49. Z. Xiao, J.G. Cleary, and B. Unger. Time-ordered forward deduction: A bottom-up evaluation strategy for starlog. Technical Report 98/625/16, Department of Computer Science, University of Calgary, 1998.

On the Verification of Finite Failure

Roberta Gori and Giorgio Levi

Dipartimento di Informatica, Università di Pisa,
Corso Italia 40, 56125 Pisa, Italy
Phone: +39-050-887248
Fax: +39-050-887226
{gori,levi}@di.unipi.it

Abstract. We first define a new fixpoint semantics which correctly models finite failure and is and-compositional. We then consider the problem of verification w.r.t. finite failure and we show how Ferrand's approach, using both a least fixpoint and greatest fixpoint semantics, can be adapted to finite failure. The verification method is not effective. Therefore, we consider an approximation from above and an approximation from below of our semantics, which give two different finite approximations. These approximations are used for effective program verification.

Keywords: Abstract interpretation, Logic programming, Program verification, Finite failure.

1 Introduction

Assume we have a semantics defined as least fixpoint of a continuous operator F on the lattice of "interpretations" and an interpretation I which specifies the expected program semantics. The program is partially correct w.r.t. I iff $\mathsf{lfp}(\mathsf{F}) \subseteq \mathrm{I}$. A sufficient partial correctness condition, which can be verified without actually computing the fixpoint is $\mathsf{F}(\mathrm{I}) \subseteq \mathrm{I}$.

In the case of logic programs, this is the approach taken by declarative debugging (diagnosis) [21,22], where the semantics is the least Herbrand model. The approach has been extended to model other observable properties such as correct answers [12], computed answers and their abstractions [7]. In [23,17], this technique has been recently related to other techniques used in logic program verification by showing that all the existing methods [4,11,2] can be reconstructed as instances of a general verification technique based on the above defined sufficient condition, where the semantic evaluation function (and the notion of interpretation) can be chosen by using abstract interpretation techniques [9,10] so as to model pre- and post-conditions, call correctness and specifications by means of assertions. The overall idea is that the property one wants to verify is simply an abstract semantics on a suitable abstract domain.

There is one interesting and specific property of logic programs, finite failure, which is not an abstraction of none of the semantics used in the above mentioned techniques and/or verification frameworks. Diagnosis or verification of finite failure is somewhat related to the diagnosis of missing answers in [13], where the

G. Nadathur (Ed.): PPDP'99, LNCS 1702, pp. 311–327, 1999.

actual semantics is the greatest fixpoint of the standard ground immediate consequences operator (i.e. the complement of a set of atoms which contains the finite failure set and some atoms whose execution does not terminate).

However, if we want to verify properties of finite failures, we need to start from a fixpoint semantics modeling finite failure.

Unfortunately all the semantics defined for finite failure so far are not adequate for our purposes. The (ground) finite failure set $\mathsf{FF_P}$ (the set of ground atoms which finitely fail in P) [3] does not model non ground failure. The Non-Ground Finite Failure set $\mathsf{NGFF_P}$ (the set of finitely failed non ground atoms in P) [16] was proved in [14] to be correct w.r.t. finite failure and and-compositional (i.e. the failure of conjunctive goals can be derived from the the behavior of atomic goals only). However, $\mathsf{NGFF_P}$ has no fixpoint characterization.

Our first step was then the development of a fixpoint definition for $\mathsf{NGFF_P}$. The fixpoint semantics defined in [15] is derived from a semantics which extends with infinite computations the trace semantics in [8], by defining a Galois insertion modeling finite failure. The corresponding abstract fixpoint semantics correctly models finite failure and is and-compositional.

In this paper we take this semantics (shortly described in Section 2) as the basis for a verification method (defined in Section 3), which extends to finite failure Ferrand's approach [13], which uses two semantics (a least fixpoint and a greatest fixpoint semantics) and two specifications. In particular, we apply Ferrand's approach using a least fixpoint semantics ($\mathsf{T_P^{ff}} \uparrow \omega$) and a $\mathsf{T_P^{ff}} \downarrow \omega$ semantics. We obtain a nice interpretation for the verification w.r.t. $\mathsf{T_P^{ff}} \downarrow \omega$ semantics, i.e. $\mathsf{T_P^{ff}} \downarrow \omega$ models the unsolvable atomic goals as introduced in [5]. The verification method is not effective. We consider therefore an approximation from above (Section 4.1) and an approximation from below (Section 4.2), which give two different finite approximations of the Non-Ground Finite Failure set and of the success set, the set of atoms which have a successful derivation.

Finally, in Section 5, we make the techniques of Section 3 effective by using the approximations from above and from below of Section 4 applied to the least fixpoint semantics and to the $\mathsf{T_P^{ff}} \downarrow \omega$ semantics respectively.

2 A Fixpoint Semantics for Finite Failure

As already mentioned, the finite failure semantics operator of definition 3 is systematically derived from a trace semantics which models successful and infinite derivations by using abstract interpretation techniques. A Galois insertion modeling finite failure is defined on an abstract domain suitable to model finite failure and to make the abstract operator complete (i.e. precise). Here we just give the semantics for finite failure, together with some technical definitions, which are needed to achieve a better understanding.

The reader is assumed to be familiar with the terminology of and the basic results in the semantics of logic programs [1,18] and with the theory of abstract interpretation as presented in [9,10]. Moreover, we will denote by $\mathbf{x}$ and $\mathbf{t}$ a tuple of distinct variables and a tuple of terms respectively, while $\mathbf{B}$ and $\mathbf{G}$ will denote a (possible empty) conjunction of atoms. By $\vartheta_1 :: \ldots :: \vartheta_n :: \ldots$ we indicate a (possibly infinite) sequence of substitution such that $\forall i \geq 1$ $\mathrm{dom}(\vartheta_i) = \mathrm{dom}(\vartheta_{i+1})$ and $\vartheta_i \leq \vartheta_{i+1}$. When we consider a sequence of substitutions for a goal $\mathbf{G}$ we assume all the substitutions in the sequence to be relevant for $\mathbf{G}$.

Finite failure is a downward closed property, i.e., if $\mathbf{G}$ finitely fails then $\mathbf{G}\vartheta$ finitely fails too. Moreover it enjoys a kind of "upward closure". Namely, if the goal $\mathbf{G}$ does not finitely fail, then there exists a (possibly infinite) sequence of substitutions $\vartheta_1 :: \ldots :: \vartheta_n :: \ldots$, such that for every $\mathbf{G}'$ which finitely fails, there exists a j, such that $\mathbf{G}'$ does not unify with $\mathbf{G}\vartheta_h$, for $h > j$.

Note that the above mentioned sequence of substitutions can be viewed as the one computed by an infinite or successful derivation for the goal $\mathbf{G}$. If we cannot find such a sequence for the goal $\mathbf{G}$, then $\mathbf{G}$ finitely fails. Now, suppose we know that a given set C of goals finitely fails. We can infer that an instance $\mathbf{G}\vartheta$ of a goal $\mathbf{G}$ finitely fails if for all sequences of substitutions $\vartheta_1 :: \ldots\ldots :: \vartheta_n :: \ldots$, there exists a $\mathbf{G}' \in C$ such that $\forall\, i$, $\mathbf{G}'$, unifies with $\mathbf{G}\vartheta_i$.

The intuition behind the above remarks can be formalized by an operator on *Goals*, where *Goals* is the domain of goals of a program P.

Definition 1. *Let* $C \subseteq$ *Goals and* $\mathbf{G} \in$ *Goals.*

$$\mathrm{up}^{ff}_{\mathbf{G}}(C) = C \cup \{\mathbf{G}\vartheta \mid \textit{for all (possibly infinite) sequences of relevant substitutions for the goal } \mathbf{G}\ \vartheta_1 :: \ldots\ldots :: \vartheta_n :: \ldots,\ \textit{there exists a } \mathbf{G}' \in C \textit{ such that } \forall\, i,\ \mathbf{G}',\ \textit{unifies with } \mathbf{G}\vartheta\vartheta_i \}.$$

$\mathrm{up}^{ff}_{\mathbf{G}}$ is a closure operator, i.e., it is monotonic w.r.t. set inclusion, idempotent and extensive. Note that $\bigcup_{p(\mathbf{x})} \mathrm{up}^{ff}_{p(\mathbf{x})}$, $p(\mathbf{x})$ predicate in P, is a closure operator too.

The *extended Herbrand base* B_V for P is the set of atoms built with the predicate symbols of P (Π_P) on the domain of terms with variables T. Let $\mathbf{S}$ be the domain of downward closed subsets of B_V, which are also closed with respect to $\bigcup_{p(\mathbf{x})} \mathrm{up}^{ff}_{p(\mathbf{x})}$. $\langle \mathbf{S}, \subseteq \rangle$ is our semantic domain. $\langle \mathbf{S}, \subseteq \rangle$ is a complete lattice where the least upper bound of $X_1, X_2 \in \mathbf{S}$ is the set $\bigcup_{p(\mathbf{x})} \mathrm{up}^{ff}_{p(\mathbf{x})}(X_1 \cup X_2)$, while the glb is intersection.

The next operator, given two atoms $p(\mathbf{t})$ and $\mathbf{A}$, defines all the instances of $p(\mathbf{t})$ which do not unify with $\mathbf{A}$.

Definition 2. *Let* $p(\mathbf{t}), \mathbf{A} \in B_V$.

$$\mathrm{NUnif}_{p(\mathbf{t})}(\mathbf{A}) = \{\, p(\mathbf{t})\gamma \mid p(\mathbf{t})\gamma \textit{ is not unifiable with } \mathbf{A} \,\}$$

Let us now define the fixpoint operator.

Definition 3. *Let* $I \in \mathbf{S}$.

$$
\begin{aligned}
T_P^{ff}(I) = \{\, p(\tilde{t}) \mid\ & \textit{for every clause defining the procedure } p, \\
& p(\mathbf{t}) :- \mathbf{B} \in P \\
& p(\tilde{t}) \in up^{ff}_{p(\mathbf{x})}(Nunif_{p(\mathbf{x})}(p(\mathbf{t})) \cup \\
& \qquad \{p(\mathbf{t})\tilde{\vartheta} \mid \tilde{\vartheta} \textit{ is a relevant substitution for } p(\mathbf{t}), \\
& \qquad\qquad \mathbf{B}\tilde{\vartheta} \in up^{ff}_{\mathbf{B}}(C) \qquad \}) \\
& \textit{where } C = \{\mathbf{B}\sigma \mid \mathbf{B} = B_1, \ldots, B_n \ \ \exists\ B_i\sigma \in I\}
\end{aligned}
$$

Note that $T_P^{ff}(I)$ includes atoms such that for each clause either they do not unify with the head of the clause or, after unification, the body of the clause $\mathbf{B}\tilde{\vartheta}$ belongs to the $up^{ff}_{\mathbf{B}}$ closure of the goals $\mathbf{B}\sigma$ which finitely fail according to I (that is, if $\mathbf{B} = B_1, \ldots, B_n$ there exists $B_i\sigma \in I$).

T_P^{ff} is monotonic and continuous. Unfortunately T_P^{ff} is not finitary. In the next sections, we will define approximations of such an operator which will allow us to derive information on finite failure in an effective way.

By defining the ordinal powers $T_P^{ff} \uparrow i$ in the usual way, our semantics will be $lfp(T_P^{ff}) = lub(\{\, T_P^{ff} \uparrow i \mid i < \omega\}) = up^{ff}_{p(\mathbf{x})}(\cup_{i<\omega} T_P^{ff} \uparrow i)$.

Example 1. Assume $\Sigma_P = \{f, a\}$ and P_1 be the program

$$
\begin{aligned}
P_1 :\ & q(a) :- p(X) \\
& p(f(X)) :- p(X)
\end{aligned}
$$

$$
\begin{aligned}
T_{P_1}^{ff} \uparrow 1 = T_{P_1}^{ff}(\emptyset) = \{\ & q(f(X)), q(f(f(X))), \ldots \\
& q(f(a)), q(f(f(a))), \ldots \\
& p(a) \qquad\qquad \},
\end{aligned}
$$

$$
\begin{aligned}
T_{P_1}^{ff}(T_{P_1}^{ff} \uparrow 1) = \{\ & q(f(X)), q(f(f(X))), \ldots \\
& q(f(a)), q(f(f(a))), \ldots \\
& p(a), p(f(a)) \qquad\qquad \},
\end{aligned}
$$

$$\vdots$$

$$
\begin{aligned}
lfp(T_{P_1}^{ff}) = \{\ & q(f(X)), q(f(f(X))), \ldots \\
& q(f(a)), q(f(f(a))), \ldots \\
& p(a), p(f(a)), p(f(f(a))), \ldots \}.
\end{aligned}
$$

Consider now

$$
\begin{aligned}
P_2 :\ & q(a) :- p(X) \\
& p(f(X)) :- p(a)
\end{aligned}
$$

$$\begin{aligned}
T^{ff}_{P_2} \uparrow 1 = \{ \ & q(f(X)), q(f(f(X))), \ldots \\
& q(f(a)), q(f(f(a))), \ldots \\
& p(a) \qquad\qquad\qquad \},
\end{aligned}$$

$$\begin{aligned}
T^{ff}_{P_2} \uparrow 2 = \{ \ & q(f(X)), q(f(f(X))), \ldots \\
& q(f(a)), q(f(f(a))), \ldots \\
& p(X), p(f(X)), \ldots \\
& p(a), p(f(a)), \ldots \qquad \},
\end{aligned}$$

$$\vdots$$

$$\begin{aligned}
lfp(T^{ff}_{P_2}) = \{ \ & q(X), q(f(X)), q(f(f(X))), \ldots \\
& q(a), q(f(a)), q(f(f(a))), \ldots \\
& p(X), p(f(X)), \ldots \\
& p(a), p(f(a)), \ldots \qquad \}.
\end{aligned}$$

Finally, consider

$$\begin{aligned}
P_3 : p(f(X), f(f(X))) &: -p(X, f(X)) \\
q(f(Y), f(Y)) &: -q(Y, Y)
\end{aligned}$$

$$\begin{aligned}
lfp(T^{ff}_{P_3}) = \{ \ & p(f^n(X), f^m(X)), \ \ m \neq n+1, \\
& p(t_1, t_2), \ \ t_1 \text{ or } t_2 \text{ ground terms} \\
& q(f^n(X), f^m(X)), \ \ m \neq n, \\
& q(t_1, t_2), \ \ t_1 \text{ or } t_2 \text{ ground terms}\}.
\end{aligned}$$

As we already pointed out, this fixpoint semantics was automatically derived by abstract interpretation from the operational semantics of (possibly infinite) trace via a fair selection rule. This assures us that $lfp(T^{ff}_P)$ really models the non ground atoms that have a finite failure. Note that $lfp(T^{ff}_P)$ gives a direct fixpoint characterization for the set of non ground atoms which finitely fail in P, $NGFF_P$ [16]. Moreover the following theorem shows how this automatic derivation also allows to define simpler conditions than the one presented in [14] for and-compositionality.

Theorem 1. *Let* $\mathbf{G} \in$ *Goals.*

- $lfp(T^{ff}_P) = lfp(T^{ff}_Q)$ *iff every goal* $\mathbf{G}$ *has the same behavior w.r.t. finite failure in the program* P *and in the program* Q.
- *the goal* $\mathbf{G}$ *finitely fails in* P *iff*

$$\mathbf{G} \in up^{ff}_G(\{ \mathbf{G}\vartheta \mid \mathbf{G} = B_1, \ldots, B_n, \ \textit{and} \ \exists\, B_i\vartheta \in lfp(T^{ff}_P)\})$$

The first property (correctness) assures that $lfp(T^{ff}_P)$ correctively models finite failure. While the second property (and-compositionality) tells us how to infer the behavior of conjunctive goals from information on the finite failure of atomic goals only.

Example 2. Consider the program P_3 of example 1. The goal $(p(H,V), q(H,V))$ finitely fails in P_3, since $(p(H,V), q(H,V)) \in up^{ff}_{(p(H,V),q(H,V))}(\mathcal{C})$, where

$$\mathcal{C} = \{\ p(f^n(X), f^m(X)), q(f^n(X), f^m(X)), m \neq n+1,$$
$$p(f^n(X), f^m(X)), q(f^n(X), f^m(X)), m \neq n,$$
$$p(t_1, t_2), q(t_1, t_2)\ \ t_1 \text{ or } t_2 \text{ ground terms}\}$$

This is true, because, for all possible sequences of substitutions $\vartheta_1 :: \ldots \vartheta_n :: \ldots$ for $(p(H,V), q(H,V))$, there exists a $(p(H,V), q(H,V))\sigma \in \mathcal{C}$ which unifies with each $(p(H,V), q(H,V))\vartheta_i$.

3 Using Expected Least Fixpoint and $T^{ff}_P \downarrow \omega$ Semantics in Program Verification

Once we have a fixpoint semantics modeling finite failure, we can state the usual condition $T^{ff}_P(S) \subseteq S$, which is a sufficient condition for partial correctness since it implies $NGFF_P = lfp(T^{ff}_P) \subseteq S$, where S is the intended Non-Ground Finite Failure set. The above condition is not effective because, as already noted, T^{ff}_P is not finitary and S is an infinite set. We will tackle this problem later, by using finite computable approximations of the semantics. For the time being, we want to show that we can define stronger verification conditions, by using Ferrand's approach using two intended semantics.

The semantics considered in [13] is based on the standard ground immediate consequences operator T_P. Two different sets of expected properties are considered.

- a set of properties S to be verified by the $lfp(T_P)$ (partial correctness means $lfp(T_P) \subseteq S$).
- a set of properties S' to be verified by the $gfp(T_P)$ ($S' \subseteq gfp(T_P)$).

The standard sufficient condition for partial correctness based on S ($T_P(S) \subseteq S$) allows us to reason about the ground success set. In addition, there exists a new sufficient condition ($S' \subseteq T_P(S)$), which originally was viewed as a condition somewhat related to sufficiency or missing answers (according to declarative debugging). The same condition allows us to reason about the behavior modeled by the complement of the greatest fixpoint of T_P, which strictly includes the (ground) finite failure set.

However, S' cannot be thought as the complement of the intended ground finite failure set, since the inclusion is strict. Remember also that the ground finite failure set does not fully characterize finite failure (for non-ground conjunctive goals).

As the ground immediate consequences operator T_P, our fixpoint operator T^{ff}_P is not co-continuous. Moreover, $T^{ff}_P \downarrow \omega$ has an interesting characterization, since, by theorem 2, it models unsolvable atomic goals [5].

Then we apply Ferrand's approach to our least fixpoint semantics and to $T^{ff}_P \downarrow \omega$ thus obtaining stronger results. In fact, let S be the expected Non-Ground Finite Failure set (which fully characterizes finite failure). The condition

$T_P^{ff}(S) \subseteq S$ guarantees that the actual Non-Ground Finite Failure set ($\mathrm{lfp}(T_P^{ff})$) is indeed included in the intended one.

The following theorem shows that the complement (w.r.t. B_V) of $T_P^{ff} \downarrow \omega$ has a very interesting characterization as the set of atoms which have a successful derivation.

Theorem 2. *$p(t) \in B_V$ has a successful derivation if and only if $p(t) \notin T_P^{ff} \downarrow \omega$.*

We can then provide a specification S' of the complement of the set of atoms which are intended to succeed and derive another meaningful sufficient condition $S' \subseteq T_P^{ff}(S')$, which will guarantee that S' is indeed included in $T_P^{ff} \downarrow \omega$, i.e. that the actual set of successful atoms is included in the intended one.

As already mentioned, the above sufficient conditions can be turned into effective conditions, by taking finite approximations of the semantics (and finitary abstract versions of T_P^{ff}).

Using two semantics and two specifications will allow us to use two different (related) abstractions. In particular, in the next section, we will introduce an upward approximation and a downward approximation of NGFF_P, both somehow related to depth k abstraction. The idea of considering upward and downward approximations for verification and debugging has recently been proposed in [6]. In Section 5, we will apply this idea by using the upward approximation of the least fixpoint semantics and the downward approximation of the $T_P^{ff} \downarrow \omega$ semantics.

4 Towards Effective Approximations of $\mathrm{lfp}(T_P^{ff})$ and $T_P^{ff} \downarrow \omega$

The semantics of Section 2 is not decidable. In order to infer that an atom belongs to $T_P^{ff} \uparrow i+1$, we may need to look at infinitely many elements of $T_P^{ff} \uparrow i$.

It is therefore interesting to define an abstraction of $\mathrm{lfp}(T_P^{ff})$ and of $T_P^{ff} \downarrow \omega$ on an abstract domain which gives a "correct" approximation of the set of atoms which finitely fail in P and of the set of atoms which have a successful derivation. The natural idea is to "approximate" an infinite set of atoms by means of a finite set of atoms whose depth is not greater than k.

We consider here the definition of depth given by Marriott and Sondergaard in [19] for finite expressions, i.e. $\mathrm{Exp} = T \cup B_V$. Let N be the set of natural numbers not including 0, Seq denote the set of all finite sequences of natural numbers, and $\epsilon \in \mathrm{Seq}$ denote the empty sequence. The length of a sequence $s \in \mathrm{Seq}$ is denoted by $|s|$.

Definition 4. *Let $e \in \mathrm{Exp}$, $s \in \mathrm{Seq}$, $|s| > 0$. The subexpression of e at s, $e[s]$ is recursively defined by*

- $e[is] = e_i[s]$ *if* $e = f(e_1, \ldots, e_n)$ *otherwise* $\perp$,
- $e[\epsilon] = e$.

The positions of e, $\mathrm{Pos}(e) = \{s \in \mathrm{Seq} \mid e[s] \neq \perp\}$. If $|s| = k$, $e[s]$ is a level k subexpression of e. Then $\mathrm{depth}(e) = \max\{\,|s| \mid s \in \mathrm{Pos}(e)\}$.

The previous definition on atoms naturally extends to *Goals*. As we will show in the following, for $\mathrm{lfp}(T_P^{ff})$ and $T_P^{ff} \downarrow \omega$ there exist two useful ways of defining correct approximations. Namely, we can take approximations which represent either subsets or supersets of $\mathrm{lfp}(T_P^{ff})$ (or $T_P^{ff} \downarrow \omega$).

The two approximations are defined on the same domain (the above defined domain of atoms whose depth is not greater than k). Of course they will define two different abstractions.

For the sake of simplicity here we consider an upward and a downward approximation for $\mathrm{lfp}(T_P^{ff})$ only. But since our approximations are based on an abstract domain and an abstract fixpoint T_P^{ff} operator the same approximations can be applied also to $T_P^{ff} \downarrow \omega$.

In the next section we will first consider a new depth k abstraction, which can be used as a upward approximation, i.e. an abstraction in the usual sense.

4.1 Approximating $\mathrm{lfp}(T_P^{ff})$ from Above

In general, an upward approximation of a semantics on the depth k domain is expected to have the following properties.

1. For every goal $p(\mathbf{t})$ belonging to the concrete semantics, for every choice of k, $p(\mathbf{t})$ belongs also to the concretization of the abstract semantics.
2. For every goal $p(\mathbf{t})$, which does not belong to the concrete semantics, there exists a k such that $p(\mathbf{t})$ does not belong to the concretization of the abstract semantics.

The first property guarantees correctness. The second property tells us that we can always improve the precision by choosing a better (greater) k. This property should hold at least for the majority of goals.

In the case of the finite failure semantics, property 1 it is easy to achieve by using the standard abstraction on the depth k domain [20]. Achieving property 2 is instead a rather difficult task. Finite failure, in fact, is a universal property. In order to infer that an atom finitely fails, we need to know whether its instances (with arbitrary depth) finitely fail. Unfortunately, on the standard depth k domain, the property of finite failure becomes existential for a "cut" atom. By correctness, in fact, we can infer that a cut atom finitely fails, if we find one instance which finitely fails.

Example 3. Consider the program

$$P : p(f(X)) : -p(X).$$

All the ground instances of $p(X)$ finitely fail. For any k, by correctness, the cut atom $p(f^k(V))$ should belong to our abstraction. This is because there exists at least a ground instance $p(X)\vartheta$ of $p(X)$ of depth greater than k which finitely fails. $p(X)\vartheta$ must belong to the concretization of our abstraction. According to our abstraction, in addition to $p(f^k(X))$ and all its instances, also $p(X)$ and all its instances finitely fail.

As it is shown by the previous example, if an atom $p(\mathbf{t})$ has an SLD tree (via a fair selection rule) with just infinite derivations, which rewrite the atom $p(\mathbf{t})$ infinitely many times (called *perpetual* in [14]), we can not find a k such that $p(\mathbf{t})$ does not belong to the concretization of the abstract semantics on the depth k domain. Note, in fact, that all the ground instances of such an atom finitely fail. Then condition 2 does not hold for a very large class of goals.

We are therefore forced to define a more complex abstract interpretation on a new depth k domain, for which property 2 holds.

The abstract domain First consider the set $\tilde{V}$ of variables, disjoint from the set V of program variables. Consider also Ψ', the domain of non-idempotent substitutions ψ', such that $dom(\psi') \cup range(\psi') \subseteq V$ and $\forall \mathbf{t}, x/\mathbf{t} \in \psi'\ Var(\mathbf{t}) \cap dom(\psi') \neq \emptyset$. We define the domain of substitutions $\Psi = \Psi' \cup \epsilon$. In the following $\psi, \tilde{\psi} \in \Psi$.

Definition 5. *The abstract domain* D^{up} *consists of atoms of the form* $p(\mathbf{t})\psi$, $p \in \Pi_P$ *such that:*

1. $depth(p(\mathbf{t})\psi) \leq k + 1$.
2. $\psi \in \Psi$.
3. *if* $\psi = \epsilon$, $\forall \sigma, \sigma' \in Pos$, $p(\mathbf{t})\sigma \in \tilde{V}$ *implies* $|\sigma| = k$ *and* $(\sigma \neq \sigma' \Rightarrow p(\mathbf{t})\sigma \neq p(\mathbf{t})\sigma')$.
4. *if* $\psi \neq \epsilon$, $Var(p(\mathbf{t})\psi) \subseteq V$.

Each concrete atom is abstracted by considering the following function α_a on atoms.

Definition 6.

$$\alpha_a(p(\mathbf{t})) = \begin{cases} p(\tilde{\mathbf{t}})\tilde{\psi} & depth(p(\mathbf{t})) > k+1 \textit{ and the set} \\ & \mathcal{M} = \{\, p(\mathbf{t}')\psi \mid \psi \in \Psi,\ \exists i\ p(\mathbf{t}) = p(\mathbf{t}')\underbrace{\psi \cdot \psi \cdot \ldots}_{i}, \\ & \qquad depth(p(\mathbf{t}')\psi) \leq k+1\} \\ & \textit{is not empty}, p(\tilde{\mathbf{t}})\tilde{\psi} \in \mathcal{M} \textit{ and } \forall p(\mathbf{t}')\psi \in \mathcal{M}, \\ & depth(p(\tilde{\mathbf{t}})\tilde{\psi}) \leq depth(p(\mathbf{t}')\psi) \\ & \\ p(\mathbf{t}'') & \textit{otherwise} \end{cases}$$

where $\mathbf{t}''$ *is obtained by replacing each subterm rooted at depth greater than* k *by a new fresh variable belonging to* $\tilde{V}$.

The function α_a extends naturally to *Goals*.

Example 4. Let $k = 2$. Consider now $\alpha_a(p(f(g(a)))) = p(f(W))$, $W \in \tilde{V}$ and $\alpha_a(p(f(g(X)))) = p(f(Y))\{Y/g(Y)\} = \alpha_a(p(f(g(g(g(X))))))$. Note that $\alpha_a(p(f(f(g(X))))) = p(f(W))$, $W \in \tilde{V}$. The predicate $p(f(f(f(X))))$ will be approximated by $p(f(X))\{X/f(X)\}$. $\alpha_a(q(f(f(a)), f(a))) = q(f(W), f(a))$, $W \in \tilde{V}$ and $\alpha_a(q(f(f(f(X))), f(f(Y)))) = q(X, Y)\{X/f(X), Y/f(Y)\}$, $\alpha_a(q(f(f(X))), f(X)) = q(f(X), X)\{X/f(X)\}$.

Definition 7 (partial order). *Let* $\psi, \psi' \in \Psi$. *Consider two abstract atoms* $p(t)\psi$, $p(t')\psi'$.
$p(t)\psi \leq p(t')\psi'$ *if there exists an idempotent substitution* ϑ, $dom(\vartheta) = V$, $range(\vartheta) = V \cup \tilde{V}$, *and an* i *such that*

$$p(t)\psi\vartheta = p(t')\underbrace{\psi'\psi'\ldots}_{i} \text{ and } dom(\psi) \cap dom(\vartheta) = \emptyset$$

The abstraction function First we define the optimal version of the up_G^{ff} operator.

Definition 8.

$$\begin{aligned} up_G^{ff^{up}}(C) = C \cup \{ G\tilde{\vartheta} \mid\ & \forall\vartheta \textit{ idempotent substitution} \\ & \textit{and } \forall\psi \in \Psi \textit{ which satisfies} \\ & dom(\vartheta) \cap dom(\psi) = \emptyset,\ depth(G\tilde{\vartheta}\vartheta\psi) \leq k+1, \textit{ and} \\ & Var(G\tilde{\vartheta}\vartheta\psi) \subseteq \tilde{V} \cup dom(\psi) \\ & G\tilde{\vartheta}\vartheta\psi \in C \qquad \} \end{aligned}$$

Let $\mathbf{S}^{up}$ be the downward closed (w.r.t. to the order on abstract atoms) subset of the depth k atoms which are also closed with respect to $\bigcup_{p(x)} up_{p(x)}^{ff^{up}}$. $\langle \mathbf{S}^{up}, \subseteq \rangle$ is our semantics domain. $\langle \mathbf{S}^{up}, \subseteq \rangle$ is a complete lattice where the least upper bound of $X_1, X_2 \in \mathbf{S}^{up}$ is the set $\bigcup_{p(x)} up_{p(x)}^{ff^{up}}(X_1 \cup X_2)$, while the glb is simply the intersection.

Definition 9. *Let* $X \in \mathbf{S}$

$$\alpha^{up}(X) := \bigcup_{p(x)} up_{p(x)}^{ff^{up}}(\{ \alpha_a(q(t)) \mid q(t) \in X\})$$

Lemma 1. α^{up} *and its adjoint* γ^{up} *form a Galois connection.*

For the sake of simplicity, we assume that k is always greater than the depth of the head of the clauses in the program P. Therefore the $Nunif_{p(x)}^{up}$ operator becomes

Definition 10. *Let* $k > depth(\mathbf{A})$.

$$\begin{aligned} Nunif_{p(t)}^{up}(\mathbf{A}) = \{ p(\tilde{t})\psi \mid\ & p(\tilde{t})\psi \in D^{up},\ p(\tilde{t}) \leq p(t) \textit{ and there exists an } i \\ & \textit{such that } p(\tilde{t})\underbrace{\psi\,\psi\,\ldots}_{i} \textit{ does not unify with } \mathbf{A}\} \end{aligned}$$

and the abstract fixpoint operator is

Definition 11. *Let* $I \in \mathbf{S}^{up}$ *and* $k > depth(\mathbf{A})$, $\mathbf{A}$ *any head of a clause in* P.

$T_P^{ff^{up}}(I) = \{ p(\tilde{t})\psi \mid p(\tilde{t})\psi \in D^{up}$ *for every clause defining* p,

$$\begin{aligned}
&\mathtt{p}(\mathbf{t}) : -\mathbf{B} \in \mathtt{P},\\
&\mathtt{p}(\tilde{\mathbf{t}})\psi \in \mathtt{up}^{ff^{up}}_{\mathtt{p}(\mathbf{x})}(\mathtt{Nunif}^{up}_{\mathtt{p}(\mathbf{x})}(\mathtt{p}(\mathbf{t})) \cup\\
&\qquad \{\alpha_a(\mathtt{p}(\mathbf{t})\tilde{\vartheta}) \mid \mathtt{depth}(\mathtt{p}(\mathbf{t})\tilde{\vartheta}) \leq 2\mathtt{k},\\
&\qquad \tilde{\vartheta} \textit{ relevant substitution for } \mathtt{p}(\mathbf{t}),\\
&\qquad \alpha_a(\mathbf{B}\tilde{\vartheta}) \in \mathtt{up}^{ff^{up}}_{\mathbf{B}}(C) \quad \})\\
&\textit{where } C = \{\mathbf{B}\sigma \mid \mathbf{B} = \mathtt{B}_1, \ldots, \mathtt{B}_n \ \ \exists\ \mathtt{B}_i\sigma \in \mathtt{I}\}.
\end{aligned}$$

Note that $\mathtt{lfp}(\mathtt{T}^{ff^{up}}_{\mathtt{P}})$ is now effectively computable since $\mathtt{T}^{ff^{up}}_{\mathtt{P}}$ is finitary.

Example 5. Let $W \in \tilde{V}$, $\mathtt{k} = 2$ and consider $\mathtt{P}_1$ in example 1,

$$\mathtt{lfp}(\mathtt{T}^{ff^{up}}_{\mathtt{P}_1}) = \{\mathtt{q}(\mathtt{f}(\mathtt{X})), \mathtt{q}(\mathtt{X})\{\mathtt{X}/\mathtt{f}(\mathtt{X})\}, \mathtt{q}(\mathtt{f}(W)), \mathtt{q}(\mathtt{f}(\mathtt{a})), \mathtt{p}(\mathtt{a}), \mathtt{p}(\mathtt{f}(\mathtt{a})), \mathtt{p}(\mathtt{f}(W))\}$$

Consider $\mathtt{P}_2$ in example 1.

$$\begin{aligned}
\mathtt{lfp}(\mathtt{T}^{ff^{up}}_{\mathtt{P}_2}) = \{ &\mathtt{q}(\mathtt{f}(\mathtt{a})), \mathtt{q}(\mathtt{a}), \mathtt{q}(\mathtt{X}), \mathtt{q}(W), \mathtt{q}(\mathtt{f}(\mathtt{X})), \mathtt{q}(\mathtt{X})\{\mathtt{X}/\mathtt{f}(\mathtt{X})\},\\
&\mathtt{p}(\mathtt{a}), \mathtt{p}(\mathtt{X}), \mathtt{p}(\mathtt{f}(\mathtt{a})), \mathtt{p}(\mathtt{f}(W)), \mathtt{p}(\mathtt{f}(\mathtt{X})), \mathtt{p}(\mathtt{X})\{\mathtt{X}/\mathtt{f}(\mathtt{X})\}\}.
\end{aligned}$$

Finally, consider

$$\begin{aligned}
\mathtt{P}_4 : \ &\mathtt{q}(\mathtt{a}) : -\mathtt{p}(\mathtt{X})\\
&\mathtt{p}(\mathtt{X}) : -\mathtt{s}(\mathtt{f}(\mathtt{f}(\mathtt{a})))\\
&\mathtt{s}(\mathtt{f}(\mathtt{f}(\mathtt{a})))
\end{aligned}$$

For $\mathtt{k} = 2$,

$$\begin{aligned}
\mathtt{lfp}(\mathtt{T}^{ff^{up}}_{\mathtt{P}_4}) = \{ &\mathtt{q}(\mathtt{X}), \mathtt{q}(\mathtt{a}), \mathtt{q}(\mathtt{f}(\mathtt{X})), \mathtt{q}(\mathtt{f}(\mathtt{a})), \mathtt{q}(\mathtt{f}(W)), \mathtt{q}(\mathtt{X})\{\mathtt{X}/\mathtt{f}(\mathtt{X})\},\\
&\mathtt{p}(\mathtt{X}), \mathtt{p}(\mathtt{a}), \mathtt{p}(\mathtt{f}(\mathtt{X})), \mathtt{p}(\mathtt{f}(\mathtt{a})), \mathtt{p}(\mathtt{f}(W)), \mathtt{p}(\mathtt{X})\{\mathtt{X}/\mathtt{f}(\mathtt{X})\},\\
&\mathtt{s}(\mathtt{a}), \mathtt{s}(\mathtt{f}(\mathtt{a})), \mathtt{s}(\mathtt{f}(W)), \mathtt{s}(\mathtt{X})\{\mathtt{X}/\mathtt{f}(\mathtt{X})\} \qquad \}
\end{aligned}$$

which is not equal to $\alpha^{up}(\mathtt{lfp}(\mathtt{T}^{ff}_{\mathtt{P}_4})) = \mathtt{lfp}(\mathtt{T}^{ff^{up}}_{\mathtt{P}_4})$, for $\mathtt{k} = 3$.

4.2 Approximating $\mathtt{lfp}(\mathtt{T}^{ff}_{\mathtt{P}})$ from Below

We consider the depth $\mathtt{k}$ domain, i.e. the domain of atoms whose depth is not greater than $\mathtt{k}+1$.

We first need to define the optimal version of the $\mathtt{up}^{ff}_{\mathtt{G}}$ operator

Definition 12. *Let* $\mathtt{C}$ *be a set of goals whose depth is not greater than* $\mathtt{k}$,

$$\begin{aligned}
\mathtt{up}^{ff^{bl}}_{\mathtt{G}}(\mathtt{C}) = \mathtt{C}\ \cup\ &\\
&\{\, \mathbf{G}\vartheta \mid \mathtt{depth}(\mathbf{G}\vartheta) \leq \mathtt{k}+1 \textit{ and}\\
&\quad \forall \vartheta' \textit{ such that } \mathtt{depth}(\mathbf{G}\vartheta\vartheta') \leq \mathtt{k}+2\\
&\quad \textit{there exists a } \overline{\mathbf{G}} \in \mathtt{C} \textit{ which unifies with } \mathbf{G}\vartheta\vartheta'\} \cup\\
&\{\, \mathbf{G}\vartheta \mid \mathtt{depth}(\mathbf{G}\vartheta) > \mathtt{k}+1 \textit{ and there exists a } \overline{\mathbf{G}} \in \mathtt{C}\\
&\quad \textit{which unifies with } \mathbf{G}\vartheta\}.
\end{aligned}$$

Let S^{bl} be the downward closed subset of the depth k atoms which are also closed with respect to $\bigcup_{p(x)} up^{ff^{bl}}_{p(x)}$. $\langle S^{bl}, \subseteq \rangle$ is our semantic domain. It is a complete lattice where the least upper bound of $X_1, X_2 \in S^{bl}$ is the set $\bigcup_{p(x)} up^{ff^{bl}}_{p(x)}(X_1 \cup X_2)$, while the glb is simply intersection.

The abstraction function just selects the atoms which have a depth not greater than $k+1$.

Definition 13. *Let* $X \in S$ *and* $X^a \in S^{bl}$.
$\alpha^{bl}(X) := \{ p(t) \mid p(t) \in X \text{ and } depth(p(t)) \le k+1 \}$
$\gamma^{bl}(X^a) := \{ p(t)\vartheta \mid p(t) \in X^a \}$

Lemma 2. $< \alpha^{bl}, \gamma^{bl} >$ *is a* reversed *Galois insertion, i.e.,*
$\alpha^{bl}(\cap X_i) = \cap(\alpha^{bl}(X_i))$.

The above lemma holds since α^{bl} just selects those atoms whose depth is not greater than k.

The optimal Nunif operator is defined in the usual way.

Definition 14.

$$Nunif^{bl}_{p(t)}(A) = \{ p(t)\vartheta \mid depth(p(t)) \le k+1 \text{ and } p(t)\vartheta \textit{ does not unifies with } \mathbf{A}\}$$

and the optimal abstract fixpoint operator turns out to be

Definition 15. *Let* $I \in S^{bl}$.

$$\begin{aligned} T^{ff^{bl}}_P(I) = \{ p(\tilde{t}) \mid\ & depth(p(\tilde{t})) \le k+1 \textit{ and} \\ & \textit{for every clause defining } p,\ p(t) :- \mathbf{B} \in P, \\ & p(\tilde{t}) \in up^{ff^{bl}}_{p(x)}(Nunif^{bl}_{p(x)}(p(t)) \cup \\ & \quad \{p(t)\tilde{\vartheta} \mid depth(p(t)\tilde{\vartheta}) \le k+1, \\ & \quad\quad \tilde{\vartheta} \textit{ is a relevant substitution for } p(t), \\ & \quad\quad \mathbf{B}\tilde{\vartheta} \in up^{ff^{bl}}_{\mathbf{B}}(C) \quad \}) \\ & \textit{where } C = \{\mathbf{B}\sigma \mid \mathbf{B} = B_1, \ldots, B_n \ \exists\ B_i\sigma \in I\}. \end{aligned}$$

As in the case of upward approximation, $lfp(T^{ff^{bl}}_P)$ is effectively computable.

Example 6. Consider the program P_1 of example 1. For $k = 2$,

$lfp(T^{ff^{bl}}_{P_1}) = \{q(f(X)), q(f(a)), p(a), p(f(a))\}$, while for $k = 3$,
$lfp(T^{ff^{bl}}_{P_1}) = \{q(f(f(X))), q(f(f(a))), q(f(X)), q(f(a)), p(a), p(f(a)), p(f(f(a)))\}$.

Consider P_2 of example 1. For $k = 2$,

$$lfp(T^{ff^{bl}}_{P_2}) = \{q(f(X)), q(f(a)), q(a), q(X), p(a), p(X), p(f(X)), p(f(a))\}.$$

Finally, $\mathsf{lfp}(T_{P_3}^{ff^{bl}}) = \alpha^{bl}(\mathsf{lfp}(T_{P_3}^{ff}))$. Of course this is not always the case.As shown in the next example.

$$\begin{aligned} P_5 : \ & q(a) :- p(X) \\ & p(X) :- s(f(f(a))) \\ & s(f(f(b))) \end{aligned}$$

For $k = 2$, $\mathsf{lfp}(T_{P_5}^{ff^{bl}}) = \{q(f(X)), q(f(a)), q(f(b)), q(b), s(a)s(f(a)), s(b), s(f(b))\}$ which is not equal to $\alpha^{bl}(\mathsf{lfp}(T_{P_5}^{ff})) = \mathsf{lfp}(T_{P_5}^{ff^{bl}})$, for $k = 3$.

5 Abstract Finite Failure Verification

As already mentioned, we will use the upward abstraction α^{up} of the least fixpoint of T_P^{ff} and the downward abstraction α^{bl} of the $T_P^{ff} \downarrow \omega$ and two corresponding specifications

- $S_{\alpha^{up}}$ is the α^{up} abstraction of the intended Non-Ground Finite Failure set.
- $S'_{\alpha^{bl}}$ is the α^{bl} abstraction of the intended set of atoms which either finitely fail or (universally) do not terminate. Alternatively, $S'_{\alpha^{bl}}$ can be viewed as the complement of the set of atoms (of depth $\leq k$) which have a successful derivation.

Definition 16. *Let* P *be a program.* P *is correct w.r.t. the finitely failed atoms not deeper than* k *if*

c_1 $\alpha^{up}(\mathsf{lfp}(T_P^{ff})) \subseteq S_{\alpha^{up}}$.
c_2 $S'_{\alpha^{bl}} \subseteq \alpha^{bl}(T_P^{ff} \downarrow \omega)$.

The previous conditions assure us that not only the program is correct w.r.t. finitely failed atoms not deeper than k, but also that the set of depth k successful atoms is correct w.r.t. the complement (w.r.t. $\alpha^{bl}(B_v)$) of $S'_{\alpha^{bl}}$.

The following theorem gives us sufficient effectively computable conditions for c_1 and c_2 to hold.

Theorem 3. *Let* P *be a program. If the following conditions* sc_1 *and* sc_2 *hold*

sc_1 $T_P^{ff^{up}}(S_{\alpha^{up}}) \subseteq S_{\alpha^{up}}$.
sc_2 $S'_{\alpha^{bl}} \subseteq T_P^{ff^{bl}}(S'_{\alpha^{bl}})$.

then P *is correct w.r.t. the finitely failed atoms not deeper than* k.

Note that, as was the case for abstract diagnosis [7], correctness is defined in terms of abstractions of the concrete semantics, while the sufficient conditions are given in terms of the (approximated) abstract operators.

The following examples show that, by using both sc_1 and sc_2, we can get more precise verification conditions.

Example 7. Consider the following program for list concatenation.

$$
\begin{aligned}
P_1 : \ & \mathtt{append}([\,], X, X) :- \mathtt{list}([\,]). \\
& \mathtt{append}([X|Y], Z, T) :- \mathtt{append}(Y, Z, [X|T]). \\
& \mathtt{list}([\,]). \\
& \mathtt{list}([X|Y]) :- \mathtt{list}(Y).
\end{aligned}
$$

Consider now a specification $S_{\alpha^{up}}$ on the D^{up} domain defined, for a given k, as

$$
\begin{aligned}
\{ \ \mathtt{append}(X_1, X_2, X_3) \ & | \ X_i \in D^{up} \text{ and there exists a } j \text{ such that} \\
& \quad X_j \text{ is not a list}\} \cup \\
\{\alpha_{aux}(\mathtt{append}(X_1, X_2, X_3)) \ & | \text{ each } X_i \text{ is a list but} \\
& \quad X_3 \text{ is not unifiable with } X_1 \cdot X_2\} \cup \\
\{\alpha_{aux}(\mathtt{list}(X)) \ & | \ X \text{ is not a list}\}
\end{aligned}
$$

where $\alpha_{aux}(p(\mathbf{t}))$ replaces each subterm of $\mathbf{t}$ of depth greater than k with a new fresh variable belonging to $\tilde{V}$.
It is easy to see that $T^{ff^{up}}_{P_1}(S_{\alpha^{up}}) \subseteq S_{\alpha^{up}}$. Hence, according to theorem 3, $\alpha_{up}(\mathrm{lfp}(T^{ff}_{P_1})) \subseteq S_{\alpha^{up}}$ holds and the program is correct w.r.t. the intended depth k finite failure set.

Consider now the specification $S'_{\alpha^{bl}}$ which is the intended complement of the depth k set of atoms which have a successful derivation, which, for a given k, is

$$
\begin{aligned}
\{(\mathtt{append}(X_1, X_2, X_3)) \ & | \ \mathrm{depth}(X_i) \leq k \ \ \exists \text{ a } j \ X_j \text{ is not a list}\} \cup \\
\{(\mathtt{append}(X_1, X_2, X_3)) \ & | \ \mathrm{depth}(X_i) \leq k \ \ X_i \text{ is a list but} \\
& \quad X_3 \text{ is not unifiable with } X_1 \cdot X_2\} \cup \\
\{ \ \mathtt{list}(X) \ & | \ \mathrm{depth}(X) \leq k \ \text{ and } X \text{ is not a list}\}
\end{aligned}
$$

Note that in this case $S'_{\alpha^{bl}} \not\subseteq T^{ff^{bl}}_{P_1}(S'_{\alpha^{bl}})$, for any $k \geq 1$. $\mathtt{append}([\ ], a, a)$ belongs to $S'_{\alpha^{bl}}$ yet $\mathtt{append}([\,], a, a)$ does not belong to $T^{ff^{bl}}_{P_1}(S'_{\alpha^{bl}})$.
Something goes wrong in this case.

$\mathtt{append}([\,], a, a)$ should fail according the intended specification. However, in P_1 $\mathtt{append}([\,], a, a)$ has a successful derivation. This means that, in this case, $S'_{\alpha^{bl}} \not\subseteq \alpha^{bl}(T^{ff}_{P_1} \downarrow \omega)$.

Example 8. As in example 7, assume that P_2 is the program obtained from P_1, by replacing the first clause of P_1 by

$$\mathtt{append}([\,], X, X) :- \mathtt{list}(X).$$

Assume $S_{\alpha^{up}}$ and $S'_{\alpha^{bl}}$ as in Example 7. Now, for a given k, $T^{ff^{up}}_{P_2}(S_{\alpha^{up}}) \subseteq S_{\alpha^{up}}$. Moreover also $S'_{\alpha^{bl}} \subseteq T^{ff^{bl}}_{P_2}(S'_{\alpha^{bl}})$. This implies that P_2 is correct w.r.t. the depth k finite failure. This means that the depth k finite failure set satisfies the expected $S_{\alpha^{up}}$ and also that the depth k set of successful atoms in P_2 satisfies the complement of $S'_{\alpha^{bl}}$.

sc_1 and sc_2 are just sufficient conditions. Hence, if they do not hold we can not conclude that we have a bug in the program. However this is often the case and conditions violations can be viewed as warnings about possible errors.

For example, assume that sc_1 does not hold. We can say that there exists a $p(t)$, such that for all instances of the clauses defining $p(t)$, $p(t) :- B_1, \ldots, B_n$, the goal $\alpha_{up}(B_1, \ldots, B_n)$ finitely fails in $S_{\alpha^{up}}$, yet $p(t) \notin S_{\alpha^{up}}$. There might be a missing clause, which would allow $p(t)$ to either succeed or have an infinite derivation, as required by $p(t) \notin S_{\alpha^{up}}$.

Assume sc_2 does not hold.

This means that there exist a $p(t) \in S'_{\alpha^{bl}}$, an instance of a clause $p(t) : -B_1, \ldots, B_n$, and an i, such that $\forall h \in S'_{\alpha^{bl}}$, h does not unify with $B_i\sigma$. There might be an error in the clause, which corresponds to a missing successful derivation of $p(t)$.

Example 9. Let P_3 be the program obtained from P_1 of example 7, by removing the first clause. Assume $k > 3$. $T_{P_3}^{ff^{up}}(S_{\alpha^{up}}) \not\subseteq S_{\alpha^{up}}$. Note, in fact, that $append([\,],[a],[a]) \in T_{P_3}^{ff^{up}}(S_{\alpha^{up}})$, yet $append([\,],[a],[a]) \notin S_{\alpha^{up}}$. This means that some clause for the procedure $append$ is missing, which would cause $append([\,],[a],[a])$ to have a successful or infinite derivation.

Consider now P_2 as in example 8. $S'_{\alpha^{bl}} \not\subseteq T_{P_2}^{ff}(S'_{\alpha^{bl}})$. For example, $append([\ ],a,a)$ belongs to $S'_{\alpha^{bl}}$ yet $append([\ ],a,a)$ does not belong to $T_{P_2}^{ff}(S'_{\alpha^{bl}})$. The problem here is that there is a wrong clause, $append([\,],X,X) : -list([\,])$, which forces $append([\,],a,a)$ to have a successful derivation, while $append([\,],a,a)$ is expected to have a finite failure.

Let us finally note that the above notions are related with the notions of error and co-error as defined in [13].

6 Conclusion

In this paper we have introduced a new fixpoint semantics which models finite failure. This semantics is considered as the basis for a verification method, which extends to finite failure Ferrand's approach [13], which uses two semantics (a least fixpoint and a greatest fixpoint semantics) and two specifications. We apply Ferrand's approch using a least fixpoint semantics and a $T_P^{ff} \downarrow \omega$ sematics. By defining an approximation from above and an approximation from below, which give two different finite approximations of the Non-Ground Finite Failure set and of the success set, we make the extension of Ferrand's verification method to finite failure effective.

One may wonder whether there exist other abstract domains which can be used to derive meaningful sufficient conditions for effective verification of finite failure. One idea which we are currently pursuing is to use the abstract domain of assertions as defined in [23,17]. In this case the abstract domain is a set of assertions which are formulas in a logic language. This would allow us to express the intended behavior using a very natural and intuitive formalism. As it is shown in [23,17], the proof that a verification condition holds, boils down to proving that a formula is valid in a particular model. An interesting result is that whenever the assertion language is decidable [24] the verification conditions can be effectively checked.

References

1. K. R. Apt. Introduction to Logic Programming. In J. van Leeuwen, editor, *Handbook of Theoretical Computer Science*, volume B: Formal Models and Semantics, pages 495–574. Elsevier and The MIT Press, 1990.
2. K. R. Apt and E. Marchiori. Reasoning about Prolog programs: from modes through types to assertions. *Formal Aspects of Computing*, 6(6A):743–765, 1994.
3. K. R. Apt and M. H. van Emden. Contributions to the theory of logic programming. *Journal of the ACM*, 29(3):841–862, 1982.
4. A. Bossi and N. Cocco. Verifying correctness of logic programs. In J. Diaz and F. Orejas, editors, *Proc. TAPSOFT'89*, pages 96–110, 1989.
5. M. Bruynooghe, H. Vandecasteele, D.A. de Waal, and M. Denecker. Detecting unsolvable queries for definite logic programs. In Palamidessi, Glaser, and Meinke, editors, *Proc. 10th Int'l Conf. and Symp. Principle of Declarative Programming*, Lecture Notes in Computer Science, pages 118–133. Springer-Verlag, 1998.
6. F. Bueno, P. Deransart, W. Drabent, G. Ferrand, M. Hermenegildo, J. Maluszynsky, and G. Puebla. On the role of semantic approximations in validation and diagnosis of constraint logic programs. In Mariam Kamkar, editor, *Proceedings of the Third International Workshop on Automatic Debugging, AADEBUG'97*, 1997.
7. M. Comini, G. Levi, M. C. Meo, and G. Vitiello. Abstract diagnosis. *Journal of Logic Programming*, 39(1-3):43–93, 1999.
8. M. Comini and M. C. Meo. Compositionality properties of *SLD*-derivations. *Theoretical Computer Science*, 211(1-2):275–309, 1999.
9. P. Cousot and R. Cousot. Abstract Interpretation: A Unified Lattice Model for Static Analysis of Programs by Construction or Approximation of Fixpoints. In *Proc. Fourth ACM Symp. Principles of Programming Languages*, pages 238–252, 1977.
10. P. Cousot and R. Cousot. Systematic Design of Program Analysis Frameworks. In *Proc. Sixth ACM Symp. Principles of Programming Languages*, pages 269–282, 1979.
11. W. Drabent and J. Maluszynski. Inductive Assertion Method for Logic Programs. *Theoretical Computer Science*, 59(1):133–155, 1988.
12. G. Ferrand. Error Diagnosis in Logic Programming, an Adaptation of E. Y. Shapiro's Method. *Journal of Logic Programming*, 4:177–198, 1987.
13. G. Ferrand. The notions of symptom and error in declarative diagnosis of logic programs. In P. A. Fritzson, editor, *Automated and Algorithmic Debugging, Proc. AADEBUG '93*, volume 749 of *Lecture Notes in Computer Science*, pages 40–57. Springer-Verlag, 1993.
14. R. Gori and G. Levi. Finite failure is and-compositional. *Journal of Logic and Computation*, 7(6):753–776, 1997.
15. R. Gori and G. Levi. On finite failure. Technical report, Dipartimento di Informatica, Università di Pisa, 1997.
16. G. Levi, M. Martelli, and C. Palamidessi. Failure and success made symmetric. In S. K. Debray and M. Hermenegildo, editors, *Proc. North American Conf. on Logic Programming'90*, pages 3–22. The MIT Press, 1990.

17. G. Levi and P. Volpe. Derivation of proof methods by abstract interpretation. In Palamidessi, Glaser, and Meinke, editors, *Proc. 10th Int'l Conf. and Symp. Principle of Declarative Programming*, Lecture Notes in Computer Science, pages 102–117. Springer-Verlag, 1998.
18. J. W. Lloyd. *Foundations of Logic Programming.* Springer-Verlag, 1987. Second edition.
19. K. Marriott and H. Søndergaard. On Describing Success Patterns of Logic Programs. Technical Report 12, The University of Melbourne, 1988.
20. T. Sato and H. Tamaki. Enumeration of Success Patterns in Logic Programs. *Theoretical Computer Science*, 34:227–240, 1984.
21. E. Y. Shapiro. Algorithmic program debugging. In *Proc. Ninth Annual ACM Symp. on Principles of Programming Languages*, pages 412–531. ACM Press, 1982.
22. E. Y. Shapiro. *Algorithmic Program Debugging.* The MIT Press, 1983.
23. P. Volpe. *Derivation of proof methods for logic programs by abstract interpretation.* PhD thesis, Universita' di Napoli, 1998.
24. P. Volpe. A first-order language for expressing aliasing and type properties of logic programs. In G. Levi, editor, *Proceeding of the Joint International Symposium SAS'98*, 1998.

Localizing and Explaining Reasons for Non-terminating Logic Programs with Failure-Slices

Ulrich Neumerkel* and Fred Mesnard

Iremia, Université de la Réunion,
15, avenue René Cassin - BP 7151 -
97 715 Saint Denis Messag. Cedex 9 France
ulrich@complang.tuwien.ac.at
fred@univ-reunion.fr

Abstract. We present a slicing approach for analyzing logic programs with respect to non-termination. The notion of a failure-slice is presented which is an executable reduced fragment of the program. Each failure-slice represents a necessary termination condition for the program. If a failure-slice does not terminate it can be used as an explanation for the non-termination of the whole program. To effectively determine useful failure-slices we combine a constraint based static analysis with the dynamic execution of actual slices. The current approach has been integrated into a programming environment for beginners. Further, we show how our approach can be combined with traditional techniques of termination analysis.

1 Introduction

Understanding the termination behavior of logic programs is rather difficult due to their complex execution mechanism. Two different intertwined control flows (AND and OR) cause a complex execution trace that cannot be followed easily in order to understand the actual reason for termination or non-termination. The commonly used *procedure box model* introduced by [2] for debugging, produces a huge amount of detailed traces with no relevance to the actual termination behavior. Similarly, the notion of proof trees is not able to explain non-termination succinctly.

Current research in termination analysis of logic programs focuses on the construction of termination proofs. Either a class of given queries is verified to guarantee termination, or —more generally— this class is inferred [9]. In both cases that class of queries is a sufficient termination condition and often smaller than the class of actually terminating queries. Further this class is described in a separate formalism different from logic programs. Explanations why a particular query does not terminate are not directly evident.

* On leave of: Technische Universität Wien, Institut für Computersprachen

G. Nadathur (Ed.): PPDP'99, LNCS 1702, pp. 328–341, 1999.

We present a complementary approach, that is able to localize and explain reasons for non-termination using a newly developed slicing technique based on the notion of failure-slices. Failure-slices expose those parts of the program that may cause non-termination; under certain conditions, non-termination can be proved.

Slicing [15] is an analysis technique to extract parts of a program related to or responsible for a particular phenomenon (e.g. a wrong value of a variable). Originally, slicing was developed for imperative languages by Weiser [15,16] who observed that programmers start debugging a program by localizing the area where the error has to be. Using program analysis techniques, this process can be partially automated, simplifying the comprehension of the program. Only recently, slicing has been adopted to logic programming languages by Zhao [17], Gyimóthy [5], and Ducassé [14]. While these approaches focus on explaining (possibly erroneous) solutions of a query, we will present a slicing technique for explaining non-termination properties. It is an implementation of a previously developed informal reading technique used in Prolog-courses [11,12] which is used within a programming environment for beginners [13].

In contrast to most other programming paradigms, there are two different notions of termination of logic programs - existential [8] and universal termination. A query terminates existentially, if one (or no) solution can be found. Universal termination requires the complete SLD-tree being finite [4]. While existential termination is easy to observe, it turned out to be rather difficult to reason about. On the other hand, universal termination, while difficult to observe, is much easier to treat formally. Further, universal termination is more robust to typical program changes that happen during program development. Universal termination is sensitive only to the computation rule but insensitive to clause selection. As has been pointed out by Plümer [7] the conjunction of two universally terminating goals always terminates. Further, reordering and duplicating clauses has no influence. For this reasons, most research on termination focused on universal termination. We will consider universal termination with the leftmost computation rule, as used for Prolog programs.

Example. The following example contains an erroneous data base causing universal non-termination of the given query. Its non-termination cannot be easily observed by inspecting the sequence of produced solutions. Glancing over the first solutions suggests a correct implementation. But in fact, an infinite sequence of redundant solutions is produced. The failure-slice on the right, generated automatically by the presented method, locates the reason for non-termination by hiding all irrelevant parts. The remaining slice has to be changed in order to make the program terminating.

The failure-slice helps significantly in understanding the program's termination property. It shows for example that clause reordering in ancestor_of/2 does not help here since this would lead to the same slice. Further it becomes evident, that the first rule in ancestor_of/2 is not responsible for termination. Often beginners have this incorrect belief confusing universal and existential termination.

% original program	% failure-slice
← ancestor_of(Anc, leopold_I).	← ancestor_of(Anc, leopold_I).
child_of(karl_VI, leopold_I).	~~child_of(karl_VI, leopold_I) ← false.~~
child_of(maria_theresia, karl_VI).	~~child_of(maria_theresia, karl_VI) ← false.~~
child_of(joseph_II, maria_theresia).	~~child_of(joseph_II, maria_theresia) ← false.~~
child_of(leopold_II, maria_theresia).	~~child_of(leopold_II, maria_theresia) ← false.~~
child_of(leopold_II, franz_I).	child_of(leopold_II, franz_I).
child_of(marie_a, maria_theresia).	~~child_of(marie_a, maria_theresia) ← false.~~
child_of(franz_I, leopold_II).	child_of(franz_I, leopold_II).
ancestor_of(Anc,Desc) ←	~~ancestor_of(Anc,Desc) ← false,~~
child_of(Desc,Anc).	~~child_of(Desc,Anc).~~
ancestor_of(Anc,Desc) ←	ancestor_of(Anc,Desc) ←
child_of(Child, Anc),	child_of(Child, Anc),
ancestor_of(Child, Desc).	ancestor_of(Child, Desc), **false.**

This example shows also some requirements for effectively producing failure-slices. On the one hand we need an analysis to identify the parts of a program responsible for non-termination. On the other hand, since such an analysis can only approximate the minimal slices, we need an efficient way to generate all slices which then are tested for termination by mere execution for a certain time. With the help of this combination of analysis and execution we often obtain explanations also when classical termination analysis cannot produce satisfying results.

Contents. The central notions failure-slice and minimal explanation are presented in Section 2. Some rules are given in Section 3 that must hold for minimal explanations. Section 4 presents our implementation. Finally we discuss how our approach is adapted to handle some aspects of full Prolog. A complete example is found in the appendix. We conclude by outlining further paths of development.

2 Failure-Slices

In the framework of the leftmost computation rule, the query $\leftarrow G$ terminates universally iff the query $\leftarrow G$, false fails finitely. Transforming a program with respect to this query may result in a more explicit characterization of universal termination. However, the current program transformation frameworks like fold/unfold are not able to reduce the responsible program size in a significant manner. We will therefore focus our attention towards approximations in the form of failure-slices.

Definition 1 (Program point). *The clause* $h \leftarrow g_1, \ldots, g_n$ *has a program point* p_i *on the leftmost side of the body and after each goal. A clause with* n *goals has therefore the following* $n+1$ *program points:* $h \leftarrow p_i, g_1 p_{i+1}, \ldots, g_n p_{i+n}$. *We label all program points of a program in some global order starting with the initial query. Program points in the query are defined analogously. We denote the set of all program points in program* P *with query* Q *by* $p(P, Q)$.

Definition 2 (Failure-slice).

A program S is called a failure-slice of a program P with query Q if S contains all clauses of P and the query Q with the goal "false" inserted at some program points. We represent a failure-slice by the subset of program points where "false" has not been inserted (i.e., where "true" has been inserted).

The trivial failure-slice is $p(P, Q)$, therefore the program itself. For a program with n program points there are $|\mathcal{P}(p(P, Q))| = 2^n$ possible failure-slices.

Example 1. For predicate list_invdiff/3 the set of program points $p(P, Q)$ is the set of integers $\{0, 1, 2, 3, 4, 5\}$. On the right, the slice $\{0, 2, 4\}$ is shown.

← /*P0*/ list_invdiff(Xs, [1,2,3], []). % P5	← list_invdiff(Xs, [1,2,3], []), false.
list_invdiff([], Xs, Xs). % P1	list_invdiff([], Xs, Xs) ← false.
list_invdiff([E|Es], Xs0, Xs) ← % P2	list_invdiff([E|Es], Xs0, Xs) ←
list_invdiff(Es, Xs0, Xs1), % P3	list_invdiff(Es, Xs0, Xs1), false,
Xs1 = [E|Xs]. % P4	Xs1 = [E|Xs].

Definition 3 (Partial order). *A failure-slice S is smaller than T if $S \subset T$.*

Theorem 1. *Let P be a definite program with query Q and let S and T be failure-slices of P, Q with $S \subseteq T$. If Q does not left-terminate in S then Q does not left-terminate in T.*

Proof. Consider the SLD-tree for the query Q in S. Since Q does not terminate, the SLD-tree is infinite. The SLD-tree for T contains all branches of S and therefore will also be infinite. □

Definition 4 (Sufficient explanation). *A sufficient explanation E is a subset of $\mathcal{P}(p(P, Q))$ such that for every non-terminating slice $S \notin E$, there is a non-terminating slice $T \in E$ such that $T \subset S$. The trivial sufficient explanation is $\mathcal{P}(p(P, Q))$.*

Example 2. A sufficient explanation of list_invdiff/3 is $\{\{0,1\}, \{5\}, \{0,2\}, \{0,2,4\}\}$. The slices $\{0,1\}$ and $\{5\}$ are terminating and therefore cannot help to explain non-termination. Slice $\{0,2,4\}$ is a superset of $\{0,2\}$. Some other non-terminating slices are $\{0, 2, 3\}, \ldots, \{0, 1, 2\}, \ldots, \{0, 1, 2, 3, 4, 5\}$. We note that there always exists a unique smallest sufficient explanation gathering all the minimal failure-slices.

Definition 5 (Minimal explanation). *The minimal explanation is the sufficient explanation with minimal cardinality.*

The minimal explanation contains only non-terminating slices that form an anti-chain (i.e., that are not included in each other). In our example, $\{\{0,2\}\}$ is the minimal explanation since all other non-terminating slices are supersets of $\{0,2\}$.

The minimal explanation is an adequate explanation of non-termination, since it contains all minimal slices that imply the non-termination of the whole program with the given query. It helps to correct the program, because in all minimal slices some parts highlighted by the minimal explanation must be changed in order to avoid non-termination. As long as the highlighted part remains completely unchanged, the very same non-terminating failure-slice can be produced. Further, in our experience, minimal explanations are very small compared to the set of possible explanations. For example, the minimal explanation of the program in the appendix contains one out of 128 possible slices.

Proposition 1. *Q left-terminates w.r.t. P iff the minimal explanation of P, Q is empty.*

The undecidability of termination therefore immediately implies that minimal explanations cannot be determined in general. For this reason we approach the problem from two different directions. First, we focus on determining small slices. Second, we try to obtain *a proof of (universal) non-termination* for each slice in the explanation. If all slices are non-terminating, the minimal set has been calculated.

Currently, we use a simple loop checker for proving universal non-termination that aborts signaling non-termination if a subsuming variant A of an atom A' that occurred in an earlier goal is considered. While this loop check may incorrectly prune some solutions ([1], e.g., ex. 2.1.6), it is sufficient to prove universal non-termination.

The first major obstacle when searching for a non-terminating failure slice is the large search space that has to be considered whereas the size of the minimal explanation is typically very small. For a program with n points there are 2^n different slices, most of them being not interesting, either because they are terminating or because there is a smaller slice that describes the same properties.

3 Failure Propagation

In order to narrow down the set of potential slices, we formulate some criteria that must hold for slices in the minimal explanation. With the help of these rules, many slices are removed that can never be part of the minimal explanation. These rules are directly implemented, by imposing the corresponding constraints on the program points that are represented with boolean variables.

Throughout the following rules we use the following names for program points. An *entry/exit point* of a predicate is a program point immediately before/after a goal for that predicate in some clause body or the initial query. A *beginning/ending point* is the first/last program point in a clause.

Right-propagating rules

Program points that will never be used do not occur in a slice of the minimal explanation. The following rules determine some of them. These rules encode the leftmost computation rule.

R1: Unused points. *In a clause, a failing program point p_i implies the next point p_{i+1} to fail.*

R2: Unused predicates. *If all entry points of a predicate fail, all corresponding beginning program points fail.*

R3: Unused points after failing definition. *If in all clauses of a predicate the ending program points fail, then all corresponding exit points fail.*

R4: Unused points of recursive clauses. *If in all clauses that do not contain a direct recursion the ending points fail, then all ending points fail.* A predicate can only be true, if its definition contains at least one non recursive clause.

Left-propagating rules

Program points that are only part of a finite failure branch cannot be part of a slice in the minimal explanation.

L1: Failing definitions. *If all beginning program points of a predicate fail then all entry points fail.*

L2: Propagation over terminating goals. *A failing program point p_{i+1} implies p_i to fail if g_{i+1} terminates.* Note that safe approximations of the termination of a goal are described below.

L3: Left-propagation of failing exit points. *If all exit points of a predicate except those after an tail-recursion fail, then all ending points fail.*

Local recursions

Some infinite loops can be immediately detected by a clausewise inspection. Currently we consider only direct left recursions.

M1: Local left recursion. *In a clause of the form $h \leftarrow g_1, ..., g_n, g, ...$ a failure is inserted after goal g, if for all substitution θ, $g\theta$ is unifiable with h, and the sequence of goals $g_1, ..., g_n$ can never fail.* Also in this case it is ensured that the program never terminates.

Example 3. In the following clause, rule M1 sets the program point after the recursive goal unconditionally to false. Thereby also the end point is set to false due to rule R1.

ancestor_of(Anc,Desc) ←	ancestor_of(Anc,Desc) ←
ancestor_of(Child, Desc),	ancestor_of(Child, Desc), **false**,
child_of(Child, Anc).	~~child_of(Child, Anc), false.~~

A detailed example that shows the usage of the other rules is given in the appendix.

Proposition 2 (Soundness of propagating rules). *If a slice is eliminated with the above rules, this slice does not occur in the minimal explanation.*

Proof. For the right propagating rules R1-R4 it is evident that the mentioned program points will never be used with the leftmost computation rule. Therefore the program points may be either true or false, the minimal explanation therefore will contain false.

The left propagating rules prune some finite failure branches. The minimal explanation will not contain these branches. The main idea is therefore to ensure that all infinite parts are preserved.

L1: When all beginning program points fail, a finite failure branch is encountered. By setting all entry points to false, only this finite branch is eliminated.

L2: A terminating goal with a subsequent false generates a finite failure branch, which thus can be eliminated completely.

L3: Consider first the simpler case, when all exit points of a predicate fail. In this case, all ending points may be true or false, without removing a branch. A minimal slice therefore will contain just false at these places.

The ending point in a tail-recursive clause has no impact on the failure branch generated by the predicate, as long as all exit points are false.

M1: This rule describes a never terminating local left recursion. The minimal explanation may thus contain this loop. The subsequent points after the loop are therefore not needed in a minimal slice. □

While the presented rules can be used to generate a sufficient explanation, they are still too general to characterize a minimal explanation. In particular, since all rules except M1 do not take information about the arguments into account.

Safe Approximation of Termination

Rule L2 needs a safe approximation for the termination property. If the call graph of a (sliced) predicate does not contain cycles, the predicate will always terminate. For many simple programs (like perm/2 described in the annex), the minimal explanation can already be determined with this simple approximation that does not take the information about data flow into account.

For many recursive predicates, however, this very coarse approximation leads to imprecise results, yielding a large sufficient explanation. We sketch the approach we are currently evaluating to combine our constraint based termination analysis [9] with rule L2. We recall that the mentioned termination prover infers for each predicate p a boolean term C_t called its *termination condition*. If the boolean version of a goal $\leftarrow p(\tilde{t})$ entails C_t then universal left-termination of the original goal $\leftarrow p(\tilde{t})$ is ensured.

In order to apply rule L2 w.r.t. P, Q, we first tabulate [10] the boolean version of P, Q. Then, if all boolean call patterns for p entail C_t, rule L2 can be safely applied to such goals.

4 Implementation

Our implementation uses finite domain constraints to encode the relations between the program points. Every program point is represented by a boolean 0/1-variable where 0 means that the program point fails. In addition every predicate has a variable whose value indicates whether that predicate is always terminating or not. We refer to the appendix for a complete example.

4.1 Encoding the Always-Terminating Property

While it is possible to express cycles in finite domains directly, they are not efficiently reified in the current CLP(FD) implementation of SICStus-Prolog [3]. For this reason we use a separate pass for detecting goals that are part of a cycle. These goals are (as an approximation) not always-terminating.

A predicate is now always-terminating if it contains only goals that are always-terminating. The encoding in finite domain constraints is straightforward. Each predicate gets a variable AlwTerm. In the following example we assume that the predicates r/0 and s/0 do not form a cycle with q/0. So only q/0 forms a cycle with itself.

q ← (P0) r, (P1) s, (P2) q (P3).

AlwTermQ ⇔ (¬P0 ∨ AlwTermR) ∧ (¬P1 ∨ AlwTermS) ∧ (¬P2 ∨ 0)

If a separate termination analysis is able to determine that q/0 terminates for all uses in P, Q, the value of AlwTermQ can already set accordingly.

4.2 Failure Propagation

The rules for minimal explanations can be encoded in a straightforward manner. For example rule R1 is encoded for predicate q/1 as follows:
¬P0 ⇒ ¬P1, ¬P1 ⇒ ¬P2, ¬P2 ⇒ ¬P3.

4.3 Labeling and Weighting

Since we are interested in obtaining minimal explanations, we use the number of program points as a weight to ensure that the smallest slices are considered first. The most straightforward approach simply tries to maximize the number of failing program points. To further order slices with the same number of program points, we prefer those slices that contain a minimal number of predicates. Therefore we use three weights in the following order.

1. minimal number of program points that succeed
2. minimal number of predicates
3. minimal number of clauses

These weights lead naturally to an implementation in finite domain constraints. By labeling these weights in the above order, we obtain minimal solutions first. Further only those solutions that are no extension to already found minimal slices are considered.

4.4 Execution of Failure-Slices

With the analysis so far we are already able to reduce the number of potentially non-terminating failure-slices. However, our analysis just as any termination analysis is only an approximation to the actual program behavior. Since failure-slices are executable we execute the remaining slices to detect potentially non-terminating slices. With the help of the built-in time_out/3 in SICStus Prolog a goal can be executed for a limited amount of time. In most situations the failure-slices will detect termination very quickly because the search space of the failure is significantly smaller than the original program.

Instead of compiling every failure-slice for execution we use a single enhanced program —a generic failure-slice— which is able to emulate all failure-slices in an efficient manner.

Generic failure-slice. All clauses of the program are mapped to clauses with a further auxiliary argument that holds a failure-vector, a structure with sufficient arity to hold all program points. At every program point n a goal arg(n,FVect,1) is inserted. This goal will succeed only if the corresponding argument of the failure-vector is equal to 1.

```
p(...) ←     slicep(...,FVect) ←
                arg(n1,FVect,1),
q(...),      sliceq(...,FVect),
                arg(n2,FVect,1),
...,            ...,
                arg(ni,FVect,1),
r(...).      slicer(...,FVect),
                arg(ni+1,FVect,1).
```

4.5 Proof of Non-termination

Slices that are part of a minimal explanation must all be non terminating. To this end, we execute the slice with a simple loop checker under a timeout. Since our loop checker is significantly slower than direct execution, we use it as the last phase in our system.

5 Full Prolog

In this section we will extend the notion of failure-slices to full Prolog. To some extent this will reduce the usefulness of failure-slices for programs using impure features heavily.

5.1 Finite Domain Constraints

Failure-slices are often very effective for CLP(FD) programs. Accidental loops often occur in parts that set up the constraints. For the programmer it is difficult to see whether the program loops or simply spends its time in labeling. Since labeling is usually guaranteed to terminate, removing the labeling from the program will uncover the actual error. No special treatment is currently performed for finite domain constraints. However, we remark that certain non-recursive queries effectively do not terminate in SICStus Prolog (or require a very large amount of time) like ← S # >0, S # > T, T # > S. Examples like this cannot be detected with our current approach. If such goals appear in an non-recursive part of the program, they will not show up in a failure-slice.

5.2 DCGs

Definite clause grammars can be sliced in the same way as regular Prolog predicates. Instead of the goal false, the escape {false} is inserted.

← phrase(rnaloop, Bases).
rnaloop ⟶
{Bs = [_,_,_|_]},
complseq(Bs), {false},
~~list([_,_,_|_])~~,
~~list(Bs)~~.

~~list([]) ⟶ {false}~~,
~~[]~~.
~~list([E|Es]) ⟶ {false}~~,
~~[E]~~,
~~list(Es)~~.

~~complseq([]) ⟶ {false}~~,
~~[]~~.
complseq([B|Bs]) ⟶
complseq(Bs), {false},
~~[C]~~,
~~{base_compl(C,B)}~~.

~~base_compl(0'A,0'T) ← false~~.
~~base_compl(0'T,0'A) ← false~~.
~~base_compl(0'C,0'G) ← false~~.
~~base_compl(0'G,0'C) ← false~~.

5.3 Moded Built-Ins

Built-ins that can only be used in a certain mode like is/2 pose no problems, since failure-slices do not alter actual modes.

5.4 Cut

The cut operator is a heritage of the early years of logic programming. Its semantics prevents an effective analysis because for general usages cuts require to reason about existential termination. Existential termination may be expressed in terms of universal termination with the help of the cut operator. A goal G terminates existentially if the conjunction G, ! terminates universally. For this reason, goals in the scope of cuts and all the predicates the goal depends on must not be sliced at all. A simple cut at the level of the query therefore prevents slicing completely.

C1: Goals in front of cuts and all its depending predicates must not contain failure points. There must be no loop check in this part.

C2: In the last clause of a predicate, failure points can be inserted anywhere. By successively applying this rule, the slice of the program may be still reduced.
C3: In all other clauses failures may only be inserted after all cuts.

Notice that these restrictions primarily hinder analysis when using deep cuts. Using recommended shallow cuts [6] does not have such a negative impact. In the deriv-benchmark for example, there are only shallow cuts right after the head. Therefore, only program points after the cuts can be made to fail besides from clauses at the end.

d(U+V,X,DU+DV) ←
!,
d(U,X,DU), false,
~~d(V,X,DV)~~.
~~d(U-V,X,DU-DV) ← false~~,
~~!~~,
~~d(U,X,DU)~~,
~~d(V,X,DV)~~.

5.5 Negation

Similar to cuts Prolog's unsound negation built-in \+/1 "not" is handled. The goal occurring in the "not" and all the predicates it depends on must not contain any injected failures. Similarly "if-then-else" and if/3 are treated. The second order predicates setof/3 and findall/3 permit a more elaborate treatment. The program point directly after such goals is the same as the one within findall/3 and setof/3. Therefore, failure may be propagated from right to left.

5.6 Side effects

Side effects must not be present in a failure-slice. However, this does not exclude the analysis of predicates with side effects completely. When built-ins only produce side effects that cannot affect Prolog's control (e.g. a simple write onto a log file provided that Prolog does not read that file, or reading something once from a constant file) still some failure-slice may be produced. Before such side effecting goals a failure is injected, therefore ensuring that the side effect is not part of the failure-slice. We note that the classification into harmless and harmful side effects relies on the operating system environment and is therefore beyond the scope of a programming language.

6 Summary

To summarize our approach, slicing proceeds in the following manner:

1. The call graph is analyzed to detect goals that are part of a cycle.

2. A predicate fvectPQ_weights(FVect,Weights) is generated and compiled. It describes the relation between the program points in P with respect to the query Q with the help of finite domain constraints. All program points are represented as variables in the failure-vector FVect. FVect therefore represents the failure-slice. Weights is a list of values that are functions of the program points. Currently three weights are used: The number of predicates, the number of clauses and the number of succeeding program points.
3. The generic failure-slice is generated and compiled.
4. Now the following query is executed to find failure-slices.
   ← fvectPQ_weights(FVect, Weights),
   FVect =.. [_|Fs],
   labeling([], Weights),
   labeling([], Fs),
   time_out(slicePQ(...,FVect), t, time_out),
   loopingslicePQ(...,FVect,Result).

   Procedurally the following happens:
   (a) fvectPQ_weights/2 imposes the constraints within FVect and Weights.
   (b) An assignment for the weights is searched, starting from minimal values.
   (c) An assignment for the program points in the failure vector is searched. A potential failure-slice is thus generated.
   (d) The failure-slice is actually run for a limited amount of time to discard some terminating slices.
   (e) The loop checker is uses to determine if non-termination can be proven.

The analysis thus executes on the fly while searching for failure-slices.

7 Conclusion and Future Work

We presented a slicing approach for termination that combines both static and dynamic techniques. For the static analysis we used finite domain constraints which turned out to be an effective tool for our task. Usual static analysis considers a single given program. By using constraints we were able to consider a large set of programs *at the same time*, thereby reducing the inherent search space considerably. Since failure-slices are executable their execution helps to discard terminating slices.

Tighter integration of termination proofs. Our approach might be further refined by termination proofs. In principle, any system for proving termination could be integrated in our system to test whether a particular slice terminates. In this manner some more terminating slices can be eliminated from a sufficient explanation. There are however several obstacles to such an approach. First, most termination proofs are rather costly, in particular, when a large set of slices is detected as terminating. We consider using a constraint based approach as presented in [9] that will be parameterized by the program points. We expect a significantly more efficient implementation than those that tests for termination at the latest possible moment. On the other hand, the precision of the analysis should not suffer from this generalization.

Stronger rules constraining sufficient explanations. In another direction we are investigating to formulate strong rules to constrain the search space of sufficient explanations. In particular in programs as ancestor_of/2, there is still an exponential number of slices that must be tested dynamically. We envisage the usage of dependencies between alternate clauses to overcome this problem.

Argument slicing. The existing slicing approaches [17,5,14] all perform argument slicing. We have currently no implementation of argument slicing. While it improves program understanding, argument slicing does not seem to be helpful for further reducing the number of clauses or program points. It appears preferable to perform argument slicing after a failure-slice has been found.

Acknowledgments. The initial work on failure-slices was done within INTAS project INTAS-93-1702.

References

1. R. N. Bol. Loop Checking in Logic Programming. Thesis, Univ. Amsterdam, 1991.
2. L. Byrd. Understanding the control flow of Prolog programs. Logic Programming Workshop, Debrecen, Hungary, 1980.
3. M. Carlsson, G. Ottosson and B. Carlson. An Open-Ended Finite Domain Constraint Solver. PLILP'97 (H. Glaser, P. Hartel and H. Kuchen Eds.), 191–206, LNCS 1292, Springer-Verlag, 1997.
4. P. Deransart and J. Maluszynski. A Grammatical View of Logic Programming. MIT-Press, 1993.
5. T. Gyimóthy and J. Paakki. Static slicing of logic programs. AADEBUG 95 (M. Ducassé Ed.), 87–103, IRISA-CNRS, 1995.
6. R. A. O'Keefe. The Craft of Prolog. MIT-Press, 1990.
7. L. Plümer. Termination Proofs for Logic Programs, LNAI 446, Springer, 1990.
8. T. Vasak, J. Potter. Characterization of Termination Logic Programs, IEEE SLP, 140–147, 1986.
9. F. Mesnard. Inferring Left-terminating Classes of Queries for Constraint Logic Programs. JICSLP'96 (M. Maher Ed.), 7–21, MIT-Press, 1996.
10. F. Mesnard and S. Hoarau. A tabulation algorithm for CLP. *Proc. of the 1st International Workshop on Tabling in Logic Programming, Leuven*, 1997. Revised report `www.univ-reunion.fr/~gcc`.
11. U. Neumerkel. Mathematische Logik und logikorientierte Programmierung, Skriptum zur Laborübung, 1993-1997.
12. U. Neumerkel. Teaching Prolog and CLP. Tutorial. PAP'95 Paris, 1995 and ICLP'97 Leuven, 1997.
13. U. Neumerkel. GUPU: A Prolog course environment and its programming methodology. Proc. of the Poster Session at JICSLP'96 (N. Fuchs and U. Geske Eds.), GMD-Studien Nr. 296, Bonn, 1996.
14. St. Schoenig, M. Ducassé. A Backward Slicing Algorithm for Prolog. SAS 1996 (R. Cousot and D. Schmidt Eds.), 317–331, LNCS 1145, Springer-Verlag, 1996.
15. M. Weiser. Programmers Use Slices When Debugging. CACM 25(7), 446–452, 1982.
16. M. Weiser. Program Slicing. IEEE TSE 10(4), 352–357, 1984.
17. J. Zhao, J. Cheng, and K. Ushijima. Literal Dependence Net and Its Use in Concurrent Logic Programming Environment: Proc. Workshop on Parallel Logic Programming FGCS'94, pp.127–141, Tokyo, 1994.

A Failure-Slices for perm/2

% Original program
perm([], []). % P1
perm(Xs, [X|Ys]) ← % P2
del(X, Xs, Zs), % P3
perm(Zs, Ys). % P4

del(X, [X|Xs], Xs). % P5
del(X, [Y|Ys], [Y|Xs]) ← % P6
del(X, Ys, Xs). % P7

← perm(Xs, [1,2]). % P0, P8

% First failure-slice {2,6}
~~perm([], []) ← false~~.
perm(Xs, [X|Ys]) ←
del(X, Xs, Zs), false,
~~perm(Zs, Ys), false~~.

~~del(X, [X|Xs], Xs) ← false~~.
del(X, [Y|Ys], [Y|Xs]) ←
del(X, Ys, Xs), false.

← perm(Xs, [1,2]), false.
% does not terminate

% 2nd failure-slice {2,3,5}
~~perm([], []) ← false~~.
perm(Xs, [X|Ys]) ←
del(X, Xs, Zs),
perm(Zs, Ys), false.

del(X, [X|Xs], Xs).
~~del(X, [Y|Ys], [Y|Xs]) ← false~~,
~~del(X, Ys, Xs), false~~.

← perm(Xs, [1,2]), false.
% terminates

% Determination of failure-slices to be tested for termination/non-termination
← fvectPQ_weights(FVect,Wghts), FVect=..[_|Ps], labeling([],Wghts), labeling([],Ps).
% FVect = s(0,1,0,0,0,1,0,0), Wghts = [3,2,2]. % {2,6} does not terminate
% FVect = s(0,1,1,0,1,0,0,0), Wghts = [4,2,2]. % {2,3,5} terminates; deleted
% FVect = s(0,1,1,0,1,1,0,0), Wghts = [5,2,3]. % {2,3,5,6} ⊃ {2,6}; not considered
% FVect = s(0,1,1,0,1,1,1,0), Wghts = [6,2,3]. % {2,3,5,6,7} ⊃ {2,6}; not considered
% ⇒ The minimal explanation $E = \{\{2,6\}\}$

% Definition of the failure-vector
fvectPQ_weights(s(P1, P2, P3, P4, P5, P6, P7), [NPoints, NPreds, NClauses]) ←
domain_zs(0..1, [P1, P2, P3, P4, P5, P6, P7]),
P0 = 1, P8 = 0, % Given Query

% R1: unused points in clause
¬P2 ⇒ ¬P3, ¬P3 ⇒ ¬P4, ¬P6 ⇒ ¬P7,
% R2: unused predicates
/*perm/2:*/ ¬P0 ∧ ¬P3 ⇒ ¬P1 ∧ ¬P2, /*del/3:*/ ¬P2 ∧ ¬P6 ⇒ ¬P5 ∧ ¬P6,
% R3: failing definition
/*perm/2:*/ ¬P1 ∧ ¬P4 ⇒ ¬P8 ∧ ¬P4, /*del/3:*/ ¬P5 ∧ ¬P7 ⇒ ¬P3 ∧ ¬P7,
% R4: right propagation into recursive clause
/*perm/2:*/ ¬P1 ⇒ ¬P4, /*del/3:*/ ¬P5 ⇒ ¬P7,

% L1: failing definition
/*perm/2:*/ ¬P1 ∧ ¬P2 ⇒ ¬P3 ∧ ¬P0, /*del/3:*/ ¬P5 ∧ ¬P6 ⇒ ¬P2 ∧ ¬P7,
% L2: over (always) terminating goals
¬P4 ∧ AlwTermPerm ⇒ ¬P3, ¬P8 ∧ AlwTermPerm ⇒ ¬P0,
¬P3 ∧ AlwTermDel ⇒ ¬P2, ¬P7 ∧ AlwTermDel ⇒ ¬P6,
% L3: failing exit points
¬P8 ⇒ ¬P1 ∧ ¬P4, ¬P3 ⇒ ¬P5 ∧ ¬P7,

% Always terminating
AlwTermPerm ⇔ (¬P2∨AlwTermDel) ∧ (¬P3∨0), AlwTermDel ⇔ (¬P6∨0),

% Weights:
NPreds #= min(1,P1+P2) + min(1,P5+P6),
NClauses #= P1+P2+P5+P6,
NPoints #= P0+P1+P2+P3+P4+P5+P6+P7+P8.

Modular Termination Proofs for Prolog with Tabling

Sofie Verbaeten[1], Konstantinos Sagonas[2*], and Danny De Schreye[1]

[1] Department of Computer Science, K.U.Leuven, Belgium
{sofie,dannyd}@cs.kuleuven.ac.be
[2] Computing Science Department, Uppsala Universitet, Sweden
kostis@csd.uu.se

Abstract. Tabling avoids many of the shortcomings of SLD(NF) execution and provides a more flexible and efficient execution mechanism for logic programs. In particular, tabled execution of logic programs terminates more often than execution based on SLD-resolution. One of the few works studying termination under a tabled execution mechanism is that of Decorte *et al.* They introduce and characterise two notions of universal termination of logic programs w.r.t. sets of queries executed under SLG-resolution, using the left-to-right selection rule; namely the notion of quasi-termination and the (stronger) notion of LG-termination. This paper extends the results of Decorte *et al* in two ways: (1) we consider a mix of tabled and Prolog execution, and (2) besides a characterisation of the two notions of universal termination under such a mixed execution, we also give modular termination conditions. From both practical and efficiency considerations, it is important to allow tabled and non-tabled predicates to be freely intermixed. This motivates the first extension. Concerning the second extension, it was already noted in the literature in the context of termination under SLD-resolution (by e.g. Apt and Pedreschi), that it is important for programming in the large to have modular termination proofs, i.e. proofs that are capable of combining termination proofs of separate programs to obtain termination proofs of combined programs.

1 Introduction

The extension of SLD-resolution with a tabling mechanism [4,15,18], avoids many of the shortcomings of SLD(NF) execution and provides a more flexible and often considerably more efficient execution mechanism for logic programs. In particular, tabled execution terminates more often than execution based on SLD. So, if a program and query can be proven terminating under SLD-resolution (by one of the existing techniques surveyed in [5]), then they will also trivially terminate under SLG-resolution, the resolution principle of tabulation [4]. However, since there are programs and queries which terminate under SLG-resolution and not

* This research was conducted during the author's stay at the K.U.Leuven, Belgium.

G. Nadathur (Ed.): PPDP'99, LNCS 1702, pp. 342–359, 1999.

under SLD-resolution, more effective proof techniques can be found. This paper is one of the few works studying termination of tabled logic programs.

We base our approach on the work of Decorte *et al* [8]. There, two notions of universal termination of a tabled logic program w.r.t. a set of queries executed under SLG-resolution using the left-to-right selection rule (called LG-resolution in the sequel) are introduced and characterised. Namely, the notion of quasi-termination and the (stronger) notion of LG-termination. We extend the results of [8] in two ways: (1) we consider a mix of LG-resolution and LD-resolution, i.e. a mix of tabled and Prolog execution, and (2) besides a characterisation of the two notions of universal termination under such a mixed execution schema, we also give modular termination conditions, i.e. conditions on two programs P and R, where P extends R, ensuring termination of the union $P \cup R$. The motivation for extension (1) will be given in the next section. There, examples from context-free grammar recognition and parsing are given, which show that, from the point of view of efficiency, it is important to allow tabled and non-tabled predicates to be freely intermixed. Extension (2) was already motivated in the literature in the context of termination under SLD-resolution (see for instance [3]). Indeed, it is important for programming in the large, to have modular termination proofs, i.e. proofs that are capable of combining termination proofs of separate programs to obtain termination proofs of combined programs.

The rest of the paper is structured as follows: In the next section we present examples which motivate the need to freely mix tabled and Prolog execution. In Section 3, we introduce some necessary concepts and present a definition of SLG-resolution. Section 4 introduces a first notion of termination under tabled evaluation: *quasi-termination*. In addition, a characterisation for quasi-termination is given which generalises the characterisation given in [8] to the case where Prolog and tabled execution are intermixed. Then, a modular termination condition is given for the quasi-termination of the union $P \cup R$ of two programs P and R, where P extends R. In Section 5, the stronger notion of *LG-termination* is defined and characterized, and a method for obtaining modular proofs for LG-termination is presented. We conclude with discussing related and future work. We refer to the full version of the paper, [17], for more results and examples and for the proofs of all the theorems, propositions and statements made here.

2 Mixing Tabled and Prolog Execution: Some Motivation

It has long been noted in the literature that tabled evaluation can be used for context-free grammar recognition and parsing: tabling eliminates redundancy and handles grammars that would otherwise infinitely loop under Prolog-style execution (e.g. left recursive ones). The program of Fig. 1 where all predicates are tabled, provides such an example. This grammar, recognizing arithmetic expressions containing additions and multiplications over the integers, is left recursive — left recursion is used to give the arithmetic operators their proper associativity — and would be non-terminating for Prolog-style execution. Under tabled execution, left recursion is handled correctly. In fact, one only needs to

$$
\begin{array}{ll}
expr(Si, So) & \leftarrow expr(Si, S1), S1 = ['+'|S2], term(S2, So) \\
expr(Si, So) & \leftarrow term(Si, So) \\
term(Si, So) & \leftarrow term(Si, S1), S1 = ['*'|S2], primary(S2, So) \\
term(Si, So) & \leftarrow primary(Si, So) \\
primary(Si, So) & \leftarrow Si = ['('|S1], expr(S1, S2), S2 = [')'|So] \\
primary(Si, So) & \leftarrow Si = [I|So], integer(I)
\end{array}
$$

Fig. 1. A tabled program recognizing simple arithmetic expressions.

table predicates *expr*/2 and *term*/2 to get the desired termination behaviour; we can and will safely drop the tabling of *primary*/2 in the sequel.

To see why a mix of tabled with Prolog execution is desirable in practice, suppose that we want to extend the above recognition grammar to handle exponentiation. The most natural way to do so is to introduce a new nonterminal, named *factor*, for handling exponentiation and make it right recursive, since the exponentiation operator is right associative. The resulting grammar is as below where only the predicates *expr*/2 and *term*/2 are tabled. Note that, at least

$$
\begin{array}{ll}
expr(Si, So) & \leftarrow expr(Si, S1), S1 = ['+'|S2], term(S2, So) \\
expr(Si, So) & \leftarrow term(Si, So) \\
term(Si, So) & \leftarrow term(Si, S1), S1 = ['*'|S2], factor(S2, So) \\
term(Si, So) & \leftarrow factor(Si, So) \\
factor(Si, So) & \leftarrow primary(Si, S1), S1 = ['\wedge'|S2], factor(S2, So) \\
factor(Si, So) & \leftarrow primary(Si, So) \\
primary(Si, So) & \leftarrow Si = ['('|S1], expr(S1, S2), S2 = [')'|So] \\
primary(Si, So) & \leftarrow Si = [I|So], integer(I)
\end{array}
$$

as far as termination is concerned, there is no need to table the new nonterminal. Indeed, Prolog's evaluation strategy handles right recursion in grammars finitely. In fact, Prolog-style evaluation of right recursion is more efficient than its tabled-based evaluation: Prolog has linear complexity for a simple right recursive grammar, but with tabling implemented as in XSB the evaluation could be quadratic as calls need to be recorded in the tables using explicit copying. Thus, it is important to allow tabled and non-tabled predicates to be freely intermixed, and be able to choose the strategy that is most efficient for the situation at hand.

By using tabling in context-free grammars, one gets a recognition algorithm that is a variant of Early's algorithm (also known as active chart recognition algorithm) whose complexity is polynomial in the size of the input expression/string [9]. However, often one wants to construct the parse tree(s) for a given input string. The usual approach is to introduce an extra argument to the nonterminals of the input grammar — representing the portion of the parse tree that each rule generates — and naturally to also add the necessary code that constructs the parse tree. This approach is straightforward, but as noticed in [19], using the same program for recognition as well as parsing may be extremely unsatisfactory from a complexity standpoint: in context-free grammars recognition is polynomial while parsing is exponential since there can be exponentially many parse trees for a given input string. The obvious solution is

$$R: \begin{cases} s(Si, So) \leftarrow a(Si, S), S = [b|So] \\ a(Si, So) \leftarrow a(Si, S), a(S, So) \\ a(Si, So) \leftarrow Si = [a|So] \end{cases}$$

$$P: \begin{cases} s(Si, So, PT) \leftarrow a(Si, S), S = [b|So], PT = spt(Pa, b), a(Si, S, Pa) \\ a(Si, So, PT) \leftarrow a(Si, S), a(S, So), PT = apt(P, P'), a(Si, S, P), a(S, So, P') \\ a(Si, So, PT) \leftarrow Si = [a|So], PT = a \end{cases}$$

Fig. 2. A tabled program recognizing and parsing the language $a^n b$.

to use two interleaved versions of the grammar as in the example program of Fig. 2. Note that only $a/2$, i.e. the recursive predicate of the 'recognition' part, R, of the program (consisting of predicates $s/2$ and $a/2$), needs to be tabled. This action allows recognition to terminate and to have polynomial complexity. Furthermore, the recognizer can now be used as a filter for the parsing process in the following way: only after knowing that a particular part of the input belongs to the grammar and having computed the exact substring that each nonterminal spans, do we invoke the parsing routine on the nonterminal to construct its (possibly exponentially many) parse trees. Doing so, avoids e.g. cases where it may take exponential time to fail on an input string that does not belong in the given language: an example for the grammar under consideration is the input string a^n. On the other hand, tabling the 'parsing' part of the program (consisting of predicates $s/3$ and $a/3$) does not affect the efficiency of the process complexity-wise and incurs a small performance overhead due to the recording of calls and their results in the tables. Finally, note that the construction is modular in the sense that the 'parsing' part of the program, P, depends on the 'recognition' part, R, but not vice versa — we say that P *extends* R.

3 Preliminaries

We assume familiarity with the basic concepts of logic programming [13,1]. Throughout the paper, P will denote a definite logic program and we restrict ourselves in this class. By $Pred_P$, we denote the set of predicates occurring in P, and by Def_P we denote the set of predicates defined in P (i.e. predicates occurring in the head of a clause of P). By Rec_P, resp. $NRec_P$, we denote the set of (directly or indirectly) recursive, resp. non-recursive, predicates of the program P (so $NRec_P = Pred_P \setminus Rec_P$). If $A = p(t_1, \ldots, t_n)$, then we denote by $Rel(A)$ the predicate symbol p of A; i.e. $Rel(A) = p$.

The *extended Herbrand Universe*, U_P^E, and the *extended Herbrand Base*, B_P^E, associated with a program P, were introduced in [10]. They are defined as follows. Let $Term_P$ and $Atom_P$ denote the set of respectively all terms and atoms that can be constructed from the alphabet underlying P. The variant relation, denoted $\approx$, defines an equivalence. U_P^E and B_P^E are respectively the quotient sets $Term_P/\approx$ and $Atom_P/\approx$. For any term t (or atom A), we denote its class in U_P^E (B_P^E) as $\tilde{t}$ ($\tilde{A}$). However, when no confusion is possible, we omit the tildes. If $\Pi \subseteq Pred_P$, we denote with B_Π^E the subset of B_P^E consisting of (equivalence classes of) atoms based on the predicate symbols of Π. So B_P^E can be seen as an abbreviation of $B_{Pred_P}^E$.

Let P be a program and p, q two predicate symbols of P. We say that p *refers to* q in P iff there is a clause in P with p in the head and q occurring in the body. We say that p *depends on* q in P, and write $p \sqsupseteq q$, iff (p, q) is in the reflexive, transitive closure of the relation refers to. Note that, by definition, each predicate depends on itself. We write $p \simeq q$ iff $p \sqsupseteq q$, $q \sqsupseteq p$ (p and q are mutually recursive or $p = q$). The *dependency graph* G of a program P is a graph where the nodes are labeled with the predicates of $Pred_P$. There is a *directed arc* from p to q in G iff p refers to q. Finally, we will say that a program P *extends* a program R iff no predicate defined in P occurs in R.

In analogy to [2], we will refer to SLD-derivations (see [13]) following the left-to-right selection rule as LD-derivations. Other concepts will adopt this naming accordingly. For a program P and set $S \subseteq B_P^E$, we denote by $Call(P, S)$ the subset of B_P^E such that $B \in Call(P, S)$ whenever an element of B is a selected atom in an LD-derivation for some $P \cup \{\leftarrow A\}$, with $\tilde{A} \in S$. Throughout, we will assume that in any derivation of a query w.r.t. a program, representants of equivalence classes are systematically provided with fresh variables, to avoid the necessity of renaming apart. In the sequel, we abbreviate computed answer substitution with c.a.s. Our termination conditions are based on the following concept of finitely partitioning level mapping.

Definition 1. ((finitely partitioning) level mapping)
Let P be a program and $L \subseteq B_P^E$. A level mapping *on L is a function $l : L \rightarrow \mathbb{N}$. A level mapping l on L is* finitely partitioning *on $C \subseteq L$ iff for all $n \in \mathbb{N}$: $\sharp(l^{-1}(n) \cap C) < \infty$, where $\sharp$ is the cardinality function.*

3.1 SLG-Resolution

We present a non-constructive definition of SLG-resolution that is sufficient for our purposes, and refer to [4,15] for more constructive formulations of (variants) of tabled resolution.

By fixing a *tabling* for a program P, we mean choosing a set of predicates of P which are tabled. We denote this tabling as Tab_P. The complement of this set of tabled predicates is denoted as $NTab_P = Pred_P \setminus Tab_P$.

Definition 2. (pseudo SLG-tree, pseudo LG-tree) *Let P be a definite program, $Tab_P \subseteq Pred_P$, $\mathcal{R}$ a selection rule and A an atom. A* pseudo SLG-tree *w.r.t. Tab_P for $P \cup \{\leftarrow A\}$* under *$\mathcal{R}$ is a tree τ_A such that:*

1. *the nodes of τ_A are labeled with goals along with an indication of the selected atom according to $\mathcal{R}$,*
2. *the arcs are labeled with substitutions,*
3. *the root of τ_A is $\leftarrow A$,*
4. *the children of the root $\leftarrow A$ are obtained by resolution against all matching program clauses in P, the arcs are labeled with the corresponding mgu used in the resolution step,*

5. *the children of a non-root node labeled with the goal* $\mathbf{Q}$ *where* $\mathcal{R}(\mathbf{Q}) = B$ *are obtained as follows:*
   (a) *if* $Rel(B) \in Tab_P$, *then the (possibly infinitely many) children of the node can only be obtained by resolving the selected atom* B *of the node with clauses of the form* $B\theta \leftarrow$ *(not necessarily in* P*), the arcs are labeled with the corresponding mgu used in the resolution step (i.e.* θ*),*
   (b) *if* $Rel(B) \in NTab_P$, *then the children of the node are obtained by resolution of* B *against all matching program clauses in* P, *and the arcs are labeled with the corresponding mgu used in the resolution step.*

If $\mathcal{R}$ *is the leftmost selection rule,* τ_A *is called a* pseudo LG-tree *w.r.t.* Tab_P *for* $P \cup \{\leftarrow A\}$.
We say that a pseudo SLG-tree τ_A *w.r.t.* Tab_P *for* $P \cup \{\leftarrow A\}$ *is* smaller *than another pseudo SLG-tree* τ_A' *w.r.t.* Tab_P *for* $P \cup \{\leftarrow A\}$ *iff* τ_A' *can be obtained from* τ_A *by attaching new sub-branches to nodes in* τ_A.
A (computed) answer clause *of a pseudo SLG-tree* τ_A *w.r.t.* Tab_P *for* $P \cup \{\leftarrow A\}$ *is a clause of the form* $A\theta \leftarrow$ *where* θ *is the composition of the substitutions found on a branch of* τ_A *whose leaf is labeled with the empty goal.*

Intuitively, a pseudo SLG-tree (in an SLG-forest, see Definition 3 below) represents the tabled computation (w.r.t. Tab_P) of all answers for a given subgoal labeling the root node of the tree. The trees in the above definition are called *pseudo* SLG-trees because there is no condition yet on which clauses $B\theta \leftarrow$ exactly are to be used for resolution in point 5a. These clauses represent the answers found (possibly in another tree of the forest) for the selected tabled atom. This interaction between the trees in an SLG-forest is captured in the following definition.

Definition 3. (SLG-forest, LG-forest) *Let* P *be a definite program,* $Tab_P \subseteq Pred_P$, $\mathcal{R}$ *be a selection rule and* T *be a (possibly infinite) set of atoms such that no two different atoms in* T *are variants of each other.* $\mathcal{F}$ *is an* SLG-forest w.r.t. Tab_P for P and T under $\mathcal{R}$ *iff* $\mathcal{F}$ *is a set of minimal pseudo SLG-trees* $\{\tau_A \mid A \in T\}$ *w.r.t.* Tab_P *where*

1. τ_A *is a pseudo SLG-tree w.r.t.* Tab_P *for* $P \cup \{\leftarrow A\}$ *under* $\mathcal{R}$,
2. *every selected tabled atom* B *of each node in every* $\tau_A \in \mathcal{F}$ *is a variant of an element* B' *of* T, *such that every clause resolved with* B *is a variant of an answer clause of* $\tau_{B'}$ *and vice versa, for every answer clause of* $\tau_{B'}$ *there is a variant of this answer clause which is resolved with* B.

Let S *be a set of atoms. An* SLG-forest for P and S w.r.t. Tab_P under $\mathcal{R}$ *is an SLG-forest w.r.t.* Tab_P *for a minimal set* T *with* $S \subseteq T$. *If* $S = \{A\}$, *then we also talk about the SLG-forest for* $P \cup \{\leftarrow A\}$.
An LG-forest *is an SLG-forest containing only pseudo LG-trees.*

Point 2 of Definition 3, together with the imposed minimality of trees in a forest, now uniquely determines these trees. So we can drop the designation "pseudo" and refer to (S)LG-trees in an (S)LG-forest.

Note that, if $Tab_P = \emptyset$, the (S)LG-forest of $P \cup \{\leftarrow A\}$ consists of one tree: the (S)LD-tree of $P \cup \{\leftarrow A\}$. We use the following artificial tabled program to illustrate the concepts that we introduced.

Example 1. Let P be the following program, with $Tab_P = \{member/2\}$. Let

$$\begin{array}{ll} intersection(Xs, Ys, Z) & \leftarrow member(Xs, Z), member(Ys, Z) \\ member([Z|Zs], Z) & \leftarrow \\ member([X|Zs], Z) & \leftarrow member(Zs, Z) \end{array}$$

$S = \{intersection(Xs, Ys, a)\}$. Then, $Call(P, S) = S \cup \{member(Zs, a)\}$ and the LG-forest for P and S is shown in Fig. 3. Note that there is a finite number of LG-trees, all with finite branches, but the trees have infinitely branching nodes.

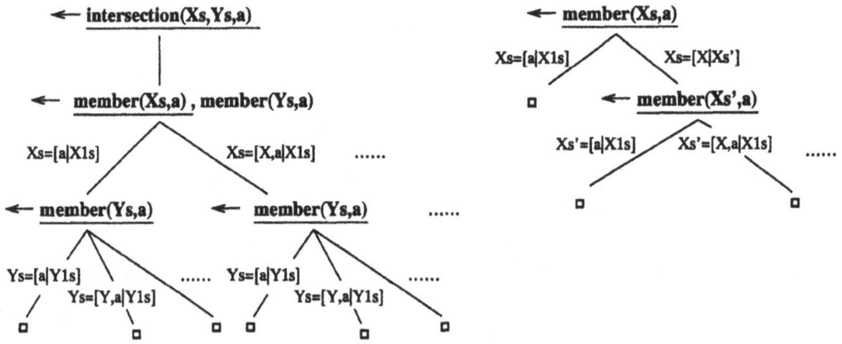

Fig. 3. The LG-forest for $P \cup \{\leftarrow intersection(Xs, Ys, a)\}$.

Note that we can use the notions of LD-derivation and LD-computation (as they appear for instance in the definition of the call set $Call(P, S)$) even in the context of SLG-resolution, as the set of call patterns and the set of computed answer substitutions are not influenced by tabling; see e.g. [12, Theorem 2.1].

4 Quasi-Termination

A first basic notion of (universal) termination under a tabled execution mechanism is quasi-termination. It is defined as follows (see [8, Definition 3.1] for the case $Tab_P = Pred_P$).

Definition 4. (quasi-termination) *Let P be a program, $Tab_P \subseteq Pred_P$ and $S \subseteq B_P^E$. P* quasi-terminates w.r.t. *Tab_P* and *S iff for all A such that $\tilde{A} \in S$, the LG-forest w.r.t. Tab_P for $P \cup \{\leftarrow A\}$ consists of a finite number of LG-trees without infinite branches. Also, P* quasi-terminates w.r.t. *S iff P quasi-terminates w.r.t. $Pred_P$ and S.*

Note that it is not required that the LG-trees are finitely branching in their nodes. In the next section, we introduce and provide conditions for the stronger notion of *LG-termination* which requires that the LG-forest consists of a finite number of finite trees (i.e. trees with finite branches *and* which are finitely branching). Recall the program P and set S of Example 1. P quasi-terminates w.r.t. $\{member/2\}$ and S. Note that P doesn't LG-terminate w.r.t. $\{member/2\}$ and S.

Many works (see [5] for a survey) address the problem of LD-termination: A program P is said to be *LD-terminating* w.r.t. a set $S \subseteq B_P^E$ iff for all A such that $\tilde{A} \in S$, the LD-tree of $P \cup \{\leftarrow A\}$ is finite (see for instance [6]). It can be easily shown that, if P LD-terminates w.r.t. S, then P quasi-terminates w.r.t. Tab_P and S (for every $Tab_P \subseteq Pred_P$). As shown in Example 1, the notion of LD-termination is strictly stronger than the notion of quasi-termination.

Since quasi-termination requires that there are only finitely many LG-trees in the LG-forest of a query, there can only be a finite number of tabled atoms in the call set of that query. More formally: *If a program P quasi-terminates w.r.t. Tab_P and S, then, for every $A \in S$, $Call(P, \{A\}) \cap B_{Tab_P}^E$ is finite.*

In [8], the special case where $Tab_P = Pred_P$, i.e. where all predicates occurring in P are tabled, is considered. If $Tab_P = Pred_P$, an LG-tree cannot have infinite branches. So, P quasi-terminates w.r.t. a set S iff for all A such that $\tilde{A} \in S$, the LG-forest for $P \cup \{\leftarrow A\}$ consists of a finite number of LG-trees. In [8, Lemma 3.1] the following equivalence was proven: *P quasi-terminates w.r.t. S iff for every $A \in S$, $Call(P, \{A\})$ is finite.* We want to note that none of the directions (if nor only-if) hold in case that the tabled predicates of the program P are a strict subset of $Pred_P$. We refer to [17] for two counterexamples, one for each direction.

4.1 Characterisation of Quasi-Termination

In order to state a necessary and sufficient condition for quasi-termination, we need to make an assumption on the set Tab_P of tabled predicates of the program P. If the assumption is not satisfied, the condition is sufficient (but not necessary).

Definition 5. (well-chosen tabling (w.r.t. a program)) *Let P be a program, $Pred_P = Tab_P \sqcup NTab_P$ and G be the predicate dependency graph of P. The tabling Tab_P is called* well-chosen w.r.t. *the program P iff for every $p, q \in NTab_P$ such that $p \simeq q$, exactly one of the following two conditions holds:*

$C_1(p, q)$: *no cycle of directed arcs in G containing p and q contains a predicate from Tab_P.*

$C_2(p, q)$: *all cycles of directed arcs in G containing p and q contain at least one predicate from Tab_P.*

In particular, if $NTab_P \subseteq \{p \in Pred_P \mid p$ is a non-recursive or only directly recursive predicate$\}$ or if $NTab_P = \emptyset$ (i.e. $Tab_P = Pred_P$), then the tabling Tab_P is well-chosen w.r.t. P.

The next theorem provides a necessary and sufficient condition for quasi-termination of a program P w.r.t. a tabling and a set of atoms, in case the tabling is well-chosen w.r.t. P.

Theorem 1. (characterisation of quasi-termination in case the tabling is well-chosen) *Let P be a program, $Tab_P \subseteq Pred_P$ and $S \subseteq B_P^E$. Suppose the tabling Tab_P is well-chosen w.r.t. P. Then, P quasi-terminates w.r.t. Tab_P and S iff there is a level mapping l on B_P^E such that for every $A \in S$, l is finitely partitioning on $Call(P,\{A\}) \cap B_{Tab_P}^E$, and such that*

- *for every atom A such that $\tilde{A} \in Call(P,S)$,*
- *for every clause $H \leftarrow B_1,\ldots,B_n$ in P, such that $mgu(A,H)=\theta$ exists,*
- *for every $1 \le i \le n$ and for every LD-c.a.s. θ_{i-1} for $\leftarrow (B_1,\ldots,B_{i-1})\theta$:*

$$
\begin{aligned}
&l(A) \ge l(B_i\theta\theta_{i-1})\\
&\textit{and}\\
&l(A) > l(B_i\theta\theta_{i-1}) \textit{ if } Rel(A) \simeq Rel(B_i) \in NTab_P\\
&\qquad\qquad\textit{and } C_2(Rel(A), Rel(B_i)) \textit{ does not hold.}
\end{aligned}
$$

Note that [8, Theorem 3.1] is an instance of this theorem, with $Tab_P = Pred_P$. We illustrate the intuition behind Theorem 1 with the following example.

Example 2. Consider the following three propositional programs P, P' and P'':

$$
P: \begin{cases} p \leftarrow q \\ q \leftarrow r \\ r \leftarrow q \end{cases} \qquad P': \begin{cases} p \leftarrow q \\ q \leftarrow r \\ r \leftarrow p \end{cases} \qquad P'': \begin{cases} p \leftarrow q \\ q \leftarrow r \\ r \leftarrow p \\ r \leftarrow q \end{cases}
$$

with $Tab_P = Tab_{P'} = Tab_{P''} = \{p\}$ and $S = \{p\}$. The LG-forests for $P \cup \{\leftarrow p\}$, $P' \cup \{\leftarrow p\}$ and $P'' \cup \{\leftarrow p\}$ are shown in Fig. 4. P and P'' do not quasi-terminate

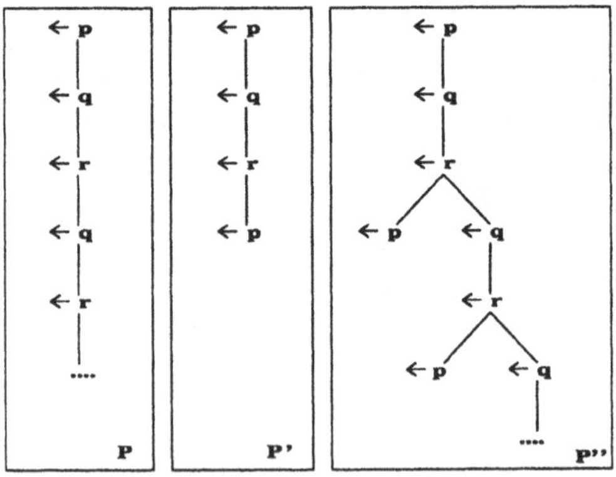

Fig. 4. The LG-forests for $P \cup \{\leftarrow p\}$, $P' \cup \{\leftarrow p\}$, and $P'' \cup \{\leftarrow p\}$.

w.r.t. $\{p\}$, whereas P' does.
Note that for programs P and P', the tablings are well-chosen. Also note that, because the programs are propositional, every level mapping will be finitely partitioning on the whole Herbrand base.
Let's first consider program P. For this program condition $C_1(q,r)$ holds. Also

note that there is no level mapping l such that $l(q) > l(r)$ and $l(r) > l(q)$. Hence, the condition in Theorem 1 can not be satisfied and P does not quasi-terminate w.r.t. $\{p\}$.
Consider next program P' for which condition $C_2(q,r)$ holds. Let l be the following level mapping $l(p) = l(q) = l(r) = 0$. With this level mapping, P' satisfies the condition of Theorem 1 and hence, P' quasi-terminates w.r.t. $\{p\}$.
Finally, note that for the program P'', the tabling is not well-chosen w.r.t. P''.

In case the tabling for a program is not well-chosen (like for the program P'' of Example 2), the condition of Theorem 1 is sufficient (but not necessary) for proving quasi-termination.

4.2 Modular Proofs for Quasi-Termination

We now present a proposition which gives a modular proof for the quasi-termination of the union $P \cup R$ of two programs P and R, such that P extends R. If $Pred_{P \cup R} = Tab_{P \cup R} \sqcup NTab_{P \cup R}$, let

$$Tab_P = Tab_{P\cup R} \cap Pred_P \ , \ NTab_P = NTab_{P\cup R} \cap Pred_P,$$
$$Tab_R = Tab_{P\cup R} \cap Pred_R \ , \ NTab_R = NTab_{P\cup R} \cap Pred_R.$$

Proposition 1. *Suppose P and R are two programs, such that P extends R. Let $S \subseteq B^E_{P\cup R}$. If*

- *R quasi-terminates w.r.t. Tab_R and $Call(P \cup R, S)$,*
- *there is a level mapping l on B^E_P such that for every $A \in S$, l is finitely partitioning on $Call(P \cup R, \{A\}) \cap B^E_{Tab_P}$, and such that*
  - *for every atom A such that $\tilde{A} \in Call(P \cup R, S)$,*
  - *for every clause $H \leftarrow B_1, \ldots, B_n$ in P such that $mgu(A, H) = \theta$ exists,*
  - *for every $1 \leq i \leq n$ and for every LD-c.a.s. θ_{i-1} in $P \cup R$ for $\leftarrow (B_1, \ldots, B_{i-1})\theta$:*

$$l(A) \geq l(B_i\theta\theta_{i-1})$$
and
$$l(A) > l(B_i\theta\theta_{i-1}) \text{ if } Rel(A) \simeq Rel(B_i) \in NTab_P \text{ and } C_2(Rel(A), Rel(B_i)) \text{ does not hold.}$$

then, $P \cup R$ quasi-terminates w.r.t. $Tab_{P\cup R}$ and S.

The program and query of Example 1 can be proven to quasi-terminate by applying Proposition 1 (see [17]). In [17] we give three more propositions for proving quasi-termination in a modular way. They all consider special cases of Proposition 1: in the first of these propositions, no defined predicate of P is tabled, in the second one all the defined predicates in P are tabled, and in the last one, P and R extend each other.

Note that the above modular termination conditions prove the quasi-termination of $P \cup R$ without constructing an appropriate level mapping which satisfies the condition of Theorem 1. We refer to [17] where modular termination conditions for quasi-termination are given which construct (from simpler level mappings) a level mapping such that $P \cup R$ and this level mapping satisfy the condition for quasi-termination of Theorem 1.

5 LG-Termination

The notion of quasi-termination only partially corresponds to our intuitive notion of a terminating execution of a query against a tabled program. This notion only requires that the LG-forest consists of only a finite number of LG-trees, without infinite branches, yet these trees can have infinitely branching nodes. To capture this source of non-termination for a tabled computation, the following stronger notion is introduced (see [8, Def. 4.1] for the special case where $Tab_P = Pred_P$).

Definition 6. (LG-termination) *Let P be a program, $Tab_P \subseteq Pred_P$ and $S \subseteq B_P^E$. P* LG-terminates w.r.t. *Tab_P* and *S iff for every atom A such that $\tilde{A} \in S$, the LG-forest w.r.t. Tab_P for $P \cup \{\leftarrow A\}$ consists of a finite number of finite LG-trees.*

As already noted, the program P of Example 1 does not LG-terminate w.r.t. $\{member/2\}$ and $\{intersection(Xs, Ys, a)\}$. Obviously, the notion of LG-termination is (strictly) stronger than the notion of quasi-termination. Also, LD-termination implies LG-termination.

Consider two tablings for a program P; one with set of tabled predicates equal to $Tab_1 \subseteq Pred_P$, the other with set of tabled predicates equal to $Tab_2 \subseteq Pred_P$. Suppose $Tab_1 \subseteq Tab_2$ (hence $NTab_1 \supseteq NTab_2$). The next proposition studies the relationship between the LG-termination of P w.r.t. these two tablings. We note that it does not hold for quasi-termination; see [17] for a counterexample.

Proposition 2. *Let P be a program. Let $Pred_P = Tab_1 \sqcup NTab_1$ and $Pred_P = Tab_2 \sqcup NTab_2$. Suppose $Tab_1 \subseteq Tab_2$. Let $S \subseteq B_P^E$. If P LG-terminates w.r.t. Tab_1 and S, then P LG-terminates w.r.t. Tab_2 and S.*

We now relate the notions of quasi-termination and LG-termination in a more detailed way: By definition, quasi-termination only corresponds to part of the LG-termination notion; it fails to capture non-termination caused by an infinitely branching node in an LG-tree. Note that if an LG-forest contains a tree with an infinitely branching node, then there is an LG-tree in the forest which is infinitely branching in a node which contains a goal with a recursive, tabled atom at the leftmost position. This observation leads to the following lemma. Let us denote the set of tabled, recursive predicates in a program P with TR_P:

$$TR_P = Tab_P \cap Rec_P.$$

Lemma 1. *Let P be a program, $Tab_P \subseteq Pred_P$ and $S \subseteq B_P^E$. P LG-terminates w.r.t. Tab_P and S iff P quasi-terminates w.r.t. Tab_P and S and for all $A \in S$ the set of (LD-)computed answers for atoms in $Call(P, \{A\}) \cap B_{TR_P}^E$ is finite.*

It follows from the proof of this lemma (see [17]) that, if P LG-terminates w.r.t. Tab_P and S, the set of computed answers for atoms in $Call(P, \{A\})$ is finite for all $A \in S$. We now present a characterisation of LG-termination.

5.1 Characterisation of LG-Termination

First (in Theorem 2), we will characterise LG-termination of a program P in terms of quasi-termination of the program P^a, which is obtained by applying the answer-transformation (Definition 7) on P. However, we will also characterise LG-termination in a more direct way (Theorem 3).

Lemma 1 gives the intuition behind the answer-transformation that we are about to present. The answer-transformation forms the basis of the characterisation of LG-termination in Theorem 2; LG-termination of a program P will be shown to be equivalent with quasi-termination of the program P^a, obtained by applying the answer-transformation to P.

Definition 7. (a(nswer)-transformation) *Let P be a program with tabling $Tab_P \subseteq Pred_P$. The* a-transformation *is defined as follows:*

- *For a clause $C = H \leftarrow B_1, \ldots, B_n$ in P, we define*

$$C^a = H \leftarrow B_1, B_1^*, \ldots, B_n, B_n^*$$

with B_i^* defined as follows (suppose $B_i = p(t_1, \ldots, t_n)$):
if $p \simeq Rel(H)$ and $p \in Tab_P$, then $B_i^* = p^a(t_1, \ldots, t_n)$, where p^a/n is a new predicate, else $B_i^* = \emptyset$.
Let $TR_P^a = \{p^a/n \mid p/n \in TR_P\}$ (recall that $TR_P = Tab_P \cap Rec_P$).
- *For the program P, we define*

$$P^a = \{C^a \mid C \in P\} \cup \{p^a(X_1, \ldots, X_n) \leftarrow \ \mid p^a/n \in TR_P^a\}.$$

- *The set of tabled predicates of the program P^a is defined as*

$$Tab_{P^a} = Tab_P \cup TR_P^a.$$

It is easy to see that $Call(P, S) = Call(P^a, S) \cap B_P^E$. Also, if we denote with $cas(P, \{p(\bar{t})\})$ the set of computed answer substitutions of $P \cup \{\leftarrow p(\bar{t})\}$, then $cas(P, \{p(\bar{t})\}) = cas(P^a, \{p(\bar{t})\})$ for all $p(\bar{t}) \in B_P^E$. It is important to note that, if we have a query $p(\bar{t}) \in B_{TR_P}^E$ to a program P, then $p(\bar{t})\sigma$ is a computed answer if $p^a(\bar{t})\sigma \in Call(P^a, \{p(\bar{t})\})$. This is in fact the main purpose of the transformation.

We want to mention that a similar transformation, namely the solution-transformation, is introduced in [8, Definition 4.2] in order to relate the concepts of LG-termination and quasi-termination. But, as opposed to the answer-transformation, the solution-transformation introduces much more "overhead" in the sense that a clause $C = H \leftarrow B_1, \ldots, B_n$ is transformed into a clause $C_{sol} = H \leftarrow B_1, sol(B_1), \ldots, B_n, sol(B_n)$ where $sol/1$ is a new tabled predicate. Notice that in contrast, the answer-transformation only keeps track of the computed answers of *recursive, tabled* body atoms (and not of all body atoms).

Example 3. Let P be the program of Example 1, with $Tab_P = \{member/2\}$. The a-transform, P^a, of P is shown in Fig. 5; $Tab_{P^a} = \{member/2, member^a/2\}$.

$$\begin{array}{ll} intersection(Xs, Ys, Z) & \leftarrow member(Xs, Z), member(Ys, Z) \\ member([Z|Zs], Z) & \leftarrow \\ member([X|Zs], Z) & \leftarrow member(Zs, Z), member^a(Zs, Z) \\ member^a(L, Z) & \leftarrow \end{array}$$

Fig. 5. The a-transformation of P from Example 1.

The following theorem is a generalisation of [8, Theorem 4.1] (there, the previously mentioned solution-transformation of [8, Definition 4.2] is used to relate LG-termination and quasi-termination in case $Tab_P = Pred_P$).

Theorem 2. (characterisation of LG-termination in terms of quasi-termination) *Let P be a program, $Tab_P \subseteq Pred_P$ and $S \subseteq B_P^E$. P LG-terminates w.r.t. Tab_P and S iff P^a quasi-terminates w.r.t. Tab_{P^a} and S.*

Example 4. (Ex. 3 ctd.). The LG-forest of $P \cup \{\leftarrow intersection(Xs, Ys, a)\}$ w.r.t. Tab_P was shown in Fig. 3. Note that the trees are infinitely branching and hence, P does not LG-terminate w.r.t. Tab_P and $\{intersection(Xs, Ys, a)\}$.
In Fig. 6, the LG-forest of the program P^a and $\{intersection(Xs, Ys, a)\}$ w.r.t. Tab_{P^a} is shown. Note that there are infinitely many LG-trees in the forest; P^a doesn't quasi-terminate w.r.t. Tab_{P^a} and $\{intersection(Xs, Ys, a)\}$.

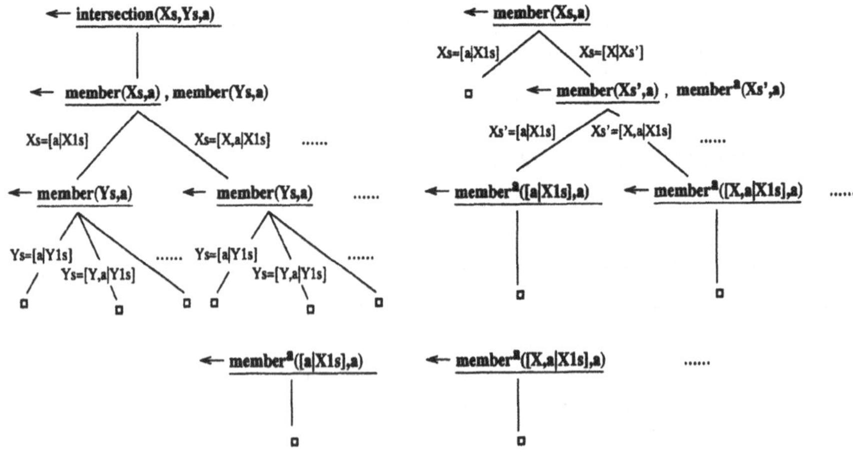

Fig. 6. The LG-forest for $P^a \cup \{\leftarrow intersection(Xs, Ys, a)\}$.

Theorem 2 provides a way to prove LG-termination of a program w.r.t. a set of queries. Namely, it is sufficient to prove quasi-termination of the a-transformation of the program w.r.t. the set of queries. To prove quasi-termination, we can use the results of Section 4.1: the condition of Theorem 1, which is necessary and sufficient in case the tabling is well-chosen[1], and which is sufficient in the general case. However, the condition of this theorem on P^a can be weakened; i.e. some of the decreases "$l(A) \geq l(B_i\theta\theta_{i-1})$" need not be checked because they can always be fulfilled. In particular, we only have to require the non-strict decrease for recursive, tabled body atoms B_i (to obtain an LG-forest with only finitely many LG-trees) or for body atoms B_i of the form $p^a(t_1, \ldots, t_n)$ (to obtain LG-trees which are finitely branching); the conditions on non-tabled predicates remain the same. The following theorem presents these optimised conditions and characterises LG-termination of a program in case the tabling is well-chosen. If the tabling is not well-chosen, the condition is sufficient (but not necessary).

Theorem 3. (characterisation of LG-termination in case the tabling is well-chosen) *Let P be a program, $Tab_P \subseteq Pred_P$ and $S \subseteq B_P^E$. Suppose the tabling Tab_P is well-chosen w.r.t. P. Then, P LG-terminates w.r.t. Tab_P and S iff there is a level mapping l on $B_{P^a}^E$ such that for every $A \in S$, l is finitely partitioning on $Call(P^a, \{A\}) \cap B^E_{TR_P \cup TR_P^a}$, and such that*

- *for every atom A such that $\tilde{A} \in Call(P^a, S)$,*
- *for every clause $H \leftarrow B_1, \ldots, B_n$ in P^a, such that $mgu(A, H) = \theta$ exists,*
- *for every B_i such that $Rel(B_i) \simeq Rel(H)$ or $Rel(B_i) \in TR_P^a$,*
- *for every LD-c.a.s. θ_{i-1} in P^a for $\leftarrow (B_1, \ldots, B_{i-1})\theta$:*

$$\begin{aligned}&l(A) \geq l(B_i\theta\theta_{i-1})\\ &\textit{and}\\ &l(A) > l(B_i\theta\theta_{i-1}) \textit{ if } Rel(A) \simeq Rel(B_i) \in NTab_P\\ &\qquad\qquad\qquad \textit{and } C_2(Rel(A), Rel(B_i)) \textit{ does not hold.}\end{aligned}$$

Example 5. Recall the recognition part of the grammar program of Fig. 2, where

$$R: \begin{cases} s(Si, So) \leftarrow a(Si, S), S = [b|So] \\ a(Si, So) \leftarrow a(Si, S), a(S, So) \\ a(Si, So) \leftarrow Si = [a|So] \end{cases}$$

$Tab_R = \{a/2\}$. We show that R LG-terminates w.r.t. $\{a/2\}$ and $S = \{s(si, So)\}$ where si is a ground list consisting of atoms and So is a variable. Consider the following a-transformation, R^a, of R ($Tab_{R^a} = \{a/2, a^a/2\}$) shown below. When

$$R^a: \begin{cases} s(Si, So) \leftarrow a(Si, S), S = [b|So] \qquad\qquad a^a(Si, So) \leftarrow \\ a(Si, So) \leftarrow a(Si, S), a^a(Si, S), a(S, So), a^a(S, So) \\ a(Si, So) \leftarrow Si = [a|So] \end{cases}$$

applying Theorem 3, we only have to consider the second clause of R^a. Note that,

[1] Note that if Tab_P is well-chosen w.r.t. P, then also Tab_{P^a} is well-chosen w.r.t. P^a.

for all $a(t1,t2) \in Call(R^a, \{s(si, S0)\})$, $t1$ is a sublist of si and $t2$ is a variable. Also, for all $a^a(v1,v2) \in Call(R^a, \{s(si, So)\})$, $v1$ is a sublist of si and $v2$ is a (strict) sublist of $v1$. Consider the trivial level mapping l (mapping everything to 0) on $Call(R^a, \{s(si, So)\}) \cap B^E_{\{a/2, a^a/2\}}$. Since this set is finite, l is obviously finitely partitioning on this set. R and S, together with l, satisfy the conditions of Theorem 3. Hence, R LG-terminates w.r.t. $\{a/2\}$ and S.

5.2 Modular Proofs for LG-Termination

Similarly to the case of quasi-termination (Section 4.2), we want to be able to obtain modular termination proofs for LG-termination of the union $P \cup R$ of two programs P and R, where P extends R. Note that, because of Theorem 2 and because $(P \cup R)^a = P^a \cup R^a$ (if P extends R), we can use the modular conditions for quasi-termination of Section 4.2. However, as we already noted in Section 5.1, we can give optimised conditions which require less checking for decreases between the values under the level mapping of the head and body atoms. Due to space limitations, in this paper we will only consider the case of two programs P and R, where P extends R, and no defined predicate symbol of P is tabled. Proposition 3 will give modular conditions for LG-termination of $P \cup R$ in that case, without using Theorem 2. The general case, the case in which all defined predicate symbols of P are tabled and the case in which the two programs extend each other are treated in the full version of the paper [17].

Proposition 3. *Let P and R be two programs, such that P extends R and such that $Def_P \subseteq NTab_P$. Let $S \subseteq B^E_{P \cup R}$. If*

- *R LG-terminates w.r.t. Tab_R and $Call(P \cup R, S)$,*
- *there is a level mapping l on B^E_P such that*
  - *for every atom A with $\tilde{A} \in Call(P \cup R, S)$,*
  - *for every clause $H \leftarrow B_1, \ldots, B_n$ in P such that $mgu(A, H) = \theta$ exists,*
  - *for every B_i, $i \in \{1, \ldots, n\}$, with $Rel(B_i) \simeq Rel(A)$,*
  - *for every LD-c.a.s. θ_{i-1} in $P \cup R$ for $\leftarrow (B_1, \ldots, B_{i-1})\theta$:*

$$l(A) > l(B_i\theta\theta_{i-1})$$

then, $P \cup R$ LG-terminates w.r.t. $Tab_{P \cup R}$ and S.

Example 6. Recall program R of Example 5. Let P be the parsing part of the grammar program of Fig. 2 which is also shown below. As already noted in Section 2, P extends R, and the only tabled predicate in $P \cup R$ is $a/2$ — see Section 2 for why this tabling is sufficient.

$$P: \begin{cases} s(Si, So, PT) \leftarrow a(Si, S), S = [b|So], PT = spt(Pa, b), a(Si, S, Pa) \\ a(Si, So, PT) \leftarrow a(Si, S), a(S, So), PT = apt(P, P'), a(Si, S, P), a(S, So, P') \\ a(Si, So, PT) \leftarrow Si = [a|So], PT = a \end{cases}$$

Let $S = \{s(si, So, PT)\}$ where si is a ground list of atoms, and So, PT are distinct variables. We show, by using Proposition 3, that $P \cup R$ LG-terminates w.r.t. $\{a/2\}$ and S.

- R LG-terminates w.r.t. $\{a/2\}$ and $Call(P \cup R, S)$.
  Note that, if $a(t1, t2) \in Call(P \cup R, S)$, then either $t1$ is a sublist of si and $t2$ is a variable, or $t1$ and $t2$ are both sublists of si. In Example 5, we proved that R LG-terminates w.r.t. this first kind of queries. To prove that R LG-terminates w.r.t. the second kind of queries, we can again apply Theorem 3. Due to space limitations, we omit the proof here.
- Note first that, if $a(t1, t2, PT) \in Call(P \cup R, S)$, then $t2$ is a (strict) sublist of $t1$, $t1$ is a sublist of si and PT is a variable. Let l be the following level mapping on $Call(P \cup R, S) \cap B^E_{\{a/3\}}$: $l(a(t1, t2, PT)) = \| t1 \|_l - \| t2 \|_l$, where $\| \ \|_l$ is the list-length norm. Because of the remark above, l is well-defined. Note that we only have to consider the recursive clause for $a/3$ in the analysis.
  - Consider the fourth body atom in the recursive clause for $a/3$. If this clause is called with $a(ti, to, PT)$, with to a (strict) sublist of ti, then the fourth body atom is called as $a(ti, t, P)$ where to is a (strict) sublist of t and t is a (strict) sublist of ti. Hence, $l(a(ti, to, PT)) = \| ti \|_l - \| to \|_l > \| ti \|_l - \| t \|_l = l(a(ti, t, P))$.
  - Consider the last body atom. If the clause is called with $a(ti, to, PT)$, with to a (strict) sublist of ti, then the last body atom is called as $a(t, to, P')$ where to is a (strict) sublist of t and t is a (strict) sublist of ti. Hence, $l(a(ti, to, PT)) = \| ti \|_l - \| to \|_l > \| t \|_l - \| to \|_l = l(a(t, to, P'))$.

We conclude that $P \cup R$ and S satisfy the condition of Proposition 3, so $P \cup R$ LG-terminates w.r.t. $\{a/2\}$ and S.

6 Related and Future Work

Our work is based on, and significantly extends, the results of [8]. In [8], the two notions of (universal) termination under tabled execution, namely quasi-termination and LG-termination, are introduced and characterised. As opposed to [8], where it is assumed that all predicates in the program are tabled, we here consider programs with a mix of tabled and Prolog execution, thereby providing a termination framework for 'real' tabled programs. We further extend the applicability of this framework by presenting modular termination conditions: conditions ensuring termination of the union $P \cup R$ of two programs P and R, where P extends R.

Termination proofs for (S)LD-resolution (such as e.g. those surveyed in [5]) are sufficient to prove termination under a tabled execution mechanism, but, since there are quasi-terminating and LG-terminating programs, which are not LD-terminating, more effective proof techniques can and need to be found. Besides [8], there are only relatively few works studying termination under tabling. In the context of well-moded programs, [14] presents a sufficient condition for a program to have the bounded term-size property, which implies LG-termination. [11] provides another sufficient condition for quasi-termination in the context of functional programming. In parallel with the work reported on in this paper, an orthogonal extension of the work of [8] was investigated in [16]. Namely, in [16] the constraint-based approach of [7] for automatically proving LD-termination was extended to the case of quasi-termination and LG-termination. More specifically, in the context of simply moded, well-typed programs and queries, sufficient conditions for quasi-termination and LG-termination (in the case that $Tab_P = Pred_P$) are given. These conditions allow reasoning fully at the clause level, contrary to those in the current paper which are stated for sets of calls. An integration of these two extensions of [8] is straightforward.

A topic for future research is to extend our results to *normal* logic programs executed under a mix of Prolog and tabled execution. Another, with an arguably more practical flavour, is to investigate how the termination conditions presented here can form the basis of a compiler that automatically decides on — or at least guides a programmer in choosing — a tabling (i.e. a set of tabled predicates) for an input program such that quasi-termination of the program is ensured.

Acknowledgements

Sofie Verbaeten is Research Assistant of the Fund for Scientific Research - F.W.O. Flanders, Belgium. Konstantinos Sagonas was supported by GOA "LP+, a second generation logic programming language". Danny De Schreye is Senior Research Associate of F.W.O. Flanders. Thanks to the anonymous referees for valuable comments.

References

1. K. Apt. Logic programming. In J. van Leeuwen, editor, *Handbook of theoretical computer science, Vol. B.* Elsevier Science Publishers, 1990.
2. K. Apt and D. Pedreschi. Reasoning about termination of pure Prolog programs. In *Information and Computation*, 106(1):109–157, 1993.
3. K. Apt and D. Pedreschi. Modular termination proofs for logic and pure Prolog programs. In *Advances in Logic Programming Theory*, pages 183–229. 1994.
4. W. Chen and D. S. Warren. Tabled evaluation with delaying for general logic programs. *J. ACM*, 43(1):20–74, 1996.
5. D. De Schreye and S. Decorte. Termination of logic programs: the never-ending story. *Journal of Logic Programming*, 19 & 20:199–260, 1994.
6. D. De Schreye, K. Verschaetse, and M. Bruynooghe. A framework for analysing the termination of definite logic programs with respect to call patterns. In *Proc. FGCS'92*, pages 481–488, ICOT Tokyo, 1992. ICOT.
7. S. Decorte, D. De Schreye and H. Vandecasteele. Constraint-based automatic termination analysis for logic programs. *ACM TOPLAS.* To appear.
8. S. Decorte, D. De Schreye, M. Leuschel, B. Martens, and K. Sagonas. Termination Analysis for Tabled Logic Programming. In N. Fuchs, editor, *Proceedings of LOPSTR'97*, number 1463 in LNCS, pages 107–123. Springer, 1997.
9. J. Early. An efficient context-free parsing algorithm. *CACM*, 13(2):94–102, 1970.
10. M. Falaschi, G. Levi, M. Martelli, and C. Palamidessi. Declarative modelling of the operational behaviour of logic languages. *Theor. Comp. Sc.*, 69(3):289–318, 1989.
11. C. K. Holst. Finiteness Analysis. In J. Hughes, editor, *Proceedings of the 5th ACM Conference on Functional Programming Languages and Computer Architecture (FPCA)*, number 523 in LNCS, pages 473–495. Springer-Verlag, 1991.

12. T. Kanamori and T. Kawamura. OLDT-based abstract interpretation. *Journal of Logic Programming*, 15(1 & 2):1–30, 1993.
13. J. Lloyd. *Foundations of logic programming.* Springer-Verlag, 1987.
14. L. Plümer. *Termination proofs for logic programs.* Number 446 in LNAI. Springer-Verlag, 1990.
15. H. Tamaki and T. Sato. OLD Resolution with Tabulation. In E. Y. Shapiro, editor, *Proceedings ICLP'86*, LNCS 225, pages 84–98. Springer Verlag, 1986.
16. S. Verbaeten and D. De Schreye. Termination analysis of tabled logic programs using mode and type information. Technical Report 277, Department of Computer Science, K.U.Leuven. Available at http://www.cs.kuleuven.ac.be/~sofie.
17. S. Verbaeten, K. Sagonas, and D. De Schreye. Modular termination proofs for Prolog with tabling. Technical Report, Department of Computer Science, K.U.Leuven, 1999. Available at http://www.cs.kuleuven.ac.be/~sofie.
18. L. Vieille. Recursive query processing: the power of logic. *Theor. Comp. Sc.*, 69(1):1–53, 1989.
19. D. S. Warren. Notes for "Programming in Tabled Prolog". Early draft available at http://www.cs.sunysb.edu/~warren/, 1998.

Declarative Program Transformation: A Deforestation Case-Study

Loïc Correnson[1], Etienne Duris[2], Didier Parigot[1], and Gilles Roussel[3]

[1] INRIA-Rocquencourt - Domaine de Voluceau,
BP 105 F-78153 Le Chesnay Cedex
{Loic.Correnson,Didier.Parigot}@inria.fr
[2] Cedric CNAM -
18, allée Jean Rostand F-91025 Evry Cedex
duris@iie.cnam.fr
[3] Institut Gaspard Monge -
5, bd Descartes F-77454 Marne-la-Vallée Cedex 2
roussel@univ-mlv.fr

Abstract. Software engineering has to reconcile modularity with efficiency. One way to grapple with this dilemma is to automatically transform a modular-specified program into an efficient-implementable one. This is the aim of deforestation transformations which get rid of intermediate data structure constructions that occur when two functions are composed. Beyond classical compile time optimization, these transformations are undeniable tools for generic programming and software component specialization.
Despite various and numerous research works in this area, general transformation methods cannot deforest some non-trivial intermediate constructions. Actually, these recalcitrant structures are built inside *accumulating parameters* and then, they follow a construction scheme which is independent from the function scheme itself. Known deforestation methods are too much tied to fixed recursion schemes to be able to deforest these structures.
In this article, we show that a fully declarative approach of program transformation allows new deforestation sites to be detected and treated. We present the principle of the *symbolic composition*, based on the attribute grammar formalism, with an illustrative running example stemming from a typical problem of standard functional deforestations.

Keywords: Program transformation, deforestation, attribute grammars, functional programming, partial evaluation.

1 Introduction

More than a decade ago, P. Wadler said *"Intermediate data-structures are both the basis and the bane of modular programming."* [29]. Indeed, if they allow functions to be composed, these data-structures also have a harmful cost from efficiency point of view (allocation and deallocation). To get the best of both

G. Nadathur (Ed.): PPDP'99, LNCS 1702, pp. 360–377, 1999.

worlds, *deforestation* transformations were introduced. These source-to-source transformations fuse two pieces of a program into another one, where intermediate data-structure constructions have been eliminated.

The main motivation for deforestation transformations was, for a long time, compiler optimization. More recently, with the emergence of component-based software development, that requires both automatic software generation and component specialization, deforestation transformations find new interest again, just as partial evaluation or more generally high level source-to-source program transformations [6,4].

Since 1990, different approaches have been developed in order to improve the efficiency of deforestation transformations. Wadler's algorithm [29], based on Burstall and Darlington *unfold/fold* strategy [1], has been improved and extended by several works [2,12,25,27]. Another approach, the *deforestation in calculational form* [11,26,16,28,13], was based on algebraic notions. This latter aims at using categorial *functors* to capture both function and data-type patterns of recursion [18] to guide the deforestation process.

With a large degree of formalisms or notations, all these methods are able to deforest function compositions like the following:

```
let lengapp l1 l2 = length (append l1 l2)
let length x = case x with          let append l1 l2 = case l1 with
  cons head tail →                    cons head tail →
    1 + (length tail)                   cons head (append tail l2)
  nil → 0                             nil → l2
```

Intuitively, these techniques process in three steps. First, they *expose* constructors to functions (unfolding).

```
let lengapp l1 l2 = case l1 with
  cons head tail →
    length (cons head (append tail l2))
  nil → length l2
```

Next, they apply a kind of *partial evaluation* to these terms (application to constructors), that carries out the elimination of intermediate data structure.

```
let lengapp l1 l2 = case l1 with
  cons head tail →
    1 + (length (append tail l2))
  nil → length l2
```

Finally, recursive *function calls* could be reintroduced or recognized[1] (folding).

```
let lengapp l1 l2 = case l1 with
  cons head tail →
    1 + (lengapp tail l2)
  nil → length l2
```

[1] Depending on the deforestation method, this step is implicit or not in the process.

In the resulting *lengapp* function definition, the *conses* of the intermediate list have been removed.

Even if each technique is particular in its algorithm implementation or in its theoretical underlying formalism (rewriting rule system [29], `foldr/build` elimination rule [11], fold normalization [26], hylomorphisms fusion [13]), they are more or less based on these three steps [8].

Major characteristics of these methods are, on the one hand, to expose data-structure producers to data-structure consumers in order to find partial evaluation application sites and, on the other hand, to detect and drive this deforestation process by following a general recursion scheme[2], that comes from the function or the data structure recursive definitions.

Unfortunately, all these methods fail in the deforestation of a class of intermediate data structures. This concerns functions that build — part of — their result inside an accumulating parameter, that is, a data which is neither directly the result nor the pattern matched syntactic argument of the function, but an auxiliary argument. Given a pair of functions to be fused, when the producer function collects its result in an accumulating parameter, the constructors in that parameter are *protected* from the consumer. In this case, no deforestation normally occurs.

As a first striking example, let us consider the function *rev* which reverses a list. In the following definition, parameter y is initialized with the value *nil*:

$$
\begin{array}{l}
\texttt{let}\ rev\ x\ y = \texttt{case}\ x\ \texttt{with}\\
\quad cons\ head\ tail \rightarrow\\
\qquad rev\ tail\ (cons\ head\ y)\\
\quad nil \rightarrow y
\end{array}
$$

The classical functional composition of this function with itself leads to the function definition `let` $revrev\ x\ y\ z = rev\ (rev\ x\ y)\ z$, where the list built by the inner *rev* is the intermediate data structure consumed by the outer *rev*. As far as we know, no general[3] existing deforestation method allows this composition to be transformed in a program that solely constructs the final list (x itself). Indeed, applying the previously presented three steps to this example leads to:

$$
\begin{array}{l}
\texttt{let}\ revrev\ x\ y\ z\ = \texttt{case}\ x\ \texttt{with}\\
\quad cons\ head\ tail \rightarrow\\
\qquad revrev\ tail\ (cons\ head\ y)\ z\\
\quad nil \rightarrow rev\ y\ z
\end{array}
$$

During the transformation process, the partial evaluation step has never been applied, so the intermediate list is still constructed in *revrev* function. The only

[2] This recursion scheme can be exploited very simply (syntactically) or more sophistically (using abstract categorial representations such as functors).

[3] This particular example could be deforested with a dedicated method [26] that cannot be applied, for instance, to *rev* (*flat* t l) h (cf. section 2).

difference with respect to the classical function composition is that the outer *rev* is now applied as soon as the inner inverted list is constructed (in y): instead of applying *rev* to the result of the first *rev* call, it is applied to the y accumulating parameter when it contains the whole inverted list.

The reason of this problem is that, since the deforestation methods are based on function and data-structure recursion schemes, they are only able to guide a deforestation process which is strongly tied to these fixed recursion schemes. Thus, they cannot detect nor treat *unfaithful* constructions in accumulating parameters. This approach could be viewed as not declarative enough.

On the opposite, a distinctive feature of attribute grammars is that they are fully declarative specifications [19]. They allow a uniform representation of all computations (as well results as parameters) by simple oriented equations. More precisely, they distinguish synthesized (bottom-up computed) and inherited (top-down computed) attributes. By this way, constructions computed in inherited attributes (those of accumulating parameters) become accessible by a deforestation process. Actually, since the operational semantics of an attribute grammar rests on the resolution of an oriented equation system,[4] the recursion scheme of the represented function is no more explicitly required.

Translating our example into attribute grammars, our deforestation method, namely the *symbolic composition*, produces a new attribute grammar that no more constructs the intermediate list. This attribute grammar could then be translated back, by well-known techniques (by the way of functional evaluators [21,15]) into the following function definitions:

$$\texttt{let}\ \mathit{revrev}\ x\ y\ z = \mathit{f2}\ x\ (\mathit{rev}\ y\ (\mathit{f1}\ x\ z))$$

$$(1)\quad \begin{array}{ll} \texttt{let}\ \mathit{f2}\ x\ t = \texttt{case}\ x\ \texttt{with} & \texttt{let}\ \mathit{f1}\ x\ z\ = \texttt{case}\ x\ \texttt{with} \\ \quad \mathit{cons\ head\ tail} \rightarrow & \quad \mathit{cons\ head\ tail} \rightarrow \\ \quad\quad \mathit{f2\ tail}\ t & \quad\quad \mathit{cons\ head}\ (\mathit{f1\ tail}\ z) \\ \quad \mathit{nil} \rightarrow t & \quad \mathit{nil} \rightarrow z \end{array}$$

The intermediate list has been completely discarded in these functions, even if a useless traversal (*f2*) of the tree remains. In fact, in the particular case of attribute grammars, a copy rule elimination could even discard this traversal [23].

The remainder of this article is structured as follows. First, section 2 presents syntactic notations, both for functional and attribute grammar languages. Next, section 3 describes a translation from functional programs into equivalent attribute grammars. Essentially, it transforms accumulating parameters into inherited attributes and breaks explicit recursions into oriented equation systems. Then, section 4 shows the basic principles of the symbolic composition, detailed on an illustrative running example. In conclusion, we discuss related works and we sketch future — and current — works related to a generalized formalization of this technique and its implementation.

[4] The equation system constituted by all attribute occurrence definitions.

2 Language Syntaxes and Notations

Rather than the confusing example *revrev* of introduction[5], we will illustrate our transformations by the deforestation example of the composition of *rev* with *flat*, where the function *flat* computes the list of the leaves of a given binary tree (cf. Fig. 1). The list constructed by *flat* before to be consumed by *rev* is then the intermediate data structure to be eliminated. This example constitutes a typical problem since, as far as we know, no known deforestation method is able to deal with. Nevertheless, this example represents the class of functions where the data-structure producer builds its result with an accumulating variable.

let *flat t l* = **case** *t* **with**
  node left right →
    flat left (*flat right l*)
  leaf n → *cons n l*

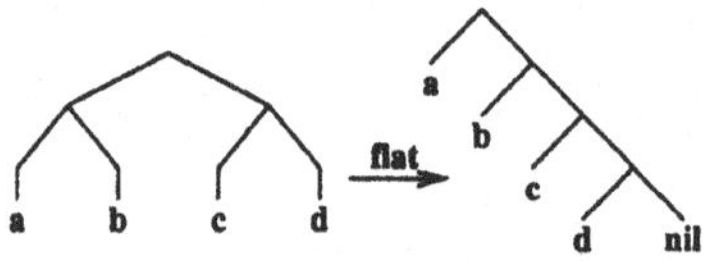

Fig. 1. Function definition for *flat*

To present the basic steps of our transformations in a simple and clear way, we deliberately restrict ourselves to a sub-class of first order functional programs with the syntax[6] presented in Fig. 2. Nested pattern-matching are not allowed, but are easy to split in several separated functions. Moreover, the statements *if-then-else* can be taken into account with *Dynamic Attribute Grammars* [22].

To bring our attribute grammar notation, presented in Fig. 3, closer to functional specifications, algebraic type definitions will be used instead of classical context free grammars [3,9,8]. This notation is not the classical one, but is a minimal form for explanatory purpose. Thus, a grammar production is represented as a data-type constructor followed by its parameter variables, that is, a pattern (for example: *cons head tail*).

[5] We prefer the *revflat* rather than the *revrev* example for explanatory purpose, because it involves two different functions and then avoids name confusions.

[6] Notation $\overline{x}$ stands for $x_1 \dots x_n$.

$$
\begin{array}{lll}
prog & ::= & \{def\}^+ \\
def & ::= & \texttt{let}\ f\ \overline{x} = exp \\
 & | & \texttt{let}\ f\ \overline{x} = \texttt{case}\ x_k\ \texttt{with}\ \{pat \rightarrow exp\}^+ \\
pat & ::= & \mathrm{c}\ \overline{x} \\
exp & ::= & Constant \\
 & | & x \in Variables \\
 & | & g\ \overline{exp} \quad \textit{Function or constructor call}
\end{array}
$$

Fig. 2. Functional language

$$
\begin{array}{lll}
\mathit{block} & ::= & \mathbf{aglet}\ f = \{f\ \overline{x} \rightarrow \overline{\mathit{semrule}}\}\{\mathit{pat} \rightarrow \overline{\mathit{semrule}}\}^{*} \\
\mathit{semrule} & ::= & \mathit{occ} = \mathit{exp} \\
\mathit{occ} & ::= & x.a \mid f.\mathit{result} \\
\mathit{exp} & ::= & \mathit{Constant} \\
 & \mid & y.b \in \mathit{Attribute\ occurrences} \\
 & \mid & x \in \mathit{Variables} \\
 & \mid & g\ \overline{\mathit{exp}} \quad \mathit{Attribute\ grammar\ or\ constructor\ call}
\end{array}
$$

Fig. 3. Attribute grammar notation

As previously said, a characteristic feature of attribute grammars is to distinguish two sorts of attributes: the *synthesized* ones are computed bottom-up over the structure and the *inherited* ones are computed top-down. Since our transformations will consider type-checked functional programs as input, this induces information about the generated attribute grammars. Thus, the sort and the type of attributes are directly deduced from the type-checked input program and could be implicit.

Furthermore, the notion of *attribute grammar profile* is introduced (in Fig. 3, $f\ \overline{x}$ is the profile of f). It represents how to call the attribute grammar and allows result and arguments to be specified.

The occurrence of an attribute a on a pattern variable x is noted $x.a$, even if this pattern variable is the constructor of the current pattern itself[7]. For instance, according to the syntax in Fig. 3, the function *rev* could be specified by the attribute grammar in Fig. 4. This figure contains also an intuitive illustration for the application *rev* (*cons a* (*cons b* (*cons c nil*))) *nil*.

With this notation, the name *rev* stands all at the same time for the attribute grammar, for the profile constructor and for a synthesized attribute. Variable x, the list to be reversed, is the pattern-matched argument and h is the parameter. The attribute *result* is the only synthesized of the profile. Variable x, and all

[7] In CFG terms, it plays the role of the left hand side (parent) of the production.

aglet *rev* =
  rev x h →
    rev.result = *x.rev*
    x.h = *h*
  cons head tail →
    cons.rev = *tail.rev*
    tail.h = *cons head cons.h*
  nil →
    nil.rev = *nil.h*

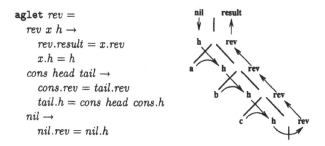

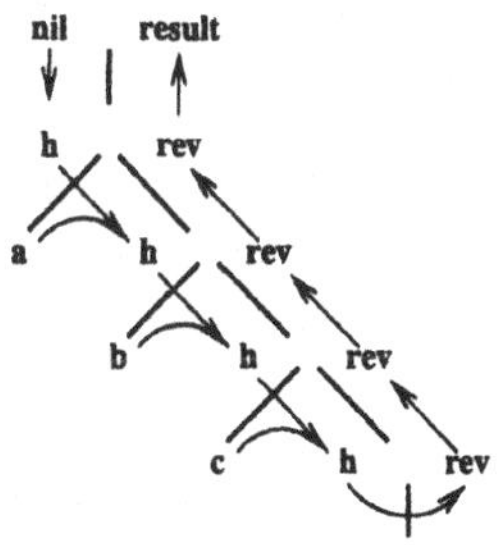

Fig. 4. Attribute grammar *rev*

pattern-matched (sub-)list, have two attributes: *rev* synthesized and *h* inherited. Each oriented equation defines an attribute for a given pattern variable.

3 Translation FP-to-AG

The intuitive idea of the translation FP-to-AG, from a functional program into its attribute grammar notation, is the following. Each functional term associated with a pattern has to be dismantled into a set of oriented equations, called *semantic rules*. Parameters in functional programs become explicit attributes attached to pattern variables, called attribute occurrences, that are defined by the semantic rules. Then, explicit recursive calls become implicit on the underlying data structure and semantic rules make the data-flow explicit. FP-to-AG is decomposed into a *preliminary transformation* and a *profile symbolic evaluation*.

These are notations used in further definitions and transformations.

$\stackrel{def}{=}$	: local definition in an algorithm
$x.a = exp$	: semantic rule defining $x.a$
$[x := y]$	: substitution of x by y
Σ	: a set of semantic rules
Π	: a pattern with its set of semantic rules
$\mathcal{C} \vdash A \Rightarrow B$	: transformation from A into B according to the context $\mathcal{C}$
$\mathcal{E}[e]$	: a term containing e as a sub-expression.

Preliminary Transformation The aim of the preliminary transformation, presented in Fig. 5, is to draw the general shape of the future attribute grammar. It introduces the attribute grammar profile, with its semantic rules, and a unique semantic rule per each constructor pattern.

The attribute *result* is defined as a synthesized attribute of the profile and it stands for the expected result of the function (rule *Let'*). For function with **case**-statement the result is computed through attributes on the pattern-matched variable (rule *Let*): one is synthesized, named by the function name itself, and each supplementary argument of the function profile yields a semantic rule defining an inherited attribute attached to the pattern-matched variable.

Each function call $(f\ \overline{a})$ is translated into a dotted notation $(f\ \overline{b}).result$ (rule *App*). This rule distinguishes between function and type constructor calls[8]. Thus, each expression appearing in a pattern is transformed into a single semantic rule which defines the synthesized attribute computing the result (rule *App*). This induces some renaming (rule *Pattern*).

The application of the preliminary transformation to the function *flat* (Fig. 1) leads to the result shown in Fig. 7.

Profile Symbolic Evaluation The result of the preliminary transformation is not yet a real attribute grammar. Each function definition in the initial program has been translated into one *block* (cf. Fig. 3) which contains the profile of the

[8] This distinction is performed from type information of the input functional program.

$$\frac{\forall i \quad \overset{exp}{\vdash} a_i \Rightarrow b_i \quad ; \quad f \textit{ is a function name}}{\overset{exp}{\vdash} (f\ \overline{a}) \Rightarrow (f\ \overline{b}).result} \quad (App)$$

$$\frac{\overset{exp}{\vdash} e \Rightarrow e'}{f, \{x_j\}_{j\neq k}, x_k \overset{pat}{\vdash} c\ \overline{y} \rightarrow e \Rightarrow c\ \overline{y} \rightarrow c.f = e'[x_k := c][x_j := c.x_j]_{\forall j \neq k}} \quad (Pattern)$$

$$\frac{\begin{array}{c}\forall i \quad f, \{x_j\}_{j\neq k}, x_k \overset{pat}{\vdash} p_i \rightarrow e_i \Rightarrow \Pi_i \\ \overline{\Pi} \overset{def}{=} \begin{pmatrix} f\ \overline{x} \rightarrow \\ \quad f.result = x_k.f \\ \quad x_k.x_j = x_j \quad (\forall j \neq k) \end{pmatrix} \cup \Pi_i \end{array}}{\overset{let}{\vdash} \mathtt{let}\ f\ \overline{x} = \mathtt{case}\ x_k\ \mathtt{with}\ \overline{p \rightarrow e} \Rightarrow \mathtt{aglet}\ f = \overline{\Pi}} \quad (Let)$$

$$\frac{\overset{exp}{\vdash} e \Rightarrow e'}{\overset{let}{\vdash} \mathtt{let}\ f\ \overline{x} = e \Rightarrow \mathtt{aglet}\ f = f\ \overline{x} \rightarrow f.result = e'} \quad (Let')$$

Constants and variables are left unchanged by the transformation.

$\overset{exp}{\vdash} e \Rightarrow e'$	means that the equation e is translated into equation e'.
$env \overset{pat}{\vdash} p \rightarrow e \Rightarrow p \rightarrow \mathcal{R}$	means that the expression associated with the pattern p is translated into the set of semantic rules $\mathcal{R}$, with respect to the environment *env*.
$\overset{let}{\vdash} \mathcal{D} \Rightarrow \mathcal{B}$	means that the function definition $\mathcal{D}$ is translated into the *block* $\mathcal{B}$.

Fig. 5. Preliminary transformation

$$\frac{\begin{pmatrix} f\ \overline{x} \rightarrow \\ \quad f.result = \varphi \\ \quad \Sigma_f \end{pmatrix} \in \mathcal{P} \qquad \begin{array}{l} \sigma \overset{def}{=} [x_i := a_i] \\ \Sigma \overset{def}{=} \begin{cases} u = \mathcal{E}[\sigma(\varphi)] \\ \sigma(\Sigma_f) \\ \Sigma_{aux} \end{cases} \end{array} \qquad Check_{PSE}(c, f, \Sigma)}{\mathcal{P} \vdash \begin{pmatrix} c\ \overline{y} \rightarrow \\ \quad u = \mathcal{E}[(f\ \overline{a}).result] \\ \quad \Sigma_{aux} \end{pmatrix} \Rightarrow \begin{pmatrix} c\ \overline{y} \rightarrow \\ \quad \Sigma \end{pmatrix}} \quad (PSE)$$

$\mathcal{P} \vdash p \rightarrow \Sigma_1 \Rightarrow p \rightarrow \Sigma_2$ means that in the program $\mathcal{P}$ the set of equations Σ_1 of a pattern p is transformed into Σ_2.

Fig. 6. Profile symbolic evaluation (*PSE*)

```
aglet flat =
  flat t l →
    flat.result = t.flat
    t.l = l
  node left right →
    node.flat = (flat left (flat right node.l).result).result
  leaf n →
    leaf.flat = cons n leaf.l
```

Fig. 7. The function *flat* after the preliminary transformation

function and its related patterns. But explicit recursive calls have been translated into the form $(f\ \overline{a}).result$. Now, these expressions have to be transformed into a set of semantic rules, breaking explicit recursions by attribute naming and attachment to pattern variables. Then, these semantic rules will implicitly define the recursion *à la* attribute grammar. This transformation is achieved by the profile symbolic evaluation (*PSE*) presented in Fig. 6.

Everywhere an expression $(f\ \overline{a}).result$ occurs, the profile symbolic evaluation projects the semantic rules of the attribute grammar profile f. The application of this transformation must be done with a depth-first application strategy. Nevertheless, the predicate $Check_{PSE}$ ensures that the resulting attribute grammar is well formed. Essentially, it verifies that each attribute is defined once and only once. Then, in the context of well-defined input functional programs, $Check_{PSE}$ forbids non-linear terms such as $g\ (f\ y\ 1)\ (f\ y\ 2)$. Moreover, in a first approach, terms like $(x.a).b$ are not allowed but they will be treated in section 4, to detect composition sites. Finally, $Check_{PSE}$ prevents cyclic treatments with the condition $c \neq f$ and all these conditions allow FP-to-AG to terminate.

$$\frac{\begin{array}{c}\text{In the pattern } c\ \overline{y} \rightarrow e \\ e \text{ is linear for each } y_i\end{array} \qquad \begin{array}{c}\text{No terms } (x.a).b \\ \text{occurs in } \Sigma\end{array} \qquad c \neq f}{Check_{PSE}(c, f, \Sigma)}$$

Wherever $Check_{PSE}(c, f, \Sigma)$ is not verified, the expression $(f\ \overline{a}).result$ is simply rewritten in the function call $(f\ a)$.

$$\frac{\begin{array}{l}\begin{pmatrix}\underline{flat\ t\ l} \rightarrow \\ \quad flat.result = t.flat \\ \quad t.l = l\end{pmatrix} \in \mathcal{P} \qquad \Sigma \stackrel{def}{=} \begin{cases} node.flat = (flat\ left\ right.flat).result \\ right.l = node.l \end{cases} \\ \sigma \stackrel{def}{=} [t := right][l := node.l] \qquad\qquad\qquad Check_{PSE}(node, flat, \Sigma)\end{array}}{flat \vdash \begin{array}{l} node\ left\ right \rightarrow node.flat = (flat\ left\ (\underline{flat}\ right\ node.l).\underline{result}).result \\ \quad \Rightarrow node\ left\ right \rightarrow \Sigma\end{array}}$$

Fig. 8. Example of *PSE* application for the pattern *node left right*

```
aglet flat =
  flat t l →
    flat.result = t.flat
    t.l = l
  node left right →
    node.flat = left.flat
    left.l = right.flat
    right.l = node.l
  leaf n →
    leaf.flat = cons n leaf.l
```

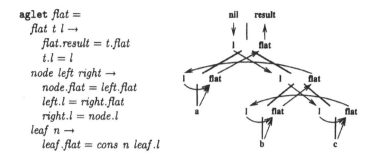

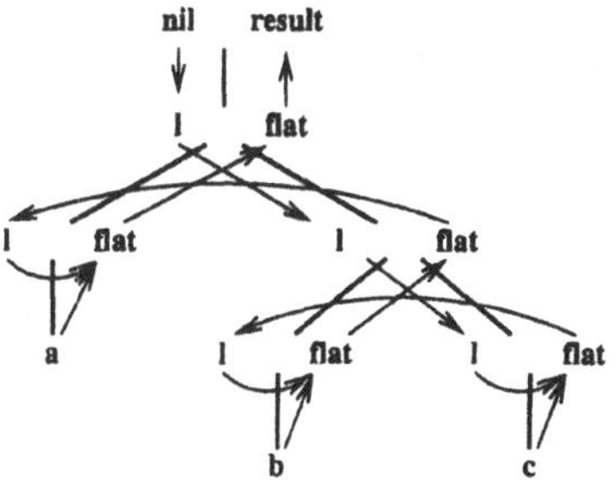

Fig. 9. Attribute grammar produced by FP-to-AG from function *flat*

The application[9] of the profile symbolic evaluation on the semantic rule for the *leaf* pattern is presented in Fig. 8. Finally, complete applications of the profile symbolic evaluation for the function *flat* leads to the well-formed attribute grammar given in Fig. 9. This figure gives also an illustrative example of *flat* application on the tree *node* (*leaf a*) (*node* (*leaf b*) (*leaf c*)).

The same algorithm applied to the function *rev* (given in introduction) yields the attribute grammar in Fig. 4. Then, the successive application of preliminary transformation and profile symbolic evaluation to an input functional program leads to a real attribute grammar. This is the translation FP-to-AG.

The cost of the preliminary transformation is linear with respect to the depth of input functional terms. Each function definition yields a profile block, with one semantic rule per each argument of the function. Furthermore, for each initial pattern case, a semantic rule defines an attribute occurrence that represents the value of the function in this case. These equations contain function calls that will be dismantled by the profile symbolic evaluation. The required number of application of this step is proportional to the number of recursive calls it contains. In this sense, the cost of FP-to-AG linearly depends on the size and the depth of the input functional program terms.

4 Symbolic Composition

It is now possible to apply attribute grammar deforestation methods to functional programs translated by FP-to-AG. Our technique, the symbolic composition, is based on the classical descriptional composition of two attribute grammars due to Ganzinger and Giegerich [10], but extends its application conditions and exploits the particular context stemming from translated functional programs. In order to describe our symbolic composition, we first present a natural extension of profile symbolic evaluation which is useful in the application of the symbolic composition.

[9] Underlined terms show where the rule is being applied.

$$\frac{\begin{pmatrix} f\ \overline{x} \rightarrow \\ \quad f.w = \varphi \\ \quad \Sigma_f \end{pmatrix} \in \mathcal{P} \qquad \begin{array}{l} \sigma \stackrel{def}{=} [x_i := a_i][f.h := \varphi_h] \\ \Sigma \stackrel{def}{=} \begin{cases} u = \mathcal{E}[\sigma(\varphi)] \\ \sigma(\Sigma_f) \\ \Sigma_{aux} \end{cases} \end{array} \qquad Check(c, f, \Sigma)}{\mathcal{P} \vdash \begin{pmatrix} c\ \overline{y} \rightarrow \\ \quad u = \mathcal{E}[(f\ \overline{a}).w] \\ \quad (f\ \overline{a}).h = \varphi_h \\ \quad \Sigma_{aux} \end{pmatrix} \Rightarrow \begin{pmatrix} c\ \overline{y} \rightarrow \\ \quad \Sigma \end{pmatrix}} \quad (SE)$$

Fig. 10. Symbolic Evaluation

It is important to note here that even if the final results of symbolic composition are attribute grammars, the objects that will be manipulated by intermediate transformations are more *blocks* of attribute grammars rather than complete attribute grammars. Furthermore, the expressions of the form $(x.a).b$, previously avoided (cf. predicate $Check_{PSE}$ in *PSE*), will be temporarily authorized by a similar *Check* predicate in the symbolic composition process.

Symbolic Evaluation Profile symbolic evaluation (*PSE*) can be generalized into a new symbolic evaluation (*SE*), presented in Fig. 10. This later performs both profile symbolic evaluation and partial evaluation on finite terms. The idea of this transformation is to recursively project semantic rules on finite terms and to eliminate intermediate attribute occurrences that are defined and used in the produced semantic rules.

Indeed, rather than only project terms of the profile (function name) as in *PSE*, that is, on expressions $(f\ \overline{a}).result$, the symbolic evaluation *SE* will project terms related to each expression $(f\ \overline{a}).w$, were f stands as well for a type constructor as for an attribute grammar profile. Since these expressions could be coupled with inherited attribute occurrence definitions like $(f\ \overline{a}).h = \varphi_h$, corresponding to parameters of the function represented by w, these definitions must also be taken into account by the transformation.

To illustrate the use of symbolic evaluation as partial evaluation, consider the term `let` $g\ z = rev\ (cons\ a\ (cons\ b\ nil))\ z$. Applying FP-to-AG to this term yields the following attribute grammar profile:

aglet $g\ z \rightarrow$
$\quad g.result = (cons\ a\ (cons\ b\ nil)).rev$
$\quad (cons\ a\ (cons\ b\ nil)).h = z$

Then, the symbolic evaluation (Fig. 10) could be applied on these terms. The first step of this application is presented in Fig. 11. Two other steps of this transformation lead to $g.result = (cons\ b\ (cons\ a\ z))$.

So, symbolic evaluation performs *partial evaluation* on finite terms.

$$\frac{\begin{pmatrix} cons\ head\ tail \rightarrow \\ \quad cons.rev = tail.rev \\ \quad tail.h = cons\ head\ cons.h \end{pmatrix} \in \mathcal{P} \quad \begin{array}{l} \sigma = [head := a][tail := cons\ b\ nil][cons.h := z] \\ \Sigma = \left\{ \begin{array}{l} g.result = (cons\ b\ nil).rev \\ (cons\ b\ nil).h = cons\ a\ z \end{array} \right. \\ Check(g, cons, \Sigma) \end{array}}{\mathcal{P} \vdash\ g\ z \rightarrow \left\{ \begin{array}{l} g.result = (cons\ a\ (cons\ b\ nil)).rev \\ (cons\ a\ (cons\ b\ nil)).h = z \end{array} \right\} \Rightarrow g\ z \rightarrow \Sigma}$$

Fig. 11. Example of *SE* application for *rev* (*cons a* (*cons b nil*)) *z*

This generalization of the profile symbolic evaluation, into the symbolic evaluation used as a partial evaluation mechanism, implies that the complexity of this transformation directly relies on those of the treated terms. Practically, the number of symbolic evaluation applications must be arbitrary limited in order to prevent infinite loop, for instance in partial evaluation of an infinite list reversal. Nevertheless, at any stage of this process, a part of the computation has been symbolically performed.

Composition Getting back to our running example, consider the definition of the function *revflat* which flattens a tree and then reverses the obtained list.

$$\texttt{let}\ revflat\ t\ l\ h = rev\ (flat\ t\ l)\ h$$

Intuitively, in the context of attribute grammar notation, this composition involves the two sets of attributes $Att_{flat} = \{flat\ ,\ l\}$ and $Att_{rev} = \{rev\ ,\ h\}$.

More generally, consider an attribute grammar $\mathcal{F}$ (e.g., *flat*), producing an intermediate data structure to be consumed by another attribute grammar $\mathcal{G}$ (e.g., *rev*). Two sets of attributes are involved in this composition. The first one, $Att_{\mathcal{F}}$, contains all the attributes used to construct the intermediate data-structure. The second one, $Att_{\mathcal{G}}$, contains the attributes of $\mathcal{G}$.

As in the descriptional composition of classical attribute grammars [10], the idea of the symbolic composition is to project the attributes of $Att_{\mathcal{G}}$ (e.g., Att_{rev}) everywhere an attribute of $Att_{\mathcal{F}}$ (e.g., Att_{flat}) is defined. This global operation brings the equations that specify a computation over the intermediate data-structure on its construction. The basic step of this projection (*Proj*) is presented in Fig. 12. Then, the application of the symbolic evaluation will eliminate the useless constructors.

From the complexity point of view, the projection step is essentially similar to the classical descriptional composition [10], that is, quadratic: the composition of two attribute grammars, respectively using n and m attributes, leads to $m * n$ attributes in the resulting attribute grammar, with as much semantic rules.

However, a point remains undefined: how to find the application sites for the projection steps *Proj*? As attended, the predicate $Check_{PSE}$ is temporarily relaxed in *Check*, authorizing expressions like $(x.a).b$. In fact, all these expressions are precisely the sites where deforestation could be performed (e.g., $(t.flat).rev$).

With this relaxed predicate *Check* and from the definition of the function *revflat*, we obtained the blocks presented in Fig. 13 (first is for the *revflat* profile, and others correspond to attribute grammars *flat* and *rev*). In the blocks building the intermediate data structure, potential application sites for the projection step *Proj* are underlined, and a $*$ highlights the construction to be deforested.

Fig. 14 shows the projection step for the pattern *leaf* and all applications of this steps yield the blocks in the left part of Fig. 15.

Now, symbolic evaluation could be tried on annotated sites, performing the real deforestation. The first annotated site is not a potential site for the symbolic evaluation application, since l is neither an attribute grammar (profile) call nor a type pattern constructor. In this case, as wherever *Check* is not verified, the computational context is reintroduced in the form of an attribute grammar (function) call ($rev\ l\ (t.l).h$). This functional call retrieval, together with linearity and distinct pattern ($c \neq f$) conditions of the *Check* predicate avoid infinite unfolding and ensure termination of the process (with the arbitrary limit for symbolic evaluation application mentioned in the partial evaluation discussion).

On the other hand, a symbolic evaluation step is successfully applied on the second annotated site, actually eliminating a *cons* construction. Finally, new attributes are created by renaming attributes $a.b$ into a_b (when $a \in Att_{\mathcal{F}}$ and $b \in Att_{\mathcal{G}}$). More precisely, $(x.a).b$ is transformed into $x.a\_b$.

Then, the basic constituents of the symbolic composition are defined:

$$\textit{Symbolic Composition} = \textit{renaming} \circ (\textit{SE}) \circ (\textit{Proj})$$

Thus, for the function *revflat*, the symbolic composition leads to the deforested attribute grammar presented in the right part of Fig. 15, where four attributes have been generated. Producing a functional evaluator for this attribute grammar yields the functions[10] *revflat*, *f1* and *f2* presented in Fig. 16.

The function *f1*, corresponding to attributes *l_h* (its result) and *flat_h* (its argument), performs the construction of a list. The function *f2*, corresponding to

[10] Functions *f1* and *f2* respectively correspond to the traversal (*passes*) determined by the attribute grammar evaluator generator.

$$\frac{a \in Att_{\mathcal{F}} \quad \overline{s} = Att\_S_{\mathcal{G}} \quad \overline{h} = Att\_H_{\mathcal{G}}}{Att_{\mathcal{G}}, Att_{\mathcal{F}} \vdash x.a = e \Rightarrow \begin{cases} (x.a).s = (e).s & \forall s \in \overline{s} \\ (e).h = (x.a).h & \forall h \in \overline{h} \end{cases}} \quad (Proj)$$

$Att_{\mathcal{G}}, Att_{\mathcal{F}} \vdash eq \Rightarrow \Sigma$ means that, while considering $\mathcal{G} \circ \mathcal{F}$, the equation eq is transformed into the set of equations Σ.

$Att\_S_{\mathcal{G}}$	is the set of synthesized attributes of $Att_{\mathcal{G}}$.
$Att\_H_{\mathcal{G}}$	is the set of inherited attributes of $Att_{\mathcal{G}}$.

Fig. 12. Projection step

$$
\begin{array}{l}
\mathit{revflat}\ t\ l\ h \rightarrow \\
\quad \mathit{revflat.result} = (t.\mathit{flat}).\mathit{rev} \\
\quad (t.\mathit{flat}).h = h \\
\quad \underline{t.l = l}
\end{array}
$$

$$
\begin{array}{ll}
\mathit{node}\ \mathit{left}\ \mathit{right} \rightarrow & \mathit{cons}\ \mathit{head}\ \mathit{tail} \rightarrow \\
\quad \underline{\mathit{node.flat} = \mathit{left.flat}} & \quad \mathit{cons.rev} = \mathit{tail.rev} \\
\quad \underline{\mathit{left}.l = \mathit{right.flat}} & \quad \mathit{tail}.h = \mathit{cons}\ \mathit{head}\ \mathit{cons}.h \\
\quad \underline{\mathit{right}.l = \mathit{node}.l} & \mathit{nil} \rightarrow \\
\mathit{leaf}\ n \rightarrow & \quad \mathit{nil.rev} = \mathit{nil}.h \\
\quad \underline{\mathit{leaf.flat} = \mathit{cons}\ n\ \mathit{leaf}.l} \quad * &
\end{array}
$$

Fig. 13. Blocks for *revflat* before projection steps

$$
\frac{\mathit{flat} \in \mathit{Att}_{\mathit{flat}} \qquad \begin{array}{l}\overline{s} = \mathit{Att\_S}_{\mathit{rev}} = \{\mathit{rev}\} \\ \overline{h} = \mathit{Att\_H}_{\mathit{rev}} = \{h\}\end{array}}{\mathit{Att}_{\mathit{rev}}, \mathit{Att}_{\mathit{flat}} \vdash \mathit{leaf.flat} = \mathit{cons}\ n\ \mathit{leaf}.l \Rightarrow \left\{\begin{array}{l}(\mathit{leaf.flat}).\mathit{rev} = (\mathit{cons}\ n\ \mathit{leaf}.l).\mathit{rev} \\ (\mathit{cons}\ n\ \mathit{leaf}.l).h = (\mathit{leaf.flat}).h\end{array}\right.}
$$

Fig. 14. Example of *Proj* application for the pattern *leaf n*

attributes *flat_rev* (its result) and *l_rev* (its argument), only propagates its argument along the tree. Then, the second parameter in the call *f2 t* (*rev l* (*f1 t h*)) corresponds to the semantic rule $t.l\_rev = (rev\ l\ t.l\_h)$ in the profile of the attribute grammar. Indeed, since $t.l\_h$ stands for the call (*f1 t h*) and since $t.l\_rev$ corresponds to the second argument of *f2*, the later stands for *rev l* (*f1 t h*).

The intermediate list is *no more constructed* and *revflat* is deforested. This achieves the presentation of our declarative deforestation methods on this typical example. Of course, this technique works equally well for simpler functions, without intermediate construction in accumulating parameters.

5 Conclusion

This paper shows that a fully declarative approach of program transformation could resolve a tenacious problem of deforestation: to deforest in accumulating parameters. The symbolic composition presented in this paper comes from a large comparison of deforestation techniques [8] and from the establishment that fixed recursion schemes, provided by data type specifications, are not flexible enough to catch all intermediate data structure constructions in function compositions. Several approaches attempted to abstract these recursion schemes in order to refine their manipulation, for instance by categorial representation [28,13]. We were first surprised that these elaborate methods do not succeed in deforestations performed in the context of attribute grammar transformations. But two points differentiate them. First, attribute grammars are using

```
revflat t l h →
   revflat.result = (t.flat).rev
   (t.flat).h = h
   (t.l).rev = (l).rev    } l is neither a function
   (l).h = (t.l).h        } nor a constructor call
node left right →
   (node.flat).rev = (left.flat).rev
   (left.flat).h = (node.flat).h
   (left.l).rev = (right.flat).rev
   (right.flat).h = (left.l).h
   (right.l).rev = (node.l).rev
   (node.l).h = (right.l).h
leaf n →
   (leaf.flat).rev = (cons n leaf.l).rev   } SE site
   (cons n leaf.l).h = (leaf.flat).h       }
```

```
aglet revflat =
  revflat t l h →
    revflat.result = t.flat_rev
    t.flat_h = h
    t.l_rev = (rev l t.l_h)
  node left right →
    node.flat_rev = left.flat_rev
    left.flat_h = node.flat_h
    left.l_rev = right.flat_rev
    right.flat_h = left.l_h
    right.l_rev = node.l_rev
    node.l_h = right.l_h
  leaf n →
    leaf.flat_rev = leaf.l_rev
    leaf.l_h = cons n leaf.flat_h
```

Fig. 15. Attribute grammar *revflat* before and after symbolic evaluation and renaming

```
let revflat t l h = f2 t (rev l (f1 t h))
let f1 t h = case t with          let f2 t l = case t with
  node left right →                 node left right →
    f1 right (f1 left h)              f2 left (f2 right l)
  leaf n → cons n h                 leaf n → l
```

Fig. 16. Functions corresponding to the deforested attribute grammar *revflat*

fully declarative specifications, independently of any evaluation method, thanks to an operational semantics based on equation systems and dependencies resolution. Next, this declarative approach led them to use inherited attributes instead of supplementary arguments in order to specify top-down propagations or computations; this allows all computations — particularly intermediate data structure constructions — to be uniformly specified, and then, uniformly treated by transformations. This reinforces our conviction that the declarative formalism of attribute grammars is simple and appropriate for this kind of transformations.

Moreover, symbolic composition extends the descriptional composition: first, it could now be used as a partial evaluation mechanism and next, it could be applied to terms with function compositions, and not only to a sole composition of two distinct attribute grammars (attribute coupled grammars [10]) that are isolated of all context. For the attribute grammars community, this stands as the main contribution of this paper.

Nevertheless, as we wanted the presentation in this paper to be intuitive and convincing, accepted programs were limited by attribute grammar restrictions. For instance, non-linear terms, forbidden by the *Check* predicates, or higher order specifications are not addressed in this presentation for technical reasons due to the attribute grammar formalism. We now have formalized a complete system that includes and extends both symbolic composition and the declarative essence of attribute grammar formalism. *Equational semantics*, fully detailed in [7], is able to encode an abstract representation of the operational semantics of a program. It supports simple transformations that could be combined into more complex ones. Its prototype implementation, EQS, is available and performs deforestation and partial evaluation (at `http://www-rocq.inria.fr/~correnso/agdoc/index.html`). Coupled with a FP-to-EQS translation, similar to FP-to-AG, EQS is able to deforest higher order functional programs, even authorizing some non-linear terms. Since EQS formalization is highly theoretical and language independent, the method and the transformation pipeline we have presented in this paper could be viewed as an intuitive presentation of these current — and future — works.

Finally, these works are involved in a more general study addressing genericity and reusability problems. The goal is to provide a set of high level transformational tools, able to abstract a given program and then to specialize it for several distinct contexts. We have compared [6] some attribute grammars tools [17,24,23,5] with similar approaches in different programming paradigms (*polytypic* programming [14], *adaptive* programming [20]). Again, it appears in this context that declarative aspects of attribute grammars bring them particularly suitable for program transformations and that they should be viewed more as an abstract representation of a specification than as a programming language.

References

1. R. M. Burstall and J. Darlington. A transformation system for developing recursive programs. *Journal of the ACM*, 24(1):44–67, January 1977.
2. W. N. Chin and S. C. Khoo. Better consumers for deforestation. In *Prog. Lang.: Impl., Logic and Programs (PLILP'95)*, LNCS # 982, Springer-Verlag, 1995.
3. L. M. Chirica and D. F. Martin. An order-algebraic definition of Knuthian semantics. *Mathematical Systems Theory*, 13(1):1–27, 1979.
4. C. Consel. Program adaptation based on program specialization. In *Workshop on Partial Evaluation and Semantics-Based Program Manipulation. PEPM'99*, San Antonio, Texas, January 1999. ACM press.
5. L. Correnson. Généricité dans les grammaires attribuées. Rapport de stage d'option, École Polytechnique, 1996.
6. L. Correnson, E. Duris, D. Parigot, and G. Roussel. Generic programming by program composition (position paper). In *Workshop on Generic Programming (WGP'98)*, Marstrand, Sweden, June 1998.
7. L. Correnson, E. Duris, D. Parigot and G. Roussel. Equational Semantics. In *International Static Anaysis Symposium*, Veneszia, Italy, September 1999.
8. E. Duris. *Contribution aux relations entre les grammaires attribuées et la programmation fonctionnelle.* PhD thesis, Université d'Orléans, October 1998.
9. H. Ganzinger, R. Giegerich, and M. Vach. MARVIN: a tool for applicative and modular compiler specifications. Forschungsbericht 220, Fachbereich Informatik, University Dortmund, July 1986.

10. R. Giegerich. Composition and evaluation of attribute coupled grammars. *Acta Informatica*, 25:355–423, 1988.
11. A. Gill, J. Launchbury, and S. L. Peyton Jones. A short cut to deforestation. In *Functional Programming and Computer Architecture (FPCA'93)*, Copenhagen, Denmark, June 1993. ACM Press.
12. G. W. Hamilton. Higher order deforestation. In *Prog. Lang.: Impl., Logics and Programs (PLILP'96)*, LNCS # 1140, Aachen, September 1996. Springer-Verlag.
13. Z. Hu, H. Iwasaki, and M. Takeishi. Deriving structural hylomorphisms from recursive definitions. In *International Conference on Functional Programming (ICFP'96)*, Philadelphia, May 1996. ACM Press.
14. P. Jansson and J. Jeuring. PolyP - a polytypic programming language extension. In *Principles of Programming Languages (POPL'97)*, January 1997. ACM Press.
15. T. Johnsson. Attribute grammars as a functional programming paradigm. In *Functional Programming and Computer Architecture (FPCA'87)*, LNCS # 274, Portland, September 1987. Springer-Verlag.
16. J. Launchbury and T. Sheard. Warm fusion: Deriving build-cata's from recursive definitions. In *Functional Programming Languages and Computer Architecture (FPCA'95)*, La Jolla, CA, 1995. ACM Press.
17. C. Le Bellec, M. Jourdan, D. Parigot, and G. Roussel. Specification and Implementation of Grammar Coupling Using Attribute Grammars. In *Prog. Lang.: Impl., Logic and Programs (PLILP '93)*, LNCS # 714, Tallinn, August 1993. Springer-Verlag.
18. E. Meijer, M. M. Fokkinga, and R. Paterson. Functional programming with bananas, lenses, envelopes and barbed wire. In *Functional Programming and Computer Architecture (FPCA'91)*, LNCS # 523, Cambridge, September 1991. Springer-Verlag.
19. J. Paakki. Attribute grammar paradigms — A high-level methodology in language implementation. *ACM Computing Surveys*, 27(2):196–255, June 1995.
20. J. Palsberg, B. Patt-Shamir, and K. Lieberherr. A new approach to compiling adaptive programs. In *European Symposium on Programming (ESOP'96)*, Linkoping, Sweden, 1996. Springer Verlag.
21. D. Parigot, E. Duris, G. Roussel, and M. Jourdan. Attribute grammars: a declarative functional language. Research Report 2662, INRIA, October 1995.
22. D. Parigot, G. Roussel, M. Jourdan, and E. Duris. Dynamic Attribute Grammars. In *Prog. Lang.: Impl., Logics and Programs (PLILP'96)*, LNCS # 1140, Aachen, September 1996. Springer-Verlag.
23. G. Roussel. *Algorithmes de base pour la modularité et la réutilisabilité des grammaires attribuées*. PhD thesis, Université de Paris 6, March 1994.
24. G. Roussel, D. Parigot, and M. Jourdan. Coupling Evaluators for Attribute Coupled Grammars. In *Compiler Construction (CC' 94)*, LNCS # 786, Edinburgh, April 1994. Springer-Verlag.
25. H. Seidl and M. H. Sørensen. Constraints to stop deforestation. *Science of Computer Programming*, 32(1-3):73-107, September 1998.
26. T. Sheard and L. Fegaras. A fold for all seasons. In *Functional Programming and Computer Architecture (FPCA'93)*, Copenhagen, Denmark, June 1993. ACM Press.
27. M. H. Sørensen, R. Glück, and N. D. Jones. Towards unifying deforestation, supercompilation, partial evaluation, and generalized partial computation. In *European Symposium on Programming (ESOP'94)*, LNCS # 788, Springer-Verlag, 1994.

28. A. Takano and E. Meijer. Shortcut deforestation in calculational form. In *Functional Programming Languages and Computer Architecture (FPCA'95)*, La Jolla, CA, 1995. ACM Press.
29. P. Wadler. Deforestation: Transforming Programs to Eliminate Trees. In *European Symposium on Programming (ESOP '88)*, LNCS # 300, Nancy, March 1988. Springer-Verlag.

A Semantic Account of Type-Directed Partial Evaluation

Andrzej Filinski *

BRICS – Basic Research in Computer Science –
Centre of the Danish National Research Foundation,
Dept. of Computer Science, University of Aarhus, Denmark
andrzej@brics.dk
www.brics.dk

Abstract. We formally characterize partial evaluation of functional programs as a normalization problem in an equational theory, and derive a type-based normalization-by-evaluation algorithm for computing normal forms in this setting. We then establish the correctness of this algorithm using a semantic argument based on Kripke logical relations. For simplicity, the results are stated for a non-strict, purely functional language; but the methods are directly applicable to stating and proving correctness of type-directed partial evaluation in ML-like languages as well.

1 Introduction

The goal of partial evaluation (PE) is as follows: given a program $\vdash p : S \times D \to R$ of two arguments, and a fixed "static" argument $s : S$, produce a *specialized* program $\vdash p_s : D \to R$ such that for all "dynamic" $d : D$, $\mathit{Eval}(p_s d) = \mathit{Eval}(p\,(s, d))$. That is, running the specialized program on the dynamic argument is equivalent to running the original program on both the static and the dynamic one.

In a functional language, it is of course trivial to come up with such a p_s: just take $p_s = \lambda d.\, p\,(s, d)$. That is, the specialized program simply invokes the original program with a constant first argument. But such a p_s is likely to be suboptimal: the knowledge of s may already allow us to perform some simplifications that are independent of d. For example, consider the power function:

$$\mathit{power}\,(n, x) \overset{\text{rec}}{=} \textbf{if } n = 0 \textbf{ then } 1 \textbf{ else } x \times \mathit{power}(n-1, x)$$

Suppose we want to compute the third power of several numbers. We can achieve this using the trivially specialized program:

$$\mathit{power}_3 = \lambda x.\, \mathit{power}(3, x)$$

But using a few simple rules derived from the semantics of the language, we can safely transform power_3 to the much more efficient

$$\mathit{power}_3' = \lambda x.\, x \times (x \times (x \times 1))$$

* Part of this work was carried out at the Laboratory for Foundations of Computer Science, University of Edinburgh, supported by a EuroFOCS research fellowship.

G. Nadathur (Ed.): PPDP'99, LNCS 1702, pp. 378–395, 1999.

Using further arithmetic identities, we can also easily eliminate the multiplication by 1. On the other hand, if only the argument x were known, we could not simplify much: the specialized program would in general still need to contain a recursive definition and a conditional test – in addition to the multiplication. (Note that, even when x is 0 or 1, the function as defined should still diverge for negative values of n.)

To facilitate automation of the task, partial evaluation is often expressed as a two-phase process, usually referred to as *off-line* PE [14]:

1. A *binding-time annotation* phase, which identifies all the operations that can be performed using just the static input. This can be done either mechanically by a *binding-time analysis* (often based on abstract interpretation), or – if the intended usage of the program is clear and the annotations are sufficiently intuitive and non-intrusive – as part of the original program.
2. A *specialization* phase, which takes the annotated program and the static input, and produces a simplified p_s, in which all the operations marked as static have been eliminated.

The annotations must of course be consistent, i.e., a subcomputation in the program cannot be classified as static if its result can not necessarily be found from only the static input. But they may be conservative by classifying some computations as dynamic even if they could in fact be performed at specialization time. Techniques for accurate binding-time analysis have been studied extensively [14]. In the following we will therefore limit our attention to the second phase, i.e., to efficiently specializing programs that are already binding-time separated.

A particularly simple way of phrasing specialization is as a general-purpose simplification of the trivially specialized program $\lambda d.p(s,d)$: contracting β-redexes and eliminating static operations as their inputs become known. What makes this approach attractive is the technique of "reduction-free normalization" or "normalization by evaluation", already known from logic and category theory [2,3,7]. A few challenges arise, however, with extending these results to a programming-language setting. Most notably:

- *Interpreted* base types and their associated static operations. These need to be properly accounted for, in addition to the β-reduction.
- Unrestricted recursion. This prevents a direct application of the usual strong-normalization results. That is, not every well-typed term even has a normal form; and not every reduction strategy will find it when it does exist.
- Call-by-value languages, and effects other than non-termination. In such a setting, the usual $\beta\eta$-conversions are actually unsound: unrestricted rearrangement of side effects may completely change the meaning of a program.

We will treat the first two concerns in detail. The call-by-value case uses the same principles, but for space reasons we will only briefly outline the necessary changes.

The paper is organized as follows: Section 2 introduces our programming language, the notion of a binding-time separated signature, and our desiderata for a partial evaluator; Section 3 presents the type-directed partial evaluation algorithm; and Section 4 shows its correctness with respect to the criteria in Section 2. Finally, Section 5 presents a few variations and extensions, and Section 6 concludes and outlines directions for further research.

2 A Small Language

2.1 The Framework and One-Level Language

Our prototypical functional language has the following syntax of types and terms:

$$\sigma ::= b \mid \sigma_1 \to \sigma_2$$
$$E ::= l \mid c_{\sigma_1,\ldots,\sigma_n} \mid x \mid \lambda x^{\sigma}.E \mid E_1\,E_2$$

Here b ranges over a set of base types listed in some signature Σ, l over a set $\Xi(b)$ of literals (numerals, truth values, etc.) for each base type b, and c over a set of (possibly polymorphic) function constants in Σ. Adding finite-product types would be completely straightforward throughout the paper, but we omit this extension for conciseness.

A typing context Γ is a finite mapping of variable names to well-formed types over Σ. The typing rules for terms are then standard:

$$\frac{l \in \Xi(b)}{\Gamma \vdash_{\Sigma} l : b} \qquad \frac{\Sigma(c_{\sigma_1,\ldots,\sigma_n}) = \sigma}{\Gamma \vdash_{\Sigma} c_{\sigma_1,\ldots,\sigma_n} : \sigma} \qquad \frac{\Gamma(x) = \sigma}{\Gamma \vdash_{\Sigma} x : \sigma}$$

$$\frac{\Gamma, x{:}\,\sigma_1 \vdash_{\Sigma} E : \sigma_2}{\Gamma \vdash_{\Sigma} \lambda x^{\sigma_1}.E : \sigma_1 \to \sigma_2} \qquad \frac{\Gamma \vdash_{\Sigma} E_1 : \sigma_1 \to \sigma_2 \qquad \Gamma \vdash_{\Sigma} E_2 : \sigma_1}{\Gamma \vdash_{\Sigma} E_1\,E_2 : \sigma_2}$$

An *interpretation* of a signature Σ is a triple $\mathcal{I} = (\mathcal{B}, \mathcal{L}, \mathcal{C})$. $\mathcal{B}$ maps every base type b in Σ to a predomain (i.e., a bottomless cpo, usually discretely ordered). Then we can interpret every type phrase σ over Σ as a domain (pointed cpo):

$$[\![b]\!]^{\mathcal{B}} = \mathcal{B}(b)_{\perp}$$
$$[\![\sigma_1 \to \sigma_2]\!]^{\mathcal{B}} = [\![\sigma_1]\!]^{\mathcal{B}} \to [\![\sigma_2]\!]^{\mathcal{B}}$$

where the interpretation of an arrow type is the full continuous function space. We also define the meaning of a typing assignment Γ as a labelled product of the domains interpreting the types of individual variables,

$$[\![\Gamma]\!]^{\mathcal{B}} = \prod\nolimits_{x \in \mathsf{dom}\,\Gamma} [\![\Gamma(x)]\!]^{\mathcal{B}}.$$

Further, for any base type b and literal $l \in \Xi(b)$, the interpretation must specify an element $\mathcal{L}_b(l) \in \mathcal{B}(b)$; and for every type instance of a polymorphic constant, an element $\mathcal{C}(c_{\sigma_1,\ldots,\sigma_n}) \in [\![\Sigma(c_{\sigma_1,\ldots,\sigma_n})]\!]^{\mathcal{B}}$. Then we interpret a well-typed term $\Gamma \vdash_{\Sigma} E : \sigma$ as a (total) continuous function $[\![E]\!]^{\mathcal{I}} : [\![\Gamma]\!]^{\mathcal{B}} \to [\![\sigma]\!]^{\mathcal{B}}$,

$$
\begin{aligned}
[\![l]\!]^{\mathcal{I}}\rho &= \mathbf{val}^{\perp}\,\mathcal{L}_b(l)\\
[\![c_{\sigma_1,\ldots,\sigma_n}]\!]^{\mathcal{I}}\rho &= \mathcal{C}(c_{\sigma_1,\ldots,\sigma_n})\\
[\![x]\!]^{\mathcal{I}}\rho &= \rho x\\
[\![\lambda x^{\sigma}.E]\!]^{\mathcal{I}}\rho &= \lambda a^{[\![\sigma]\!]^{\mathcal{B}}}.[\![E]\!]^{\mathcal{I}}(\rho[x\mapsto a])\\
[\![E_1\,E_2]\!]^{\mathcal{I}}\rho &= [\![E_1]\!]^{\mathcal{I}}\rho([\![E_2]\!]^{\mathcal{I}}\rho)
\end{aligned}
$$

(We use the following notation: $\mathbf{val}^{\perp}\,x$ and $\mathbf{let}^{\perp}\;y \Leftarrow x\;\mathbf{in}\;f\,y$ are lifting-injection and the strict extension of f, respectively; $b \to x \,[\!]\, y$ chooses between x and y based on the truth value b.)

When $\vdash_{\Sigma} E : b$ is a closed term of base type, we define the partial function $Eval_{\mathcal{I}}$ by $Eval_{\mathcal{I}}(E) = n$ if $[\![E]\!]^{\mathcal{I}}\emptyset = \mathbf{val}^{\perp}\,n$ and undefined otherwise.

Definition 1 (standard static language). *We define a simple functional language (essentially PCF [17]) by taking the signature Σ_{s} as follows. The base types are* int *and* bool*; the literals, $\Xi(\mathsf{int}) = \{\ldots,\text{-}1,0,1,2,\ldots\}$ and $\Xi(\mathsf{bool}) = \{\mathsf{true},\mathsf{false}\}$; and the constants,*

$$
\begin{aligned}
+,-,\times &: \mathsf{int}\to\mathsf{int}\to\mathsf{int} & \qquad \mathsf{if}_{\sigma} &: \mathsf{bool}\to\sigma\to\sigma\to\sigma\\
=,< &: \mathsf{int}\to\mathsf{int}\to\mathsf{bool} & \mathsf{fix}_{\sigma} &: (\sigma\to\sigma)\to\sigma
\end{aligned}
$$

(We write the binary operations infixed for readability.) The interpretation of this signature is also as expected:

$$
\begin{aligned}
\mathcal{B}_{\mathrm{s}}(\mathsf{bool}) &= \mathbf{B} = \{tt, ff\}\\
\mathcal{B}_{\mathrm{s}}(\mathsf{int}) &= \mathbf{Z} = \{\ldots,-1,0,1,2,\ldots\}\\
\mathcal{C}_{\mathrm{s}}(\star) &= \lambda x^{\mathbf{Z}_{\perp}}.\lambda y^{\mathbf{Z}_{\perp}}.\mathbf{let}^{\perp}\;n\Leftarrow x\;\mathbf{in}\;\mathbf{let}^{\perp}\;m\Leftarrow y\;\mathbf{in}\;\mathbf{val}^{\perp}\;m\star n \quad {\scriptstyle \star\in\{+,-,\times,=,<\}}\\
\mathcal{C}_{\mathrm{s}}(\mathsf{if}_{\sigma}) &= \lambda x^{\mathbf{B}_{\perp}}.\lambda a_1^{[\![\sigma]\!]}.\lambda a_2^{[\![\sigma]\!]}.\mathbf{let}^{\perp}\;b\Leftarrow x\;\mathbf{in}\;b\to a_1\,[\!]\,a_2\\
\mathcal{C}_{\mathrm{s}}(\mathsf{fix}_{\sigma}) &= \lambda f^{[\![\sigma]\!]\to[\![\sigma]\!]}.\bigsqcup\nolimits_{i\in\omega} f^i\,\perp_{[\![\sigma]\!]}
\end{aligned}
$$

It is well known (computational adequacy of the denotational semantics for call-by-name evaluation [17]) that with this interpretation, $Eval_{\mathcal{I}_{\mathrm{s}}}$ is computable.

2.2 The Binding-Time Separated Language

Assume now that the signature Σ is partitioned according to binding times, $\Sigma = \Sigma_{\mathrm{s}}, \Sigma_{\mathrm{d}}$. We will write type and term constants from the static part overlined, and the dynamic ones underlined. For simplicity, we require that the dynamic base types do not come with any new literals, i.e., $\Xi(\underline{b}) = \emptyset$. (If needed, they can be added as dynamic constants.) However, some base types will be persistent, i.e., have both static and dynamic versions with the same intended meaning. In that case, we also include *lifting functions* $\$_b : \overline{b} \to \underline{b}$ in the dynamic signature.

We say that a type τ is *fully dynamic* if it is constructed from dynamic base types only,

$$\tau ::= \underline{b} \mid \tau_1 \rightarrow \tau_2$$

We also reserve Δ for typing assumptions assigning fully dynamic types to all variables. All term constants in Σ_{d} must have fully dynamic types, and in particular, polymorphic dynamic constants must only be instantiated by dynamic types, e.g., $\Sigma_{\mathrm{d}}(\underline{\mathsf{if}}_{\tau}) = \underline{\mathsf{bool}} \rightarrow \tau \rightarrow \tau \rightarrow \tau$.

We will always take the language from Definition 1 with the standard semantics $\mathcal{I}_{\mathrm{s}}$ as the static part. The dynamic signature typically also has some intended *evaluating interpretation* $\mathcal{I}_{\mathrm{d}}^{\mathrm{e}}$; in particular, when Σ_{d} is merely a copy of Σ_{s}, we can use $\mathcal{I}_{\mathrm{s}}$ directly for $\mathcal{I}_{\mathrm{d}}^{\mathrm{e}}$ (interpreting all lifting functions as identities). Later, however, we will also introduce a "code-generating", *residualizing* interpretation.

Example 1. Here are the four different binding-time annotations for the function *power* : int $\rightarrow$ int $\rightarrow$ int (abbreviating int as ι):

$$
\begin{aligned}
&power_{ss} : \bar{\iota} \rightarrow \bar{\iota} \rightarrow \bar{\iota} = \lambda x^{\bar{\iota}}.\overline{\mathsf{fix}}_{\bar{\iota}\rightarrow\bar{\iota}}\,(\lambda p^{\bar{\iota}\rightarrow\bar{\iota}}.\lambda n^{\bar{\iota}}.\overline{\mathsf{if}}_{\bar{\iota}}\,(n \mathbin{\overline{\equiv}} 0)\,1\,(x \mathbin{\overline{\times}} p\,(n \mathbin{\overline{-}} 1)))\\
&power_{sd} : \bar{\iota} \rightarrow \underline{\iota} \rightarrow \underline{\iota} = \lambda x^{\bar{\iota}}.\underline{\mathsf{fix}}_{\underline{\iota}\rightarrow\underline{\iota}}\,(\lambda p^{\underline{\iota}\rightarrow\underline{\iota}}.\lambda n^{\underline{\iota}}.\underline{\mathsf{if}}_{\underline{\iota}}\,(n \mathbin{\underline{\equiv}} \$\,0)\,(\$\,1)\,(\$\,x \mathbin{\underline{\times}} p\,(n \mathbin{\underline{-}} \$\,1)))\\
&power_{ds} : \underline{\iota} \rightarrow \bar{\iota} \rightarrow \underline{\iota} = \lambda x^{\underline{\iota}}.\overline{\mathsf{fix}}_{\bar{\iota}\rightarrow\underline{\iota}}\,(\lambda p^{\bar{\iota}\rightarrow\underline{\iota}}.\lambda n^{\bar{\iota}}.\overline{\mathsf{if}}_{\underline{\iota}}\,(n \mathbin{\overline{\equiv}} 0)\,(\$\,1)\,(x \mathbin{\underline{\times}} p\,(n \mathbin{\overline{-}} 1)))\\
&power_{dd} : \underline{\iota} \rightarrow \underline{\iota} \rightarrow \underline{\iota} = \lambda x^{\underline{\iota}}.\underline{\mathsf{fix}}_{\underline{\iota}\rightarrow\underline{\iota}}\,(\lambda p^{\underline{\iota}\rightarrow\underline{\iota}}.\lambda n^{\underline{\iota}}.\underline{\mathsf{if}}_{\underline{\iota}}\,(n \mathbin{\underline{\equiv}} \$\,0)\,(\$\,1)\,(x \mathbin{\underline{\times}} p\,(n \mathbin{\underline{-}} \$\,1)))
\end{aligned}
$$

Note how the fixed-point and conditional operators are classified as static or dynamic, depending on the binding time of the second argument.

2.3 Static Normal Forms and PE

Definition 2 (static normal forms). *Among the well-typed, purely dynamic terms $\Delta \vdash_{\Sigma_{\mathrm{d}}} E : \tau$, we distinguish those in* normal *and* atomic *form:*

$$
\frac{\Delta \vdash^{\mathrm{at}} E : \underline{b}}{\Delta \vdash^{\mathrm{nf}} E : \underline{b}}
\qquad
\frac{\Delta, x\!:\tau_1 \vdash^{\mathrm{nf}} E : \tau_2}{\Delta \vdash^{\mathrm{nf}} \lambda x^{\tau_1}.E : \tau_1 \rightarrow \tau_2}\, x \notin \mathrm{dom}\,\Delta
$$

$$
\frac{l \in \Xi(\bar{b})}{\Delta \vdash^{\mathrm{at}} \$_b l : \underline{b}}
\qquad
\frac{\Sigma_{\mathrm{d}}(\underline{c}_{\tau_1,\ldots,\tau_n}) = \tau}{\Delta \vdash^{\mathrm{at}} \underline{c}_{\tau_1,\ldots,\tau_n} : \tau}
\qquad
\frac{\Delta(x) = \tau}{\Delta \vdash^{\mathrm{at}} x : \tau}
$$

$$
\frac{\Delta \vdash^{\mathrm{at}} E_1 : \tau_1 \rightarrow \tau_2 \qquad \Delta \vdash^{\mathrm{nf}} E_2 : \tau_1}{\Delta \vdash^{\mathrm{at}} E_1\,E_2 : \tau_2}
$$

In particular, such terms contain no static constants nor β-redexes. (Incidentally, this also means that if we had included polymorphic lets in the source language, they would simply get unfolded in the resulting normal forms.)

We can now define a notion of normalization based on (undirected) equality, rather than on (directed) reduction [3]. Since lambda-abstracting a dynamic-type term over a dynamic-type variable still yields a dynamic term, it suffices to be able to compute normal forms of closed terms:

Definition 3 (static equivalence and normalization). *Let $\mathcal{I}_s$ be an interpretation of Σ_s. We say that two terms $\vdash_{\Sigma_s,\Sigma_d} E : \sigma$ and $\vdash_{\Sigma_s,\Sigma_d} E' : \sigma$ are* statically equivalent wrt. *$\mathcal{I}_s$, written $E =^{\mathcal{I}_s} E'$, if for all $\mathcal{I}_d$ interpreting Σ_d, $[\![E]\!]^{\mathcal{I}_s,\mathcal{I}_d} = [\![E']\!]^{\mathcal{I}_s,\mathcal{I}_d}$. A* static-normalization function *is then a computable partial function NF on well-typed terms such that*

1. *If $\vdash_{\Sigma_s,\Sigma_d} E : \tau$ and $NF(E) = \tilde{E}$ then $\vdash^{\mathsf{nf}}_{\Sigma_d} \tilde{E} : \tau$ and $\tilde{E} =^{\mathcal{I}_s} E$.*
2. *If also $\vdash_{\Sigma_s,\Sigma_d} E' : \tau$ and $E' =^{\mathcal{I}_s} E$ then $NF(E') \equiv NF(E)$ (α-equivalence).*

We further say that such a normalization function is complete *if whenever an $\tilde{E}$ satisfying the conditions in (1) exists, $NF(E)$ is defined.*

Example 2. One can check that a complete static-normalization function *NF* for our language must have the following properties:

$$\begin{aligned} NF(\$\,(power_{ss}\,3\,4)) &\equiv \$\,81 \\ NF(\lambda x^{\underline{\mathsf{int}}}.\,power_{ds}\,x\,3) &\equiv \lambda x^{\underline{\mathsf{int}}}.\,x \mathbin{\underline{\times}} (x \mathbin{\underline{\times}} (x \mathbin{\underline{\times}} \$\,1)) \\ NF(\lambda x^{\underline{\mathsf{int}}}.\,power_{ds}\,x\,\text{-}2) &\quad \text{undefined} \end{aligned}$$

Note first that ordinary evaluation is just a special case of static normalization. The second example shows how static normalization achieves the partial-evaluation goal of the introduction. Finally, some terms have no static normal form at all; in that case, the normalization function must diverge.

There are two basic ways to compute normal forms. The usual one is based on term rewriting, repeatedly locating and contracting β-redexes and applications of static constants (and possibly η-expanding the final result). But there is an alternative technique, *normalization by evaluation*, which utilizes the existing mechanism of complete-program evaluation (defined only for closed terms of base type) as the normalization engine for general terms. This is the subject of the next section.

3 A Normalization-by-Evaluation Algorithm

We now present Type-Directed Partial Evaluation (TDPE), an efficient algorithm for computing static normal forms.

3.1 Representing Programs as Data

To compute normal forms, we need a way of representing them as program outputs. Assume therefore that we have base cpos rich enough to contain unique representations of all well-formed dynamic types, variable names, and (open) static-normal form terms, i.e., sets T, $\mathcal{V}$, and Λ with injective operations

$$\begin{aligned} BASE_b &: T & CST &: \mathcal{V} \times T^* \to \Lambda \\ ARR &: T \times T \to T & VAR &: \mathcal{V} \to \Lambda \\ LIT_b &: \mathcal{B}_s(b) \to \Lambda & LAM &: \mathcal{V} \times T \times \Lambda \to \Lambda \\ & & APP &: \Lambda \times \Lambda \to \Lambda \end{aligned}$$

(where T^* is the set of finite lists of elements from T). Using these, we can define injective *representation functions* for types and terms, such that $\ulcorner\tau\urcorner \in T$ for any dynamic type τ, and $\ulcorner E\urcorner \in \Lambda$ for $\Delta \vdash^{\mathrm{nf}}_{\Sigma_d} E : \tau$, by equations such as

$$\ulcorner\tau_1 \to \tau_2\urcorner = ARR(\ulcorner\tau_1\urcorner, \ulcorner\tau_2\urcorner) \quad \ulcorner\lambda x^\tau . E\urcorner = LAM(x, \ulcorner\tau\urcorner, \ulcorner E\urcorner) \quad \ulcorner\$_b l\urcorner = LIT_b(\mathcal{L}_b(l))$$

We do not need to require a priori that all elements of T and Λ represent well-formed types and terms (although this is easy to achieve), let alone well-typed ones, or ones in normal form. For example, we could simply take all of T, $\mathcal{V}$, and Λ as the type of finite character strings. Or, even more radically, Gödel-code everything in terms of integer arithmetic only.

To account for potentially diverging normalizations, we must now turn the set of term representations into a pointed cpo. To also model the generation of "new" variable names, however, we will not work with elements of $\Lambda_\perp$ directly, but instead introduce a term-family representation,

$$\hat{\Lambda} = \mathcal{N} \to \Lambda_\perp$$

where $\mathbf{N} \subseteq \mathcal{N}$. The intent is that for $e \in \hat{\Lambda}$ and $i \in \mathbf{N}$, if $e\,i = \mathbf{val}^\perp \ulcorner E\urcorner$ then all bound variables of E will belong to the set $\{\mathsf{g}_i, \mathsf{g}_{i+1}, \ldots\} \subseteq \mathcal{V}$.

We also define wrapper functions to conveniently build representations of lambda-terms without committing to particular choices of bound-variable names:

$$\begin{aligned}
\widehat{LIT}_b &: \mathcal{B}_s(b) \to \hat{\Lambda} = \lambda n.\, \lambda i.\, \mathbf{val}^\perp\, LIT_b(n) \\
\widehat{CST} &: \mathcal{V} \times T^* \to \hat{\Lambda} = \lambda(c, \mathbf{t}).\, \lambda i.\, \mathbf{val}^\perp\, CST(c, \mathbf{t}) \\
\widehat{VAR} &: \mathcal{V} \to \hat{\Lambda} = \lambda v.\, \lambda i.\, \mathbf{val}^\perp\, VAR(v) \\
\widehat{LAM} &: T \times (\mathcal{V} \to \hat{\Lambda}) \to \hat{\Lambda} = \lambda(t, \varepsilon).\, \lambda i.\, \mathbf{let}^\perp\, l \Leftarrow \varepsilon\, \mathsf{g}_i\, (i+1)\ \mathbf{in}\ \mathbf{val}^\perp\, LAM(\mathsf{g}_i, t, l) \\
\widehat{APP} &: \hat{\Lambda} \times \hat{\Lambda} \to \hat{\Lambda} = \\
&\qquad \lambda(e_1, e_2).\, \lambda i.\, \mathbf{let}^\perp\, l_1 \Leftarrow e_1\, i\ \mathbf{in}\ \mathbf{let}^\perp\, l_2 \Leftarrow e_2\, i\ \mathbf{in}\ \mathbf{val}^\perp\, APP(l_1, l_2)
\end{aligned}$$

(These definitions would not be needed in a setting with support for higher-order abstract syntax. But one of our goals is to show rigorously that all the variable-name manipulations can be done efficiently by the normalization algorithm itself, without relying on higher-level operations such as capture-avoiding substitution or higher-order matching.)

Example 3. Let $t = ARR(BASE_{\mathsf{int}}, BASE_{\mathsf{int}})$. Then

$$\begin{aligned}
&\widehat{LAM}\,(t, \lambda v^{\mathcal{V}}.\, \widehat{APP}\,(\widehat{VAR}\,v, \widehat{LIT}_{\mathsf{int}}\,3))\,7 \\
&\quad = \mathbf{val}^\perp\, LAM(\mathsf{g}_7, t, APP(VAR(\mathsf{g}_7), LIT_{\mathsf{int}}(3))) = \mathbf{val}^\perp \ulcorner\lambda \mathsf{g}_7^{\mathsf{int}\to\mathsf{int}}.\, \mathsf{g}_7\, (\$\, 3)\urcorner
\end{aligned}$$

That is, we can apply an element of $\hat{\Lambda}$ constructed using the wrapper functions to a starting index and obtain the representation of a concrete lambda-term.

3.2 The Residualizing Interpretation

We now define a non-standard interpretation $\mathcal{I}_{\mathrm{d}}^{\mathrm{r}} = (\mathcal{B}_{\mathrm{d}}^{\mathrm{r}}, \emptyset, \mathcal{C}_{\mathrm{d}}^{\mathrm{r}})$ of the dynamic signature Σ_{d}, based on representations of syntactic program fragments and operations constructing such representations. We will abbreviate $[\![-]\!]^{\mathcal{I}_{\mathrm{s}}, \mathcal{I}_{\mathrm{d}}^{\mathrm{r}}}$ as $[\![-]\!]_{\mathrm{r}}$. For the interpretation of Σ_{d}'s types, we take

$$\mathcal{B}_{\mathrm{d}}^{\mathrm{r}}(\underline{b}) = \hat{\Lambda}.$$

This allows us to define for any dynamic τ a pair of continuous functions, often called *reification*, $\downarrow^{\tau} : [\![\tau]\!]_{\mathrm{r}} \to \hat{\Lambda}$, and *reflection*, $\uparrow_{\tau} : \hat{\Lambda} \to [\![\tau]\!]_{\mathrm{r}}$, as follows:

$$\begin{array}{ll} \downarrow^{\underline{b}} = \lambda t^{\hat{\Lambda}}.t & \downarrow^{\tau_1 \to \tau_2} = \lambda f^{[\![\tau_1]\!]_{\mathrm{r}} \to [\![\tau_2]\!]_{\mathrm{r}}}.\widehat{LAM}\,(\ulcorner\tau_1\urcorner, \lambda v^{\mathcal{V}}.\downarrow^{\tau_2}(f\,(\uparrow_{\tau_1}(\widehat{VAR}\,v)))) \\ \uparrow_{\underline{b}} = \lambda e^{\hat{\Lambda}}.e & \uparrow_{\tau_1 \to \tau_2} = \lambda e^{\hat{\Lambda}}.\lambda a^{[\![\tau_1]\!]_{\mathrm{r}}}.\uparrow_{\tau_2}(\widehat{APP}\,(e, \downarrow^{\tau_1} a)) \end{array}$$

Informally, reification constructs a syntactic representation of a "well-behaved" semantic value, while reflection constructs such values from pieces of syntax. For the residualizing interpretations of Σ_{d}'s term constants we now take

$$\begin{aligned} \mathcal{C}_{\mathrm{d}}^{\mathrm{r}}(\underline{c}_{\tau_1,\ldots,\tau_n}) &= \uparrow_{\Sigma_{\mathrm{d}}(c_{\tau_1,\ldots,\tau_n})}(\widehat{CST}\,(c, [\ulcorner\tau_1\urcorner, \ldots, \ulcorner\tau_n\urcorner])) \\ \mathcal{C}_{\mathrm{d}}^{\mathrm{r}}(\$_b) &= \lambda x^{\mathcal{B}_{\mathrm{s}}(b)_{\perp}}.\mathbf{let}^{\perp}\ n \Leftarrow x\ \mathbf{in}\ \widehat{LIT}_b\, n \end{aligned}$$

That is, a general dynamic constant is simply interpreted as the reflection of its type-annotated name, while a lifting function forces evaluation of its argument and constructs a representation of the literal result. (It is this forcing of static subcomputations that may cause the whole specialization process to diverge.)

Example 4. Applying the reification function to the residualizing meaning of a term not in static normal form, we obtain:

$$\begin{aligned} &\downarrow^{(\underline{\mathsf{int}}\to\underline{\mathsf{int}})\to\underline{\mathsf{int}}}([\![(\lambda x^{\overline{\mathsf{int}}}.\lambda f^{\underline{\mathsf{int}}\to\underline{\mathsf{int}}}.f\,(\$_{\mathsf{int}}\,(x \mathbin{\overline{+}} 1)))\,2]\!]_{\mathrm{r}}\,\emptyset) \\ &\quad = \downarrow^{(\underline{\mathsf{int}}\to\underline{\mathsf{int}})\to\underline{\mathsf{int}}}([\![\lambda f.f\,(\$_{\mathsf{int}}\,(x \mathbin{\overline{+}} 1))]\!]_{\mathrm{r}}\,(\emptyset[x \mapsto [\![2]\!]_{\mathrm{r}}\,\emptyset])) \\ &\quad = \downarrow^{(\underline{\mathsf{int}}\to\underline{\mathsf{int}})\to\underline{\mathsf{int}}}(\lambda\varphi^{\hat{\Lambda}\to\hat{\Lambda}}.[\![f\,(\$_{\mathsf{int}}\,(x \mathbin{\overline{+}} 1))]\!]_{\mathrm{r}}\,(\emptyset[x \mapsto \mathbf{val}^{\perp}\,2, f \mapsto \varphi])) \\ &\quad = \downarrow^{(\underline{\mathsf{int}}\to\underline{\mathsf{int}})\to\underline{\mathsf{int}}}(\lambda\varphi.\varphi\,(\mathcal{C}_{\mathrm{d}}^{\mathrm{r}}(\$_{\mathsf{int}})\,(\mathcal{C}_{\mathrm{s}}(+)\,(\mathbf{val}^{\perp}\,2)\,(\mathbf{val}^{\perp}\,1)))) \\ &\quad = \downarrow^{(\underline{\mathsf{int}}\to\underline{\mathsf{int}})\to\underline{\mathsf{int}}}(\lambda\varphi.\varphi\,(\mathcal{C}_{\mathrm{d}}^{\mathrm{r}}(\$_{\mathsf{int}})\,(\mathbf{val}^{\perp}\,3))) = \downarrow^{(\underline{\mathsf{int}}\to\underline{\mathsf{int}})\to\underline{\mathsf{int}}}(\lambda\varphi.\varphi\,(\widehat{LIT}_{\mathsf{int}}\,3)) \\ &\quad = \widehat{LAM}\,(\ulcorner\underline{\mathsf{int}} \to \underline{\mathsf{int}}\urcorner, \lambda v^{\mathcal{V}}.\downarrow^{\underline{\mathsf{int}}}\Big((\lambda\varphi.\varphi\,(\widehat{LIT}_{\mathsf{int}}\,3))\,(\uparrow_{\underline{\mathsf{int}}\to\underline{\mathsf{int}}}(\widehat{VAR}\,v))\Big)) \\ &\quad = \widehat{LAM}\,(ARR(BASE_{\mathsf{int}}, BASE_{\mathsf{int}}), \lambda v^{\mathcal{V}}.\widehat{APP}\,(\widehat{VAR}\,v)\,(\widehat{LIT}_{\mathsf{int}}\,3)) \end{aligned}$$

And applying this value to 7 as the first bound-variable index gives us precisely the normal-form term from Example 3 at the end of the previous section.

3.3 The Algorithm

So far, we have looked at a semantic property: from the interpretation of a lambda-term in a non-standard denotational semantics of the dynamic signature, we can apparently recover that term's normal form. But this semantic result also forms the basis of an eminently practical normalization *algorithm*, obtained by pulling back the components of the residualizing semantics to the level of program syntax.

We say that a *realization* Φ of a signature Σ in a programming language given by Σ_{pl} is a substitution assigning to every type constant of Σ, a type over Σ_{pl}, and to every term constant of Σ, a Σ_{pl}-term. (For simplicity, we assume that the literals of Σ's base types are also literals of the corresponding Σ_{pl}-types.)

Suppose now that $\Sigma_{\text{s}} \subseteq \Sigma_{\text{pl}}$, $\mathcal{I}_{\text{pl}}$ agrees with $\mathcal{I}_{\text{s}}$, and Σ_{pl} also has some distinguished base types typ and exp with $\mathcal{B}_{\text{pl}}(\mathsf{typ}) = T$ and $\mathcal{B}_{\text{pl}}(\mathsf{exp}) = \Lambda$, as well as the associated (strict) constructor constants. Note that $[\![\mathsf{int} \to \mathsf{exp}]\!] = \hat{\Lambda}$ (with $\mathcal{N} = \mathbf{Z}_\perp$). Then we can realize the base types of $(\Sigma_{\text{s}}, \Sigma_{\text{d}})$ in Σ_{pl} by

$$\Phi^{\text{r}}(\overline{b}) = b \qquad\qquad \Phi^{\text{r}}(\underline{b}) = \mathsf{int} \to \mathsf{exp}$$

so that $[\![\sigma\{\Phi^{\text{r}}\}]\!]^{\mathcal{B}_{\text{pl}}} = [\![\sigma]\!]_{\text{r}}$. Further, for any τ, we can define closed Σ_{pl}-terms,

$$\mathit{name}_\tau : \mathsf{typ} \qquad \mathit{reify}_\tau : \tau\{\Phi^{\text{r}}\} \to \mathsf{int} \to \mathsf{exp} \qquad \mathit{reflect}_\tau : (\mathsf{int} \to \mathsf{exp}) \to \tau\{\Phi^{\text{r}}\}$$

such that $[\![\mathit{name}_\tau]\!]^{\mathcal{I}_{\text{pl}}}\emptyset = \mathbf{val}^\perp \ulcorner\tau\urcorner$, $[\![\mathit{reify}_\tau]\!]^{\mathcal{I}_{\text{pl}}}\emptyset = \downarrow^\tau$, and $[\![\mathit{reflect}_\tau]\!]^{\mathcal{I}_{\text{pl}}}\emptyset = \uparrow_\tau$. And using those, we can define realizations of the term constants from $(\Sigma_{\text{s}}, \Sigma_{\text{d}})$:

$$\begin{aligned}
\Phi^{\text{r}}(\overline{c}_{\sigma_1,\ldots,\sigma_n}) &= c_{\sigma_1\{\Phi^{\text{r}}\},\ldots,\sigma_n\{\Phi^{\text{r}}\}} \\
\Phi^{\text{r}}(\underline{c}_{\tau_1,\ldots,\tau_n}) &= \mathit{reflect}_{\Sigma_{\text{d}}(\underline{c}_{\tau_1,\ldots,\tau_n})}\,(\lambda i.\,\mathsf{CST}\,(c, [\mathit{name}_{\tau_1}, \ldots, \mathit{name}_{\tau_n}])) \\
\Phi^{\text{r}}(\$_b) &= \lambda n.\,\lambda i.\,\mathsf{LIT}_b\, n \quad (\text{given } \mathcal{C}_{\text{pl}}(\mathsf{LIT}_b) = \lambda x.\,\mathbf{let}^\perp\; n \Leftarrow x \;\mathbf{in}\; \mathbf{val}^\perp\, \mathit{LIT}_b(n))
\end{aligned}$$

so that $[\![E\{\Phi^{\text{r}}\}]\!]^{\mathcal{I}_{\text{pl}}} = [\![E]\!]_{\text{r}}$. Note in particular that the realizations of static base types and constants are exactly the corresponding constructs from the programming language. This means that we can even use the usual syntactic sugar (such as **letrec** for applications of $\overline{\mathsf{fix}}$) in the static parts of programs to be specialized.

We can use this realization to express our normalization algorithm:

Definition 4 (TDPE). *For any dynamic type τ, we define the partial function $\mathit{TDPE}_\tau : \{E \mid \vdash_{\Sigma_{\text{s}},\Sigma_{\text{d}}} E : \tau\} \rightharpoonup \{E \mid \vdash^{\text{nf}}_{\Sigma_{\text{d}}} E : \tau\}$ by*

$$\mathit{TDPE}_\tau(E) = \tilde{E} \text{ if } \mathit{Eval}_{\mathcal{I}_{\text{pl}}}(\mathit{reify}_\tau\, E\{\Phi^{\text{r}}\}\, 0) = \ulcorner\tilde{E}\urcorner\,.$$

This *TDPE* is clearly computable; we will show in Section 4 that it is indeed a complete static-normalization function.

Note that we can view TDPE an instance of "cogen-based specialization" [13], in which a "compiler generator" is used to syntactically transform a (binding-time annotated) program $\vdash p : S \times D \to R$ into its *generating extension* $\vdash p^\dagger : S \to \mathsf{exp}$, with the property that for any $s : S$, $\mathit{Eval}(p^\dagger\, s) = \ulcorner p_s \urcorner$. That is, we effectively take

$$p^\dagger = \lambda s^S.\,\mathit{reify}_{D \to R}\,(\lambda d^D.\,p\{\Phi^{\text{r}}\}\,(s, d))\,0\,.$$

TDPE shares the general high efficiency of cogen-based PE [12]. Formulating the task in terms of static normalization over a binding-time separated signature, however, permits a very precise yet concise syntactic characterization of the specialized program p_s. Also, unlike traditional cogens, TDPE does not require any binding-time annotation of lambdas and applications in the source program.

As a further advantage, the signatures and realizations can be very conveniently expressed in terms of parameterized modules in a Standard ML-style module system. The program to be specialized is simply written as the body of a functor parameterized by the signature of dynamic operations. The functor can then be applied to either an evaluating (Φ^{e}) or a residualizing (Φ^{r}) structure. That is, the cogen pass does not even require an explicit syntactic traversal of the program, making it possible to enrich the static fragment of the language (e.g., with pattern matching) without any modification to the partial evaluator itself.

It is also worth noting that the τ-indexed families above can be straightforwardly defined even in ML's type system: consider the type abbreviation

$$\mathit{tdpe}(\alpha) \equiv \mathsf{typ} \times (\alpha \to \mathsf{int} \to \mathsf{exp}) \times ((\mathsf{int} \to \mathsf{exp}) \to \alpha)\,.$$

Then for any dynamic type τ, we can construct a term of type $\mathit{tdpe}(\tau\{\Phi^{\mathrm{r}}\})$ whose value is the triple $(\mathit{name}_\tau, \mathit{reify}_\tau, \mathit{reflect}_\tau)$. We do this by defining once and for all two ML-typable terms

$$\mathit{base} : \mathit{tdpe}(\mathsf{int} \to \mathsf{exp}) \qquad \mathit{arrow} : \forall \alpha, \beta.\, \mathit{tdpe}(\alpha) \times \mathit{tdpe}(\beta) \to \mathit{tdpe}(\alpha \to \beta)\,,$$

with which we can then systematically construct the required value. The technique is explained in more detail elsewhere [18].

Finally, the dynamic polymorphic constants (e.g., $\underline{\mathrm{fix}}$) now take explicit representations of the types at which they are being instantiated as extra arguments. In the evaluating realization, these extra arguments are ignored; but the residualizing realization uses them to construct the name-reflect-reify triple for $\Sigma(\underline{c}_{\tau_1,\ldots,\tau_n})$ given corresponding triples for $\tau_1, \ldots, \tau_n$.

3.4 Applications

Despite its apparent simplicity, TDPE has been successfully used for several nontrivial examples; see Danvy's tutorial for an overview [6]. Many of these actually use the slightly more complicated call-by-value version [4] (see Section 5.4). Because it exploits the highly-optimized evaluation mechanism of a functional language, such a partial evaluator is typically much faster than one representing and manipulating the source program as an explicit value.

Let us just mention here that in addition to stand-alone, source-to-source PE, the TDPE framework can be particularly naturally employed as a "semantic back-end" for executable language specifications. That is, if we explicitly parameterize such a specification by the signature of runtime operations (including conditionals, fixed points, etc.), we can instantiate this signature with either the runtime realization, yielding an interpreter, or with the residualizing signature, yielding a compiler [8,11]. Amusingly, the specializer does not even need the actual *text* of the specification, only its representation as an already compiled module.

4 Showing Correctness

In this section, we sketch a correctness proof for the TDPE algorithm, i.e., that it computes static normal forms when they exist. For the case without static constants, essentially the same algorithm can actually be extracted directly from the standard (syntactic) proof of strong normalization for the simply typed lambda-calculus [1]; but it is not clear if this approach can be extended to a richer programming-language setting.

Instead, our proof uses the technique of semantic logical relations, structured similarly to Gomard and Jones's proof of Lambda-mix [14, 8.8], but accounting more rigorously for potential divergence and for the generation of "fresh" variable names. It also admits a richer type structure for the dynamic language. (We can still treat the untyped variant as a special case; see Section 5.1.)

4.1 Properties of the Term-Family Representation

Let some evaluating dynamic interpretation $\mathcal{I}_{\mathrm{d}}^{\mathrm{e}}$ of Σ_{d} be given. We abbreviate $[\![-]\!]^{\mathcal{I}_{\mathrm{s}},\mathcal{I}_{\mathrm{d}}^{\mathrm{e}}}$ as $[\![-]\!]_{\mathrm{e}}$ (and $[\![-]\!]^{\mathcal{I}_{\mathrm{s}},\mathcal{I}_{\mathrm{d}}^{\mathrm{r}}}$ as $[\![-]\!]_{\mathrm{r}}$ as before).

Definition 5 (partial meaning relation, $\succ$). *For any Δ, let*

$$\sharp\Delta = \max(\{i+1 \mid \mathrm{g}_i \in \mathrm{dom}\,\Delta\} \cup \{0\})$$

(so if $i \geq \sharp\Delta$ then $\mathrm{g}_i \notin \mathrm{dom}\,\Delta$). Then for any Δ, τ, $s \in \{\mathrm{nf}, \mathrm{at}\}$ (as used in Definition 2), $\delta \in [\![\Delta]\!]^{\mathcal{I}_{\mathrm{d}}^{\mathrm{e}}}$, $e \in \hat{\Lambda}$, and $a \in [\![\tau]\!]^{\mathcal{I}_{\mathrm{d}}^{\mathrm{e}}}$, we define a relation by

$$e @^{\Delta} \delta \succ^{s}_{\tau} a \iff \forall i \geq \sharp\Delta.\, e\,i = \bot \vee \exists E.\, e\,i = \mathbf{val}^{\bot}\ulcorner E \urcorner \wedge \Delta \vdash^{s}_{\Sigma_{\mathrm{d}}} E : \tau \wedge [\![E]\!]^{\mathcal{I}_{\mathrm{d}}^{\mathrm{e}}}\delta = a$$

This roughly expresses that "$[\![e]\!]\delta = a$", but taking into account variable renaming, partiality, and simplification: for all sufficiently large starting indices i, if $e\,i$ converges, it must represent a normal-form term with the right meaning. We check that this relation is semantically well behaved:

Definition 6 (admissibility). *We say that a relation $R \subseteq A \times A'$ between two pointed cpos is* admissible *(or* inclusive*) if it is chain-complete (i.e., for all chains $(a_i)_i$ and $(a'_i)_i$, if $\forall i.\, (a_i, a'_i) \in R$ then also $(\bigsqcup_i a_i, \bigsqcup_i a'_i) \in R$) and* pointed *(i.e., $(\bot_A, \bot_{A'}) \in R$).*

Lemma 1 ($\succ$ is admissible). *For any Δ, $\delta \in [\![\Delta]\!]^{\mathcal{I}_{\mathrm{d}}^{\mathrm{e}}}$, τ, and $s \in \{\mathrm{nf}, \mathrm{at}\}$, the relation $\{(e, a) \mid e\,@^{\Delta}\,\delta \succ^{s}_{\tau} a\}$ is admissible.*

Proof. Straightforward, noting that admissible relations are closed under arbitrary intersection, and that any chain in $\Lambda_{\bot}$ is eventually constant. □

Although the output of TDPE is a closed program, we still need to account for the typing and meaning of open program fragments as they are being constructed and put into context:

Definition 7 (Kripke structure). *A* world *is a pair* (Δ, δ) *where* $\delta \in [\![\Delta]\!]^{\mathcal{I}^{\mathrm{e}}_{\mathrm{d}}}$. *Such worlds are partially ordered by*

$$(\Delta', \delta') \geq (\Delta, \delta) \iff \forall x \in \operatorname{dom} \Delta.\, \Delta'(x) = \Delta(x) \wedge \delta' x = \delta x$$

Lemma 2 ($\succ$ is Kripke). *If* $e @^{\Delta} \delta \succ^{s}_{\tau} a$ *and* $(\Delta', \delta') \geq (\Delta, \delta)$, *then also* $e @^{\Delta'} \delta' \succ^{s}_{\tau} a$.

Proof. Follows easily from standard weakening properties of the typing relation (if $\Delta \vdash E : \tau$ then $\Delta' \vdash E : \tau$) and denotational semantics ($[\![E]\!]\delta' = [\![E]\!]\delta$). □

Lemma 3 (meanings of term families). *The wrapper functions have the following properties:*

1. *If* $\Delta(v) = \tau$ *then* $\widehat{VAR}\, v @^{\Delta} \delta \succ^{\mathrm{at}}_{\tau} \delta v$.
2. *If* $n \in \mathcal{B}_{\mathrm{s}}(b)$ *then* $\widehat{LIT}_b\, n @^{\Delta} \delta \succ^{\mathrm{at}}_{\underline{b}} \mathbf{val}^{\perp}\, n$
3. $\widehat{CST}\,(c, [\ulcorner\tau_1\urcorner, \ldots, \ulcorner\tau_n\urcorner]) @^{\Delta} \delta \succ^{\mathrm{at}}_{\Sigma_{\mathrm{d}}(\underline{c}_{\tau_1,\ldots,\tau_n})} \mathcal{C}^{\mathrm{e}}_{\mathrm{d}}(\underline{c}_{\tau_1,\ldots,\tau_n})$
4. *If for all* $v \notin \operatorname{dom} \Delta$ *and* $a \in [\![\tau_1]\!]^{\mathcal{I}^{\mathrm{e}}_{\mathrm{d}}}$, $\varepsilon v @^{\Delta, v:\tau_1} \delta[v \mapsto a] \succ^{\mathrm{nf}}_{\tau_2} f a$ *then* $\widehat{LAM}\,(\ulcorner\tau_1\urcorner, \varepsilon) @^{\Delta} \delta \succ^{\mathrm{nf}}_{\tau_1 \to \tau_2} f$.
5. *If* $e_1 @^{\Delta} \delta \succ^{\mathrm{at}}_{\tau_1 \to \tau_2} f$ *and* $e_2 @^{\Delta} \delta \succ^{\mathrm{nf}}_{\tau_1} a$ *then* $\widehat{APP}\,(e_1, e_2) @^{\Delta} \delta \succ^{\mathrm{at}}_{\tau_2} f a$

Proof. Straightforward verification in all cases. (For case 4, we exploit the fact that $[\![\tau_1]\!]^{\mathcal{I}^{\mathrm{e}}_{\mathrm{d}}}$ is always non-empty; this shortcut can be avoided by using a slightly more complicated world structure throughout the proof.) □

4.2 Soundness of TDPE

We prove soundness by formally relating the standard and the residualizing interpretations of types and terms.

Definition 8 (logical relation, $\sim_\sigma$). *For any type* σ *and world* (Δ, δ), *we define a relation* $a @^{\Delta} \delta \sim_{\sigma} a'$, *where* $a \in [\![\sigma]\!]_{\mathrm{r}}$ *and* $a' \in [\![\sigma]\!]_{\mathrm{e}}$ *by:*

$$\begin{aligned} n @^{\Delta} \delta \sim_{\overline{b}} n' &\iff n = n' \\ e @^{\Delta} \delta \sim_{\underline{b}} n' &\iff e @^{\Delta} \delta \succ^{\mathrm{nf}}_{\underline{b}} n' \\ f @^{\Delta} \delta \sim_{\sigma_1 \to \sigma_2} f' &\iff \forall (\Delta', \delta') \geq (\Delta, \delta). \\ &\qquad \forall a, a'.\, a @^{\Delta'} \delta' \sim_{\sigma_1} a' \Rightarrow f a @^{\Delta'} \delta' \sim_{\sigma_2} f' a' \end{aligned}$$

We first check the standard requirements:

Lemma 4 ($\sim_\sigma$ is admissible). *For any σ, the relation $\{(a, a') \mid a \mathbin{@^\Delta} \delta \sim_\sigma a'\}$ is admissible.*

Proof. Simple induction on σ. For $\underline{b}$, use admissibility of $\succ$ (Lemma 1). □

Lemma 5 ($\sim_\sigma$ is Kripke). *If $e \mathbin{@^\Delta} \delta \sim_\sigma a$ and $(\Delta', \delta') \geq (\Delta, \delta)$, then also $e \mathbin{@^{\Delta'}} \delta' \sim_\sigma a$.*

Proof. This is a standard result about Kripke logical relations; the proof is by a simple induction on σ, using Lemma 2 for the base case $\sigma = \underline{b}$. □

We obtain our main correctness result from two lemmas:

Lemma 6 (soundness, type part). *For any dynamic type τ,*

1. *If $a \mathbin{@^\Delta} \delta \sim_\tau a'$ then $\downarrow^\tau a \mathbin{@^\Delta} \delta \succ_\tau^{\mathrm{nf}} a'$.*
2. *If $e \mathbin{@^\Delta} \delta \succ_\tau^{\mathrm{at}} a'$ then $\uparrow_\tau e \mathbin{@^\Delta} \delta \sim_\tau a'$.*

Proof. Straightforward induction on τ, using the properties of the wrapper functions from Lemma 3. □

Lemma 7 (soundness, term part). *Let (Δ, δ) be a world, and let $\rho \in [\![\Gamma]\!]_{\mathrm{r}}$ and $\rho' \in [\![\Gamma]\!]_{\mathrm{e}}$. Then for any well-typed term $\Gamma \vdash_{\Sigma_{\mathrm{s}}, \Sigma_{\mathrm{d}}} E : \sigma$, if $\forall x \in \mathrm{dom}\,\Gamma.\, \rho x \mathbin{@^\Delta} \delta \sim_{\Gamma(x)} \rho' x$ then $[\![E]\!]_{\mathrm{r}} \rho \mathbin{@^\Delta} \delta \sim_\sigma [\![E]\!]_{\mathrm{e}} \rho'$.*

Proof. This is the usual Kripke logical relations lemma, proved by straightforward induction on E. The only non-standard case is that of $E = \underline{c}_{\tau_1, \ldots, \tau_n}$, for which we need Lemma 6(2). For $E = \overline{\mathsf{fix}}_\sigma$, we use fixed-point induction, i.e., Lemma 4 together with the chain-based construction of $\mathcal{C}_{\mathrm{s}}(\mathsf{fix}_\sigma)$ in Definition 1. □

Theorem 1 (soundness). *TDPE is a static-normalization function.*

Proof. Observe first that $TDPE_\tau(E) = \tilde{E}$ iff $\downarrow^\tau ([\![E]\!]_{\mathrm{r}} \emptyset) 0 = \mathbf{val}^\perp \ulcorner \tilde{E} \urcorner$. Now, by Lemma 7, since empty environments are vacuously related, $[\![E]\!]_{\mathrm{r}} \emptyset \mathbin{@} \emptyset \sim_\tau [\![E]\!]_{\mathrm{e}} \emptyset$. And thus by Lemma 6(1), $\downarrow^\tau ([\![E]\!]_{\mathrm{r}} \emptyset) \mathbin{@} \emptyset \succ_\tau^{\mathrm{nf}} [\![E]\!]_{\mathrm{e}} \emptyset$, which, by the definitions of $\succ_\tau$ and $\sharp$, gives us precisely that $\vdash_{\Sigma_{\mathrm{d}}}^{\mathrm{nf}} \tilde{E} : \tau$ and $[\![\tilde{E}]\!]^{\mathcal{I}_{\mathrm{d}}^\circ} = [\![E]\!]^{\mathcal{I}_{\mathrm{s}}, \mathcal{I}_{\mathrm{d}}^\circ}$.

For the second part, if $E' =^{\mathcal{I}_{\mathrm{s}}} E$ then in particular $[\![E']\!]_{\mathrm{r}} = [\![E]\!]_{\mathrm{r}}$. And thus by the observation above, we must have $TDPE_\tau(E') = TDPE_\tau(E)$. □

4.3 Completeness of TDPE

To supplement the above partial-correctness result, we can also show that if a suitable $\tilde{E}$ exists, the algorithm will actually find it. This proof uses a much simpler logical-relation argument, capturing the intuition that the algorithm necessarily converges when applied to a term containing no static constants:

Definition 9 (totality predicate). *For any dynamic type τ, we define a predicate $T_\tau \subseteq [\![\tau]\!]^{\mathcal{I}_d^r}$ by*

$$T_{\underline{b}} = \{e \in \hat{\Lambda} \mid \forall i.\, ei \neq \bot\}$$
$$T_{\tau_1 \to \tau_2} = \{f \in [\![\tau_1]\!]^{\mathcal{I}_d^r} \to [\![\tau_2]\!]^{\mathcal{I}_d^r} \mid \forall a \in T_{\tau_1}.\, fa \in T_{\tau_2}\}$$

As before, we then obtain the result from two main lemmas:

Lemma 8 (completeness, type part). *For any dynamic type τ,*

1. *If $a \in T_\tau$ then for all $i \geq 0$, $\downarrow^\tau a\, i \neq \bot$.*
2. *If for all $i \geq 0$, $ei \neq \bot$ then $\uparrow_\tau e \in T_\tau$.*

Proof. Straightforward induction on τ, by inspection of the definitions of the wrapper functions. □

Lemma 9 (completeness, term part). *Let $\delta \in [\![\Delta]\!]^{\mathcal{I}_d^r}$. Then for any well-typed term $\Delta \vdash_{\Sigma_d} E : \tau$, if $\forall x \in \operatorname{dom} \Delta.\, \delta x \in T_{\Delta(x)}$ then $[\![E]\!]^{\mathcal{I}_d^r} \delta \in T_\tau$.*

Proof. Standard induction on E, using Lemma 8(2) for dynamic constants. □

Theorem 2 (completeness). *TDPE is a complete static-normalization function.*

Proof. Suppose $\vdash_{\Sigma_s, \Sigma_d} E : \tau$ has the static normal form $\vdash_{\Sigma_d} \tilde{E} : \tau$. Then in particular $[\![E]\!]_r = [\![E]\!]^{\mathcal{I}_s, \mathcal{I}_d^r} = [\![\tilde{E}]\!]^{\mathcal{I}_d^r}$. By Lemma 9, $[\![\tilde{E}]\!]^{\mathcal{I}_d^r}\emptyset \in T_\tau$, and thus by Lemma 8(1), $\downarrow^\tau ([\![E]\!]_r \emptyset) 0 = \downarrow^\tau ([\![\tilde{E}]\!]^{\mathcal{I}_d^r} \emptyset) 0 \neq \bot$, so $TDPE_\tau(E)$ is defined. □

5 Variations and Extensions

5.1 Lambda-Mix

We can use the previous results to show correctness of partial evaluation for languages like the one used for Lambda-mix [14, 8.8]. Here, the dynamic language is untyped. Or, more precisely, it has a single type $\underline{d}$ of dynamic values, and operators:

$$\frac{\Gamma, x{:}\,\underline{d} \vdash E : \underline{d}}{\Gamma \vdash \underline{\lambda} x.\, E : \underline{d}} \qquad \frac{\Gamma \vdash E_1 : \underline{d} \qquad \Gamma \vdash E_2 : \underline{d}}{\Gamma \vdash E_1 \mathbin{\underline{@}} E_2 : \underline{d}}$$

To model this in our typed framework, we let the dynamic signature Σ_d contain the single base type $\underline{d}$, and constants $\underline{\phi} : (\underline{d} \to \underline{d}) \to \underline{d}$ and $\underline{\psi} : \underline{d} \to \underline{d} \to \underline{d}$. We can then treat dynamic lambda-abstraction and application as abbreviations:

$$\underline{\lambda} x.\, E \equiv \underline{\phi}(\lambda x^{\underline{d}}.\, E) \qquad \text{and} \qquad E_1 \mathbin{\underline{@}} E_2 \equiv \underline{\psi}\, E_1\, E_2$$

In the evaluating dynamic semantics $\mathcal{I}_d^e$ of Σ_d, the type constant $\underline{d}$ is interpreted as a solution to the domain equation

$$D \cong (D \to D) \oplus \mathbf{Z}_\bot \oplus \mathbf{B}_\bot\,,$$

and $\underline{\phi}$ and $\underline{\psi}$ as the evident embedding and projection functions for the first summand. In the residualizing interpretation $\mathcal{I}_{\mathrm{d}}^{\mathrm{r}}$, on the other hand, $\underline{d}$ is the domain of syntactic term families, and the constants are reflected according to their types, as usual. In particular, $\mathit{reify}_{\underline{d}}$ is simply the identity.

The soundness result for TDPE then gives us that if $\vdash_{\Sigma_{\mathrm{s}},\Sigma_{\mathrm{d}}} E : \underline{d}$ and $\mathit{Eval}_{\mathcal{I}_{\mathrm{s}},\mathcal{I}_{\mathrm{d}}^{\mathrm{r}}}(E) = \ulcorner\tilde{E}\urcorner$ then $\vdash^{\mathrm{nf}}_{\Sigma_{\mathrm{d}}} \tilde{E} : \underline{d}$ and $\mathit{Eval}_{\mathcal{I}_{\mathrm{d}}^{\mathrm{e}}}(\tilde{E}) = \mathit{Eval}_{\mathcal{I}_{\mathrm{s}},\mathcal{I}_{\mathrm{d}}^{\mathrm{e}}}(E)$. With a little more work we also obtain a similar statement for non-closed terms.

Note finally that normalizing a term of type $\underline{d}$ a priori yields a simply-typed term over Σ_{d}, rather than an untyped one. In a static normal form, however, any occurrence of the constant $\underline{\phi}$ will be applied to a syntactic lambda-abstraction, and $\underline{\psi}$ will be applied to two arguments. Thus, the output of the partial evaluator can always be directly expressed in terms of the underlined abstraction and application operators.

5.2 Gensym-Like Name Generation

The term-family representation from Section 3.1 constructs terms in which the names of bound variables are derived from the number of enclosing lambdas; this convention is sometimes known as *de Bruijn levels* (not to be confused with de Bruijn *indices*). Although this is probably the simplest choice in a purely functional setting, there is nothing canonical about it. To more precisely capture the informal concept of newly-generated "fresh" variable names, we could instead take:

$$\hat{\Lambda} = \mathcal{N} \to (\Lambda \times \mathcal{N})_{\perp}$$

$$\widehat{VAR} = \lambda v.\, \lambda i.\, \mathbf{val}^{\perp}\, (VAR(v), i)$$

$$\widehat{LAM} = \lambda(t, \varepsilon).\, \lambda i.\, \mathbf{let}^{\perp}\; (l, i') \Leftarrow \varepsilon\, \mathrm{g}_i\, (i+1)\; \mathbf{in}\; \mathbf{val}^{\perp}\, (LAM(\mathrm{g}_i, t, l), i')$$

$$\widehat{APP} = \lambda(e_1, e_2).\, \lambda i.\, \mathbf{let}^{\perp}\; (l_1, i') \Leftarrow e_1\, i\; \mathbf{in}\; \mathbf{let}^{\perp}\; (l_2, i'') \Leftarrow e_2\, i'\; \mathbf{in}\; \mathbf{val}^{\perp}\, (APP(l_1, l_2), i'')$$

(with analogous extensions for constants and literals). This scheme generates terms in which all bound-variable names are distinct. Then, after changing the conditional meaning relation to read:

$$e\, @^{\Delta}\, \delta \succ^{s}_{\tau} a \iff$$
$$\forall i \geq \sharp\Delta.\, e\, i = \perp \vee \exists E, i' \geq i.\, e\, i = \mathbf{val}^{\perp}\, (\ulcorner E \urcorner, i') \wedge \Delta \vdash^{s}_{\Sigma_{\mathrm{d}}} E : \tau \wedge [\![E]\!]\delta = a.$$

we can check that Lemma 3 still holds, and therefore all the remaining constructions and proofs go through without further modifications.

5.3 On-Line Type-Directed Partial Evaluation

Although TDPE generally works on binding-time separated signatures, it is actually possible to give an on-line formulation, in which it is not necessary to explicitly annotate all base types and operations. Conceptually, we instead take $\mathcal{B}^{\mathrm{r}}_{\mathrm{d}}(b) = \mathcal{N} \to (\mathcal{B}_{\mathrm{s}}(b) + \Lambda)_{\perp}$. (In practice, when Λ is a conveniently inspectable type, it suffices to take $\mathcal{B}^r_d(b) = \hat{\Lambda}$ and explicitly recognize Λ-values that represent literals.) The arithmetic operators then produce a static result if if both arguments are static, and dynamic otherwise, possibly coercing one argument in the process. A similar extension works for conditionals.

This scheme enables "opportunistic" simplifications, in cases where an operand is sometimes, but not always, statically known (or where a static analysis cannot prove that it is known). Note, however, that we must still annotate occurrences of fix as static or dynamic, or otherwise prevent fruitless infinite expansion of a recursive function. For example, it is often possible to explicitly identify a particular function parameter as the one controlling the recursion, and only unfold calls in which that argument is a literal [5].

Of course, the price of these potential improvements is that the amount of simplification is less predictable: the output will still be in long $\beta\eta$-normal form, but it is no longer evident from the original program which operations will be performed statically, and which ones must remain in the specialized program.

5.4 Call-by-Value and Effects

For practical applications, a call-by-value variant of TDPE is usually preferable, and indeed the technique was first presented in this setting [4]. Let us briefly sketch the necessary changes from the call-by-name case here.

To give a denotational semantics of an ML-like language, we consider an interpretation $\mathcal{I}$ to also explicitly include a *monad* for modeling effectful computations. We usually want to be able to use any monad in the evaluating interpretation; thus the notion of static equality must be safe for any dynamic effect. That is, instead of computing normal forms based on the strong $\beta\eta$-lambda-calculus, we now need a normalization-by-evaluation algorithm for Moggi's computational lambda-calculus λ_c [15].

Fortunately, much as a single residualizing interpretation of dynamic type and term constants suffices to compute call-by-name static normal forms sound for any dynamic interpretation, it turns out that a single "maximally general" residualizing interpretation of effects can be used to compute call-by-value normal forms suitable for any dynamic monad.

A particularly natural such residualizing monad is that of continuations with answer type $\hat{\Lambda}$, which can be straightforwardly related to any dynamic monad for the purpose of the logical relation in Section 4.2. Moreover, we can still construct the corresponding residualizing realization Φ^r, as long as our programming language contains Scheme-style first-class continuations and state [10]. Incidentally, this construction also allows disjoint-union types (sums) to be naturally added to the language. The details are still under investigation, however, and will be reported in a forthcoming paper.

6 Conclusions and Future Work

We have given an account of type-directed partial evaluation that separates the specification of the problem (computation of static normal forms) from its implementation (normalization by evaluation); in previous work these tended to be intertwined. We also presented a correctness proof for the implementation, using logical relations over a simple denotational model of the binding-time separated language. To keep the details manageable, we restricted our scope to a purely functional language; but both the algorithm and the proof techniques extend to call-by-value languages with effects as well.

Future work falls in two classes. First, there are a number of natural extensions to the framework and results in essentially the form they are presented here. In addition to the directions already mentioned in Section 5, one can also consider polyvariant specialization, run-time code generation, and other classical PE concepts in the context of TDPE.

Second, it would be interesting to investigate how TDPE relates to more general work on linguistic support for staged computation, especially recent developments based on modal logics [9,16]. For example, it might be possible to generalize the notion of static normalization to such settings, and consider normalization-by-evaluation algorithms for type systems more expressive than simple types.

Acknowledgments

I want to thank Olivier Danvy for many deep and fruitful discussions about TDPE. I am also grateful to Daniel Damian, Bernd Grobauer, Zhe Yang, and the PPDP'99 reviewers for their careful reading and insightful comments on various drafts of this manuscript.

References

1. Ulrich Berger. Program extraction from normalization proofs. In M. Bezem and J. F. Groote, editors, *Typed Lambda Calculi and Applications*, number 664 in Lecture Notes in Computer Science, pages 91–106, Utrecht, The Netherlands, March 1993.
2. Ulrich Berger and Helmut Schwichtenberg. An inverse of the evaluation functional for typed λ-calculus. In *Proceedings of the Sixth Annual IEEE Symposium on Logic in Computer Science*, pages 203–211, Amsterdam, The Netherlands, July 1991.
3. Thierry Coquand and Peter Dybjer. Intuitionistic model constructions and normalization proofs. *Mathematical Structures in Computer Science*, 7:75–94, 1997.
4. Olivier Danvy. Type-directed partial evaluation. In *23rd ACM Symposium on Principles of Programming Languages*, pages 242–257, St. Petersburg Beach, Florida, January 1996.
5. Olivier Danvy. Online type-directed partial evaluation. In Masahiko Sato and Yoshihito Toyama, editors, *Proceedings of the Third Fuji International Symposium on Functional and Logic Programming*, pages 271–295, Kyoto, Japan, April 1998.
6. Olivier Danvy. Type-directed partial evaluation. Lecture Notes BRICS LN-98-3, Department of Computer Science, University of Aarhus, Aarhus, Denmark, December 1998. To appear in LNCS.

7. Olivier Danvy and Peter Dybjer, editors. *Preliminary Proceedings of the APPSEM Workshop on Normalization by Evaluation*, Chalmers, Sweeden, May 1998. BRICS Note NS-98-1.
8. Olivier Danvy and René Vestergaard. Semantics-based compiling: A case study in type-directed partial evaluation. In *Eighth International Symposium on Programming Language Implementation and Logic Programming*, number 1140 in Lecture Notes in Computer Science, pages 182–197, Aachen, Germany, September 1996.
9. Rowan Davies and Frank Pfenning. A modal analysis of staged computation. In *23rd ACM Symposium on Principles of Programming Languages*, pages 258–270, St. Petersburg Beach, Florida, January 1996.
10. Andrzej Filinski. Representing monads. In *Proceedings of the 21st ACM SIGPLAN-SIGACT Symposium on Principles of Programming Languages*, pages 446–457, Portland, Oregon, January 1994.
11. William L. Harrison and Samuel N. Kamin. Modular compilers based on monad transformers. In *Proceedings of the IEEE International Conference on Computer Languages*, pages 122–131, Chicago, Illinois, May 1998. IEEE Computer Society.
12. Simon Helsen and Peter Thiemann. Two flavors of offline partial evaluation. In J. Hsiang and A. Ohori, editors, *Advances in Computing Science – ASIAN'98*, number 1538 in Lecture Notes in Computer Science, pages 188–205, Manilla, The Philippines, December 1998.
13. Carsten Kehler Holst and John Launchbury. Handwriting cogen to avoid problems with static typing. In *Draft Proceedings, Fourth Annual Glasgow Workshop on Functional Programming*, pages 210–218, Skye, Scotland, 1991.
14. Neil D. Jones, Carsten K. Gomard, and Peter Sestoft. *Partial Evaluation and Automatic Program Generation*. Prentice Hall International Series in Computer Science. Prentice-Hall, 1993.
15. Eugenio Moggi. Computational lambda-calculus and monads. In *Proceedings of the Fourth Annual Symposium on Logic in Computer Science*, pages 14–23, Pacific Grove, California, June 1989. IEEE.
16. Eugenio Moggi, Walid Taha, Zine El-Abidine Benaissa, and Tim Sheard. An idealized MetaML: Simpler and more expressive. In *8th European Symposium on Programming Languages and Systems*, number 1576 in Lecture Notes in Computer Science, pages 193–207, Amsterdam, The Netherlands, March 1999.
17. Gordon D. Plotkin. LCF considered as a programming language. *Theoretical Computer Science*, 5(3):223–255, December 1977.
18. Zhe Yang. Encoding types in ML-like languages. In *International Conference on Functional Programming*, pages 289–300, Baltimore, Maryland, September 1998.

A Parameterized Unfold/Fold Transformation Framework for Definite Logic Programs*

Abhik Roychoudhury[1], K. Narayan Kumar[1,2], C.R. Ramakrishnan[1], and I.V. Ramakrishnan[1]

[1] Dept. of Computer Science, SUNY Stony Brook,
Stony Brook, NY 11794, USA
{abhik,kumar,cram,ram}@cs.sunysb.edu
[2] Chennai Mathematical Institute,
92 G.N. Chetty Road, Chennai, India
kumar@smi.ernet.in

Abstract. Given a program P, an unfold/fold program transformation system derives a sequence of programs $P = P_0, P_1, \ldots, P_n$, such that P_{i+1} is derived from P_i by application of either an unfolding or a folding step. Existing unfold/fold transformation systems for definite logic programs differ from one another mainly in the kind of folding transformations they permit at each step. Some allow folding using a single (possibly recursive) clause while others permit folding using multiple non-recursive clauses. However, none allow folding using *multiple recursive* clauses that are drawn from some previous program in the transformation sequence. In this paper we develop a *parameterized* framework for unfold/fold transformations by suitably abstracting and extending the proofs of existing transformation systems. Various existing unfold/fold transformation systems can be obtained by instantiating the parameters of the framework. This framework enables us to not only understand the relative strengths and limitations of these systems but also construct new transformation systems. Specifically we present a more *general* transformation system that permits folding using multiple recursive clauses that can be drawn from any previous program in the transformation sequence. This new transformation system is also obtained by instantiating our parameterized framework.

1 Introduction

Some of the most extensively studied transformation systems for definite logic programs are the so called *unfold/fold* transformation systems. At a high level unfold and fold transformations can be viewed as follows. Definite logic programs consist of definitions of the form A:– ϕ where A is an atom and ϕ is a positive boolean formula over atoms. Unfolding replaces an occurrence of A in

* The work of Abhik Roychoudhury, C.R. Ramakrishnan and I.V. Ramakrishnan was partially supported by NSF grants CCR-9711386 and EIA-9705998. The work of K. Narayan Kumar was partially supported by NSF grant CDA-9805735.

G. Nadathur (Ed.): PPDP'99, LNCS 1702, pp. 396–413, 1999.

a program with ϕ while folding replaces an occurrence of ϕ with A. Folding is called *reversible* if its effects can be undone by an unfolding, and *irreversible* otherwise. An unfold/fold transformation system for definite logic programs was first described in a seminal paper by Tamaki and Sato [20]. In the flurry of research activity that followed, a number of unfold/fold transformation systems were developed. Kanamori and Fujita [8] proposed a transformation system that was based on maintaining counters to guide folding. Maher described a system that permits only reversible folding [10]. The basic Tamaki-Sato system itself was extended in several directions (e.g., to handle folding with multiple clauses [7], negation [1,18,19]) and applied to practical problems (e.g., [2,3,12]). (See [11] for an excellent survey of research on this topic over the past decade).

Correctness of Unfold/Fold Transformations Correctness proofs for unfold/fold transformations consider *transformation sequences* of the form $P_0, P_1, \ldots$, where P_0 is an initial program and P_{i+1} is obtained from P_i by applying an unfolding or folding transformation. The proofs usually show that all programs in the transformation sequence have the same least Herbrand model. It is easy to verify that transforming P_i to P_{i+1} using unfolding or folding is *partially correct*, i.e., the least model of P_{i+1} is a subset of that of P_i. It is also easy to show, by induction on the structure of the proof trees, that unfolding transformation is *totally* correct, i.e., it *preserves* the least model. However, as illustrated below, indiscriminate folding may introduce circularity in definitions, thereby replacing finite proof paths with infinite ones.

Consider the sequence of programs in Figure 1. In the figure, P_1 is derived by unfolding the occurrence of `q(X)` in the first clause of P_0. P_2 is derived from P_1 by folding the literal `q(X)` in the body of the second clause of predicate p into `p(X)` using the clause `p(X) :- q(X)` in P_0. Alternatively, consider the transformation sequence in figure 2. By folding `q(X)` in the second clause of p in P_1 (using the second clause defining q in P_1), we obtain program P_2'. Now folding `q(X)` in the second clause of q in P_2' (using second clause of p in P_1), we get program P_3', whose least model differs from that of P_0.

Transformation Systems with Irreversible Folding If the folding transformation is reversible, then since its effect can be undone by an unfolding, any partially correct unfold/fold transformation sequence is also totally correct. However, for reversibility, folding at step i of the transformation can *only* use the clauses in P_i.

`p(X):-q(X).`
`q(a).`
`q(f(X)):-q(X).`
	`p(a).`
	`p(f(X)):-q(X).`
	`q(a).`
	`q(f(X)):-q(X).`
		`p(a).`
		`p(f(X)):-p(X).`
		`q(a).`
		`q(f(X)):-q(X).`

Program P_0	Program P_1	Program P_2

Fig. 1. An example of correct unfold/fold transformation sequence

Therefore reversibility is a *restrictive* condition that seriously limits the power of unfold/fold systems by disallowing many correct folding transformations, such as the one used to derive P_2 from P_1. Hence almost all research on unfold/fold transformations have focused on constructing systems that permit irreversible folding. In such systems folding at step i can use clauses that are not in P_i. For example, in the original and extended Tamaki-Sato systems [20,21] folding always uses clauses in P_0 whereas in the Kanamori-Fujita system [8] the clauses can come from any P_j ($j \leq i$). But ensuring total correctness of irreversible transformation sequences is difficult. In order to ensure that folding is still totally correct, these systems permit folding using only clauses with certain (syntactic) properties. For instance, the original Tamaki-Sato system permits folding using a single clause only (*conjunctive* folding) and this clause is required to be non-recursive. In [7] the above system was extended to allow folding with multiple clauses (*disjunctive* folding) but all the clauses are required to be be non-recursive. Kanamori and Fujita [8] as well Tamaki and Sato in a later paper [21] gave two different approaches for conjunctive folding using recursive clauses. But the design of a transformation system that allows folding in the presence of both disjunction *and* recursion has remained open so far. We will describe such a system in this paper.

To generalize in this direction one needs to first understand the strengths and limitations of the above systems. The key observation is that, although the book-keeping needed to determine permissible foldings appear radically different in the different systems, there is a striking similarity in how the transformations are proved correct. Essentially, these systems associate some *measure* with different program elements, namely, atoms and clauses to determine whether folding is permissible in that step (e.g., "foldable" flag in [20], descent levels/strata numbers in [21], and counters in [8]). Moreover, they ensure that each transformation step maintains an invariant relating proofs in the derived program to the various measures (e.g., the notions of rank-consistency in [8,20], weight-consistency in [7] and μ-completeness in [21]). This raises another interesting question: can we exploit the similarities in the correctness proofs of irreversible unfold/fold systems to develop an abstract framework. Such a framework will specify the obligations that must be satisfied to ensure total correctness and hence can simplify construction of unfold/fold systems to the extent that one is relieved of the burden of giving correctness proofs. We propose such a framework in this paper.

Program P_0	Program P_1	Program P_2'	Program P_3'

`p(X):-q(X).`
`q(a).`
`q(f(X)):-q(X).`
	`p(a).`
	`p(f(X)):-q(X).`
	`q(a).`
	`q(f(X)):-q(X).`
		`p(a).`
		`p(f(X)):-q(f(X)).`
		`q(a).`
		`q(f(X)):-q(X).`
			`p(a).`
			`p(f(X)):-q(f(X)).`
			`q(a).`
			`q(f(X)):-p(f(X)).`

Fig. 2. An example of incorrect unfold/fold transformation sequence

Summary of Results In this paper, we develop a general transformation framework for definite logic programs parameterized by certain abstract measures by suitably abstracting and extending the measures used in [7,8,20,21] (see Section 2). We relax the invariants needed in the proofs to permit *approximation* of measure values. This is the key idea that enables us to fold using multiple recursive clauses. We prove the correctness of transformations in the framework based only on the properties of the abstract measures. We show that various existing unfold/fold transformation systems can be derived from the framework by instantiating these abstract measures (see Section 3). We also show how the framework can be extended to include the Goal Replacement transformation (see Section 4).

The parameterized framework presented in this paper is useful for understanding the strengths and limitations of existing transformation systems. It also enables the construction of new unfold/fold systems. As evidence we obtain SCOUT (Strata and COunter based Unfold/fold Transformations), a transformation system that permits disjunctive folding using recursive clauses. The development of SCOUT was based on two crucial observations made possible by the framework. First, when instantiating the framework to obtain the Kanamori-Fujita system, it is easy to see that the counters (the measure used in their system) may come from any linearly ordered set; this permits us to incorporate stratification into the counters to obtain a system that generalizes the extended Tamaki-Sato system [21] as well as the Kanamori-Fujita system. Secondly, the framework enables us to maintain approximate counters; we can hence generalize the combination of the Kanamori-Fujita and the extended Tamaki-Sato systems to fold using multiple recursive clauses.

2 A Parameterized Transformation Framework

We now describe our parameterized unfold/fold transformation framework and illustrate the abstractions by drawing analogies to the Kanamori-Fujita system.

We assume familiarity with the standard notions of terms, models, substitutions, unification, most general unifier (mgu), definite clauses, SLD resolution, and proof trees [9]. We will use the following symbols (possibly with primes and subscripts): P to denote a definite logic program; $M(P)$ its least Herbrand model; C and D for clauses; A, B to denote atoms and literals and σ for mgu.

2.1 Unfolding and Folding

The unfolding and folding rules are defined as follows:

Rule 1 (Unfolding) Let C be a clause in P_i and A an atom in the body of C. Let $C_1, \ldots, C_m$ be the clauses in P_i whose heads are unifiable with A with most general unifier $\sigma_1, \ldots, \sigma_m$. Let C'_j be the clause that is obtained by replacing $A\sigma_j$ by the body of $C_j\sigma_j$ in $C\sigma_j$ $(1 \leq j \leq m)$. Assign $(P_i - \{C\}) \cup \{C'_1, \ldots, C'_m\}$ to P_{i+1}. □

Rule 2 (Folding) Let $\{C_1, \dots, C_m\} \subseteq P_i$ where C_l denotes the clause $A{:-}\ A_{l,1}, \dots, A_{l,n_l}, A'_1, \dots, A'_n$, and $\{D_1, \dots, D_m\} \subseteq P_j$ $(j \le i)$ where D_l is the clause $B_l{:-}\ B_{l,1}, \dots, B_{l,n_l}$. Further, let:
1. $\forall 1 \le l \le m\ \exists \sigma_l\ \forall 1 \le k \le n_l\ A_{l,k} = B_{l,k}\sigma_l$
2. $B_1\sigma_1 = B_2\sigma_2 = \cdots = B_m\sigma_m = B$
3. $D_1, \dots, D_m$ are the only clauses in P_j whose heads are unifiable with B.
4. $\forall 1 \le l \le m$, σ_l substitutes the internal variables[1] of D_l to distinct variables which do not appear in $\{A, B, A'_1, \dots A'_n\}$.

Then $P_{i+1} := (P_i - \{C_1, \dots, C_m\}) \cup \{C'\}$ where $C' \equiv A{:-}\ B, A'_1, \dots, A'_n$. □

$D_1, \dots, D_m$ are the *folder* clauses, $C_1, \dots, C_m$ are the *folded* clauses, and B is the *folder* atom. A folding step is *conjunctive* whenever both the folder and folded clauses are singleton sets and is *disjunctive* otherwise. Note that in the latter step a set of folded clauses is *simultaneously* replaced by a single clause using a set of folder clauses. We say that $P_0, P_1, \dots, P_n$ is an unfold/fold transformation sequence if the program P_{i+1} is obtained from P_i $(i \ge 0)$ by application of an unfold or a fold rule. Partial correctness of an unfold/fold transformation sequence (Theorem 1) is established by showing that a proof T of any ground atom $A \in M(P_{i+1})$, has a corresponding proof T' in P_i. This can be proved by induction on the structure of T.

Theorem 1 (Partial Correctness) *Let $P_0, P_1, \dots, P_i$ be a program transformation sequence where $M(P_j) = M(P_0)$ for all $0 \le j \le i$. If P_{i+1} is obtained from P_i by applying either unfolding or folding, then $M(P_{i+1}) \subseteq M(P_i)$.* □

2.2 Measures, Measure-Consistent Proofs and Total Correctness

Total correctness of an unfold/fold transformation sequence is established by inducting on some well-founded order to construct a proof in P_{i+1} for any atom A in $M(P_i)$. To see the subtleties in showing total correctness, consider transforming P_i to P_{i+1} using a conjunctive folding step. To construct a proof of A (the head of the folded clause) in P_{i+1}, we need a proof of B (the folder atom) in P_{i+1}. But the existence of such a proof can be established (by induction hypothesis) only if B is less than A in the well-founded order on which we are inducting. Note that if the folder clause is picked from P_j, $j < i$, we cannot use simple well-founded orders like size of proof trees in P_i, since proof of B in P_i can be larger in size than the proof of A in P_i. Here we develop an abstract formulation of certain well-founded orders (which we call *measures*) on which we can induct to establish total correctness.

It is worth noting that we do not attempt to translate every proof of A in P_i to a proof of A in P_{i+1}. Instead, following [8,20,21] we consider a "special proof" called *strongly measure-consistent proof* (see Definition 6) of A in P_i and construct a proof of A in P_{i+1}. The induction proof for establishing total correctness is completed by showing that the proof of A in P_{i+1} thus constructed is itself strongly measure consistent.

[1] Variables appearing in the body of a clause, but not its head

Recall that irreversible folding steps need to be constrained in order to preserve the semantics. In order to enforce these constraints, we maintain some book-keeping information as we perform the transformations, formalized using the following notions of *Measure structure*, *Atom measure*, and *Clause measure*.

Definition 1 (Measure Structure) *A Measure Structure is a 4-tuple* $\mu = \langle \mathcal{M}, \oplus, \prec, \mathcal{W} \rangle$ *where* $\langle \mathcal{M}, \oplus \rangle$ *is a commutative group with* $\mathbf{0} \in \mathcal{M}$ *as its identity element,* $\prec$ *is a linear order on* $\mathcal{M}$, $\oplus$ *is monotone w.r.t.* $\prec$, *and* $\mathcal{W}$ *is a subset of* $\{x \in \mathcal{M} \mid \mathbf{0} \preceq x\}$, *over which* $\prec$ *is well-founded.*

We will refer to $\mathcal{M}$, the first component of the measure structure, as the *measure space*. We let $\preceq$ denote $\prec$ or $=$. Moreover, we use $\ominus$ to denote the inverse operation of the group $\langle \mathcal{M}, \oplus \rangle$. We also use $\ominus$ as a binary operator, $a \ominus b$ meaning $a \oplus (\ominus b)$ (where $(\ominus b)$ is the inverse of b). The Kanamori-Fujita system [8] keeps track of integer counters. Thus the measure structure is $\langle \mathbb{Z}, +, <, \mathbb{N} \rangle$, where $\mathbb{Z}$ and $\mathbb{N}$ are the set of integers and natural numbers respectively, $+$ denotes integer addition, and $<$ is the arithmetic comparison operator.

Definition 2 (Atom Measure) *An atom measure* α *of a program* P *w.r.t. a measure structure* μ *is a partial function from the Herbrand base of* P *to* $\mathcal{W}$ *such that it is total on the least Herbrand model of* P. *For our purposes, it suffices to use the same atom measure for each program in a transformation sequence.*

In the Kanamori-Fujita system, the atom measure of any P_i in the transformation sequence is the number of nodes in the shortest proof tree of A in the initial program P_0. The proof of total correctness for folding will induct on the atom measure, relating the atom measure of A (the head of the folded clauses) with the atom measure of B (the folder atom).

Definition 3 (Clause Measure) *A clause measure* $(\gamma_{lo}, \gamma_{hi})$ *of a program* P *w.r.t. a measure structure* μ *is a pair of total functions from clauses of* P *to* $\mathcal{M}$ *such that* $\forall C \in P \; \gamma_{lo}(C) \preceq \gamma_{hi}(C)$.

In the Kanamori-Fujita system, γ_{lo} and γ_{hi} are the same and map each clause to its corresponding counter value. However, as we will see later, to allow disjunctive folding we will need the two distinct functions γ_{lo} and γ_{hi}. Henceforth, we denote the clause measure of a program P_i by $(\gamma_{lo}^i, \gamma_{hi}^i)$. We will now develop the idea of "special proofs" mentioned earlier. For that purpose, we need the definition:

Definition 4 (Ground Proof of an Atom) *Let* T *be a tree, each of whose nodes is labeled with a ground atom. Then* T *is a ground proof in program* P, *if every node* A *in* T *satisfies the condition :* $A{:}{-}\; A_1, ..., A_n$ *is a ground instance of a clause in* P, *where* $A_1, ..., A_n$ $(n \geq 0)$ *are the children of* A *in* T.

Consider transforming P_i to P_{i+1} by a folding step (see figure below). C and D are the folded and folder clauses respectively and $j < i$.

.....	.....	.....
$D:$ q:– $q_1, ..., q_k$	$C:$ p:– $q_1, ..., q_k, q_{k+1}, ..., q_n$	$C':$ p:– q, $q_{k+1}, ..., q_n$
.....	.....	.....
Program P_j	Program P_i	Program P_{i+1}

In order to show that $p \in M(P_i) \Rightarrow p \in M(P_{i+1})$ by induction on $\prec$, we would like to show that $\alpha(q) \prec \alpha(p)$. The atoms p and q are related by what is shared between the bodies of the clauses C and D. Hence we attempt to relate their measures via the measures of bodies of C and D. Suppose D satisfies : (i) $\alpha(q) \preceq \sum_{1\le i\le k} \alpha(q_i)$, then we can relate $\alpha(q)$ to the sum of the measures of the body atoms of the folded clause C (since $k \le n$). Further if C satisfies : (ii) $\alpha(p) \succeq \sum_{1\le i\le n} \alpha(q_i)$, then we can establish that $\alpha(q) \preceq \alpha(p)$. If either (i) or (ii) is a strict relationship then we can establish that $\alpha(q) \prec \alpha(p)$. Relations (i) and (ii) form the basis for the notions of *weak* and *strong measure consistency*.

Definition 5 (Weakly Measure Consistent Proof) *A ground proof T in program P_i is weakly measure consistent w.r.t. atom measure α and clause measure $(\gamma^i_{lo}, \gamma^i_{hi})$ if every ground instance A:– $A_1, ..., A_n$ of a clause $C \in P_i$ used in T satisfies $\alpha(A) \preceq \gamma^i_{hi}(C) \oplus \sum_{1\le l\le n} \alpha(A_l)$.*

Definition 6 (Strongly Measure Consistent Proof) *A ground proof T in program P_i is strongly measure consistent w.r.t. atom measure α and clause measure $(\gamma^i_{lo}, \gamma^i_{hi})$ if every ground instance A:– $A_1, ..., A_n$ of a clause $C \in P_i$ used in T satisfies $\forall 1 \le l \le n\ \alpha(A_l) \prec \alpha(A)$ and $\alpha(A) \succeq \gamma^i_{lo}(C) \oplus \sum_{1\le l\le n} \alpha(A_l)$*

Definition 7 (Measure Consistent Proof) *A ground proof T in program P_i is said to be measure consistent w.r.t. atom measure α and clause measure $(\gamma^i_{lo}, \gamma^i_{hi})$, if it is strongly and weakly measure consistent w.r.t. α and $(\gamma^i_{lo}, \gamma^i_{hi})$.*

We point out that our abstract notion of measure consistency relaxes the concrete notion of rank consistency of [8]. While rank consistency of [8] imposes a strict equality constraint on $\alpha(A)$, measure consistency only *bounds it from above and below.* As we will show later, this facilitates maintenance of approximate information. This is the central idea that permits us to do disjunctive folding using recursive clauses. For proving total correctness, we need :

Definition 8 (Measure consistent Program) *A program P is measure consistent w.r.t. atom measure α and clause measure $(\gamma_{lo}, \gamma_{hi})$, if for all $A \in M(P)$, we have : (1) All ground proofs of A in P are weakly measure consistent w.r.t. α and $(\gamma_{lo}, \gamma_{hi})$ (2) A has a ground proof in P which is strongly measure consistent w.r.t. α and $(\gamma_{lo}, \gamma_{hi})$*

We are now ready to define the abstract conditions on folding and constraints on how the clause measures are to be updated after an unfold/fold step. For each clause C obtained by applying an unfold/fold transformation on program P_i, we derive a lower bound on $\gamma^{i+1}_{hi}(C)$ and an upper bound on $\gamma^{i+1}_{lo}(C)$, denoted by

$GLB^{i+1}(C)$ and $LUB^{i+1}(C)$ respectively. We will see later that the conditions on when the rules become applicable, as well as these bounds will be based on the requirements of the proof of total correctness.

We assume that for any atom A (not necessarily ground), $\alpha_{min}(A)$ denotes a lower bound on the measure of any provable ground instantiation of A *i.e.* $\forall\theta\ \alpha_{min}(A) \preceq \alpha(A\theta)$. We use α_{min} in the folding condition of rule 4 below.

Rule 3 (Measure Preserving Unfolding) Let P_{i+1} be obtained from P_i by an unfolding transformation as described in Rule 1. Then, $\forall 1 \leq j \leq m$

$$\gamma_{lo}^{i+1}(C'_j) \preceq GLB^{i+1}(C'_j) = \gamma_{lo}^{i}(C) \oplus \gamma_{lo}^{i}(C_j) \tag{1}$$

$$\gamma_{hi}^{i+1}(C'_j) \succeq LUB^{i+1}(C'_j) = \gamma_{hi}^{i}(C) \oplus \gamma_{hi}^{i}(C_j) \tag{2}$$

The clause measure of all other clauses in P_{i+1} are inherited from P_i. □

Rule 4 (Measure Preserving Folding) Let P_{i+1} be obtained from P_i by a folding transformation as described in Rule 2, such that $\forall 1 \leq l \leq m.\ \gamma_{hi}^{j}(D_l) \prec \gamma_{lo}^{i}(C_l) \oplus \sum_{1\leq k\leq n} \alpha_{min}(A'_k)$.[2] Then,

$$\gamma_{lo}^{i+1}(C') \preceq GLB^{i+1}(C') = \min_{1\leq l\leq m} (\ \gamma_{lo}^{i}(C_l) \ominus \gamma_{hi}^{j}(D_l)\ ) \tag{3}$$

$$\gamma_{hi}^{i+1}(C') \succeq LUB^{i+1}(C') = \max_{1\leq l\leq m} (\gamma_{hi}^{i}(C_l) \ominus \gamma_{lo}^{j}(D_l)) \tag{4}$$

and the clause measure of all other clauses in P_{i+1} are inherited from P_i. □

It should be noted that the above rules do not prescribe *unique* values for upper and lower clause measures for the clauses generated by the transformations. Instead, they only specify bounds of these values; the values themselves are chosen only when instantiating the framework to a concrete system.

Observe from the definition of atom measures that we can always assign **0** to α_{min}. However, by setting a more accurate estimate of α_{min}, we can allow more folding steps. As an example, consider any conjunctive folding step where the folded clause $C \in P_i$ has more body atoms than the folder clause $D \in P_j$, and $\gamma_{lo}^{i}(C) = \gamma_{hi}^{j}(D)$. Such a folding step will not be allowed if $\forall A\ \alpha_{min}(A) = \mathbf{0}$.

The Need for Approximate Clause Measures : In the Kanamori-Fujita system, a counter (corresponding to our clause measure) is associated with every clause. Roughly speaking, the counter associated with a clause $C \in P_i$ where $C \equiv A{:-}\ A_1, \ldots, A_n$ indicates the number of interior nodes in the smallest proof tree in P_0 that derives $A_1, \ldots, A_n$ from A. Thus, it is the amount saved (in terms of proof tree size, compared to the smallest proof in P_0) whenever C is used in a proof in P_i. The folding rule is applicable provided the savings accrued in the folded clause is more than that in the folder clause.

To see why a single counter is inadequate for disjunctive folding, consider the following example:

[2] Intuitively, if the clause measure of C_l "exceeds" the clause measure of D_l then we can fold C_l using D_l.

Program P_i	Program P_{i+1}
C_1: `p :- r, t.` (x_1)	
C_2: `p :- s, t.` (x_2)	C': `p :- q, t.` (?)
C_3: `q :- r.` (x_3)	C_3: `q :- r.` (x_3)
C_4: `q :- s.` (x_4)	C_4: `q :- s.` (x_4)

P_{i+1} is obtained from P_i by folding $\{C_3, C_4\}$ into $\{C_1, C_2\}$. Now, the savings due to C' in a proof of P_{i+1} depends on whether C_3 or C_4 is used to resolve q in that proof. Since this information is unknown at transformation time, we can only keep approximate information about savings. In our framework we choose to approximate the savings by the closed interval $[\gamma_{lo}, \gamma_{hi}]$.

We now have the necessary machinery for establishing total correctness of a sequence of unfold/fold transformations.

Lemma 1 (Preserving Weak Measure Consistency) *Let $P_0, \ldots, P_i$ be a transformation sequence of measure consistent programs such that $M(P_0) = M(P_j)$ for all $0 \leq j \leq i$. Let P_{i+1} be obtained from P_i by applying measure-preserving unfolding or measure-preserving folding. Then, all ground proofs of P_{i+1} are weakly measure consistent.*

Proof Sketch. The proof proceeds by induction on the size of ground proofs of P_{i+1}. Let T be a ground proof of some ground atom A in P_{i+1}, and let A:– $A_1, \ldots, A_n$ (where $n \geq 0$) be the ground instance of a clause $C \in P_{i+1}$ that is used at the root of the proof T. Then the subproofs of $A_1, \ldots, A_n$ in T are weakly measure consistent by induction hypothesis.

Hence, it suffices to show that, $\alpha(A) \preceq \gamma_{hi}^{i+1}(C) \oplus \sum_{1 \leq l \leq n} \alpha(A_l)$. To show this, we consider three cases: (1) C was inherited from P_i. (2) C was obtained from P_i by unfolding; and (3) C was obtained from P_i by folding. In each of these three cases, we can show the above inequality by assuming $M(P_{i+1}) \subseteq M(P_i)$ (which follows from theorem 1). □

Theorem 2 (Total Correctness) *Let $P_0, P_1, \ldots, P_i$ be a transformation sequence of measure consistent programs such that $M(P_0) = M(P_j)$ for all $0 \leq j \leq i$. Let P_{i+1} be obtained from P_i by applying measure-preserving unfolding or measure-preserving folding. Then,* (i) *$M(P_{i+1}) = M(P_i)$ and* (ii) *P_{i+1} is a measure-consistent program.*

Proof. By theorem 1, we have $M(P_{i+1}) \subseteq M(P_i)$, and by lemma 1 we know that all ground proofs of P_{i+1} are weakly measure consistent. Hence it is sufficient to prove that (1) $M(P_i) \subseteq M(P_{i+1})$ and (2) $\forall A \in M(P_{i+1})$, A has a strongly measure consistent proof in P_{i+1}.

Consider any ground atom $A \in M(P_i)$. Since P_i is measure consistent, A has a strongly measure consistent proof T in P_i. We now construct a strongly measure consistent proof T' of A in P_{i+1}. Construction of T' proceeds by induction on atom measures. Let C be a clause used at the root of T. Let A:– $A_1, \ldots, A_n$ (where $n \geq 0$) be the ground instantiation of C at the root of T. Since T is strongly measure consistent $\alpha(A_i) \prec \alpha(A)$, for all $1 \leq i \leq n$. Hence, we have strongly measure consistent proofs $T'_1, ..., T'_n$ of $A_1, ..., A_n$ in P_{i+1}. We construct T' by considering the following cases:

Case 1: C is *inherited* from P_i into P_{i+1}

T' is constructed with A:– $A_1, ..., A_n$ at its root and $T'_1, ..., T'_n$ as its children. This proof T' is strongly measure consistent.

Case 2: C is *unfolded.*

Let A_1 be the atom in the body of C which is unfolded. Let the clause used to resolve A_1 in T be C_1 and the ground instance of C_1 used be A_1:– $A_{1,1}, ..., A_{1,l_1}$. By definition of unfolding, A:– $A_{1,1}, ..., A_{1,l_1}, A_2, ..., A_n$ is a ground instance of a clause C'_1 in P_{i+1} with $\gamma_{lo}^{i+1}(C'_1) \preceq \gamma_{lo}^i(C) \oplus \gamma_{lo}^i(C_1)$. Also, $\alpha(A_{1,j}) \prec \alpha(A_1) \prec \alpha(A)$, for all $1 \leq j \leq l_1$. Thus, we have strongly measure consistent proofs $T'_{1,1}, ..., T'_{1,l_1}$ of $A_{1,1}, ..., A_{1,l_1}$ in P_{i+1}. The proof T' is now constructed by applying A:– $A_{1,1}, ..., A_{1,l_1}, A_2, ..., A_n$ at the root, and putting $T'_{1,1}, ..., T'_{1,l_1}, T'_2, ..., T'_n$ as the children. Since T is strongly measure consistent,

$$\begin{aligned} & \alpha(A) \succeq \gamma_{lo}^i(C) \oplus \textstyle\sum_{1 \leq j \leq n} \alpha(A_j) \text{ and } \alpha(A_1) \succeq \gamma_{lo}^i(C_1) \oplus \textstyle\sum_{1 \leq j \leq l_1} \alpha(A_{1,j}) \\ \Longrightarrow\ & (\alpha(A) \oplus \alpha(A_1)) \succeq \gamma_{lo}^i(C) \oplus \gamma_{lo}^i(C_1) \oplus \textstyle\sum_{1 \leq j \leq n} \alpha(A_j) \oplus \textstyle\sum_{1 \leq j \leq l_1} \alpha(A_{1,j}) \\ \Longrightarrow\ & \alpha(A) \succeq \gamma_{lo}^{i+1}(C'_1) \oplus \textstyle\sum_{2 \leq j \leq n} \alpha(A_j) \oplus \textstyle\sum_{1 \leq j \leq l_1} \alpha(A_{1,j}) \end{aligned}$$

Hence, T' is a strongly measure consistent proof in P_{i+1}.

Case 3: C is *folded.*

Let C (potentially with other clauses) be folded, using folder clauses from P_j, $j \leq i$, to clause C' in P_{i+1}. Assume that $A_1, ..., A_k$ are the instances of the folded atoms in C. Then, C' has a ground instance of the form A:– $B, A_{k+1}, ..., A_n$ where B:– $A_1, ..., A_k$ is a ground instance of a folder clause $D \in P_j$.[3] Since $M(P_i) = M(P_j)$ and $A_1, ..., A_k$ are provable in P_i they must also be provable in P_j. Moreover, since $D \in P_j$, $B \in M(P_j) = M(P_i)$. Since P_j is measure consistent, $\alpha(B) \preceq \gamma_{hi}^j(D) \oplus \sum_{1 \leq l \leq k} \alpha(A_l)$.

Now, by the strong measure consistency of T,

$$\begin{aligned} \alpha(A) & \succeq \gamma_{lo}^i(C) \oplus \textstyle\sum_{1 \leq l \leq k} \alpha(A_l) \oplus \textstyle\sum_{k+1 \leq l \leq n} \alpha(A_l) \\ & \succeq \gamma_{lo}^i(C) \oplus (\alpha(B) \ominus \gamma_{hi}^j(D)) \oplus \textstyle\sum_{k+1 \leq l \leq n} \alpha(A_l) \qquad \cdots\cdots (*) \\ & \succeq (\gamma_{lo}^i(C) \ominus \gamma_{hi}^j(D)) \oplus \alpha(B) \oplus \textstyle\sum_{k+1 \leq l \leq n} \alpha_{min}(A_l) \\ & \succ \alpha(B) \text{ (by condition of measure preserving folding)} \end{aligned}$$

Now, by induction hypothesis, B has a strongly measure consistent proof T'_B in P_{i+1}. We construct T', the proof of A in P_{i+1}, with A:– $B, A_{k+1}, ..., A_n$ at its root, and $T'_B, T'_{k+1}, ..., T'_n$ as its children. To show that T' is strongly measure consistent, note that $\gamma_{lo}^{i+1}(C') \preceq (\gamma_{lo}^i(C) \ominus \gamma_{hi}^j(D))$ according to the definition of measure preserving folding, as C and D are folded and folder clauses. Combining this with (*) we get,

$$\alpha(A) \succeq \gamma_{lo}^{i+1}(C') \oplus \alpha(B) \oplus \textstyle\sum_{k+1 \leq l \leq n} \alpha(A_l)$$

This completes the proof. □

[3] Recall that in the folding transformation, all clauses in P_j whose head is unifiable with B are folder clauses.

Note that by applying measure preserving unfolding/folding to program P_i, we can generate a clause which is also inherited from P_i. It is straightforward to adjust the clause measures of P_{i+1} that will still ensure that P_{i+1} remains measure consistent (details are omitted).

3 Constructing Concrete Unfold/Fold Systems by Instantiating the Framework

To construct a concrete unfold/fold transformation system from our abstract framework, the following parameters need to be instantiated :

1. a measure structure μ;
2. atom measure α and α_{min};
3. clause measure $(\gamma_{lo}, \gamma_{hi})$ for clauses in the initial program P_0 such that P_0 is measure consistent; and
4. functions to compute the clause measure of new clauses obtained by the transformations such that they satisfy the constraints imposed by equations (1) through (4) (refer Rules 3 and 4).

Note that there are *no further* proof obligations. Once the above four elements are defined, total correctness of the transformation system is *guaranteed* by the framework.

3.1 Existing Unfold/Fold Systems

We first show how our framework can be instantiated to obtain the Kanamori-Fujita and the extended Tamaki-Sato systems. To the best of our knowledge, these are the only two existing systems that allow folding using recursive clauses. However in both of these systems folding is conjunctive.

The Kanamori-Fujita System [8]: This system can be obtained as an instance of our framework as follows:

1. $\mu = \langle \mathbb{Z}, +, <, \mathbb{N} \rangle$. This measure structure corresponds to the use of integer counters in [8].
2. $\alpha(A)$ = number of nodes in the smallest proof of A in P_0, and for any atom A, $\alpha_{min}(A) = 1$. Thus, $\alpha(A)$ denotes the *rank* of A described in [8].
3. $\forall C \in P_0\ \gamma^0_{lo}(C) = \gamma^0_{hi}(C) = 1$. Since all clause measures are 1, it follows immediately from the definition of atom measures that the smallest proofs of any ground goal G are strongly measure consistent, and all proofs in P_0 are weakly measure consistent. Hence P_0 is measure consistent.
4. $\forall C \in P_{i+1} - P_i$ (i.e., new clauses in P_{i+1}), $\gamma^{i+1}_{lo}(C) = GLB^{i+1}(C)$ and $\gamma^{i+1}_{hi}(C) = LUB^{i+1}(C)$. Under the given measure structure, it is immediate that the above definition is identical to the computation on counters in [8].

Furthermore, the measure preserving folding rule (Rule 4) is applied only when both folder and folded clauses are singleton sets. It is easy to see a one-to-one correspondence between the conditions on unfold/fold transformations of the above instantiation and the Kanamori-Fujita system.

The Extended Tamaki-Sato System [21]: In this system all the predicate symbols are partitioned into n strata. In the initial program a predicate from stratum j is defined using only predicates from strata $\leq j$. We can obtain this system as an instance of our framework as follows:

1. $\mu = \langle \mathbb{Z}^n, \oplus, \prec, \mathbb{N}^n \rangle$ where $\oplus$ denotes coordinate-wise integer addition of n-tuples of integers, and $\prec$ denotes the lexicographic $<$ order over n-tuples of integers. The n-tuples in the measure structure will correspond to the n strata of the original program.
2. $\alpha(A) = \min(\{w(T) \mid T \text{ is a proof of } A \text{ in } P_0\})$, where $w(T)$ is the *weight* of the proof T defined as an n-tuple $\langle w_1, \ldots, w_n \rangle$ such that $\forall 1 \leq j \leq n$, w_j is the number of nodes of predicates from stratum j in T. $\alpha(A)$ corresponds to the notion of *weight-tuple measure* of A defined in [21].
   For any atom A, $\alpha_{min}(A) = \mathbf{0} = \langle 0, \ldots, 0 \rangle$.
3. $\forall C \in P_0$, $\gamma_{lo}^0(C) = \gamma_{hi}^0(C) = \langle w_1, \ldots, w_n \rangle$, where $C \equiv A{:}-\ A_1, \ldots, A_n$ and for $1 \leq j \leq n$, $w_j = 1$ if the predicate symbol of A is from stratum j, and 0 otherwise.
   For any $A \in M(P_0)$, the proof T that defines $\alpha(A)$ (item 2 above) is strongly measure consistent. Weak measure consistency of ground proofs in P_0 is established by induction on their size.
4. $\forall C \in P_{i+1} - P_i$, $\gamma_{hi}^{i+1}(C) = LUB^{i+1}(C)$ and $\gamma_{lo}^{i+1}(C) = approx(GLB^{i+1}(C))$. The function *approx* reduces a measure as follows. Let $u = \langle u_1, \ldots, u_n \rangle$ and k_{min} be the smallest index k such that $u_k > 0$. Then $approx(u) = \langle u'_1, \ldots, u'_n \rangle$ where $u'_{k_{min}} = 1$ and is 0 elsewhere.

As in the Kanamori-Fujita system, here also the measure preserving folding rule is applied only when both folder and folded clauses are singleton sets.

To establish the correspondence between the above instantiation and the extended Tamaki-Sato system, recall that the latter associates a descent level with each clause of every program in a transformation sequence. If a clause C in P_i has the descent level k, then with the above instantiation, $\gamma_{lo}^i(C) = \langle l_1, \ldots, l_n \rangle$ where $l_k = 1$ and 0 elsewhere; i.e. the only non-zero entry in its lower clause measure appears in the kth position. Thus our lower clause measure precisely captures the information that is kept track of by the extended Tamaki-Sato system.

Assigning Measure Structures and Clause Measures Observe that our framework does not prescribe exact values to the clause measures. Instead it bounds the clause measures from above and below. So an important aspect of our instantiation involves assigning values to the clause measures that satisfy these constraints. From an abstract point of view, the Kanamori-Fujita system uses a relatively coarse measure space ($\mathbb{Z}$) but within this space it maintains accurate clause measures (integer counters). Our instantiation reflects this by not relaxing the bounds while updating the clause measures (see step 4 of the instantiation). On the other hand, the extended Tamaki-Sato system uses a more fine-grained measure space ($\mathbb{Z}^n$). But this measure space is not completely utilized since clause measures are the descent level of clauses, which can be simply represented by an integer. Therefore in step 4 of our instantiation we accordingly loosened the bound. As far as the Gergatsoulis-Katzouraki [7] and original Tamaki-Sato systems [20] are concerned, first note that they do not permit folding using recursive clauses. These systems use coarse measure spaces. Moreover they do not even fully utilize these measure spaces as is evident from the lesser amount of book keeping performed by them. By choosing a coarse measure structure and relaxing the bounds along lines similar to the extended Tamaki-Sato system we have been able to instantiate these two systems as well. Details are omitted.

3.2 SCOUT— A New Unfold/Fold System

We now construct SCOUT, an unfold/fold transformation system for definite logic programs that allows disjunctive folding using recursive clauses. It incorporates the notion of strata from the extended Tamaki-Sato system into the counters of the Kanamori-Fujita system. Thus with every clause it maintains a *pair* of stratified counters as the clause measure. The instantiation is as follows. We assume that the predicate symbols appearing in the initial program P_0 are partitioned into n strata, as in the extended Tamaki-Sato system.

1. $\mu = \langle \mathbb{Z}^n, \oplus, \prec, \mathbb{N}^n \rangle$ where $\oplus$ denotes coordinate-wise integer addition of n-tuples of integers, and $\prec$ denotes the lexicographic $<$ order over n-tuples of integers.
2. $\alpha(A)$ is defined exactly as in the instantiation of the extended Tamaki-Sato system above. For any atom A we set $\alpha_{min}(A) = \langle w_1, \ldots, w_n \rangle$ where $w_j = 1$ if A is from stratum j and 0 elsewhere.
3. Clause measure of clauses in P_0 is defined exactly as in the instantiation of the extended Tamaki-Sato system above. Therefore the proofs of measure consistency are also identical.
4. $\forall C \in P_{i+1} - P_i$, $\gamma_{lo}^{i+1}(C) = GLB^{i+1}(C)$ and $\gamma_{hi}^{i+1}(C) = LUB^{i+1}(C)$.

SCOUT provides a solution to two important (and orthogonal) problems that have thus far remained open: folding using clauses that have disjunctions as well as recursion, and combining the stratification-based (extended) Tamaki-Sato system with the counter-based Kanamori-Fujita system thereby obtaining a single system that strictly subsumes either of them even when restricted to conjunctive folding (See [13] for a formal proof of this claim).

It is interesting to note that by simple inspection of the instantiations, one can see that when the number of strata is 1 and only conjunctive folding is permitted, SCOUT collapses to the Kanamori-Fujita system. Collapsing SCOUT to other existing unfold/fold systems by varying the number of strata and extending the parameters (e.g. measure structure) remains an interesting open problem.

4 Goal Replacement

Augmenting an unfold/fold transformation system with the goal replacement rule makes it more powerful. In this section we incorporate goal replacement to our parameterized framework. Goal replacement allows semantically equivalent conjunctions of atoms to be freely interchanged. We formally define it below. For a conjunction of atoms $A_1, ..., A_n$, we use the notation $vars(A_1, ..., A_n)$ to denote the set of variables in $A_1, ..., A_n$.

Rule 5 (Goal Replacement) Let C be a clause $A\text{:-}\ A_1, \ldots, A_k, G$ in P_i, and G' be an atom such that $vars(G) = vars(G') \subseteq vars(A, A_1, ..., A_k)$. Suppose for all ground instantiation θ of G, G' we have $P_i \vdash G\theta \Leftrightarrow P_i \vdash G'\theta$. Then $P_{i+1} := (P_i - \{C\}) \cup \{C'\}$ where $C' \equiv A\text{:-}\ A_1, \ldots, A_k, G'$. □

Note that although we replace a single atom G by another atom G' (where G and G' do not contain any internal variables), we can replace conjunctions of atoms using a sequence of folding, goal replacement and unfolding transformations.

The above transformation is partially correct (a formal proof appears in [13]). However, if goal replacement is applied to a measure consistent program P_i it is totally correct. But then we also need to ensure that the resulting program P_{i+1} is measure consistent. If this is ensured, then even if goal replacement is interleaved with irreversible folding total correctness will be preserved. Formally,

Rule 6 (Measure Preserving Goal Replacement) Suppose program P_{i+1} is obtained from program P_i by applying the goal replacement transformation as described in Rule 5. Let there exist $\delta, \delta' \in \mathcal{M}$ (where measure structure is $\mu = \langle \mathcal{M}, \oplus, \prec, \mathcal{W} \rangle)$ such that for all ground instantiation θ of G, G', we have: *(i)* $\delta \preceq \alpha(G\theta) \ominus \alpha(G'\theta) \preceq \delta'$ *(ii)* $\gamma^i_{lo}(C) \oplus \delta \oplus \sum_{1 \le p \le k} \alpha_{min}(A_p) \succ \mathbf{0}$. Then

$$\gamma^{i+1}_{lo}(C') \preceq \gamma^i_{lo}(C) \oplus \delta \tag{5}$$
$$\gamma^{i+1}_{hi}(C') \succeq \gamma^i_{hi}(C) \oplus \delta' \tag{6}$$

The clause measures of the other clauses of P_{i+1} are inherited from P_i. □

We now present a formal proof of total correctness and preservation of measure consistency of the above rule.

Theorem 3 *Let P_{i+1} be derived from P_i by applying measure preserving goal replacement as described in rule 6. If P_i is measure consistent, then $M(P_i) = M(P_{i+1})$ and P_{i+1} is also measure consistent.*

Proof. Since measure preserving goal replacement is a special case of the goal replacement transformation in rule 5, we have $M(P_{i+1}) \subseteq M(P_i)$ by partial correctness of rule 5. Therefore it is sufficient to prove that : (1) all ground proofs of P_{i+1} are weakly measure consistent (2) $M(P_i) \subseteq M(P_{i+1})$ (3) $\forall B \in M(P_{i+1})$ there exists a strongly measure consistent proof of B in P_{i+1}. We prove proof obligation (1) separately. Proof obligations (2) and (3) are proved by showing that : $\forall B \in M(P_i)$ there exists a strongly measure consistent proof of B in P_{i+1}. This is sufficient since we know $M(P_{i+1}) \subseteq M(P_i)$.

First, we prove that all ground proofs of P_{i+1} are weakly measure consistent. The proof proceeds by induction on the size of ground proofs in P_{i+1}. Let T be a ground proof of a ground atom B in P_{i+1}. If the clause used at the root of T is not the new clause C', then the proof follows by induction hypothesis and the measure consistency of P_i. If the clause used at the root of T is C', then let the ground instance of C' used at the root of T be $A\theta$:– $A_1\theta, \ldots, A_k\theta, G'\theta$. By induction hypothesis, the proofs of $A_1\theta, \ldots, A_k\theta, G'\theta$ in T are weakly measure consistent. It suffices to show that $\alpha(A) \preceq \gamma_{hi}^{i+1}(C') \oplus \sum_{1\leq l\leq k} \alpha(A_l\theta) \oplus \alpha(G'\theta)$ Now, $G'\theta \in M(P_{i+1}) \Rightarrow G'\theta \in M(P_i)$. Hence by rule 5 we have $G\theta \in M(P_i)$. Also, $\forall 1 \leq l \leq k\ A_l\theta \in M(P_i)$ (as $M(P_{i+1} \subseteq M(P_i))$. Then, $A\theta$:– $A_1\theta, \ldots A_k\theta, G\theta$ is a ground instantiation of C which appears at the root of some ground proof in P_i. Since P_i is measure consistent we have

$$
\begin{aligned}
\alpha(A) &\preceq \gamma_{hi}^{i}(C) \oplus \textstyle\sum_{1\leq l\leq k} \alpha(A_l\theta) \oplus \alpha(G\theta) \\
&\preceq \gamma_{hi}^{i}(C) \oplus \textstyle\sum_{1\leq l\leq k} \alpha(A_l\theta) \oplus (\ \alpha(G'\theta) \oplus \delta'\ ) \\
&\preceq \gamma_{hi}^{i+1}(C') \oplus \textstyle\sum_{1\leq l\leq k} \alpha(A_l\theta) \oplus \alpha(G'\theta)
\end{aligned}
$$

Now, we prove that $\forall B \in M(P_i)$ there is a strongly measure consistent proof of B in P_{i+1}. Since P_i is measure consistent, it suffices to translate a strongly measure consistent proof T of B in P_i to a strongly measure consistent proof T' of B in P_{i+1} for all $B \in M(P_i)$. We do this translation by induction on the atom measures. If the clause used at the root of T is not C (where C is the clause in P_i that is replaced) then the proof follows from the definition of strong measure consistency and induction hypothesis. Let C be the clause used at the root of T (a strongly measure consistent proof of A in P_i) and let $A\theta$:– $A_1\theta, \ldots, A_k\theta, G\theta$ be the ground instance of C used. Then, by strong measure consistency of T, $\alpha(A_l\theta) \prec \alpha(A\theta)$ for all $1 \leq l \leq k$. By induction hypothesis, we then have strongly measure consistent ground proofs $T_1', \ldots, T_k'$ of $A_1\theta, \ldots, A_k\theta$ in P_{i+1}. Also, by strong measure consistency of T

$$
\begin{aligned}
\alpha(A) &\succeq \gamma_{lo}^{i}(C) \oplus \textstyle\sum_{1\leq l\leq k} \alpha(A_l\theta) \oplus \alpha(G\theta) \\
&\succeq \gamma_{lo}^{i}(C) \oplus \textstyle\sum_{1\leq l\leq k} \alpha(A_l\theta) \oplus (\ \alpha(G'\theta) \oplus \delta\ ) \quad \cdots\cdots (*) \\
&\succeq (\ \gamma_{lo}^{i}(C) \oplus \textstyle\sum_{1\leq l\leq k} \alpha_{min}(A_l\theta) \oplus \delta\ ) \oplus \alpha(G'\theta) \\
&\succ \alpha(G'\theta) \text{ (By condition (ii) of rule 6)}
\end{aligned}
$$

Then, by induction hypothesis, $G'\theta$ has a proof $T_{G'\theta}'$ in P_{i+1}. The ground proof T' is constructed with $A\theta$:– $A_1\theta, \ldots, A_k\theta, G'\theta$ at the root (this is a ground instance of C', the new clause in P_{i+1}) and $T_1', \ldots, T_k', T_{G'\theta}'$ as its children. To show that this proof T' is measure consistent, note that $\gamma_{lo}^{i+1}(C') \preceq \gamma_{lo}^{i}(C) \oplus \delta$. Combining this with (*), we get

$$
\alpha(A) \succeq \gamma_{lo}^{i+1}(C') \oplus \sum_{1\leq l\leq k} \alpha(A_l\theta) \oplus \alpha(G'\theta)
$$

This completes the proof. □

Observe that, similar to the goal replacement transformation in [8,20,21] the conditions under which rule 6 may be applied are not testable at transformation time. For testability we need to (1) determine whether G and G' are semantically equivalent, and (2) estimate δ and δ' such that the clause measures of P_{i+1} can be computed.

Semantic equivalence is undecidable in general and can be conservatively approximated using program analysis. To estimate δ and δ' observe that any δ' which dominates the atom measure of all ground atoms satisfies the conditions of Rule 6. However, such a δ' may not always exist in the given measure structure. In such cases, we can extend the measure structure $\mu = \langle \mathcal{M}, \oplus, \prec, \mathcal{W} \rangle$ to $\langle \mathbb{Z} \times \mathcal{M}, \oplus', \preceq', \mathbb{N} \times \mathcal{W} \rangle$, where $\forall z_1, z_2 \in \mathbb{Z}$ and $\forall m_1, m_2 \in \mathcal{M}$ $(z_1, m_1) \oplus' (z_2, m_2) = (z_1 + z_2, m_1 \oplus m_2)$, and $\preceq'$ is the lexicographic ordering of pairs from $\mathbb{Z} \times \mathcal{M}$. Atom measures in this extended measure space are of the form $(0, w)$ (where $w \in \mathcal{W}$). We set $\delta' = (1, \mathbf{0})$, which is lexicographically greater than all atom measures. Also, in certain cases we can define a lower bound of δ as follows. Let B be the atom in the body of a clause in P_i that is replaced and let $\{C_1, \ldots, C_n\}$ be the clauses in P_i that unify with B. Then, $\delta \preceq \min_{1 \leq k \leq n}(\gamma^i_{lo}(C_k) - \alpha_{min}(hd(C_k)))$, where $hd(C_k)$ is the head atom of C_k (for details see [14]).

The above steps define a procedure to add goal replacement to any arbitrary unfold/fold system instantiated in our framework. More importantly, this is done by simply manipulating the measures; the proofs of correctness of the augmented transformation system follow immediately from the proofs of our framework.

5 Conclusion

The development of a parameterized framework for unfold/fold transformations has several important implications. It enables us to compare existing transformation systems and modify them without redoing the correctness proofs (e.g., extending measures for goal replacement in Section 4). It also facilitates the development of new transformations systems. For instance, we derived SCOUT which permits folding using multiple recursive clauses. Such a transformation system is particularly important for verifying parameterized concurrent systems (such as a n-process token ring for arbitrary n) using logic program evaluation and deduction [4,16].

In [15], we have extended the work reported in this paper to obtain generalized unfold/fold transformation systems for normal logic programs. Aravindan and Dung [1] developed an approach to parameterize the correctness proofs of the original Tamaki-Sato system with respect to various semantics based on the notion of *semantic kernels*. Incorporating the idea of semantic kernel into our framework yields a framework that is parameterized with respect to the measure structures as well as semantics.

In future, it would be interesting to study whether we can develop similar parameterized unfold/fold transformation frameworks for other programming paradigms such as functional and concurrent constraint programming languages [5,17] as well as process algebraic specification languages (*e.g.* CCS) [6].

Acknowledgements

We would like to thank the anonymous referees for their valuable comments. We thank Alberto Pettorossi and Maurizio Proietti for useful discussions and pointers to earlier work. We also thank Sandro Etalle for relevant references, Taisuke Sato for providing us with a copy of his technical report [21], and David S. Warren for his comments about an earlier draft of this paper.

References

1. C. Aravindan and P.M. Dung. On the correctness of unfold/fold transformations of normal and extended logic programs. *Journal of Logic Programming*, pages 295–322, 1995.
2. A. Bossi, N. Cocco, and S. Dulli. A method of specializing logic programs. *ACM TOPLAS*, pages 253–302, 1990.
3. D. Boulanger and M. Bruynooghe. Deriving unfold/fold transformations of logic programs using extended OLDT-based abstract interpretation. *Journal of Symbolic Computation*, pages 495–521, 1993.
4. B. Cui, Y. Dong, X. Du, K. Narayan Kumar, C.R. Ramakrishnan, I.V. Ramakrishnan, A. Roychoudhury, S.A. Smolka, and D.S. Warren. Logic programming and model checking. In *Proceedings of PLILP/ALP, LNCS 1490*, pages 1–20, 1998.
5. S. Etalle, M. Gabrielli, and M.C. Meo. Unfold/fold transformations of CCP programs. In *Proceedings of CONCUR*, 1998.
6. Nicoletta De Francesco and Antonella Santone. A transformation system for concurrent processes. *Acta Informatica*, 35(12):1037–1073, 1998.
7. M. Gergatsoulis and M. Katzouraki. Unfold/fold transformations for definite clause programs. In *Proceedings of PLILP, LNCS 844*, pages 340–354, 1994.
8. T. Kanamori and H. Fujita. Unfold/fold transformation of logic programs with counters. In *USA-Japan Seminar on Logics of Programs*, 1987.
9. J.W. Lloyd. *Foundations of Logic Programming, Second Edition*. Springer-Verlag, 1993.
10. M. J. Maher. Correctness of a logic program transformation system. Technical report, IBM T.J. Watson Research Center, 1987.
11. A. Pettorossi and M. Proietti. *Transformation of logic programs*, volume 5 of *Handbook of Logic in Artificial Intelligence*, pages 697–787. Oxford University Press, 1998.
12. A. Pettorossi, M. Proietti, and S. Renault. Reducing nondeterminism while specializing logic programs. In *Proceedings of POPL*, pages 414–427, 1997.
13. A. Roychoudhury, K. Narayan Kumar, C.R. Ramakrishnan, and I.V. Ramakrishnan. A generalized unfold/fold transformation system for definite logic programs. Technical Report 98/37, Dept. of Computer Science, SUNY Stony Brook, 1998.
14. A. Roychoudhury, K. Narayan Kumar, C.R. Ramakrishnan, and I.V. Ramakrishnan. Proofs by program transformations. *Accepted for LOPSTR*, 1999.
15. A. Roychoudhury, K. Narayan Kumar, and I.V. Ramakrishnan. Beyond Tamaki-Sato style unfold/fold transformations for normal logic programs. Technical Report 99/21, Dept. of Computer Science, SUNY Stony Brook, 1999.
16. A. Roychoudhury, C. R. Ramakrishnan, I. V. Ramakrishnan, and S. A. Smolka. Tabulation based Induction proofs with applications to Automated Verification. In *Workshop on Tabulation in Parsing and Deduction*, pages 83–88, 1998.

17. David Sands. Total correctness by local improvement in the transformation of functional programs. *ACM TOPLAS*, 18(2):175–234, 1996.
18. H. Seki. Unfold/fold transformation of stratified programs. *In Theoretical Computer Science*, pages 107–139, 1991.
19. H. Seki. Unfold/fold transformation of general logic programs for well-founded semantics. *In Journal of Logic Programming*, pages 5–23, 1993.
20. H. Tamaki and T. Sato. Unfold/fold transformations of logic programs. In *Proceedings of International Conference on Logic Programming*, pages 127–138, 1984.
21. H. Tamaki and T. Sato. A generalized correctness proof of the unfold/ fold logic program transformation. Technical report, Ibaraki University, Japan, 1986.

Widening Sharing

Enea Zaffanella[1], Roberto Bagnara[2], and Patricia M. Hill[3]*

[1] Servizio IX Automazione, Università degli Studi di Modena, Italy.
zaffanella.enea@unimo.it
[2] Dipartimento di Matematica, Università degli Studi di Parma, Italy.
bagnara@cs.unipr.it
[3] School of Computer Studies, University of Leeds,
Leeds, LS2 9JT, U.K.
hill@scs.leeds.ac.uk

Abstract. We study the problem of an efficient *and* precise sharing analysis of (constraint) logic programs. After recognizing that neither plain Sharing nor its non-redundant (but equivalent) abstraction scale well to real programs, we consider the domain proposed by C. Fecht [12,13]. This domain consists of a combination of *Pos* with a quite weak abstraction of Sharing. While verifying that this domain is truly remarkable, in terms of both precision and efficiency, we have revealed significant precision losses for several real programs. This loss concerns groundness, pair-sharing, linearity, but not freeness. (Indeed, we have proved that a wide family of abstractions of Sharing do not incur precision loss on freeness.) We define a simple domain for sharing analysis that supports the implementation of several widening techniques. In particular, with this domain it is straightforward to turn Fecht's idea into a proper widening. More precise widenings are also considered. However, in spite of thorough experimentation we found that the first widening we propose is hard to improve on, provided *Pos* is included in the domain. We show that when *Pos* is not included, a widening based on cliques of sharing pairs is preferred.

Keywords: Mode Analysis, Sharing Analysis, Widening.

1 Introduction

For (constraint) logic programs, the main purpose of sharing analysis is to detect pair-sharing; that is, which *pairs* of variables are definitely independent. In a previous work [3] we observed that the Sharing domain of Jacobs and Langen [15] is redundant for pair-sharing. This achievement has important theoretical consequences (some of which will be exploited in the present work) and also a practical interest. In fact, it allows to keep sharing-sets as small as possible without any precision loss and to replace the *star-union* operation, whose complexity is exponential, by *self-bin-union*, which is quadratic. Even though significant speed-ups

* This research was partly supported by EPSRC, grant GR/M05645.

G. Nadathur (Ed.): PPDP'99, LNCS 1702, pp. 414–431, 1999.

have been observed in practice (up to three orders of magnitude on the analysis of real programs), the problem of scalability of the analysis, both in terms of precision (that is, the number of pairs that are detected as being definitely independent) and of resource usage, was still to be solved.

In this paper we address this problem. However, in order to give the right focus to the present work, we need to explain in detail what we aim at.

1.1 Analyses and Analyzers

The experimental part of our work is devoted to the construction of *practical*, *precise* and *efficient* data-flow analyzers for constraint logic-based languages. Some issues connected with the emphasized words deserve clarification.

A "practical analyzer" is one that has a chance to be turned into a useful tool. On one hand this means that compromising assumptions about the languages and the programs to be analyzed must be avoided as far as possible. Researchers in our area (including the present authors) have often made assumptions that are falsified by the implemented languages and their programs. This state of affairs can be justified in a relatively immature field, but this is no longer the case for the data-flow analysis of logic programs. Therefore we believe that we should now rid ourselves of most, if not all, limiting assumptions. We must take into account, for instance, that implemented languages perform unification that omits the *occur-check*; that programmers do exploit "nasty constructs" such as `assert/1` and `call/1`; that real programs make use of all kinds of built-ins provided by the language; as well as libraries, foreign language interfaces etc.

Many applications of data-flow analysis, such as semantics-based programming environments, need very precise information about a program's behavior in order, say, to assist the programmer during development, debugging, and certification. In the literature there are several papers reporting on the experimental evaluation of data-flow analyzers. In some of them one can find analysis' times well under the second for non-trivial, lengthy programs. What can one conclude from the fact that a program of several thousands lines can be analyzed in a couple of seconds on a desktop computer? If one excludes the possibility outlined above that special assumptions have been exploited so that the results cannot be generalized, the answer is probably that more precision is attainable. One of the important applications of data-flow analysis is in computer-assisted program verification or certification. In this field, what is not done by the computer must be done by hand. Who will spend hours to complete proofs by hand when the computer can do them in the same or even double the time? Similar remarks hold also for optimized compilation, if one takes into account that (1) only *production versions* deserve to be compiled with the optimization passes turned on, (2) a production version is compiled once and used thousands, perhaps millions of times, and (3) computers do work overnight.

So we do not participate in the race for the fastest ever analysis, especially when done (as is often the case) at the expense of precision. The real problem is how to increase precision yet avoid the concrete effects of exponential complexity. Consider groundness analysis, for instance. The cruder domains do not pose any efficiency problem. In contrast, the more refined domains for groundness, such as *Pos*, work perfectly until you bump into a "nasty" program clause (i.e., with more than, say, fifty variables for which the analyzer knows too little at that point of the analysis). When this happens, *Pos* will exhaust your computer's memory. One would like to have a more *linear*, or *stable* behavior. The right solution, as indicated by Cousot and Cousot [11], is not to revert to the simpler domains. We should use instead complex domains together with widening/narrowing operators. With such techniques we can try to limit precision losses to those cases where the cost of the complexity implied by these refined domains exceeds the available resources.

Ideally, it should be possible to endow data-flow analyzers with a *knob*. The user could then "rotate the knob" in order to control the complexity/precision ratio of the system. The widening/narrowing approach can make this possibility a reality. Unfortunately, the design of widening operators tends somewhat to escape the realm of theoretical analysis, and thus, in the authors' opinion, it has not been studied enough. Indeed, the development of successful widening operators requires, perhaps more than other things, extensive experimentation.

1.2 Fecht's Work

C. Fecht [12,13] proposed a domain $\downarrow SH$ for sharing analysis based on an abstraction of the usual Jacobs and Langen domain *SH* [15]. This domain is the same as *SH* but the concretization of a set of variables in $\downarrow SH$ is equivalent to the concretization of its powerset in *SH*. The advantage of $\downarrow SH$ is not just that an element can be normalized by removing all but the maximal sets, thereby reducing its size, but because it enables more efficient (but less precise) abstract operations than those used for *SH* and its non-redundant version SH^{ρ} [3]. Moreover, for computing the abstract unification in $\downarrow SH$, Fecht describes two useful optimizations that improve efficiency without losing any further precision.

One of the problems with the domain $\downarrow SH$ is that it does not capture ground dependencies. These are important for tracking sharing dependencies and, hence, sharing. Fecht solved this by deriving the ground dependencies through the *Pos* component of the combined domain $Pos + \downarrow SH$ and also $Pos + \downarrow SH + Lin$. Fecht tested both these domains and showed that, with his benchmarks, they compared favorably with equivalent ones using *SH* for the sharing and ground dependencies. He reported a negligible loss of precision and demonstrated that large programs could be analyzed using both $Pos + \downarrow SH$ and $Pos + \downarrow SH + Lin$ in a reasonable time scale. The results, although inconclusive, demonstrated real promise for an analyzer based on the $\downarrow SH$ approach. We say the results were inconclusive. The reason for this is that only a few non-trivial programs were tested and, for most of these, precision was not compared. (Fecht's *SH* analyzer could not cope with large programs possibly due to the problem that there was no redundancy elimination.) We note that Fecht did not present the domain $\downarrow SH$

as a widening[1] and did not discuss how a widening based on his domain might be achieved.

1.3 Combining Domains

In Fecht's work, and also in the work presented here, the combination of a sharing domain with *Pos* is the simplest possible. For any operation of the analysis, abstract mgu in particular, the *Pos* component is evaluated first. All sharing groups containing at least one variable that is definitely ground according to the resulting *Pos* formula are removed from the sharing component. This combination is made particularly efficient by the ready availability of definite groundness information allowed by the GER representation introduced in [5], where obtaining the set of definitely ground variables (and also the classes of groundness-equivalent variables) is a constant-time operation. Note that, theoretically speaking, more sophisticated combinations of *Pos* with Sharing are possible [8].

Following several other authors, we observed in [3], that, from a practical point of view, sharing analysis without freeness or linearity does not make sense. Both these properties allow, in a significant proportion of cases, to dispense with costly operations (such as star-union or, better, self-bin-union [4]) increasing the precision of sharing information at the same time, and this with very little overhead. Moreover, freeness is a useful property in itself. For details on how the combination with freeness is realized, we refer the reader to [17,19]. See [7] for the combination of both freeness and linearity information.

1.4 Experimental Results

We have compared the domain of Fecht *enhanced with freeness information*, that is $Pos{+}{\downarrow}SH{+}Free{+}Lin$, with the same domain where $\downarrow SH$ is substituted by the non-redundant sharing domain SH^{ρ} [3]. The precision of the analysis is measured by summing results over the success-patterns, for goal-independent (GI) analysis, and in both the call- and success-patterns, for goal-dependent (GD) analysis, for each procedure. For the domains tested, that is, $Pos{+}{\downarrow}SH{+}Free{+}Lin$, abbreviated as P+DSH+F+L, and $Pos{+}SH^{\rho}{+}Free{+}Lin$, abbreviated as P+NSH+F+L, the precision results consist of: the total number of definitely non-sharing pairs of program variables, NSP, the total number of definitely ground variables, GV, and the total number of definitely linear variables that are possibly not ground, LV. The freeness results are not compared because, as we have shown in [19], freeness is not affected, neither by abstracting SH to $\downarrow SH$, nor by redundancy elimination.

The comparison involved all the 92 Prolog programs in our current test-suite. On 73 of them there was no difference in precision. This is really remarkable considering that the $\downarrow SH$ approximation is rather crude.

[1] Indeed the approach of Fecht falls under the category "use a simpler domain" which, as clearly explained in [11], is both contrary and inferior to the approach "use a complex domain with widening" that is advocated in this paper.

	Goal-Independent						Goal-Dependent					
	P+DSH+F+L			P+NSH+F+L			P+DSH+F+L			P+NSH+F+L		
Program	NSP	GV	LV	NSP	GV	LV	NSP	GV	LV	NSP	GV	LV
aqua_c	10749	$\star$406	2753	?	?	?	16306	$\star$1186	2028	?	?	?
bmtp	1451	136	972	1461	136	976						
bryant	784	10	146	1088	10	223	1033	141	58	1781	141	58
caslog	6456	$\star$466	1588	7027	$\star$474	1615	11073	$\star$1625	1079	?	?	?
cg_parser	136	31	159	138	31	160						
dpos_an	92	40	76	95	40	76	183	76	53	183	76	53
lg_sys	7274	645	2260	7334	645	2261						
nand	473	23	182	475	23	182	1341	481	70	1341	481	70
nbody	261	52	104	262	52	104	477	151	41	478	151	41
oldchina	2185	285	1163	2193	285	1166	3985	802	760	?	?	?
quot_an	288	37	160	288	37	160	639	159	122	646	159	122
reg	774	42	272	796	42	284	207	67	52	207	67	52
rubik	70	$\star$55	110	73	$\star$76	93	174	$\star$110	124	201	$\star$200	103
scc	63	0	37	63	0	37	503	174	46	506	174	46
sfecht	28	0	14	85	0	31	221	0	47	278	0	64
simple_an	370	27	139	373	27	139	572	82	76	639	82	76
slice	427	126	453	428	126	453						
spsys	788	81	386	800	81	394						
trs	32	6	22	53	6	22	73	$\star$12	20	104	$\star$12	20

Table 1. *Pos* + $\downarrow$ *SH* + *Free* + *Lin* vs *Pos* + SH^{ρ} + *Free* + *Lin*: precision.

The combined domain *Pos* + $\downarrow$ *SH* + *Lin* is isomorphic to ASub + *Pos* (where ASub is the pair-sharing domain of Søndergaard [18]), and the domain *Pos*+$\downarrow$ *SH* is exactly the domain ASub^{+} defined by Cortesi and Filé in [9]. However, they considered this domain only *en passant* and only from a theoretical point of view. In other words, Fecht has the whole merit for having trusted on this domain from a precision/efficiency perspective.

The results for the remaining 19 programs are summarized in Table 1. The blank entries in the goal-dependent columns are for those program whose goal-dependent analysis is pointless. This usually happens because the program contains a procedure call to an unknown procedure (e.g., by means of `call/1`). The CHINA analyzer (i.e., our system [1]) promptly recognizes these cases and reverts to a goal-independent analysis. This is one of the reasons why focusing only on goal-dependent analyses is, in our opinion, a mistake. The other reason being that the ability of analyzing libraries once and for all is desirable and, more generally, so is the separate analysis of different program modules, especially in very large projects. Focusing only on goal-independent analyses is the opposite mistake: GD analyses, when possible, are more precise than GI ones. For these reasons, we insist in presenting experimental results for both.

A star symbol ($\star$) in the GV column signifies that one of the widenings we employ on the GER representation of *Pos* fired. This is a widening imposing a limit on the number of ROBDD nodes simultaneously allocated. It makes approximations of the R (ROBDD) component when this limit is reached[2], while retaining full precision on the G (definitely ground variables) and the E (classes of equivalent variables) components [2,5]. The scarcity of stars in this and the following tables, shows how seldom this widening is actually required.[3]

Apart from `sfecht`, which is a synthetic benchmark designed in order to show that arbitrary precision losses are possible with $\downarrow SH$, Table 1 illustrates how heavy precision penalties can be incurred by $\downarrow SH$ even on real programs. Most notably, for `bryant` we see a precision loss as high as 28% on goal-independent analysis (GI) and 42% on goal-dependent analysis. In addition, `simple_an` loses 10% (GD), while `trs` loses 40% (GI) and 30% (GD). Note that, for these programs, the *Pos* widening fires only on the GD analysis of `trs`. The `rubik` program shows an interesting phenomenon: here the *Pos* widening fires incurring a precision loss of exactly 1 ground variable (a critical one indeed), but SH^{ρ} saves the day by recovering the lost groundness information. A similar thing happens for `caslog`. Thus, the widely held opinion (now proved in [8]) that Sharing does not help *Pos* on groundness does not carry through when widenings are considered.

While space limitations do not allow to report full timing information, we can easily confirm Fecht's claim: the speedup is dramatic. Just a few examples: the fixpoint computation time in seconds for `bmtp`, `caslog`, `lg_sys`, and `spsys` drops from 15.6, 614.7, 735.9, and 2.2, to 0.8, 2.0, 3.3, and 0.6, respectively. All the experiments described in this paper were performed on a PC equipped with an AMD K6@400MHz, 128MB of main memory, and running Linux 2.2.1.

1.5 The Present Work

The objective of this work, after having recognized that Fecht's approach incurs significant precision loss on several real programs, is to improve the state of the art in mode analysis, in general, and sharing analysis in particular.

We moved from the observation that, when the sharing-sets become large, then they are at the same time heavy to manipulate and, at least for a subset of the variables involved, light as far as information content is concerned. We thus introduce a new representation for set-sharing made of two components. They are both sharing-sets. However, while the second one is interpreted in the usual way, the first component records worst-case sharing assumptions of sets of variables.

We define the operations required for the analysis with this representation, and we prove them correct. We also introduce two safe optimizations that turn out to be very effective in practice.

We then show how the proposed representation supports a variety of widenings. One of those is a simple adaptation of Fecht's idea. Others are much more sophisticated and involve only a limited precision loss. However, in spite of thorough experimentation (of which only a tiny fraction can be reported here) we found that the first widening we propose is hard to improve on, provided *Pos*

[2] That is, by approximating $x \wedge y$ with x or with y, $x \vee y$ with *true* and so forth.

[3] Indeed, the newest version of CHINA avoids also the widening for the `caslog` program.

is included in the domain. This suggests that what is lost by this widening is mostly constituted by ground dependencies, and these can be recovered (and improved) by the *Pos* component. We show that when *Pos* is not included, a widening based on cliques of sharing pairs is preferred. Since some authors advocate the use of Sharing without coupling it with *Pos* (we do not share this view), this is an important message for them.

Among the contributions of this paper we would like to stress the following: we present a data-flow analysis for groundness, freeness, pair-sharing, and linearity, with unprecedented levels of precision *and* efficiency. With the implementation described in this paper, the CHINA analyzer is able to honor one of its most important design goals: never crash (e.g., by exhausting all the available memory), always terminate with a correct result and in reasonable time.

The paper is structured as follows: In Section 2 we briefly recall the required notions and notations, even though we assume general acquaintance with the topics of abstract interpretation, sharing analysis and groundness analysis. Section 3 introduces a simple domain for sharing analysis that supports the implementation of several widening techniques. In particular, with this domain it is straightforward to turn Fecht's idea into a proper widening. This is done in Section 4, after the introduction of an infinite family of widenings and the proof of their safety. More precise widenings are also considered. The experimental evaluation of the proposed approach is presented in Section 5. Section 6 concludes with some final remark. The reader is referred to [19] for full proofs of all the results presented in this paper, and for more material on this subject.

2 Preliminaries

For any set S, $\wp(S)$ denotes the power set of S and $\# S$ is the cardinality of S. A monotone and idempotent self-map $\rho\colon P \to P$ over a poset $\langle P, \preceq\rangle$ is called a *closure operator* (or *upper closure operator*) if it is also *extensive*, namely $\forall x \in P : x \preceq \rho(x)$. In this paper, we assume there is a fixed and finite set of variables of interest denoted by VI. If t is a first-order term over VI, then $vars(t)$ denotes the set of variables in t. *Bind* denotes the set of equations of the form $x = t$ where $x \in VI$ and t is a first-order term over VI. Note that we do not impose the *occur-check* condition $x \notin vars(t)$, since we have proved in [14] that this is not required to ensure correctness of the operations of Sharing and its derivatives. The following definition is a simplification of the standard definition for the Sharing domain [10,14,15] where the set of variables of interest is fixed and finite.

Definition 1. (The *set-sharing* domain SH.) *The set SH is defined as $SH \stackrel{\mathrm{def}}{=} \wp(SG)$, where $SG \stackrel{\mathrm{def}}{=} \{\, S \in \wp(VI) \mid S \neq \varnothing \,\}$.*

We now introduce the required abstract operations over SH.

Definition 2. (Some abstract operations over SH.) *The binary function* $\mathrm{proj}\colon SH \times \wp(VI) \to SH$ *projects an element of SH onto a subset of VI: if $sh \in SH$ and $V \in \wp(VI)$, then* $\mathrm{proj}(sh, V) \stackrel{\mathrm{def}}{=} \{\, S \cap V \mid S \in sh, S \cap V \neq \varnothing \,\}$.

For each $sh \in SH$ *and each* $V \in \wp(VI)$, *the extraction of the* relevant component of sh with respect to V *is encoded by the function* rel: $\wp(VI) \times SH \to SH$ *defined as* $\mathrm{rel}(V, sh) \stackrel{\mathrm{def}}{=} \{\, S \in sh \mid S \cap V \neq \varnothing \,\}$.

For $sh \in SH$ *and* $V \in \wp(VI)$, *the exclusion of the* irrelevant component of sh with respect to V *is encoded by the function* $\overline{\mathrm{rel}}$: $\wp(VI) \times SH \to SH$ *defined as* $\overline{\mathrm{rel}}(V, sh) \stackrel{\mathrm{def}}{=} sh \setminus \mathrm{rel}(V, sh)$.

The star-union *function* $(\cdot)^\star \colon SH \to SH$, *is given, for each* $sh \in SH$, *by* $sh^\star \stackrel{\mathrm{def}}{=} \{\, S \in SG \mid \exists n \geq 1 \,.\, \exists T_1, \ldots, T_n \in sh \,.\, S = T_1 \cup \cdots \cup T_n \,\}$.

For each $sh_1, sh_2 \in SH$, *the* binary union *function* bin: $SH \times SH \to SH$ *is given by* $\mathrm{bin}(sh_1, sh_2) \stackrel{\mathrm{def}}{=} \{\, S_1 \cup S_2 \mid S_1 \in sh_1, S_2 \in sh_2 \,\}$.

We also use the self-bin-union *function* sbin: $SH \to SH$ *which is given by* $\mathrm{sbin}(sh) \stackrel{\mathrm{def}}{=} \mathrm{bin}(sh, sh)$

The function amgu *captures the effects of a binding on an SH element. Let* $(x = t) \in Bind$, $sh \in SH$, $V_x = \{x\}$, $V_t = vars(t)$, *and* $V_{xt} = V_x \cup V_t$. *Then*

$$\mathrm{amgu}(sh, x = t) \stackrel{\mathrm{def}}{=} \overline{\mathrm{rel}}(V_{xt}, sh) \cup \mathrm{bin}\bigl(\mathrm{rel}(V_x, sh)^\star, \mathrm{rel}(V_t, sh)^\star\bigr).$$

The domain SH captures *set-sharing*. However, the property we wish to detect is *pair-sharing* and, for this, it has been shown that SH includes unwanted redundancy [3].

Definition 3. (Redundancy.) *Let* $sh \in SH$ *and* $S \in SG$. S *is* redundant for sh *if and only if* $\# S > 2$ *and* $\mathrm{pairs}(S) = \bigcup \{\, \mathrm{pairs}(T) \mid T \in sh, T \subset S \,\}$ *where* $\mathrm{pairs}(S) \stackrel{\mathrm{def}}{=} \{\, P \in \wp(S) \mid \# P = 2 \,\}$.

Definition 4. (The domain SH^ρ.) *The function* $\rho \colon SH \to SH$ *is given, for each* $sh \in SH$, *by* $\rho(sh) \stackrel{\mathrm{def}}{=} sh \cup \{\, S \in SG \mid S \text{ is redundant for } sh \,\}$. *Then* $SH^\rho = \rho(SH) = \{\, \rho(sh) \mid sh \in SH \,\}$.

We use the notation $sh_1 =_\rho sh_2$ and $sh_1 \subseteq_\rho sh_2$ to denote $\rho(sh_1) = \rho(sh_2)$ and $\rho(sh_1) \subseteq \rho(sh_2)$, respectively. The advantage of SH^ρ is that we can replace the star-union operation in the definition of the amgu by self-bin-union without loss of precision [3]. In particular, it is shown that

$$\mathrm{amgu}(sh, x = t) =_\rho \overline{\mathrm{rel}}(V_{xt}, sh) \cup \mathrm{bin}\Bigl(\mathrm{sbin}\bigl(\mathrm{rel}(V_x, sh)\bigr), \mathrm{sbin}\bigl(\mathrm{rel}(V_t, sh)\bigr)\Bigr). \quad (1)$$

3 A New Representation for Set-Sharing

We introduce here a new representation for set-sharing. It is made up of two components: one is the original set-sharing domain while the other represents all possible subsets of each of its elements and, for this reason, is called a *clique-set*.

Definition 5. (Clique-set.) *A* clique-set *is an element of* CL *and* $CL \stackrel{\mathrm{def}}{=} SH$.

An element of a clique-set is called a *clique*.

Definition 6. (Sharing-sets representation for clique-sets.) *The (overloaded) functions* $\downarrow : SG \to SH$ *and* $\downarrow : CL \to SH$ *are given, for each* $C \in SG$ *and each* $cl \in CL$*, by* $\downarrow C \stackrel{\text{def}}{=} \wp(C) \setminus \{\varnothing\}$ *and* $\downarrow cl \stackrel{\text{def}}{=} \bigcup_{C \in cl} \downarrow C$. *Observe that* $\downarrow$ *is an upper closure operator over* SH. *If* $cl \in CL$ *and* $C \in SG$ *then we say that* C *is* down-redundant *in* cl *if there exists* $C' \in cl$ *such that* $C \subset C'$.

The addition or removal of down-redundant elements to or from a clique-set makes no difference to the sharing-sets that it represents. So, a clique represents a *worst case*[4] pair-sharing condition on the set of variables it contains.

In an implementation, as we need to keep the clique-sets as small as possible, down-redundant cliques are removed via a *normalization* function.

Definition 7. (Normalization of clique-sets.) *The normalization function* $|\cdot| : CL \to CL$ *is given, for each* $cl \in CL$*, by*

$$|cl| \stackrel{\text{def}}{=} cl \setminus \{\, C \in cl \mid C \text{ is down-redundant for } cl \,\}.$$

We now define abstract unification over clique-sets and state its soundness.

Definition 8. (Abstract unification over cliques.) *For each* $V \in \wp(VI)$ *and each* $cl \in CL$*, the function* $\overline{\mathrm{rel}}^{\mathrm{CL}} : \wp(VI) \times CL \to CL$ *is given by*

$$\overline{\mathrm{rel}}^{\mathrm{CL}}(V, cl) \stackrel{\text{def}}{=} \{\, C \setminus V \mid C \in cl \,\} \setminus \{\varnothing\}.$$

The function $\mathrm{amgu}^{\mathrm{CL}} : CL \times Bind \to CL$ *is given, for each* $cl \in CL$ *and each* $(x = t) \in Bind$*, by*

$$\mathrm{amgu}^{\mathrm{CL}}(cl, x = t) \stackrel{\text{def}}{=} \overline{\mathrm{rel}}^{\mathrm{CL}}(V_{xt}, cl) \cup \mathrm{bin}\bigl(\mathrm{sbin}(cl_x), \mathrm{sbin}(cl_t)\bigr),$$

where $cl_x = \mathrm{rel}(V_x, cl)$, $cl_t = \mathrm{rel}(V_t, cl)$, $V_x = \{x\}$, $V_t = vars(t)$, *and, finally,* $V_{xt} = V_x \cup V_t$.

Theorem 1. *For each* $cl \in CL$ *and each* $(x = t) \in Bind$*,*

$$\mathrm{amgu}\bigl(\downarrow cl, x = t\bigr) \subseteq_\rho \downarrow \mathrm{amgu}^{\mathrm{CL}}(cl, x = t).$$

Because cliques represent their downward closure, $\mathrm{amgu}^{\mathrm{CL}}$ introduces down-redundant cliques when both the relevant components are non-empty. As already observed (without proof) and implemented by Fecht, there are two optimizations for computing the $\mathrm{amgu}^{\mathrm{CL}}$ that enable useful efficiency improvements. These are reformulated in Section 3.1 for the domains defined here.

We next define our new sharing domain for widening.

[4] While this terminology is due to Langen [16], our definition differs from the one he used.

Definition 9. (The SH^{W} representation.) *The set SH^{W} is given by*

$$SH^{W} \stackrel{\text{def}}{=} \{ (cl, sh) \mid cl \in CL, sh \in SH \}$$

and is ordered by $\sqsubseteq$ defined as follows, for each $shw, (cl_1, sh_1), (cl_2, sh_2) \in SH^{W}$:

$$(cl_1, sh_1) \sqsubseteq (cl_2, sh_2) \iff (cl_1 \subseteq cl_2) \wedge (sh_1 \subseteq sh_2).$$

It can be seen that SH^{W} is a complete lattice.

The sharing-set represented by an element of SH^{W} is given by the function $\mathcal{I}(\cdot)\colon SH^{W} \to SH$ defined, for each $(cl, sh) \in SH^{W}$, by $\mathcal{I}\bigl((cl, sh)\bigr) \stackrel{\text{def}}{=} \downarrow cl \cup sh$. The normalization of an element of SH^{W} is given by $|\cdot|\colon SH^{W} \to SH^{W}$ defined, for each $(cl, sh) \in SH^{W}$, by $|(cl, sh)| \stackrel{\text{def}}{=} \bigl(|cl|, sh \setminus \downarrow cl\bigr)$.

The normalization removes unnecessary elements from a description in SH^{W}. We now define an upper closure operator ϱ inducing an equivalence relation on the elements of SH^{W}.

Definition 10. (The $\varrho(SH^{W})$ domain.) *The function $\varrho\colon SH^{W} \to SH^{W}$ is given, for each $shw \in SH^{W}$ with $shw \stackrel{\text{def}}{=} (cl, sh)$, by $\varrho(shw) \stackrel{\text{def}}{=} \bigl(\rho(\downarrow cl), \rho(\mathcal{I}(shw))\bigr)$. Then ϱ is an upper closure operator for SH^{W} [19]. We will use the notation $shw_1 =_{\varrho} shw_2$ to denote $\varrho(shw_1) = \varrho(shw_2)$ and $shw_1 \sqsubseteq_{\varrho} shw_2$ to denote $\varrho(shw_1) \sqsubseteq \varrho(shw_2)$.*

The ordering $\sqsubseteq_{\varrho}$ is used for modeling the relative precision between widenings in Section 4. When $shw_1 =_{\varrho} shw_2$, shw_1 and shw_2 behave the same way as far as representing pair-sharing and groundness is concerned.

Proposition 1. *If $shw \in SH^{W}$, then $\mathcal{I}(shw) =_{\rho} \mathcal{I}\bigl(\varrho(shw)\bigr)$ and $shw =_{\varrho} |shw|$.*

Definition 11. (Operations over SH^{W}.) *For each $(cl, sh), (cl_i, sh_i) \in SH^{W}$, $i = 1, 2$, and each $V \in \wp(VI)$, the functions $\mathrm{rel}^{W}, \overline{\mathrm{rel}}^{W}\colon \wp(VI) \times SH^{W} \to SH^{W}$ and $\cup^{W}, \mathrm{bin}^{W}\colon SH^{W} \times SH^{W} \to SH^{W}$, the functions $\mathrm{sbin}^{W}\colon SH^{W} \to SH^{W}$ and $\mathrm{amgu}^{W}\colon SH^{W} \times Bind \to SH^{W}$ are defined as follows:*

$$\begin{aligned}
\mathrm{rel}^{W}\bigl(V, (cl, sh)\bigr) &\stackrel{\text{def}}{=} \bigl(\mathrm{rel}(V, cl), \mathrm{rel}(V, sh)\bigr),\\
\overline{\mathrm{rel}}^{W}\bigl(V, (cl, sh)\bigr) &\stackrel{\text{def}}{=} \bigl(\overline{\mathrm{rel}}^{CL}(V, cl), \overline{\mathrm{rel}}(V, sh)\bigr),\\
(cl_1, sh_1) \cup^{W} (cl_2, sh_2) &\stackrel{\text{def}}{=} \bigl(cl_1 \cup cl_2, sh_1 \cup sh_2\bigr),\\
\mathrm{bin}^{W}\bigl((cl_1, sh_1), (cl_2, sh_2)\bigr) &\stackrel{\text{def}}{=} \bigl(\mathrm{bin}(cl_1, cl_2) \cup \mathrm{bin}(cl_1, sh_2) \cup \mathrm{bin}(sh_1, cl_2),\\
&\qquad \mathrm{bin}(sh_1, sh_2)\bigr),\\
\mathrm{sbin}^{W}\bigl((cl, sh)\bigr) &\stackrel{\text{def}}{=} \mathrm{bin}^{W}\bigl((cl, sh), (cl, sh)\bigr)\\
&= \bigl(\mathrm{sbin}(cl) \cup \mathrm{bin}(cl, sh), \mathrm{sbin}(sh)\bigr),\\
\mathrm{amgu}^{W}(shw, x = t) &\stackrel{\text{def}}{=} \overline{\mathrm{rel}}^{W}(V_{xt}, shw)\\
&\qquad \cup^{W} \mathrm{bin}^{W}\Bigl(\mathrm{sbin}^{W}\bigl(\mathrm{rel}^{W}(V_x, shw)\bigr),\\
&\qquad\qquad \mathrm{sbin}^{W}\bigl(\mathrm{rel}^{W}(V_t, shw)\bigr)\Bigr),
\end{aligned}$$

where $V_x = \{x\}$, $V_t = vars(t)$, *and* $V_{xt} = V_x \cup V_t$.

The next two theorems, proven in [19], state the correctness of $\mathrm{amgu}^{\mathrm{W}}$ and that normalization does not affect the correctness or precision of $\mathrm{amgu}^{\mathrm{W}}$.

Theorem 2. *For each* $shw \in SH^{\mathrm{W}}$ *and each* $(x = t) \in Bind$,

$$\mathrm{amgu}\bigl(\mathcal{I}(shw), x = t\bigr) \subseteq_\rho \mathcal{I}\bigl(\mathrm{amgu}^{\mathrm{W}}(shw, x = t)\bigr).$$

Theorem 3. *For each* $shw \in SH^{\mathrm{W}}$ *and each* $(x = t) \in Bind$,

$$\mathrm{amgu}^{\mathrm{W}}(shw, x = t) =_\varrho \mathrm{amgu}^{\mathrm{W}}\bigl(|shw|, x = t\bigr).$$

In general, $=_\varrho$ is not a congruence for $\mathrm{amgu}^{\mathrm{W}}$ and precision may be lost when the first component of *shw* is non-empty and the second component of *shw* contains redundant elements. Further work on this aspect is ongoing.

In Eq. (1), the basic amgu operation is defined using the SH^ρ domain. However, when we have freeness and linearity information it has been proven that we can avoid one or both of the self-bin-unions occurring as components of the binary union operation. The question arises as to whether this optimization can be applied when we have the $\mathrm{amgu}^{\mathrm{W}}$ operation for the SH^{W} domain. That is, can we avoid the corresponding $\mathrm{sbin}^{\mathrm{W}}$ operations under the same linearity and freeness conditions? The answer is *yes*, we can generalize Theorem 2 and show that such an optimization is sound. However, the optimization may lose precision and further work on this aspect is ongoing.

3.1 Optimizations

We can optimize the computation of $\mathrm{amgu}^{\mathrm{W}}$ in two ways. To explain these, we need some extra notation. Let: $shw = (cl, sh) \in SH^{\mathrm{W}}$ and $x = t \in Bind$; $V_x = \{x\}$, $V_t = vars(t)$, and $V_{xt} = V_x \cup V_t$; $shw_x = (cl_x, sh_x) = \mathrm{rel}^{\mathrm{W}}(V_x, shw)$ and $shw_t = (cl_t, sh_t) = \mathrm{rel}^{\mathrm{W}}(V_t, shw)$; and, finally,

$$shw_{\mathrm{rel}} = (cl_{\mathrm{rel}}, sh_{\mathrm{rel}}) = \mathrm{bin}^{\mathrm{W}}\bigl(\mathrm{sbin}^{\mathrm{W}}(shw_x), \mathrm{sbin}^{\mathrm{W}}(shw_t)\bigr).$$

Theorem 4. *If neither* $shw_x = (\varnothing, \varnothing)$ *nor* $shw_t = (\varnothing, \varnothing)$, *then*

$$\overline{\mathrm{rel}}^{\mathrm{W}}(V_{xt}, shw) = \bigl(\overline{\mathrm{rel}}(V_{xt}, cl) \cup cl', \overline{\mathrm{rel}}(V_{xt}, sh)\bigr),$$

where $cl' \subseteq {\downarrow}\, cl_{\mathrm{rel}}$.

Theorem 5. *Suppose that* $C_x = \bigcup cl_x$, $C_t = \bigcup cl_t$, $S_x = \bigcup sh_x$, $S_t = \bigcup sh_t$, $A_{xt} = \mathrm{bin}\bigl(\mathrm{sbin}(sh_x), \mathrm{sbin}(sh_t)\bigr)$, $B_{xt} = \mathrm{bin}(sh_x, sh_t)$, $B_x = \mathrm{bin}(cl_x, sh_x)$, *and* $B_t = \mathrm{bin}(cl_t, sh_t)$. *Let also*

$$shw_{\mathrm{rel}}^{\mathrm{opt}} \stackrel{\mathrm{def}}{=} \begin{cases} \bigl(\{C_x \cup C_t \cup S_x \cup S_t\}, \varnothing\bigr), & \text{if } cl_x \neq \varnothing, cl_t \neq \varnothing; \\ \bigl(\{C_x \cup S_t\} \cup B_x \cup B_{xt}, A_{xt}\bigr), & \text{if } cl_x \neq \varnothing, cl_t = \varnothing; \\ \bigl(\{C_t \cup S_x\} \cup B_t \cup B_{xt}, A_{xt}\bigr), & \text{if } cl_x = \varnothing, cl_t \neq \varnothing; \\ (\varnothing, A_{xt}), & \text{if } cl_x = \varnothing, cl_t = \varnothing. \end{cases}$$

Then,

$$shw_{\mathrm{rel}} =_{\varrho} \begin{cases} shw_{\mathrm{rel}}^{\mathrm{opt}}, & \text{if } shw_x \neq (\varnothing,\varnothing), shw_t \neq (\varnothing,\varnothing); \\ (\varnothing,\varnothing), & \text{otherwise.} \end{cases}$$

Both these results are proven in [19]. These can then be combined to provide the following optimization (also proven in [19]) for the computation of $\mathrm{amgu}^{\mathrm{W}}$.

Corollary 1. *Assuming the notation used in* Theorem 5, *then*

$$\begin{aligned} &\mathrm{amgu}^{\mathrm{W}}(shw, x = t) \\ &=_{\varrho} \begin{cases} \bigl(\overline{\mathrm{rel}}(V_{xt}, cl), \overline{\mathrm{rel}}(V_{xt}, sh)\bigr) \cup^{\mathrm{W}} shw_{\mathrm{rel}}^{\mathrm{opt}}, & \text{if } shw_x \neq (\varnothing,\varnothing), shw_t \neq (\varnothing,\varnothing); \\ \overline{\mathrm{rel}}^{\mathrm{W}}(V_{xt}, shw), & \text{otherwise.} \end{cases} \end{aligned}$$

Observe that this result applies to the basic $\mathrm{amgu}^{\mathrm{W}}$ operation as given in Definition 11. When one or both of the self-bin-unions here is omitted due to available freeness and linearity information, then $=_{\varrho}$ in the corollary becomes $\sqsubseteq_{\varrho}$ and we may lose further precision. Further work on this subject is ongoing.

4 Widening Set-Sharing

We can now define a family of *unary* widenings over SH^{W}.

Definition 12. (Widening for SH^{W}.) *The function* $\nabla\colon SH^{\mathrm{W}} \to SH^{\mathrm{W}}$ *is a* widening for SH^{W} *if, for each* $shw \in SH^{\mathrm{W}}$, *we have* $shw \sqsubseteq_{\varrho} \nabla\, shw$.

The following result establishes the safety of such widening operators.

Theorem 6. *For each* $shw \in SH^{\mathrm{W}}$ *and each* $(x = t) \in Bind$ *we have*

$$\mathrm{amgu}^{\mathrm{W}}(shw, x = t) \sqsubseteq_{\varrho} \mathrm{amgu}^{\mathrm{W}}\bigl(\nabla\, shw, x = t\bigr).$$

The obvious corollary is that any analysis using these widenings, possibly a different widening at each step of the analysis, is correct. After widening we always normalize the resulting description to provide a smaller representation. Moreover, it is also shown in [19] that similar results hold for each of the component operators, such as $\mathrm{bin}^{\mathrm{W}}$, for $\mathrm{amgu}^{\mathrm{W}}$. Thus we can (and do) safely widen and normalize within the actual computation of $\mathrm{amgu}^{\mathrm{W}}$. The analyzer has the freedom of using whichever widening suits its current needs. Those needs can be dictated by a number of heuristics. Of course, really useful widenings are *guarded* by some applicability condition. The simplest conditions are those based on the cardinality of the sets in the SH^{W} description. For example, for each widening ∇ and for suitable choices of $f\colon \mathbb{N}^2 \to \mathbb{N}$ and $n \in \mathbb{N}$, one can define

$$\nabla_{f,n}(cl, sh) \stackrel{\mathrm{def}}{=} \begin{cases} \nabla(cl, sh), & \text{if } f(\#\, cl, \#\, sh) > n, \\ (cl, sh), & \text{otherwise.} \end{cases}$$

We order the widenings in the obvious way. If ∇_1 and ∇_2 are two widenings and for all *shw*, $\nabla_1(shw) \sqsubseteq_\varrho \nabla_2(shw)$, then let $\nabla_1 \sqsubseteq_\varrho \nabla_2$, meaning that ∇_1 is more precise than ∇_2.

At the top end of the scale of widenings we have two *panic widenings*. They are defined by

$$\nabla^p(cl, sh) \stackrel{\text{def}}{=} \Bigl(cl \cup \bigl\{\bigcup sh\bigr\}, \varnothing\Bigr),$$
$$\nabla^P(cl, sh) \stackrel{\text{def}}{=} \Bigl(\bigl\{\bigcup cl \cup \bigcup sh\bigr\}, \varnothing\Bigr).$$

The panic widenings are present in the CHINA implementation, with very strict guards, only to obey the "never crash" motto: no real program we have access to makes them fire.

At the other extreme we have very soft widenings.

Definition 13. (Cautious widening.) *A widening* $\nabla \colon SH^{\mathrm{W}} \to SH^{\mathrm{W}}$ *is called a* cautious widening *if, for each* $shw \in SH^{\mathrm{W}}$,

$$\mathcal{I}(\nabla\, shw) =_\rho \mathcal{I}(shw).$$

Thus, a widening is cautious if it is invariant with respect to the set-sharing representation. In particular, it never introduces new pair-sharings nor new singletons in the description. However, information is lost as soon as the operations for the analysis given by Definition 11 are considered. For example, consider two elements of SH^{W}: $shw_1 \stackrel{\text{def}}{=} \bigl(\varnothing, \{x, y, z, xy, xz, yz\}\bigr)$ and $shw_2 \stackrel{\text{def}}{=} \bigl(\{xyz\}, \varnothing\bigr)$ so that we have $\mathcal{I}(shw_1) =_\rho \mathcal{I}(shw_2)$ but $\varrho(shw_1) \neq \varrho(shw_2)$. While sharing between y and z is not contemplated in $\mathrm{rel}^{\mathrm{W}}\bigl(\{x\}, shw_1\bigr) = \bigl(\varnothing, \{x, xy, xz\}\bigr)$, the same does not hold for $\mathrm{rel}^{\mathrm{W}}\bigl(\{x\}, shw_2\bigr) = shw_2$.

A useful cautious widening is the *gentle widening*, defined as follows. Consider $shw \in SH^{\mathrm{W}}$, and let us define the undirected graph $G \stackrel{\text{def}}{=} (N, E)$ such that $N \stackrel{\text{def}}{=} \bigl\{\, x \bigm| \{x\} \in \mathcal{I}(shw) \,\bigr\}$ and $E \stackrel{\text{def}}{=} \bigl\{\, (x, y) \bigm| \{x, y\} \in \mathcal{I}(shw), x, y \in N, x \neq y \,\bigr\}$. Then

$$\nabla^G\, shw \stackrel{\text{def}}{=} \bigl(\{C_1, \ldots, C_k\}, sh\bigr),$$

where $C_1, \ldots, C_k$ are all the maximal cliques of G. Note that, although the problem of enumerating all the maximal cliques of an undirected graph is NP-complete, this does not seem to be a problem for the graphs arising during the analysis of even the biggest real programs. For the experimentation we used the algorithm by Bron and Kerbosch [6], which is *Algorithm 457* in the ACM collection, even though more efficient algorithms are present in the literature.

Of intermediate precision is the widening based on Fecht's idea, which we will call *Fecht's widening*. It is simply given by

$$\nabla^F(cl, sh) \stackrel{\text{def}}{=} (cl \cup sh, \varnothing).$$

	Goal-Independent						Goal-Dependent					
	P+WSH+F+L			P+NSH+F+L			P+WSH+F+L			P+NSH+F+L		
Program	NSP	GV	LV	NSP	GV	LV	NSP	GV	LV	NSP	GV	LV
aqua_c	11147	⋆406	2757	?	?	?	16364	⋆118 8	2028	?	?	?
caslog	6553	⋆474	1615	7027	⋆474	1615	11338	⋆1739	1062	?	?	?
oldchina	2193	285	1166	2193	285	1166	3985	802	760	?	?	?
quot_an	288	37	160	288	37	160	639	159	122	646	159	122

Table 2. *Pos*+ SH^{w} + *Free*+ *Lin* vs *Pos*+ SH^{ρ} + *Free*+ *Lin* using ∇^F_{100}: precision.

This widening is not cautious. However, it does not introduce new pairs. As it can introduce new singletons, it may destroy ground dependencies, and this is why this kind of widening is better coupled with *Pos*.

5 Experimental Evaluation

For the experimental evaluation of the Fecht's widening ∇^F, precision is compared with respect to the non-redundant sharing domain SH^{ρ}. In fact, this approach is almost always as precise as the optimal one using SH^{ρ}.

For this and the following experiments, the widening was guarded by a size threshold of 100 on the second component (i.e., the normal sharing part). In other words, immediately before each abstract mgu operation the analyzer operated redundancy elimination, as usual. If after this the operand (cl, sh) was such that $\# sh > 100$, then (cl, sh) was substituted by $\nabla^F(cl, sh)$. Let us call this guarded widening ∇^F_{100}. The results are reported in Table 2. Note that only the programs where the analysis with SH^{w} gives different results from the analysis with SH^{ρ} are reported in the table. Thus, for all the programs in the test-suite, the analysis with SH^{w} using the (rather drastic) widening ∇^F_{100} gives the same results obtainable (at a much higher cost) with SH^{ρ}, apart from those in Table 2. For `aqua_c` we obtain termination in reasonable time, as with Fecht's technique but with higher precision. The same holds for the GD analysis of `caslog` and `oldchina`. However, while the GI analysis of `oldchina` is "optimal" (meaning "as precise as SH^{ρ}"), this is not the case for `caslog`. Non-optimality happens also for the GD analysis of `quot_an`.

Obviously, ∇^F_{100} is never less precise than Fecht's domain. What is surprising, however, is that it is almost as efficient. The timings and the number of applications of the widening are reported in Table 3 for all the programs such that at least one timing was above 0.4 seconds. The first observation to be made is that the widening comes into play only a few times on the test-suite. On average, it is safe to say that on 99.9% of cases the sharing-sets remain of reasonable size (100 groups or less in this experiment). Table 3 says that this definition of "reasonable" makes sense: for those programs where widening does not take place the difference in performance between Fecht's domain and our SH^{w} with the ∇^F_{100} widening is very limited. Analysis of `aqua_c` shows that limiting precision

Program	Goal-Independent P+DSH+F+L T	Goal-Independent P+WSH+F+L T	Goal-Independent P+WSH+F+L #W	Goal-Dependent P+DSH+F+L T	Goal-Dependent P+WSH+F+L T	Goal-Dependent P+WSH+F+L #W
action	0.1	0.1	1	1.1	1.4	1
aircraft	0.2	0.2	0	0.7	0.7	0
aqua_c	10.4	10.9	56	48.6	40.7	3
bmtp	0.8	0.9	6			
bryant	0.1	0.1	0	0.6	1.4	1
caslog	2.0	2.5	17	17.7	19.2	22
chat80	0.9	1.0	2	4.3	4.9	6
chat_parser	0.4	0.4	1	1.7	1.8	1
dpos_an	0.2	0.2	0	0.5	0.8	1
eliza	0.1	0.1	0	0.2	0.4	1
41g_sys	3.3	3.9	23			
log_interp	0.2	0.4	2	0.7	0.9	1
mixtus	0.9	0.9	4			
oldchina	1.2	1.4	11	7.7	8.3	4
parser_dcg	0.2	0.1	0	0.7	0.6	0
peephole1	0.1	0.1	0	0.4	0.7	1
pets_an	0.8	0.9	4	4.5	4.5	1
peval	0.2	0.3	3	0.4	0.5	1
plaiclp	0.7	0.7	3			
press	0.1	0.1	0	0.4	0.7	0
quot_an	0.3	0.4	0	1.3	1.7	1
read	0.1	0.1	0	0.3	0.6	1
reg	0.4	0.4	4	0.4	0.4	1
sdda	0.1	0.1	1	0.2	0.4	2
sim	0.2	0.3	2	0.7	0.8	2
simple_an	0.1	0.2	0	0.6	0.9	2
slice	0.6	0.7	2			
spsys	0.6	0.7	5			
trs	0.2	0.3	2	0.5	0.6	1
unify	0.1	0.1	0	0.5	0.7	0

Table 3. $Pos + \downarrow SH + Free + Lin$ vs $Pos + SH^{W} + Free + Lin$ using ∇^F_{100}: timings (T) and number of (sharing) widenings (#W).

may cost (less precision means more self-bin-unions to perform, thus even less precision, ...).

The results on the precision of ∇^F_{100} are so good that we are left with a ridiculous test-suite for checking how much we can improve by using a more cautious widening. Our experimentation showed that the gentle widening ∇^G_{100} improves over ∇^F_{100} only on quot_an. The same does, but at a lower price, a bigger widening ∇^g that is defined as ∇^G apart from the fact that singletons are disregarded. In other words, the undirected graph considered for ∇^g, given

	Goal-Independent						Goal-Dependent					
	SH^{W}, ∇^{F}_{100}		SH^{W}, ∇^{g}_{100}		SH^{ρ}		SH^{W}, ∇^{F}_{100}		SH^{W}, ∇^{g}_{100}		SH^{ρ}	
Program	T	NSP	T	NSP	T	NSP	T	NSP	T	NSP	T	NSP
`aqua_c`	4.1	10703	15.0	10899	?	?	27.6	15754	37.8	15754	?	?
`bryant`	0.2	1066	0.2	1066	0.2	1066	1.0	1033	1.0	1781	0.9	1781
`caslog`	2.1	6506	4.5	6539	744.4	7027	17.9	11054	21.8	11054	?	?
`chat80`	0.6	2536	1.1	2536	9.1	2536	4.4	3923	7.7	3926	285.7	5111
`eliza`	0.1	49	0.1	49	0.1	49	0.3	109	0.5	113	0.5	113
`lg_sys`	2.7	7328	7.9	7334	725.1	7334						
`oldchina`	0.9	2187	2.6	2189	5.0	2193	5.9	3936	9.5	3936	?	?
`pets_an`	0.6	2525	1.3	2563	19.8	2569	3.7	4664	5.3	4664	1006.5	4710
`quot_an`	0.3	288	0.4	288	0.3	288	1.4	639	3.2	646	3.1	646
`simple_an`	0.1	373	0.1	373	0.1	373	0.8	572	1.3	639	17.6	639
`slice`	0.6	426	0.9	428	0.8	428						

Table 4. SH^{W} with ∇^{F}_{100} vs SH^{W} with ∇^{g}_{100} vs plain SH^{ρ}: timings and precision.

$shw \in SH^{W}$, is $G \stackrel{\text{def}}{=} (N, E)$ such that $E \stackrel{\text{def}}{=} \{ (x, y) \mid \{x, y\} \in \mathcal{I}(shw), x \neq y \}$ and $N \stackrel{\text{def}}{=} \{ x \mid (x, y) \in E \text{ or } (y, x) \in E \}$.

Now, suppose we perform sharing analysis *without* combining the sharing domain with *Pos*. Then using a more or less precise widening makes a difference. In Table 4 are reported the results (fixpoint time and number of definitely not-sharing pairs) for SH^{W} with ∇^{F}_{100}, SH^{W} with ∇^{g}_{100}, and plain SH^{ρ}. The GD analysis of `bryant` is particularly eloquent example of the superiority of more cautious widenings when *Pos* is not used.

6 Conclusion

We believe we have made a significant step forward towards the solution of the problem of practical, precise, and efficient sharing analysis of (constraint) logic programs. We have studied a new representation for set-sharing that allows for the incorporation of a variety of widenings. Extensive experimentation has shown that one of these widenings, which is based on an idea of C. Fecht, provides seemingly hard to beat precision and performance, when combined with *Pos*. When this combination is not performed, we have also shown that "more cautious" widenings offer more precision at an acceptable extra-cost.

We are now studying how to increase precision of the analysis beyond the limits of set-sharing. This includes more precise tracking of freeness and linearity, and the efficient incorporation of structural information into the analysis domain.

References

1. R. Bagnara. *Data-Flow Analysis for Constraint Logic-Based Languages.* PhD thesis, Dipartimento di Informatica, Università di Pisa, Corso Italia 40, I-56125 Pisa, Italy, March 1997. Printed as Report TD-1/97.

2. R. Bagnara. Widening *Pos*: Simple, effective, and rarely needed. Unpublished short note, 1998.
3. R. Bagnara, P. M. Hill, and E. Zaffanella. Set-sharing is redundant for pair-sharing. In P. Van Hentenryck, editor, *Static Analysis: Proceedings of the 4th International Symposium*, volume 1302 of *Lecture Notes in Computer Science*, pages 53–67, Paris, France, 1997. Springer-Verlag, Berlin.
4. R. Bagnara, P. M. Hill, and E. Zaffanella. Set-sharing is redundant for pair-sharing. *Theoretical Computer Science*, 1999. To appear.
5. R. Bagnara and P. Schachte. Factorizing equivalent variable pairs in ROBDD-based implementations of *Pos*. In A. M. Haeberer, editor, *Proceedings of the "Seventh International Conference on Algebraic Methodology and Software Technology (AMAST'98)"*, volume 1548 of *Lecture Notes in Computer Science*, pages 471–485, Amazonia, Brazil, 1999. Springer-Verlag, Berlin.
6. C. Bron and J. Kerbosch. Finding all cliques of an undirected graph. *Communications of the ACM*, 16(9):575–577, 1973.
7. M. Bruynooghe, M. Codish, and A. Mulkers. Abstract unification for a composite domain deriving sharing and freeness properties of program variables. In F. S. de Boer and M. Gabbrielli, editors, *Verification and Analysis of Logic Languages, Proceedings of the W2 Post-Conference Workshop, International Conference on Logic Programming*, pages 213–230, Santa Margherita Ligure, Italy, 1994.
8. M. Codish, H. Søndergaard, and P. J. Stuckey. Sharing and groundness dependencies in logic programs. Submitted for publication.
9. A. Cortesi and G. Filé. Comparison and design of abstract domains for sharing analysis. In D. Saccà, editor, *Proceedings of the "Eighth Italian Conference on Logic Programming (GULP'93)"*, pages 251–265, Gizzeria, Italy, 1993. Mediterranean Press.
10. A. Cortesi and G. Filé. Sharing is optimal. *Journal of Logic Programming*, 38(3):371–386, 1999.
11. P. Cousot and R. Cousot. Comparing the Galois connection and widening/narrowing approaches to abstract interpretation. In M. Bruynooghe and M. Wirsing, editors, *Proceedings of the 4th International Symposium on Programming Language Implementation and Logic Programming*, volume 631 of *Lecture Notes in Computer Science*, pages 269–295, Leuven, Belgium, 1992. Springer-Verlag, Berlin.
12. C. Fecht. An efficient and precise sharing domain for logic programs. In H. Kuchen and S. D. Swierstra, editors, *Programming Languages: Implementations, Logics and Programs, Proceedings of the Eighth International Symposium*, volume 1140 of *Lecture Notes in Computer Science*, pages 469–470, Aachen, Germany, 1996. Springer-Verlag, Berlin. Poster.
13. C. Fecht. Efficient and precise sharing domains for logic programs. Technical Report A/04/96, Universität des Saarlandes, Fachbereich 14 Informatik, Saarbrücken, Germany, 1996.
14. P. M. Hill, R. Bagnara, and E. Zaffanella. The correctness of set-sharing. In G. Levi, editor, *Static Analysis: Proceedings of the 5th International Symposium*, volume 1503 of *Lecture Notes in Computer Science*, pages 99–114, Pisa, Italy, 1998. Springer-Verlag, Berlin.
15. D. Jacobs and A. Langen. Static analysis of logic programs for independent AND parallelism. *Journal of Logic Programming*, 13(2&3):291–314, 1992.
16. A. Langen. *Static Analysis for Independent And-Parallelism in Logic Programs*. PhD thesis, Computer Science Department, University of Southern California, 1990. Printed as Report TR 91-05.

17. K. Muthukumar and M. Hermenegildo. Compile-time derivation of variable dependency using abstract interpretation. *Journal of Logic Programming*, 13(2&3):315–347, 1992.
18. H. Søndergaard. An application of abstract interpretation of logic programs: Occur check reduction. In *Proceedings of the 1986 European Symposium on Programming*, volume 213 of *Lecture Notes in Computer Science*, pages 327–338. Springer-Verlag, Berlin, 1986.
19. E. Zaffanella, R. Bagnara, and P. M. Hill. Widening Sharing. Submitted for publication. Available at `http://www.cs.unipr.it/~bagnara/`, 1999.

Author Index

Lecture Notes in Computer Science

For information about Vols. 1–1616
please contact your bookseller or Springer-Verlag

Vol. 1617: N.V. Murray (Ed.), Automated Reasoning with Analytic Tableaux and Related Methods. Proceedings, 1999. X, 325 pages. 1999. (Subseries LNAI).

Vol. 1618: J. Bézivin, P.-A. Muller (Eds.), The Unified Modeling Language. Proceedings, 1998. IX, 443 pages. 1999.

Vol. 1619: M.T. Goodrich, C.C. McGeoch (Eds.), Algorithm Engineering and Experimentation. Proceedings, 1999. VIII, 349 pages. 1999.

Vol. 1620: W. Horn, Y. Shahar, G. Lindberg, S. Andreassen, J. Wyatt (Eds.), Artificial Intelligence in Medicine. Proceedings, 1999. XIII, 454 pages. 1999. (Subseries LNAI).

Vol. 1621: D. Fensel, R. Studer (Eds.), Knowledge Acquisition Modeling and Management. Proceedings, 1999. XI, 404 pages. 1999. (Subseries LNAI).

Vol. 1622: M. González Harbour, J.A. de la Puente (Eds.), Reliable Software Technologies – Ada-Europe'99. Proceedings, 1999. XIII, 451 pages. 1999.

Vol. 1623: T. Reinartz, Focusing Solutions for Data Mining. XV, 309 pages. 1999. (Subseries LNAI).

Vol. 1625: B. Reusch (Ed.), Computational Intelligence. Proceedings, 1999. XIV, 710 pages. 1999.

Vol. 1626: M. Jarke, A. Oberweis (Eds.), Advanced Information Systems Engineering. Proceedings, 1999. XIV, 478 pages. 1999.

Vol. 1627: T. Asano, H. Imai, D.T. Lee, S.-i. Nakano, T. Tokuyama (Eds.), Computing and Combinatorics. Proceedings, 1999. XIV, 494 pages. 1999.

Col. 1628: R. Guerraoui (Ed.), ECOOP'99 - Object-Oriented Programming. Proceedings, 1999. XIII, 529 pages. 1999.

Vol. 1629: H. Leopold, N. García (Eds.), Multimedia Applications, Services and Techniques - ECMAST'99. Proceedings, 1999. XV, 574 pages. 1999.

Vol. 1631: P. Narendran, M. Rusinowitch (Eds.), Rewriting Techniques and Applications. Proceedings, 1999. XI, 397 pages. 1999.

Vol. 1632: H. Ganzinger (Ed.), Automated Deduction – Cade-16. Proceedings, 1999. XIV, 429 pages. 1999. (Subseries LNAI).

Vol. 1633: N. Halbwachs, D. Peled (Eds.), Computer Aided Verification. Proceedings, 1999. XII, 506 pages. 1999.

Vol. 1634: S. Džeroski, P. Flach (Eds.), Inductive Logic Programming. Proceedings, 1999. VIII, 303 pages. 1999. (Subseries LNAI).

Vol. 1636: L. Knudsen (Ed.), Fast Software Encryption. Proceedings, 1999. VIII, 317 pages. 1999.

Vol. 1637: J.P. Walser, Integer Optimization by Local Search. XIX, 137 pages. 1999. (Subseries LNAI).

Vol. 1638: A. Hunter, S. Parsons (Eds.), Symbolic and Quantitative Approaches to Reasoning and Uncertainty. Proceedings, 1999. IX, 397 pages. 1999. (Subseries LNAI).

Vol. 1639: S. Donatelli, J. Kleijn (Eds.), Application and Theory of Petri Nets 1999. Proceedings, 1999. VIII, 425 pages. 1999.

Vol. 1640: W. Tepfenhart, W. Cyre (Eds.), Conceptual Structures: Standards and Practices. Proceedings, 1999. XII, 515 pages. 1999. (Subseries LNAI).

Vol. 1641: D. Hutter, W. Stephan, P. Traverso, M. Ullmann (Eds.), Applied Formal Methods – FM-Trends 98. Proceedings, 1998. XI, 377 pages. 1999.

Vol. 1642: D.J. Hand, J.N. Kok, M.R. Berthold (Eds.), Advances in Intelligent Data Analysis. Proceedings, 1999. XII, 538 pages. 1999.

Vol. 1643: J. Nešetřil (Ed.), Algorithms – ESA '99. Proceedings, 1999. XII, 552 pages. 1999.

Vol. 1644: J. Wiedermann, P. van Emde Boas, M. Nielsen (Eds.), Automata, Languages, and Programming. Proceedings, 1999. XIV, 720 pages. 1999.

Vol. 1645: M. Crochemore, M. Paterson (Eds.), Combinatorial Pattern Matching. Proceedings, 1999. VIII, 295 pages. 1999.

Vol. 1647: F.J. Garijo, M. Boman (Eds.), Multi-Agent System Engineering. Proceedings, 1999. X, 233 pages. 1999. (Subseries LNAI).

Vol. 1648: M. Franklin (Ed.), Financial Cryptography. Proceedings, 1999. VIII, 269 pages. 1999.

Vol. 1649: R.Y. Pinter, S. Tsur (Eds.), Next Generation Information Technologies and Systems. Proceedings, 1999. IX, 327 pages. 1999.

Vol. 1650: K.-D. Althoff, R. Bergmann, L.K. Branting (Eds.), Case-Based Reasoning Research and Development. Proceedings, 1999. XII, 598 pages. 1999. (Subseries LNAI).

Vol. 1651: R.H. Güting, D. Papadias, F. Lochovsky (Eds.), Advances in Spatial Databases. Proceedings, 1999. XI, 371 pages. 1999.

Vol. 1652: M. Klusch, O.M. Shehory, G. Weiss (Eds.), Cooperative Information Agents III. Proceedings, 1999. XI, 404 pages. 1999. (Subseries LNAI).

Vol. 1653: S. Covaci (Ed.), Active Networks. Proceedings, 1999. XIII, 346 pages. 1999.

Vol. 1654: E.R. Hancock, M. Pelillo (Eds.), Energy Minimization Methods in Computer Vision and Pattern Recognition. Proceedings, 1999. IX, 331 pages. 1999.

Vol. 1655: S.-W. Lee, Y. Nakano (Eds.), Document Analysis Systems: Theory and Practice. Proceedings, 1998. XI, 377 pages. 1999.

Vol. 1656: S. Chatterjee, J.F. Prins, L. Carter, J. Ferrante, Z. Li, D. Sehr, P.-C. Yew (Eds.), Languages and Compilers for Parallel Computing. Proceedings, 1998. XI, 384 pages. 1999.

Vol. 1657: T. Altenkirch, W. Naraschewski, B. Reus (Eds.), Types for Proofs and Programs. Proceedings, 1999. VIII, 207 pages. 1999.

Vol. 1661: C. Freksa, D.M. Mark (Eds.), Spatial Information Theory. Proceedings, 1999. XIII, 477 pages. 1999.

Vol. 1662: V. Malyshkin (Ed.), Parallel Computing Technologies. Proceedings, 1999. XIX, 510 pages. 1999.

Vol. 1663: F. Dehne, A. Gupta. J.-R. Sack, R. Tamassia (Eds.), Algorithms and Data Structures. Proceedings, 1999. IX, 366 pages. 1999.

Vol. 1664: J.C.M. Baeten, S. Mauw (Eds.), CONCUR'99. Concurrency Theory. Proceedings, 1999. XI, 573 pages. 1999.

Vol. 1666: M. Wiener (Ed.), Advances in Cryptology – CRYPTO '99. Proceedings, 1999. XII, 639 pages. 1999.

Vol. 1667: J. Hlavička, E. Maehle, A. Pataricza (Eds.), Dependable Computing – EDCC-3. Proceedings, 1999. XVIII, 455 pages. 1999.

Vol. 1668: J.S. Vitter, C.D. Zaroliagis (Eds.), Algorithm Engineering. Proceedings, 1999. VIII, 361 pages. 1999.

Vol. 1671: D. Hochbaum, K. Jansen, J.D.P. Rolim, A. Sinclair (Eds.), Randomization, Approximation, and Combinatorial Optimization. Proceedings, 1999. IX, 289 pages. 1999.

Vol. 1672: M. Kutylowski, L. Pacholski, T. Wierzbicki (Eds.), Mathematical Foundations of Computer Science 1999. Proceedings, 1999. XII, 455 pages. 1999.

Vol. 1673: P. Lysaght, J. Irvine, R. Hartenstein (Eds.), Field Programmable Logic and Applications. Proceedings, 1999. XI, 541 pages. 1999.

Vol. 1674: D. Floreano, J.-D. Nicoud, F. Mondada (Eds.), Advances in Artificial Life. Proceedings, 1999. XVI, 737 pages. 1999. (Subseries LNAI).

Vol. 1675: J. Estublier (Ed.), System Configuration Management. Proceedings, 1999. VIII, 255 pages. 1999.

Vol. 1976: M. Mohania, A M. Tjoa (Eds.), Data Warehousing and Knowledge Discovery. Proceedings, 1999. XII, 400 pages. 1999.

Vol. 1677: T. Bench-Capon, G. Soda, A M. Tjoa (Eds.), Database and Expert Systems Applications. Proceedings, 1999. XVIII, 1105 pages. 1999.

Vol. 1678: M.H. Böhlen, C.S. Jensen, M.O. Scholl (Eds.), Spatio-Temporal Database Management. Proceedings, 1999. X, 243 pages. 1999.

Vol. 1679: C. Taylor, A. Colchester (Eds.), Medical Image Computing and Computer-Assisted Intervention – MICCAI'99. Proceedings, 1999. XXI, 1240 pages. 1999.

Vol. 1680: D. Dams, R. Gerth, S. Leue, M. Massink (Eds.), Theoretical and Practical Aspects of SPIN Model Checking. Proceedings, 1999. X, 277 pages. 1999.

Vol. 1682: M. Nielsen, P. Johansen, O.F. Olsen, J. Weickert (Eds.), Scale-Space Theories in Computer Vision. Proceedings, 1999. XII, 532 pages. 1999.

Vol. 1683: J. Flum, M. Rodríguez-Artalejo (Eds.), Co,puter Science Logic. Proceedings, 1999. XI, 580 pages. 1999.

Vol. 1684: G. Ciobanu, G. Păun (Eds.), Fundamentals of Computation Theory. Proceedings, 1999. XI, 570 pages. 1999.

Vol. 1685: P. Amestoy, P. Berger, M. Daydé, I. Duff, V. Frayssé, L. Giraud, D. Ruiz (Eds.), Euro-Par'99. Parallel Processing. Proceedings, 1999. XXXII, 1503 pages. 1999.

Vol. 1687: O. Nierstrasz, M. Lemoine (Eds.), Software Engineering – ESEC/FSE '99. Proceedings, 1999. XII, 529 pages. 1999.

Vol. 1688: P. Bouquet, L. Serafini, P. Brézillon, M. Benerecetti, F. Castellani (Eds.), Modeling and Using Context. Proceedings, 1999. XII, 528 pages. 1999. (Subseries LNAI).

Vol. 1689: F. Solina, A. Leonardis (Eds.), Computer Analysis of Images and Patterns. Proceedings, 1999. XIV, 650 pages. 1999.

Vol. 1690: Y. Bertot, G. Dowek, A. Hirschowitz, C. Paulin, L. Théry (Eds.), Theorem Proving in Higher Order Logics. Proceedings, 1999. VIII, 359 pages. 1999.

Vol. 1691: J. Eder, I. Rozman, T. Welzer (Eds.), Advances in Databases and Information Systems. Proceedings, 1999. XIII, 383 pages. 1999.

Vol. 1692: V. Matoušek, P. Mautner, J. Ocelíková, P. Sojka (Eds.), Text, Speech and Dialogue. Proceedings, 1999. XI, 396 pages. 1999. (Subseries LNAI).

Vol. 1693: P. Jayanti (Ed.), Distributed Computing. Proceedings, 1999. X, 357 pages. 1999.

Vol. 1694: A. Cortesi, G. Filé (Eds.), Static Analysis. Proceedings, 1999. VIII, 357 pages. 1999.

Vol. 1695: P. Barahona, J.J. Alferes (Eds.), Progress in Artificial Intelligence. Proceedings, 1999. XI, 385 pages. 1999. (Subseries LNAI).

Vol. 1696: S. Abiteboul, A.-M. Vercoustre (Eds.), Research and Advanced Technology for Digital Libraries. Proceedings, 1999. XII, 497 pages. 1999.

Vol. 1697: J. Dongarra, E. Luque, T. Margalef (Eds.), Recent Advances in Parallel Virtual Machine and Message Passing Interface. Proceedings, 1999. XVII, 551 pages. 1999.

Vol. 1698: M. Felici, K. Kanoun, A. Pasquini (Eds.), Computer Safety, Reliability and Security. Proceedings, 1999. XVIII, 482 pages. 1999.

Vol. 1699: S. Albayrak (Ed.), Intelligent Agents for Telecommunication Applications. Proceedings, 1999. IX, 191 pages. 1999. (Subseries LNAI).

Vol. 1701: W. Burgard, T. Christaller, A.B. Cremers (Eds.), KI-99: Advances in Artificial Intelligence. Proceedings, 1999. XI, 311 pages. 1999. (Subseries LNAI).

Vol. 1702: G. Nadathur (Ed.), Principles and Practice of Declarative Programming. Proceedings, 1999. X, 434 pages. 1999.

Vol. 1704: Jan M. Żytkow, J. Rauch (Eds.), Principles of Data Mining and Knowledge Discovery. Proceedings, 1999. XIV, 593 pages. 1999. (Subseries LNAI).

Vol. 1705: H. Ganzinger, D. McAllester, A. Voronkov (Eds.), Logic for Programming and Automated Reasoning. Proceedings, 1999. XII, 397 pages. 1999. (Subseries LNAI).

Vol. 1707: H.-W. Gellersen (Ed.), Handheld and Ubiquitous Computing. Proceedings, 1999. XII, 390 pages. 1999.